WORLD WAR II IN COLONIAL AFRICA

THE DEATH KNELL OF COLONIALISM

by

Richard E. Osborne

Riebel-Roque Publishing Company

Indianapolis, Indiana

Library of Congress Catalog Card Number 00 091681

ISBN 0-9628324-5-6

Published and printed in the U.S.A.
Book design and production by Steve Miller

RIEBEL-ROQUE PUBLISHING COMPANY
6027 Castlebar Circle
Indianapolis, IN 46220

Distributed by:
SEVEN HILLS BOOK DISTRIBUTORS, INC.
1531 Tremont St.
Cincinnati, Ohio 45214

Other books by author:

TOUR BOOK FOR ANTIQUE CAR BUFFS
CASABLANCA COMPANION
WORLD WAR II SITES IN THE UNITED STATES

INTRODUCTION

This book tells two stories at the same time. The first is the history of the involvement of the ENTIRE continent of Africa during World War II, and the second is the history of the beginning stages of the process of de-colonizations that occurred in the years immediately following the war. Historians have long known that the two events were interrelated. Here, in this book, the reader will find the details of that interrelationship..

Many books have been written on the various aspects of World War II in Africa, especially the long and difficult military struggles in North Africa. But, seldom has a book told ALL of the wartime events in Africa and how they related to each other, to the wars in Europe, Asia, and the Americas, and to the demise of colonialism. What is more, the waters around Africa—the Mediterranean Sea, the South Atlantic Ocean, and the Indian Ocean—were battle grounds, too, where many events happened that were related to the war in Africa.

Also related here is the story of Africans fighting overseas in Europe and Asia, and of the Africans at home who made the transition from the primitive life-styles of the rural villages and farms into the booming war-related economies in the cities. The combined effects of having served in the white man's armies and worked in the white man's factories made lasting and inalterable impressions on hundreds of thousands of Africans, and became a major factor in their struggle for self-advancement and self-determination that was to come in the postwar years.

It is hoped that the reader of this book gains an understanding of how truly worldwide the war was and how it accelerated a process of major political change with regard to the colonial world that, otherwise, would have taken decades to achieve.

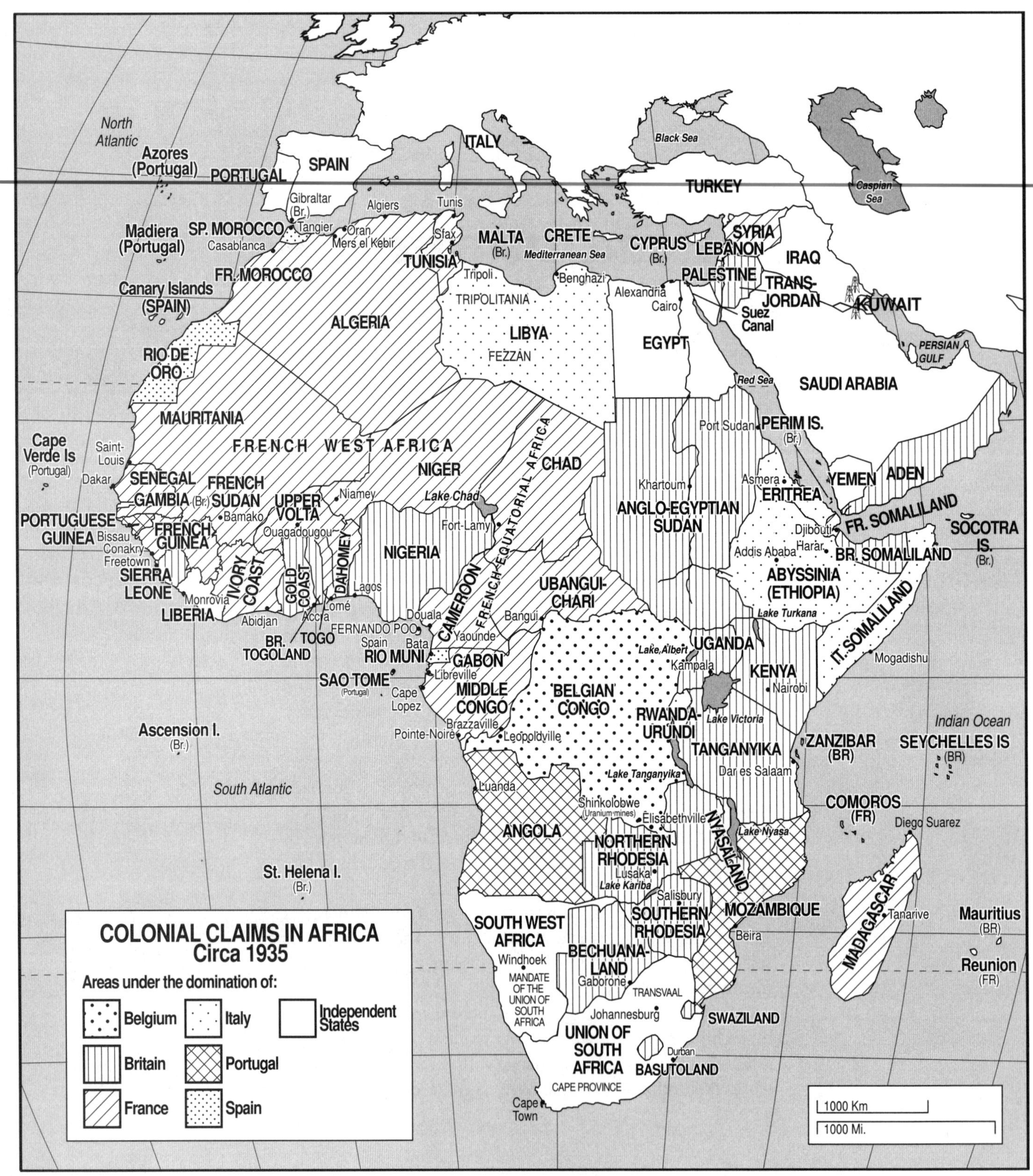

Colonial Africa in 1939.

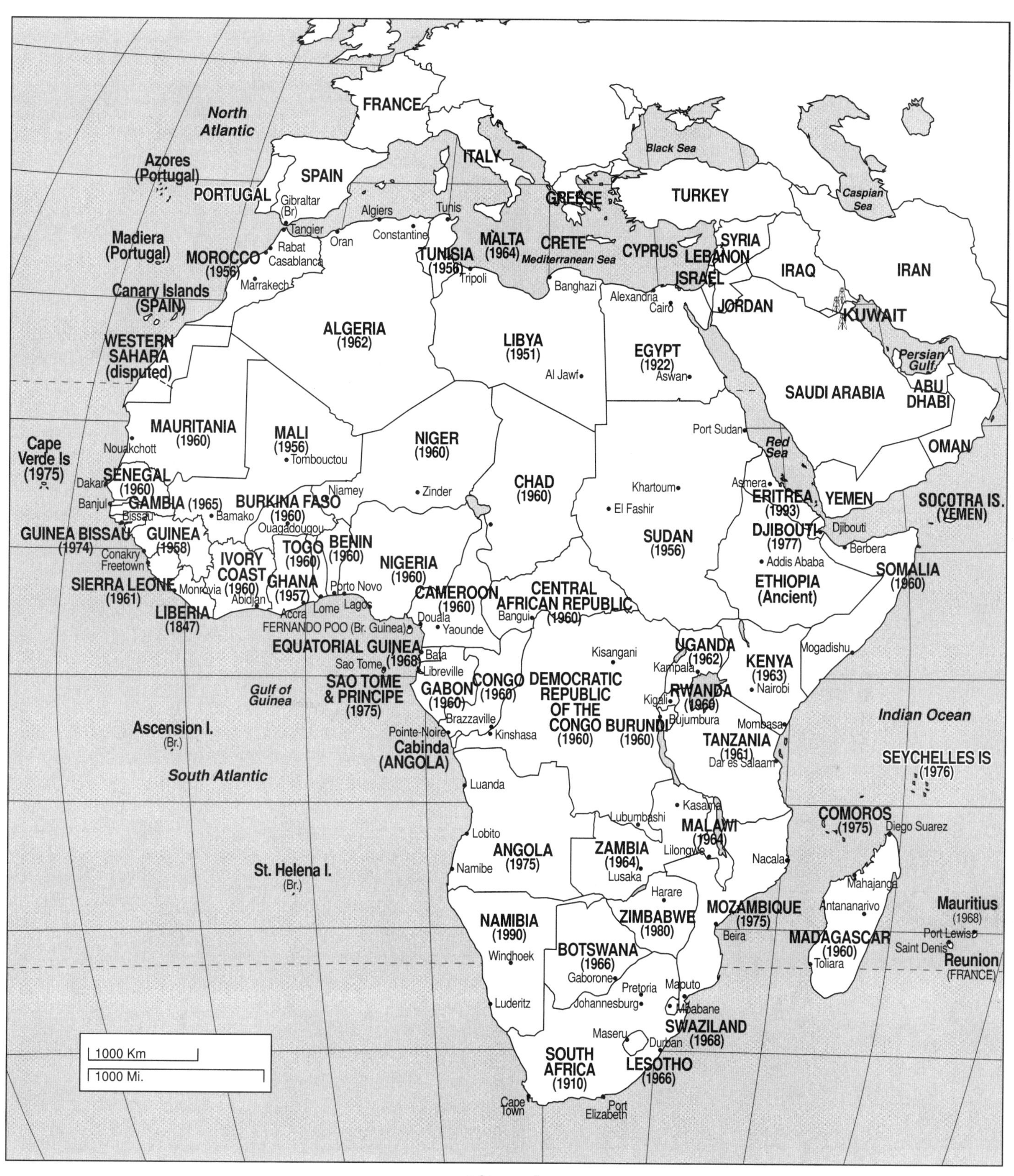

Africa today.

TABLE OF CONTENTS

Chapter 1
THE FIRST EAST AFRICAN WAR (1935-36)

FASCISM'S FIRST VICTIM—ETHIOPIA

It was in colonial Africa that the first shots of Fascist aggression were fired. The exact date was October 3, 1935 when Fascist Italy launched an unprovoked invasion of the independent Christian nation of Ethiopia in East Africa. This was an act of pure aggression and a move by Benito Mussolini, the dictator of Italy and the creator of Fascism, to spread Fascist control to another country by force of arms. For the next ten years aggressions of this sort by Fascist-like nations would be repeated over and over again causing death and misery to tens of millions of people. It was called World War II.

Italy already controlled two colonies in East Africa, Eritrea and Italian Somaliland. Between them lay Ethiopia. Mussolini wanted to conquer Ethiopia solely for the purpose of combining it with his two existing colonies to create one large and united colonial holding. If that could be accomplished Italy's colonial holdings in East Africa would became almost as large as those of Great Britain's East African colonial holdings at this point and put Italy's interests in that part of the world on a par with those of Britain. Furthermore, the acquisition of Ethiopia would be a fulfillment of the promise Mussolini had made to his people over the years to expand Italy's living space and regain for Italy the glory and power of its Roman past. He called it a "Place in the sun." The Italian people wanted it, too, and believed their "Duce" (leader) could make good his promise.

It must be remembered that this was still the age of colonialism. The thinking of these days was that a nation's possession of colonies gave that nation additional wealth, political clout, and considerable prestige within the world community. Colonies provided for geographic expansion, a source for human and material resources, a captive market for exports, and a place to which its citizens could migrate and spread the national culture. This had been a part of the European socio/political thinking for almost a hundred years and it was ingrained into the thinking of virtually all of the European political leaders of the 1930s.

THE ITALIANS HAD TRIED ONCE BEFORE TO CONQUER ETHIOPIA

The Italians had tried once before to conquer Ethiopia, but with disastrous results. In 1896 Italian troops invaded Ethiopia from Eritrea hoping, at that time, to add the kingdom to its colonial empire. But, the Italian Army was resoundingly defeated by determined native force at the town of Adowa. The Italians lost 12,000 men. Of these, 1705 had been captured as prisoners of war, and Italy was obliged to pay Ethiopia 10 million lire for their return. It was a humiliating defeat for a modern European nation. The Italians never forgot it and longed for revenge. So when, in the early 1930s, Mussolini began making demands on Ethiopia and the possibility of a war with Ethiopia loomed once again, the Italian people were with him.

By 1935, the Italian people, like most of the other peoples of the western world, were caught up in a scenario of gloom. The Great Depression had spread across the globe ravaging the economies of virtually every nation in the world. Russian Communism was another threat to world stability and, in Germany, there was Adolf Hitler, a daring and clever dictator who was aggressively threatening the peace of Europe by arming the German nation once again.

HITLER AND MUSSOLINI NOT YET FRIENDS

At this point in time Hitler posed a threat to Italy's interests in central and southern Europe, and Hitler and Mussolini were more adversaries than friends. Their well-known friendship of World War II would come later, and in part, due to events in Ethiopia. At this time, the mid-1930s, Italy was an ally of sorts with Germany's two most powerful adversaries in Europe, France and Britain. These three nations had concluded

The Italian air base at Gura, Eritrea, with extensive workshops and repair facilities, was built in 1935 as part of the Italian military buildup in preparation for the invasion of Ethiopia.

a mutual assistance pact six months earlier, in April 1935 at Stresa, designed to restrain Hitler. A month earlier Hitler had shocked Europe by announcing that he would impose military conscription in Germany and rebuild Germany's army to a strength of 36 divisions. This was not only a challenge to the peace of Europe but a direct violation of the 1919 Versailles Peace Treaty imposed upon Germany by the victorious Allies of World War I. Italy was one of those World War I Allies that had imposed the restrictions.

MUSSOLINI MAKES WAR PLANS

The Stresa alliance played nicely into Mussolini's hands. He could see that France and Britain would be most reluctant to weaken their newly-formed united front against Germany by breaking with Italy over the Ethiopian question. This opened the door, in Mussolini's mind, for Italy to take action.

Furthermore, by conquering all, or even part, of Ethiopia, that victory would lift the spirits of his depression-racked people, and convince them that they were truly a great warrior race, as he had been telling them for over a decade. Furthermore, a successful military conquest would prove to the world, and to Germany, that Italy was truly a world power.

To insure popular support for his coming adventure in Africa, Mussolini's government began telling the Italian people that with Italy in control of Ethiopia all sorts of good things would happen for Italy. He claimed millions of Italians could emigrate to East Africa, acquire land that was either unused or misused, and live comfortable lives in a land of plenty. The people were further tantalized with tales of untapped resources such as coal, oil, platinum, and gold. Overtures were made to Italian business interests ensuring that they would also benefit. To entice Italian young men to join the army, recruiting posters appeared all over Italy showing handsome bare-breasted Ethiopian women implying that they, too, might be considered spoils of the conquest.

For Mussolini personally, a success of this magnitude would solidify his own popularity at home and prove to the world that both he and Fascism were to be taken seriously and given their due respect.

Toward these ends Mussolini formulated a plan. He began building up, slowly but noticeably, his military forces in both Eritrea and Italian Somaliland. New military facilities and roads were built, especially in Eritrea, from which the main attack into Ethiopia was to be launched. Supplies and equipment were purchased all over East Africa and the Red Sea area, creating a seller's market for those who had items to sell that the Italians wanted.

New recruits from ethnic Italian communities overseas were sought for an "international" brigade in the Army. Mussolini let it be known that his two sons, Vittorio and Bruno, and his son-in-law, Galeazzo Ciano, would serve in the armed forces. This started a rush among Mussolini's most loyal followers to follow Mussolini's lead and encourage their sons to join the armed forces.

In all, seven Army divisions, six "Blackshirt" Divisions (Fascist Party members), and two Eritrean Divisions were made ready along with about a dozen smaller independent units including a battalion of Libyan army regulars and a smaller group of Libyan volunteers.

In both Eritrea and Italian Somaliland dozens of "bande" units were hired by the Italians. These were traditional bands of mounted and armed tribesmen who sold their services to the highest bidder. The Italians had long used them to keep the peace in certain parts of their empire.

The Italians set up a new government agency called the "Political Office" with the expressed purpose of winning, by whatever means necessary, supporters inside Ethiopia. The Italians were well aware of the age-old rivalries and feuds that existed in Ethiopia and hoped to entice, bribe, or threaten some of the various factions into supporting Italy. For this purpose 1 million Maria Theresa silver dollars, coins accepted worldwide, were minted in Italy and assigned to the Political Office. If some of the factions that came forward proved reliable enough, they would be given arms.

Since the annual dry season began in October 1935, all had to be ready by then.

AN ARTIFICIAL CRISIS MADE IN ROME

Other nations took notice and questioned Mussolini's motives. When the time was right, he announced that Italy had serious grievances with Ethiopia and intended to resolve them to Italy's satisfaction. Most of these grievances were in Mussolini's imagination and were concocted by his propagandists. To press his case, Mussolini began making unreasonable demands against Ethiopia, meddling in Ethiopia's internal affairs, and seeking out clan leaders and others who would support an Italian takeover. He also painted Ethiopia as an aggressor threatening the security of Italy's colonies. Mussolini gambled that if and when a military showdown came with Ethiopia, his modern army could easily defeat the weak and poorly equipped army of Ethiopia. The major powers of the world, mired down as they were with other problems, would do nothing more than protest Italy's actions, and would take no military action to save Ethiopia. Since Britain, with her own colonial interests in the area, was the most likely adversary, Mussolini pointed out that Britain had, in the past, not hesitated using military force to build her empire. Mussolini hedged his bet further by placing strong and threatening Italian military forces in eastern Libya close to the Egyptian border, in northern Eritrea on The Anglo-Egyptian Sudan border, and in southern Italian Somaliland on the border with British-controlled Kenya. The message was clear. If Britain interfered with Italy's plans, Italian forces could invade Egypt, The Sudan, Kenya, or all three with a command from Rome.

BRITISH TRY APPEASEMENT

Mussolini's fears of Britain lessened when, in September 1935, the British government came through with an offer of appeasement. The British told Mussolini secretly that they would accept his taking parts of northern Ethiopia if he would keep the peace in the area.

As a show of force the British Home Fleet was mobilized and sent to the Mediterranean. The Italians countered by moving naval units from the Dodecanese Islands, one of their colonial territories in the eastern Mediterranean, to Italian bases to better protect the homeland.

The League of Nations sought to mediate the situation by recommending Ethiopia give up certain territories and make significant economic concessions to the Italians.

Mussolini rejected all proposals because now he was more convinced than ever that the British would eventually back down and that he could have <u>all</u> of Ethiopia and on his terms. He further reckoned that after Ethiopia had been conquered, he could make amends, as others had done who had temporarily disturbed the international order, and then bide his time while the episode faded into history. All the while he could claim, and prove by example, that the Ethiopian people were better off under Italian guidance and that ancient scourges such as disease, abject poverty, slavery and cannibalism would be brought to an end.

Ethiopia was virtually helpless in the face of Mussolini's threats and military power. That country had very little political clout on the world stage and no powerful ally who, through mutual interests, would come to its aid militarily.

ETHIOPIA LOOKS TO AMERICA FOR HELP

In a desperate attempt to gain support from America, the Ethiopians approached America's Standard Oil Company and offered them substantial oil and mineral concessions in hopes that such an involvement with the United States would strengthen Ethiopia's political position. Standard Oil Company was interested and sent a representative, Francis W. Rickett, to Addis Ababa. Rickett negotiated directly with the Emperor on August 29, 1935, and gained oil and mineral concessions over half of the country for 75 years.

By the time Rickett returned to the United States, the U.S. government had learned of the deal and disapproved it. Through the State Department the Standard Oil Company was pressured to renege on the deal on the grounds that it might draw America into the Ethiopian/Italian conflict and would hamper the efforts of the European nations who were trying to bring about a peaceful solution to the crisis.

It must be remembered, too, that America was in the depths of the Depression and isolationism was very strong both in Congress and in the general public. Only a few months earlier, in May 1935, Congress had passed a restrictive neutrality law designed to keep America out of wars just like the one that was now brewing in East Africa. The mood of the American people in 1935 was to stay out of foreign entanglements.

ETHIOPIA MOBILIZES, WAR BEGINS

On September 28, 1935, Ethiopia's Emperor, Haile Selassie, seeing that an Italian invasion was imminent, ordered his armed forces to mobilize for war.

Mussolini pounced on this, declaring that the mobilization of Ethiopia's armed forces was clearly an act of war that threatened Italy's colonies. By twisting the issues, Mussolini now claimed that Ethiopia was the aggressor.

On October 1 an Eritrean bande unit crossed the border into Ethiopia and occupied the strategic Moussa Ali mountain pass. The local Ethiopian officials had no way of communicating this fact to Addis Ababa but, by chance, a French pilot flying from Djibouti to Addis Ababa noticed the incursion

(Above) Ethiopian Army officers in full dress uniforms. Note that they are barefooted. The whole Ethiopian Army was barefooted. (Left) Emperor Haile Selassie of Ethiopia. Called "the Black Napoleon" by his western admirers. (Below) Haile Abba Mersa, one of several clan leaders who came to his country's defense. Abba Mersa was killed in action.

and, upon landing, sent word to the palace. Haile Selassie made a few last-minute changes in his military leadership and then spent most of the next 24 hours praying at the Church of Miriam on Mount Entotto.

In Italy, Mussolini played his next card. He boldly announced that his patience with Ethiopia was at an end and that decisive action had to be taken. This was on October 2, 1935. The next day Italian forces invaded Ethiopia.

Haile Selassie responded to the invasion by calling his people to arms and ordering his Christian nation to pray for victory. He promised his soldiers that after a final victory over the Italians they would be given free land in Eritrea and Italian Somaliland as a reward for their services. Haile Selassie's messages were transmitted across the primitive landscape by runners and drums. Ethiopians responded by the thousands. They picked up their antiquated rifles, spears, and bows and arrows and went out to meet the Italian Army. The world watched in amazement as these two terribly unequal armies approached one another.

The Ethiopian Army was a loose collection of regular army soldiers, draftees, irregular units raised by tribal or clan leaders, foreign volunteers, and hired mercenaries. It was said that the further the Army was from Addis Ababa, Ethiopia's capital, the less cohesive it was. It was not uncommon for commanders to quarrel among themselves and for one unit to fight with another. Commanders were prone to take independent action and, as events would show, even refuse to fight. Furthermore, some commanders defected to the enemy. The best unit in the Ethiopian Army was the Imperial Guards. Its men were well-trained, well-equipped, and well-fed. However, they had a constant problem because soldiers from other units often tried to steal their weapons and supplies.

Despite the obvious handicaps that plagued the Ethiopian Army, most of the rank and file soldiers were motivated and fought well—bonded together by a sense of patriotism for their country and the fear of becoming colonial subjects.

ETHIOPIA STANDS ALONE

Virtually everywhere in the world community, sympathies were with the Ethiopians. But Mussolini guessed right. No nation offered to come to Ethiopia's aid with military force. All that was offered were scathing condemnations of Italy's behavior and encouragement for Ethiopia.

The Italians did have one ally in the region, Yemen, an in-

THE POPE SPEAKS OUT

From the Vatican, Pope Pius XII spoke out on the war in Ethiopia. Since the conflict was between two Christian nations, he could hardly side with one nation or the other on the basis of religion. Instead he chose to speak out in favor of the policy of colonialization. The Italian media reported that His Holiness had said "a defeat of the Italian undertaking would be to the detriment of the interests of the European colonizers of Africa."

dependent kingdom on the southern tip of the Arabian Peninsula. Yemen and Italy had a long history of friendly relations. When the troubles started in Ethiopia, the Italians actively recruited Yemenis for their army because Yemenis had a reputation for being good soldiers. As a result, several thousand Yemenis fought in the Ethiopian campaign with the Italians.

Yemen's neighbor, Saudi Arabia, was also friendly toward Italy but did not send men to fight in Ethiopia. Saudi Arabia had, since the 1920s, been trying to reduce British influence in the Arabian Peninsula and had befriended Italy as a political counterbalance toward that end. Saudi Arabia was one of the nations that ignored the League of Nations' sanctions against Italy and conducted on-going trade with that country throughout the East African War.

The pilots of Ethiopia's six-plane air force. Third from the left is Ludwig Weber, a German and Haile Selassie's personal pilot. Later in the war two black American pilots, Hubert Julian and John Robinson, came to Ethiopia, violating America's neutrality laws to do so, and flew in the Ethiopian Air Force. Unlike Ethiopia's soldiers, Ethiopia's airmen wore shoes.

LEAGUE OF NATIONS ORDERS SANCTIONS

The League of Nations soon acted by calling for sanctions against both nations to minimize the effects of the war. These sanctions, though, were full of holes and both nations could get almost anything they wanted—and could pay for—from someone. The biggest hole of all was the port of Djibouti in French Somaliland, one of Ethiopia's northern neighbors. Years earlier the French had built a railroad from Djibouti to Addis Ababa and thereafter operated it under the direction of a French-owned company. It was the only railroad in either country and Ethiopia's main outlet to the sea. France had proclaimed her neutrality in the Ethiopian/Italian War, but the sentiments of the French government and people were overwhelmingly in support of Ethiopia. Therefore, the French officials at Djibouti turned a blind eye to war materials and individuals going to and from Ethiopia via the railroad. The Italians, of course, knew this, and since the railroad was owned and operated by the French, did not interfere with its operation for fear of creating political complications with Paris. The Italians had to plan on conquering Ethiopia without cutting off that country's main avenue of supply.

Additional men and supplies trickled into Ethiopia from the neighboring British colonies of The Sudan, British Somaliland, and Kenya. These supplies usually came by animal caravan, making them slow-moving and limited in scope.

THE MILITARY CONQUEST OF ETHIOPIA

On the morning of October 3, 1935, four Italian army divisions, with tanks, armored cars, mobile artillery, personnel carriers, and aircraft protection overhead crossed the Eritrean/Ethiopian border at two points south of Asmara, the capital of Eritrea. Accompanying the Italians were the two Eritrean divisions, along with smaller Eritrean units all commanded by Italian officers. It was the beginning of a decade in colonial Africa during which black men would fight black men.

In the east a second invasion of Ethiopia took place from Italian Somaliland across the emptiness of the Ogaden Desert. This was a much smaller force of six battalions of Somali soldiers. It too was a two-pronged attack. The northern force advanced on Wal Wal down the Wal Wal-Mogadishu Road, and the southern force advanced across country toward Nagele in southern Ethiopia.

In Rome, on this momentous day, Mussolini spoke to the Italian people from his balcony at the Piazza Venezia and told them of the invasion. In an impassioned speech he repeated one of his favorite themes, telling the cheering throng, "Now, we too want our place in the sun." The crowd was ecstatic.

There was no formal declaration of war, no immediate opposition from the ill-prepared Ethiopians and the weather was good. The northern arm of the advance from Eritrea headed for Adowa, which was captured on October 6 with only token resistance by the Ethiopians. On October 15 the Italians took Aksum, the capital of the legendary Queen of Sheba. From the Italian point of view, it was a magnificent way to start a war. The horrible defeat of 1896 had been avenged.

The Italian forces from Eritrea, which was the main arm of the invasion, advanced down the Asmara-Dessie road which lead, eventually, to Addis Ababa, the Ethiopian capital and heart of the nation.

Back in Italy the people were, almost to a man, behind their Duce. Mussolini's leadership had produced spectacular results once again. Italy's King Victor Emmanuel III spoke favorably of the invasion as did many prominent Italian politicians. Even several Cardinals of the Roman Catholic Church, following the Pope's lead, announced their approval of Italy's actions. As a sop to local and world opinion, the Italian government announced that as the Italian Army ad-

An Italian woman donates her wedding ring to the government to help finance the Ethiopian war.

vanced it was performing humanitarian acts for the long-oppressed Ethiopian people. There were several accounts of the Italian soldiers encountering slaves who were liberated, fed, and cared for by the Army.

Mussolini, ever the opportunist, took advantage of the situation to ask for additional sacrifices from his people to insure victory. One thing he specifically called for was that women donate their gold jewelry to the Italian treasury to help finance the war. The response was overwhelming.

To make sure that the world witnessed Italy's coming victory, some 200 Italian and about 40 foreign journalists were invited to cover the war. Journalists from Britain, France, Germany, and the United States were among those who went to East Africa as guests of the Italian government.

THE ITALIAN ADVANCE STALLS

The Italian Army advanced against very little opposition for about two weeks, then stalled due to a number of unforeseen problems caused mainly by the decrepit condition of the Ethiopian roads. This was not altogether unexpected by the Italians. They had road-building units ready to go to work immediately when called upon. However, some stretches of road proved to be worse than expected and totally impassible for heavily laden trucks. The road-builders rushed forward to repair the roads but the task was monumental. This took time and cost lots of fuel to operate the huge road-building machinery. As a result, a fuel shortage soon developed adding to the Italian's woes.

The Italian propagandists turned the problem with the roads into a positive theme by announcing that the Italian Army was building roads for the benefit of the Ethiopian people and the country as it advanced.

Propaganda, though, does not move supplies. To accomplish this the Italians reverted to animal power, but there were not enough animals. So, the Army's quartermasters launched an emergency program throughout East Africa and the Middle East buying up pack animals wherever they could be found. Suddenly, it was a seller's market throughout the region and the prices of camels, horses, mules, and donkeys shot up. Many of the animals purchased by the Italians came from the neighboring British and French colonies. The Anglo-Egyptian Sudan proved to be an excellent source for camels.

During the latter part of October a bedraggled Ethiopian clan leader, Haile Selassie Gugsa, arrived at the Italian-occupied town of Adigrat with about 1200 poorly armed tribesmen. Just prior to the invasion, Italian agents had enlisted Gugsa's help in overthrowing the Emperor, a bitter enemy. At that time, Gugsa claimed he could raise tens of thousands of men, so his arrival with a much smaller force was a great disappointment to the Italians. But, the Italian propagandists were put to work to salvage the situation. They claimed that Gugsa had arrived with over 120,000 men ready and eager to fight for the Italians, and to show Italy's gratitude toward Gugsa he was taken to Asmara, given a fancy new uniform, a parade, and appointed Governor of the Province of Tigre once it was captured.

Meanwhile, the Italian advance inched forward. On November 12, 1935 they met their first meaningful opposition from the Ethiopian Army near the fortified town of Makalle. The Ethiopians had set up a clever ambush in a dry and rocky gorge on the Italian's left flank. The Italian column entered the gorge unaware and were set upon by withering machine gun and rifle fire from three sides. The Italians took heavy losses and were pinned down until nightfall when the fighting stopped. During the night, the Ethiopians withdrew. The battered Italians discovered this the next morning and began a retreat to Makalle over the next four days. The ferocity of the encounter, though, had surprised the Italians and they were now more cautious. Foreign observers reported that the Ethiopians fought bravely and that their morale was high.

Back in Rome the government was having to make excuses to the Italian people for the slow pace of the advance. Behind the closed doors of the government offices, Mussolini was in trouble. Some leading party members believed that the invasion had become a fiasco and began speaking about a negotiated peace settlement. There were even those who felt Mussolini might fall from power.

Foreign leaders too, saw clearly what was happening and

AVENGED AT LAST

Soon after the war ended in Ethiopia the Italians erected a monument at Adowa commemorating the 1896 battle and inscribed "To the Dead of Adowa. Avenged at Last."

Left: A heavily-laden Italian army truck has to be pulled along a road by manpower. Right: The Italians were forced to resort to the age-old mode of transportation in Ethiopia—pack animals.

urged Mussolini to seek peace. Mussolini, though, was not about to give in. He placed the major blame on his field commander General Emilio de Bono and "fired" him by giving him a face-saving promotion to Field Marshal and bringing him home. In his place he appointed the more aggressive, chain smoking, General Pietro Badoglio who had been a young Italian soldier at the time of the 1896 defeat at Adowa.

During the month of November 1935, Mussolini had another thing to worry about—the British elections. So far the British, who controlled the Suez Canal, had kept it open to Italian and Ethiopian shipping as called for in previous international agreements. But, in Britain, the Labour Party announced that if they won the elections they would close the Canal to Italy. The voters went to the polls on November 14, 1935, and returned the Conservatives to power. Mussolini's luck was still with him.

General Pietro Badoglio took command of the Italian forces in the north after General Emilio de Bono failed to meet Mussolini's expectations.

On December 8, 1935, the British and French offered Mussolini a secret deal—two-thirds of Ethiopia if Italy would end the aggression. The secret deal remained secret only one day before being leaked to the public. All parties were greatly embarrassed, especially Mussolini because the mere suggestion of such a proposal implied that his promise of an easy victory now did not look so easy.

Mussolini's reaction was to get tough with his own people and escalate the war. He ordered Badoglio to resume the attack and authorized him to use poison gas, bacterial warfare, and bomb hospitals if necessary. Badoglio chose to use mustard gas, a gas that causes burns and blisters on the skin and lungs and is often fatal. The use of mustard gas had been outlawed by international convention, but the Italians were desperate enough to ignore that agreement. The first use of mustard gas came two days before Christmas 1935, when it was dropped from airplanes in canisters on Ethiopian troops at the Takkaze River near Mai Timchet. Later, it was sprayed from planes making it much more deadly. When word of this reached the outside world there was an outcry of rage against the Italians. The Italian government, however, denied that it was using poison gas and offered various explanations for the detailed accounts and photos of dead bodies that soon appeared in the world press. They claimed that some of the bodies were those of people who had died of leprosy. Other Italian claims stated that it was the Ethiopians who were using poison gas—which was supplied to them by the British—and that the dead Ethiopians in the newspaper photographs had accidently been killed by their own people.

NEWS COVERAGE OF THE ETHIOPIAN WAR

News reports coming from Ethiopia were seldom firsthand. Neither side permitted foreign correspondents to get too close to the battle areas. Those reporting news from the Italian side were kept miles behind the front and had to be content with receiving and interpreting the news releases from the official Italian sources. The most reliable news came from Addis Ababa, where restrictions and censorship were fairly loose. The Ethiopian government promised the foreign correspondents that they could go to the front, but it never happened. The correspondents had to be content with official reports from the Ethiopian government and interviews from returning soldiers, Red Cross workers, and others who had been up front. The correspondents hung out at hotels, the railroad station, bars, and other places looking for someone who might have the latest news.

On the southern front the Italian advance from Italian Somaliland, under the command of General Rodolfo Graziani, had been steady and virtually unopposed until November 2, when advanced units encountered a well-armed band of Ethiopians at a Mullah's stone fort outside the town of Gorrahei. The Italians attacked the fort and, in a bombing raid, mortally wounded the Ethiopian commander, General Afework. He died two days later. With Afework's death the morale and cohesiveness of the Ethiopian forces in the east deteriorated and they retreated in disorder. The Italians entered the town of Gorrahei on November 7 to find it deserted and burned. There was also a store of some 500 rifles abandoned by the fleeing Ethiopians. The Italians advanced rapidly out of Gorrahei until they encountered another well-armed band of Ethiopians at the junction of the Tug Fafan and Tug Jerrer Rivers. Rather than attack, the Italians chose to retreat to Gorrahei. In the next few days there were several skirmishes and, in one encounter, the Ethiopians destroyed three Italian tanks. On November 11, the Emperor himself flew to the front to stiffen the resolve of his forces. He did this by handing out medals and honors, especially to those men who had destroyed the tanks. He also handed out punishment in the form of lashings and bayonet stabs to those who had shown cowardice.

AMERICAN BLACKS RECRUITED FOR SERVICE IN ETHIOPIA

In late 1935, several black American organizations began attempts to recruit black Americans for service in Ethiopia. Rallies were held in several big cities. The greatest effort was made in New York City's Harlem. The results were not very successful. First of all, the American Neutrality Act of 1935 made it illegal for Americans to join the armies of any belligerent nation, and secondly, travel to Ethiopia was very expensive.

Some volunteers, though, did come forward, but the organizations were unable to finance their travel and only very few black Americans ever made it to Ethiopia. When the civil war started in Spain (July 1936) some of those individuals who had volunteered for service in Ethiopia volunteered to fight in Spain. The organizations calling for volunteers for Spain were much better financed, so a sizeable number of the black Americans went to Spain. There, they became members of the famous "Abraham Lincoln" and "George Washington" International Brigade.

THE ITALIAN ADVANCE RESUMES IN THE NORTH

Badoglio pressed his troops hard and the Italian advance resumed against determined but futile Ethiopian resistance. Some Ethiopian units fought to the last man, but the firepower of the modern Italian Army proved decisive time and again.

As the reports of victories reached Rome, Mussolini began handing out medals and promotions most generously. Many of these went to members of his Black Shirt Legions so that the conquest of Ethiopia would appear to be more of a Fascist Party victory than strictly a victory of the army.

BLACKSHIRT LEGIONS

Black Shirt Legions were military units formed by the Fascist Party and comprised of Party members only. Their first loyalty was to Mussolini personally, but, in a combat situation, they were attached to the army and operated under the direction of Italian Army commanders. The Black Shirts had the best of equipment and high morale and were considered elite units.

One of the medals Mussolini handed out went to one of his closest friends, Roberto Farinacci, a member of the Black Shirt Legion. Farinacci had been wounded. He was "fishing" in a lake with hand grenades when one of the grenades went off in his hand. Farinacci lost his hand.

In early December the Italians were approaching the town of Dessie and bombed it several times in preparation for their attack. On one occasion a hospital was destroyed and many patients killed. Foreign correspondents broadcast this to the world, and once again condemnation came down upon the Italians. During one raid Haile Selassie was in Dessie and it was reported that he ran to a machine gun and began firing at the Italian planes. This incident was widely disseminated by the world press and the Ethiopian government made use of it in its propaganda by showing the Emperor, in a variety of photos and drawings, manning the machine gun.

A GLIMMER OF HOPE FOR THE ETHIOPIANS

In mid December 1935, the Ethiopians went on the offensive. The Italians were now deep into Ethiopia on both the northern and southern fronts and were dependent on long and difficult supply lines. The Ethiopians' supply lines reaching back to Addis Ababa were much shorter. The front

Ethiopian soldiers fought bravely, and at times to the last man.

had also moved into the mountainous uplands, Ethiopia's most populous and productive region. In the mountainous terrain the Italian tanks and armored cars were of less value to the Italians and hostilities became more like those of a guerilla-type war. This was an advantage to the small units of the Ethiopian Army. The Ethiopians knew the area and could make effective use of hit-and-run tactics.

The Ethiopian offensive took place at Tembien, in the mountains of southern Tigre Province. Two Ethiopian armies coordinated their efforts and tried to force the Italians back. The fighting lasted until the last week in January 1936, but the Italians held on. The Italians suffered 1100 dead and wounded, and the Ethiopians, 8000.

On February 10, Badoglio launched a counterattack on the Ethiopian forces entrenched at Amba Aradam using almost his entire force of 200,000 men. The Ethiopian force was estimated to be 60,000. After five days of hard fighting, during which the Italians used massive amounts of artillery weapons, aircraft, and mustard gas, they succeeded in encircling the Ethiopian force and decimating it. Some 12,000 Ethiopians were killed. The Ethiopian commander, Ras Mulugueta, who was also the country's War Minister, escaped the encirclement, but was later killed as he tried to make good his escape. Mulugueta had come upon the body of his son who had just been killed. As he bent over the body he was struck down by a sniper's bullet.

The main Ethiopian force, the nucleus of the two armies, still remained in the Tembien area, and were a threat to any further Italian advance. The Battle of Tembien was not over.

Meanwhile, on the southern front, General Graziani's force launched an attack during January, and succeeded in forcing the Ethiopian defender to give up considerable ground. At this point Graziani was closer to Addis Ababa then Badoglio. Back in Italy, people were making bets as to who would be the first to reach the Ethiopian capital.

On February 27, Badoglio's forces attacked the main Ethiopian force at Tembien. The Ethiopians were well entrenched on a mountain top and the Italians had to fight their way up the steep mountain slopes. The Italians used heavy artillery, aerial bombardment, and—once again—mustard gas. The battle lasted three days before the Ethiopians finally broke and ran. Only the Emperor's personal guard unit held its position until it was overrun.

FASTING AND THE LEAGUE OF NATIONS

The Ethiopians now were in need of any help they could get. On March 1, 1936 the government called for eight days of fasting and, to show his unity with the people, the Emperor set out on foot for the northern front to personally direct the course of the war. Along the way he made himself visible to as many people as possible. On March 20 and again on March 23 the Ethiopian delegates at the League of Nations in Geneva presented the assembly with what they claimed was "unquestionable" evidence of Italian aggression, atrocities, and the use of poison gas. But the League was slow to act. The Ethiopian war was no longer the main issue in Europe. It had been pushed aside by new international concerns resulting from the London Naval Conference between Britain and Germany. This was a bilateral agreement between Britain and Germany which limited the size of the German Navy by a percentage formula with that of the British Navy. In the agreement, the British, French, and Americans (who were beginning to creep out of their isolationist foreign policy) gave their consent for the Germans to build small, fast battleships which would become known as "Pocket Battleships." These new warships would outclass many of the older warships belonging to some of the lesser allies. The London Naval Conference was seen by many as yet another crack in the united front of the Allied Powers in the face of Fascist aggression, and another example of appeasement.

An American bubble gum card showing Emperor Haile Selassie manning the machine gun at Dessie.

On April 8, the League finally got around to the Ethiopian problem and assigned a committee to investigate Ethiopia's claims, causing still more delay.

BACK IN ETHIOPIA

Ethiopian tradition dictated that the Emperor should lead his forces in battle. To this end, Haile Selassie went to the northern front in late March 1936. He set up headquarters in a cave and gathered his generals and clan leaders around him. Together they planned a major offensive against the Italians in the Mai Ceu area, 150 miles north of Dessie. Unfortunately, tradition and personal honor superseded good judgement and critical phases of the attack were assigned to

ETHIOPIAN PLANS FOR GUERILLA WARFARE

Part of Ethiopia's war planning was the possibility of having to conduct prolonged guerilla warfare against an invader. The Ethiopians knew that their army was no match for any of the modern European armies but they saw in a prolonged guerilla war the hope that an invader could be worn down and eventually defeated, either militarily, politically or both.

This, in fact, was much the way it happened. Even after the Italians claimed victory in May 1936 small bands of Ethiopian fighters held out in remote and mountainous areas harassing the Italians until 1941 when the country was reconquered by the British. During the interim there were areas of Ethiopia that never came under Italian control.

clan leaders who expected such roles in spite of the fact that their troops had little or no training in modern military tactics. Furthermore, spies soon revealed the plan of attack to the Italians.

The offensive began on March 31, 1936, with attacks on the Italian flanks. Haile Selassie, himself, again manned a machine gun. Some progress was made but at a terrible cost in human life. Then, the main attack, a massive frontal assault, an ancient Ethiopian military tradition, was launched. The Italians had six divisions ready and waiting, commanded personally by Badoglio. It was a desperate and costly venture. The Italians held their ground and used all the firepower at their command to mow down row upon row of charging Ethiopian soldiers. The Ethiopians were slaughtered in great numbers, and in the end, the attack failed.

This was the last great battle of the war. The Ethiopians had lost the nucleus of their army by now and were severely short of both ammunition and food. But hopes rose as rumors spread among the Ethiopians that Britain was about to intervene in the war on their side. Unfortunately for the Ethiopians, the rumors were false.

On April 2, Haile Selassie realized that the offensive was a failure and that his army was being destroyed. Therefore, he ordered a retreat. The Italians pursued the retreating Ethiopians with a vengeance. They were attacked from the air and on the flanks by horse-mounted cavalrymen, some of them Ethiopian turncoats fighting for the Italians. The retreat turned into a rout. Several top government officials were killed or captured as were several clan leaders. An attempted stand at Dessie failed to materialize and the road to Addis Ababa lay open to the Italians. The Italians took Dessie and from there on to Addis Ababa the Italians' transportation problems were diminished because the road between the two cities, called "The Imperial Highway," was the best in the country. General Badoglio, unimpressed by both the name and the road itself, called it "a bad cart track." Nevertheless, it was built to take motor vehicles and the Italians could retire some of their slow-moving pack animals and advance in motorized columns.

ITALIAN VICTORY ON THE SOUTHERN FRONT

In the south Graziani's forces succeeded in breaking through the formidable Ethiopian defenses at Dagghabur. In the western press those defenses had been touted as the Ethiopian "Maginot Line." They were nothing of the sort but they did delay the Italian advance for sixteen days. Once the Italians broke through on April 30, the Ethiopians retreated in disorder and the road into the heartland of Ethiopia lay open from the south and east. That same day Haile Selassie returned to Addis Ababa and made preparations to flee his country.

THE LEAGUE OF NATIONS

On April 20, 1936, as Ethiopian forces were in full retreat on the northern front and fighting their last major defensive battle to the east of the capital, the League of Nations acted. The League issued a meaningless appeal to both Italy and Ethiopia "for the prompt cessation of hostilities and the restoration of peace." It was a worthless gesture. An Italian victory was close at hand in Ethiopia.

HAILE SELASSIE FLEES

On the morning of May 2, 1936, Emperor Haile Selassie boarded a French train at a secret location outside Addis Ababa and traveled up the French rail line to the safety of Djibouti, in French Somaliland. As soon as it was known that Haile Selassie had fled, some of his top government officials, some clan leaders, and some chieftains also left for Djibouti. However, some did not and chose to remain and fight—or, perhaps, to strike a deal with the Italians that would allow them to continue to rule in their local areas. Early on, the Italians had let it be known that such things were possible.

On May 4, Haile Selassie boarded a British warship and was taken first to Palestine and then to London. In Addis Ababa, following Haile Selassie's departure, anarchy and looting erupted with many soldiers and policemen joining in. The various embassies called in their citizens and placed armed guards around their compounds. Westerners banded together to help each other. On one occasion the British sent a unit of Sikh soldiers to the U. S. Embassy to help protect it.

Indian merchants took up arms and barricaded themselves and their families in their homes and shops. At the railroad station the French railroad workers did likewise. At the airport every flight out was filled with both Ethiopians and foreigners fleeing the city. Still others fled into the surrounding countryside.

On the evening of May 4 the first Italian units, Eritrean askaris, entered the outskirts of the city.

On May 5, Badoglio's forces entered the city from the north. In some European quarters it was believed that Badoglio could have entered the city two or three days earlier but that he hesitated, letting the world see what savages the Ethiopians really were by ravaging their own capital city.

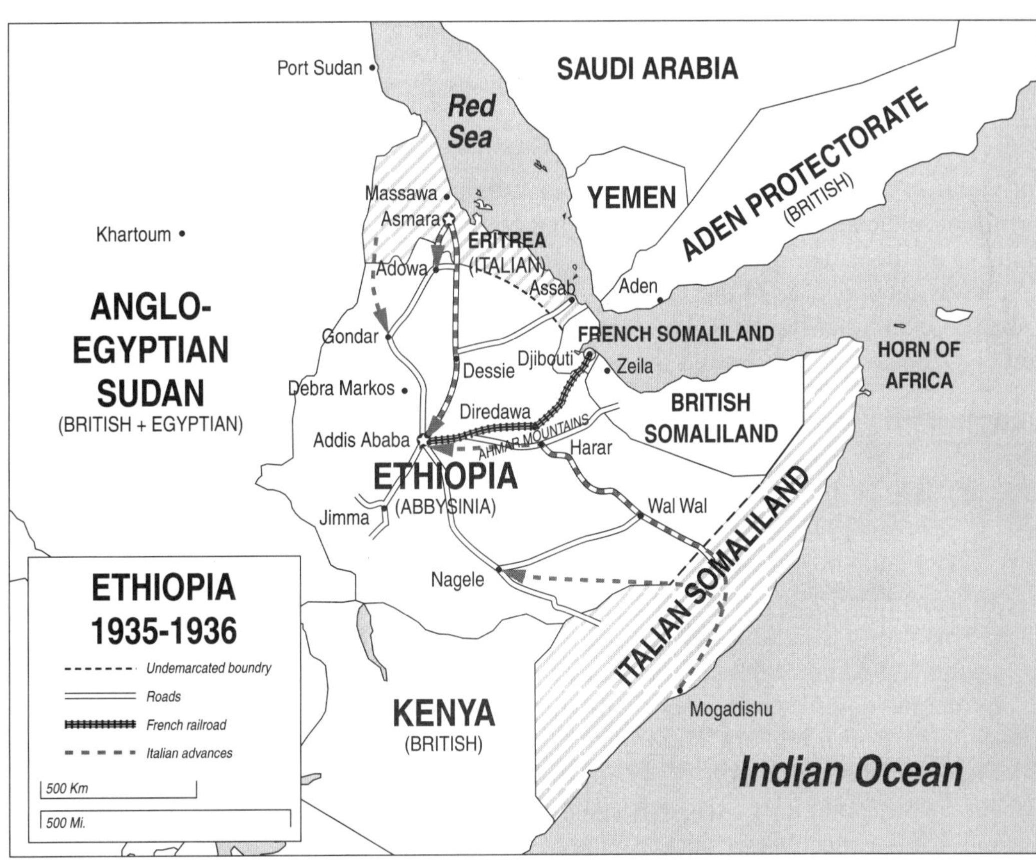

The Italian conquest of Ethiopia was a two-front offensive, one from Eritrea in the north and one from Italian Somaliland in the south and east. It took eight months.

When the main Italian force finally marched into Addis Ababa it was in formation with all their troops and armor on display. The march route had been given to the world press in time for them to set up their cameras at advantageous locations. It was claimed in Rome that the citizens of Addis Ababa welcomed the Italians with open arms. In reality Badoglio ordered his troops to bring about law and order in the most brutal fashion. Looters, arsonists, and others causing mayhem were to be shot on sight. During the next three days some 1,500 people were killed as the Italians restored order.

Badoglio was praised as a great hero back in Italy and was promoted to Governor-General and Viceroy of Abyssinia—Italy's new name for Ethiopia. These were positions Badoglio did not covet.

On the morning of May 9, 1936, Mussolini staged a great parade in Rome to celebrate the conquest of Ethiopia. He appeared again on his balcony at the Piazza Venezia before a jubilant throng of half a million people and proclaimed the conquest and annexation of Ethiopia, and the assumption by King Victor Emmanuel III of the additional title of Emperor of Abyssinia. Mussolini also proclaimed that henceforth the three Italian colonial possessions of Eritrea, Abyssinia, and Italian Somaliland would be united into one colonial federation known as Italian East Africa.

MAY 9, 1936: HIGH POINT OF COLONIALISM IN AFRICA

No one knew it at the time, but May 9, 1936, marked the high water mark for colonialism in Africa. It lasted for about five years and then began to decline.

That same day Haile Selassie arrived at Haifa, Palestine. His arrival was something of an embarrassment to the British and no high level British officeholder wanted to greet him at the dock. That job was assigned to the city's mayor and a district commissioner. Selassie and his small entourage were then whisked away unceremoniously and put up at the King David Hotel rather than at the British High-Commissioner's residence, which would have been protocol for a reigning head of state.

In Geneva, the League of Nations announced that Ethiopia would continue to be considered as a member. On May 12, Italy resigned from the League in protest.

FIGHTING STILL RAGED IN ETHIOPIA

Despite Mussolini's victory claims, the war in Ethiopia had

not ended. Graziani's forces were still encountering determined opposition as they approached Addis Ababa from the east. It was not until May 8 that he was able to take the city of Harar, 230 miles east of Addis Ababa. The Ethiopian Army was not beaten yet. Units withdrew successfully to the mountains west of Harar to fight another day. Elsewhere in Ethiopia small bands of soldiers were coming together in remote areas planning to do the same.

It was not until May 21 that Graziani's forces entered Addis Ababa. Upon his arrival Badoglio promptly resigned as Governor-General and Viceroy and the positions were given to Graziani. Graziani was also promoted to Field Marshal.

Both men were brought back to Rome for a brief victory celebration and given a hero's welcome. Then Badoglio was sent off to a comfortable Army post in Italy and Graziani went back to Ethiopia. Mussolini did not want them to remain in Rome too long lest they steal his glory.

EGYPTIANS COME TO RESENT THE TREATY OF 1936

The military treaty of 1936 would still be in effect in September 1939 when Britain went to war against Germany and in June 1940 when Britain went to war against Italy. The British would use the treaty to build numerous bases in Egypt and make Egypt into the strongest British military bastions in the Middle East. This would become a thorn in the side of the Egyptians in that British military strength became overwhelming and that Egypt could very likely become a battle ground between the British and the Axis Powers. Using the war as their excuse, and citing the treaty as their justification, the British would tend, under the stress of war, to treat Egypt once again as a protectorate interfering frequently with their internal affairs and foreign policies. The Egyptian politicians, led by young King Farouk, who came of age and ascended to the throne in July 1937, would counter this influence by maintaining strong diplomatic ties with Germany and Italy and engaging in a constant struggle of trying to outmaneuver the British on internal matters and foreign affairs.

The Egyptians even took on some of the trappings of the fascist world. Most notably was the creation of a paramilitary force called the "Blue Shirts" in emulation of the "Black Shirts" of Italy and the "Brown Shirts" of Germany.

The Wafdist Party, Egypt's largest and strongest political party and the party that had brought about Egyptian independence in 1922, had negotiated the now-hated military treaty of 1936 with the British. Not surprisingly, as the treaty became more and more resented so did the Wafdists. In the eyes of many Egyptians the Wafdists were now seen as puppets of the British. So devastating was this that a large group of dissidents in the Wafdist Party broke away and formed a new party, the "Saadist Party."

MUSSOLINI WANTED MORE

Flush with victory, the greedy Mussolini now wanted more. He told close associates at different times during May 1936 that he saw no reason why an army of one million blacks could not be raised in Italian East Africa, supported by a local arms and munitions industry, and thereby dominate all of East Africa. He also said that it should be a goal of Italy to acquire The Sudan which has a common border with Libya. That way the Italians would have a land link and supply line between Italian East Africa and the Mediterranean and would not be dependent on the British-controlled Suez Canal.

Mussolini's ambitions toward The Sudan were no secret in London and Cairo. The British and Egyptians had previously agreed that they would control The Sudan and they wanted no Italian interference. To strengthen their position in the face of the Italian threat, Britain and Egypt concluded a twenty-year military agreement on August 26, 1936. They declared that in the event of a military threat to either of their respective interests in The Sudan, the Egyptians would allow the British to use Egyptian ports, airfield, roads, railroads, rivers, etc. for military purposes. The contents of the agreement were made public so Mussolini could take note.

Sometime later Mussolini tempered his ambitions regarding a million-man black army telling his associates that perhaps 300,000 men would be enough. For public consumption, though, the Italian press spoke frequently of a two million-man black army-to-be.

PROBLEMS STILL IN ETHIOPIA

Upon his return to Addis Ababa Graziani inherited a bundle of problems. There were two large Ethiopian forces still fighting in the south. One was under Ras Imru in the Gore area close to the Sudanese border, a region of dense tropical forests. Ras Imru had been appointed Regent of Ethiopia by Haile Selassie in his absence. The other force was under Ras Desta in the Sidamo area near the Kenyan border and Lake Abaya in a mountainous region. Both of these forces intended to carry out guerilla-type warfare but both were acting independently. This weakened their effect, but on the other hand, forced Graziani to prepare two separate expeditions to deal with them. Furthermore, the rainy season had just begun making the primitive roads of southern Ethiopia impassable for motorized vehicles, so any military action there had to be postponed until the rainy season ended in October 1936.

In the meantime there was plenty to do in the Addis Ababa

Prince Amedeo Umberto, Duke of Aosta and Viceroy of Abyssinia.

area. A number of major and minor war-leaders had not yet surrendered and, in the Ethiopian culture, surrendering was a formal affair. The Political Office of the Italian Army had to negotiate with each of these leaders and organize a formal ceremony for each in which the leader would formally lay down his arms and submit to the new central authority in Addis Ababa.

One of the more important surrender ceremonies occurred on June 24, 1936, when one of the most powerful war-leaders, Ras Kebbede Mangasha Atikim and the Moslem leader, Sultan Abba Jobir II, surrendered. Other ceremonies followed, but Addis Ababa was still not a safe place for Europeans. On July 28, 1936, Abba Petros, one of the still-defiant military leaders, launched a four-pronged attack on Addis Ababa. Fighting lasted three days in and around the city and ended in defeat for the Ethiopians when Abba Petros was captured and executed.

With the rainy season still in progress Graziani went about his overall mission of pacifying the country as best he could. In an effort to suppress Ethiopian nationalism, he jailed or executed many members of the Ethiopian intelligentsia and some of the leaders of the Coptic Church. These things brought more international scorn upon Italy, but were effective in subduing the country.

By November 1936, the rainy season had ended and Italian forces resumed military operations against the Ethiopian guerrillas in the south. Italian military successes came in rapid order, and Mussolini could sense that victory was at hand. In December 1936, he announced that all of Ethiopia had been pacified. It had not. It was not until mid-February 1937 that organized resistance in the south was eliminated. Most of the Ethiopian leaders, including Regent Ras Imru, were killed in action, or captured and shot.

In a last desperate move by the Ethiopians an assassin attempted to kill Marshal Graziani at a public ceremony in Addis Ababa on February 19, 1937. Graziani survived but was wounded. Out of revenge, the Black Shirts went on a three-day orgy of massacres killing some 3,000 Ethiopians all over the country, including about 100 priests. After this horrible reign of terror, there was a period of calm throughout the country. But then, Graziani made a grievous mistake. In early May 1937, a large cache of weapons was discovered hidden at Debra Libanos, Ethiopia's most famous monastery. On May 20, 1937, Italian soldiers, acting under Graziani's orders, raided the monastery and summarily executed 297 monks. As might be expected, the Ethiopians were outraged. Uprising sprang up all over the country and were especially strong in the north. The Italians, though, were handicapped in putting them down because the rainy season had come again. When the rainy season stopped in November 1937, the revolts in the north intensified. Graziani was in trouble.

The year's developments in Ethiopia were a great disappointment to Mussolini and it was costing too much. By now Italy was deeply involved with its military intervention in the Spanish Civil War which was draining the treasury. In October 1937, Mussolini had to devalue the lire, raise the national sales tax and place a 10% tax levy on publicly-owned corpo-

GRAZIANI'S FATE

In 1939, Graziani's career was revived when he was made Chief of the Army Staff. In 1940, the year Italy entered the war, he became Commander-in-Chief of Italian armed forces in Libya. The Italians suffered a series of major defeats by the British in late 1940, in early 1941, and in February 1941. After the loss of Benghazi, Libya, Graziani resigned and was replaced by General Italo Garibaldi.

Field Marshal Rodolfo Graziani.

Graziani faded into the background once again until after the fall of Mussolini in July 1943. Upon Mussolini's rescue by the Germans in September 1943, and the resurrection of his Fascist government, Graziani became Minister of War in that government. At the end of the war Graziani was captured by Italian Partisans and was almost certainly destined for a summary execution. He was saved, however, by two operatives of the U.S. Office of Strategic Services (OSS, forerunner to the CIA) and turned over to the postwar Italian government. He was tried for war crimes by the Italian government and, in May 1950, sentenced to 19 years in prison. He was released three months later, though, after having been given amnesty. After that, he went into politics and became a leader of the Italian Social Movement Party. Graziani died in 1955 at the age of 73.

Italians building a new bridge on the road between Addis Ababa, the capital of Ethiopia and Asmara, the capital of Eritrea.

rations. He placed part of the blame on Graziani and recalled him to Italy in December 1937. Graziani was given a hero's welcome, but was then shoved into the background. In Ethiopia the King's cousin, Prince Amedeo Umberto, Duke of Aosta, a more moderate administrator, became Viceroy.

The Duke had no choice but to try to subdue the new uprisings. This required the services of some 60,000 Italian troops and their newly-acquired, but not too reliable, Ethiopian askari units. Slowly the Duke's forces began to get the upper hand in the north, but soon it was June 1938 and the rains began again. For two more years the on-again-off-again battles raged in Ethiopia, tying down tens of thousands of Italian troop. They were still raging when the British and their allies invaded Ethiopia in January 1941, at the beginning of the Second Ethiopian War. All the while the Italians continued to use poison gas—but always denying it.

ITALY ATTEMPTS TO COLONIZE ITS NEW EMPIRE.

The Italian government made a determined effort to convince Italians to emigrate to Italian East Africa and partake of the great adventure and opportunities Mussolini had promised. An on-going propaganda campaign existed in Italy for this purpose. There was a reasonable flow of emigration to Eritrea and Italian Somaliland but Ethiopia was a different matter. The on-going fighting in Ethiopia was no secret and not many Italian civilians wanted to take the risks of relocating to such an unsettled land. Furthermore, the improvements in that colony's infrastructure were materializing very slowly. Due to the chronic shortage of finances such things as roads, schools, safe-water systems, electricity and other necessities for a European life-style were still inadequate in many places. The Italian government was aware of these problems so only certain areas were improved to the point where immigrants would be attracted. The bulk of Ethiopia thus remained undeveloped and unpopulated by Italians.

One endeavor the Italians undertook was to improve the roads. In order to control the country the Italians needed good roads over which their motorized military units could travel in all types of weather. Many Ethiopian laborers were conscripted to work on the roads under quite harsh conditions. Those who slacked off or failed to perform were beaten, put on short rations, or imprisoned.

As the selected areas of Ethiopia were developed Italian immigration increased. Most were from southern Italy, where unemployment was high and the standard of living low. Those people made good settlers, though, because they were hard workers and more racially tolerant than northern Italians.

Addis Ababa was one of the areas where significant improvements were made and many Italians settled there.

Improving the lot of the natives was secondary to the Italians, but some progress was made. Many natives were put to

WHITE WOMEN NEEDED IN ITALIAN EAST AFRICA

Not too surprisingly Italian women were more reluctant to set out for the pioneering life in Italian East Africa than men. This caused two problems; a shortage of white women in the colonies and an increase in the number of mulattos. To help resolve this problem, the Italian courts began sending convicted prostitutes to the colonies. The program worked well. In April 1938, an investigating committee headed by Mussolini's close friend, Roberto Farinacci, went to East Africa to report on various matters, including the prostitutes. Farinacci reported that 90% of the women had given birth to white children or were currently pregnant.

The supply of prostitutes was limited, so the Italian government actively recruited foreign white women to go to East Africa. Italian women were deemed more valuable at home and were discouraged from emigrating unless it was with their husband. Many of the foreign women who responded to the program were French women. The French government objected to this, and French women going to Italian East Africa by way of the port of Djibouti, French Somaliland were, more often than not, intercepted and sent home.

work in jobs that had not existed before, but their wages were much lower than those of Europeans. This, though, helped to eliminate the age-old barter systems that still existed, and aided in spreading the monetary system.

Some effort was made to bring more primary education to the Ethiopian people. Missionary schools and Islamic schools that had existed before were encouraged to continue their work, and some new schools were built. The curriculum was basic, and stressed things Italian and western and downplayed things Ethiopian and African. Care was taken, however, not to stimulate a sense of Ethiopian nationalism in the educational system.

THE EFFECTS OF THE ETHIOPIAN WAR ELSEWHERE

The consequences of the Ethiopian war were felt both in eastern Africa and in Europe. In eastern Africa tens of thousands of Ethiopian refugees and defeated soldiers fled into the surrounding British colonies. Virtually all of them had to be sheltered and fed. With them came thousands of head of livestock, which helped ease the food problem but, on the other hand, created a problem in pasturing. Among the refugees were a small number of renegades, bandits, and other troublemakers to add to the problems. The situation was most acute in Kenya and British Somaliland. In northern Kenya, a unique problem arose as members of the Merille, Toposa, and Danyiro tribes crossed into Kenya and encountered their traditional enemy, the Turkana tribe. Members of the three Ethiopian tribes began stealing the Turkana's women and cattle, and a tribal war threatened. The local Kenyan police force was not large enough to handle the problem, so units of the King's African Rifles (KAR), Kenya's main defense force, had to be called in to help. In British Somaliland the British Somaliland Camel Corps, that colony's defense force, was not large enough to handle all of the refugees either, so additional KAR units had to be sent there from Kenya.

With so many units of the KAR and the entire British Somaliland Camel Corps doing humanitarian duties, the security of the British colonies became a concern in London. None of the colonies were protected well enough to counter an Italian invasion, if such a scenario came about.

In Paris, the French government had similar concerns about their colony of French Somaliland, because the Italians began to look more covetously toward that colony. Italy had long-standing claims on the colony and now, with Ethiopia an Italian possession, the Italians wanted the French-owned Addis Ababa-to-Djibouti railroad, and the seaport of Djibouti for their own.

In Europe Mussolini announced on June 1, 1936, that Italian East Africa would be reorganized into five provinces, the remainder of the country pacified, and projects begun to make the colony ready for more Italian settlers and business interests.

Haile Selassie addressing the League of Nations on June 30, 1936. This was one of the most widely seen photos of 1936. Selassie's pathetic appeal for help personified the weakness of both the League of Nations and the victorious Allies of World War I and their inability to stop armed Fascist aggression.

Two days later, Haile Selassie arrived at Southhampton aboard the ocean liner "Orford." His arrival aboard a commercial ship rather than a British warship was another diplomatic disassociation for the British. Selassie was greeted by huge crowds at both dockside and upon his arrival at Waterloo Station in London. Conspicuously absent, however, were high British dignitaries. Fortunately, the Ethiopian Ambassador to Britain, Dr. Martin, was on hand to greet the Emperor and took him to the Ethiopian Embassy in London. In the days that followed, Selassie met privately with Foreign Secretary Anthony Eden, other members of the British government and several foreign statesmen. King Edward VIII, however, did not invite his fellow monarch to Buckingham Palace, and when Selassie was invited to lunch at the House of Commons, Prime Minister Stanley Baldwin made a point not to meet him. A few days later Baldwin's Chancellor of the Exchequer, future Prime Minister and leading advocate of Britain's appeasement policy, Neville Chamberlain, announced that the British government was ready to discontinue sanctions against Italy.

One place where Haile Selassie was welcome was at the League of Nations. He asked to address the League and was told he was welcome to do so on June 30, 1936. The day before, in an attempt to influence League opinion, the Italian government, after months of speaking about its future black army, suddenly reversed itself and announced that Italy did not intend to recruit Ethiopians for military service. Few members believed it.

In an impassioned speech, publicized around the world, Selassie pleaded with the League members to live up to its ideals and restore his nation to him. He spoke in his native tongue, Amharic, and told his listeners, "It is us today. It will be you tomorrow." Selassie ended his speech with the question, "What reply shall I have to take back to my people?."

The members smiled and applauded, but five days later they voted to end all sanctions against Italy. Mussolini had guessed right. After the conquest of Ethiopia, the world powers would want to quickly rid themselves of the uncomfortable defeat and move on to other issues.

HAILE SELASSIE IN EXILE

Haile Selassie gathered his family about him, bought a small villa in England and prepared for a life in exile. Money and weather soon proved to be problems. He had to sell the imperial silverware to raise money to pay off some of his obligations. Then, Empress Menen fell ill due to the harsh British winter and had to return, more-or-less permanently, to Palestine for her health. Some of their children went with her and some remained in England. The family travelled back and forth between Britain and Palestine frequently. Haile Selassie, too, became ill during several of the British winters, and travelled to Palestine for his health as well as to be with his family.

Other relatives and high ranking members of the former government congregated in Jerusalem near the Rechov Habashim, the Ethiopian convent and church on the Street of the Abyssinians. The Emperor was able to send the former government members some money, but almost all had to accept employment to survive.

GERMANY AND ITALY GROW CLOSER

The Ethiopian war was a major factor in bringing Germany and Italy closer together. All through the crisis, Hitler openly supported Mussolini and took the opportunity to remind the world that Germany, too, had demands in Africa regarding the return of her former colonies.

The British saw in Hitler's demands for the return of German colonies another area in which Hitler's ambitions might be quelled by appeasement. A commission called the "Plymouth Committee" was formed to study the question of returning Germany's colonies to her. On June 9, 1936 the committee reported their finding stating that the return of Germany's colonies would not be a good idea, at least not immediately. The idea came up in Britain again in October 1937 but was again rejected by the House of Commons. One of the strongest arguments against returning Germany's colonies to her was her current treatment of the Jews. It was only logical to presume that because of the way the Germans were treating the Jews, they would, likewise, mistreat black and brown people under their control.

There were some leaders within the British government that suggested that Hitler might be appeased on the colonial issue by giving him all or parts of some of the Portuguese African colonies or the Belgian Congo. Word of this reached Prime Minister Antonio Salazar of Portugal, and caused a temporary strain in Portuguese/British relations until the British gave assurances that it would not happen. This was particularly disturbing to the Portuguese because one of the reasons they entered World War I in 1916 on the Allied side was to prevent their colonies from becoming bargaining chips by the victorious powers after the war.

Mussolini found another friend and potential ally during this time—Japan. Japan had accomplished in the Chinese province of Manchuria in 1932 what Italy had in Ethiopia in 1936. That is, conquered the region and added it to its empire in the face of adverse world opinion. In Japan's case, Manchuria was proclaimed an independent nation with the new name of Manchukuo, but the world saw that it was nothing more than a puppet state beholden to Tokyo. Most nations of the world refused to grant diplomatic recognition to Manchukuo as an independent nation. Japan and Italy, though, saw an opportunity for mutual support and friendship. In November 1937, they concluded an agreement whereby Japan would withdraw its embassy in Addis Ababa, thereby acknowledging Italy's conquest of Ethiopia, while Italy would set up a consulate in Manchukuo acknowledging that country's independence.

For Mussolini, he now had a new set of friends and there was no going back to his relationships with Britain and France. London's and Paris's support of sanctions against Italy, and their covert support of Ethiopia, could not be easily forgiven.

Before the summer of 1936 had ended civil war erupted in Spain and the Italians and Germans found themselves on the same side, supporting the Spanish rebels under General Francisco Franco. And, before the end of the year, Italy and Germany formalized their new-found friendship by forming the infamous "Axis" alliance.

MUSSOLINI THE CONQUEROR

Things were going very well for Mussolini. Italy, in his mind, was truly moving into the exclusive ranks of the world's great powers—and he could rightfully boast that it was all his doing. He had conquered Ethiopia, befriended a powerful ally whose political philosophy and ambitions were almost carbon copies of his own, and was involved deeply in Spain on what appeared to be the winning side. He had all of this but still wanted more.

In March 1937, Mussolini made a much-publicized trip to Libya, Italy's Arab colony in North Africa. On March 16, he made an important speech directed to the entire Islamic world telling them that Italy was now their new friend and mentor, and hinted that he would help the Arabs rid themselves of British and French imperialism. This, of course affected colonial Africa with its millions of Moslems. It also indicated that Mussolini was not finished yet with his conquests.

Mussolini's ambitions in the Arab world were not well-received by the Arabs. They could readily see that Mussolini's scheme would only replace British and French imperialism with Italian imperialism. Furthermore, Mussolini's earlier claim that he was "the protector of Islam" was seen by most Arabs as ludicrous and was widely ridiculed in the Arab world. The Arabs, like everyone else under the thumb of the European powers, wanted self-determination and/or independence. But, from the point of view of Arabs in French-controlled lands, experience had shown that if it was their lot to have a European master, then a French master was better than an Italian master. All this changed, however, in June 1940, when France was militarily defeated by Germany and Italy. At that time, Mussolini's claim took on more meaning.

In Arab lands controlled by the British, the opinions of the Arabs was mixed. This was especially true in Egypt where large numbers of people saw Italy as a sort of savior plotting to oust the hated British.

During the summer of 1937, Mussolini boasted frequently of Italy's might. He referred to the conquest of Ethiopia calling it one of the great military conquests of all times over an army that many believed was undefeatable. He further boasted that the Italian Army was the equal of any army in Europe.

In his heart, though, Mussolini knew that the Ethiopian war had been a "cheap" war. Only 1573 Italians had been killed. In contrast, Italy lost some 600,000 soldiers in World War I.

Nevertheless, Mussolini had ample proof of his successes. The Italian people were more supportive of him than ever before, he had a new colonial empire, and he had thumbed his nose at the League of Nations and gotten away with it.

AMERICA'S POSITION

American foreign policy continued to be one of neutrality and opposition to naked aggression, but with the facts as they were that policy, due to the lesson of Ethiopia, began to fade rapidly. In early 1937, the Roosevelt Administration sent a new ambassador to Italy, William Phillips, who had been Assistant Secretary of State. Phillips was not unsympathetic toward Italian Fascism and Mussolini, and had written favorably of both. Phillips, too, was one of the leading proponents in Washington who saw Mussolini as a moderating influence on Hitler. With Phillips's appointment, Washington was sending Mussolini a signal that the United States wanted improved relations with Italy, and that the unpleasant business in Ethiopia could now be pushed into the background. In the months that followed, Phillips wrote a series of favorable reports on Fascism and Mussolini, most of which were read by Roosevelt. Throughout the remainder of 1937, American relations with Italy showed a marked improvement.

THE "EASTER AGREEMENT"—A TRADE OFF—ETHIOPIA FOR SPAIN

On April 1, 1938, Britain and Italy signed a comprehensive agreement that resolved some of their differences. Negotiations for this agreement had been under way for months. Britain wanted Italy to withdraw her troops from the civil war in Spain as part of a larger international agreement under which all foreigners fighting in Spain on both sides would leave. Italy agreed to withdraw her troops but, of course, there was a price. That price was that the British recognize Italy's conquest of Ethiopia. Ex-Emperor Haile Selassie, living in exile in England, bitterly resented the British using his country as a bargaining chip but his pleas were ignored by the

HOW THE "AXIS" GOT ITS NAME

Webster's New Lexicon Dictionary defines "axis" as "a line, real or imaginary, around which things rotate, the earth's axis runs through the poles...."

During October 1936, Mussolini and Hitler met at Hitler's mountain retreat, the Berghof at Berchtesgaden, Germany, and secretly agreed on many issues of common interest regarding their respective foreign policies. Previously, in July 1936, Mussolini and Hitler had reached a gentlemen's agreement giving Hitler a free hand with regard to his designs on Austria. Now, with the October agreement, a new political order was about to emerge in Europe which Italy and Germany planned to dominate. On November 1, 1936, Mussolini spoke to the Italian people to tell them of the coming new order. In his speech he chose a unique and colorful way to describe how the other nations of Europe would soon be subject to the wills of Italy and Germany. Mussolini said that across the map of Europe there is a north/south political line running from Berlin to Rome and that "this vertical line between Rome and Berlin is not a partition, but rather an axis round which all European states animated by the will to collaboration and peace can also collaborate (with Germany and Italy)."

The world press quickly picked up on the word "axis" because it was descriptive of Hitler's and Mussolini's mutual political ambitions and it also fit nicely into headlines. Soon it was being spelled with a capital "A." As a general European war grew nearer in the coming months and the major Allies of World War I gathered together to renew their World War I-era alliance, those nations were, once again, referred to as "The Allies." Their enemy, rather than being called "The Central Powers," as was the case in World War I, was now "The Axis."

Chamberlain government. Britain agreed to the deal and later in the year all foreigners, including the Italians, left Spain. This was not a great concession on the part of the Italians because, by now, the Spanish rebels, now known as the Nationalists, had conquered most of Spain and a Nationalist victory was almost a certainty.

The British lived up to their part of the Easter Agreement and recognized Ethiopia as an Italian colony. Britain was also obliged, under the agreement, to ask the League of Nations to put the question of recognizing Italy's claims to Ethiopia on the agenda for the coming summer session. This was done April 9, 1938.

On May 12, 1938, after debating that issue, the League passed a resolution stating that League members were free to recognize Italy's claims in Ethiopia as they desired. In the days and weeks that followed, most of the major nations of the world joined Britain in recognizing Ethiopia as an Italian colony.

Mussolini had won again.

Chapter 2

THE LAST YEARS OF PEACE IN COLONIAL AFRICA (1936-39)

A RIGID AND STRUCTURED COLONIAL SYSTEM

With the end of the First East African War in 1936, peace returned to colonial Africa. It would last a little over three years and then be followed by six more years of war. When peace eventually returned, colonial Africa would be an entirely difference place.

GRADUAL AND SIGNIFICANT CHANGES

The years 1936-39 saw some gradual and significant changes in colonial Africa. For several preceding decades, modern medicine and various methods of controlling famines had come to benefit a significant number of Africans, so that, by the late 1930s, the native population was increasing rapidly. With increased numbers, improved medical care, and a more stable food supply, there came a strong desire for more upward mobility among the people. This signaled the need for more jobs, more land, and more direct participation in local affairs. But, the Great Depression spread across the land and had a counter-productive effect. The Great Depression brought about joblessness and a significant internal movement of peoples. Farmers, miners, plantation workers, and others who lost their livelihood began migrating to urban areas in hopes of finding work. But, there was little work to be found and wages were low for the work that was available. The result was large-scale unemployment in the cities, and the emergence of shanty towns and squatter settlements. By being thrown together in the cities, though, and with time on their hands, the people learned that they all had common needs and that, by organizing their efforts, could address some of their needs. Therefore, native organizations sprang up for a multitude of purposes. Most of them were peaceful and sought to improve the lot of their members or their community.

This new restlessness of the natives was of concern to all of the colonial powers. Generally, the colonial administrators tried to ignore it when they could, suppress it when possible, and deal with it only when absolutely necessary. But, time, numbers, and circumstances were on the side of the African people. Their time to be heard was at hand.

JEWS TO AFRICA

One of the major questions with regards to Africa in the late 1930s was the prospect of Jews coming to Africa in relatively large numbers. With the rise of the Nazis in Germany, thousands of refugees, most of them Jews, streamed out of Germany (and later Austria and Czechoslovakia) into other parts of Europe. The question thus arose as to what to do with these people. Many eyes looked to areas outside Europe for a solution. Sending Jews out of Europe was not a new concept. In modern times both the Czars and Communists in Russia had made attempts to send Jews to Siberia, and thousands of Jews had emigrated on their own to the New World. The Jews themselves, through their Zionist organizations, foresaw a time when great numbers of Jews would leave Europe for a new homeland in Palestine. But Palestine was a British mandated territory, and there were restrictions on Jewish immigration. Furthermore, the Palestinian Arabs did not want to see Jews migrating to their homeland and demonstrated against this by carrying out acts of terrorism against both Jews and the British. This strife was on-going in Palestine all during this time period.

Therefore, places other than Palestine were sought out and considered as possible home lands for the European Jews. Quite understandably, the vast and sparsely settled lands of Africa offered a possible solution. But, there were problems. Numerous and strong objections came from colonial leaders in both Europe and Africa, and settlers and others already in the colonies. Then, there was the cost factor. Who would pay for the transportation and the enormous start-up costs it would take to transplant tens, or even hundreds, of thousands of European Jews into a primitive land like Africa?

While the politicians, intellectuals and the Jewish organizations debated, some European Jews moved to Africa on their own. Their numbers were small, usually in the hundreds, or even less, at any given place or time. The Union of South Africa, Kenya, the Rhodesias, Nyasaland, Tanganyika, Mauritius, and other colonies admitted Jews. The French, however, were the most resistant to Jews settling in their colonies, fearing that they would take jobs from the white settlers and natives alike and that economic, and perhaps even political and racial, problems would follow. This was quite ironic because France itself had generously opened its doors to refugees of all descriptions and, by the late 1930s, had more refugees than any other country in Europe.

Emigration to the Portuguese and Spanish colonies was not popular among the Jews themselves, because of the atmosphere of religious intolerance that had persisted in those Iberian-dominated lands ever since the Inquisition.

From the other side of the Atlantic came suggestions from the American President, Franklin D. Roosevelt, that Jews might settle in the Belgian Congo, or The Cameroons, or perhaps, in southwestern Ethiopia once that area was pacified. Roosevelt also approached the British and suggested that they approach their traditional friends, the Portuguese, to see if there might not be a place for Jews in Angola.

An Egyptian poster critical of the German/Soviet Pact of August 23, 1939, shows Hitler and Stalin wearing the same boot. Egypt, a Moslem country, was genuinely fearful of Communism, but not necessarily so of Fascism.

Whether or not Roosevelt was serious remains a question. The President was prone to make statements that the American Jewish community liked to hear because they were, for the most part, his loyal supporters.

From Germany came suggestions, too, that Africa might be a place for the Jews. One of Nazidom's primary theorists on this issue was Alfred Rosenberg, who openly supported the concept of a Jewish state somewhere in Africa, and even hinted that Germany might cooperate in such an undertaking. German propaganda supported Rosenberg's remarks.

The problem of refugees in Europe was becoming so great that an international conference was held on the subject in July 1938, at Evian-les-bains, France. During the conference, Africa was widely discussed, but very little was accomplished. The conference proved to be something of an international embarrassment because it revealed how really unwelcome the Jews were around the world, and how few countries were willing to take them in large numbers.

JEWS TO MADAGASCAR?

By far, the most often-mentioned area of Africa for possible Jewish settlement was the French controlled island of Madagascar off the east coast of Africa in the Indian Ocean. Madagascar was first suggested as a possible Jewish homeland in the late 1800s by a Jewish leader, Theodore Herzl. The idea became the subject of several books and pamphlets, and was discussed off-and-on thereafter. From the viewpoint of many Europeans Madagascar had a lot to offer. It was thousands of miles from Europe where the Jews would be out of sight and out of mind and there would be no neighbors to complain of their presence. Furthermore, the effect on the small European community that already existed in Madagascar was considered inconsequential, and the indigenous people, about 3.8 million Malagachies, were docile and cooperative. It was also known that there was anthropological evidence indicating that the people in northern Madagascar had been exposed to ancient Jewish culture and were, in fact, a racial mix of Semitic and indigenous peoples. It was further suggested that the Jews could bring the Malagachie people into the modern-day world community and, in the exchange, the Malagachies could pay their way by becoming good workers and servants.

Not only was Madagascar talked about, it was investigated, first-hand, on several occasions. In 1926, France and Poland sent a joint investigative team to the island to see if it were suitable for white settlers, a euphemism, many thought, for Polish Jews. After an initial visit, the project was dropped, having made no report. The next year the Japanese government sent an inspection team to the island to see if it was suitable for the resettlement of Japanese. The team came and left and nothing more was heard of this effort.

In 1937, the Polish government tried again and sent an inspection team, which included both Poles and Jews. This team made a thorough study of the island and came to some conclusions. By this date, the island was fairly prosperous and well-developed. It had an adequate local food supply and a good export business in coffee, vanilla, tobacco, manioc (tapioca), oil seed,

A new recruit for the King's African Rifles (KAR) makes his mark, a thumb print, on the recruiting documents.

perfume plants, spices, beef, graphite, mica, wild raffia, and sisal. There were 16,000 miles of good roads, 534 miles of railroads, mail service, and rudimentary phone and telegraph services. There were about 26,000 French people on the island, but few of them were settlers. They lived mostly in the larger cities in the temperate highlands. Most Frenchmen came as government officials or tradesmen, were well-paid while on the island, stayed only a few years, then left. There were also about 8,000 East Indians, 3,000 Chinese, and 3,000 other foreigners. Most of the island's internal trade was in the hands of the East Indians and Chinese. Population density was only six people per square mile. Missionaries were active on the island, and about 600,000 natives had been Christianized. These were the attributes that Madagascar had to offer. The Polish commission also reported on its detriments, including a failed attempt at European colonization in the late 1800s. At that time the French government made an attempt to settle French war veterans in Madagascar, but tropical diseases doomed the effort. Many of the Frenchmen died, and many others got too sick to work. Thereafter, Madagascar got the reputation as being a very unhealthy place for Europeans, and the French government made no further organized attempts to bring white settlers to the island. And very few Frenchmen who came as settlers did so on their own. It was also reported that the best land was already in the hands of the few settlers and natives, and that a redistribution of those lands would, almost certainly, create an economic, and possibly a political, upheaval. The Polish commission concluded that only about 40,000 to 60,000 Europeans could be successfully settled in the island's highland where the climate was more temperate. The report was published and then shelved in Warsaw. Poland made no attempt to send settlers to Madagascar.

COLONIAL POLICIES IN AFRICA

The war in Ethiopia had almost no effect on the colonial policies of the ruling European powers. Their respective colonial policies and administrations had long been established, and were well entrenched.

British colonial policy was the most flexible and progressive. The British allowed different types of administration to evolve in their respective colonies, depending upon what was deemed best for both Britain and the colony in question. This was reflected in the British government in London, which had three separate offices concerned with colonial affairs: the Secretaries of State for Dominion Affairs, for India and Burma, and for Colonies.

The French, Belgians, Portuguese and Spanish took a different approach. They practiced what was called "Direct Rule" whereby all major decisions were made in the mother country, and passed down to the colonies. These nations developed standardized policies that they then tried to impose

After several months of training the African recruits were shaped into a disciplined and effective fighting force. Here, a Ugandan unit of the KAR marches at a ceremony.

A British recruiting poster of mid-1939 for the Royal Tank Regiment of the Territorial Army.

throughout their respective colonies, regardless of local conditions. This, naturally, caused problems in some areas which were addressed as they appeared.

The French had a unique situation. The political scene in France was very fluid and governments changed with an alarming regularity. If a conservative government was in power in Paris the tendency was to hold the line against change and enforce the existing policies. If a liberal government was in power, it tended to give in to change. And, because of the unsettled nature of French politics, especially during the 1930s when the French governments changed on average of three times a year, colonial edict from Paris see-sawed back and forth. Because of the more stable and enlightened policies of the British it was not uncommon for blacks to migrate from French colonies to British colonies where conditions were often better for them.

In the Belgian, Portuguese, and Spanish colonies, the norm was to continually hold the line against change. The thinking in these countries was, as it had been from the beginning of the colonial period, that colonies existed for the benefit of the mother country and the gulf between the citizens of the mother county and their colonial subjects was unbridgeable and was not likely to change.

Racial segregation was practiced in all colonies with the Europeans always at the top, non-black-non-Europeans and people of mixed race sometimes in the middle and sometimes not, and the blacks always at the bottom. There were ways for individuals to work their way up in economic, military and political circles, but the social gulfs between whites, browns, and blacks was rigid and considered—by the whites—to be permanent.

Collective punishment of the natives had been practiced by all the colonial powers from the beginning of the colonial period. It usually consisted of confiscating land or stock, burning dwellings, or some combination thereof. This did not change in the 1930s although it was less frequent.

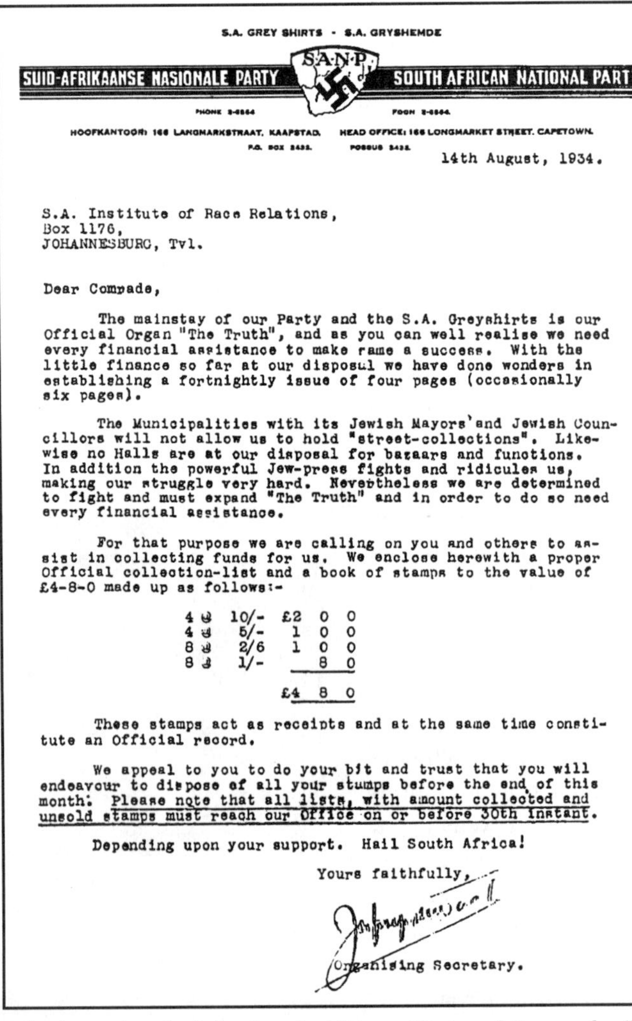

S.A. GREY SHIRTS - S.A. GRYSHEMDE

SUID-AFRIKAANSE NASIONALE PARTY — S.A.N.P. — SOUTH AFRICAN NATIONAL PARTY

HOOFKANTOOR: 166 LANGMARKSTRAAT, KAAPSTAD. HEAD OFFICE: 166 LONGMARKET STREET, CAPETOWN.

14th August, 1934.

S.A. Institute of Race Relations,
Box 1176,
JOHANNESBURG, Tvl.

Dear Comrade,

The mainstay of our Party and the S.A. Greyshirts is our Official Organ "The Truth", and as you can well realise we need every financial assistance to make same a success. With the little finance so far at our disposal we have done wonders in establishing a fortnightly issue of four pages (occasionally six pages).

The Municipalities with its Jewish Mayors and Jewish Councillors will not allow us to hold "street-collections". Likewise no Halls are at our disposal for bazaars and functions. In addition the powerful Jew-press fights and ridicules us, making our struggle very hard. Nevertheless we are determined to fight and must expand "The Truth" and in order to do so need every financial assistance.

For that purpose we are calling on you and others to assist in collecting funds for us. We enclose herewith a proper Official collection-list and a book of stamps to the value of £4-8-0 made up as follows:-

4 @ 10/- £2 0 0
4 @ 5/- 1 0 0
8 @ 2/6 1 0 0
8 @ 1/- 8 0
£4 8 0

These stamps act as receipts and at the same time constitute an Official record.

We appeal to you to do your bit and trust that you will endeavour to dispose of all your stamps before the end of this month. Please note that all lists, with amount collected and unsold stamps must reach our Office on or before 30th instant.

Depending upon your support. Hail South Africa!

Yours faithfully,

Organising Secretary.

The letter head of the South African National Party, the "Grey Shirts'" political arm, boldly displays the swastika. Notice at the bottom of the letter their salute, "Hail South Africa" is displayed. The "Grey Shirts" continued using the swastika into the postwar years even after Nazi Germany had been defeated.

The colonial powers also used the colonies to punish or banish their own. It was not uncommon for out-of-favor politicians and military men who got into trouble at home to be assigned to the colonies. Then too, in some countries, ordinary criminals convicted of crimes were offered a choice of jail or Africa.

BRITISH COLONIAL RULE IN THE LATE 1930s

In the late 1930s, the British continued to tinker with, and adjust, their colonial policies.

The cost of maintaining colonies was always an issue for the British, and there were on-going discussions on this in both Parliament and the colonial offices. The cost factor, coupled with the foreign policy of appeasement then being followed by the London government, gave rise to open discussion, in the late 1930s, on the possibility of returning to Germany those colonies mandated to Britain by the League of Nations following World War I, in order to save money and reduce Britain's colonial commitments. However, this was a political bombshell. There was strong opposition to this among the British general public, especially with Hitler on the rise in Germany. It was well remembered that, during World War I, the British paid a high price to protect their own colonies in Africa, and conquer those of the Germans, and they did not want it to happen again. British military leaders, too, warned against the prospect of German submarine and air bases appearing on the coasts of the South Atlantic and Indian Oceans. The general consensus in Britain was that it was best to keep the Germans out of Africa, even if it cost a lot of money to do so.

With the problems of Africa always in the background, the question of national and colonial defense had to be addressed as world tensions mounted in the late 1930s. The British government was, at this time, steadily increasing the strength of the British armed forces and, during March 1939, announced that the British Territorial Army would be increased from twelve to twenty-six divisions.

There had always been the understanding that the colonies should do whatever they could to defend themselves. This was true more than ever in the late 1930s, and on-going programs were improved and expanded to acquire and train native troops to serve in local defense units, under British officers. Every British colony had a substantial native police force and some sort of a para-military unit trained for both police work and defense. In East Africa there was the sizeable "King's African Rifles" (KAR), in West Africa the 8,000-man "Royal West African Frontier Force," in British Somaliland the small but mobile "Somaliland Camel Corps," in Northern Rhodesia the "Northern Rhodesian Regiment," and in The Sudan the 5,000-man "Sudan Defence Force."

There were also training facilities and plans in place to quickly build up a native "army" if and when the need arose.

The "Wapiti," the first plane built in South Africa.

The primary defense of the colonies, though, was as always, dependent on the huge British Navy which could, in almost any scenario, control the seacoast and major waterways of any colony and deposit Royal Marines or British soldiers at any trouble spot on relatively short notice.

The British colonies, of course, were expected to help the mother country if they were able to do so. This was the case in 1937, when Nigeria, one of the Empire's most prosperous colonies, was able to contribute 75,000 pounds to Britain's re-armament program.

To help the over-all economic situation within their empire, the British government made adjustments and improvements whenever they were deemed necessary or cost-effective. A major move in this direction was the creation, in 1937, of the "Colonial Empire Marketing Board," whose mission was to assist the colonies in finding markets for their exports. This effort was welcomed in the colonies.

There had always been some degree of native unrest in the colonies and the late 1930s were no different. During these years, there were miners' strikes in the copper mines of Northern Rhodesia, labor unrest in the cocoa industry in Gold Coast, and peasant farmers protesting in Nigeria. Most of the issues were Depression-related, and concerned economic matters and/or working conditions. There was virtually no unrest caused by political issues or the question of colonial independence—and the British wanted to keep it that way. To this end the British discouraged blacks from going abroad for higher education, fearing that they might return as nationalistic-minded troublemakers. The British satisfied the natural instinct to seek higher education by providing several colleges for natives at various places in Africa. There was Gordon College at Khartoum, Sudan, Achimota College in the Gold Coast, and Makerere College in Kenya. Britain was the only colonial power to provide higher education for its colonial subjects.

All in all, the British genuinely felt that their native populations were better off under their rule than under the rule of any other colonial power.

On the matter of independence, it was a foregone conclusion that certain colonies were on the irreversible path to independence. This had been addressed years earlier with the creation of the British Commonwealth, under which Britain and those colonial entities that had reached independence could continue to act as a political and economic bloc for the good of its members. Colonies that had reached independence were called Dominions and those close to independence were labelled Crown Colonies. Membership in the Commonwealth was voluntary. In Africa, two countries had gained full independence from Britain, The Union of South Africa and Egypt. South Africa chose to participate in the Commonwealth but Egypt did not. Egypt, though, did maintain strong ties with Britain through individual treaties and agreements.

Other British colonial entities in Africa on the road to independence, or in some cases autonomy, were the former German colonies mandated to Britain's control by the League of Nations after World War I. Guiding a mandated territory toward independence or autonomy was a requirement set forth by the League, but there were no time limits. That was a matter to be considered in each individual case.

As for the remainder of the British colonies, their futures were generally undetermined. For the colonies where blacks would ultimately rule, the thinking in London was that it would take at least three generations before independence for these areas could even be considered.

THE PRINCE OF WALES AND BLACKS

It was not publicly acknowledged, but it was common knowledge in Britain that the future King of England, Edward, Prince of Wales, was very prejudiced against blacks. His biographer, Philip Ziegler, wrote of him: "He believed that the black man was inevitably inferior to the white and was wholly unfitted to govern. He was ill at ease with them socially and...found any sort of physical contact repulsive. In this attitude he was abetted by his (future) wife."

THE UNION OF SOUTH AFRICA

The Union of South Africa, commonly referred to as South Africa, was a unique part of British Africa in that it was a Dominion within the British Commonwealth and therefore independent in every way except for its ties to Britain, all of which were voluntary. South Africa was a productive land. It was economically self-sufficient, and enjoyed a very healthy export business in food, hides, wool, and minerals. This included gold, of which South Africa was the world's largest producer in the late 1930s. The country had 13,213 miles of railroad, the most in sub-Saharan Africa; a system of well-maintained paved highways, and a secondary highway system of gravel and dirt roads, some of which were impassable at certain times of the year. Rural electrification was steadily spreading, and the country had a good phone system. Two airlines connected South Africa with the rest of the world, Imperial Airways and South African Airways.

South Africa had two capitals; Pretoria, the seat of the administrative branch of the government, and Cape Town, the seat of the legislature.

In 1939, South Africa was a nation of 10.1 million people, of which 7 million were natives, 815,000 of mixed race called "colored," 231,000 Asians and 2.1 million Europeans. Of the 2.1 million Europeans, 39% were English-speakers, mostly the descendants of early British settlers, and 56% spoke a dialect of Dutch called Afrikaans. These people were called Afrikaners and were the descendants of early Dutch (Boer) settlers.

The white Europeans had, from the earliest days of settlement, ruled the country politically and shut out all of the non-whites. But the white community was divided, mainly as the result of the bitter Second Boer War (1899-1902), during which the British conquered the independent Boer nations known as the Orange Free State and the South African Republic (also called the Transvaal). By 1910, though, the healing process had progressed to the point where the Boer states and British provinces were united, given independence and dominion status within the British Commonwealth and named the Union of South Africa. The new nation was also proclaimed bi-lingual. The Afrikaners, however, were divided. A sizeable minority of Afrikaners harbored ongoing resentment against the English-speakers and, at the same time, usually professed far right political views which included strict segregation of the races.

An equally sizeable minority of Afrikaners openly and aggressively pursued a policy of cooperation with the English-speakers, arguing that the two peoples must learn to live together in peace, and that the Afrikaners, because of their greater numbers and higher birth rate, could eventually come to rule in the country by peaceful means. In between were the remainder of Afrikaner society which swung one way or the other politically, depending on issues and events.

Economically, most of the Afrikaners remained close to the land and were, fundamentally, a community of farmers, shop owners, and small town business people. The economic elite of South Africa was, almost exclusively, English-speakers.

By the late 1930s, these divisions still existed and the political scene in South Africa had become dominated by two political parties. The United Party, which was currently in power, was led by General B. M. Hertzog, an English-speaker with conservative views and General Jan Christian Smuts, an

Afrikaner and former officer in the Boer Army, with strong conciliatory views toward the English-speakers.

The National Party, the opposition party, was the home of the unreconciled Afrikaners, as well as many of the non-committed. Its leader was the Reverend Dr. Daniel F. Malan, an Afrikaner with far-right political views. There were several smaller political parties which, at times, could tip the balance of power by forming a coalition government with one or the other of the major parties.

However, all the European factions, the English-speakers included, agreed on one thing. That was that the white man should rule and that there should be well-defined lines of segregation between the races. The word "apartheid," which was to become so prevalent in the politics of South Africa during the latter part of the 20th Century, was not in use at this time in South Africa, but the fundamentals for it were in place.

The political left in the white community was very small and the extreme left, including the Communists, were almost non-existent. Communism, though, had made some inroads into the black community.

THE ANC

The African National Congress (ANC), which was to become very powerful in the latter part of the 20th century and eventually change South Africa into a multi-racial nation, existed during this time but was very weak. It had been founded in 1912 and was traditionally led by black leaders educated in mission schools. Two of its first five leaders were black clergymen, giving it a Christian image. The ANC worked for reform within the South African system, and rejected Socialism and Communism. However, the white community was never that certain about this claim, especially in 1927, when an admitted Communist, James Gumede, was elected its president. In the early 1930s the ANC declined rapidly in membership and began to lose its religious base because by this time the South African black community was greatly divided over religion. Hundreds of separate black Christian churches and cults had sprung up and these religious differences reflected adversely in the leadership and membership of the ANC. Membership in the ANC dropped to the point where the organization could no longer afford to hold an annual convention. By 1936, the ANC's leaders began to disassociate the organization from religious matter and it began to revive, albeit slowly. The ANC continued to grow during the early war years but was not a strong or disruptive force. In the latter 1940s, though, the ANC would grow rapidly and eventually become a major political force in South Africa.

These factors combined to make the everyday politics of South Africa permanently right of center. In this atmosphere, it is not surprising that during the 1930s, Fascism found fertile ground. Several Fascist-like organizations evolved among the Afrikaners.

In 1932, before Hitler came to power in Germany, Hermann Bohle, an engineering professor at the University of Cape Town, founded the "National Socialist (Nazi) Party of South Africa." He had excellent connections in Germany. His son, Ernest Bohle, was head of the Ausslandsorgainsation (AO), a department of the German government that kept in touch with Germans living overseas. Ernest Bohle grew up in South Africa, but migrated to Germany when he was sixteen and became involved in Nazi politics. The AO attempted to compile personal dossiers on every German citizen living overseas and in South Africa that information was dutifully provided by Hermann Bohle. Hermann Bohle also had solid contacts with the German embassy in Pretoria, and was thus able to contact every newly-arrived German and give them his sales pitch with regards to his political party. Not surprisingly, he reported back to the German embassy on those who harbored anti-Nazi sympathies. This was passed on to Germany, and some of the relatives of the German immigrants were punished for the behavior of those in South Africa. Bohle's party, though, remained small, but did manage to establish branches in most of the big cities. It also published a pro-Nazi newspaper called "Der Deutsch-Afrikaner" (The German-Afrikaner). The paper got many articles and photos from Germany, and German firms doing business in South Africa were pressured to advertise in the paper.

The AO worked closely with the "Deutsch Arbeitsfront"

THE COMMUNIST'S PROPOSAL FOR SOUTH AFRICA

At the 6th Congress of the Communist Internationale in Moscow in 1928, a resolution was passed calling for South Africa to be divided into several black republics with each republic given majority rule. The South African black community, though, was too poorly organized to help itself even with whatever external aid might be forthcoming from the communists. Knowing this, the Communists further suggested that educated black Americans be sent to South Africa to help train and organize the South African blacks. This suggestion was widely known in South Africa and, from that point on, any black American entering South Africa, for any reason whatsoever, was closely watched by the police.

(German Labor Front-DAF) which was based in Germany but had branches in South Africa. The DAF was less political than the AO, and had a traditional labor-oriented program calling for workers' rights and cooperation with management. The DAF also offered its members unemployment compensation and illness and death benefits. German-South Africans who had little interest in politics and did not want to join one of the other right wing political organizations were urged to join this organization.

And there was still more influence in South Africa coming directly from Germany. The "Deutsch Akademie" in Munich, actively promoted and organized visitor exchanges between Germany and South Africa. Another German organization, the "Goethe Institute," provided classes on German culture in Pretoria and Kingwilliamstown. An Afrikaner organization, the "Kultuurraad," based in the Orange Free State, promoted Germanic culture and sent students to study in Germany.

Several months after Hitler's assumption of power in Germany in 1933, an organization called the "South African Gentile National-Socialist Movement" evolved. Its leader was a German South African hairdresser named Louis Weichardt. The members wore Nazi Party style uniforms with grey shirts, and were generally referred to as "The Grey Shirts." They used the Nazi-style salute, held Nazi-style rallies and parades, and defiled Jewish homes and businesses. They also formed a political party, the "South African National Party" (not to be confused with the mainstream National Party) which was ineffectual at the polls.

There soon followed a rival and more radical organization, the "Black Shirts." They evolved in The Orange Free State under one Mannie Wessels. The "Black Shirts" called themselves "Storm Troopers," but were plagued by low membership and internal squabbling. The "Black Shirts" remained a minor force on the South African political scene. Both "shirt" organizations, though, received secret funds from Germany, and the German press chronicled their activities.

The "Grey Shirts" and "Black Shirts" were, actually, the second and third "shirts" organization in South Africa. In 1934, the National Party, the country's main opposition party, created the first of the "shirt" organization, by creating a youth movement patterned somewhat after the Hitler Youth in Germany. These were the "Orange Shirts." This movement floundered, though and was never a serious political factor.

German-South African youths were targets in yet another way. There were a number of German language schools throughout South Africa which were infiltrated by local pro-Nazi sympathizers. These people were able to adjust the schools' curriculum to be more pro-German and pro-Nazi. "Reading Circles" were established to study Nazi-approved publications, and a more elite organization, the "Lehrerbund" came into being to train certain young persons in Nazi ideology and practices.

These fascist-like organizations all used some Nazi trappings and some of them printed newspapers. By the late 1930s, the swastika and pro-Nazi, anti-Semitic publications were common sights to the citizens of South Africa, as were German newspapers and periodicals.

There then arose yet another neo-Fascist, pro-Afrikaner organization called the "Afrikaner Cultural Union." This organization was mainly cultural, but with pro-Afrikaner political overtones.

In 1938, still another Fascist-like organization emerged within the Afrikaner community as a result of the 100th year enactment of the famous Boer trek into the wilderness of 1838. An organization replicating the wagon guards on the trek, the "Ossewabrandwag" (Ox-wagon Sentinels or OB), came in to being as part of the pageantry of the celebration. Its members found a common identity and continued on after the celebration ended as a far right wing political organization under the leadership of Oswald Pirow, a pro-Nazi Afrikaner.

The OB grew rapidly and became the dominant, and most dangerous, Fascist organization in South Africa during the war. It took on Nazi trappings, organized secret commando and other paramilitary units, and developed a political platform calling for a totalitarian, sovereign, and ethnic Afrikaner state.

COMMANDO

The word "Commando" was first used in the Boer War (1899-1902) in South Africa to describe soldiers specially trained in hit and run attacks. British Prime Minister Winston Churchill suggested that it be used again during World War II to describe soldiers trained for the same purposes.

The OB was openly anti-British, anti-Communist, anti-Semitic and had strong connections to the Dutch Reform Church. Several leaders of that Church came out in support of the OB, and even preached from the pulpit that Afrikaners were both racially superior to all other peoples, and were the protectors of the only true religion. The slogan of the OB was "One People, One Country, One Tongue."

Soon, riots, assassinations and other mayhem were being carried out by the OB. These activities, though, were to bring about its own weakening. A sizeable number of OB members saw the organization as becoming too militant, and the leadership became divided. The leadership, though, was able to keep the organization whole, but had to tone down its militant activities. The OB's antics also spread a cloud over the National Party of which many of the OB were members. In the national elections of 1938 the voters showed their disgust for the OB and returned the United Party to power with 73% of the vote—the largest majority in South African history.

Hitler inadvertently helped the United Party election prospects when, in March 1938, just before the South African elections, he made repeated demands for the return of South West Africa, Germany's former colony which had been mandated to South Africa by the League of Nations. Their continued control of South West Africa was one issue that united all South Africans, and made it even easier for the electorate to vote against the National Party which was perceived as being friendly toward Germany.

In November 1938, Oswald Pirow, who was both the leader of the OB and the Defence Minister in the Hertzog government, went to Germany and met with Hitler. In their discussion, Hitler suggested that Europe's Jews might be moved onto reservations somewhere in southern Africa. Pirow was bitterly opposed to this and returned home disappointed with Hitler in this respect.

Despite the neo-Nazi behavior of their most radical elements, and a natural feeling of Germanic kinship, the Afrikaners, as a whole, did not want to see South Africa become a vassal state of Germany, nor even a German ally. Their goal was Afrikaner independence. It was very much like the Dutch/German relationship in Europe where the Dutch wanted to remain totally independent of the Germans. This strong feeling of Afrikaner independence had shown itself during World War I when many Afrikaners volunteered for service in the South African Army and fought in Europe and elsewhere against Germany and Germany's allies. By the late 1930s, that feeling of independence had not changed, and there were still many Afrikaners in the South African Army ready and willing to fight Germany, or anybody else, who threatened South Africa's interests.

When South Africa gained its independence, a permanent South African Army, Navy and Air Force was established as well and a permanent "Council of Defence" in the government and a military college. In the late 1930s, the leaders of South Africa, like those in Europe, could see the possibility of a coming war and took steps to improve their defenses. One hundred modern warplanes were ordered from Britain and in 1937, a five-year program was begun to train up to 1,000 pilots for the South African Air Force (SAAF). The SAAF had two bases, one at Roberts Heights near Pretoria and one at Cape Town. Air Force reservists were trained at the Roberts Heights base.

In 1938, South Africa began to build its own aircraft. The first plane produced was the "Wapiti," a multi-purpose biwing pursuit plane.

Later the South African aircraft industry produced a version of the Avro "Tutor," a trainer, and the Hawker "Hartebeest," a light bomber. During these early years the South Africans made the airframes only and imported the engines.

Blacks and coloreds (the term used at the time in South Africa for people of mixed race) were recruited for service in the South African armed forces for use as service personnel, but were not allowed to carry arms.

Near Pretoria, a huge munitions plant was constructed to insure that South Africa would be self-sufficient in that important military need. South Africa was fortunate enough to have sizeable deposits of iron ore and coal which, over the years, had spawned a small steel industry. Furthermore, there were additional deposits of iron ore and coal in adjacent Southern Rhodesia and further north in Northern Rhodesia.

The country had a military draft system for white males between the ages of seventeen and twenty-five. Each year 50% of those eligible were called up for military training. Men who completed their training were automatically enrolled in a reserve organization called the "Citizens Force Reserve."

South Africa's Navy was small and suited for defensive purposes only. It had a naval station and dry dock facilities at Simon's Town and an active naval reserve.

As for international trade, South Africa was the only economic powerhouse in southern Africa, and as such, traded with all the major countries of the world, including Germany. By the late 1930s, South African business interests had made deep inroads into all of the neighboring territories including the Portuguese colony of Mozambique, which had become an economic satellite of South Africa.

In South West Africa, though, there existed an area of conflict with Germany. Hitler wanted this former German colony back and was quite vocal about it. The South Africans had no intention of giving up their mandate on the colony, so a political stalemate developed that was a permanent strain on the relations between South Africa and Germany.

One South African leader that thought South West Africa should be returned to Germany under a German mandate was Oswald Pirow, leader of the OB. His stance only complicated the German/South African relationship because, being a government minister, his position was opposite that of his government. Several years later, though, Pirow changed his mind and stated that Germany's colonial claims should be satisfied elsewhere.

Despite the problem concerning South West Africa, Germany was one of South Africa's biggest trading partners. German cars and other consumer goods were popular, and the South African government had no qualms about buying German military hardware. In the late 1930s the SAAF purchased a number of bombers from Germany. At that time 14% of South Africa's trade was with Germany, and, in 1936, the Germans named one of their merchant ships, the "Pretoria," in honor of South Africa.

During these years the South Africans had no great fear of German aggression and, at times, displayed isolationist tendencies. Many South Africans believed that if war erupted in Europe between Germany and Britain, South Africa should remain neutral. This attitude was formalized in 1938, when Prime Minister Hertzog put the question to his cabinet. The cabinet agreed with the public sentiment of the day and voted that South Africa should remain neutral in such a war. This cabinet vote was to have a profound influence on Hertzog's political career one year later.

Both Germany and South Africa, in the late 1930s, shared another common bond—laws against minorities, including Jews. From the earliest days of settlement in South Africa, there had been laws regulating the blacks and, in the years before World War I, laws evolved to stop the influx of East Indians and Chinese. In the 1920s, these laws were extended to limit the influx of Jews from countries other than the British Commonwealth. For a variety of reasons, relatively large numbers of Eastern European Jews, especially Lithuanian Jews, had already migrated to South Africa in the early years of the twentieth century. These people were unwelcome because of their foreign and clannish ways and, after the Bolshevik Revolution of 1917, for their alleged sympathies for Communism. They also had arrived desperately poor and took jobs at lower wages from white residents. The image of Jews was tarnished again in 1922, when it was revealed that several Jews had served as the leaders of the black miners in the "Rand Revolt," an unsuccessful attempt by white miners to stave off replacement by lower-paid black miners.

During the 1920s and 30s, the hate book "Protocols of the Elders of Zion," which purported to expose a Jewish plot to take over the world by economic means, circulated widely in South Africa. The book was generally regarded as a forgery but, everywhere the book circulated, there were those who believed it.

South African Jews, which amounted to only 4% of the white population, supported the United Party at the polls time and again and liked General Jan Christian Smuts personally because he was a friend of Chaim Weizmann, the famous Zionist leader. From the viewpoint of the conservative Afrikaners, though, the support of Zionism was seen, like elsewhere around the world, as a show of lack of loyalty to the home country. Many Afrikaners, rightly or wrongly, further accused the South African Jewish population of being influence by their orthodox Litvak (Lithuanian) tradition which was self-serving, and another example of Jewish loyalty to a foreign interest.

In 1930, while a National Party government was in power, a quota act was passed with bi-partisan support limiting immigration from the nations of eastern Europe to 50 people per year. This was aimed at the Jews. The dividing line in central Europe was the Polish/German border. Polish, Lithuanian, and other eastern Jews were covered by the quota system but German Jews were not. Suddenly, in 1936, the question of Jewish immigration came charging to the fore. With Germany actively expelling Jews, some of them migrated to South Africa and their numbers alarmed the political right and anti-Semites. In 1932, five German Jews had immigrated to South Africa. In 1936, that number surged to 2,579 out of a total immigration from Germany of 3,344. This brought the Jewish population in South Africa to about 95,000 out of a population of some 2 million whites.

During that year an ugly incident occurred at Cape Town when the chartered ship "Stuttgart" arrived with 537 German Jews seeking to immigrate. The "Grey Shirts" led a mob which tried, unsuccessfully, to prevent the Jews from disembarking. This brought the Jewish immigration question to the fore, and pressures from the political right, as well as from within the United Party, mounted on Hertzog to act to stem the immigration. The result was the passage of the "Aliens Act" of 1937, which empowered the Immigration Selection Board to accept or reject immigrants on the basis of "assimilability." This had the desired effect of greatly reducing Jewish immigration. By the end of 1937, the number of immigrating Jews had dropped to 954, and by 1940 the number was 218.

Certain members of Dr. Malan's National Party wanted still stronger controls. In Parliament, they introduced amendments to restrict even further the immigration of Jews. Ironically, at this time, a grass-root boycott of German goods had begun in South Africa because of the Nazi excesses in Europe. The Nationalists used the boycott to their advantage claiming that the Jews had instigated it and that it was hurting the South African economy. This ploy, and the mountain of anti-Semitic propaganda produced by the nation's political right, failed to influence Parliament, and none of the amendments passed. In Germany, Hitler personally praised Dr. Malan for his efforts. German Jews continued to come to South Africa, but in reduced numbers.

"HOGGENHEIMER"

Beginning around 1930, the Afrikaner press, and to a lesser degree, the English-speaking press, began using a cartoon character named "Hoggenheimer" to represent the South African Jew. He was a fat, ludicrous, cigar-smoking, money-hungary Jewish capitalist who displayed no patriotism or loyalty toward South Africa. Hoggenheimer became a popular character in newspapers, magazines and posters.

In 1938, the National Party, still pursuing its anti-Jewish stance, sent a delegation to Germany to study Germany's "achievements," as they called them, on managing the Jewish question there. This did not result in any changes in South Africa's Jewish policies, but was simply another example of anti-Semitic activity by the political right.

In 1939, the right-wingers scored a success on the race issue when legislation was passed to further restrict the immigration of East Indians and Asians.

The Jewish issue in South Africa did not go away. It was still a hotly debated subject when World War II erupted.

As for South Africa's blacks, the late 1930s brought some changes. Most South Africans considered them improvements, others did not. In 1937 the "Native Representation Act" was passed creating the "Native Representative Council" which was given the authority to advise the national Parliament on matters concerning black affairs. The Council had no vote in Parliament, but now, at least, it had a voice. The Council met for the first time in December 1937.

Blacks could not vote in national elections, but there were local elections held concerning native affairs, and blacks did vote there. Those who voted, though, had a pay a poll tax of one pound.

Primary and secondary education for the blacks in South Africa was still mostly in the hands of the missionaries, but a college for non-whites was established at Fort Har.

There were on-going talks between Britain and South Africa to transfer the control of several adjoining areas from British control to South African control. These included the colonies of Basutoland, Bechuanaland, and Swaziland, all of which had substantial black populations and very small white populations. The blacks generally opposed the transfer because British rule was less repressive than South African rule. This issue was too complicated to be resolved quickly and lingered throughout the war.

EGYPT A PROBLEM FOR THE BRITISH

With the war in Ethiopia concluded, and the threat of an Italian attack on Egypt greatly diminished, many Egyptian politicians began, in 1937, to call upon Britain to terminate the 1936 military treaty that permitted the British virtually unlimited military activity in Egypt. However, the British refused, citing that the treaty was for twenty years duration and that the mounting crises with Germany and Italy still posed a threat to Egypt.

In December 1937, young King Farouk found an excuse to dismiss the Wafdist government of Mustafa al-Nahas, which had signed the treaty, and call for new elections. The British objected to this, but Farouk's hand was strengthened by the fact that the Wafdists had lost much of their popular support, and the King had the constitutional power to dismiss governments, for just cause, as he saw fit.

The national elections held during April 1938 were rigged by King Farouk's supporters, and a little-known politician from a minor party, Muhammad Mahmud, became Prime Minister. The British questioned the honesty of the election but took no action. The King was wise enough, though, in his appointment of Mahmud to pick a man who was Oxford-educated and pro-British in many ways while, at the same time, completely loyal to Farouk. The main benefit to the King and his cohorts was that the Wafdists were now out of office and punished, and the new prime minister was beholden to the King for his office. The King won yet another political skirmish in that the Wafdists now turned on the British, criticizing them for acquiescing to the formation of a weak government. The Wafdists attack on the British was also motivated by the fact that they needed to redeem themselves in the eyes of the Egyptian people to dispel the image of them as British puppets.

Mahmud remained in office until August 12, 1939, when he resigned for health reasons. Just by circumstance this was a very critical time in Europe. The beginning of World War II was only weeks away. To replace Mahmud, the King appointed one of his trusted advisors, Ali Maher, as Prime Minister. Maher was, like Mahmud, loyal to the King but much less pro-British. The British, facing a crisis of monumental proportions in Europe, where Germany was on the verge of invading Poland, did nothing in Cairo. This proved to be a mistake. When World War II started the British had a government in Cairo headed by a man they hardly knew, who was politically weak, and in no way loyal to them.

FRENCH COLONIAL RULE IN THE LATE 1930s

French colonial rule in the late 1930s was, as it had always been, standardized and from the top down. France's colonial policies had not changed significantly since 1919. At the top was the government's colonial office in Paris and at the bottom were the tribal chiefs and other natural leaders among the natives. In between was a large bureaucracy that had considerable authority of its own over colonial matters, but was in a near-continual state of flux due to the unstable political atmosphere in France and the frequent change of governments. On the plus side of the ledger, the French government had established a school for colonial administrators, the "Ecole Colonial," soon after the end of World War I, and was able, over the years, to turn out well-educated professional colonial administrators. These individuals were usually dedicated public servants who, because of their common training, tended to bring standardization and stabilization to the empire, despite the flow of ever-changing directives from Paris.

Africans had a say in French politics in that native representatives were allowed to serve in the French Assembly in Paris. On occasion Africans also served in the Premier's cabinet.

World War I poster praising the courage and skills of colonial troops.

One of the major changes occurring in the French Empire in the late 1930s came in June 1936, when a very liberal government, known as the "Popular Front," came to power in Paris and legalized trade unions for colonial subjects. This was a great economic and political leap forward for the native populations. Unions sprang up quickly, and so did strikes and other labor problems. Colonial officials and subsequent conservative governments in Paris tried to modify and contain the new unions with varying degrees of success. When France went to war in September 1939, the muddled labor situation throughout the French Empire was a weak link in the French war effort.

Of all the colonial powers, France had the largest Moslem population because of their control of French Morocco, Algeria, and Tunisia in North Africa. In sub-Saharan Africa there were sizeable Moslem communities in French West Africa and particularly in Senegal. There they were organized into an ethnic faction called the "Mouride." This was a group of some 100,000 members who pursued primarily economic interests and, by the late 1930s, had managed to gain control of about one-third of Senegal's groundnut production, the country's leading export.

Tariffs on foreign goods in French colonies were among the highest in Africa. This policy had been established in the 1920s to help stimulate colonial businesses and industrial development, and safeguard markets for French goods. As was usual with high tariffs, imported non-French goods in the French colonies were high priced and scarce. The high tariffs were also a deterrent to inter-colonial trade. The French could not impose high tariffs in mandated territories, because the League of Nations had decreed, from the start, that mandated territories must maintain open door trade policies.

Of all the colonial powers in Europe the French were the most racially tolerant. This was reflected in France itself, where the French people displayed a nonchalant attitude toward racial differences, and in Africa, where a man of mixed race, Felix Eboue, had become governor of the colony of Chad. Eboue would play a significant role in the French civil war in Africa in 1940.

As war threatened in the summer of 1939, the French people remembered with gratitude that some 449,000 colonial soldiers had fought for France during World War I, and 187,000 more had served in labor battalions. Actually, Africans had been used in the French armed forces since the mid-1800s.

It was comforting for the French to know that this manpower reserve of over 100 million colonial subjects was still available, because France's potential adversary, Germany, had a population much larger than France and could mobilize more European soldiers than France. The French took comfort, too, in knowing that an abundance of raw materials and food would be available from the empire, whereas Germany would have to rely on its own resources.

To this end, the French government, as early as the 1920s, required colonial subjects in several colonies to perform national service, including military training, for periods of up to three years.

During April of 1938, an experienced and able French politician, Georges Mandel, became Minister of Colonies in Paris. With war clouds mounting in Europe, he secured permission from the government to pursue an aggressive policy to improve the defenses of the French colonies and to prepare the colonies to come to the aid of France herself, as they had done during World War I.

Mandel's first step was to prepare the French people for this effort. In that regard, his ministry initiated a campaign throughout France reminding the French people how important the colonies were to France's security and well-being. A movie entitled "Regards sur l'Empire" was produced, showing the Empire's wealth of workers, soldiers, food, minerals, and other resources.

Meanwhile, Mandel was instrumental in convincing

Japan bombs Pearl Harbor → US Enters War
↳ Germany declares war on U.S.
Italy Controlled - Eritrea + Italian Somaliland
French Somaliland - port Djibouti
Jews to Madagascar (?)
Colonies vs Dominion

Wafd Party (Egypt) - Anti British
Black Shame - Using African troops in European theatre
Appeasment Policy for Italians over Ethiopia
Germany appeasment policy over Rhineland Czecholavikia
↳ Poland breaks appeasment
*Anti-semintism thraughout Europe
Soviet - German Non-Agression agreement
French Surrender
↳ Spilt - Vichy + Free-French
↳ Petain vs de Guella
British vs French
↳ Naval Tensions (bombardment of French ships)
Italy invades Egypt through Libiya
↳ British sucess
↳ German help later (Romell Desert Korps)
Ethiopian Theatre
↳ wins back capital Addis Ababa
↳ Emperor Halie Selassies
Land - Lease Act
Egytian/Libya
↳ Tobruk
↳ Tripoli
↳ El Aghelia
} Romell (wins/loses)
Paris Potocols (not ratified)
German invasion of S.U. (decreases German presure of Africa)
Atlantic Charter

France's military leaders to allow the colonial army to create its own chief of staff with the authority to organize colonial defenses, conscript and train colonial soldiers for service in the French Army, improve roads and seaports and take charge of other matters concerning colonial defense. These developments were begun, and ended a long period of stagnation, during which colonial defenses had been badly neglected. These efforts were well underway when France went to war seventeen months later. When that time came, ten of the French Army's 80 divisions were African; three North African and seven West African.

BELGIAN COLONIAL RULE IN THE LATE 1930s

Belgium had only one colony in Africa, the Belgian Congo, and two mandated territories, the former German colonies of Rwanda and Urundi. The latter were assigned to Belgium after World War I by the League of Nations. The three colonial entities adjoined each other to create a huge, strategically located colonial holding in the heart of sub-Saharan Africa. Rwanda and Urundi were densely populated but the Belgian Congo, which was 78 times the size of Belgium, only had a population about the same as Belgium's.

The Belgian Congo was rich in resources, and produced gold, diamonds, copper, tin, zinc, manganese, rubber (mostly wild), gum copal, cotton, jute substitute, coal, timber, cobalt, and uranium. The last two commodities were found, at least in the late 1930s, in very few places in the world, making the Belgian Congo sources of primary commercial and political importance. Cobalt is a metal absolutely necessary for an industrialized society, because without it certain types of high grade steels and metal working tools could not be made. Smaller amounts of cobalt came from Northern Rhodesia, Canada, French Morocco, and Burma, but together, without the Belgian Congo's output, they could not meet the world's needs. The United States had no domestic source for cobalt, so the U. S. government stockpiled the metal and the Belgian Congo was its primary source.

Uranium, in the late 1930s, was something of a novelty, and a material about which little was known. Most of the world's supply of uranium came from the Shinkolobwe Mine in Upper Katanga, which was owned by a Belgian company called Union Miniere. Uranium ore was shipped to Belgium and refined at a Union Miniere plant near Brussels. Uranium had no major commercial uses in the late 1930s but that would change drastically near the end of the war when it became the principle ingredient in atomic bombs.

The Belgian Congo was a major exporter of food. This included palm oil, palm kernels, coffee, and sugar. In this area of the economy the United States was a major player because of the presence of Lever Brothers Company, an American company, which had huge palm-oil plantations in the colony.

"...THE MOST IMPORTANT SOURCE OF URANIUM IS BELGIAN CONGO."

On August 2, 1939, thirty-one days before World War II began in Europe, Dr. Albert Einstein, the world's most famous scientist, wrote a two-page letter to President Roosevelt telling him of recent discoveries in the field of nuclear physics concerning the element uranium. Einstein wrote that the discoveries indicated that, "in the immediate future... extremely powerful bombs of a new type may thus be constructed." Einstein went on to write, "A single bomb of this type, carried by boat and exploded in a port, might very well destroy the whole port together with some of the surrounding territory."

In his letter, Einstein tells of the availability of uranium and states, "...the most important source of uranium is Belgian Congo."

Roosevelt realized the importance of the letter and carried the project forward. On October 10, 1939, the President replied to Einstein thanking him for bringing this important matter to his attention, and saying that he had set up a committee to study the subject. This, of course, was the beginning of the "Manhattan Project" and America's entry into the atomic age.

Communications within the Belgian Congo were difficult. The main means of transportation between Leopoldville, the colonial capital at the mouth of the Congo River, and Stanleyville, in the northeast, was via river steamer on the Congo River. There was no rail connection between these two cities, and the roads were primitive. Communications with Katanga and Kasai Provinces in the south, where the mines were, was even more difficult. Again there were no railroads and only primitive roads. And, as the upper reaches of the Congo River and its tributaries became shallower and made impassable because of rapids and falls, river steamers could not reach all of these important areas. The main outlet to the world for the people and mineral wealth of the southern provinces of the Belgian Congo was via two railroads. One led south-eastward into British controlled Northern and Southern Rhodesia, and on to seaports on the Indian Ocean in Portuguese-controlled Mozambique. The other led westward to the port of Lobito on the South Atlantic coast of Portuguese Angola.

The administration of the Belgian Congo was, perhaps, the most rigid and non-progressive in Africa. Colonial policy and budgets were controlled from Brussels by the "Conseil Colonial," and native affairs were managed by a permanent government commission established for the protection of the natives. The Belgians looked upon their rich colony as a treasured asset that existed primarily to serve the needs of the mother country. Europeans lived primarily in three parts of the country; Leopoldville, the capital, Elizabethville, the largest city, and the mining areas of Katanga and Kasai Provinces in southern Belgian Congo. Their main reasons for being in the Belgian Congo were administrative or economic. There were no plans in Brussels to make the colony into a future homeland for Belgian settlers, nor to displace the natives for such purposes. For the Belgians, the Belgian Congo was an economic enterprise. As a result, several large Belgian companies controlled the colony's economy and accounted for 40-50% of the colony's tax revenues.

The up-lifting of the native people, some of whom were the most primitive in Africa, was a low priority. This was left mostly to the missionaries. In 1925, the Roman Catholic Church was given a monopoly on native education in the colonies, and the Church did a good job with the resources it had. Some 56% of native children attended grade school, which was a higher percent than in the French colonies to the north. High schools were also available, and there were programs in place to educate natives in the skilled trades and to be civil servants, teachers, journalists, accountants, and medical assistants. Beyond high school, though, there was no higher education in the colony for the natives, and going abroad for higher learning was discouraged by the administration.

THE KIMBANGUISTES

Religious organizations other than the Catholic Church were allowed to send missionaries to the Belgian Congo, and the Jehovah's Witnesses was one group that became active. From their preachings a native religious movement called the Kimbanguistes sprang up in the 1930s which twisted basic Christian doctrine, adopted the apocalyptic vision of the Witnesses, vilified the white man and predicted that on the day of the apocalypse everyone on earth would be killed except for the true believers. The survivors would then turn white and take control of the Congo and live happily ever after under a divinely guided utopian political system.

The religion preached that there was a god with three sons, one black, one white and one Asiatic. The latter two sons committed terrible atrocities against the black son, which was the source of the present-day misery of the black man. All would be made right for the black man on the day of the apocalypse, but in the meantime, blacks were instructed to break off all contact with white and Asian men, and not obey their rules. This brought into play civil disobedience, and the acceptance of martyrdom. The colonial authorities blamed the Jehovah's Witnesses for the rise of the Kimbanguistes, and expelled them from the colony. But the damage was done. The Kimbanguistes became very strong in the Stanleyville area of northeastern Belgian Congo. Persistent repressions by the colonial government backfired because it showed the evil ways of the white man, and only served to bring to the faith more adherents.

The Kimbanguistes movement survived World War II and went on into the post war years to become an important factor in the independence movement in the Belgian Congo.

In the 1930s, a native religious sect called the Kimbanguistes sprang up in the eastern Belgian Congo. It became very racist against whites, and had bizarre beliefs about a coming apocalypse. The colonial authorities tried to stamp it out, but were unsuccessful. The Kimbanguistes also sought to control their own political future, which further brought the sect into conflict with the authorities. At one point, in 1939, the sect's leader and prophet, Simon Mpadi, sent word, through German contacts, to Hitler, asking him to send the mighty German Army to the Belgian Congo to liberate his followers. Hitler did not respond.

As World War II approached, the Kimbanguistes movement continued to thrive but was, for the most part, peaceful. Their presence, though, constituted the closest thing to an active nationalist movement that existed in the Belgian Congo.

Most Belgian authorities believed it would be at least 100 years before the people of the Congo would be anywhere near being able to govern themselves, and the administration's policies indicated that they would prolong it even longer if they could.

In most parts of the Belgian Congo the natives were virtually ignored by the colonial administrators, and left to their own resources so long as they caused no problems. There were some 6,100 tribes or tribal remnants in the Belgian Congo, and up to 1917, anarchy reigned in many places. The Belgians stepped in, defined territorial boundaries, found cooperative chiefs, purged non-cooperative chiefs, and combined some tribes for administrative purposes. The Belgians divided the colony into 550 "sectors," each with its own appointed and salaried "chief," who was paid by a formula which depended on how efficiently he ran his sector. Each chief had a council and a court system. Those members, and all other positions where Africans served, were appointed by the Colonial government. There were no elections at the native level. This system worked well, and the Belgians were able to maintain law and order with a relatively small police force.

The colony had a small native army called the "Force Publique." It consisted of 15,000 askaris and Belgian officers (mostly Flemish) and was used mainly for internal peacekeeping. Askari recruits were required to make a complete break with their tribes and swear loyalty to the Force. They were well treated and well paid by African standards. Service in the Force was a prestigious occupation by native standards.

In 1937, there were discussions in Brussels about creating an air force in the Belgian Congo, but this did not materialize.

In the mining areas, the natives were treated very differently than in the rest of the Belgian Congo, but still in a paternalistic manner. The mine owners wanted to keep their workers, so native workers were offered three-year contracts, fair wages, housing, generous rations, medical services, eight to nine hour workdays with four days off per month. They were encouraged to bring their families during their length of service. During the Depression, when production at the mines declined dramatically, the mine owners, with the cooperation of colonial administrators, took steps to keep from laying off their workers. Hours were shortened and miners were kept on the payroll even when their labor was not needed. This lasted only so long, and eventually large numbers of miners had to be laid off. During the mid-1930s, the miners fell on hard times. By the late 1930s, though, the worst of the bad times had passed and many miners were called back to work because production in the mines began to increase.

One of the programs undertaken by the colonial government during the Depression was, in 1933, the instigation of a program of compulsory national service. This was a program to keep laid-off miners, plantation workers, and impoverished farmers partially employed—and out of the big cities or from wandering aimlessly around the colony looking for work. The program called for sixty days service per year by every able-bodied male for such things as the building of roads, bridges, public buildings, and planting and harvesting cash crops. Sometimes the natives were paid and sometimes not. Many natives still lived outside the economy and transacted their local affairs by barter. This program was not popular with the natives. They saw it as a failure of the white man's economy, and brought into question the whole concept of the white man's role in Africa. The program, nevertheless, was kept in place by the administration, even as economic conditions improved, because its effect was good for the colony. During the war, it was expanded to meet the pressing needs of a wartime economy.

This program of mandatory public service did not, as in the French colonies, include military training. Neither were natives recruited for service in the Belgian Army in Europe, not even as laborers. The Belgians believed that the less the natives knew about firearms and military matters, the better. Actually, natives were forbidden by law to own firearms. They also had to have permits to travel, and could not drink alcoholic beverages stronger than beer.

In the Rwanda and Urundi mandates, the Belgians showed more concern for the natives. This was because the League was looking over their shoulder and, like every mandate-holder, had to report annually to the League on conditions in their mandated territories. The Belgians did not attempt to economically exploit Rwanda and Urundi. Most of their efforts there were directed toward preserving the native cultures, providing a minimal amount of welfare services, and keeping the peace. Native laborers from the mandates, though, were an important source of workers for the mines in Katanga and Kasai Provinces.

PORTUGUESE COLONIAL RULE IN THE LATE 1930s

Portugal was the oldest colonial nation in Europe, and in the late 1930s, had the fourth largest colonial empire in the world. It was also, perhaps, the most peaceful of the colonial empires. Native uprisings, riots, rebellions and the like were rare. Portuguese colonial rule had been, from its inception, a rule from the top with all major policies and budget decisions being made in Lisbon, and standardized as much as possible throughout the empire. The Portuguese had a slogan regarding their colonial mission. It was to "Christianize, colonize, and civilize."

In the early 1930s, Portugal underwent some radical political changes because of internal problems and the Depression. Also, an economics professor-turned-prime minister, Antonio Salazar, came to power. Portugal, at the time, was a dictatorship under Army General Antonio Carmona, who had assumed the office of the President and assigned Salazar, first as Finance Minister and later as Prime Minister, to run the government. Salazar was a devoted technocrat, a strong Roman Catholic, and a lifelong bachelor after having taken a vow of chastity in his youth as the result of a failed love affair.

Salazar devoted his life to the affairs of state of Portugal, and ruled for thirty years. Using the dictatorial powers assigned to him by General Carmona, Salazar was able to minimize the adverse effects of the Depression on Portugal, and bring about an economic recovery which was among the fastest in Europe. The cost, though, was the loss of personal freedoms for the people, and the absence of any political opposition.

Salazar saw the colonies as assets that should contribute to improving the conditions of Portugal and the Portuguese people. Heretofore, that goal had not been attained. Economic development in the Portuguese colonies lagged behind other colonies in Africa, because the Portuguese lacked the capital it took to exploit the business opportunities available. Furthermore, Portuguese colonial policy had been to discourage foreign investments in the colonies, because the presence of foreigners in the colonies might politically contaminate the natives.

There was no thought of guiding the colonies toward ultimate independence so, as far as Salazar was concerned, the relationship between the mother country and the colonies was permanent. Portugal, although she had been a combatant on

Dr. Antonio de Oliveira Salazar, ruler of Portugal for thirty years.

the Allied side in World War I, had not been assigned any mandated territory, so Salazar did not have to answer to the League of Nations for any of his colonial policies. Portuguese law, though, had several built-in safeguards to provide for the protection and welfare of the natives. By law, there was to be no forced labor in the colonies, but by the same law, able-bodied male natives were required to work for at least six months per year at some endeavor. If they could not, or would not find work, the colonial governments had the authority to conscript them for work on public projects for the required period. Each native worker had to carry a work card showing his yearly work records.

Early in his term of office, Salazar found another way to make use of native labor. He devised a plan whereby natives could be contracted for work abroad. This was not new for the Portuguese. It had been done before. Through coercion, economic necessity, and/or the six months per year work requirement many natives were induced into signing work contracts abroad. Under most of the contracts the Portuguese government collected the workers' pay checks, took out taxes, and then passed the balance on to the workers.

The Union of South Africa was a major customer for these contracts, and many natives from Portuguese colonies, especially Mozambique, went to South Africa to work in the mines. Many contract workers also came from the Portuguese-owned Cape Verde Islands, where there was chronic unemployment. Many Cape Verdeans were sent to the Western Hemisphere, including the United States. Upon returning home, they brought with them hard currency which greatly helped the colonial economies and contributed to Salazar's overall success in bringing Portugal rapidly out of the Depression. During 1938-39, a drought devastated agriculture in the Cape Verde Islands, and the people turned, more than ever, to the contract labor system for employment. These years saw an increased number of Cape Verde workers going abroad.

Another program Salazar implemented throughout the empire was a program to slowly educate the natives in the ways of European work ethics, while at the same time spreading Christianity. The small group of "advanced" natives that already existed, approximately 37,000, were to be used as middlemen in this venture and, for their services, were brought into the Portuguese colonial ruling circles. Together with the Portuguese already in the colonies, and those who would come later, it was hoped that an assimilated ruling class would develop that would secure long-time economic and political stability within the respective colonies. In the long run this proved difficult to accomplish because the whites, especially new immigrants, tended to keep themselves segregated from all of the natives, "advanced" or not.

Salazar continued a program already in place designed to whiten the colonies by offering individuals accused of crimes in Portugal the option of going to jail or taking meaningful employment in the colonies. This offered the accused a second chance to become a productive tax-paying member of society, and kept him from having to be supported by the state while in jail. In this regard, Salazar further stimulated the economy of the Cape Verde Island by building a huge prison camp at Tarrafal for offenders, primarily political prisoners, from all over the empire. This provided much-needed jobs for the islanders and kept these undesirables out of Portugal.

Employment opportunities were not much better in the colonies, so the displaced unemployed from Portugal took whatever work was available, even at low wages. This displaced Africans, but on Salazar's books it still looked good because unemployed whites were entitled to various types of government compensation and unemployed blacks were not.

In 1939, Salazar found another way to save money. He struck a deal with the Vatican giving the Catholic Church the exclusive rights to provide primary education for the natives throughout the Portuguese Empire. The Portuguese government provided some financial support but the bulk of the cost came from the pockets of the faithful. This program went smoothly most places except in Portuguese Guinea, where much of the population was Moslem. Moslem parents refused to send their children to the Catholic schools, so they had to rely on their own resources to educate their children.

In September and October 1939, soon after World War II started in Europe, President Carmona toured the Portuguese Empire. Upon returning home he praised his Prime Minister for doing an excellent job in making the colonies economically sound, peaceful, and loyal.

SPANISH COLONIAL RULE IN THE LATE 1930s

Spanish colonial rule, like that of most of the other Colonial Powers was one of centralized and paternalistic control from Madrid. In 1904, the principle of Patronato de Indegenas had been established by the Spanish government of the day, which legally decreed that blacks were morally, mentally, and legally under age and were to be treated as minors before the law for their entire lives. Those few blacks and people of mixed race who were able to obtain a certain level of education could apply for, and receive, Emancipation Cards which brought them out from under the "Patronato de Indegenas" system. Few, however, were able to do this.

Then, beginning in the early 1920s, Spain became engulfed in two decades of political turmoil which culminated in the tragic and bloody Spanish Civil War of 1936-39. During that time, attention given to Spain's colonies from Madrid was minimal, and financial support was nil. The one exception was Spanish Morocco, which was nearest to Spain on the southern shore of the Strait of Gibraltar. Because of its strategic location and economic importance Madrid treated Spanish Morocco as an extension of Spain. This became even more apparent after the civil war began in July 1936. The Moorish population of Spanish Morocco quickly sided with General Francisco Franco, the leader of the Nationalist (pro-Fascist) rebels, and all of Spanish Morocco went over to the Nationalist's side without a struggle. Furthermore, many Moroccans went to Spain to fight in Franco's Nationalist Army. After final victory in 1939, Franco rewarded his Moroccan followers generously.

As for the lesser and more remote colonies, they were treated like poor relatives, both before and during the civil war. This forced the local administrators and commercial interests to take matters into their own hands, and opened the door for wide spread corruption. The island of Fernando Poo was, perhaps, the best example. This small but fertile island was, by the 1930s, a plantation colony specializing in the export of cocoa, palm products, and hardwoods. The local Bubi tribesmen, though, refused to work on the plantations, so the owners, with the cooperation of the local administrators, brought in unsuspecting workers from the Kru tribe in Liberia. Working conditions for the imported workers were horrible and their conditions bordered on slavery. In the early 1930s, an international scandal erupted over the conditions on Fernando Poo, and the League of Nations sent an investigating team. The team could do little other than expose the problem to the world, and they shamed the local Spanish authorities into improving conditions to some degree.

When the civil war began in Spain, there were some military skirmishes between Nationalist and Loyalist factions in Rio Muni and Rio de Oro, but the Nationalist, quickly prevailed in both colonies. The Franco regime, engulfed in the war, thereafter paid little attention to the colonies except to announce that the Patronato de Indegenas system would remain in place. Actually, it remained in place throughout World War II and well into the postwar years.

After the final victory of the Nationalists in early 1939, the Spanish brand of Fascism came to Spain's African colonies. This was of concern to the western Allies because now Fascism had outposts in western and central Africa through Spain, as well as in North and East Africa through Italy. But the Spanish government did not pursue its advantage. In fact, Franco further weakened these outposts militarily and politically when, in 1939, he ordered them to become self-supporting. This showed that Madrid was not interested in spending its resources to make the Spanish colonies into centers of Fascism in Africa. On the contrary, with loose ties to Madrid, the door was still open for the local administrators and commercial interests to manage things for their own benefit.

Generalissimo Francisco Franco, leader of the Nationalists rebels in Spain during the Spanish Civil War, and future dictator of Spain.

In August 1939, just days before hostilities began in Europe, Spain and Germany signed a secret agreement that in the event of war, German tankers and supply ships could lay at anchor in various Spanish harbors and supply German submarines. Three harbors in Spain were designated, one in Spanish Morocco, and one in the Canary Islands off the west coast of Africa.

Therefore, with the onset of World War II, the Spanish colonies in Africa, other than Spanish Morocco and the Canary Islands, were benign political and military entities, and glaring examples of a neglectful colonial rule.

LIBERIA IN TROUBLE

During the Great Depression, the independent country of Liberia had fallen on extremely hard times, and the government went bankrupt. At times the country was on the verge of anarchy. During this time various European leaders suggested that the country be taken over by the League of Nations. The United States objected to this, and Liberia remained independent. As the Depression waned, conditions gradually improved in Liberia.

JEWS TO ITALIAN EAST AFRICA AND LIBYA

On September 1, 1938, Mussolini issued a decree requiring all foreign-born Jews living in Italy, who had arrived since the end of World War I, to leave the country by March 1, 1939. This applied to about 25,000 people, and was a concession by Mussolini to his newfound friend, Adolf Hitler.

Many of the Jews in question were German Jews who had found sanctuary in Italy. This situation had become an embarrassment to the Nazis, since German Jews were living freely in the homeland of Germany's principal ally. Mussolini understood Hitler's concern and, therefore, issued the decree. It did not apply to Italian-born Jews who were Italian citizens nor to Jews already in the Italian colonies. Not surprisingly, some of the expelled foreign Jews elected to go to Libya and Italian East Africa.

Chapter 3

GERMAN CLAIMS IN COLONIAL AFRICA

"RETURN OUR COLONIES"—A. HITLER

During the 1800s, when the various major European powers were scrambling for African colonies, the Germans were one of the major contenders. They had great hopes of acquiring what they called "Mittel Afrika." This was to be a giant colonial holding across the central part of Africa, stretching from Nigeria to the Cape Provinces on the Atlantic coast, across Africa, encompassing the entire Congo Basin, and spreading out on the west coast of Africa between Italian Somaliland and Portuguese Mozambique.

The German dream of Mittel Afrika was dashed, however, by the other European powers. Almost no one wanted Germany to gain and control so much of the African continent. There was one exception, though, the two independent Afrikaner nations of The Orange Free State and The South African Republic (Transvaal) in southern Africa. The ethnic Dutch Afrikaners were the only other Germanic people in Africa and would have welcomed the prospect of their German brethren controlling huge land areas to the north. The Boer War of 1899-1902 ended the independence of these two southern African nations, and the Afrikaner people were forcibly incorporated into the Union of South Africa, a part of the British Empire. There the Afrikaners became an out-of-power political minority, but their aspirations for a significant Germanic presence on the African continent remained strong.

On the Atlantic coast, Belgium took the heart of Mittel Afrika by proclaiming rights to the Belgian Congo. The other colonial powers acknowledged Belgium's claim, thus shutting out the Germans. The French took land north of that, and the Portuguese took the area to the south. Spain took a small enclave called Rio Muni. On the Atlantic coast, only Togo (also called Togoland), the Kameroons, and the sparsely-settled and mostly desert wasteland of South West Africa, were actually acquired by Germany. In East Africa, the British took ownership of Kenya and Uganda leaving Germany a cluster of three colonies; Tanganyika, Rwanda, and Urundi.

There were always those in the German leadership who questioned the wisdom of Germany acquiring overseas colonies, mainly because, in order to protect such colonies, a large and modern navy was required. But, Germany's potential enemies, Britain and France, already had huge navies to protect their overseas empires, and Germany, by acquiring an empire, would be forced to compete in that league. The obvious question in the German leadership was, was it worth it? Might it not be better for Germany to spend its resources on its army because Germany, situated as it was in Central Europe, was surrounded by neighbors with powerful land armies? Then too, there was the never-dormant German dream of expanding by land eastward where a navy was of little value.

The Germans found some hope for protecting their colonies in 1885 when, at the Berlin Conference of that year, the major powers agreed to neutralize all of the colonies in the "Congo Basin", in that, in the event of a European war those colonies would remain neutral and not go to war against each other. The "Congo Basin" was not geographically defined, but it was Germany's understanding that it included five of Germany's six African colonies, Kameroons, Togo, Rwanda, Urundi, and Tanganyika. One reason given for the Berlin Agreement was that it was in the best interest of all Europeans that the white men show unity of purpose in the eyes of the black men.

"BANG! BANG! YOU'RE DEAD"

During the war Hitler told a few of his associates that as a child he and his neighborhood playmates played war games based on the Boer War. The Boers were the "good guys" and the British were the "bad guys." In 1899 Hitler was ten years old.

World War I soon proved that the Berlin Agreement was not worth the paper it was written on. When the war started, the British and French navies quickly gained control of the world's seas, and maintained it throughout the war. Germany's navy was of little value in protecting her colonies. This proved those in the German leadership who had questioned the wisdom of having overseas colonies to be right. With the German colonies defenseless and ripe for the taking, the temptation was too strong for the Allies to resist. One by one, the German colonies were taken by the Allies. The one exception was Tanganyika, where an on-going struggle was maintained by a handful of determined and resourceful German soldiers who were able to conduct a brilliant fighting retreat for all four years of the war.

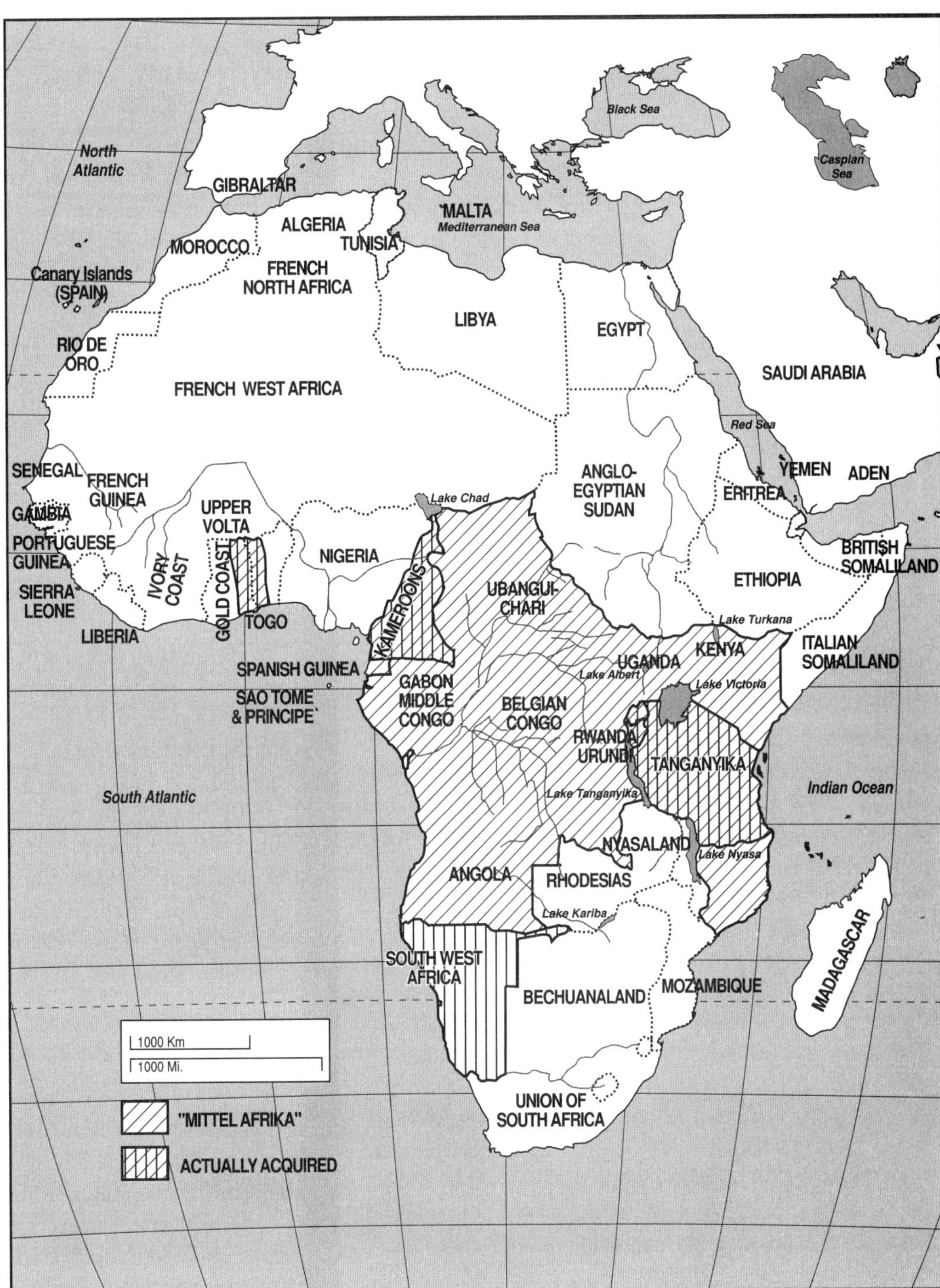

Germany's dream and Germany's reality. Germany dreamed of a huge colonial holding in the heart of Africa that spread from coast to coast. They called it "Mittel Afrika." What Germany received was considerably less.

To justify their invasions of the German colonies and the obvious violation of the Berlin Agreement, the Allies argued that the Germans had brought it upon themselves in several ways. The Allies argued that from the beginning of the war, the Germans had used their powerful radio stations in Africa to contact and direct German submarines at sea, and by doing so, had been the first to violate the Berlin Agreement. The fact that the Allies were also using their radio stations in Africa for military purposes was ignored. Then, in 1914, a bloody rebellion occurred in South Africa started by Afrikaners who objected to South Africa's entry into the war. The South Africans and British blamed the rebellion, in part, on German subversive activities from the adjacent German colony of South West Africa. To further justify their actions in taking the German colonies, the Allies argued that adherence to the provisions of the Berlin Agreement was voluntary in the first place and not obligatory.

GERMAN COLONIAL RULE

Germany ruled their colonies from a centralized colonial office in Berlin, and were tough taskmasters as far as the natives were concerned. Group punishment, beatings, and arbitrary confinement were widely practiced by the German colonial administrators.

The colonies were relatively peaceful and productive, and the Germans recruited modest-sized native armies in their larger colonies. Those military units remained in Africa, and did not go to Europe.

The fighting in Africa during World War I was considered to be a side show by both the Germans and Allies, yet it was a nasty little war. It was a very fluid war and not at all like the trench warfare that was going on in Europe. Both sides were plagued by long and difficult marches, disease, lack of supplies, inadequate or non-existent maps, hot and humid weather, mud, and, at times, angry bees, charging rhinoceroses, biting insects of many descriptions, and other perils of the jungle.

Both sides used substantial numbers of native troops. Of the German forces, 96% were black.

World War I in Africa went badly for Germany, and when it ended she was forced to give up all of her colonies to the Allies. When the victorious Allies convened at Versailles, in 1919, to write the peace treaty, they confirmed that Germany's colonial empire was lost to her forever, and was to be distributed among the war's victors as a part of the spoils of war. To make it easier and more justifiable to strip Germany of her colonies, the Germans were denounced at Versailles as unworthy colonial masters. One report said that the Germans were "...cruel, brutal, arrogant, and utterly unsuited for intercourse with primitive people; lustful, and malicious in their attitude toward subject races."

The German delegation at Versailles tried to save the colonies by arguing that colonies should be retained because Germany had proven herself to be a capable colonial ruler, and that the colonies were needed to insure Germany's economic well-being in the coming years. The German delegation accepted, though, the concept that the colonies might be retained under a mandate from a governing authority such as the League of Nations. This argument did not prevail. In the final analysis, the Germans were required to give up their colonies completely. This was stated very clearly in Article 119 of the Versailles Treaty, which read:

> *"Germany renounces in favor of the Principle Allied and Associated Powers all her rights and titles over her overseas possessions."*

When the German colonies were divided among the Allies, they were generally given to those who had conquered them under mandates from the League of Nations.

Many German assets in the colonies, both public and private, were ordered sold at auction to raise money to help Germany pay the huge reparations debt that had been levied upon her. Some of the people and corporations that owned property in the colonies, however, were able to buy back some of their assets thru middlemen—mostly East Indians or Greeks.

As for the German citizens who lived in the colonies, Article 122 of the Versailles treaty provided:

> *"The government exercising authority over such territories may make such provisions as it thinks fit with reference to the repatriation from them of German nationals and to the conditions upon which German subjects of European origin shall, or shall not, be allowed to reside, hold property, trade, or exercise a profession in them."*

HITLER'S EARLY POSITION ON COLONIES

Hitler began his political career in 1919, and from the beginning spoke out on the lost German colonies. But, he was not consistent. He swung both ways on the issue. Knowing it was a sensitive issue with the German people, though, he frequently railed, in his speeches, against the injustices heaped upon Germany by the victorious Allies of World War I and the League of Nations for taking away Germany's colonies. It was a marvelous attention-getter. In his more thoughtful moments, however, when he contemplated the realities of war and politics, he could see that Germany's having an overseas colonial empire would be a very costly undertaking and hardly worth it. He put these thoughts in writing twice. First in his book Mein Kampf (1924), he stated that the Germany of old should have followed a policy of "...renunciation of world trade and colonies; renunciation of a German war fleet; concentration of all the state's instruments of power on the land army." Then, in 1928, he wrote on the subject again in his second, but unpublished, book. Hitler was not yet in power in 1928, but felt the need to express the Nazi Party's position in book form on a critical issue of the day—the control of South Tyrol, an area in dispute between Austria and Italy. The South Tyrol issue suddenly faded into the background before Hitler finished his book, so he chose not to publish it.

Nevertheless, while expounding on the South Tyrol issue, Hitler also wrote on the issue of colonies. He recalled that in the early days of colonialism "...we let ourselves be swept along by the great colonial waves of the Nineteenth Century, strengthened perhaps by romanic memories of the old Hansa (Hanseatic League, 13th-16th century German trading colonies which existed eastward along the southern coast of the Baltic Sea), as well as driven by the peaceful economic policy to shelve the exclusive promotion of the land army and take up the construction of a fleet. This policy...was calamitous...(Germany's future) lay and lies for us in Europe, just as exactly as the course of our decline will always be of a purely continental character."

Most of the mandatory powers were most lenient in this matter. Some Germans, of course, returned home, but there was no great exodus of Germans back to Europe.

THE COLONIAL ISSUE IN POST WORLD WAR I GERMANY

In Germany, in the early 1920s, the loss of the colonies was not an issue that was widely discussed because there were so many other traumatic events that commanded the German people's and the German government's attention. But memories of the lost empire were kept alive. In every school in Germany, maps posted on the walls showed the youth of Germany the empire that once was.

HITLER'S "BROWN SHIRTS"

Horst Wessel, one of Hitler's first Storm Troopers, "Brown Shirts." Wessel was killed in a street fight and elevated, by the Nazis, to the rank of a martyr.

Hitler was a talented public speaker and rose rapidly within the Nazi Party to become one of the party's leaders, and its principle speaker. The party soon became known for its raucous and flamboyant public meetings—meetings that, at times, degenerated into fist fights and other mayhem. To keep order at the meetings, Hitler created a guards unit called the Sturmabteilungen (Storm Troopers or SA). To give these men a para-military appearance, he instructed that they be dressed in appropriate uniforms. In searching about for those uniforms Hitler discovered that there were surplus army brown shirts available at bargain prices. These shirts had been destined for use by the colonial soldiers in the African colonies, but had never been shipped due to the Allied naval blockade of Germany. The Nazis bought a supply of the shirts to outfit their Storm Troopers who soon became known as "Brown Shirts."

TOGO

Togo was the first area of Africa colonized by the Germans in 1844. By 1914, the colony was a prosperous, self-supporting protectorate of about one million people, exporting maize, yams, cocoa, copra, cotton, palm kernels, and palm oil. It had no standing army and only a para-military police force of about 560 men.

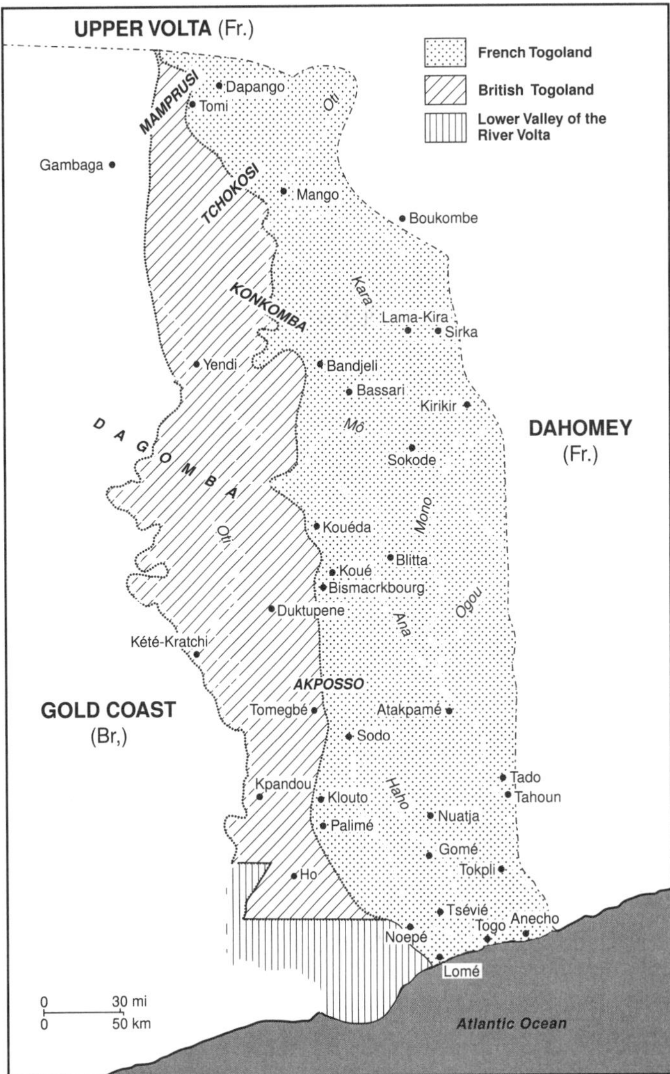

The former German protectorate of Togo was divided between the British colony of Gold Coast and the French colony of Dahomey.

It is believed that the first shots of World War I were fired in Lome, the capital of Togo, on August 15, 1914, by an unidentified black man in a British uniform. Sometime later the spot was marked with a plaque. This being the case, it can be argued that World War I in Africa lasted longer than it did in Europe.

With the beginning of hostilities in Europe, Togo's governor, Duke Freidrich zu Machlemberg, proposed to his British neighbors in Gold Coast and French neighbors in Dahomey that they agree not to fight each other and become an outstanding example of the spirit of the 1885 Treaty of Berlin. Both neighbors rejected Machlemberg's plea. In desperation he turned to the United States to intervene, but his plea was ignored by Washington.

Within a short time the British invaded Togo from the west while the French invaded from the east and together they conquered the colony in three weeks. This would be the shortest and least bloody conflict in Africa during World War I. Togo was the first German colony conquered.

Commercial life quickly returned to normal, and the colony remained occupied territory for the rest of the war.

When the German colonies were distributed after the war among the victorious Allies, Togo was divided roughly in two with the halves being given respectively to Gold Coast and Dahomey as mandated territories.

The division of the colony split the largest tribe, the Ewes, in two but this was of little concern to the British and French. The French were unhappy with the settlement so, in 1920, the dividing line in Togo was redrawn to give France more of the coast line and Britain more of the interior.

In the years that followed there was no consideration given to reuniting the colony, or returning it to Germany.

KAMEROONS (Cameroons)

The word Kameroons comes from the Portuguese word "cameroes" (prawns) which existed in abundance in the colony when the white man first arrived. Other than prawns, the colony had little to offer. It was hot and humid, and very unhealthy for Europeans. It soon gained the reputation as being the "white man's grave." Both Britain and France were active in nearby areas and had designs on the Kameroons, but they hesitated in acting. The Germans took advantage of the delay and jumped into the area and began making treaties with the tribes along the coast in the Duala area. The British renounced their interests in the colony but the French did not. The Germans, nevertheless, advanced inland, staking their claims as they went. Some of that land had also been claimed by France.

German Chancellor Otto von Bismarck was not enthusiastic about acquiring the colony, but saw it as a possible bargaining chip in some future negotiation. This paid off, in a round-about way, in 1911. In that year, the French were seeking international approval of their position in Morocco, so the Germans and French struck a deal whereby Germany would recognize France's position in Morocco in exchange for France's renouncing its claims in the Kameroons. This enlarged the colony to 190,000 square miles, and committed the Germans, more than ever, to the Kameroons.

By the outbreak of World War I in 1914, the colony had been pacified and was moderately productive. There was a small army called the "Schutztruppe" consisting of 1,500 askaris and 200 German officers and NCOs. There was also a police force of 1,255 natives and forty Europeans. Both were equipped and trained for internal security only. To the west, in British-controlled Nigeria, the British mustered 7,737 askaris, 252 white officers and 118 NCOs from Nigeria, Gold Coast, Sierra Leone, and Gambia with the clear intention of invading and occupying the Kameroons. To the east, in French Equatorial Africa, the French mustered a smaller force and agreed that it be placed under British command. The conquest of the Kameroons was to be a British affair.

In mid-August 1914, the British launched their invasion from Nigeria, and the French force moved in from the east. The Schutztruppe was no match for this overwhelming force so, after some delaying actions, withdrew into the interior. Duala, the capital of the Kameroons, fell to the Allies on September 27, 1914. The Allies pursued the retreating Germans into the interior, where the German had asked the tribes to come to their aid. Only one out of several dozen tribes heeded the call and took up arms on behalf of the Germans. In the next few months the German force was beaten down by a combination of combat, fatigue, lack of supplies, and disease. When the last remnants of the German force surrendered, it was noted that the askaris in the Schutztruppe had remained loyal to their German officers to the end.

For the remainder of World War I, the Kameroons was Allied occupied territory.

When the division of the German colonies took place in 1919, Britain was given only a small strip of land along the eastern border of Nigeria, and put it under the administration of Nigeria. The French took the remainder, and both were under League of Nations mandates. Unlike Togo, the division of the Kameroons was made primarily on the basis of tribal areas, so that as many tribes as possible could remain whole. The French set up their new area as a separate colony called the "Cameroons" within the colonial federation of French Equatorial Africa. Yaounde became the capital of the French Cameroons, and Duala its chief seaport.

In the years between the wars, the French lived up to the conditions of the mandate and made an effort to advance the colony toward future autonomy or independence. The French made a serious effort to eradicate sleeping sickness in the colony, encouraged native farming, and improved the educational system. Elections were held at the native levels for various low-level posts held by natives, and several natives were appointed to the colony's Administrative Council and Chamber of Commerce. Commercial enterprises, primarily plantations, were allowed to prosper, and by the late 1930s the Cameroons was an exporter of cocoa, palm kernels and oil, bananas, and wild rubber. Many of the plantations were still in German hands, and much of the exports went to Germany.

SOUTH WEST AFRICA

South West Africa was Germany's largest colony in Africa. It was a sparsely-settled area, and mostly desert. The Germans acquired it in the late 1800s, and its first Imperial Commissioner, who arrived in 1885, was Dr. Ernst Goering, father of Hermann Goering, Germany's #2 Nazi. Hermann was not yet born, and spent no time in South West Africa. Dr. Goering was arrogant and high handed, and was not liked by the natives. The feeling was reciprocal. A small colonial army, the Schutztruppe was formed consisting of about

January 1939. The German citizens of Swakopmund, South West Africa, boldly display Nazi flags on the sixth anniversary of Hitler's rise to power.

3,200 white soldiers and local white volunteers. Black soldiers were not recruited.

From 1904 to 1908, the Germans undertook a military campaign to pacify the colony. This led to a bloody struggle against the indigenous native leaders, but the Germans prevailed.

Over the years, friendly, but unofficial, relations developed between the Germans in South West Africa and the more conservative elements of the Afrikaner society in South Africa. This was of concern to the English-speakers in South Africa, and their cooperative Afrikaners allies, but little could be done about it.

In August 1914, when World War I started in Europe, London asked South African Prime Minister, General Louis Botha, a pro-British Afrikaner, to mobilize the South African Army and occupy German South West Africa. The primary targets in South West Africa were the radio stations being used to communicate with German submarines at sea. Botha agreed, knowing it would be an unpopular war with his constituents. He was right. This was one of the major factors of the ugly Afrikaner-inspired protests that occurred that month. Botha, nevertheless, proceeded to make preparations to invade South West Africa, and the Afrikaners in the South African Army obediently followed his orders. The first actions took place in September 1914, but had to be halted abruptly. So many South African Afrikaner civilians opposed the invasion that a full-scale anti-British rebellion broke out in the Orange Free State in October 1914. Botha was forced to divert the bulk of his army from South West Africa to the Orange Free State to quell the rebellion. It took until December of that year for 30,000 men of the South African Army to subdue the well-organized rebel forces of 11,500 in the Orange Free State.

Botha then turned his full attention, again, on the Germans in South West Africa. The South African Army consisted of some 50,000 white soldiers, supported by 33,000 black service personnel. Botha personally led the invasion. This force, which was far superior to anything the Germans could muster, soon occupied all of South West Africa.

In 1919, when the League of Nations mandates were being assigned, South Africa was given the mandate over South West Africa. A large percentage of the German population remained, however, but were very resentful of the South African rule. This would not diminish rapidly.

South Africa was one of those colonial powers that opposed the League of Nations, concept that the mandated territories should be led toward future autonomy or independence. There was great pressure among the Afrikaners in South Africa to annex South West Africa at sometime in the future, thereby swelling the Germanic population of South Africa and facilitating an eventual Afrikaner political takeover. Not surprisingly, the English-speakers opposed annexation of South West Africa, but they were not supportive of the League of Nations' goal of independence for South West Africa, either. For them the future of South West Africa remained undecided.

The South African government filed the required annual reports to the League of Nations on its management of South West Africa, but as the League's influence declined, those reports became increasingly meaningless.

By the late 1930s, conditions had changed little in South West Africa from the early 1920s. South African police and para-military units kept the peace, and the colony remained sparsely settled. Windhoek, the capital, had only 19,000 people, and the 1936 census showed a total population for the colony of only 360,000 with a European population of 31,000, of which some 9,600 people still spoke German as their first language. And the attitude of the German-speakers had not changed. They still resented South African control.

The South Africans, complying with the League of Nations' mandate and, of course, for their own interests, did improve conditions in South West Africa during the 1920s and 1930s. In addition to about seventy missionary schools, the South African government added sixty government supported schools, including four high schools. There were also German schools supported by the local German communities. One area where South Africa directly violated a League of Nations ruling, though, was in the matter of tariffs. The League had called for an open-door economic policy for all mandated territories, but the South Africans imposed their own tariff regulations on South West Africa. This included granting Germany a favored nation status in South West Africa as also existed in South Africa.

The main occupation of the natives was the raising of livestock and the colony exported hides, butter, and meat. Diamonds, vanadium ore and several other ores were also exported. A railroad was built connecting Windhoek with Cape Town.

With the rise of National Socialism (Nazism) in Germany, politically sympathetic organizations sprang up almost immediately in South West Africa, including a local Nazi Party. The Nazis in Germany quickly recognized their opportunities in South West Africa, and sent hundreds of pounds of pro-Nazi and anti-Semitic propaganda to the German consulate in Windhoek. It was so voluminous that much of it had to be stored for quite a while so that it could be handed out evenly.

In South Africa in the early 1930s, the political parties were undergoing a painful realignment, and little attention was given to the problems in South West Africa except for one action in 1934, which outlawed the South West African Nazi Party.

By 1937, the political situation in South Africa had stabilized, and the Pretoria government turned its attention once again to the problems of South West Africa. On April 4, 1937, the South African government issued a proclamation for South West Africa making it illegal for any colonial subject, which included the South West African Germans, to give allegiance to any foreign head of state other than the King of England. This only served to aggravate the confrontational atmosphere that existed in the colony.

Then the South African Afrikaner extremists stirred the pot by calling for the return of South West Africa to Germany. Their political opponents in South Africa saw an entirely different future for South West Africa, and called for the nationalization of South West Africa's diamond mines as a first step toward the eventual annexation of South West Africa by South Africa. The United Party, which was in power in South Africa, was in a no-win situation. The Party was an amalgamation of political factions, stretching from far right to far left as a result of the political re-alignments of the 1930s. Making any substantial changes in South West Africa would alienate one group or the other within the party. The government leaders therefore chose to do nothing, and did what they could to maintain the status quo in South West Africa. As a sop to everyone in the party, and as a means of diverting attention, the government leaders tightened the racial laws pertaining to South West Africa. Part of this process was the limiting of Jewish immigration into the mandated territory.

The German government saw potential political gains in the situation in South West Africa and, in the mid-1930s, began sending agents there with plans to instigate a boycott against British goods, and encourage the German population to speak out on the return of the colony to Germany. In Germany, an organization called "The Colonial Society" was formed for the specific purpose of working toward the return of South West Africa to Germany. The Society began making personal contacts with various German individuals and groups in South West Africa, giving them the feeling that someone in Germany was directly interested in their plight. These things had their effect, and the German population of South West Africa became more and more openly pro-Nazi. One such pro-Nazi demonstration occurred during January 1939, the sixth anniversary of Hitler's rise to power, when the German citizens of Swakopmund boldly flew German flags from the homes and places of business.

Hitler did not disappoint the citizens of Swakopmund. On January 30, 1939, he went before the Reichstag in Berlin and once again demanded the return of South West Africa and the other former German colonies. A few days later, German Foreign Minister Joachim von Ribbentrop issued a formal statement on Germany's position toward the lost colonies.

The people of South West Africa were clearly excited by the rhetoric from Berlin. Rumors began to circulate in both South West Africa and South Africa that German young men in South West Africa were practicing throwing hand grenades in the desert, and that there were plans in motion to build secret airfields in remote areas of the colony. Other rumors hinted of the existence of kangaroo courts meting out Nazi-style justice within the German community.

In March 1939 Germany, took over the remainder of Czechoslovakia in Europe and transformed it into a colonial-style possession called "The Protectorate of Bohemia-Moravia." This was Germany's first colonial acquisition since World War I. In South Africa, it stimulated the extremist Afrikaners in the National Party to, once again, call for the return of South West Africa to Germany so that it, like Czechoslovakia, could become a German protectorate.

In late 1938, rumors spread throughout South West Africa that a German "Strength Through Joy" cruise ship was on its way to South West Africa with 2,000 German troops aboard disguised as tourists, and that they intended to take over the colony by force. The ship did not materialize but the rumor frightened enough English-speaking residents that some of them made preparations to, or did flee, into South Africa. Some even sold their properties and left permanently. Rumors of a German takeover continued to persist even after the "Strength Through Joy" scare had faded.

By April 1939, rumors had intensified to the point where the South African authorities actually feared that a "putsch" (local take-over) might be attempted. Smuts, who was then Minister of Justice in the Hertzog government, was sufficiently alarmed that he sent additional policemen to the colony to keep order. The putsch did not materialize, but neither did its threat abate. In August 1939, just days before World War II erupted in Europe, Smuts confided to an associate that strong rumors of a putsch still persisted in South West Africa.

GERMAN EAST AFRICA

German East Africa consisted of the colonies of Tanganyika, Rwanda, and Urundi. Tanganyika, bordering on the Indian Ocean, was the largest and, by far, the most valuable of the three. Rwanda and Urundi were two small colonies on the western edge of Tanganyika bordering the Belgian Congo. Rwanda and Urundi were very similar to each other in that both were ancient kingdoms dominated by the Tutsi tribe. The more numerous Hutu tribe also occupied the area, but were historically subservient to the Tutsi. Both colonies were heavily populated, but there were no modern cities of any size, and no modern infrastructure. This made Rwanda and Urundi unappealing to Europeans, and very few whites settled there. The Germans allowed the Tutsi to continue to rule in their time-honored way, as long as the colonies were peaceful and they paid the required taxes to the colonial treasury in Dar es Salaam, Tanganyika.

It was Tanganyika that got all the attention. The last areas there were pacified in 1907. A majority of the Europeans, mostly Germans, settled in the northern part of the country which had the healthiest climate. Plantations were begun, mines opened, and two railroads built connecting the interior to the sea. The Germans also built hospitals and medical dispensaries throughout the colony.

The colony became nearly self-sufficient in food, produced its own leather goods, had a small manufacturing facility to make rubber tires out of locally grown wild rubber, and produced a motor fuel called "trebol" from coconuts.

"I WANT A SNOW-CAPPED MOUNTAIN"

In 1910, the British and Germans agreed to a change in the border between Kenya, to the north, and Tanganyika. This was at the request of Germany's Kaiser Wilhelm. Nowhere in his empire did he have a snow-capped mountain, so the British agreed to give him Mount Kilimanjaro.

As in their other colonies, the Germans created a police force and a para-military peace-keeping force using German officers and native enlisted men. The Germans also employed Arabs in these forces. They allowed both the askaris and the Arabs to bring their wives to cook for them and tend to their needs. Most askaris brought wives, but the Arabs preferred to bring young boys.

The Tanganyikan askaris were well-trained by their German officers, and were considered to be the best-trained native soldiers on the continent.

When World War I began, Tanganyika was invaded by British and South African forces from the north. The South African force was the larger of the two, and was commanded by General Jan Christian Smuts. The Germans put up a very good initial defense but, because of their fewer numbers and lack of supplies, had to begin a retreat. That retreat lasted four years. During the summer of 1916, the British scored a number of victories in Tanganyika which were credited to Smuts. These came at a time when Britain sorely needed a victory, and Smuts became famous in Britain. Furthermore, about this time, a small Belgian force invaded Tanganyika from the west and captured the important railroad town of Tabora.

That same year the Belgians also captured the German colonies of Rwanda and Urundi with little opposition.

The German defenders and their askaris, under the brilliant leadership of General Paul von Lettow-Vorbeck, eventually retreated southward into Portuguese Mozambique. Since Portugal was a member of the Allies during that war, they were confronted there by the small Portuguese colonial army with the British still in pursuit at the rear. While in Mozambique the Germans were able to capture a sizeable amount of arms and ammunition, which allowed them to carry on their struggle.

The Portuguese and British pursued Lettow-Vorbeck's small force for months until it retreated northward again and re-entered Tanganyika. The Portuguese broke off the chase, but the British continued. When the war ended, the German force was in the British colony of Nyasaland, still a viable fighting force and still with the British in pursuit. One reason for the durability of the German force was that each German soldier was allowed seven native carriers. In the British and South African armies each European soldier had only one carrier. In Lettow-Vorbeck's force the carriers could carry everything the soldier possessed and even carry him if he fell ill or was wounded. Here too, the carriers were allowed to bring their wives. To improve the harmony within his force, Lettow-Vorbeck encouraged his German soldiers to learn Swahili so they could better communicate with both their carriers and askaris.

This sizeable body of people lived successfully off the land, killing and eating the abundant wild game. Hippopotamus meat was a favorite. When wild game could not be had the band's pack donkeys were eaten.

Lettow-Vorbeck's military exploits made him a national hero back in Germany, and during World War II General Irwin Rommel's heroic leadership in northern Africa would be compared with that of Lettow-Vorbeck.

For the South Africans, they too had a World War I hero. He was General Jan Christian Smuts, commander of the South African forces in German East Africa. Smuts went on to represent South Africa at the Versailles Peace Conference, where he was a strong advocate of Germany's colonies not being returned. Upon returning home he began a very successful political career that continued throughout the rest of his life.

When the German colonies were parcelled out at Versailles, it was only natural the British would be given the mandate over Tanganyika. A small parcel of land, known as the Kionga triangle in southeastern Tanganyika, was given to Portuguese Mozambique. Rwanda and Urundi were mandated to Belgium, and administratively attached to the Belgian Congo, and were governed from Leopoldville. A vice governor-general resided in Usumbura, Urundi and each native ruler had a staff of resident Belgian advisers. White settlement in Rwanda and Urundi was not encouraged by the Belgian government nor by the Belgian Congo colonial administration.

Next door, though, Tanganyika was given its own colonial government by the British. That government retained the original German-created administrative structure that allowed the natives a measure of self-government. This was a wise policy because it suited both the German community and the native leaders. Tanganyika was affiliated with Kenya, Uganda and British-controlled Zanzibar to form the colonial federation known as British East Africa.

Many of the German settlers stayed on in Tanganyika and resumed their pre-war occupations. The British discouraged further white settlement in the colony, claiming that they were attempting to live up to the League of Nations' ideal by preserving the colony for its people and its future. In reality, the British did not want more white settlers in Tanganyika because many of them would probably be Germans.

The British made improvements in Tanganyika and maintained the economic open door policy called for under the mandate. Because of the open door policy the colony continued to do a considerable amount of business with Germany. The colony's German planters and merchants took the lead in this endeavor.

There were no native reserves in Tanganyika. The land was considered publicly owned. This was not the case in neighboring Kenya, where the reserve system for native had been long established.

Sleeping sickness, malaria, and tuberculosis were problems in Tanganyika so the British devoted much of their colonial budget to eradicating these diseases. The German community, as well as many tribal chiefs, eagerly cooperated in this effort. Fifty hospital were established during the inter-war years in Tanganyika, along with 297 dispensaries. The latter were run mostly by trained natives.

The devilish tsetse fly had long plagued both domestic and wild animals in Tanganyika, so here too, the British made inroads in reducing that pest.

In education, the British encouraged missionary schools and set up government-operated primary schools in native villages. By 1936, there were 74 government-supported village schools with half of them administered and run solely by natives.

By the late 1930s, Tanganyika was a relatively prosperous colony and one of the better developed areas in sub-Saharan Africa. The colony had a big export in sisal, coffee, cotton, and other items including gold. The 1935 census showed that the colony was home to 3.1 million natives, 33,000 Asians and 8500 Europeans. It had 1,400 miles of railroads, 17,000 miles of road fit for motor traffic, 46 government-owned and six privately-owned airfields.

Like all the other colonies, Germany wanted Tanganyika, Rwanda, and Urundi back. To play on the German people's sympathies, a propaganda poster appeared in Germany in 1936 showing Germany's lost snow-capped mountain, Kilimanjaro.

The Nazi government in Germany did not want Germans to leave the former colonies because they would be much needed there if and when Germany regained them. To this end, an organization sprang up in 1938 in Nairobi, Kenya, the capital of British East Africa, called the Tanganyika League. Its main purpose was to discourage Germans from leaving East Africa.

GERMAN EFFORTS IN THE 1920s-30s TO REGAIN THEIR COLONIES

In 1926, when Germany was being considered for membership in the League of Nations, the question of the German colonies came to the fore. The Germans argued that, as a member of the League of Nations, they would be entitled to act as a mandatory power as were the other major nations of the world and that their colonies should be returned to them under League of Nations mandates. The majority of the members did not support this point of view, but agreed that if and when Germany might acquire new colonies they, then, could certainly qualify for a League of Nation mandate under German control. For the present, though, the former German colonies would remain under the existing mandates.

The German government was obliged to accept this condition and proceeded to join the League of Nations. Thereafter, the question of the lost colonies was not actively pursued by the German government.

Hitler and his Nazis, who were still contending for power, were relatively quiet, too, about the colonial question at this time. With Germany in the League of Nations and coming back into the good graces of most nations, Hitler, who was by now a leading politician in Germany, was making friendly overtures toward Britain. In response to these overtures, there were important individuals in Britain who suggested that the question of the German colonies be re-opened and that some, or perhaps all of them, might be returned to Germany. The British government of the day did not support this point of view, and put a firm halt to these prospects by announcing that the question of the German colonies was not negotiable.

COLONIES FOR BRITAIN'S FRIENDSHIP

One of the reasons Hitler did not press for the return of the German colonies in the 1920s was that he saw them as a bargaining chip (as had Bismarck) with which he might gain Britain's friendship and cooperation. He detailed this quite succinctly in Mein Kampf when he wrote:

> *"No sacrifice would have been too great to gain England's alliance... It would have meant renunciation of colonies and impotence on the sea and refraining from interference with British industry by our competition."*

This poster appeared in Germany in 1936 to remind the German people of the loss of Mt. Kilimanjaro in Tanganyika, their empire's only snow-capped mountain.

But, the cat was out of the bag. It was clear that the British were not united on this issue. Hitler took note of this interesting development and filed it away for future use.

Soon after Hitler came to power in January 1933, he was curious enough about East Africa to send a scientific mission there to see how suitable it was for large-scale settlement of Europeans. The mission returned in 1934 with disappointing news. It concluded that the area was not suitable for such a venture. The mission's report read, in part:

> *"It had not yet been proved that the European is physically capable of performing continuous heavy manual work in the tropical highlands and of maintaining himself throughout the generations."*

The report was suppressed in Germany, but later, in 1939, was leaked and published outside Germany.

While the scientific mission was still in Africa, Nazi Germany left the League of Nations in November of 1933. Hav-

A MOVIE: "THE RIDERS OF GERMAN EAST AFRICA"

In 1934, the Reichskolonialbund financed a German movie with the above title as part of its propaganda campaign regarding the lost colonies. Part of the movie was shot, in secret and illegally, in Tanganyika. The movie tells of two friends in East Africa, a Britisher (played by Peter Voss) and a German (played by Sepp Rist). They are good friends before World War I, and participate in a series of adventures in East Africa together and fall in love with the same girl. When World War I starts they find themselves on opposite sides. The Britisher, a desent fellow, is forced to go along with his cruel, scotch-drinking, "Tipperary"-singing companions and burn the homes of German settlers. The lady-in-question is threatened with a fate worse than death by the British, but is saved at the last minute by Rist's Arab side-kick, Mustapha (played by Rudolf Klicks, a German Mickey Rooney-type). Mustapha, unfortunately, is killed in the process.

When the war ends, the Britisher and German renew their friendship as before, but the German wins the final victory by getting the girl.

In December 1939, four months after World War II started, Dr. Joseph Goebbels, Germany's Propaganda Minister and movie czar, had second thoughts about the movie and banned any further showing of the film in Germany because it was too sympathetic toward the British. After the war the Allies continued the ban on the movie in Germany, calling it military propaganda.

ing broken with the League, Hitler no longer felt the need to be quiescent on the issue of the lost colonies and a new round of demands began to flow from Berlin for the return of Germany's colonies.

That same year, 1933, Hitler appointed retired Army General Franz von Epp to head an organization called the "Reichskolonialbund" (Reich Colonial League—RKB) whose mission was to continually press for the return of Germany's colonies. Through the RKB, the official government line of the colonial question was that the German colonies had been taken by the League of Nations for temporary management and that Germany had never surrendered ownership.

Germany's continuing propaganda about the return of the lost colonies had its effect, once more, in Britain. Again, responsible British leaders brought up the possibility of returning Germany's colonies. And, once again the British government was forced to step in and make an official statement that the question was "not a discussible issue."

During April 1939 the British government had reason to believe that Germany might make good its claim on the colony of Tanganyika and take it back by force of arms. The War Office received what appeared to be credible reports that a German aerial invasion of that colony, launched from Italian East Africa, would take place on April 20, Hitler's birthday. The landing site was purported to be the airfield at Arusha just eighty miles southwest of Mt. Kilimanjaro. Such a dramatic event would, the London officials feared, possibly induce the German population of the colony to rebel against the British colonial authorities. And, even if it was a failure it would serve to solidify German public opinion at home behind the Fuhrer and draw world attention to Hitler's colonial demands. This appeared to be very similar to the successful tactic used by Hitler in 1936 to regain control of the Rhineland.

Orders went out from London to the governor of Tanganyika to scrape together what forces he could to meet the expected German invasion. That force consisted of one brigade of KAR troops. The KAR men blocked the airfield with vehicles, wagons, oxcarts, and other objects, took up defensive positions around the airfield, and waited. April 20 came and went without an invasion. The troops held their positions for a few more days and were then withdrawn. Thereafter, the incident was considered to be a hoax or a clever ploy by the Germans.

THE 1936 OLYMPICS—MAKING A GOOD IMPRESSION

During the year 1936, all eyes were on Germany, because Germany was host to both the winter and summer Olympics of that year. The Nazis wanted to make a good impression on the thousands of foreign visitors who came for the games so they began to temper their behavior. Persecution of the Jews subsided, caustic rhetoric against Austria, which Hitler was hoping to annex, was reduced, and Hitler renounced the several passages in his book, Mein Kampf, which called for German territorial and colonial expansion at the expense of others. It sounded too good to be true. It was. Once the games were over and the visitors went home the Nazi reverted to their pre-Olympia aggressive behavior.

During the Olympic "spring" Neville Chamberlain, a prominent member of the British Parliament and a contender for the post of Prime Minister, was so impressed with the new German attitude that he announced from the floor of Parliament on April 6, 1936, that there was a clear distinction between British colonies and those assigned to Britain under mandate. He stated that conditions might develop that would justify an open debate on the future of the mandated lands. This time there was no counter response from the British government. Hitler was impressed, but withheld pursuing the matter until the summer Olympics were over. This was a wise decision because by maintaining his silence on the issue, Hitler allowed the debate in Britain to expand unhindered.

HITLER SNUBS JESSIE OWENS

At the Olympics, Hitler made it point to personally congratulate gold medal winners. But, when the American black athlete Jessie Owens won four gold medals, Hitler conveniently walked out of the stadium rather than greet Owens. This racial snub was duly noted by many people in Africa.

Hitler greeting Norwegian skater, gold medal winner and future movie star, Sonja Heine at the winter Olympics in Germany.

Following Chamberlain's lead, other liberal politicians in Britain spoke out in favor of discussing the return of the German colonies. Proposals were put forward to encourage the Dominions of South Africa, Australia, and New Zealand, all of whom had received Germany colonial lands under mandate, to cooperate in the matter. If they chose not to, certain liberals in Britain suggested that Britain might compensate Germany by giving her some of Britain's own colonies. Others spoke up suggesting that Belgium give back Rwanda and Urundi and that Portugal give back the Kionga Triangle awarded her from Tanganyika. These proposals did not sit well in Brussels and Lisbon, and the British government was obliged to step in and make the statement that such proposals, most certainly, did not represent British governmental policy.

The discussion in Britain was not all one-sided. Conservatives, such as Winston Churchill, spoke out, saying—as they had said all along—that the re-emergence of Germans in Africa and other parts of the world would pose a decided and expensive challenge to the security of the British Empire and its lines of communication. Also, the conservatives argued, that with the re-acquisition of their colonies, the Germans would be encouraged to build a larger navy, which would pose a greater threat to the British Navy and violate the recent British/German Naval Agreement of 1935, which fixed a ratio between the size of the British Navy vis a vis the German Navy.

During this time, virtually nothing was heard from France on the issue of the German colonies, because the French political scene was in constant turmoil. Weak coalition governments came and went in Paris with alarming regularity, and the French were simply not capable of resolving major and controversial issues.

Hitler saw in this situation an opportunity to possibly bring about the rapprochement with Britain that he had always hoped for. Hitler's idea of rapprochement with Britain was that Britain and Germany would come to an understanding whereby Germany would not interfere with the British Empire and Britain would allow Germany a free hand to settle old scores on the Continent. This would negate the British-French alliance and allow Hitler to acquire "lebensraum" (living room) in the east as he had promised his people he would do. Hitler knew he would have to pay a price for such an agreement, and surely saw that an appropriate bargaining chip to lay on the table before the British would be a renunciation of his demands for the return of the German colonies. Hitler felt he could justify this to his people because of Bismarck's similar attitude toward the colonies.

Hitler thought that the time was right to pursue this possibility, so he send his best diplomat, Joachim von Ribbentrop, to London as the German Ambassador. Von Ribbentrop had negotiated the 1935 Naval Agreement with Britain to Hitler's satisfaction, so now maybe he could negotiate a second successful agreement in London.

Meanwhile Hitler sent his trusted aide, Hans Frank, to Rome in September 1936, to obtain Mussolini's support on whatever was to develop with Britain. Mussolini readily agreed to support Germany's position on the colonies, whatever it might be.

The debate in Britain over the German colonies continued, off and on, over the next year. In March 1937, the South African government, speaking for itself, officially announced that it would not consider entering into discussions on returning South West Africa to Germany. That closed the issue on South West Africa as far as London was concerned, but the future of the other former German colonies were still open for consideration.

In May 1937, Neville Chamberlain became Prime Minister and began to give signs that his policy toward Hitler and the other world dictators would be one of appeasement. Hitler was encouraged. But then, Hitler's own actions were to doom von Ribbentrop's efforts in London. All during 1937, Hitler's aggressive behavior toward his neighbors, his on-going military buildup in Germany, and his increased persecution of the Jews belied his real intentions. The treatment of the Jews revealed that Hitler was a racist of the first order, and that the native peoples of Africa would, almost certainly, be badly treated if they came under the control of the Nazis. No one could forget Hitler's true feelings toward black people. He spelled them out for all the world to read in Mein Kampf. Hitler wrote:

"One hears from time to time that a negro has become a lawyer, teacher, tenor or the like. This is a sin against all reason; it is criminal lunacy to train a born semi-ape to become a lawyer. It is a sin against the Eternal Greatness of train Hottentots and Kaffirs to intellectual professions."

Hitler further doomed the prospect of rapprochement with Britain when, on September 7, 1937, he brought up, once again, the question of lebensraum for the German people and, specifically, the question of food. Hitler said that the current German living space was... :

"...too small to guarantee an undisturbed, assured and permanent supply of food... the thought of being permanently dependent on the accident of a good or bad harvest is intolerable... the attitude to this demand by other Powers is simply incomprehensible."

Considering that food production was one of the great industries in overseas colonies, Hitler's comments were construed to be a resumption of his demands on the colonies.

By the fall of 1937, the debate in Britain on Germany's colonies had crystallized around the conservative view, and in October of that year, the question of discussing the return of the German colonies was formally brought before the House of Commons and resoundingly rejected. The British had taken a stand. Discussions on returning the German colonies had ended.

In Germany, this was unacceptable to Hitler and the demands for the return of the colonies resumed. On November 5, 1937, he told his military leaders privately that the "lebensraum" needed by Germany could only be acquired by force. On the 21st of that month, Hitler again addressed the German people telling them that their living space was "too small" and that the colonies must be returned to satisfy Germany's needs. The resumption of Hitler's hard line on the colonies sounded alarm bells among the appeasement-minded leaders in London and Paris who now felt it necessary to revise their positions. Nine days later Britain and France made a very surprising joint announcement on the question of the Germany colonies. It read in part:

"...the question (of the German colonies) was one that could not be considered in isolation and, moreover, would involve a number of other countries. It was agreed that the subject would require much more extended study."

Suddenly, the British position on the colonies, supported now by France, had softened. This was an example of the appeasement policy Britain and France were beginning to pursue. There would be others.

From South Africa, Justice Minister Smuts felt obliged to speak out on his country's non-appeasement policy toward South West Africa, stating that it was still the same and would not change regardless of the position taken by the Chamberlain government in London.

ITALY SUPPORTS GERMANY ON THE COLONIAL ISSUE

During December 1937, Mussolini supported his friend, Hitler, and did as the Fuhrer had been urging him to do—leave the League of Nations. In a speech to the Italian people soon afterwards explaining this action, Mussolini put part of the blame for Italy's leaving the League of Nations on other nations, which attempted to wreck, not only Germany's colonial aspirations, but Italy's as well. Mussolini said:

"We had not forgotten, and shall not forget, the opprobrious attempt at economic strangulation (sanctions) of the Italian people perpetrated at Geneva (over Ethiopia)... In these circumstances our presence at the door of Geneva could not be tolerated any longer..."

The next day Hitler publicly thanked Mussolini for his action, and stated that Germany would never return to the League of Nations because the League had been ineffectual in solving world problems.

Few could disagree with Hitler's assessment of the League of Nations. By now the League was seen as a failure by virtually everyone. Italy's departure made it even more so. As for the colonial mandates granted by the League, they too were of little value. Without a powerful organization to enforce them, the former German colonies had become, more or less, cast adrift and were being administered independently by the mandated powers.

And Hitler intended to take full advantage of the situation. In early 1938, Nazi planners began making secret plans on how Germany might re-acquire its colonies, and possibly the colonies of others, by whatever means necessary. The planners looked covetously at the mineral-rich Belgian Congo and the sprawling French Equatorial Africa. These plans would slowly emerge in the coming years. The dream of Mittel Afrika had not died.

1938: THE AXIS GROWS STRONGER. AMERICA BEGINS TO EMERGE FROM ISOLATIONISM

On January 7, 1938 the Italian government announced that it would begin a program to enlarge its navy, which included the building of new battleships. Part of the reason given for the expansion was the need to protect Italy's colonial empire. This action would greatly alter the balance of power in the Mediterranean and pose an increased threat with regards to the Suez Canal, which the Italians had long coveted.

Twenty-one days later, the American President, Franklin D. Roosevelt, addressed the American people and called for a massive armaments program to improve the capabilities of the U. S. Armed Forces. This represented a major policy change for the United States. The American giant was beginning to emerge from two decades of isolation to participate in an arms race. Roosevelt's timing was good. The American people had become fully aware of what was happening in the world, and were supportive of the idea.

In early February 1938, Hitler dismissed some of the army generals who had shown a lack of enthusiasm for his aggressive policies. He then created a centralized command over the German armed forces called the "Oberkommando der Wehrmacht" (OKW) and assumed its top post himself. Hitler was now Chairman of the Nazi Party, President of Germany, Chancellor of Germany and Supreme Commander of the German armed forces. Of such things are dictators made.

On both February 6 and 20, 1938, Hitler addressed the Reichstag, and each time demanded the return of the colonies. He also demanded that the German people of Austria and the Sudetenland (a crescent-shaped area along the western border of Czechoslovakia populated half by Germans and half by Czechs) be given self-determination—a Nazi euphemism for a Nazi takeover. Hitler was in the home stretch of his campaign to annex both of these territories to provide the German people with "lebensraum." Before the year ended, he would accomplish both of these goals and the world would ask, "Where would it all end?."

HITLER'S LAST TERRITORIAL DEMAND IN EUROPE—BUT NOT IN AFRICA

In March 1838, Hitler successfully carried out one of his life-long dreams by annexing his native Austria to Germany. This had been accomplished peacefully, primarily because Austria, which had tried to follow a strictly neutral course since world War I, had no military allies and could not stand up alone against Germany's military might.

Next, in September 1938, Hitler turned his attentions to the Sudetenland of Czechoslovakia and demanded that it, with its population of ethnic Germans and Czechs, be given to Germany. The Sudetenland was a part of the newly-created state of Czechoslovakia, which had been assembled after World War I by the victorious Allies out of several provinces of the former Austro-Hungarian Empire. Czechoslovakia, however, was no political sitting-duck like Austria had been. The Czechs had firm military alliances with Britain and France that stated if any country, such as Germany, attacked her, Britain and France would be obliged to come to Czechoslovakia's defense.

Hitler could not be dissuaded on the Sudetenland issue, and threatened to use military force if necessary to accomplish his goal. Britain and France replied, just as adamantly, that they would honor their military commitments to protect Czechoslovakia.

In a desperate effort to head off a major war, French Premier Edouard Daladier and British Prime Minister Neville Chamberlain met with Hitler at Munich in late September 1938. Mussolini, who spoke German, French, and English, was invited as mediator. The Czechs were not invited. Surprisingly, and mercifully, an agreement was reached. Hitler promised that the Sudetenland would be his last territorial demand in Europe and the British and French agreed not to attack Germany if she took possession of that area. On October 1, 1938, German troops moved into the Sudetenland unopposed and the area was annexed to Germany.

The Munich Agreement was hailed, world-wide, as a great diplomatic success and a triumph for the Allied policy of appeasement. And, Mussolini, who was instrumental in brokering the deal, was hailed as a great peacemaker.

The fact that Hitler had promised to keep the peace in Europe only now heightened fears that he might turn next, with a vengeance, to the issue of the lost colonies. The British and French governments braced for this eventuality.

But, the Munich Agreement soon proved to be a cruel deception. Within a few days after the conference ended, Hitler began making territorial demands on neighboring Poland and, as with Czechoslovakia, threatened to carry them out with military force if necessary. The lands Hitler sought were areas taken from Germany after World War I, which were used, along with lands taken from Czarist Russia and the Austro-Hungarian Empire, to re-create the Polish nation, which had been conquered and divided by those three countries in the previous century.

Poland, like Czechoslovakia, had military alliances with Britain and France. Suddenly the whole diplomatic atmosphere in Europe reversed. Hitler had shown his promises to be worthless and the policy of appeasement had proven to be a failure. Britain and France announced that they would honor their military commitments to Poland, and that there would not be another Munich-like agreement. Conditions in Europe, thereafter, degenerated into a very tense diplomatic stalemate, with a major European war being a very real possibility.

As for colonial Africa, however, the German pressure was off—at least for the moment. Hitler had much greater issues to worry about than the return of colonies.

"CRYSTAL NIGHT" AND AFRICA

On November 7, 1938, another event happened in Europe that was to adversely effect the political atmosphere there and be very detrimental to Europe's Jews. There would also be reverberations in Africa. On that day a seventeen year-old Jewish youth, Herschel Grynszpan, walked into the German Embassy in Paris and shot to death Ernst vom Rath, the third secretary of the Embassy. Grynszpan's motive was that his parents had recently been expelled from Germany into Poland, forced to leave behind all their possessions, and were now living in miserable conditions in a make-shift refugee camp.

The Nazis were enraged by the assassination and used it as an excuse to send their SA thugs into the streets of Germany and carry out a swift and deadly pogrom against the Jews that still remained in Germany. One of the tactics the thugs used was to smash the windows of stores owned by Jews. In some German cities, so much broken glass littered the streets and sidewalks that the event became known as "Crystal Night." This was just the beginning. Within 24 hours some 20,000 Jews were arrested and 37 Jews killed. The Nazi government also levied a collective fine of one billion marks on Germany's Jewish community. Vom Rath's body was brought back to his hometown of Dusseldorf and given a hero's funeral. Hitler was in attendance.

Crystal Night brought renewed international attention to the plight of Europe's Jews, and most of the major powers made some sort of gesture to help the Jews. Some of those gestures involved Africa. Britain opened two of its colonies to Jewish settlers, British Guiana in South America and Tanganyika in Africa. France, likewise, opened areas within its African empire to a limited number of Jews, and the Dutch allowed some Jews to settle in their colonial possessions. Despite these and other concessions, there were still tens of thousands of homeless Jews in Europe and elsewhere.

ITALY PRESSES ITS CLAIMS IN COLONIAL AFRICA

Encouraged by Hitler's gains at Munich, Mussolini decided to renew his long-standing territorial claims to see if he could emulate Hitler's success. Mussolini had some territorial claims in Europe but the bulk of his claims were in Africa. Specifically, Mussolini, and to a certain degree, other Italian leaders before him, had sought to gain control over French-controlled Corsica, Tunisia, French Somaliland (often referred to as Djibouti), and of course the Suez Canal.

On November 30, 1938, Mussolini's campaign was launched when his Foreign Minister and son-in-law, Galeazzo Ciano, made a well-orchestrated speech before the Italian National Assembly raising, once again, Italy's old territorial claims. As Ciano's speech ended the Assembly members rose on cue and shouted out "Tunis, Djibouti, Corsica! Tunis, Djibouti, Corsica!" time and again. Coincidentally, the Italian media took up the call and the Italian Diplomatic Corps began pressing the French, British, and others to open talks on Italy's territorial demands.

The most intense Italian pressure fell on France which refused to even consider opening the proposed talks that Italy demanded. The French and British saw clearly what Mussolini was up to, and that his actions had moved Europe,

AMERICA'S—AND JOSEPH P. KENNEDY'S—PLANS FOR THE JEWS

In London, the American Ambassador, Joseph P. Kennedy, was working closely with Washington attorney George Rublee, who had connections to the White House, and with Prime Minister Chamberlain on a relocation program for Europe's Jews. The plan called for Britain to offer some part of the British Empire, most likely in Africa, as a sanctuary for the Jews. It also called for the world Jewish community to contribute $600 million dollars to cover the cost of the relocation. It was presumed that a large part of that money could come from American Jews. The "Kennedy-Chamberlain Plan," as it became known, received favorable press in both the United States and Britain. It was compared favorably as an alternative to the "Madagascar Plan." Germany, however, showed no interest in the plan. Ambassador Kennedy then began working on another supportive plan of his own, without the knowledge of the Roosevelt Administration, which he hoped would gain Germany's cooperation. Kennedy enlisted the aid of James D. Mooney, head of General Motors Corporation's operation in Europe who, in turn, made contact with Goering's principal economic representative, Dr. Helmuth Wohlthat. The three gentlemen, Kennedy, Mooney, and Wohlthat, met secretly in London and worked out a plan that they believed Hitler might accept. It called for a $1 billion gold loan to be made to Germany, a promise of the return of her colonies, and the removal of all restrictions on Germany's world trade. Germany would be required to cooperate with the relocation of the Jews, write non-aggression pacts with all of her neighbors, accept arms limitations, and participate in free trade. Kennedy and Mooney had secretly contacted a number of the world's leading industrialists and received some verbal support for their plan.

British intelligence, however, learned of the secret dealings and informed the Chamberlain government which, to say the least, was shocked at the audacity of the Americans and, as might be expected, was opposed to the plan. London informed Washington of Kennedy's and Mooney's secret dealings, and the "Kennedy-Mooney Plan" was leaked to the press. The British press denounced the plan and the Roosevelt Administration, greatly embarrassed by Kennedy's action, diplomatically but firmly did likewise. Once the plan was made public and denounced by both London and Washington, Kennedy's and Mooney's industrialist friends backed out and the plan came to naught.

and now Africa, ever closer to war. Britain and France's response, and virtually their only remaining option, was to begin building up their armed forces to protect these areas from an Italian attack. In France's case, the French Army began a program in the African colonies to recruit 20,000 black African soldiers. Within a few months the first contingent of these troops, some 7000, departed for France. They were not sent to the Italian and German borders as might have been expected. Other French troops were used for that purpose. The askaris were sent to southern France to guard the sprawling refugee camps which still held several hundred thousand refugees from the Spanish Civil War. This action released regular army soldiers for action on the Italian and German borders.

In February 1939, another 1000 West African askaris and their white officers were sent to French Somaliland (Djibouti) to beef up that colony's defenses. The message to Mussolini was clear, if he wanted Djibouti and the other French colonies, he would have to fight for them and risk an attack on Italy proper from southern France.

There was more to come. Tens of thousands more askaris were recruited in the months that followed, and by the time France fought its last battles in June 1940, there were over 80,000 black troops in France. In addition to these men the French also recruited and brought to France tens of thousands of North Africans.

The British increased their African forces, but not nearly to the degree the French did. The two Allies, however, could see that if there was to be war in Africa they would probably be in it together. So, to improve communications, the British and French established a direct liaison between their respective colonial offices in London and Paris on matters regarding colonial defense.

MUSSOLINI STRIKES AGAIN

In late March 1939, the Spanish Civil War was coming to an end with a complete and total victory for the Spanish Nationalists. Generalissimo Franco, of course, was beholden to Germany and Italy for their substantial military support and was showing signs that the new regime he would install in Madrid would be very Fascist-like in its makeup.

In Rome, Mussolini was very pleased with the outcome in Spain, and was convinced that Fascism was on the march and he intended to keep the momentum rolling. On March 26, 1939, the Italian government officially repeated its demands for Corsica, Tunisia, Djibouti, and the Suez Canal. Three days later Paris responded that it would not cede a square foot of territory to Italy. The possibility of war in both Europe and Africa loomed once again.

Then Mussolini turned his attentions to the Balkans. In early April 1939, Italian forces invaded and quickly conquered the tiny Balkan country of Albania on the eastern shore of the Adriatic Sea. Italy had been threatening Albania for some time, and this arbitrary act proved that Mussolini was willing and able to use military force to take

GERMANY ACQUIRES AN OVERSEAS POSSESSION

The permanent residents of Germany's new Antarctic colony.

In December 1938, a German expedition left Hamburg, Germany for Antarctica with the announced purpose of staking out a part of that ice-covered continent for the Third Reich. Unfortunately, all of Antarctica had already been claimed by others, but this was no deterrent to the pioneers of the new world order. During the spring of 1939, the Germans trekked over the snow and ice of Antarctica, dropping little swastika flags along the border of their new colonial territory. In June 1939, they returned to Germany in triumph to announce that Germany had its first new overseas possession. The other nations of the world simply ignored Germany's claim.

what he wanted. This was Italy's third major military triumph in four years: Ethiopia 1935-36, Spain 1936-38 and Albania 1939.

While Italy looked like a military menace on the surface, it was quite another story behind the scenes. Italy's armed forces were not really ready for a major European war. Count Ciano admitted this to the Germans on August 12 and 13, 1939, when he met with Hitler and von Ribbentrop in Germany. War over Poland was moving ever closer and Italy, because of its alliances with Germany, would be obligated to enter the war on Germany's side. This frightened Mussolini and the other Italian leaders, and they had to tell the Germans that Italy would not be able to participate in a war against Poland, Britain, and France. Ciano told the Germans that the Italian armed forces had been drained by their actions in Ethiopia, Spain, and Albania, and would not be ready for a major war until 1941. This was an accurate assessment of the Italian military situations, and the Germans knew it. On August 25, 1939, Mussolini personally confirmed to Hitler that Italy would not go to war on Germany's side over the Polish question. Hitler, though, decided to move ahead on the issue of Poland without Italy's military support.

THE GERMAN/SOVIET PACT AND MITTEL AFRIKA AGAIN

On August 23, 1939, Germany and the Soviet Union electrified the world by signing a nonaggression pact in Moscow. This was a completely unexpected event, and a masterful stoke of diplomacy by Hitler. By initiating this pact, Hitler was protecting Germany's eastern frontier from a surprise attack by the Soviets if Germany was forced to fight France and Britain in the west. Hitler was willing to pay a generous price for this security because he knew in his heart, and had already confided to a few of his closest colleagues, that one day soon Germany would have no alternative but to turn on the Soviet Union to eliminate world Communism and, at the same time, conquer its vast land area as lebensraum for the German people. Therefore, German concessions made to the Soviets now were of little consequence in the long run.

For the moment, though, the Soviet Union could have everything it asked for. Hitler gave Stalin a free hand in Eastern Europe, whereby the Soviet Union could settle all of its old scores with its neighbors without German objection or interference. This included conquering eastern Poland which had once been Czarist territory. Furthermore, Hitler agreed that the Soviet Union could expand southward, at the expense of the British, by taking India and the Persian Gulf area to become the dominant power in the Indian Ocean. All that Hitler asked was that the Soviet Union stay out of Africa and allow Germany to establish there its long-sought colonial empire of "Mittel Afrika." This was agreeable with the Soviets. Several months later, in March 1940, Hitler would tell Mussolini that one factor that facilitated the pact with the Soviet Union was that the Soviets believed him with regards to his demands for the return of the German colonies.

In the mean time German propaganda stopped calling for German lebensraum in the east and began to emphasize that that need could be met in Africa. Events would soon prove that this was, in fact, only a ploy to mollify the Soviets.

HITLER PLAYS THE COLONIES CARD ONE MORE TIME

By mid-August 1939, the date for the invasion of Poland had been set in Berlin. It would be August 26. But, Hitler would try one last time to reach a negotiated settlement. On August 25 he summoned British Ambassador Neville Henderson to the Chancellory in Berlin and told him that the German government was willing "...to approach England with a large and comprehensive offer" if Britain would allow Germany to take the land it sought in Poland. Hitler offered to "...guarantee the existence of the British Empire" providing Britain would agree to negotiate on Germany's "limited" colonial demands. It would be a quid pro quo—an empire for an empire. Furthermore, Britain must not ask for revisions on Germany's obligations with her allies. Henderson knew, and, of course, Hitler did too, that this was an attempt to split the British/French alliance.

Henderson, nevertheless, had to relay Hitler's proposals to London, and a response would take several days. Accordingly, Hitler postponed the invasion of Poland. London eventually expressed no interest in dealing separately with Hitler at this late date and rejected the offer. Other last-minute negotiations were initiated by the Germans but they too broke down. Hitler then set the new date for the invasion of to be Friday, September 1, 1939.

On that day his orders were carried out. German troops invaded Poland. Two days later Britain and France, living up to the promises they had made to Poland (but denied to Czechoslovakia), declared war on Germany. World War II had begun.

Chapter 4

EUROPE GOES TO WAR: AFRICA GOES TO WAR (SEPTEMBER 1939–JUNE 1940)

TWO CONTINENTS AFLAME

When German forces invaded Poland on September 1, 1939, the world got its first glimpse at how really powerful the German armed forces had become since 1933, the year Hitler came to power. Both their army and air force (Luftwaffe) were large, well-equipped, and well-trained. And, above all, the Army's new tactic of "Blitzkrieg" (Lightening War), was extremely effective. This tactic utilized massed tank formations, supported by intensive air cover, that smashed through the enemy's front at one or more places and created holes through which motorized infantry units could then flow. Together the tanks and motorized infantry quickly penetrated the enemy's rear and encircled large numbers of enemy troops. It was unlike anything that had been experienced in World War I. In the west, the Allied leaders were astonished and alarmed. They had been expecting a trench war similar to that of World War I, and their armies were not equipped or trained to deal with Blitzkrieg warfare.

By September 3, 1939, the British and French, after unsuccessfully playing their last desperate diplomatic cards, were obliged to honor their word to Poland and declare war on Germany. By this time it was obvious that Poland would soon be lost.

On September 4 the Polish government began to evacuate Warsaw. On the 5th Krakow, fell and on the 6th German troops entered Warsaw. By October 6 hostilities in Poland ended.

AFRICA GOES TO WAR

When Britain and France entered the war on September 3, 1939, all of their colonies, protectorates, crown colonies, and mandates went to war with them. In Africa, this meant that Tunisia, Algeria, French Morocco, French West Africa, French Equatorial Africa, French Somaliland, Madagascar, The Comoro Islands, and Reunion Island followed France into the war, while Gambia, Sierra Leone, Gold Coast, Nigeria, British Somaliland, British East Africa, Nyasaland, the Rhodesias, Bechuanaland, Swaziland, and Basutoland all went to war with Britain. The colonies of Italy, Spain, Portugal, and Belgium all remained neutral because their mother countries had all proclaimed neutrality.

The independent countries of Africa, Egypt, Liberia, and South Africa had to chose for themselves. The Egyptian government of Ali Maher broke diplomatic relations with Germany on September 7, under strong British pressure, but refused to declare war. Maher's government, instead, declared a state of siege, interned 120 German nationals, imposed censorship and price controls, broke off trade relations with Germany, and searched neutral ships in Egyptian harbors. These measures satisfied the British for the moment. The German diplomats left Cairo, and the Swedish government took over German affairs in Egypt.

Egypt's government was riddled with anti-British and pro-German individuals, and public opinion was very much against entering the war. The Egyptians had little to fear from Germany and the Egyptian leadership knew it. Berlin knew of Egypt's dilemma and had, in September 1938, at the time of the Munich Crisis, informed the Egyptian government that Germany would not retaliate against Egypt if, even under strong British pressures, it was forced to sever diplomatic relations with Germany. Before taking that action, though, the Egyptian government sought, and received, assurances from Berlin that the German government would abide by its statement of September 1938.

In Berlin, as was necessary under diplomatic protocol, the German government ordered the Egyptian legation closed. A few Egyptians were interned but soon released. The Embassy of Afghanistan took over Egyptian interests in Berlin.

As for the other independent countries, Liberia proclaimed its neutrality, and in South Africa a very unpleasant situation began to evolve.

SOUTH AFRICA GOES TO WAR BUT THE GOVERNMENT FALLS.

Entering the war was an extremely difficult question for the people and government of South Africa. As a Dominion of the British Commonwealth, he nation had moral and treaty ties to Britain, but it was not mandatory for South Africa to enter the war as a British ally.

South Africa had been through this crisis before, in 1914, and it had been a very painful experience. At that time World War I had just started in Europe, and the people of South Africa faced the same question. Many Afrikaners were against entering World War I, and took to the streets demanding that the nation stay out of the war. The protests turned into an open rebellion, and the South African Army had to be called in to restore law and order. This tragic event, which saw South Africans fighting South Africans, was in the living memory of many people, and virtually all of the nation's leaders. No one wanted it to happen again.

Yet, Prime Minister J. B. M. Hertzog had to make a decision. He, personally, was against entering the war, at least at this time. He was also mindful that the attitude of the people in the years just before the war had shown little popular support for South Africa going to war, just as had been the case in 1914. Most importantly for Hertzog was the cabinet vote of 1938, in which his own cabinet, at the time, voted to remain neutral in the event of a war between Britain and Germany.

Jan Christian Smuts became Prime Minister of South Africa on September 5, 1939, and took the nation into World War II against Germany. This was his third time as Prime Minister. He was 69 year old.

But, things had changed. Fascism's aggressive and evil ways were obviously a threat to the world order, and Britain had done the honorable thing in trying to stop it. Those efforts had failed, and now Britain had put her very existence on the line. Could

the South Africans be any less dedicated?

Former Prime Minister J. B. M. Hertzog.

Leading the pro-war faction was Jan Christian Smuts, the number two man in Hertzog's United Party. This old warrior spoke for the conscience of the nation and demanded that South Africa do the honorable thing and join Britain in the war. Smuts had many supporters throughout the nation, and his position was further supported by a broadcast from London by King George, personally appealing to the members of the Empire to support Britain in her time of need.

For the first five days of the war this issue was hotly debated in South Africa's Parliament, as well as in the media, and in the homes and businesses throughout the country. In the meantime the other Dominions acted. On September 3, the same day Britain declared war, India and the Dominions of Australia and New Zealand declared war on Germany. On the 4th, Northern Ireland declared war. Only Ireland, the renegade Dominion of the Empire, proclaimed its neutrality. Canada had not yet decided, but was visibly moving toward declaring war and did so on September 10.

On the evening of September 5, 1939, Hertzog put the issue to a vote in Parliament with his personal recommendation to remain neutral. The vote surprised nearly everyone. It was 80 to 67 in favor of war. There were five absent or abstention votes. The three native representatives in Parliament supported the majority, but their votes did not count in the final tally.

This was a crushing blow to Hertzog, and made his position as Prime Minister untenable. He could no longer lead a government under these conditions and, about 10:00 that evening, resigned. His resignation was accepted within the hour by Governor-General Sir Patrick Duncan, who then summoned Smuts to form a new government. Smuts had been prime minister twice before. Now he would be prime minister for a third time at the age of 69.

Smuts quickly formed a coalition government of members of his own United Party and the small Labour and Dominion Parties. He took the posts of Minister of Defence and Minister of the Interior (which controlled the police) unto himself. The next day, September 6, the Smuts government declared war on Germany. Soon afterwards, the German diplomatic corps assigned to South Africa travelled to Lourenco Marques, Mozambique, and departed for Germany. Likewise, the South African diplomatic delegation in Germany returned to South Africa.

THE NATAL MERCURY, THURSDAY, SEPTEMBER 7, 1939.

The English-speaking newspapers of South Africa universally supported the decision to go to war. Above is a cartoon which appeared in the Natal Mercury newspaper on September 7, 1939.

The decision to go to war was far from unanimous among the citizenry of South Africa, and a sizeable minority of the white population, primarily Afrikaners, continued to openly oppose the war. This opposition would surface in a variety of ways throughout the conflict. South Africa was in the war on the Allied side, but it was one of the alliance's weaker-willed members.

The Smuts government soon passed legislation increasing the strength of the country's armed forces. They were in pretty sorry shape. There were only 2585 white soldiers in South Africa's army, the South African Permanent Force (SAPF); 2800 in the air force and a smaller number yet in the South African Navy. There were also blacks in the armed forces, but since they were not allowed to carry arms, the small number of white men in the services was the sum total of the nation's armed forces.

Smuts had the power, under the Union Defence Act, to impose conscription, but chose not to do so at this time because of the deep divisions within the nation. Furthermore, conscription was one of the issues that sparked the rebellion of 1914, and there were rumors in the air that certain elements of the citizenry might rise again if conscription was imposed. Smuts did, however, call for volunteers. Thereto, Smuts had a problem because South African law forbad the use of the SAPF outside the territorial boundaries of the country. Smuts also let this issue stand because of the tense political atmosphere.

South Africa had a sizeable military reserve organization called the Active Citizens Force (ACF) of 13,490 member but it had not been mobilized. Furthermore, the ACF could not, like the SAPF, be sent outside of South Africa.

South Africa's Air Force had several dozen airplanes, but only four modern fighter planes—British-made Hurricanes—and 17 bombers—German-made Junker JU–86 transports which had been converted into bombers.

Hundreds of young South African men answered Smuts's call for volunteers and flocked to the recruiting offices. The Smuts government took this opportunity to pass a law authorizing "volunteers" to be sent outside of South Africa thus negating, for the most part, the home-bound nature of the armed forces.

South Africa had other military assets of note; the huge British naval base at Simonstown, in the Cape Town area, and a second naval base at Durban. South Africa, like many other parts of the British Empire, depended on the British Navy to control the high seas. The South African Navy was equipped and trained primarily for coastal defense, submarine patrol, and convoy duty.

On September 11, the South African government began registering German aliens. There were some 35,000 in the country. They had to fill out forms giving information on themselves and were ordered to notify authorities when they moved. This was rather mild treatment of German aliens. In some countries, notably Britain, large numbers were placed in internment camps and kept there for an extended period. Here again, the Smuts government took a less controversial approach.

In the deeply divided political atmosphere that existed in South Africa, rumors were a constant problem. One such rumor began circulating in November 1939, stating that German missionaries, which the government had allowed to continue operating, were preaching anti-British doctrines to the native and telling them that there would soon be a German takeover of the country. This rumor came to naught, but gave many people cause for alarm and kept tensions high in South Africa.

ANTI-WAR AFRIKANERS OPERATE IN THE OPEN

The hard-core segment of Afrikaners society in South Africa was centered in the Transvaal region and was too large and too powerful to be silenced. So, the Smuts government had to tolerate their aggravating and counterproductive activities so long as they did not cross the line into treason. The Afrikaner's leaders knew this and, having memories of the bloody rebellion of 1914, kept their activities within bounds. But, they were determined to be heard and utilized, to the limits of legality, the freedoms permitted them by the nation's constitution and the Smuts government.

The Ox wagon Sentinels (OB) took the lead within this segment of the Afrikaner community and continued preaching its prewar policies of calling for an all-Afrikaner Republic, an end to ties with the British Empire, and firm and well-defined segregation policies for blacks, colored people, Asians, and Jews. And now that their country was at war, they called for an end to that war.

Since many leaders in the National Party were members of, or sympathetic to, the OB's policies, those policies worked

GERMAN INFLUENCE IN THE NATIONAL PARTY

Just prior to the vote of January 23, 1940, Dr. Daniel Malan, leader of the National Party, held a secret meeting in his home at Cape Town with Mrs. Hans Denk, the wife of a known German agent inSouth Africa. This was on, or about, January 16. Mrs. Denk claimed that she was authorized to pass on to Malan Germany's plans for South Africa after Germany's final victory in the war. Mrs. Denk told Malan that Germany would welcome South Africa's becoming a republic, independent of the British Commonwealth, and would support South Africa's taking control of Britain's protectorates of Bechuanaland, Swaziland, and Basutoland. And, if South Africa wanted to absorb the Rhodesias, Germany would support that effort, too. Germany, of course, would expect to recover her lost colony of South West Africa. Mrs. Denk went on to offer Malan reliable communications links to Berlin.

Malan did not report this meeting to the authorities, which was a direct violation of South Africa's wartime security laws. A week later Malan's National Party members in Parliament introduced the resolution calling for South Africa's withdrawal from the war.

After the war, notes on the Malan/Denk meeting were found in the files of the German Foreign Office in Berlin, and both Malan and Mrs. Denk were ordered to appear before a bi–partisan Parliamentary select committee to explain their actions. The captured records stated that Malan was very receptive to Germany's proposals, and offered to enlist other National Party leaders, as well as ex–Prime Minister Hertzog, in supporting Germany's proposals.

Malan's defense before the select committee for not having reported the meeting at the time was that Mrs. Denk only told him things that he already knew, and therefore thought the meeting was of little value. He further stated that he believed the meetingmight have been set up by his opponents to embarrass him. Malan further claimed he took no action as a result of the meeting.

Mrs. Denk was called before the committee and claimed that she had only vague memory of the meeting and did not remember the details.

The committee decided in Malan's favor and took no action against him. In his autobiography, some years later, Malan wrote of the details of the Denk meeting, and of a second meeting with German operatives during the war.

their way into that Party's programs. This resulted, among other things, in the formation by the National Party in 1940 of a new youth movement called the "Nasionale Jeugbond" (National Youth Union—NJ). Membership in the NJ was open to all white South Africans, except Jews, ages twelve through thirty. Its constitution called for a "Christian National Boer Republic" and pledged its members' services not to South Africa, but to the Afrikaner "Volk." NJ programs called for Afrikaans to be the national language and banned intermarriages between Afrikaners and "inassimilable" whites.

The OB and NJ were, of course, extremely nationalistic but not necessarily pro-Nazi. But, the rise of the Nazi Party in Europe and German successes on the battlefield were greatly admired, and it was not surprising that Nazi-like thinking and trappings were adopted by these Afrikaner organizations. This was seen in the Transvaal where some schools began their school day with the Nazi salute and during school time the students and teachers listened together to "Zeesen Radio," the shortwave radio broadcasts from Germany. Students were told that Zeesen Radio was the only source of reliable news in South Africa.

These, and other openly pro-Nazi activities, were not done in secret and were openly discussed, pro and con, throughout South Africa and in the news media. Pro-German newspapers were widely circulated in South Africa and they, too, often mimicked Nazi views and propaganda. One of the most popular was "Die Oosterlig" published by Otto du Plessis, a high official in the National Party holding the position of Enlightenment Secretary.

Most of these things were tolerated by the Smuts government, which was able to surmount them because it had a supporting majority in Parliament and the support of the majority of the South African voters. This was proven on January 23, 1940, when a resolution was introduced in Parliament by the Nationalist, calling for South Africa to drop out of the war. That resolution was defeated by the substantial majority of 81 to 59.

Supporting the minority on this issue was ex-Prime Minister Hertzog, now the number two man in the United Party under Smuts. Hertzog was convinced that the Germans would win the war and made his views well-known.

The Smuts government did take one precaution, however, and disarmed the OB soon after the war started. This was only a half-measure because many of the OB members were able to hide their arms from the authorities.

Afrikaner sentiment against the war was very real, and the Transvaal was the center of this activity. The Transvaal National Party, a small ultra-right-wing Afrikaners political organization, organized a series of protest meetings in the Transvaal, the largest of which attracted some 5000 people in February 1940 in the Johannesburg City Hall. There, and at other meetings, spokesmen openly denounced Smuts and

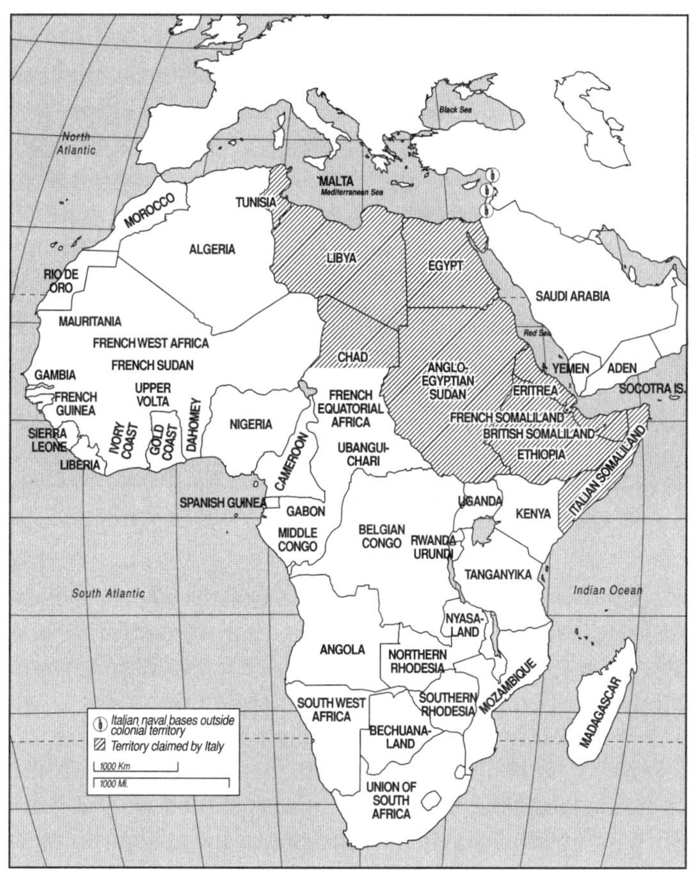

Mussolini's territorial claims in Africa, prior to Italy's entering the war.

his war policies, and decried the fact that many innocent South African young men would be killed as a result of Smuts' folly. Smuts was denounced as a foolhardy old man and a tool of the "English Jews." Some Afrikaner speakers hinted that the time might come when the Afrikaners might be forced to seize power. This meant revolution, and was treasonable rhetoric in wartime. But, both the hard-core Afrikaners and the government restrained themselves, both mindful of the 1914 rebellion.

TENSIONS IN EAST AFRICA

One of the first war-related acts by the British in East Africa was taken in Kenya and Tanganyika when those colonies' authorities ordered the internment of every German national. A parallel action had been taken in Britain. In time, the individual internees were interviewed, and those deemed not to be security risks were released while the others were held.

The real threat in East Africa was not the Germans but the Italians in Italian East Africa. With Italy being Germany's ally and Germany being at war with Britain and France this concern was unavoidable. Adding to the tensions was the fact that the Italians still had large military forces in their colonies from the days of the First East African War (1935-36). Some of these troops were engaged in battling Ethiopian guerrillas who still held out in various parts of Ethiopia, but others, the British and French feared, were available to attack them if and when Italy should join in the war. It was well-ingrained in the mind of every colonial administrator in East Africa that all during the late 1930s Mussolini had been quite vocal on settling Italy's territorial claims in Africa and had not ruled out the use of force.

Another fear among the Allies was that the Italians had recruited and trained sizeable numbers of natives for their armed forces. Also, the Italians had improved the infrastructure of their colonies by building new roads and some industry, thereby enhancing their military position in East Africa.

The British and French did not know it at the time but they had little to fear from the Italians. The Ethiopian guerrillas were tying down more Italian troops than the British and French realized, and seemed capable of continuing their struggle for a long time to come. Furthermore, the Italians had made virtually no preparations for launching military attacks into the neighboring British and French colonies, and had made only minimal preparations for defense. Furthermore, the new Italian settlers did not want war. They had, for the most part, come to Italian East Africa to establish new lives for themselves and make money. They had no interest in seeing their new homeland become a battleground. These concerns exercised a certain restraint on the military planning of the Italians.

Italian East Africa's economy was still very shaky. There were guerrillas in the bush, shortages of many necessities, and

MUSSOLINI CRITICAL OF "COLORED" TROOPS

On March 10 and 11, 1940 Mussolini met with German Foreign Minister von Ribbentrop in Rome to discuss various aspects of the war in Europe. During the conversation, Mussolini criticized the French Army for having so many "colored" troops. He told von Ribbentrop that within the French Army there are "...numerous colored elements, who are impulsive but do not stand up to fighting. No one knows what these African auxiliary troops think among themselves. They communicate between themselves in a language which the French do not understand, and their attitude, in the event of military reverses, might be a danger to France."

Mussolini might have based his opinion on his own efforts to raise a black army in Italian East Africa, especially in Ethiopia. There, the Italians had discovered that the newly–conquered Ethiopians were very reluctant to serve in the army of their conqueror.

much of the country was still very primitive. A black market had come into being and there was a high rate of corruption within the colonial administration. The latter was so prevalent that a system of middlemen, called "Pampadours," arose who would intercede on behalf of anyone who wanted a favor and the official who, with a bribe, could provide it.

Mussolini knew of these things but could do little about them. He also knew that Italian East Africa was not prepared for war. On March 31, 1940, Marshal Graziani, the Italian Army Chief of Staff, confirmed this by telling Mussolini that Ethiopia was still not sufficiently pacified, and that defenses in the north were so weak the British could easily take all of Eritrea.

The British and French could not take any chances, though, in East Africa and saw no alternative but to begin building up their own forces.

Mindful of this problem the War Office in London issued orders, in early September 1939, to the colonial administration in British East Africa authorizing a sizeable increase in the main defense force there, the "King's African Rifles" (KAR) as well as other native military units. The KAR was the primary military contingent in British East Africa, and had been an organized military entity since before World War I.

New and enlarged headquarters for the British East African Command (BEAC) were established at Kenton College in Nairobi, Kenya, under Major General D. P. Dickenson, who had been sent to British East Africa by the War Office to oversee the military buildup. Under Dickinson's direction, the recruiting of native volunteers was begun for service in the KAR and the Carrier Corps while conscription was imposed for white males.

CARRIER CORPS

The road system of sub-Saharan Africa in the 1940s was still very primitive. Therefore, the time-honored methods of carrying supplies either by animals or humans was still widely used. Both had their advantages for the military. Animals could carry more weight per unit of cost, could forage off the land, and, in a crisis, could be eaten to supplement the food supply. Men could carry less and cost more but could perform useful services such as cooking, laundry, first aid, running messages, etc. In sub-Saharan Africa, all of the colonial armies used both.

In late 1939, the main force of the KAR consisted of two brigades, the Kenya Territorial Regiment and the Northern Rhodesian Regiment. It was their duty to guard the 850 mile border of Kenya with Italian East Africa. There were also coastal defense units at the seaport of Mombasa, and a few small Royal Air Force (RAF) units.

A King's Africa Rifles (KAR) unit being moved by truck.

The British believed that if the Italians struck in East Africa, the most likely place would be a drive southward out of Italian Somaliland, along the Kenyan coast toward Mombasa. Because of this, the two regiments of the KAR were moved at once to defensive positions north of Mombasa, and opposite the Italian Somaliland border. Military transportation vehicles were in very short supply in British East Africa, so civilian vehicles had to be requisitioned to move the troops.

Once in place, the mission of the KAR was to fight a delaying action until reinforcements arrived.

During October 1939, the 22nd Indian Mountain Battalion arrived temporarily in Kenya. These men had experience in artillery weapons and, during their stay, were assigned to train members of the KAR in the use of field artillery using the Indians' guns. Heretofore, the only artillery weapons in Kenya were the stationary coastal guns defending the sea-

At the beginning of the war the only artillery pieces in Kenya were coastal guns such as these. The KAR, the colony's main defense force, had no field artillery.

port of Mombasa and the nearby British naval base of Kilindini.

In December 1939, Prime Minister Smuts of South Africa offered to send a South African brigade to Kenya, but the British authorities declined the offer on the grounds that it might provoke the Italians. Instead, the brigade remained in South Africa, but was held in readiness for a move northward on short notice.

On January 13, 1940, General Archibald Wavell, Supreme Commander of all British forces in North Africa and the Middle East, was given operational control over all British colonial forces, including those in East Africa. This was to better coordinate military activities throughout the region.

During the first few months of 1940, the British authorities organized a sizeable number of Ethiopian refugees into auxiliary units and gave them the name "Patriots." These units were trained to serve alongside British colonial forces. For the most part, these were men who had fled their homeland in the wake of the Italian invasion in 1935–36 and who were eager to fight the Italians.

In Kenya, there was another very special problem. Native nationalist movements, some of them quite militant, were more advanced than elsewhere in British East Africa, and posed a threat to wartime security. The largest and most militant of these organizations was the "Kenya African Union" (KAU). Because of wartime necessities, the Kenyan administration banned all of these organizations for the duration of the war.

THE KAU AND THE MAU MAU REBELLION

The "Kenya African Union" went underground and posed no major problems for the British in Kenya for the duration of the war. But, with the end of hostilities, it revived quickly and was soon taken over by Jomo Kenyatta, a daring and militant leader, who had lived abroad throughout the war. Kenyatta advocated the return of European-owned lands to the natives by any means necessary including violence. These measures led to the bloody Mau Mau Rebellion of 1952–57.

In the former German colony of Tanganyika, the white population was mostly German and supportive, in varying degrees, of Germany. The British authorities had dossiers on most of the German settlers there, and when war started, a sizeable number of them were rounded up as security risks and interned. Many others were closely watched.

The initial internment camp in Tanganyika was the Mbeya Hotel in Boma. Later, a permanent camp was built at Dar es Salaam and upon, completion, 268 German aliens were interned. Some German settlers fled into the neutral territories of Portuguese Mozambique or the Belgian Congo rather than risk being interned.

Once those Germans who were security risks were interned, Tanganyika was considered to be secure enough for most of the small British and KAR units who were stationed there to be sent northward into Kenya to reinforce the British forces already stationed along the border with Italian Somaliland.

Tanganyikan natives were, for the most part, not seen as security risks. Quite to the contrary, they were actively recruited in large numbers into the KAR.

INTERNMENT

The internment of enemy aliens (German citizens and others thought to be sympathetic to Germany) was carried out in most parts of the British Empire, including Britain itself, at the start of the war. This was perfectly legal under the international agreements reached at the Geneva Conference on War in 1929. Internment, however, was usually temporary. The internees, once in custody, were interviewed individually and graded as to their degree of being security risks. All but the most dangerous individuals were released with firm instructions on how to conduct themselves in public and in private, and given dates and places to report regularly to the authorities. Failure to abide by these regulations would result in the alien being lowered in grade and possibly interned again. Those not released were held in internment camps for whatever length of time the host nation determined. The camps were open to frequent inspection by officials from cooperating neutral nations, such as Switzerland, and from international relief agencies such as the Red Cross, who served as monitors.

When Britain went to war against Italy and the other Axis nations, the process was repeated throughout the empire for citizens of those nations.

In Uganda, all male enemy aliens were temporarily interned until their degree of security risk could be determined. The few British and KAR units in the colony were assigned to guard the internment camps and such places as railroads, power plants, water stations, and other vital facilities in both Uganda and Kenya. Ugandan natives, like those elsewhere in British East Africa, were not considered security risks and were actively recruited for service in the KAR.

In British Somaliland, the only defense force available there was the small, but mobile, "Somaliland Camel Corps." If the Italians attacked that colony, the mission of the Camel Corps was the same as that of the KAR in Kenya, to fight a delaying action until reinforcements arrived.

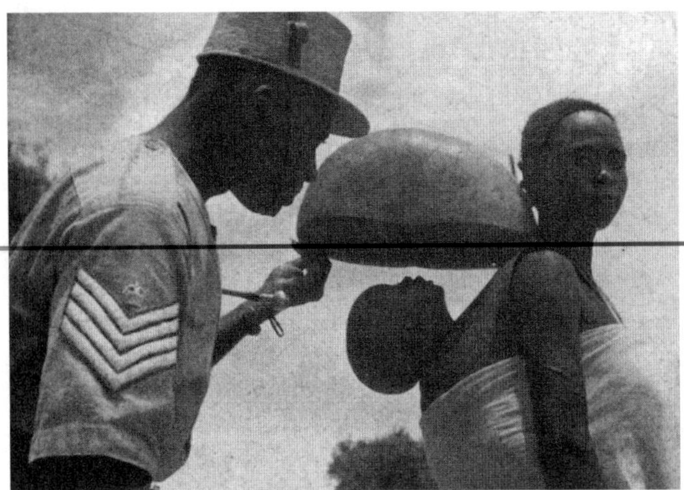

A member of the Sudan Defence Force checking on his son. Wives and children were allowed to accompany the soldiers to their duty posts.

On the northern border of Italian East Africa was the Anglo-Egyptian Sudan. This was a huge colony administered jointly by Britain and Egypt. Its capital was Khartoum. The colony had its own small army called the "Sudan Defence Force" and, under agreement between Britain and Egypt, British and/or Egyptian troops could be called in by the colony's Governor-General to aid in the colony's defense.

In September 1939, a small number of British Army units were scattered throughout the Sudan and an Egyptian Army infantry battalion was stationed at Port Sudan on the Red Sea, and two companies at Khartoum. Together, these forces were a poor match of the Italian forces south of the border.

PLENTY OF VOLUNTEERS

Native recruitment throughout British East Africa proved to be very successful. More than enough natives volunteered for military service to meet the British needs and plans for drafting natives, as had been done during World War I, were shelved. By early October 1939, some 11,000 natives had been recruited and were undergoing training and more were waiting to be called up. The white officer corps had risen to 517 and other white ranks to 1,020.

Not only were natives volunteering in large numbers for military service in British East Africa, but the same phenomenon was occurring in other British colonies in Africa. The British, therefore, decided to tap this huge pool of manpower for other purposes.

In October 1939, Dickinson met with his superior, General Sir Archibald Wavell, Commander-in-Chief Middle East, and worked out plans to create a Colonial Division of askaris for service outside Africa. The KAR, since it was the most advanced of the all the British colonial units, would be the backbone of the new division augmented by forces from British West Africa and Northern Rhodesia. Smaller units were to be formed for service in British Somaliland, Iraq, Iran, and Aden. With recruitment so strong in British East Africa, it was determined that the defense of that region could be left, primarily, in the hands of the KAR. If the Italians struck in East Africa, askari troops from British West Africa, primarily the Royal West African Frontier Forces, would be sent as reinforcements.

These plans filled the immediate manpower needs of the British, but not the need for equipment such as planes, tanks, artillery, and the like. These would have to be provided by the industrialized areas of the Empire such as Britain, South Africa, the other British Dominions, or be purchased abroad.

This lack of equipment showed itself in northern Kenya as the British forces spread out along the Italian Somaliland border. Trenches, pill boxes, mine fields, barbed wire emplacements, and reserve defensive positions were all constructed but there was virtually no supporting artillery or antitank weapons. This was of concern because it was known that some of the "Black Shirt" battalions in Italian East Africa had light tanks.

Some military hardware was received from Britain and South Africa but most of it was old, or even obsolete. The European theater of war, of course, had top priority on the newest and most modern weapons. This, though, was true also in Italian East Africa, so the armaments on both sides were, more or less, of equal quality. Consequently, when war did finally come to East Africa most of the troops, on both sides, would fight with old equipment.

One exception to this were the newly-manufactured armored cars made in South Africa. These vehicles were of great value to the British forces because the form of warfare in sub-Saharan Africa was known as "ribbon warfare," or warfare conducted along the roads. These all-wheel-drive vehicles could tackle the most primitive roads, as well as cross-country terrain and long distances. In some ways they were superior to tanks because tanks were susceptible to high wear when driven long distances. In sub-Saharan Africa, as on other battle fronts, tanks had to be trucked to the battlefields. Armored cars, on the other hand, could make it there on their own.

To satisfy their need for armored cars, the South African government contracted with the Ford Motor

A British recruiting poster for the Royal West African Frontier Force.

A South African–made Marmon–Herrington armored car in North Africa.

Company plant in Port Elizabeth to build armored cars for the South African armed forces as well as other Allied forces. The armored cars became known as the "Marmon-Herrington" armored car, because the all-wheel drive train was made by the Marmon-Herrington Corporation of Indianapolis, Indiana USA, a manufacturer of busses and heavy duty trucks. The drive trains were then shipped to a Ford Motor Company plant in Canada and assembled to a truck frame. That assembly was then sent to Port Elizabeth where the South Africans manufactured the body and assembled the completed vehicle.

After fulfilling the combat needs of the African forces, there were still tens of thousands of volunteers left over. Many of them were placed in the Army's Pioneer Companies (Engineer units). Since the KAR and the Royal West African Frontier Forces preferred to take men from their own regions, the ranks of the Pioneer Companies were filled with men from other parts of the British Empire. From Africa that meant that the men of the Pioneer Companies came from Basutoland, Bechuanaland, Swaziland, the Rhodesias, the Mauritius Islands, the Seychelles Islands, and Egypt.

One thing the British did not want to happen in British East Africa was to have miners leave their jobs for military service. To solve this problem, the British authorities conscripted some miners for the duration of the war to remain at their jobs. Labor conscription was also applied to several other segments of the economy important to the war effort.

BRITISH FORCES BUILD IN EAST AFRICA

By June 1940, British armed forces in East Africa had made considerable progress, but the overall forces available to the British were still considerably less than those in Italian East Africa.

In Kenya, the two regiments of the KAR had grown to 8,500 men and had acquired two light artillery batteries. Another military unit in Kenya was the Kenya Regiment, an all-white volunteer unit of settlers, which was used primarily to train white officers and noncommissioned officers (NCOs) for service in KAR units. Many of the members of the Kenya Regiment were older men, and veterans of World War I.

The federation of Kenya, Uganda, and Tanganyika had an armored car unit, the East African Armored Car Regiment, and a small navy known as the Royal East African Navy (REAN). The REAN had two antiquated whale catchers that had been con-

THE SISAL CONNECTION

The sisal plant. Sisal fibers were sold to the United States to make rope and twine. With the dollars earned, the British in East Africa were then able to buy war supplies from America.

Both Kenya and Tanganyika were major exporters of sisal, a natural fiber used to make rope and twine. Traditionally, it had been a good money–maker for the colonial governments and was one of the ways the colonies strived toward self–sufficiency. The biggest customer for East African sisal was the United States. Now, with British East Africa being at war, that connection was a great benefit to the British. By selling sisal to America, the British colonies accumulated dollars which they could then use to buy war equipment from the United States. Ironically, many of the sisal plantations in Tanganyika were owned by Germans and the largest, over 45,000 acres, was owned by a former German Army officer.

verted into mine sweepers and were also used as patrol vessels.

British East Africa had no air force of its own and relied on the South African Air Force (SAAF) and air units from Southern Rhodesia for its air defenses. These units, while in Kenya, were known as the Kenya Auxiliary Air Unit (KAAU). By June 1940, the KAAU had been built up to three SAAF squadrons and one Southern Rhodesian squadron, all of which were equipped with old aircraft. Back in South Africa, though, the SAAF had acquired more modern planes, and some of them were destined for use in the KAAU.

The British estimated that the Italians had a very sizeable air force of 325 combat-ready aircraft in Italian East Africa, with another 142 planes in reserve. If hostilities started in East Africa, the British plan of air attack was to strike as soon as possible in hopes of destroying large numbers of Italian aircraft on the ground.

Nairobi, Kenya's capital, also prepared for war. The city began practicing blackouts in late May 1940, and had a false air raid alarm on May 24. Many of Nairobi's public buildings were sandbagged, air raid shelters were built, and gas masks distributed.

As part of their defense strategy, the British evacuated all troops out of northern Kenya bordering Abyssinia, Italy's new name for Ethiopia. No major Italian attack was expected here, but if the Italians did choose to attack there they would find very difficult terrain, poor roads, inaccurate maps, and considerable supply problems. This tactic, however, created another problem. Soon after the KAR departed, long dormant tribal conflicts surfaced and looting, cattle rustling, and acts of banditry began among the natives. They were especially bad in the border towns of Moyale and Mandera. The disorder spread across the border into Abyssinia, and the Italians soon urged the British to reoccupy the area. The British agreed and the KAR was rushed back into the area to restore order. The Italians helped in restoring order mainly by seeing to it that cattle stolen in Kenya and transported to Abyssinia were returned.

THE SUDAN

By June 1940, British forces in the Sudan had been strengthened to some degree, but were still very weak compared to the Italian forces in Italian East Africa. Some progress had been made, though, in covert operations by British agents working inside Abyssinia. They had contacted eleven Ethiopian clan chieftains in northern Abyssinia who agreed to cooperate with the British in the event of war with Italy. An understanding was reached whereby, when war started, the chieftains would send men and draft animals to the border where the British would supply them with guns, ammunition, money, and food in order to conduct guerilla warfare against the Italians.

The RAF in Sudan had managed to build up three squadrons of old Vickers Wellesley bombers and Vickers Vincent and Gloster Gladiator bi-wing fighters, and station one squadron each at Port Sudan, Erkowit, and Summit.

During these tense month the British allowed the Italians, who were still neutral, to use their airfields in Egypt and The Sudan for their air communications to and from East Africa. This was done for several reasons. It was a deterrent to Italy's entering the war because the Italians knew this accommodation would end if and when Italy entered the war. Also, as long as this program was in force the British could expect reciprocity from the Italians. Furthermore, the British could monitor, to some degree, the number and types of war planes going to East Africa and study any changes made to the various aircraft types.

BRITISH SOMALILAND AND FRENCH SOMALILAND

By June 1940, the British forces in British Somaliland were still very weak. They consisted only of 1,475 men, mostly in the Somaliland Camel Corps, and a newly-raised company of Army reservists. In late May, as the prospects of Italy entering the war increased, a battalion of KAR troops was sent to British Somaliland. British defense for the protectorate envisioned joint military operations with French forces in neighboring French Somaliland, which were larger, and could count on reinforcements from Madagascar. The French also had a small air force in French Somaliland consisting of some twenty old war planes and several liaison aircraft. By agreement with the French, all British forces in British Somaliland would be under the field command of General Paul Legentilhomme, Governor of French Somaliland.

ADEN

The British protectorate of Aden was on the southern tip of the Arabian Peninsula but, from the British point of view, was an integral part of the defenses of East Africa. Being separated from Africa by water, Aden was relatively safe from a land attack. Residents of Aden had long been recruited by the British for labor units in the British Army, and a few Adenese served in the British Navy. Even more served in the British merchant marine. The British had a large naval base at Aden, and an RAF base at Sheik Othman, Aden. The RAF in Aden was equipped with fairly modern Bristol Blenheim fighter-bombers, which were used for war purposes as well as for punitive action against marauding tribesmen in the surrounding British colonies.

BRITISH WEST AFRICA AT THE BEGINNING OF THE WAR

British West Africa, unlike British East Africa, consisted of a number of disconnected colonies. They were Gambia,

Sierra Leone, Gold Coast, Nigeria, St. Helena's Island, and Ascension Island. As a political entity, British West Africa had a Colonial Council and a unified defense force: the Royal West African Frontier Force (RWAFF). This force, at the beginning of the war, consisted of two brigades comprised primarily of troops raised in Gambia, Sierra Leone, Gold Coast, and Nigeria. With the coming of war the size of the RWAFF was increased, trained, and organized into a reserve force for the KAR in East Africa. In British West Africa, whites were subject to military conscription, but blacks were not. Blacks, however, were asked to volunteer for service in the British Army as Pioneers (Engineers) and eventually some 100,000 enlisted. There were not enough whites in British West Africa to fill the need for white officers, so whites from East Africa and England were sent to West Africa for that purpose. From the last half of 1940 to May 1943, 18,400 West Africans served in the British 8th Army in North Africa and then went on to fight in Italy.

In the British Cameroons, the portion of the former German Kameroons which was administered by the colonial administration in Nigeria, all German-owned estates were taken over by the Nigerian colonial administration. However, in the neighboring French Cameroons, the German estates were allowed to remain in their owners' hands. During September and October 1939, many Germans from both of the Cameroons fled to the nearby Spanish island of Fernando Poo rather than face an uncertain future under the British and French.

GAMBIA AND SIERRA LEONE ON THE FRINGE OF THE EUROPEAN THEATER OF WAR

The northernmost colonies in British West Africa, Gambia and Sierra Leone, were within range of German submarines, so the British ordered that a convoy system be established to and from these colonies to safeguard shipping. Freetown, Sierra Leone's capital, was the main seaport in the region and was designated to be the primary convoy gathering point. To accomplish this, Freetown's harbor facilities had to be greatly improved so a construction program, one of the largest in Africa at the time, was begun. Freetown was a city of 61,000 people (1935 census) and already had good coastal defenses. It was also strategically located on the western bulge of Africa where the South Atlantic Ocean was its narrowest.

At first, in the fall of 1939, the only armed escorts the Royal Navy could provide for Freetown convoys was a group of seven armed merchant cruisers (merchant ships equipped with one or more deck guns). This group, known as the "Freetown Escort Force" was not always available, and some convoys had to sail unescorted. The "Freetown Escort Force," under normal conditions, accompanied convoys northward to the 20th parallel where an escort group from the "Western Approaches Force" out of England took over and escorted the convoy the rest of the way to the British Isles.

Also based at Freetown was a small force of Royal Navy trawlers which were used for antisubmarine duties and coastal defense.

Further down the coast, in Nigeria, there was no great threat from the sea, but here were other problems. That colony's tin and columbium mines were very important to the British war economy, and had to be worked to their maximum capacity. To accomplish this the British had to resort to the conscription of local laborers. To reduce the need to ship bulky tin ore and save much-needed shipping capacity for wartime needs, construction soon begun in Nigeria on a tin refinery and mill. The United States was a major customer for Nigeria's minerals, too, notably columbium. A new industrial need for columbium was just beginning because that metal was found to be essential in making high temperature-resistant parts for jet aircraft engines, which were in their very early stages of development.

In Gambia, the American had a sea plane base at Bathhurst that could be used by both military and civilian aircraft. It was one of the very few American military facilities on the African continent. With the start of hostilities this base was closed as a military base for belligerents on both sides, as was required by U.S. neutrality laws at the time.

FRENCH SUB-SAHARAN AFRICA AT THE BEGINNING OF THE WAR

The primary French colonial empire south of the Sahara Desert consisted of about a dozen colonies organized into two large colonial federations, French West Africa and French Equatorial Africa. French West Africa, with its capital at Dakar, Senegal, was the larger and, by far, the more important. French Equatorial Africa was in central Africa, straddling the Equator, with its capital, Brazzaville, Middle Congo on the Congo River opposite Leopoldville, capital of the Belgian Congo.

French West Africa had, at the start of the war, a strong economy based on a wide variety of exports, a strong intercolonial trade, and strong commercial ties with France. The infrastructure was well developed, especially in the colonies bordering the Atlantic Ocean. The colonies in the interior were less developed but, nevertheless, had valuable assets and were good sources for laborers.

French Equatorial Africa was one of the French Empire's least developed colonial holdings, and had a much weaker economy. The territory had never been favored in Paris, and it received less financial support than French West Africa and often less capable administrators.

Military conscription for both whites and blacks already existed in the French Empire prior to the beginning of hostilities, and was soon expanded. Aside from this, once France went to war many young black men stepped forward to volunteer for military service much the same as they did in the British colonies. In 1940 alone, up to June, French West Africa contributed 127,320 infantrymen to the French Army, while French Equatorial Africa contributed another 15,500 and Madagascar still another 34,000. Furthermore, many African civilians went to France to fill war-related jobs that had been vacated by Frenchmen who were called up for military service.

SOLDIERS AND "EVOLES"

Several hundred thousand natives from the French Empire had served in the French Army during World War I, and that experience had a lasting effect on them. When France went to war in 1914, conscription was decreed for both blacks and whites in the empire. Whites in the colonies were called up for eighteen months' service, and blacks for three years. Nine out of ten blacks called up, however, were rejected for medical reasons. Those who were accepted were trained for service in the French Army and sent to France or other parts of the French empire. Very few remained in their home colony.

Virtually all of those who served in Metropolitan France became "Europeanized" to some degree. A large number of veterans stayed on in France after the war taking low-paying, low-skilled jobs. To those back home, this looked appealing and induced others to migrate to France. Those who stayed in France and those who migrated there voluntarily became even more Europeanized.

Most of the World War I black soldiers, though, returned to Africa only to find themselves resented by their own people. This happened for several reasons. Those at home who had been rejected were often jealous of those who had been selected, in addition, there were those at home who resented the veterans for having served the white man in the first place. Still other returnees exhibited an air of superiority, and many had no interest in going back to their old native life-styles. Together, with the better-educated natives in the colonies, these Europeanized individuals tended to gravitate toward the European communities in the cities. There they congregated together and soon became identified as a separate class of people known as "Evoles" (evolved ones). By 1939 the Evoles were numerous, especially in French West Africa. They were influential in both the political and economic activities of the colonies, and were an element of colonial society very supportive of France.

When France went to war, the export business in West Africa surged and both the white and black communities enjoyed a measure of prosperity. Major improvements were begun at the port of Dakar for both economic and military purposes.

There was one major weakness, though, in the economic relationship between France and her empire. This was in the supply of basic minerals. The empire supplied France with only 4% of its mineral imports. This amazingly low percentage was the result of a long-standing policy in French industry, which was supported by the government, of allowing free trade to dominate the market place. It seemed that whatever the French colonies could produce in the way of minerals, those minerals could be found elsewhere at cheaper prices. As a result, mineral development throughout the empire did not progress. Oil was an outstanding example. Nowhere in the French empire (the second largest in the world) were there developed oil fields because it was always cheaper to buy oil from the United States or other suppliers. Thus, when war broke out, France was dependent on foreign sources for oil and other important materials.

ROADS ACROSS THE SAHARA

While French commercial contact with sub-Saharan Africa was done mostly by sea, there were two all-weather roads that traversed the Sahara Desert connecting Algeria with Niger and French Sudan. In late 1939, a third road was completed that connected western Algeria and French Morocco through Mauritania to Senegal and its main port, Dakar. This was a very important road because the militarily important port of Dakar could now be supplied by land from North Africa.

Also, the first railroad across the French Sahara Desert was in its beginning stages. It would run from Bou Afar, Algeria to Timbuktu, French Sudan, and then eastward into Niger. Completion of this railroad was, however, years away.

From a military point of view these roads were of great importance because men and equipment destined for the southern colonies could be shipped overland rather than by the more vulnerable sea routes. Furthermore, private commerce could go overland, too, reducing the need of the French Navy to protect seaborne commerce in time of war.

A number of problems existed in sub-Saharan French Africa with, perhaps, the biggest problem being in French Guinea. This colony was more of a liability to the French than an asset. It had still not been totally pacified, and sizeable units of the French Army were stationed there permanently to keep order. Consequently, little had been done to develop that colony. Furthermore, it was a demoralizing place for French servicemen because duty in French Guinea was used as punishment for both officers and enlisted men. Colonial administrators, too, saw duty in French Guinea as a low point in their careers. Despite the difficult conditions in French Guinea, the colony did produce some gold, coffee, cocoa, and bananas for export.

There was also trouble in French Sudan. In late 1939–early 1940, two rival Islamic sects clashed with each other over pasture rights. French Army troops had to be sent in to end the conflict and arrest the leaders of the Hamallah Sect, who were responsible for starting the conflict. Before order was restored some 400 people had been killed.

HITLER CALLS FOR PEACE. THE BEGINNING OF THE "PHONY WAR."

Having won what he wanted in Poland, Hitler went before the Reichstag in Berlin on October 6, 1939, and called for an "unconditionally guaranteed peace." He implied, but this time did not promise, that the conquest of Poland was his last territorial demand in Europe that would be detrimental to the Western Allies. He declared that a Polish state would be reconstituted—something the Western Allies would welcome—and he suggested that part of the conquered land might be used as a reserve for Europe's Jews.

In his speech he brought up, once again, Germany's demands for the return of her overseas colonies. By stressing this subject at this time, some believed that Hitler was putting his colonial claims on the table as a bargaining chip—possibly a bargaining chip for peace. If peace could be restored in the west Hitler would be in an excellent position to turn all of his attention to the east and pursue the dreams he had harbored all his political life—the elimination of Communism and the Soviet Union and the creation of a huge colonial holding in the east for the expansion of the German people. If this could be brought about, Hitler, almost certainly, would have willingly traded his demands on Germany's overseas colonies for the opportunity to gain such a prize. Such an empire would be contiguous to Germany and could be easily protected by his very powerful army and with little need fora navy. This dream was no secret. Hitler had written about it in his book, *Mein Kampf*, and spoken of it frequently. He also had reason to believe that the Western Allies might be willing to let him have his way, especially if it meant the elimination of Communism and an end to the question of the German colonies.

Hitler's peace speech was, clearly, an offer to negotiate, but the Western Powers were not interested. Hitler had lost all credibility in the West after having violated the 1938 Munich Agreement over Czechoslovakia.

With Hitler calling for peace and the Western Powers rejecting his overtures a period in the war began which became known as the phony war. There was very little military action from either side and it lasted for eight months.

Both sides took advantage of this time to build up their military strength as a means of intimidating the other. That buildup effected Africa where programs proceeded unhindered in building up native armies and gearing the various economies for a continuation of the war.

BRITAIN BUYS COCOA

As a part of their buildup for war the British government began stockpiling food. One of the items stockpiled was cocoa, and since cocoa came from West Africa the word went out to all the British and French colonies in West Africa that Britain would buy all of that product available. Sales of cocoa became very brisk in the African cocoa markets and prices shot up. The British loved cocoa.

A GERMAN BATTLESHIP PROWLS SOUTH AFRICAN WATERS

When war started in Europe the German battleship "Graf Spee" was already at sea and heading for the South Atlantic. She was one of Germany's newest and most modern warships, and had been designed to be a commerce raider. Once hostilities started in Europe the Graf Spee's mission was to sink Allied shipping in the South Atlantic.

On September 1, the day the war started, Graf Spee's support ship, "Altmark" refueled her at sea with oil recently purchased at Port Arthur, Texas. The Graf Spee then headed for the east coast of South America.

The Graf Spee first went into action in late September off the coast of Brazil, sinking several Allied ships. Then she darted eastward across the South Atlantic and first appeared in African waters at a point some 1200 miles due west of Luanda, Angola. There, in quick order, she took four British merchant ships. The first victim was the "Newton Beach," a British merchantman which the Graf Spee captured, on October 5, 1939, without a fight. A German prize crew boarded the Newton Beach with the intention of sailing her to Germany, but they never made it. The Newton Beach was intercepted by British warships four days later and sunk.

The Graf Spee sailed closer to Africa, and on October 8, sank the British steamer "Ashlea" and captured the crew.

On October 10, the Graf Spee captured the British freighter "Huntsman" and sent her, under a prize crew, successfully to Germany. On the 22nd, the German battleship sank the British steamer "Trevanion" and took more prisoners. On October 18, the Graf Spee transferred most of her prisoners to her support ship, Altmark, and the two ships continued to travel together. Near the remote island of Tristan da Cunha, the Altmark refueled the Graf Spee with more Texas oil.

The South African Air Force's German–made Junker 86 bombers which helped search for the German battleship "Graf Spee."

Because these attacks were a threat to South Africa, the South African Air Force (SAAF) joined in the search for the Graf Spee. Planes flew out of Walvis Bay and Cape Town during daylight hours. Ironically, the planes used by the SAAF were German-made Junker 86 passenger planes that had been converted into bombers. These planes had the longest range of any aircraft in the SAAF inventory.

Patrolling off South Africa's coast was a precarious undertaking for the men of the SAAF because, at this stage of the war, they had no airborne radar units nor any other devices that facilitated night flights, so the planes flew only in daylight hours. Some planes did not have radios and others did not even have bombs due to the overall shortages.

During South Africa's winter (May–August) there were days upon days of fog and low-lying clouds. Planes frequently had to fly as low as 500 feet to stay under the clouds. Furthermore, there was no air-rescue service in place, so going down at sea was usually a death sentence for the crew.

The Graf Spee felt relatively secure in African waters, because the Germans knew, full well, of the weaknesses of the Allied air and sea patrols. The greatest fear for the Germans was encountering one of the several British naval squadrons that were known to be operating in the South Atlantic and looking for them.

Knowing this, the Graf Spee headed south and rounded the Cape of Good Hope entering the Indian Ocean. The ship passed the Cape 450 miles out, which was beyond the range of the SAAF Junkers. By now, however, all merchant ships in African waters were alert to the Graf Spee's presence and were avoiding those waters or staying in port.

The Graf Spee patrolled the Indian Ocean waters off eastern South Africa and Mozambique for several days but found no targets. On November 15, 1939 she did manage to sink the small British tanker "Africa Shell" off the coast of Mozambique. The Germans took the British captain as a prisoner of war, but allowed the crew to escape in their lifeboats to shore. This action took place within sight of land. The next day the Graf Spee stopped a neutral Dutch freighter but allowed her to proceed. These two actions, the Germans reckoned, would be enough to alert the Allied that the Graf Spee was in the Indian Ocean, and that the Allies would shift their search effort away from the South Atlantic and into the Indian Ocean. This tactic worked to some degree because SAAF Junkers were dispatched from Durban to search to the east for the Graf Spee.

The Graf Spee then returned to the South Atlantic, again passing the Cape of Good Hope far out, and began working the coasts of South West Africa and Angola once more. Early in the morning on December 2 she sank the refrigerator ship "Doric Star" about 400 miles off the coast of South West Africa. Before she went down, the Doric Star was able to radio to the British authorities her location and that she was being attacked by the Graf Spee. This alerted every British and French warship in the South Atlantic to the German ship's approximate location and they converged on that area. Planes from the SAAF also joined the search.

SAAF SINKS GERMAN MERCHANT SHIP

On the morning of December 2, 1939, about 10:30, SAAF planes searching for the Graf Spee spotted a mysterious vessel 100 miles south of Cape Point. She was the German liner "Watussi" which had been trapped at Lourenco Marques, Mozambique when the war started. The Watussi's captain, knowing that virtually all of the Allied ships and planes in the region were searching for the Graf Spee, figured it was a good time for him to run to the neutral port of Rio

The sinking "Doric Star" as seen from the "Graf Spee."

The "Watussi" sinking.

de Janeiro, Brazil, the first leg of his hoped-for return to Germany. For added protection he flew the British flag. It took several hours for the South Africans to penetrate the Watussi's disguise, but once identified, the ship was ordered, by flashing lights from an SAAF Junker bomber, to change course and sail for Cape Town and surrender. The Watussi seemingly obliged and turned toward Cape Town. Soon afterwards the cruisers HMS "Sussex" and HMS "Renown" made contact with the German ship about sixty miles off Cape Point. A short time later the Watussi stopped dead in the water; her crew abandoned the ship into nine lifeboats and a motor launch. Minutes later scuttling charges went off inside the Watussi in an obvious attempt to scuttle the ship. The ship caught fire but did not sink. Since she was now a hazard to navigation the Renown finished her off with gunfire while the Sussex rescued the German survivors. This was the SAAF's first successful military action of the war. There would be others.

GRAF SPEE STILL ON THE RAMPAGE

The next day, December 3, 1939, the Graf Spee sank the "Tairoa" about fifty miles north of where the Doric Star went down. This was the last ship the Graf Spee would take in African waters.

The Graf Spee was nearing the end of her tour of duty and was given one last mission by Berlin. She was to sail westward into South American waters and rendezvous with a convoy of five German merchant ships loaded with cargos of food, and escort them home to Germany. Obediently the Graf Spee turned westward, out into the South Atlantic. There, she soon encountered a force of three British cruisers, and a running sea battle ensued in which the British warships were able to badly damage the Graf Spee. The German captain, knowing that his ship was no longer able to adequately defend herself, sought refuge in the harbor of Montevideo, Uruguay in South America. There the Graf Spee was trapped. Uruguay was a neutral country and under international law the Graf Spee could stay only a short time before being interned by the Uruguayan government for the duration of the war. If, on the other hand, she sailed out of the harbor she would have to do battle once again in damaged condition, with the British warships waiting for her offshore in international waters.

Under the circumstances the Graf Spee's captain chose to avoid both internment and battle. On December 17, 1939, he sailed his ship out of the mouth of Montevideo harbor and, while still in Uruguayan coastal waters, scuttled his ship.

With the demise of the Graf Spee, the waters of the South Atlantic and African coasts became relatively safe once more.

GERMAN TRADE WITH AFRICA ENDS

When hostilities started in Europe the British and French Naviesset up a naval blockade around Europe with the intent of stopping all waterborne commerce to and from Germany. This blockade, while slow to be implemented at first, eventually became very effective. Almost every item of commerce was declared contraband by the Allies. This included food and raw materials—the main products of colonial Africa.

By late November 1939, virtually all trade between Germany and colonial Africa had ended. This hurt some sectors of the African economy, but not for long. With the war needs of the Allies on the rise, those products which would have been sold to Germany were now sold to the Allies.

In Germany, many items from Africa soon appeared on the lists of rationed items.

BRITAIN REDUCES ECONOMIC AID TO ITS COLONIES

Due to the urgencies of the war, the British government had to inform the colonies that economic aid had to be reduced to the colonies. When the annual "Colonial Development and Welfare Act for 1940" was passed in late 1939, it contained only 5 million pounds for the entire empire. This was but a small fraction of former peacetime programs. The British leaders fully realized that this was a negative political move, because it played nicely into the hands of the various nationalistic organizations throughout the Empire. Those organizations could, thereafter, claim that Britain abandoned them in their hour of need—irrespective of Britain's hour of need.

To soften the blow, the London government blanketed the empire with propaganda declaring that every part of the empire was in this war together and that they must stand united to be victorious. The propaganda also made vague promises that rewards for these hard times would be forthcoming after victory had been achieved, and that social and political questions would be given favorable consideration.

PORTUGUESE AFRICA AT THE BEGINNING OF THE WAR

The Portuguese government in Lisbon declared its neutrality at the beginning of the war and began following a well-calculated foreign policy to support that declaration while, at the same time, staying on as friendly terms as possible with both sides in the conflict. In Europe, with Fascist Spain next door, Portugal's neutrality leaned, much of the time, toward the Axis Powers. But, in Africa where Portugal's colonies adjoined British and French colonies, that policy leaned, much of the time, toward the Allies. With regards to her overseas colonies, the facts of political reality tended to dominate the thinking in Lisbon. Portugal did not have a navy powerful enough to protect its overseas possessions but could, in most scenarios, count on the powerful British Navy to provide that protection. This was because Britain and Portugal had long-standing relationships in matters of politics and trade, and it was in the interest of Britain that Portuguese colonies remained secure, prosperous, and trading with the Allies. From Portugal's point of view, if Britain lost the war, the Portuguese colonies would be unprotected and fair game for the Axis victors. Therefore, it was in Lisbon's best interest to follow a British-oriented policy of neutrality in colonial matters. This materialized in the fact that trade between Portuguese colonies and Germany was allowed to decline because the Portuguese honored the British naval blockade of Europe. At the same time, British trade with the Portuguese colonies continued as before and accelerated in some instances.

Lisbon endeavored to maintain good relations, too, with Britain's powerful, but as yet uncommitted friend, the United States. It was through the Portuguese colony of Portuguese Guinea that the continent of Africa had its only commercial air link with America. This was via the Pan-American Airways Clipper route that flew three times a week between New York City–Lisbon–Bolama, Portuguese Guinea–Trinidad–San Juan, Puerto Rico–Miami–New York. On occasions the Pan-American Clippers would stop at Horta in the Portuguese-owned Azores Islands. Portugal wanted this connection to America to continue, as did the Americans.

In Portugal, Lisbon became a city of high intrigue during the war, with secret agents and spies from both sides operating there in sizeable numbers. Some of this spilled over into the Portuguese colonies, and Axis agents operated almost as freely in the Portuguese colonies as they did in Portugal. This was an on-going concern of the Allies, but never posed a major threat. Of the several Portuguese colonies in Africa, Mozambique had the highest level of intrigue. Most Axis and Allied nations maintained consulates in Mozambique and they became the centers of operations for spies, agents, informers, and phony business fronts. Being adjacent to South Africa, information was easily available from the many Axis sympathizers in that country. And to the north, Tanganyika was home to many Germans who were more than willing to pass on critical war information to Germany via German agents in Mozambique. Also, Allied ships called regularly at Mozambique's seaports carrying off minerals, food, and other raw materials produced all over central and southern Africa. Movement of these ships was easily monitored and relayed to German naval intelligence.

At the beginning of the war, Portugal began a program to enlarge its army and some of these forces were sent to her African colonies and the Azores. They were there for defensive purposes only, and were not a threat to Portugal's colonial neighbors.

Portugal's Cape Verde Islands posed a very special problem. Because of their strategic location off the coast of western Africa, their control would be a major asset to either side in the war. In Allied hands they would be very useful as a base for antisubmarine activities, and for naval and convoy operations. In Axis hands they would be useful for advanced submarine and air bases. And, of course, another fear in Lisbon was that if one side made a threatening move toward the Cape Verde Islands, the other side would very likely react and the islands could become a battle ground. Because of this distinct possibility the British kept a force of Royal Marines on standby in England, ready to leave on short notice, to invade and occupy the islands with—or without—Portugal's approval. Lisbon was made aware of this.

During these early stages of the war, though, neither the Axis nor the Allies made any threatening moves toward either the Cape Verde Islands or the Azores.

The United States had concerns about the Azores, too, because from there German long-range bombers could reach the U.S. east coast. Washington made these concerns known to Lisbon and watched activities in the Azores closely.

SPANISH AFRICA AT THE BEGINNING OF THE WAR

At the beginning of the war Spain declared her neutrality, which extended to her colonies. She was also obliged to honor the British blockade of Europe. This, however, was not a major problem for Madrid. Spain was still suffering the aftereffects of the bloody three-year civil war, and there were shortages of many kinds in Spain, including food. Spain herself, therefore, consumed much of the products produced by her colonies and had little to pass on to her friends, Germany and Italy.

Spain, too, had interests in Portugal's Cape Verde and Azores Islands in that if an armed conflict erupted over those islands, Portugal might be drawn into the war on the Allied side. It was remembered in Madrid that Portugal had been a combatant on the Allied side during World War I.

The Spanish government, therefore, informed Britain and France that an Allied invasion of either the Cape Verde Islands or the Azores would be seen as a threat to Spain's interests and that Spain's reaction might be to invite Axis troops into Spain to serve as Spain's protector.

Spain had already made an unusually friendly gesture toward Germany when in August 1939, just days before the war started, Madrid signed an agreement with Berlin permitting German tankers and supply ships to lay at anchor in any Spanish harbor to supply German submarines and warships. This was a very un-neutral act. International law allowed the submarines and warships of belligerent nations to use the harbors of neutral nations for a limited time and avail themselves of whatever supplies and services were available. By allowing German supply ships, though, to lay at anchor for long periods of time was beyond the intent of the international agreements. This meant that torpedoes, ammunition, spare parts, and other articles of war not normally available in neutral harbors would be available to the Germans in Spanish harbors. This arrangement was condemned by the Allies and would bring about military action within months in the Spanish-owned Canary Island.

There was yet another problem concerning Spanish nationals. These were the thousands of Spanish Republicans, both soldiers and civilians, who had fled into southern France after having lost the civil war in Spain. When World War II started most of these people were still languishing in refugee camps in southern France.

The French government decided that the men and resources necessary to guard and sustain these refugees would be better used now for the war effort and wanted to rid itself of the problem. Efforts had been made to repatriate the refugees to Spain, but the Franco government in Madrid did not want them back because of the shortages in Spain and the fact that many of these people, especially the communists, would become security risks.

The French resolved the problem by redesignating these people as internees and shipping many of them to internment camps in French North Africa, where the expense of keeping them was less. There they were mixed in with other internees and remained in those camps for years.

FURTHER WAR DEVELOPMENTS IN THE SPRING OF 1940

In Paris, the French government succumbed once again to its old nemesis, political instability. On March 20, 1940, the government of Edouard Daladier fell and a new government was formed under Paul Reynaud. As a reassurance to France's commitment in the war the new Reynaud government, eight days later, signed an agreement with Britain stating that neither nations would seek a separate peace with Germany.

In the Atlantic Ocean, German submarines had, by late March 1940, fanned out into the Atlantic and were now operating off the Strait of Gibraltar. This was a direct threat to the security of North and West Africa.

In South Africa, Field Marshal Archibald Wavell, British Commander in the Middle East, North Africa and East Africa, met with Prime Minister Smuts. Smuts told Wavell that South Africa could soon supply one infantry brigade, one antiaircraft brigade, and three South African Air Force (SAAF) squadrons for service in Kenya. This time Smuts' offer, unlike that of December 1939, was accepted. By May 1940, the first South African units began moving to Kenya.

On the morning of April 9, 1940, came the electrifying news that German troops were invading both Denmark and Norway, both neutral nations. The phony war was over and Hitler, for the first time, had shown that he was no respecter of neutrality. Denmark was quickly overrun, but in Norway Britain was able to rush in both ground and naval forces and forestall a quick German victory there. A short time later, France sent a contingent of troops to Norway. The war in Norway would go on for more than two more months.

GERMANY STRIKES IN WESTERN EUROPE

On the morning of May 10, 1940, German troops began invading Belgium, The Netherlands, and Luxembourg, all neutral nations. This was the most dramatic turn of events yet in the war. The German thrust was obviously designed as an attack against France by outflanking the heavily fortified Maginot Line which had been built by the French in the years between the wars to guard against a direct attack from Germany. The Maginot Line did not extend along the French/Belgium border, and the German intent was to drive deep into Belgium and then turn south to invade northern France.

Later that day, the British government of Neville Chamberlain resigned, his policies of appeasement an utter failure. In his place Winston Churchill, an old warrior and longtime opponent of appeasement, became Prime Minister. Churchill was also a firm believer in maintaining a strong and closely-knit empire.

Within days, large-scale British Army forces crossed the English Channel to help the French, Belgian, and Dutch forces defend against the German invasion. At this point, many Allied leaders believed that the terrible and prolonged trench warfare of World War I would be resumed. Churchill told the British people this on May 13, 1940 when, in a dramatic speech in the House of Commons, he told them, "I have nothing to offer but blood, toil, tears, and sweat."

CHURCHILL THE COLONIALIST

As a young man, Churchill spent time in South Africa, The Sudan, India, and Cuba, and thereafter considered himself something of an expert on colonial matters. He became a strong colonialist and frequently made his views known. Life Magazine said of Churchill in their January 9, 1939, issue "The Empire of his dreams is a Rudyard Kipling sort of empire—the spangles and the bugles, the palm and pine, the lesser breed without the law, the white man's burden, and all the rest of it."

It was men like Churchill that Kipling praised when he wrote:

Take up the White Man's burden–
Send forth the best ye breed–
Go bind your sons to exile
To serve your captive's need.
To wait in heavy harness,
On flattered folk and wild–
Your new caught, sullen peoples,
Half–devil and half–child....

Take of the White Man's burden–
The savage wars of peace–
Fill full the mouth of Famine
And bid the sickness cease;...

Take up the White Man's burden–
No tawdry rule of kings,
But toil of serf and sweeper–
The tale of common things.
The ports ye shall not enter,
The roads ye shall not tread,
Go make them with your living,
And mark them with your dead.

—Rudyard Kipling 1899

RAIDERS OFF CAPE TOWN

In early May 1940, a unique type of sea warfare came to African waters in the form of German "surface raiders." These were innocent-looking merchant ships that had been converted into warships. All of the ship's guns and other weapons were hidden behind ship panels and false cargo crates which could be swung open quickly for action. The raiders sailed alone following established trade routes and often under the flag of a neutral nation. Upon encountering an Allied merchant ship they would approach as closely as possible, suddenly drop their disguise, run up the German flag and attack the unsuspecting ship. Surface raiders were not new. They had been used successfully by the German Navy in World War I. In the 1930s the Nazi government began building them again in secret. Certain fast merchant ships were selected for the program, armed with guns up to 5.0 inch caliber, torpedo tubes, radar, and, at times, reconnaissance aircraft.

The German surface raider "Atlantis."

Surface raiders had been operating since early in the year but had not ventured into African waters. This, though, changed on May 3, 1940, when the raider "Atlantis," masquerading as the neutral Japanese ship "Kassi Maru," attacked the unarmed British freighter "Scientist" off Cape Town, South Africa. The Scientist was out of Durban for Liverpool with a mixed cargo of ores, jute, corn, chemicals and wattle bark. The Atlantis sailed all the way to South Africa, passing up other targets as she went, so that she could make her first attacks at this time and place, in an effort to draw off Allied naval units from the north in preparation for the coming German invasion of The Netherlands, Belgium, Luxembourg, and France. This would occur on May 10, 1940.

The Atlantis approached the Scientist, dropped its disguise, and ordered the Scientist to stop. The British ship radioed a distress signal and began to run. The distress signal was quickly jammed by the radio operators on the Atlantis which took off in pursuit of the British ship. The Scientist never had a chance. Several shells from the Atlantis's guns stopped the British ship, damaging her engine room, and her captain quickly surrendered. One man had been killed, but 77 other British seamen were taken prisoner aboard the Atlantis. They would reside in the below-deck prison cells of the Atlantis until she returned to Germany. A German boarding party boarded the Scientist and placed demolition charges to sink the ship. These charges, when they were detonated, failed to do the job, so the Atlantis finished off the British freighter with a torpedo.

The Atlantis was scheduled to sail on into the Indian Ocean, but she was not quite finished with her business off Cape Town. She resumed the Japanese disguise and headed for Cape Agulhas, Africa's southernmost point. There on May 10, 1940, guided by the Cape's powerful lighthouse, she laid 92 mines in the main shipping channel that rounded the Cape. The mines were laid at night in a straight line from twenty miles out to a point five miles off shore from Cape Agulhas lighthouse. The Atlantis then dropped an empty German life raft into the waters off Cape Agulhas marked "U–37." It was intended to deceive the British into thinking that the German submarine, U–37, laid the mines.

PLAYING THE ROLE

Masquerading as a Japanese ship was one of the Atlantis's favorite ploys because Japanese ships were quite often seen in these waters. To enhance his ship's disguise, the German captain assigned short dark-haired members of the crew to parade on deck in Japanese clothes. Some played the role of Japanese women carrying parasols and pushing baby carriages.

After depositing her mines the Atlantis turned eastward and sailed into the Indian Ocean. There, she would hopefully draw off Allied warships from the Atlantic while, at the same time, sinking more Allied merchant ships. The Germans expected the Indian Ocean to be good hunting grounds because the Allies would not expect German warships in that area, and Allied ships would be sailing alone and unarmed. Convoys in the Indian Ocean had not yet been instigated.

For ten days the mines off Cape Agulhas laid in wait but sank no ship. Then, on May 13, 1940, coast watchers in the area heard an explosion at sea about ten miles out. The next day another explosion was heard. No ships were seen to be involved. For some unknown reasons the mines had self-detonated. South African authorities rightfully suspected the explosions were from mines, but incorrectly, and without discovering the U–37 life raft, believed they were laid by a German submarine. Prime Minister Smuts believed they were laid by an Italian submarine. Several South African Junker bombers were sent to investigate, but found nothing. Meanwhile, rumors circulated throughout South Africa that their territorial waters had been mined. The SAAF searched the area for ten days and still found nothing.

Meanwhile, on May 15, 1940, the South African authorities broadcast messages in the clear for ships to avoid the area. The Germans, of course, learned of the rumors and concern in South Africa, and Radio Zeesen claimed that eight ships had been sunk by the mines, "several" minesweepers sunk in trying to remove them, and three ships were missing. Actually, no ships were sunk or damaged by the mines.

Following the Atlantis into the Indian Ocean was a second German raider, the "Orion." Her mission was to sail on into the Pacific Ocean and attack Allied shipping there. So far, the Orion had sailed down the Atlantic and rounded the Cape of Good Hope without making any attacks and without being noticed.

ALLIED DESIGNS ON THE CANARY ISLANDS

The Spanish-owned Canary Islands lie 250 miles off the coast of Morocco, and athwart the main shipping lanes between Europe and West Africa. It was obvious that if these islands should fall into German hands, German planes, submarines, and ships would dominate those shipping lanes and effectively disrupt British and French sea communication.

Such a possibility existed because the Franco government in Madrid was highly indebted to Germany for the military aid extended to the Nationalists forces during Spain's Civil War. Therefore, Spain was very friendly toward the Axis, and a possible co-belligerent in the war on Germany's side. So far, though, Spain had remained neutral, although that neutrality leaned heavily toward the Axis. If, however, Spain should enter the war, or perhaps allow Axis troops to use her territory to lay siege to Gibraltar, Britain's mighty bastion at the western end of the Mediterranean Sea the Allies would have to respond in some way. An Allied invasion of the Canary Islands was seen as one possibility. Furthermore, an unacceptable arrangement already existed in the Canarys.

Under their August 1939 Agreement with Germany, the Spanish were allowing two German tankers, "Corrientes" and "Charlotte Schliemann," to lie at anchor in the harbor at Las Palmas (the capital of the Canary Islands) to supply fuel and other supplies to German submarines. The German submarines would usually enter the harbor soon after dark, refuel during the night, and depart before dawn. This situation was intolerable for the Allies, and they took steps to correct it. On the night of May 9, a French underwater demolition team, operating from the British coal freighter "Rhin" and under the cover of darkness, attached a limpet mine to the hull of the Corrientes. Minutes later the mine exploded and the Corrientes sank to the bottom of the harbor at her moorings. Such attacks were very difficult to defend against, and the Germans knew it. The next day, May 10, the Germans launched their massive offensive on the western front in Europe, and most of the German Navy had been committed to support that attack. Therefore, the Germans made no immediate effort to replace the Corrientes.

The sinking of the Corrientes had a positive effect for Africa, because now fewer German submarines operating in African waters could not penetrate much beyond the Canary Islands.

Meanwhile, in London, more grandiose plans were being formulated with regards to the Canary Islands. In conjunction with the British Navy, a British Army force of some 10,000 men was assembled, trained, and made ready to depart Britain on short notice to invade the Canary Islands. This force would be activated only if Spanish military action was instigated against Gibraltar.

In late May and early June, the Spanish threat against Gibraltar became very real. As the Allies suffered defeat after defeat in western Europe, influential voices rose in Madrid for Spain to enter the war with the aims of acquiring Gibraltar, French Morocco, Tangier, and parts of Algeria. Generalissimo Franco and others kept their heads. Realizing that Spain was in no position to participate in a major war against Britain and France, the Madrid government took no action and the demands of the Madrid warmongers subsided. The British, feeling that they could not afford to trust the Spaniards, reacted by doubling the size of their Canary invasion force.

RAPID ALLIED COLLAPSE IN THE BENELUX COUNTRIES

The western Allies were soon to succumb to the German Blitzkrieg just as the Poles had eight months earlier. Masses of German tanks and motorized infantry smashed into the static Allied defense lines in the Low Countries and decimated the Allies' positions.

On the second day of the attack, the Germans, in a daring air assault using parachute and glider troops, captured the Belgian fort of Eben Emael, the strongest point on the Albert Canal/Muses River defense line. On May 13, 1940, the city of Liege fell to the rapidly advancing German Army. That same day, tanks of the powerful 7th Panzer Division, under General Irwin Rommel, smashed their way out of the Ardennes forest into northern France. The surprised and poorly led French 55th and 71st Divisions defending the area retreated in disorder.

During the next three weeks, the Allies suffered one disaster after the other. By May 14, 1940, most of The Netherlands was in German hands and the Dutch government fled to London. By May 18, Rommel's forces reached Amiens, only forty miles from the English Channel, after having driven due west out of the Ardennes and across northern France. This advance was driving a wedge between the Allied force in the north and those in France to the south. That same day, in the north, Antwerp fell. Two days later Rommel reached the English Channel west of Abbeville, splitting the Allied armies in two. The position of the armies in the north was untenable and on May 26, 1940, a massive and desperate withdrawal by sea began at Dunkirk. The Belgian government fled to Paris and on May 28 the Belgium Army surrendered, en masse, to the Germans. Later the Belgian government moved to London.

On June 4, 1940, the last Allied troops were rescued from Dunkirk, and Allied resistance in the north ended. Many Allied soldiers had been rescued, but the British Army lost a large percentage of its equipment. It was in no shape to return to France nor to defend England if the Germans choose to invade.

The next day, German troops launched their attack into northern France. The French Army, now outnumbered and badly demoralized, retreated on every front. By June 9, 1940, the French 10th Army, which was defending Paris, was surrounded. The end was near for France.

ITALY ENTERS THE WAR IN EUROPE AND IN AFRICA

With France on the verge of collapse, Mussolini chose this time to enter the war as Germany's ally. On June 10, 1940, Italy declared war on France and Britain and, hours later, Italian troops invaded areas of southern France. By entering the war in Europe, Italy's colonies in Africa also entered the war. Those colonies, Libya in North Africa and Italian East Africa, had hostile borders with British and French colonies, but no immediate military actions were initiated there by the Italians. All parties realized, though, that these areas could not remain quiescent indefinitely. The shooting war would, inevitably, come to Africa. The Allies were quick to respond to Italy's actions. The next day, June 11, 1940, France, Britain, Canada, Australia, New Zealand, India, and South Africa declared war on Italy.

EGYPT

On June 12 Egypt, which bordered Italian-controlled Libya on the east, broke diplomatic relations with Italy. The Egyptian government had a military alliance with Britain and was under pressure from London to declare war on Italy. The Egyptians, though, did not have the desire nor the resources to fight Italy, and chose this lesser alternative in an attempt to satisfy the British.

EGYPTIAN AND BRITISH RELATIONS STRAINED

Political relations between Egypt and Britain had been strained for several years. Many influential Egyptian political leaders, and some political organizations, wanted the British to leave their country altogether and turn over control, or at least share control, of the vital Suez Canal.

SADAT AND NASSAR

Two individuals, who would both become future Premiers of Egypt, were very active in Egypt's anti-British underground at this time. They were Anwar Sadat, who participated in terrorists activities, and Gamal Abdul Nassar, who was an anti-British operative in the pay of the German Abwehr (intelligence agency of the German armed forces).

A small Fascist-like political party, the "Misr el-Fatat," known also as the "Green Shirts," was one of the anti-British groups that functioned in Egypt. This group remained small and had little influence on political events, but was a conduit for Axis activities in the country.

Perhaps the biggest problem the British had in Egypt centered around Egypt's young King Farouk. Farouk had often shown signs of being anti-British, and secretly supported some of the anti-British activities of others.

The British, however, had no intention of reducing their role in Egypt, especially now with a war on, and saw the absolute control of the Suez Canal as vital to the security of their entire Empire. In January 1940, the British were able to strengthen their position in the country, somewhat, by bringing about the resignation of General Aziz Ali el-Hasri, Chief of Staff of the 40,000-man Egyptian Army, who was outspokenly anti-British. But this was only one small political victory. The British knew they could expect little political or military support from the Egyptian government; Premier Ali Maher had announced publicly, in late May 1940, that Egypt would not go to war against Italy if Italy were to enter the war against Britain and France. This policy was repeated on several occasions by other spokesmen for the Egyptian government. Thus, it was clear to the British that, if Britain and Italy went to war, the British would be on their own to defend the Egyptian/Libyan border, the Sudanese/Italian East African border in southern Sudan, and the Suez Canal. The Egyptians did, however, qualify their position by stating that Egyptian forces would fight to defend the country against any invader. This was a condition they would not live up to.

The British, badly in need of troops in Egypt and not being able to rely on the Egyptian Army, exercised their rights under existing Anglo-Egyptian treaties; they brought in about 30,000 Australian and New Zealander troops in February 1940, and additional Indian troops in August. It was almost a certainty now, with Italy in the war, that Egypt would become a battle ground regardless of the actions of the Egyptian governments and the will of the Egyptian people.

FRANCE SURRENDERS

On the day Italy declared war, June 10, the French government of Paul Reynaud fled Paris for Tours.

On June 13, 1940, the French government, declared Paris an open city, meaning that it would not be defended. The German took full advantage of this and marched into Paris, unopposed, on the 14th.

The Germans did not stop at Paris. They marched on into central France, and the French government had to flee again, this time to Bordeaux. There a political crisis developed. A rapidly growing number of French leaders had concluded that France was militarily defeated and should ask the Germans for an immediate armistice in order to save as much of France as possible from being occupied. An opposing faction within the government argued that the government should flee to French North Africa and continue the struggle from there. It was up to Premier Reynaud and his Cabinet to decide.

Around midnight on June 16, 1940, Reynaud's government became deadlocked on the issue, unable to decide whether to fight on or ask for an armistice. At this point, Reynaud resigned and asked French President, Albert Lebrun, to appoint someone else as Premier. Lebrun acted quickly and appointed Marshal Henri Petain, a venerated and highly respected hero of World War I. Petain favored an immediate armistice.

Within hours he formed his government, and together its members opted for an armistice. Word of this was sent immediately to the Germans and Italians. This was devastating news for the Churchill government in London and a breach of France's promise not to seek a separate peace. The British government promptly announced that it and its empire would continue to fight on. This announcement was followed by an announcement by French General Charles de Gaulle, who was in London at the time, that he, too, would continue to fight on, and called upon Frenchmen all over the empire to join him. De Gaulle was a newly-promoted one-star general, and quite low in the hierarchy of the French Army leadership. Recognizing this, he offered to serve under any French military leader of a higher rank who came forward. None did.

The Germans and Italians accepted Petain's offer. Negotiations followed, and on June 21, 1940, the government of Marshal Petain signed an armistice with Germany. On June 24 an armistice was signed with Italy. Petain announced that his government would remain in unoccupied France and that France would, henceforth, be a neutral nation.

This action eased tensions, somewhat, in Africa where French and Italian colonies bordered each other. But, Italian/British borders were still hostile and tense.

Captured French prisoners of war. Many of them can be identified as Africans by their head dress.

Thousands of French colonial troops escaped to Switzerland after the fall of France, where they became internees for the remainder of the war.

Meanwhile, German troops marched down the full length of the French Atlantic coast to the border with Spain. Fighting ended on June 25, 1940, and territorial adjustments were hastily made, leaving the Petain government in control of approximately one-third of Metropolitan France.

On July 1, 1940, the French government moved to Vichy, France in east-central France. Vichy was a beautiful town of about 20,000 people in the center of a spa resort area. The famous Vichy Water, renowned worldwide for its medicinal properties, came from there. Vichy was also a town of luxurious hotels which catered to the many tourists who came to take the waters. But, in the midst of war, the hotels were virtually empty. This, however, proved to be of great benefit to the French government, which needed lots of space quickly to house the many governmental departments and the thousands of individuals and their families associated with the government. Petain's government and its entourage, therefore, moved into the hotels. The French Assembly established itself at the Vichy casino.

Thousands of French soldiers were taken as prisoners of war (POW) by the Germans, including many Africans.

Critics of the French often claimed that African troops were regularly used as rear guards, a risky undertaking, to allow white soldiers to escape. This was not necessarily true, in that most of the troops were organized into divisions and fought as divisions.

During May and June eight North African and West African divisions were used in the front lines and suffered heavy casualties from the German tanks because they had inadequate antitank defenses. A few black soldiers were evacuated to England during the massive evacuation at Dunkirk.

The real trouble, however, began for blacks after being captured. The Germans acted horribly against them. Some black soldiers were summarily executed by German troops rather than taking them as prisoners. Still, others were executed upon reaching the prison camps. German propaganda had portrayed black French soldiers as wild savages who often fought to the death, took no prisoners, and killed enemy wounded. Many German soldiers believed this and, therefore, were afraid of them and willing to treat them in kind. During May 1940, General K. Nehring, Guderian's Chief-of-Staff, issued an order regarding black soldiers of which virtually every German soldier was aware. It read:

> *"Colonial soldiers have mutilated in bestial fashion our German wounded... all kindness would be an error. It is forbidden to send them to the rear without a guard. They are to be treated with the greatest rigor."*

On June 10 one of the worst massacres occurred at the town of Erquinvillers when German soldiers shot and killed between 400 and 500 black African soldiers. At the village of Chasselay-Montluzin another 212 were lined up and shot by firing squads. Other ugly incidents occurred during these days, but with lesser numbers of victims. Those lucky enough to remain alive in German hands were badly treated. First of all, they were segregated from white soldiers, which was permitted by the Geneva Convention, but which also reduced the number of white witnesses to atrocities. As a rule, the blacks got less food, fuel, and medical care than white POWs. Most of the black POW camps were in northeastern France and Brittany, where the weather was colder. This caused many of them to die of weather-related diseases. The black POWs were often pressed into labor gangs and sent out to work on farms, forests, factories, and the like. This was sometimes fortunate for the black soldiers in that sympathetic Frenchmen would, at times, give them food and clothing.

Conditions for black POWS in German hands gradually improved during the war because Vichy officials were eventually allowed to visit the camps, as were Red Cross workers and other humanitarian organizations. In a few cases some sick black soldiers were released to the care of the French. Some of them were even released temporarily for use in German movies because there were virtually no blacks in Germany to fill such roles.

During the height of the North African campaign in 1941, when it appeared that the Axis Powers might win, special magazines were printed for the black soldiers telling them how good the Germans would treat Africans once Germany regained its African colonies.

FRANCE BECOMES A DICTATORSHIP

In the days that followed the move to Vichy, the French leaders debated their future. It looked bleak indeed. In searching for answers as to how France had sunk so low, it was almost universally agreed that the old prewar system of government, that of democracy, had failed. It was in this atmosphere of defeat and despair that on July 10, 1940, the French Assembly decided to scrap the democratic process in France and voted dictatorial powers to Marshal Petain. Having done this, the Assembly dissolved itself and did not meet again for the remainder of the war. Petain then created a new constitution which provided for an all-powerful office of Head of State, and an administrative system whereby the Head of State and an appointed Premier would rule by decree. Petain assumed the office of Head of State and appointed Pierre Laval, a controversial and pro-Axis politician, as Premier.

Petain's government had much in common with the governments of Germany, Italy and Spain. While the Petain government proclaimed its independence and neutrality, it was obvious to all that the government at Vichy was a weak, Axis-leaning neo-puppet of Germany and Italy.

IN THE UNITED STATES

The beginning of the war in Europe was of great concern to the American government and American people, and major developments soon got underway to build up America's defenses. Overseas, however, the United States was affected very little. There was no great rush of Americans returning home from Europe, and American businesses there remained active and quickly adjusted to the new wartime conditions.

On the high seas, however, American ships, as well as other ships of neutral nations heading for certain ports in Europe, became subject to the Allied blockade. In the eastern Atlantic and Mediterranean, every ship heading for Italy was detained, because Italy was known to be a conduit of supplies for Germany. American ships were no exception. A case in point concerned the American freighter "Meanticut" which was heading for Italy with a mixed cargo. As she passed through the Strait of Gibraltar on October 12 she was ordered by the British to put into Gibraltar harbor for an inspection of her cargo. Some of her cargo was declared contraband and the Meanticut was then ordered to proceed to Oran, Algeria to off-load that cargo. This she did, and was then allowed to proceed to Italy. The inconvenience, though, cost the shipping company a fifteen-day delay in its schedule.

When Germany invaded in the west and defeated France in June, the picture for Americans in both Europe and Africa changed. Thousands of Americans now fled Europe and hundreds fled the French and Italian colonies in Africa. The American government aided in this exodus when it could. Such an incident occurred at Casablanca, French Morocco where the American destroyer "Dickerson" was at anchor. As it became evident that France was on the verge of military collapse, word was quickly spread throughout French Morocco that any American citizen who wanted to leave should report aboard the Dickerson as soon as possible. The Dickerson then departed Casablanca on June 9 and took her passengers to Lisbon. The next day they boarded the American ocean line "Washington" for home.

On June 11 President Roosevelt, acting under the authority of the American Neutrality Act of 1935, declared the entire Mediterranean and the northern end of the Red Sea war zones. This, by law, prohibited American merchant ships from sailing in these areas. It also meant that most of French North Africa, all of Libya, and all of Egypt no longer had direct sea communications with the United States.

Chapter 5

FIGHTING SPREADS TO NORTH AFRICA AND EAST AFRICA (JUNE–AUGUST 1940)

WHITE MAN AGAINST WHITE MAN, BLACK MAN AGAINST BLACK MAN

FRANCE'S GOLD WENT TO AFRICA

With the defeat of the British and French Armies in the north, the French government decided that France's gold supply, which had long been stored in the Bank of France in Paris, should be sent elsewhere for safe keeping. Since France was the custodian of Belgium's and Poland's gold, it was decided that gold should go, too. Rather than send the gold on a French ship which might be sunk or captured by the enemy, especially if the word of the transfer got out, the French asked the neutral Americans to transport the gold for them. President Roosevelt quickly agreed and sent the cruiser "Vincennes," which was then in European waters, to pick up about 1,200 tons of gold at Bordeaux and take 1,000 tons of it to Dakar, Senegal, and the remainder to the United States.

GOLD ON THE DOCK

On June 10, 1940, the "Vincennes" stopped at Casablanca, French Morocco to pick up additional gold. During that transfer, one of the containers burst open and hundreds of pounds of gold coins spilled onto the dock floor. The startled longshoremen quickly scooped up the coins, put them back in the container and took it aboard the Vincennes.

The Vincennes took the 1000 tons of gold to Dakar, as planned, and from there it was taken secretly inland to an old fortress at Kayes, French Sudan, where it was kept under heavy guard for most of the remainder of the war. The gold shipped to the United States was stored temporarily at the U.S. Military Academy in New York, and then moved on to the U. S. Gold Bullion Center at Fort Knox, Kentucky.

FIGHTING ERUPTS IN THE MEDITERRANEAN AND NORTH AFRICA

With Italy in the war the contest for the Mediterranean began—and with it control of North Africa. Italy had a powerful fleet—on paper—but the construction of the ships was substandard compared to other navies of the world. The Italian sailors knew this and called it "The Cardboard Fleet." Mussolini knew it too, but this did not keep him from boasting that the entire Mediterranean would, one day, belong to Italy. "Mare Nostra" (Our Sea), he called it.

The French had powerful naval forces in the Mediterranean, as did the British, and it was obvious that the Allies would not relinquish control of this vital waterway without a determined struggle. If that struggle were to end in a decisive victory for one side or the other, it was a foregone conclusion that control of most of North Africa would automatically fall into the hands of the victor.

Both sides were relatively well-prepared for war in the Mediterranean, and during the first twenty-four hours each would strike several times.

It was the Italians who struck first in the Mediterranean. Italy officially declared war on France and Britain around 5:00 pm on June 10. That night nine waves of Italian bombers took off from Sicily and bombed the British naval base on the island of Malta during the early morning hours of June 11. Later that day British bombers attacked Italian airfields in Libya. These were the first bombs to fall on African soil since the Ethiopian war of 1935–36. That same day, a British armored car unit crossed the Egyptian/Libyan border and destroyed several Italian trucks at the border post of Fort Capuzzo. Also that day, Italian planes bombed French targets in Corsica. That night thirteen British bombers from England bombed the Italian cities of Genoa and Turin in northern Italy. The British lost one plane.

On June 12 the British government ordered that the naval blockade, already in place against Germany, be extended to include Italy and her overseas possessions.

Fighting increased dramatically in the Mediterranean and North Africa on June 12. A British naval task force of one cruiser and several destroyers bombarded the Italian port of Tobruk, Libya. Italian ships steamed out to challenge the British ships, but the British withdrew before contact was made. Off Crete, the Italians scored the first naval victory in the Mediterranean when the Italian submarine "Bagnolini" torpedoed and sank the British light cruiser "Calipso."

EGYPT

In Cairo, the Egyptian government of Ali Maher broke diplomatic relations with Italy on June 12 and, under pressure from the British, pledged its loyalty to the Allies. Both King Farouk and Maher, though, showed signs of not wanting to offend the Italians and displayed this by deliberately delaying the ejection of Italian diplomats and interning dangerous Italian aliens.

On June 13 the Italians showed signs that they were preparing defensive positions on both the western and eastern borders of Libya. This indicated that they would not be attacking either Egypt or Tunisia in the immediate future. The British were not so sure.

On the 14th a small British force raided both Fort Capuzzo, Libya, and another frontier post, Maddalena. In both places the Italian garrisons were easily routed. The British took possession of the posts but soon withdrew. They had achieved their objective—to test the resolve of the Italian defenders.

On June 16, in retaliation for the British raids into Libya, a small Italian force crossed into Egypt and raided British and Egyptian Army positions at Sollum and Marsa Matruh, and then withdrew. Several Egyptians were killed.

The British pounced on this event to claim that it was an outright invasion of Egypt, and called upon Premier Ali Maher to live up to his previous statements that Egypt would

The British battleship "Howe" passing though the Suez Canal. The Canal is a even–level waterway with no locks or dams making Axis air and naval strikes ineffectual. The only sure way for the Axis to deny the use of the Canal to the British was to occupy it. Even the sinking of a large ship in the Canal would not block it permanently.

declare war on any invader. Maher replied that he would refuse to declare war on Italy, claiming that the Italian raid was a minor incursion that could be settled by diplomatic means. The British were not pleased.

This action and the delays in ejecting the Italian diplomates created an intolerable situation for the British. So, on June 17, the British Ambassador to Egypt, Sir Miles Lampson, called on the King, armed with instructions from London. He told Farouk that Maher must be dismissed from office because of his lack of cooperation with the British war effort. This was a clear threat to Farouk, too, that his position was in danger. All were aware that in 1914, at the beginning of World War I, a similar situation had arisen and the British had forced the abdication of the then ruler of Egypt, Khedive Abbas Hilmi.

Hearing that Maher might soon be relieved, the Wafdist Party began agitating for national elections, feeling that their party could win. But, because of the war emergency and the recent anti-British stand taken by the Wafdists, the British rejected the idea of an election and demanded that Farouk appoint a new Prime Minister who would support British interests. Farouk was very angry with the British for their blatant interference into Egyptian affairs, but his overriding need now was to protect his throne. He therefore dismissed Maher and appointed a pro-British politician, Hassan Sabry, as Prime Minister. Sabry had very little popular support, but the British were confident that he would do their bidding. The Wafdists condemned the high-handed action of the British, refused to serve in Sabry's cabinet, and resumed their anti-British rhetoric. The British demanded that the ousted

Maher not return to his previous post as an advisor to the King. Rather, Maher was offered two new opportunities, house arrest or the Ambassadorship to the United States. He chose the latter.

Sabry soon announced that Egypt's new policy would be one of supporting the British war effort, upholding public morale, and using the Egyptian Army for internal security such as the guarding of public utilities, communications systems, bridges, and the like. This satisfied the British and they dropped their demand that Egypt declare war on Italy.

Meanwhile, regarding military matters, the British began to concentrate some of their most powerful warships at Port Said, Egypt, to guard the northern entrance to the Suez Canal from a possible attack by the Italian Navy.

HITLER DISPLEASED WITH THE ITALIANS, SPEAKS OUT ON THE BRITISH EMPIRE

The Germans were quite surprised and disappointed with the Italians having taken the defensive in North Africa, and even more so when they learned that the Italians had no plans to send substantial reinforcements to Libya. Mussolini believed at this time, that with France all but defeated, Britain would soon surrender too and the war would be over. Mussolini was so confident of this that he allowed new maps to be printed in Italy showing all of Savoy, Nice, Corsica, Tunisia, The Sudan, British and French Somaliland, Cyprus, and Crete as Italian territory. Furthermore, the Italian propagandists began to tell the Italian people that the Mediterranean was now under Italian control and that the Indian Ocean soon would be.

Hitler could do little about the situation in North Africa at this time, because all of his attentions were devoted to the pending military collapse of France.

On June 13, the day that Paris was declared an open city, Hitler offered what might be seen as an olive branch to the British. It was Hitler's hope that he could terminate hostilities in western Europe, where Germany would soon reign supreme and where little else could be gained by war. Hitler reasoned that if Germany could make peace with Britain, Germany would be free to act elsewhere— most probably in the east. The Fuhrer's offer was made in a rare personal interview granted to an American journalist, Karl von Wiegand. During their conversation Hitler directed the topic toward Britain and the British Empire, and told von Wiegand, "All I have ever asked is that Germany should enjoy equal rights with Great Britain and receive back its former colonies. It has never been my intention to destroy the (British) empire." When von Wiegand's report was published, the Churchill government chose to ignore it and Hitler later expressed his disappointment to colleagues. Hitler would have no easy peace in the west.

SPAIN TAKES TANGIER

At the western end of North Africa the Spaniards made several surprising moves. On June 13 the Madrid government of Generalissimo Franco officially changed its status with regards to the war from one of neutrality to one of non-belligerency. This was a clear indication that Spain was moving closer to its Axis friends. Then, on June 14, taking advantage of the situation in France, in the Mediterranean, in Libya, and in Egypt, the Madrid government sent Spanish troops into the international enclave of Tangier and occupied that important seaport. Tangier, on the southern shore of the Strait of Gibraltar, had long been governed as an international community. This had been a constant thorn in the side of the Spanish, who claimed that Tangier was a part of their Spanish Moroccan Protectorate and should not have been internationalized in the first place. To ease public criticism, which was sure to follow, Madrid called the takeover of Tangier a "provisional occupation." Furthermore, troops of the Sultan of Morocco accompanied the Spanish troops into Tangier, giving credibility to both Spain and the Sultan's claim that Tangier was an integral part of Morocco. As for international reactions, Franco was right. Condemnations were forthcoming from all Allied, and most neutral quarters, but no one chose to take retaliatory action against Spain.

Further taking advantage of the situation, Franco instructed his ambassador to France, who was, at that moment, in the awkward position of travelling with the French government of Paul Reynaud from Tours to Bordeaux, to inform the French that Madrid wanted to open discussions on long-standing territorial claims in Africa. These claims affected French Morocco, Algeria, and French West Africa. Clearly, Spain was rattling the sword. Reynaud's reply was noncommittal and designed to put the Spanish off as long as possible.

FRENCH GOVERNMENT DECIDES AGAINST GOING TO NORTH AFRICA—HITLER APPROVES

At Bordeaux the Petain government, after deciding to seek armistices with Germany and Italy, also decided not to flee to North Africa, but to remain in metropolitan France.

In Germany, Hitler felt he had been most generous toward the French. He wanted the French to remain strong enough to protect their vast empire. If France were utterly defeated, Hitler reasoned, the French empire would be gobbled up by Britain, the United States, Japan and others. From Germany's point of view, it was better to have France in control of her empire and Germany in control of France. Therefore, Hitler had ordered that France must not be totally defeated. As for the future of France and her empire, Hitler decreed, that question would be postponed until after the war.

THE WAR IN THE MEDITERRANEAN AND NORTH AFRICA CONTINUES

During the middle two weeks of June 1940, as surrender negotiations were underway, hundreds of French ships arrived at French North African ports bringing civilians, military personnel, vital supplies and war equipment being evacuated from Metropolitan France. Most of these ships were commercial and privately owned vessels and were not attacked by the Italians.

From French North Africa General Auguste Nogues, Governor of French Morocco and Commander of French forces in North Africa, cabled General Maxime Weygand, now Minister of Defense in the Petain government, stating that French forces under his command were, like de Gaulle, "burning" to continue the fight.

Weygand's reply was that the terms of the armistices must be honored.

In Germany, Hitler phoned Mussolini and suggested that they meet the next day, June 18, in Munich to discuss the French surrender. At the meeting, the two dictators would coordinate their demands on the French and work out the terms of the armistices.

It was during this time that Mussolini received some disturbing news from Libya. The British submarine "Parthian" sank the Italian destroyer "Nembo" off Tobruk on the 17th. Then on the 19th the sub penetrated Tobruk harbor and fired two torpedoes at the cruiser "San Giorgio" but they exploded in the mud before reaching the ship. The next day Parthian, still operating in the Tobruk area, sank a second Italian submarine, the "Diamonte."

On June 19, 1940, German forces continued the march deep into France and along the French Atlantic coast. The exodus of civilians and military personnel from France to North Africa continued. Among the exodus was the nearly completed French battleship "Jean Bart" which slipped out of its dry dock at St. Nazaire and sailed to safety at Casablanca, French Morocco.

SPAIN MAKES AN OFFER

With German forces rapidly approaching his northern border, Generalissimo Franco of Spain sent a message to Hitler announcing that Spain, under certain conditions, would be willing to enter the war on the side of the Axis in much the same way as Italy had. Part of those conditions were that, at war's end, Spain would be able to increase her empire. This would be accomplished by acquiring the British bastion of Gibraltar, all of French Morocco, the seaport of

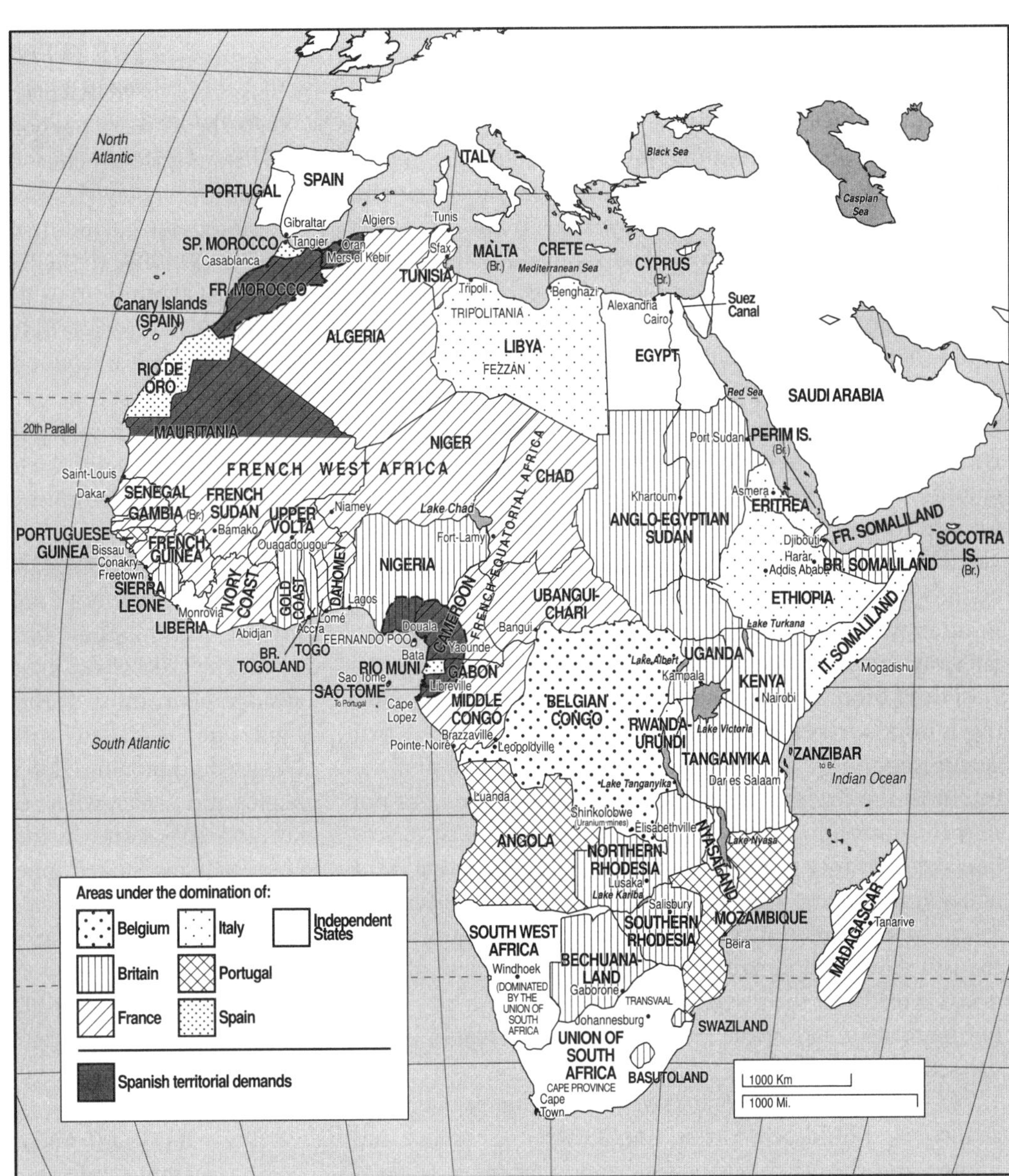

Spain's territorial demands in Africa of June 1940 for entering the war on the side of the Axis.

Oran and its environs in Algeria, an enlargement of Spain's Rio de Oro colony in West Africa by acquiring land from French West Africa down to the 20th parallel, and the enlargement of Spain's Rio Muni colony in central Africa by acquiring land from Nigeria and French Equatorial Africa. That expanded colony would extend from the mouth of the Niger River to Cape Lopez.

Franco's message was received in Berlin and promptly forwarded to Munich where Hitler and Mussolini were meeting.

HITLER AND MUSSOLINI ESTABLISH ARMISTICE TERMS FOR THE FRENCH

Hitler, Mussolini, and their top aides met in Munich on June 18 as planned. Hitler stressed that he wanted to be lenient with France to prevent Petain's government from escaping to French North Africa to carry on "a holy war," as he put it, for an indefinite period of time. Mussolini at first wanted to occupy all of France, but later agreed with Hitler's viewpoint. Mussolini, nevertheless, stressed Italy's long-standing territorial demands against France. Mussolini also laid on the table new, but not specific, demands against Algeria and French Morocco which would allow Italy to have an outlet to the Atlantic Ocean as a way of bypassing Gibraltar. Hitler reminded Mussolini that Germany, too, had historic interests in Morocco, and so did Spain.

Hitler reviewed again his territorial interests in Africa, stating that he wanted Germany's colonies back, as well as all of the Belgian Congo. This was based on the fact that Belgium was now a conquered nation and that the Congo would be considered a spoil of war for Germany and a major step toward Germany's long-held aspirations of creating "Mittel-Afrika." In the same vein Hitler said that the Netherlands was a conquered nation, too, but that Germany had no interest in the Dutch East Indies because they were too far away, and that Japan's interests there had priority.

Hitler brought up the often-discussed question of sending Europe's Jews to Madagascar. With France's defeat that island might now be easily acquired and provide a final solution to the Jewish question in Europe. This idea was not new to Mussolini. On May 25, 1940, when it became very likely that France would be defeated, the Fuhrer had sent Mussolini a memo suggesting that a place for the Jews be found somewhere in Africa. Mussolini was noncommittal on the issue then and remained the same now. Because of this, it was agreed that the placement of the Jews in Africa should not be made a part of the armistice terms but would be addressed later.

At Mussolini's insistence, it was agreed that two separate armistices should be written, one between Germany and France, and the other between Italy and France.

By the end of their meeting the Germans and Italians had worked out the conditions they would present to France for their respective armistices. They were almost identical.

As for France's future it was agreed that the Petain government must accept, at least for the moment, the fait accompli in Europe, and the fact that there would be future territorial changes in the French empire.

In his conversations with Mussolini, Hitler stressed again that he would be lenient with Britain if she, too, sought an armistice, because he wanted Britain, like France, to remain strong enough to protect whatever portion of her empire would be left to her.

Franco's note on Spain's entering the war and his accompanying demands were quickly reviewed by Hitler and Mussolini, and it was agreed that Franco should be told only that his message had been received and was under consideration.

THE EFFECTS OF FRANCE'S SURRENDER ON AFRICA

As the surrender negotiations were under way in France, the Petain government was able to convince such leaders as Nogues in French Morocco and others in various parts of the Empire, to terminate their aggressive rhetoric and accept the armistices. Only de Gaulle and a few others remained in defiance. The schism in the French leadership was now taking form and proving to be very lopsided in favor of Petain.

The armistices required many things of France that would reduce her to a second-rate military power, and subject virtually all of her future political moves to German and Italian scrutiny. To monitor the armistices, separate German and Italian armistice commissions would be sent to critical points throughout the French empire to insure that the Petain government complied with the terms to which it had agreed. In an effort to prevent a duplication of effort regarding the armistice commissions, the Germans and Italians agreed to divide the tasks of supervision among themselves. Under this arrangement, most of the French empire in Africa was assigned to the Italians with the exception that the German Navy would be allowed to send control commissions to Casablanca and Dakar, where they would work alongside the Italian armistice commissions. It was in these ports that the German Navy hoped, one day, to establish naval bases.

The French/Italian armistice required France to establish a 200 km-wide demilitarized zone within French possessions bordering Libya. This zone encompassed about half of Tunisia and reached deep into southeastern Algeria, northwestern French West Africa, and the northern part of French Equatorial Africa.

HITLER AND MUSSOLINI AGREE ON ITALIAN ATTACK ON EGYPT

On June 25 the Italians sent a peace-feeler to London, but it was promptly rejected. Because of this, Hitler advised

Mussolini that before the British would agree to Italy's peace demands the Italians would have to make a show of force against Britain, and that the best place to do that would be in Egypt. Mussolini could hardly disagree and soon began making plans for an invasion of Egypt from Libya. The Italians were in an excellent position to do so because they already had over 200,000 troops in Libya and it was known that the British had considerably fewer. Actually the British had about 36,000 troops in Egypt plus the very weak Egyptian Army.

The Italians suffered an unexpected setback in their planning on June 28, 1940, when a plane carrying Libyan Governor and Commander-in-Chief of Italian forces in North Africa, Italo Balbo, was mistakenly shot down by Italian antiaircraft gunners as it flew over Tobruk during a British air raid. Balbo was killed. Three days later Marshall Rodolfo Graziani succeeded Balbo and the planning for the invasion of Egypt resumed.

HITLER STATES AGAIN THAT THE BRITISH EMPIRE MUST SURVIVE

During the last week of June 1940, Hitler apparently came to the conclusion that the time had come to pursue his lifelong goal of creating a huge colonial empire in eastern Europe for the German people by conquering the Soviet Union. All indications were that he felt he could do this even though Britain was not totally defeated. In an atmosphere of extreme secrecy, he began discussing the possibilities of such an undertaking with his closest associates. When asked if it might not be best to eliminate Britain first, Hitler repeated what he had said before; that the British, like the French, must not be totally defeated lest the British Empire disintegrate and be acquired by others. His exact words were, "If we crush England by force of arms the British Empire will fall to pieces. But, this would be no advantage to Germany. We should spill German blood only in order that Japan, America, and others might benefit." Rather than spill more German blood over England, Hitler chose to pursue his dream in the east, and his top military commanders were obliged to go along. On July 2, 1940, he assigned an experienced Army planner, Colonel von Lossberg, to begin drawing up the first plans for the invasion of the Soviet Union.

As for Britain, Hitler felt that she could be militarily neutralized by the Luftwaffe and the German Navy for the relatively short time it would take to conquer the Soviet Union. This would leave the bulk of his mighty Army free to pursue the conquest in the east. After all, Hermann Goering had promised that he could bring the British government to the negotiating table by air power alone and Admiral Erich Raeder, Commander of the Germany Navy, believed he could starve Britain into submission by destroying her sea commerce. And, as further insurance, actual plans for an invasion of England would proceed, along with accompanying propaganda, in the event that an opportunity should present itself whereby England might actually be invaded. Then too, the Italians would keep substantial British forces tied down in Africa.

This, then, was the course Hitler would take throughout the winter of 1940/41. All other issues important to Germany, including those in Africa, would be postponed.

BRITISH NAVY ATTACKS THE FRENCH NAVY IN NORTH AFRICA

The question of the French Navy had been a burning issue with the British since the defeat of France. The French fleet, the fourth largest in the world, was still very much intact, and the French had been able to retain control of the fleet, albeit under the conditions of the armistices. The Germans and Italians promised not to acquire the French fleet, and demanded only that the majority of the warships be disarmed and remain in their home ports. Certain ships, though, remained mobilized so that the French could defend their empire.

In London the Churchill government put absolutely no faith in this arrangement. Churchill feared that all, or part of the French fleet would eventually fall into Axis hands, despite repeated French promises that they would scuttle their fleet rather than allow that to happen. If major elements of the French fleet did fall into Axis hands those ships, combined with the ships of Germany and Italy, could mount a serious challenge against the British Navy for control of the seas, and especially the control of the Mediterranean.

Furthermore, there was now deep hatred in London toward the Petain government for breaking the alliance and leaving Britain alone to face Germany and Italy. The attitude of the British leaders was that the Petain government must be punished in some manner. The conflict over the French fleet provided that opportunity.

In June, when the first signs that France was on the verge of surrendering were noticed, the British began demanding that, if such a scenario came about, the French ships would sail to either British or neutral harbors for internment, or scuttle themselves. The French refused to do any of these things and at that time began making their often-to-be-repeated promise that their ships would not, under any circumstances, fall into the hands of the Axis powers.

Churchill, though, was determined to teach the French a lesson and, since he feared the presence of the French ships in the Mediterranean, he saw an opportunity to satisfy both needs with a single action. He ordered the British Navy to carry out a surprise attack on the large French naval base east of Oran, Algeria at Mers el Kebir. There, a large part of the French Navy lay at anchor and in the process of disarming. The attack, Churchill reasoned, would not only punish the French but whatever damage was done to the French ships

The French battleship "Bretagne" sinking by the stern as a result of the attack by the British Navy of July 3, 1940, on the French naval base at Mers el Kebir, Algeria.

would reduce the potential threat to Britain's naval position in the Mediterranean.

On the morning of July 3, 1940, a powerful British naval force, commanded by Admiral Sir James Somerville, sailed into sight of the French naval base of Mers el Kebir and took up positions off shore with guns at the ready. A British delegation went ashore, met with the French base commander, Admiral Marcel Gensoul, and ordered him to choose under threat of attack, one of several options, all of which would neutralize the French ships under his command. Gensoul quickly conferred with the Petain government which was then en route to Vichy. Petain rejected all the British demands and the British delegation returned to inform Somerville. After a brief delay the British ships opened fire. The French gun replied and for the better part of an hour the navies of the two former allies blasted away at each other until the British broke off contact and departed. Losses and casualties were inflicted on both sides, but the French losses were greater.

Meanwhile, throughout the British Empire, French ships at anchor in British ports were boarded and taken over by British sailors, soldiers, and/or marines. At Alexandria, Egypt, where French and British warships were within several hundred yards of each other, the French refused to let the British board. After a tense standoff, the French finally gave in and accepted the British demand that their ships be completely disarmed.

At Mers el Kebir, one French battleship, the "Bretagne," was sunk, two other battleships badly damaged, and some 1,400 French seamen killed. Another French battleship, the "Strasbourg" was able to escape along with five destroyers and eventually made it safely to the French naval base at Toulon, France.

The British were not finished with their unpleasant task. On the 4th the British sub "Pandora," still patrolling off Algeria, sank the French sloop "Rigualt de Genouilly" off Matifou within sight of land.

The attack on Mers el Kebir was clearly an act of war and the French had every right to declare war on Britain. In addition, there were those in Petain's government who advocated that action. Petain, though, wisely hesitated. Clearly a French response was called for but it need not be as drastic as a declaration of war. Petain began exploring his options.

The next day Petain asked Hitler to suspend article #8 of the armistice agreement, which disarmed the French ships, so that the French Navy could retaliate against the British. Hitler promptly agreed.

By the evening of July 4, cooler heads had prevailed within the French government and it was realized that France was in no condition to fight a war with Britain, nor did the French leaders want to be thrust into the arms of the Axis powers as a co-belligerent. Furthermore, the French ruled out a retaliatory attack by their navy on the British Navy because losses could be expected and the French had no way of replacing lost warships. The fleet was France's most powerful weapon and it was thought best to conserve it. This thrust the job of carrying out the retaliation on the French Air Force or Army. An air raid on Gibraltar was considered, as well as some sort of raid into the British colony of Sierra Leone and/or an air attack on its capital, Freetown.

Petain and his advisors finally agreed that an appropriate retaliation for the Mers el Kebir attack would be an air attack by French planes on Gibraltar. That attack was carried out on the morning of July 5 by French planes flying from bases in French Morocco. Then in an effort to tone down the confrontation, Petain instructed the French fleet not to attack any

British warship unless it ventured to within twenty miles of a French military installation. This order was made public.

Churchill, though, was not satisfied. He felt that the French had not been punished enough and ordered a second attack—this time by aircraft—on Mers el Kebir. That attack took place on the morning of July 6 by planes from the carrier "Ark Royal." Their main target was the French battleship "Dunkerque," which was one of the most modern ships in the French Navy. Several bomb hits were scored on the ship putting her out of action for the near future.

The next day, the French responded by breaking diplomatic relations with London. The British responded to that action by announcing that their naval blockade would be extended to include unoccupied France and all French colonies that remained loyal to the Petain government. This action had worldwide consequences. First of all, it meant that France's supply of food and raw materials from her overseas colonies would all but cease—and France was already short of food. Furthermore, the extension of the blockade meant that supplies from America and other neutral nations flowing to France would now be restricted and subjected to the will of the British.

The British, however, could not blockade the air, so French commercial air operations continued throughout the French Empire. Only a very small percentage of France's commerce and military needs, though, could be met in these early days of commercial aviation.

The undeclared war between Britain and France then shifted to West Africa where the French battleship "Richelieu," laying at anchor in Dakar harbor, was attacked and damaged by torpedo bombers from the British aircraft carrier "Hermes." The Richelieu was badly damaged and could no longer move under her own power. She was towed to a convenient pier to be used as a floating battery to protect the city and harbor.

The next day planes from the Hermes attacked the battleship Jean Bart in Casablanca harbor, causing some damage to the ship.

On July 9, British and French warships encountered each other at sea in the Mediterranean and shots were exchanged. No damage, however, was suffered by either side.

By July 12, Churchill was satisfied. He announced that the British would no longer attack the French ships so long as those ships did not try to sail to Axis-controlled ports. With this, the Mers el Kebir crisis faded, but a deep wedge of distrust had been driven between the British and French. The French in Africa, where the attacks had occurred, were particularly resentful toward the British, and now more than ever, loyal to Petain. In London, Charles de Gaulle, who had not been consulted about the Mers el Kebir attacks, publicly objected to the attacks, and recruitments into the Free French fell for the next few months. Churchill got his revenge, but the price was high.

A Vichy anti–British poster from late 1940 or early 1941 shows Churchill as a world–grabbing octopus, but losing his arms with the words, "His amputations continue systematically." Note that the octopus had been bloodied several times in Africa but still holds South Africa firmly in its grip.

As for the British blockade of French ports, London later announced that food, medical supplies, and other humanitarian goods would be permitted to reach the French. Furthermore, the British did not interfere with French commercial shipping passing through the Strait of Gibraltar and down the coast of West Africa. The main reason for this was not humanitarian but simply because the British did not have the naval forces available to stop it. Another reason was that Churchill thought it best not to punish the French colonies in hopes that some of them might eventually rebel against Vichy and join de Gaulle's Free French.

Because the trade between French Africa and Metropolitan France continued, Pierre Laval, Petain's pro-German Premier, saw an opportunity to win concessions from Hitler, and indicated that Vichy would be willing to share the incoming products from Africa with Germany. There were others at Vichy who mistakenly believed that the British noninterference with this trade was intentional. This worked to soften, somewhat, the anti-British attitudes within Petain's government.

Because of the diplomatic break with Britain, the Petain government sent an order throughout the French Empire that all trade with neighboring British colonies was to cease immediately. Local trade between the native peoples was, however, allowed to continue. This latter condition opened many loopholes and the businessmen of the respective colonies soon found ways to sell goods across their colonial borders using native traders as middlemen.

Petain's order was counterproductive, though, with regards to police work. All throughout the colonial world, it had been a tradition for police forces on either side of a colonial border to cooperate with each other in the matter of ordinary crime. This cooperation now ended between the French and British colonies, allowing criminals to flee across colonial borders to relative safety. Another consequence of Petain's order was that customs revenues dropped for the colonial governments. This hurt the French as well as the British at a time when it was badly needed by both parties. Still another problem generated was that surpluses began to build, especially in the French colonies, because the French products could not be exported to long-standing customers due to the British blockade. As a result, prices fell on certain commodities in the French colonies and both traders and native producers complained. The British colonies did not have this problem because they could continue exporting their products to old as well as new customers which were relatively easy to find in a turbulent world at war. Some of their new customers were, not surprisingly, former French customers.

Another facet of Petain's order was that the French made no effort to increase border surveillance or other means of enforcement, so smuggling, which had long been a common practice, simply increased.

Petain further decreed that British subjects, both military and civilian, would not be allowed to leave French territory. This was due partly to the Mers el Kebir attack and partly to the fact that the British were making it very difficult, and at times impossible, for French citizens to leave British territory. The British wanted these Frenchmen to stay and support de Gaulle.

THE ARABS OF NORTH AFRICA

All across North Africa there was an on-going and long-standing resentment by the Arab population against the occupation of their ancient lands by the Europeans. In years past, most of the Arab states had been independent and most Arabs longed for the day when that independence would be regained. The European powers, however, had been very successful in suppressing Arab nationalism so that when the war started, Arab political movements were no great problem for the colonial authorities. With the defeat of France and the ensuing events that set the Europeans against each other, the Arabs could see that the Europeans had been pushed to the limits of their political, economic and military resources and that their abilities to maintain and control their respective colonial empires had been weakened. The hard-core Arab nationalists took advantage of this and began preaching the cause of Arab nationalism more aggressively from their secret hiding places. This activity was especially strong in Algeria.

The Italians compounded the issues by presented a mixed message to the Arabs that did little to endear the Arabs to Italy. On the one hand, the Italians vigorously suppressed all signs of nationalism in Libya, yet they had a powerful radio station in Bari, Italy that constantly broadcast propaganda to the entire Arab world advising the Arabs to throw off their British and French colonial yokes. The Italians tried to convince the Arab world that Italian colonialism was more benevolent than that of the other European powers, but the Arab people never fully believed it. Furthermore Mussolini, years earlier, had proclaimed himself the "Protector of Islam" which was generally seen by the Arabs as a pitiful joke.

As the war progressed and the Arabs became caught up in the Europeans' war, the credibility of the Europeans as a whole declined much to the advantage of the local nationalists.

THE "MEDITERRANEAN PLAN"

In late June 1940, Admiral Erich Raeder, Commander-in-Chief of the German Navy, proposed an ambitious plan to Hitler to gain Axis control of the Mediterranean Sea, and to facilitate the advance of strong German and Italian naval forces down the west coast of Africa, as well as down the Red Sea and into the Indian Ocean. As Raeder and his naval planners saw it, Italy's entry into the war split the Mediterranean into three spheres of naval influence: the British, out of Gibraltar, in the eastern Mediterranean; the Italian Home Fleet in the central Mediterranean; and the British in the western Mediterranean again out of Egypt, Cyprus, and Palestine.

Raeder's proposal, which he called the "Mediterranean Plan," called for elements of the German Navy combined with the Italian Navy, and possibly the Spanish and French Navies, to gain naval supremacy in the eastern Mediterranean by defeating the British naval and air forces there and capturing, or at least neutralizing, Gibraltar. The plan suggested that, in order to gain the cooperation of Spain and the Vichy French,

Admiral Erich Raeder, Commander-in-Chief of the German Navy, and author of "The Mediterranean Plan."

those governments might be politically played one against the other, using as bait territorial concessions in North Africa and elsewhere.

The combined Axis fleets would then move out into the central Atlantic and establish naval and air bases all along the Atlantic coast from Spain, possibly in Portugal, and down the west coast of Africa to the Spanish colony of Rio de Oro, or perhaps even to Dakar. Bases would also be established in the Canary Island and possibly the Azores. Most of the bases in question already existed but were in the hands of others. Militarily, most of the African bases were out of easy range of the British Home Fleet and England-based aircraft. Once the bases became operational in Axis hands they would service Axis submarines, surface ships, and aircraft operating in the Central and South Atlantic where sea and air supremacy would soon be gained, totally choking off Britain's seaborne commerce from the south. This would isolate Britain from a large part of her empire.

With those waters secured and Gibraltar closed, the British fleet in the eastern Mediterranean would be cut off from Britain except from the arduous communication link via the Panama Canal and around the world to the Red Sea. The combined Axis fleets would then turn their attention to eliminating all the remaining British naval, air, and land forces in the eastern Mediterranean. While the combined Axis fleets and air forces eliminated the British fleet, the "Mediterranean Plan" called for a pincers movement on the ground against Egypt. This envisioned an Italian advance into Egypt from Libya, and a combined German, Italian and possibly French advance southward out of Syria, through Palestine, and into Egypt from the east. The Suez Canal would be taken and Axis ships would then sail down the Red Sea to make contact with Italian East Africa. Later, land communications would be established with Italian East Africa with a combined German and Italian march up the Nile River Valley. From Italian East Africa, German and Italian naval and air forces could spread out into the Indian Ocean as far as the Persian Gulf. Saudi Arabia would then be virtually surrounded by Axis forces and that nation would come into the Axis camp or, at the least, be coerced into ousting the American oil companies that were developing the oil fields in the Persian Gulf area and turning those assets over to Germany and Italy to be developed.

With the Mediterranean a docile Axis lake, all the naval facilities around the Mediterranean could be converted into shipbuilding operations, since they were no longer needed as operational bases. With such resources the German and Italian Navies could rapidly expand and challenge the British Navy for control of the high sea.

The "Mediterranean Plan" also foresaw Turkey as becoming a member of the Axis, or at least a friendly neutral, and allowing Axis ships to pass through the Dardanelles into the Black Sea and be in a position to threaten the southern shores of the Soviet Union and the Balkan nations of Bulgaria and Romania. Because of the current treaty of friendship with the Soviet Union, the Soviets could be placated with offers of concessions in Afghanistan, Iran, and northern India.

It was a grand scheme and not one that Hitler quickly rejected. He seriously studied the plan and allowed it to be further developed. For the moment, though, his primary thoughts were still focused on the conquest of the Soviet Union. There was a chance that the "Mediterranean Plan" could be utilized after the Soviet Union was defeated.

HITLER COVETS THE CANARY ISLANDS

On July 11, 1940, in a conference with his generals, Hitler referred to the Canary Islands as potentially being very valuable to the Axis. He also feared that the British or Americans might take the Canaries because the British had recently (May 10, 1940) taken Iceland in the North Atlantic. The Canaries were, of course, Spanish territory, so some arrangement would have to be made with Spain. Hitler suggested that French Morocco, which Spain coveted, might be taken from France and exchanged for the Canaries. Nothing came of this proposal, but it served to reveal Hitler's expansionist thinking at the time.

About this time the Germans asked Vichy for the use of several bases in French North Africa. On July 15, the Petain government, surprisingly rejected the offer. Just as surprisingly, Hitler accepted the rejection and let the matter drop. It was apparent he still did not want to push the French too hard and he could certainly predict that the presence of German forces there would be deeply resented by the North African French. Rather than stir up more trouble with the French Hitler chose to back down.

ITALIAN TERRITORIAL DEMANDS EXPAND AND EXPAND...

On July 7, 1940, Italy's Foreign Minister, Count Galeazzo Ciano, met with Hitler to discuss issues concerning the war and

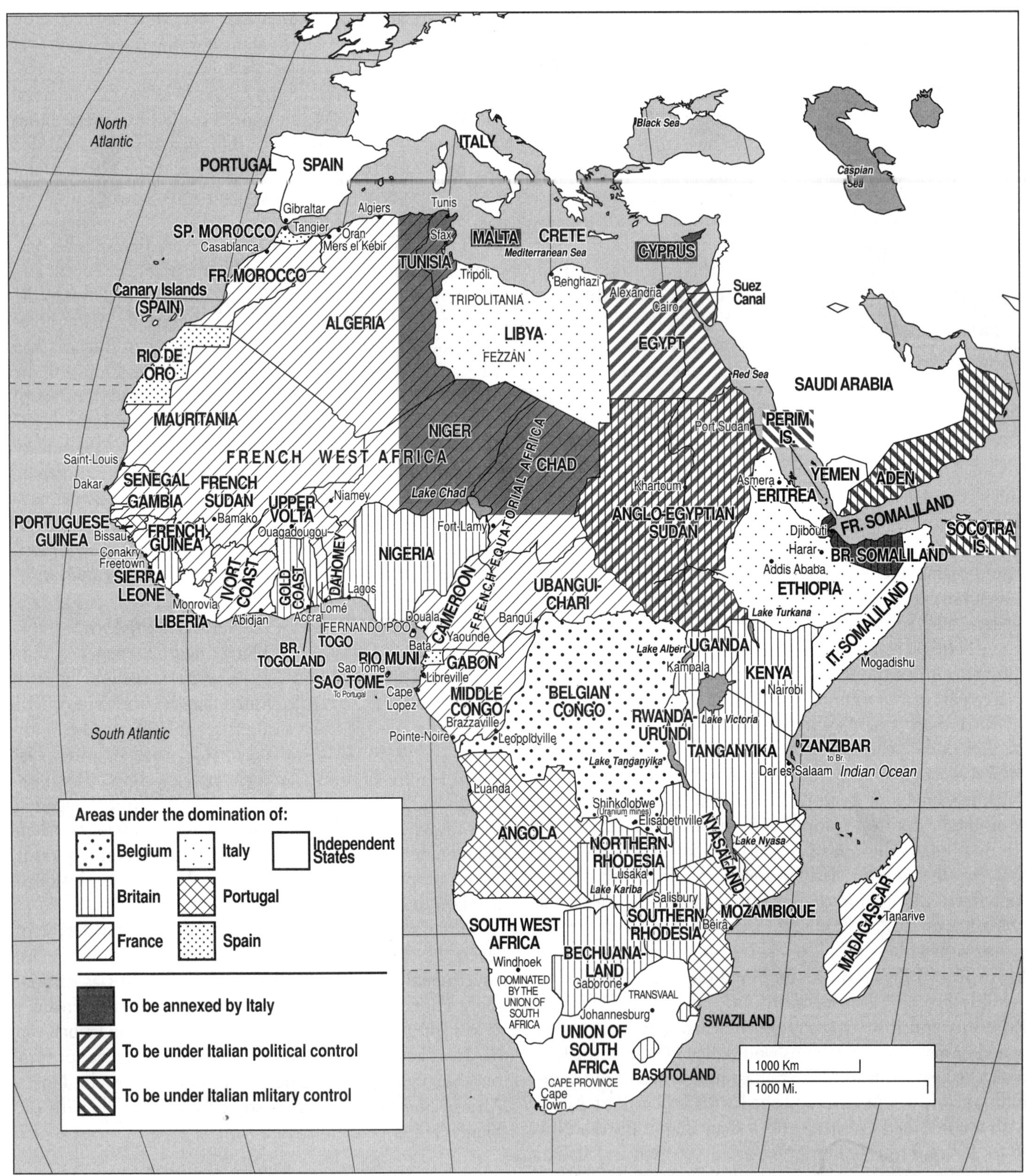

Mussolini's territorial claims in Africa after Italy's having entered the war. (For prior claims, see page 57.)

the postwar era. One of the subjects discussed was the change in Italy's territorial demands, some of which affected Africa. Ciano told Hitler that Italy was dropping demands on both Gibraltar and French Morocco, but would remain firm elsewhere. He insisted that Tunisia should become an Italian protectorate and that unspecified parts of eastern Algeria would be incorporated into that protectorate. Corsica and Malta would be annexed to Italy outright, French and British Somalilands would be annexed to Italian East Africa; The northern part of Chad in French Equatorial Africa and the eastern part of Niger in French West Africa, as far south as Lake Chad and the Nigerian border, would be annexed to Libya. Egypt and The Sudan would come under Italian control and appropriate agreements would guarantee the continuation of Egypt's nominal independence. The Paris-based Suez Canal Corporation, which owned the rights to the Suez Canal, would be liquidated and the Italians would take complete control of the Canal. Aden, on the end of the Arabian Peninsula along with the important islands of Perim and Socotra in the Gulf of Aden, would be put under Italian military occupation. Ciano also detailed Italian territorial demands in Greece, the Middle East, and Italian interests in the Persian Gulf oil. The British-controlled island of Cyprus in the Mediterranean might be given to Greece in compensation for territories taken from Greece by Italy.

Hitler's reaction to these demands is not certain. Ciano reported to Mussolini that the Fuhrer accepted the demands, but German records of the meeting state that Hitler was noncommittal.

These demands were widely publicized in Italy to raise the morale of the Italian people. Mussolini expanded on the theme of Italian expansion by suggesting that a powerful Italian-dominated economic union might be formed around the Mediterranean. This would include Italy, Spain, Portugal, Morocco, Algeria, Tunisia, Libya, (Egypt was omitted), the Middle East, Turkey, Bulgaria, and Greece. He called it the "Lire Bloc." Mussolini further noted that there were many places in the Middle East, as far east as the Persian Gulf, that might be acquired as additional Italian living space. When Mussolini spoke of these things, he not only spoke as the dictator of Italy but also as the Minister of Colonies, one of five cabinet posts he held.

As for France, Mussolini said that nation must be punished for her past indiscretions against Italy and it would be justifiable for Italy to acquire the huge French naval base at Toulon, and that important Italian works of art, most of which were in Paris, be returned to Italy.

Other Italian political leaders and some newspapers picked up on this theme of Italian expansionism and suggested that Italy might acquire Kenya and Uganda in East Africa and Nigeria in West Africa, with a railroad across the Sahara Desert connecting Nigeria and Libya. This dream of expansion soon turned into a feeding frenzy as Italian politicos and newspapers vied to outdo each other. Some suggested that the entire Cape Town to Cairo Railroad should come under Italian control, because from Kenya it ran southward through Tanganyika which, of course, would be German-controlled, and into the political sphere of South Africa which might very likely become a friend of the Axis.

There were printed reports that Switzerland might be dismembered and the Italian section annexed by Italy. The King and Count Ciano were known to favor this possibility. Italian expansion into the Balkans was also discussed with the possibility of Italy gaining territorial concessions from Yugoslavia and control of the Romanian oil fields.

Some newspapers resurrected the House of Savoy's (Italy's Royal family) ancient claims to the thrones of Cyprus and Jerusalem. With regard to the latter the papers suggested that parts of the Holy Land might be ruled by Italy in conjunction with the Vatican.

Others went further, suggesting that Italy might help the Indians free themselves from the British and that Australia and New Zealand might even be "liberated." With such a huge empire Italy would acquire a mighty Navy and gigantic merchant fleet which would propel Italy into becoming one of the world's great merchant states.

Oh, it was a wonderful dream!

THE "MEDITERRANEAN PLAN" EXPANDED

By late July it was becoming clear to the top German leaders that Britain would not surrender anytime soon, and would probably have to be defeated by force of arms. This meant that at a final peace settlement the Germans would have a greater claim on the British Empire than now. The ambitious German naval officers working on the "Mediterranean Plan," therefore, saw the need to expand the parameters of the Plan. In late July, Admiral Raeder presented Hitler with some interesting revisions to the Plan. The Navy now saw more justification for Germany to take large chunks of British Africa, specifically Kenya and Uganda along with the recovery of the former German colony of Tanganyika. To accomplish this, a combined sea and land offensive could be undertaken in this area from bases in Italian East Africa. To further protect these newly acquired German lands, the British-owned Mauritius and Seychelles Islands in the Indian Ocean might be acquired, along with the strategic French-owned Comoros Islands at the north end of the Madagascar Channel, the area's most important waterway. Furthermore, Madagascar might then be acquired and used, as had been discussed, as a future home for Europe's Jews. Raeder's plans called for Madagascar to be ruled by a German governor and a German police force to make certain the Jews remained on the island and under control.

JEWS AND INDIANS

When speaking of various schemes to relocate Europe's Jews, Hitler frequently referred to the solution the Americans had adapted for the American Indians as a possible model—the reservation system. Raeder's plans for Madagascar becoming a German-controlled Jewish homeland would have met this criteria.

A lookout tower in Kenya to warn against an Italian air attack.

There was more. Since the Belgian government-in-exile had moved to London and announced that it, too, would continue the war against Germany, this would give the Germans justification to conquer the entire Belgian Congo, as well as retake the former German colonies of Urundi and Rwanda (which had been mandated to Belgium after World War I).

Hitler listened to Raeder's revisions but was skeptical. He said he doubted that Germany could undertake such far-flung military operations while still fighting England. However, he could also see that if Germany did not act in these areas, others might. As before, Hitler did not reject the plan and allowed the Navy to keep it active.

As for Madagascar becoming a home for the Jews, this hope had all but faded in Hitler's mind. Certainly it could not be implemented in the near future. In the meantime, Heinrich Himmler, head of the SS, had proposed a plan for the Jews and Hitler had accepted it. The Plan was known as "Aufban Ost" and called for Europe's Jews to be sent to the existing ghettos in the big cities of the former part of Poland now called the General Government. From there a future determination would be made as to what to do with them.

The Italians learned of the Mediterranean Plan and on July 18, 1940, the semiofficial newspaper, "La Stampa" in Turin, referred to the plan by name in such a manner as to make its readers believe that it was an accepted part of the New Order. Reports in other Italian papers followed and stated that secret clauses in the armistices with France permitted the Plan to be implemented. Still other reports stated that the solution to the Jewish Question was near, which implied to many readers that the Jews would soon be shipped off to Madagascar. None of these things were true.

WAR ACTIVITY IN NORTH AFRICA; JULY–AUGUST 1940

While the top leaders of Germany and Italy divided up Africa on paper, the shooting war continued in North Africa but at a reduced pace now that France was no longer a combatant.

All was quiet along the Libyan/Egyptian border, but the forces on both sides were building their strengths. It was almost a certainty that fighting there would soon erupt.

EGYPTIAN ARMY PASSES THE BUCK

During these first days of the war with Italy, Italian planes made several harassing raids on Egyptian Army positions along the Egyptian/Libyan border. This was enough for the Egyptian troops. They abandoned their posts and began retreating eastward, passing upcoming British forces as they went. Every Egyptian knew that, under treaty obligations, it was Britain's job to defend Egypt—not theirs.

SEA AND AIR WAR IN THE MEDITERRANEAN AND NORTH AFRICA

On July 19, 1940, the Australian cruiser "Sydney" and five destroyers encountered two Italian cruisers, "Bartolomeo Colleoni and "Bande Nere," off the north coast of Crete, and a brief naval engagement ensued. During the battle, shells from the Sydney crippled the Bartolomeo Colleoni and the Allied destroyers moved in quickly and sent her to the bottom. The Sydney, however, was hit several times with shells from the Bande Nere which fled the scene after the Bartolomeo Colleoni had been lost. It was a welcome victory for the Allies.

On the 20th, Mussolini announced a total Italian naval blockade of all British ports in the Mediterranean and in Africa. This was a blockade in name only and would remain relatively ineffective for the remainder of the war.

On the 21st, the British sub "Rorqual," operating off Tobruk, sank two Italian freighters.

On the 25th, Italian planes bombed British military installations at Alexandria, Egypt. That same day, the Italians bombed Haifa, Palestine.

On the July 30 the Vichy French announced that their

army in North Africa had been demobilized to the point where it conformed to the demands of the German and Italian Armistice Agreements.

For the next three weeks there was no significant ground action in the region, but at sea the British sub Rorqual sank three Italian merchant ships off eastern Libya between the 14th and 21st.

By late July, the first American Lend-Lease planes began arriving in Egypt, unassembled in freighters. These consisted of P–40 fighters, A–20 fighter-bombers, B–24 heavy bombers, and C–47 transports. They were assembled in Egypt, test flown, and then sent off to serve with the RAF.

On August 20, Italy announced a naval blockade of its own. Henceforth, all British possessions in the Mediterranean, Red Sea, Gulf of Aden, and coast of South Africa would be blockaded.

On August 28, 1940, Italian planes bombed Port Said, Egypt for the first time, and on the 29th they bombed Malta again.

THE WAR IN EAST AFRICA

When Italy entered the war on June 10, 1940, the British, of course, closed the Suez Canal to all Italian shipping, thus isolating Italian East Africa from the mother country. The Italians foresaw this actions and it was one reason Mussolini left such large forces in East Africa after the conquest of Ethiopia. He knew they would have to hold out for a period of time until Britain surrendered or Italian forces could conquer Egypt and reopen the Canal.

The British and French colonies in East Africa that surrounded Italian East Africa were not built up to be as militarily strong as the Italians, because the Allied leaders knew that these colonies could always be supplied, one way or the other, in the event of a war. Both the British and French counted on the forces at hand to fight a delaying action, if attacked, until reinforcements could be sent. Thus, during the first months of war with Italy, both the Italians and Allies were playing the defensive game in East Africa. Neither side was anxious to launch a major attack on the other.

The primary British tactic, in the event of war, was for the RAF to strike immediately at Italian air facilities and, hopefully, cripple the Italian Air Force in East Africa to the point where it could not support a major ground offensive. Therefore, the British proceeded as best they could, with their limited resources, to built up their military air strength in East Africa. South Africa contributed to this buildup by sending several SAAF squadrons to British East Africa.

On the day the Italians declared war, June 10, 1940, the British put their plan into action. Within hours after the declaration of war, British Air Marshal Sir A. M. Longmore ordered nine Wellington bombers from The Sudan to attack the Italian antiaircraft batteries and fuel stores at Massawa, Eritrea. This was done with considerable success in that 780 tons of irreplaceable fuel were destroyed.

At dawn the next day, eight RAF Wellesley bombers from The Sudan bombed targets at Asmara, Eritrea, losing one aircraft to Italian antiaircraft fire. Later that day the SAAF made its first raid of the war, just six hours after South Africa declared war on Italy. In that raid, four SAAF Junker Ju–86 bombers from Eastleigh, Kenya bombed a camp of Italian irregular forces, the Bande, in Abyssinia just north of the border town of Moyale, Kenya. The Bande, local mercenaries who sold their military services, were masters of the desert and were experts at hiding themselves in the desert terrain. They proved to be very difficult to spot and attack from the air.

During the day other RAF planes from Aden and SAAF planes from Kenya flew reconnaissance missions over Italian territory.

On that same day, the second day of the war in East Africa, the Italians struck back. A lone Savoia S–81 bomber from Libya attacked British targets at Port Sudan, and that night two Italian planes from Massawa, Eritrea bombed British targets in Aden. One of the planes crashed upon returning. Also that night, British Wellesleys, again from The Sudan, bombed Massawa destroying an oil facility.

ITALIAN BOMBS

The British were surprised to discover that a relatively large number of Italian bombs failed to explode on impact. They began digging them up with the intention of reusing them only to find that the bombs had delayed fuses set to go off up to four days after being dropped.

The next day, June 12, the cross bombing continued. Nine British planes from Aden bombed an Italian airfield at Asaba, Eritrea, and later, twelve more Aden-based planes hit another Italian airfield at Diredawa, Abyssinia. Nine RAF Wellesleys from The Sudan attacked Gura, Eritrea while nine others hit Asmara again. At Gura, Italian fighter planes rose to challenge the British bombers, and shot down one bomber, and damaged a second beyond repair. One Italian fighter plane was downed and two damaged. On the Kenyan border, the Italian defenses opposite Moyale were bombed a second time by the SAAF.

After dusk five British Vincent bombers from Aden attacked the Italian airfield at Macaala, Eritrea.

The Italian Air Force fought back that day with a seven-plane raid from Asaba on the British airfield at Khormaksar, Aden and that night ten Caprioni Ca 133 bombers attacked the RAF airfield at Kassala, Sudan. Other Italian planes raided British outposts and a supply column in Kenya, and made re-

Gladiator fighter planes of the South African Air Force (SAAF) operating out of Kenya.

Italy's Savoia S–79 bomber. Some of the Italian bombers in East Africa, such as this one, had the range to attack the Suez Canal, Mombasa, Nairobi, and Dar es Salaam.

connaissance flights over Kenya and along the border between Abyssinia and The Sudan.

The next day, June 13, it was more of the same. In the early morning four Savoia S–81s from Diredawa bombed targets in Aden. All four planes were lost to British antiaircraft defenses. Three hours later nine Savoia S–79 bombers from Diredawa attacked Aden again. British fighter planes rose to challenge the Italians and succeeded in downing one bomber, while antiaircraft fire destroyed two more.

Other Italian planes struck that day at Port Sudan, Berbera, Moyale, Mandera, Erkowit, and Gebir.

Later that night, RAF Blenheims hit airfields at Macaala and Asaba, destroying three Italian aircraft on the ground. In the south, SAAF planes raided Kismayu, Jelib, and Afmadu in Italian Somaliland. At dawn the next morning three Italian Caprioni 133 bombers attacked the airfield at Wajir, Kenya, where the #237th RAF squadron, Rhodesian unit, had just arrived. The Italians damaged two of the Rhodesian's planes on the ground, destroyed 5,000 gallons of aviation fuel (the airfield's entire supply) and killed five British airmen and eleven askaris.

And so it went, day after day, on almost a daily basis in East Africa for the remainder of 1940 and well into 1941. The raids were small by European standards but, nevertheless, amounted to a war of attrition as each side attempted to wear down the other. This was a war the Italians, cut off from any significant reinforcements from Italy or Libya, could not hope to win. Air contact was maintained between Libya and Italian East Africa across hostile British-controlled Sudan, but it was minimal. The Italians made no serious attempts to resupply East Africa either by air or sea. Their great hope remained that Britain would surrender, or that Egypt and the Suez Canal would soon be conquered.

ON THE GROUND IN EAST AFRICA: THE ITALIAN FORCES

The Italian ground forces in East Africa were formidable by African standards. The Duke of Aosta commanded some 92,000 Italian troops, and an additional 200,000 native troops. These numbers rose to 330,000 when war was declared with

The three–engine Caprioni 133 bomber was designed by the Italians for colonial service and did not have many of the modern features necessary for war planes intended for use in Europe. Note that the Caprioni 133 had fixed landing gear which increased drag and reduced speed, but saved money in construction.

the activation of the reserve forces in the colony. The Duke's army had 24 medium tanks and 39 light tanks, compared to no tanks at all for the British or French. Aosta's best unit was the all-Italian Granatieri di Savoia (Savoy Grenadiers) Division from northern Italy. They were well-trained soldiers with adequate equipment and reserves. There was also a crack Blackshirt battalion of Fascist Party members, and an all-Italian volunteer unit known as the "CCNN" comprised of unemployed settlers and middle-aged men. They had good morale but lacked training and proper equipment.

OFF THE BOAT AND INTO THE ARMY

Some of the CCNN men had been in Italian East Africa only a few weeks when they were recruited. The last load of Italian settlers arrived May 19, 1940, and the colonial administrators had little or no time to deal with them. Many of the newly arrived men suddenly found themselves unemployed and joined the CCNN out of desperation.

Within the native units there was a mix of good and bad. Some Eritrean and Somali units had been well-trained and were considered to be reliable infantry units. As for the Ethiopians and most of the new recruits, the Italians simply had not had enough time to train them, and their fighting quality ranged from mediocre to poor. Tribal rivalries were a constant problem, as was the ingrained African attitude that war was a man-to-man thing. This was hard to break and the untrained men tended to run from artillery fire, armored cars, and air attacks.

The Italians had yet another force called the "Fascist Voluntary Militia for National Security." These were Italian workers who had been given some military training, primarily for self-defense against still-rebellious Ethiopians. They often worked in the more remote areas of the colony with guards posted and rifles stacked. At the first sign of trouble they dropped their work tools and took up arms to fend off marauding bands of natives.

Transportation was a big problem for the Italians. There simply were not enough trucks to carry the troops, and gasoline and truck tires were in short supply. The troops frequently had to walk where ever they went although the Italian officers usually had horses. This meant that the entire Italian army in East Africa was a slow-moving force.

WRONG SIZE—SO SORRY

Just before hostilities began in East Africa, a Japanese freighter docked at Mogadishu, Italian Somaliland, with a load of truck tires. Unfortunately, they were the wrong size and did not fit the Italian trucks.

The Italians also employed Bande units which were used primarily as scouts and skirmishers. They were led by Italian officers and, at times, did police work.

The Italians had no intelligence service and relied only on native informers. The British made good use of this by planting informers who intentionally gave the Italians false or misleading information.

When Italy entered the war, some 100,000 Italian troops were stationed in northern Abyssinia and Eritrea, 83,000 along the borders of French and British Somaliland and only 20,000 along the Kenyan border. Some 40,000 Italian troops were still engaged inside Abyssinia fighting the Ethiopian guerrillas.

GROUND ACTION SLOW TO DEVELOP IN EAST AFRICA

While fighting was quick to develop in the air, it was just the opposite on the ground. Neither side had ground units ready to strike out across the border into enemy territory.

The weather was a factor here too. The rainy season, from June through October, was just beginning. During this period, dirt roads and tracks become avenues of mud and dry gulches become fast-moving streams.

THE FIRST PRISONER OF WAR

The Italians took the first prisoner of war in the East African campaign. He was a police superintendent from the border town of Moyale who, on June 10, went out on a routine inspection tour and unknowingly wondered across the border into Abyssinia. There he was grabbed by the Italians, was told of the war, and informed that he was now a prisoner of war. The rest of Kenya learned of Italy's entry into the war around 8:45 pm from the British Broadcasting Company (BBC).

The first ground action of any consequence took place on June 13, when a small KAR unit raided the Italian border post at Dif, Italian Somaliland. The post was guarded by ten Bande mercenaries, only three of which were on duty. All three were taken prisoner and the KAR withdrew.

On June 18 the Italians attacked French positions in French Somaliland by air and with long-range artillery while infantry troops made probing raids across the border. This went on sporadically for six days until June 24, when France surrendered. No French territory was occupied by the Italians, and all of French Somaliland remained under French control.

Also on June 18, to the south, two companies of KAR moved out of the border town of El Wak, Kenya, crossed the border, and attacked the Italian garrison opposite El Wak. The Italians retreated

South African soldiers departing South Africa for East Africa.

into the bush and the KAR men burned the Italian's barracks after capturing some rations and an Italian flag.

The attack was supported from the air by a Rhodesian squadron of the RAF. Italian planes came to the defense and one of the RAF planes was lost. Its pilot and observer, though, were rescued by the KAR.

Soon, Bande irregulars began shooting at the KAR men from the bush and other Italian troops joined in. With this, the KAR retreated back across the border and the battle of El Wak was over. For the next two weeks all was quiet on the Kenyan border.

Italy's entry into the war forced the British to activate another facet of their defensive plans for East Africa, that being the call-up of reinforcements from other parts of Africa. By coincidence the first detachment of South African troops arrived at Mombasa on June 10, the day Italy declared war. More South Africans soon follow. Also ordered now to East Africa were units of the "Royal West African Defense Force" from Nigeria and Gold Coast, and units from the Rhodesias.

FRENCH SOMALILAND REMAINED LOYAL TO PETAIN

French Somaliland was a sparsely-settled colony with only 46,000 inhabitants, half of which lived in the seaport capital of Djibouti.

The Italian flag captured by KAR troops at El Wak.

By mid-June 1940, the French collapse in Europe was having reverberations throughout the French Empire, including French Somaliland. Colonial leaders throughout the empire were forced to choose whether or not to obey the orders of the legitimate government of France and accept the armistices, or disobey them and continue the struggle under the little-known general in London, Charles de Gaulle. By disobeying the Petain government the individual committed a treasonable act and would lose his military rank, his pension, and, if apprehended, possibly his life. It took a very brave man to choose for de Gaulle. But, General Paul Legentilhomme, Commander of French forces in French Somaliland, was such a man. Without hesitation he declared that he would support de Gaulle and continue the fight. By doing so he was the first soldier of rank to pledge his loyalty to de Gaulle. This gave de Gaulle and his Free French movement a much-needed boost in prestige in London.

Unfortunately for de Gaulle, Legentilhomme's fellow officers and subordinates chose to obey the Petain government, and Legentilhomme was forced to flee for his life to British territory. French Somaliland remained Vichy territory. Legentilhomme made his way to London and became one of de Gaulle's top aides. On July 15, 1940, General Germain arrived to take Legentilhomme's place. Germain was totally loyal to Petain and began, at once, to collaborate with the Italians.

An Italian Armistice Commission soon arrived in Djibouti and the Italians were granted full access to that port and the vital Djibouti-to-Addis Ababa Railroad. It would be of little value, though, to the Italians because the British had established a naval blockade of French Somaliland. That blockade was very weak at first, but strengthened with time.

Other than the railroad, no other significant demands were made by the Italians on the colonial leaders of French Somaliland.

THE ITALIANS TAKE THE OFFENSIVE IN EAST AFRICA

On the southern front in East Africa, a substantial force of Bande from Abyssinia crossed into northern Kenya on July 1 and surrounded the border town of Moyale, which was defended by a single company of the KAR. British planes came to the rescue but accidently bombed buildings still in the hands of the KAR. The Bande held their positions for a short while, then withdrew.

This was a preliminary attack for a much larger Italian offensive which was to be carried out a few days later. That Italian offensive would be carried out piecemeal but would have some success. In planning for that offensive, Marshall Pietro Badoglio, Army Chief of Staff in Rome, wanted Aosta to launch a full-scaled attack from northern Italian East Africa toward Khartoum, or perhaps Port Sudan, in conjunction with the coming Italian invasion of Egypt from Libya. Aosta, however, rejected the idea claiming that his forces were not strong enough for such an operation. Instead, he would attack and capture what he could and hopefully draw off what British forces he could. Thus, he chose the attack on Morale.

An American cartoon from the summer of 1940.

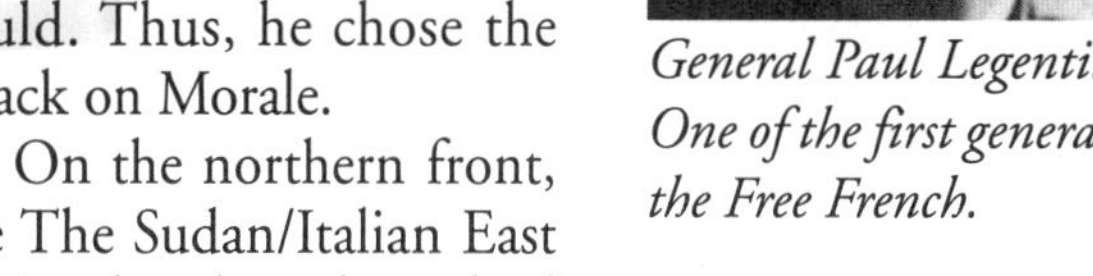

General Paul Legentilhomme. One of the first generals to join the Free French.

On the northern front, the The Sudan/Italian East Africa border, there had been virtually no ground action at all until July 3, 1940. On this date, the date of the attack on Mers el Kebir, a small British force, unaware of the Italian's coming offensive, crossed into Abyssinia and raided the Italian airfield at the border town of Medemma which was on the road to Gondar.

Also on July 3 Ethiopian Emperor Haile Selassie arrived in Khartoum, Sudan from exile in England. He had been brought to The Sudan by the British to lead a force of Ethiopians which, it was planned, would eventually be used against the Italians and become a basis for a new Ethiopian Army. In its initial stages of development, Selassie's force would be very much like an askari force. It would be under British command and would have volunteer white officers from Britain, Kenya, South Africa, Australia, and the Free French. The great majority of soldiers and some of the NCOs would be Ethiopians and Selassie would be in nominal command. It was anticipated that Haile Selassie's presence on the battlefield would inspire the Ethiopian people to resist the Italians in whatever ways they could. To further enhance Selassie's image the British government announced on July 12th that they recognized Selassie, once again, as the rightful ruler of Ethiopia and would support him in regaining his throne.

On July 4 the Italians launched their planned invasion of The Sudan. Some 8,000 Italian troops, supported by tanks, artillery, and aircraft advanced on the important junction and provincial capital of Kasala about 25 miles inside The Sudan. A second force, 250 miles to the south, forced the British out of recently-captured Medemma and advanced on the Sudanese border town of Gallabat. Both attacks were in the direction of Khartoum, and gave the British cause for alarm. Both Kasala and Gallabat were defended by company-sized units of the Sudan Defence Force and were greatly outnumbered. The Sudanese put up a brief resistance and then withdrew. A third Italian force, the smallest of the three, operating about 250

A unit of the British Somaliland Camel Corps.

ply dumps, evacuating civilians, and taking other measures to facilitate the planned invasion.

On July 12, the British government announced that it once again recognized Haile Selassie as the Emperor of Ethiopia and would assist him in liberating his country. This, of course, was made known throughout Abyssinia.

On July 28, the 1st South African Brigade, a well-equipped infantry unit, arrived at Mombasa and moved on to Gil Gil, 82 miles north of Nairobi, to set up a base of operations to undergo additional training. With the arrival of this unit, the British forces in Kenya became a more even match for the Italian forces across the border.

miles south of the Gallabat force, took the Sudanese border town of Kurmuk on the 7th. Kurmuk was held by about seventy Sudanese policemen, most of whom were captured. A forth Italian force, operating 200 miles north of the Kassala force, took the Sudanese border town of Karora. This attack was in the direction of Port Sudan. A week later, on July 13, Italian forces invaded northern Kenya and captured the town of Moyale which was still lightly defended following the Bande attack of earlier in the month. All five towns fell easily to the Italians, who then halted their advance much to the surprise of the British. But this was enough of a show of force for Aosta. He now turned his attention to British Somaliland—but it would be a month before he acted there.

A LULL IN THE EAST AFRICAN GROUND WAR

Following the Italian invasions of The Sudan and northern Kenya, a four-week lull in the ground war followed in East Africa. Air activity, though, continued almost daily with one side or the other, and often both sides, raiding each other's military targets with small groups of bombers and fighters.

While the Duke of Aosta was moving his forces across Abyssinia in preparation for a planned invasion of British Somaliland, the British in Kenya were preparing a plan of their own to invade Italian Somaliland and Abyssinia from the south.

In northern Kenya, the British undertook a large-scale program of building roads, digging wells, establishing sup-

THE ITALIANS INVADE AND CONQUER BRITISH SOMALILAND

On June 10, 1940, Italians had bombed Berbera, the capital of British Somaliland, and two of the colony's major towns, Hargeisa and Ziela. This was a portent of things to come. Italian ground forces began accumulating in the Aubarre area of Abyssinia, and in late June a small Italian force crossed the border and captured the town of Borama, just inside the British Somaliland border. The small British garrison retreated.

The British could read the Italian's intentions and sent what reinforcements they could to the colony. On July 1, 1940, an Indian battalion arrived along with a British regular army light artillery battalion. Two KAR battalions arrived on the 12th, and the famous "Black Watch" Regiment, stationed in Aden, was put on alert for transfer to British Somaliland at short notice. These forces were pitifully small compared to the Italian forces building up on the Abyssinian side of the border. Large stretches of the British Somaliland border were undefended and patrolled only by policemen and Somali scouts.

On August 3, 1940, the Italians launched their planned invasion of British Somaliland. The Italian force consisted of some 25,000 men supported by artillery, tanks, and aircraft. The British forces, outnumbered seven to one, consisted of only four battalions of assorted troops and the local

Somaliland Camel Corps. The British had no artillery or tanks but they did have air cover from bases in British Somaliland and Aden.

The Italians crossed the border at three places intending to drive on Odweina, Hargeisa and the seaport of Zeila. All that the British forces could do was to fight delaying actions and withdraw. On August 5, both Zeila and Hargeisa fell to the Italians and on the 6th Odweina fell.

On August 7, the Black Watch was brought over from Aden. Now fighting on the British side in British Somaliland were Englishmen, Somalis, Kenyans, Nyasalanders, Northern Rhodesians, and Indians. On the Italian side were Italians, Somalis, Ethiopians, and Eritreans. White officers and NCOs commanding askari units on both sides frequently wore black face, so they could not be easily distinguished by the enemy.

The Italian advance had been split into two columns, converging on the Berbera area. Thousands of Somali refugees fled ahead of the Italian advance, inundating the British positions.

While the British troops fought delaying actions, the main body of British troops fell back to Tug Argen, on the Hargeisa-Berbera road, where the terrain favored the defenders. There the British hoped to make a stand. The two enemies came together at Tug Argen on the 11th, and a five-day battle ensued in which the Somaliland Camel Corps was decimated and the other British forces suffered heavy losses. The Indians made one of the most determined stands against the Italians, until their ammunition ran out and they were forced to retreat.

On August 13, the Italian Air Force came out in force attacking the British supply columns reaching back to Berbera. By the 15th, after repeated Italian ground attacks, the British positions at Tug Argen became untenable because the Italians, with their superior numbers, were able to outflank the defenders' front. On that day the British began an orderly withdrawal to Barkasan, fifteen miles from Berbera and their last defense line in the colony. The Italians followed in close pursuit, delayed occasionally by British rear guard actions.

On August 17, the two forces met again and an eight-and-a-half hour battle ensued. The Italians, using their tanks, were able to break through the British flank forcing a retreat of the entire defense line. The British troops now streamed into Berbera setting up rear guard units and booby traps around the city.

On the 17th and 18th, the remnants of the British forces withdrew in an orderly fashion under the protective gunfire of British warships off shore and aircraft from Aden. Both military and commandeered private vessels were used to transport the men. Before departing, the badly battered Somaliland Camel Corps was disbanded. Some of the men were paid, and allowed to melt into the general population while others evacuated with the British. The British had to abandon much of their equipment, but the remaining British force of some 7000 men was evacuated safely by ship. Most of them were taken to Aden. On August 19, the Italians entered Berbera and the battle for British Somaliland was over. Casualties for the British for the entire campaign were 38 killed, 102 wounded and 120 missing. The British officers had made a concerted effort to minimize casualties during their long retreat. The heaviest losses were suffered by the Northern Rhodesians, who had been in the some of the hardest fighting. Losses for the Italians were 565 killed, 1,530 wounded and 34 missing. Losses in fuel, vehicles, and general wear and tear on all of their equipment also had to be counted against the Italians because these things were irreplaceable. The British, on the other hand, could replace their material losses.

This was the first major Italian victory over the British in the war, and raised morale in Italy and throughout the Italian Empire. Mussolini hailed the victory as an example of the invincibility of the Italian armed forces.

The Italians won another victory of sorts but did not know it. In London, Churchill was very critical of the British military operations in British Somaliland and General Wavell, Supreme Commander in Africa and the Middle East, defended them. This soured relations between the two men which only ended, sometime later, with Wavell's removal.

Italian askaris being trucked back to Abyssinia after the conquest of British Somaliland.

During the fighting in British Somaliland, the Italians received their first significant reinforcements from the north. This consisted of 36 new aircraft flown in from Libya, complete with air crews. With dwindling fuel supplies, however, the value of these planes was questionable.

No one knew it at the time, but this was the high watermark for the Italians in East Africa.

The bulk of the Italian forces were withdrawn from British Somaliland and dispersed along the northern and southern borders of Italian East Africa to face the British attacks which were, by now, expected. The British troops, likewise, were reassigned. The remnants of the Somaliland Camel Corps were sent to the southeastern part of The Sudan, which was mainly desert, and reconstituted as a mobile striking force.

BRITISH CONTINUE PLANS TO INVADE ITALIAN EAST AFRICA

On August 5 the Indian 5th Division arrived at Port Sudan and moved south toward the border with Italian East Africa. This was another well-equipped British unit, and one which was scheduled to play a major role in the British plans. Somewhat later the 1st South African Brigade moved out of its training camp at Gil Gil in Kenya and took up positions on Kenya's northern border. They were soon joined by South African reserves and service units.

On the 19th, the SAAF launched a nine-day air offensive against Mogadishu, Italian Somaliland's capital and largest city. The attackers concentrated on Italian military installations such as airfields, docks, bridges, and especially motor pools. In the nine days of bombardment many Italian trucks were destroyed, thereby decreasing the mobility of the Italian forces. On the raids of August 28 alone the SAAF claimed to have destroyed between 800 and 1,000 trucks which they discovered packed tightly together in a motor pool. Later it was discovered that the "motor pool" was a salvage yard for derelict vehicles.

The Italian Air Force retaliated, but its effort was in no way commensurate with the SAAF attacks. For whatever reasons the Italians had yet to bomb Mombasa, the main British port of supply for most of the men and equipment coming into Kenya. Mombasa was easily within range of their largest bombers and this would have been an appropriate time for them to attack. But, the Italians chose not to do so.

Chapter 6

ELSEWHERE IN AFRICA (JUNE–AUGUST 1940)

THE VIRUS OF WAR SPREADS

As could be expected, with the entry of Italy into the war, both North Africa and East Africa became instant war zones because of the presence of Italian colonies there. But, before this happened, there was another place in Africa where men were fighting and dying—her surrounding seas.

THE AFRICAN SEAS

The British unquestionably ruled most of the world's seas with their huge navy, the world's largest, and had naval bases in all parts of the globe. In the late 1930s and early 1940s, the British expanded many of their naval bases, some of which were in, or associated with, Africa. These included bases at Alexandria, Egypt; Gibraltar; Freetown, Sierra Leone; Simonstown (Cape Town), South Africa; Durban, South Africa; Kilindini (Mombasa), Kenya, and Aden.

The expansion of these bases was primarily for military purposes, but commercial needs were also a factor. It could be foreseen that if hostilities broke out British merchant shipping would be stretched to its limits which, in turn, would dictate that food and raw materials be obtained from the closest sources. That meant from Africa. Thus, the need arose for improved military and commercial shipping facilities there.

When hostilities did break out in September 1939, the Germans had submarines and sea raiders at sea ready to strike British and French shipping. The British anticipated this and immediately ordered their merchant ships to begin sailing in convoys in certain parts of the world. One such area was along the northwest coast of Africa. Experience from World War I had shown that convoys provided the safest methods of moving ships about in the face of a strong seaborne enemy. As the war progressed and Axis submarine and raider activities increased, the Allies were forced to expand their convoy system. Much of this expansion took place in African waters. But still, there were gaps in the convoys systems where merchant ships sailed alone. These gaps were favored hunting grounds for the enemy subs and raiders.

When Italy entered the war in June 1940, Allied commercial shipping through the Mediterranean ceased due to the threat of the Italian Navy and Air Force. Only a few heavily escorted military convoys would operate in the Mediterranean, mainly to supply the island fortress of Malta. The closing of the Mediterranean forced the Allies to send commercial shipping completely around Africa to supply Egypt, British East Africa, French Somaliland, Aden, the Middle East, and points in East Asia. In turn the existing convoy system in the Atlantic was expanded down the coast of West Africa, and new convoy routes were created in the Indian Ocean. The Indian Ocean convoys operated between Cape Town, Durban, Dar es Salaam, Mombasa, the Red Sea, and points in the Middle East.

The trip around Africa was an arduous journey. After reaching Cape Town, fast convoys still had a trip of six to ten weeks to reach locations in the Middle East, and slow convoys took even longer.

ABANDON THE MEDITERRANEAN?

When Italy entered the war, there were those leaders in London who suggested that the Mediterranean be abandoned altogether. Churchill was adamantly against this, claiming it could be a fatal blow to British morale at home and especially in the colonies. As a result, British warships remained at their posts in the Mediterranean and an occasional convoy was forced through to the important island base of Malta, sometimes at great cost.

INDIAN OCEAN PORTS EXPERIENCE A REVIVAL

Many of the seaports in eastern Africa on the Indian Ocean had not been used regularly for international sea trade since 1869 when the Suez Canal opened. As a result, their docking facilities, warehousing, and other necessities of maritime trade were outmoded and inadequate. The Allies now needed these ports and had to instigate a crash program to improve most of them as fast as possible. Airfields were also needed for the aircraft that would protect convoys and patrol the western reaches of the Indian Ocean. The problem of air fields was relieved, somewhat, by using sea planes that did not need airports and could land in harbors, rivers, and lakes. The British had some seaplanes available and had many more on order in the United States.

The expansion of the seaports and other construction projects brought boom times to areas of eastern Africa that had, heretofore, been economically depressed.

THE OFFSHORE ISLAND

The many offshore islands and island groups experienced a similar revival to that going on in the seaports on the African mainland. Fortunately for the Allies most of the offshore islands were colonial possessions of either Britain or France. These islands were vital to the Allies as sites for air fields and naval facilities that would support the convoy system and combat enemy naval activities.

Socotra Island. A British officer, his Bedouin guide (left), and two Adenese soldiers pause in the shade of an Adenium tree on a routine patrol of the island. The island had no electricity, roads, sanitation, or medical facilities, so the air field built there by the British had to be self–sustaining.

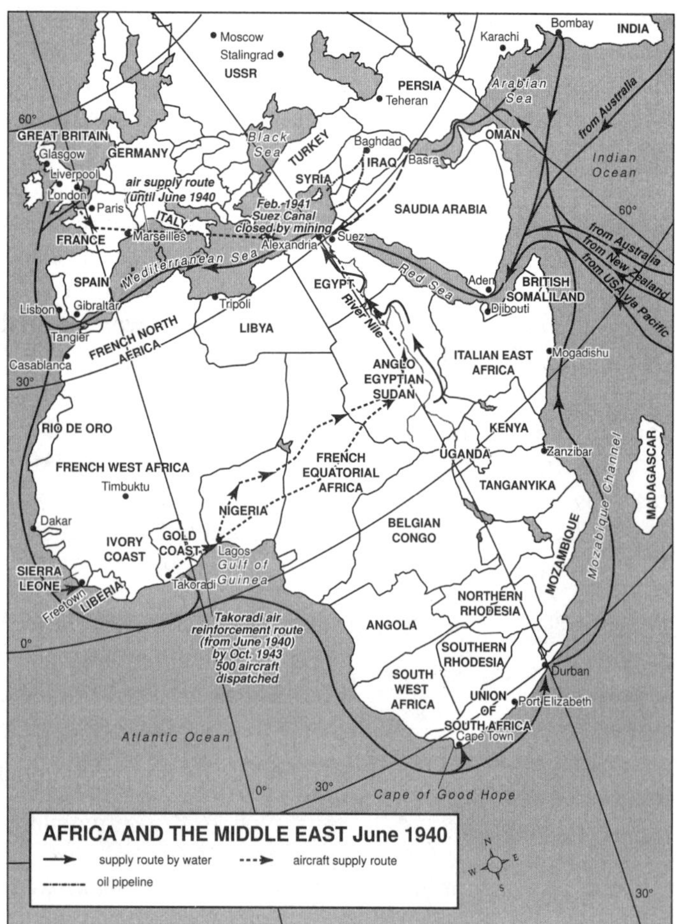

In June 1940 these were the main sea and air routes in and around Africa.

The islands and island groups in question were British-controlled Mauritius Island, Socotra Island, Seychelles Island, Diego Garcia, and French-controlled Madagascar, Comoros Island group, and Reunion Island. All of these islands were in the Indian Ocean. Sometime later, the British-owned islands of Ascension and St. Helena in the South Atlantic were put to use.

THE ITALIAN NAVY IN EAST AFRICA

In June 1940, the major naval threat to the Allies in the Indian Ocean was the presence of the Italian Navy in Italian East Africa. It was known that the Italians had at least seven destroyers, eight submarines (only four of which were operable), and two Patrol/Torpedo (PT) boats based in Eritrea, and aircraft at several locations. These military assets could, if used effectively, block the southern entrance to the Red Sea to Allied convoys. Similarly, the British had ships and planes in Aden, British Somaliland, The Sudan, and on strategic Perim Island in the middle of the Bab el-Mandeb, the narrow strait that forms the southern entrance to the Red Sea. Their job would be to see that the southern entrance to the Red Sea remained open and that Allied convoys passed through safely to Egypt.

THE SEA WAR WITH THE ITALIANS IN AFRICAN WATERS

It was the South Africans who struck the first blow against the Italians in African waters. On June 9, the day before Italy entered the war, two Italian merchant vessels, the "Timavo" and "Gerusalemme," departed Durban harbor and sailed northward, apparently heading for Italian East Africa. Since there was a strong chance that Italy would enter the war in the next day or two, SAAF Blenheim bombers were dispatched to keep track of the ships. On June 10, Italy declared war on South Africa and on the 11th South Africa declared war on Italy. On the morning of the 11th the ships were spotted 50 miles south of Madagascar, and several SAAF Blenheims went on the attack. The Timavo was damaged by bombs and machine gunfire from the planes, so her captain turned toward Madagascar and made a run for the nearest shore, where he beached his stricken ship. Meanwhile, the SAAF Blenheims began searching for the Gerusalemme but could not find her before the winter darkness set in. Meanwhile, during the night the Timavo was able to repair some of her damage and free herself from the beach and make it safely to Lourenco Marques in neutral Portuguese Mozambique. There she was interned. The Gerusalemme managed to sail on safely to her destination in Italian East Africa. The South Africans had to be content with half a victory.

The next action at sea occurred on June 16, 1940, when the Italian submarine "Galileo Galilei" sank the Norwegian tanker "James Stove" off Aden. British ships and planes converged on the area, but the submarine got away—for the moment. On the 18th, the Galileo Galilei intercepted the neutral Yugoslav merchant ship "Drava" in the Gulf of Aden, and an Italian inspection team went aboard to check her cargo for contraband that might violate the recently proclaimed Italian naval blockade. No contraband was found and the ship was allowed to proceed. This action, which happened close to shore, was spotted by a coast watcher in Aden, and the British authorities were promptly notified. Three SAAF aircraft rushed to the scene, spotted the submarine and dropped bombs. All missed. As darkness fell, the destroyer HMS "Kandahar" and sloop HMS "Shoreham" arrived, located the submerged submarine with sonar, and made an unsuccessful depth charge attack. The next morning the Galileo Galilei, running submerged, was located again about 11:30 a.m. by sonar aboard the British trawler "Moonstone." The Moonstone made two depth charge runs over the submarine, the second of which damaged her so that she had to surface. A gun battle at close range then ensued with the Italian crew using their deck cannon and machine guns and the British crew using its World War I four-pounder cannon, machine guns, and rifles. The British fire was more accurate and the submarine's captain was killed and all the other officers and ratings were wounded. With this, the Italian crewmen waved a white flag and the British stopped firing. A British crew went aboard and was able to sail the submarine to Aden under its own power.

On June 22, naval action flared again as three British destroyers, "Kandahar," "Kingston," and "Khartoum," and two British sloops encountered the Italian submarine "Toricelli" operating on the surface just north of Perim Island in the Red Sea. A very uneven 40–minute gun battle followed in which the Toricelli was sunk, but not before her guns had sent one of the British sloops to the bottom. During the battle a torpedo accidently exploded aboard the Khartoum and her captain was forced to beach his stricken ship on nearby Bare Mussa Seghir Island. The Khartoum's crew was rescued the next day, but the ship was a total loss.

On June 23 the Italian submarine "Galvani" torpedoed and sank the Indian patrol craft "Pathan" in the Gulf of Oman, killing five of her crewmen. The survivors of the Pathan had no idea that their ship was torpedoed and attributed the sinking to a contact mine. Two days later the Galvani was located by sloop HMS "Falmouth" in the same area and was sent to the bottom by a skillfully executed depth charge attack.

On the morning of June 24, 1940, the German raider Atlantis, which was now operating in the Indian Ocean, spotted the British freighter "Mandasor" near the Seychelles Islands. The Mandasor was out of Calcutta with a load of pig iron and tea for England. As the Atlantis approached flying the Norwegian flag, the captain of the "Mandasor" became suspicious and made a run for the safely of the Seychelles. The Atlantis gave chase, overtook the Mandasor, lowered the Norwegian flag, raised the German flag, and succeeded in sinking the Mandasor with gunfire. Before going down, the Mandasor was able to radio the QQQ signal, an international signal for a ship being attacked by a raider, and gave her location. The Atlantis, of course, heard the signal and departed at top speed from the area.

By July 1940, virtually all Allied shipping in the western Indian Ocean and the Red Sea was in the form of convoys. These

A busy day in Cape Town Harbor. In the distance is the ocean liner–turned–troop ship "Aquitania," in the center the ocean liner–turned–troop ship "Queen Mary," and in the foreground the "General Botha," a training ship of the South African Defence Forces.

convoys were often very lightly protected or not protected at all by escort vessels because of the worldwide shortage of such vessels. Also, the Indian Ocean had low priority for such ships compared to the more important areas of the Atlantic and Mediterranean. Raiders such as the Atlantis, nevertheless avoided convoys because of the probability that escort vessels could be present. It would not take many escort vessels to out-gun a single attacking ship. Furthermore, Allied aircraft might be in the area or nearby. Attacking convoys, then, was relegated to submarines. During July the Italians became much more cautious at sea. They sent out only one submarine on patrol, which was unsuccessful, and canceled a second patrol. In August they sent out four submarine patrols, three of which were unsuccessful. The submarine on the fourth patrol, the "Guglielmotti," made one unsuccessful attack on an unidentified warship.

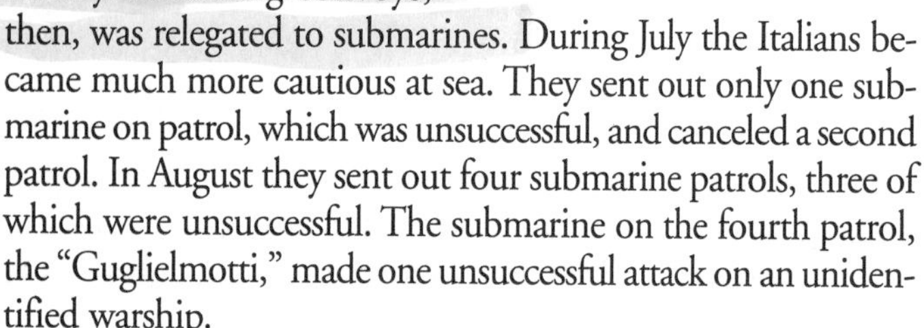

It was not until September 6, 1940, that the Italian submarines made another kill. This was in the southern end of the Red Sea when the submarine Guglielmotti torpedoed and sank the tanker "Atlas." This turned out to be a mistake, however, because the Atlas was a neutral Greek ship.

SOUTH AFRICAN PORTS VERY BUSY

With the Mediterranean all but closed to both miliary and commercial shipping, more ships than ever now rounded the southern tip of Africa. A large percentage of those ships, both Allied and neutral, put in at one of the South African ports for fuel and supplies. The South African ports were also transfer ports for military personnel going east and west. Allied ships from the east would arrive with Australians and New Zealanders who would disembark in South Africa and later reembark for other destinations. Similarly, Axis prisoners of war would arrive from the west and be transferred to ships heading for Australia and New Zealand.

The waters off South Africa were still a dangerous place because German commerce raiders were still operating in the area and, after Italy's entry into the war, there was the new threat of Italian warships and submarines rounding the Cape.

On June 10, 1940, that threat materialized when the German raider Atlantis, masquerading as the Dutch ship "Abbekerk," captured the Norwegian freighter "Tirrana" off the tip of South Africa. The Tirrana had a cargo of wool and flour, and the Germans hoped to send her on to Europe with a prize crew, but the ship did not have enough fuel for the journey. Therefore, the Tirrana, under the control of the German prize crew, tailed along behind the Atlantis as it returned to the Indian Ocean with hopes of capturing a tanker which would provide fuel for the Tirrana's voyage. The Tirrana followed the Atlantis for six weeks, but no tanker was found. Finally, the Atlantis transferred her 126 Allied prisoners to the Tirrana and she sailed on safely to Italian Somaliland.

It is quite surprising that the Atlantis could not find more targets because she was certainly operating in the right place. There were plenty of ships about. On June 15, the Officer-in-Charge at the British naval base at Simonstown (Cape Town) reported to his superiors that at that moment the British Navy was tracking 390 vessels in the area including two troop convoys.

The British and South African coastal defense forces were woefully inadequate at this stage of the war to protect such large numbers of ships with the resources available. On the other hand, neither the Germans or Italians were prepared to send submarines or additional raiders into South African waters because they were needed elsewhere. The Allies, though, did not know this, and there was great fear in South Africa that, any day, a flotilla of German or Italian submarines would appear in the area and wreak havoc with Allied shipping. In mid-June, a report was received from London that a reliable source in Cairo had reported that four Italian submarines were on their way from Italian East Africa to patrol the waters around the Cape. This proved to be false. The Italian submarines never appeared, but a mere report of that nature served to keep the South Africans tense and alert. War jitters also brought many false sighting from coast watchers and others watching the seas. One report was received of an enemy aircraft carrier off the coast. This was quite absurd because neither the German or Italian navies had aircraft carriers.

FRENCH SHIPS SAIL UNHINDERED

Immediately after the Mers el Kebir incident in North Africa, the British extended their naval blockade to include all French-controlled colonies loyal the Petain government. But the British simply did not have enough warships to enforce the blockade all around Africa, so the best they could do was to keep the French ships under surveillance. The French realized this and their sea traffic continued as usual.

On the morning of June 25, the day the French-German armistice came into effect, the uncompleted French battleship Richelieu sailed out of Dakar harbor where it had been anchored along with some British warships. The French wanted to avoid a confrontation with the British and decided to move the Richelieu to Casablanca.

As the Richelieu sailed northward along the African coast, the British cruiser "Dorsetshire" began following her. Sensing a possible confrontation with the British under these circumstances, the French quickly changed their minds and ordered the Richelieu back to Dakar.

Within a short time, the French ships sailing in African waters began sailing in convoys escorted by French warships. This occurred mostly along the northwest coast of Africa and in the Indian Ocean between Madagascar and other French ports. Almost certainly these ships were carrying illegal contraband through the British blockade, but the British were simply too weak to intercept the ships and inspect their cargos in the face of the French warship. The British, therefore, had little choice but to let the French ships pass until such time that they were powerful enough to stop them. On July 11, the Admiralty formalized the naval procedures by secretly ordering British ships to stop and inspect only French ships sailing unescorted. Individual French ships and convoys escorted by French warships would be allowed to pass.

ANOTHER RAIDER INVADES AFRICAN WATERS

In late June, the German disguised merchant raider "Thor" left Germany for a tour of duty in the South Atlantic.

On July 1, 1940, Thor took her first victim in mid-ocean, the Dutch freighter "Kertosono" which was out of Curacao with a cargo of agricultural machinery, petroleum, asphalt, and wood for Freetown, Sierra Leone. The Thor captured the Dutch ship intact and, with a prize crew, successfully sent her on to the German-controlled port of L'Orient, France.

On July 8, 1940, the Thor encountered the British freighter "Delambre" out of Rio de Janeiro heading for Freetown with a cargo of cotton, cotton seeds and hides. The Delambre was sunk and her crew taken prisoner aboard the Thor.

The next day, Thor took a third ship heading for Freetown, the Belgian freighter "Bruges" out of Argentina with a cargo of wheat. The Bruges was sunk and her crew also taken captive. This action happened at night and was successful because the Thor had radar. She was the first German raider to have that device.

MORE CARNAGE IN AFRICAN WATERS

On June 26, a German submarine struck in West African waters for the first time. The submarine "UA" torpedoed and sank the Norwegian freighter "Crux" off the coast of French Morocco. The UA travelled on south, and on July 14 torpedoed and sank the Norwegian tanker "Sarita" southwest of the Cape Verde Islands. This was the furthest south that a German submarine had penetrated so far in African waters. That same day the Thor, operating in the South Atlantic, took yet another Freetown-bound ship, the British freighter "Gracefield" out of Montevideo with a cargo of wheat and bran. Again, the British crew was taken captive.

On July 17, it happened again. Thor sank the Dutch freighter "Dela" out of Rosario, Argentina, with a cargo of grain bound for Freetown. The Dela's crew was taken captive making a total number of 194 prisoners of war aboard the Thor.

On August 3, 1940, the German submarine UA, having moved deeper into African waters, sank the Yugoslav steamship "Rad" off Dakar with torpedoes and gunfire.

During the first week in August 1940, the Italian submarine "Malaspina" penetrated West African waters and on August 12 torpedoed and sank the freighter "British Flame" east of the Azores.

By then the UA, too, had moved to the Azores and on August 15th torpedoed and sank the Greek steam ship "Aspasia" east of the islands.

On August 17, a naval action took place in the Mediterranean when a force of British warships bombarded Italian military installations at Bardia and Fort Capuzzo, Libya, near the Egyptian border. Italian planes attacked the ships but did no damage.

On August 19, a second Italian submarine, "Barbarigo," appeared in African waters off French Morocco and sank the British steamship "Aguilla" with gunfire.

On August 21, a third Italian submarine, "Dandolo," torpedoed and sank the Dutch tanker "Hermes" in the same general area. The Dandolo then moved northwest and on the 26th torpedoed and sank the British steam ship "Ilvington Court" east of the Azores.

The sea war then shifted back to the Indian Ocean when

a new menace appeared. She was the German disguised raider "Penguin." This ship, which had been assigned to work in the Indian Ocean, had sailed down the Atlantic Ocean, rounded the Cape, 360 miles offshore, and sailed into the Indian Ocean undetected by the Allies. There the Penguin experienced an excellent first day of hunting when she took three ships in six hours. The Penguin's first success was the capture of the Norwegian tanker "Filefjell," which had been spotted by the Penguin's small seaplane. The Filefjell was carrying gasoline and oil from the Persian Gulf to Cape Town. She was boarded by a German prize crew and ordered to follow the Penguin with her fate to be decided later. Minutes later the Penguin spotted the empty British tanker "British Commander" on its way to the Persian Gulf to pick up petroleum products. The British Commander was stopped and sunk but not before she put out the QQQ signal.

As the British Commander was sinking a third vessel appeared. She was the Norwegian freighter "Morviken" out of Calcutta for Cape Town. The Penguin quickly sank the Morviken and then, incredibly, a fourth Allied ship appeared. But, the Penguin's captain, knowing that the QQQ alarm had been sent, decided, for the security of his ship and crew, to steam out of the area rather than attack the newcomer. The Penguin's captain also knew that the Atlantis was working in the eastern Indian Ocean and that the QQQ signal was a danger to her also.

Before departing, the Penguin retrieved her prize crew from the Filefjell and sank her.

EVENTS IN WEST AFRICA AND EQUATORIAL AFRICA

Italy's entry into the war had far less effect on West Africa than it did on North or East Africa. In West Africa, there were no common borders with the Italian colonies except in the northeastern corner of French West Africa where the northern border of Nigeria joins southern Libya and in Equatorial Africa where the northern border of Chad also adjoins Libya. These borders with Libya were deep in the Sahara Desert, not armed on either side, and only lightly patrolled.

The economy in West Africa boomed during the first ten months of the war, and trade between British and French colonies was active. But, when France surrendered and Britain imposed the blockade on all French possessions, the economies of French West Africa and French Equatorial Africa began to suffer. As a result, many native workers were laid off and some of them simply migrated to the British colonies where jobs were plentiful.

This border-jumping was short lived, however, because it posed another possible area of conflict between the British and French. Therefore, the British colonial authorities, with London's blessing, began returning all French natives to their home colonies except those who were willing to join the Free French.

THE FRENCH AFRICAN COLONIES WAVER—THEN DECLARE FOR PETAIN

When France was undergoing the process of surrendering, the French colonial leaders were divided on whether to continue the struggle or not. One powerful colonial leader who threatened to carry on the war was the Governor-General of French Equatorial Africa, General Pierre Boisson, who resided in Brazzaville, the capital. On June 18, 1940, the day after the Petain government asked Germany for an armistice, Boisson took the very bold step of telegraphing all of his colonial governors, telling them that French Equatorial Africa would remain in the war. Boisson was known to hate the Germans from his World War I experience of being wounded, which left him with an artificial leg. He also had no great love for the British and would, almost certainly, not have served under de Gaulle's Free French. If Boisson had pursued his course he would have, in all likelihood, taken independent action.

As one French territory after the other declared for Petain, Boisson's confidence became shaky. This was especially so after all of French North Africa declared for Petain. Then, an offer came from Petain that Boisson found hard to refuse. Petain offered to promote Boisson to the newly created, and all-powerful, position of High Commissioner for all of tropical Africa, to be headquartered at Dakar. This was an emergency position whereby all political and military authority would be concentrated in one man's hands making him something of a regional dictator. In French North Africa, Maxime Weygand had been appointed High Commissioner there. As High Commissioner, Boisson would work closely with Petain's Premier, Pierre Laval, whom Boisson knew very well because he had served as Laval's "Chef de Cabinet" when Laval was Premier in the 1930s.

Boisson, though, hesitated and did not respond. Then came the British attack at Mers el Kebir. This pushed Boisson over the line and firmly into Petain's camp. Boisson accepted the position and soon moved to Dakar.

Petain's problems were not over, however. There were other French colonial leaders in tropical Africa that announced they would continue the fight. One such individual was Governor-General Leon Cayla of French West Africa, residing at Dakar. This problem was resolved with Boisson's appointment and transfer to Dakar. Cayla was, likewise, promoted to High Commissioner for Madagascar. He and Boisson were the only two High Commissioners in French Sub-Saharan Africa. Petain's two bribes had worked.

Still others in French West Africa wanted to fight on. The Governor of Senegal and the Mayor of Dakar conspired to bring a British naval force to Dakar to secure the city, and hopefully all of tropical Africa, from the Petainists. They sent a request for such a force to London on July 4, the day after the Mers el Kebir attack, asking that such a force arrive before July 10. The British were in no position to respond that fast, so the opportunity passed. The note from Dakar was filed, but not forgotten. It surfaced again in September 1940, when the British and Free French were in a position to do so with regards to Dakar, and they decided to act on it.

The anti-Petainist sentiment in Dakar was well-known in the British colonies of Nigeria and Gold Coast. The governors of both colonies informed London that they favored an immediate British occupation of Dakar and were willing to help. The governor of Gold Coast further reported that the French civil and military authorities in the French colony of Ivory Coast strongly favored continuing the war and would, probably, support an occupation of Dakar. These reports too, were filed away and not acted upon.

The British very likely would have acted at Dakar if they had the strength. The matter was discussed at length by Churchill and his Cabinet, but other priorities were more pressing and an operation against Dakar was rejected. Churchill's government did, however, on July 6, instruct the British Consul-General, who was still in residence in Dakar, to inform Governor-General Cayla that the British were willing to treat all of French tropical Africa on the same basis as the adjacent British colonies and buy large quantities of products from them to compensate for their lost markets in Europe.

Cayla hesitated in replying to Churchill's message—then came the attack of July 8 by British planes on the battleship Richelieu in Dakar harbor. This all but solidified Cayla's opinion against the British and thrust him, unceremoniously, into Petain's lap.

Even after the attack on the Richelieu there were still two important French leaders who had not formally declared for Petain. They were Governor Brunot of the French Cameroons and Governor Felix Eboure of Chad. Eboure was very unique in the French political structure because he was a mulatto, and the only nonwhite individual of such high rank in all of French Africa.

By the end of July, though, Brunot's interests in continuing the war faded and he declared for Petain. This left only Eboure undecided. It appeared, at this point in time, that de Gaulle had lost all of French Africa.

In London, the Churchill government now made a complete about face with regard to the French tropical colonies, and decided to punish them as they had punished French North Africa. The British made plans to strengthen the naval blockade against the French colonies wherever, and whenever they could and choke off all commerce between France and the French colonies. The feeling in London was that this would create a food shortage in France, and Germany would then be forced to share its food supply with the French. Furthermore, a strong British blockade would be a powerful bargaining chip in future relations with Vichy.

Germany then complicated the British/French feud by asking Vichy, on July 15, for the use of eight air bases in French Morocco from which German planes could help the French break the British blockade. This would clearly have been an escalation of the crisis and Petain did not want that. Petain refused the request on July 18.

It was at this time that Boisson, now a firm Petain loyalist, arrived at Dakar. Among his first acts as High Commissioner was to arrest those French individuals in military and civilian posts who had announced for de Gaulle. Boisson also took immediate steps to strengthen Dakar's defenses in case of a British attack.

Throughout all of these troubles, Boisson kept one important communications link open with the British. This was through the Governor of Nigeria, Sir Bernard Bourdillon, Chairman of the British West African Governors' Conference. This link remained in place until the Allied invasion of North Africa in November 1942.

NATIVE LOYALTIES

As with their colonial masters, the loyalties of the natives in the French colonies were divided, but in a different way. There were three loyalty segments within the native population in general; those who supported the Petain government, those who supported the Free French, and the largest segment of all, those who were apathetic and/or uncommitted toward the white man's problems. Permeating virtually all of the native population, though, was the feeling of nationalism and the longing for improved living and working conditions. This was to play well into de Gaulle's hands as the war progressed, because de Gaulle's policies toward the French colonies would be much more liberal and enlightened than those of Vichy. In contrast, Petain, in an effort to placate his German and Italian masters, became more repressive across the board. And, of course, the great majority of natives were well aware of Germany's racist policies and that Petain would, in all likelihood, be obliged to accept some of them. In the long run, native support would become one of de Gaulle's greatest assets in Africa.

There were early signs of this in June, July, and August 1940, in that there were a large number of pro-Free French demonstrations throughout French tropical Africa supported by a mix of whites and blacks. Demonstrations occurred in Dakar, Saint-Louis, Ouagadougon, Abidjan, Konakry, Lome, Duala, Brazzaville, Tananarive, and in the Cameroons. When Petain was able to consolidate his power he quickly put an end to such demonstrations, but the grass roots sentiment remained.

Another show of support for de Gaulle was that in some

places in French tropical Africa, local tribal leaders openly urged their young men to escape across the border into British colonies and join the Free French. The Gold Coast was a popular destination for those who chose to do so.

Another incident regarding African natives, and favorable to de Gaulle, occurred in England in July 1940, when a force of about 1,000 Ivory Coast sharpshooters, who were in the French Army, chose to go with the Free French. But, with de Gaulle's approval, these men were sent to Gold Coast and integrated into the British defense forces of that colony.

GERMAN INFLUENCE STILL STRONG IN FRENCH CAMEROONS

The French Cameroons had been a German colony until 1919, and a sizeable number of Germans had stayed on in the colony. With Germany's victories in Europe, the true sentiments of the German settlers emerged in the form of private and public rhetoric favoring Germany and open support for the possible return of the colony to Germany. The German settlers were not hesitant to predict that if Germany regained the colony, the old German system of rigid colonial rule, racial segregation, and the plantation systems would return. This upset the natives because over the years the French had proven themselves to be more of a benevolent ruler than the Germans. Now, with the Petain government subservient to Germany, the natives had few options but to support de Gaulle. Therefore, the residents of French Cameroons became polarized with the French administrators and German settlers favoring Petain, and most of the native population favoring de Gaulle.

UNOFFICIAL TRUCE BETWEEN FRENCH AND BRITISH COLONIES

With French tropical Africa firmly committed to Vichy, a tense calm began to prevail over tropical Africa. Neither the British nor the French made military moves to threaten the other but, as precautions, border posts were strengthened and both sides watched more carefully for hostile military activity in adjacent colonies. The area of greatest tension was between the British enclave of Gambia which was surrounded on three sides by the French colony of Senegal. The French, with the military forces they had nearby in Dakar, could easily have occupied Gambia at any time. But, Vichy ordered that the peace would be kept with respect to Gambia. There were, however, several border incidents between Gambia and Senegal, and contact between the Europeans in the two colonies ceased.

Dakar continued to be a very active commercial trading center for the remainder of 1940 because the British blockade was not strong enough to cut off the seaport's international trade. Ships regularly sailed between Dakar, and unoccupied France, and North Africa as well as across the Atlantic to points in the Western Hemisphere. All knew, however, that this would not last if Britain remained in the war.

In other parts of West Africa, intercolonial trade continued despite Petain's order that it stop. Some trading arrangements were simply too well-established and too vitally important to the local economies to be suddenly halted by a decree from faraway Vichy. A case in point was the cattle trade between the French colonies of French West Africa and the British colonies of Gold Coast, Sierra Leone, and Nigeria. French cattle had long been the primary source of meat in those British colonies, and to halt it would have caused hardships on both sides. The officials on both sides of the borders, therefore, turned a blind eye to the cross-border cattle trading and, as a result, no meat shortage developed in the British colonies and no cattle glut on the French side. Going the other way from the British colonies were supplies of veterinarian supplies, including vaccines, to keep the French cattle healthy. Similarly, the ground nut trade from the British colonies to the French colonies was important to the French and it, too, continued.

In the fall of 1940, Boisson made a halfhearted effort to stop the cross-border cattle trade by sending additional border patrol personnel to Upper Volta, the northern neighbor of Gold Coast. The flow of cattle out of Upper Volta into Gold Coast was successfully stopped, but not that out of Niger and French Equatorial Africa into Nigeria. Boisson's efforts were thwarted when the cross-border cattle trade with Nigeria simply increased with the extra cattle then being shipped on to Gold Coast.

In the French colony of Ivory Coast, Governor Horace Crocicchia went over the line, though, and made a secret deal, on his own, with the British to supply cattle and fish in exchange for fuel and spare parts. His activities were eventually discovered in Dakar and Crocicchia was dismissed.

SOUTH AFRICA

The entrance of Italy into the war and the fall of France served to strengthen the hand of the pro-Axis elements in South Africa, while at the same time dividing the Afrikaner community. The Afrikaner hard core continued their public criticism of Smuts and South Africa's participation in the war, while moderate and liberal Afrikaners flocked to join the armed forces and take jobs in war plants. The hard core Afrikaners showed their disapproval by calling the independent-minded kinfolk "liberal stooges" and "Red lice." Some who spoke out too strongly in favor of the Allies were even excommunicated from the hard-core dominated Dutch Reform Church.

Some members of the pro-Axis Ox-Wagon Sentinels (OB) began plotting subversive activities but were discovered by the police and jailed.

During the summer of 1940, J. B. M. Hertzog, the ex-

Prime Minister of South Africa and former leader of the United Party who had been replaced by Smuts, turned coat and went over to the National Party, taking with him a few of his close associates. Similarly, two of the most prominent leaders of the small ultra-right-wing Afrikaners Party also left that party and joined the National Party. Working closely with these new-found supporters Daniel Malan, the National Party leader, agreed to rename the party as the "Reunited National Party" to reflect the union of Hertzog's faction and the Afrikaner Party leaders with the National Party. But, the platform of the Reunited National Party was basically the same as that of the National Party had been, which was: to take South Africa out of the war and demand a separate peace with Germany and Italy; to withdraw from the British Commonwealth, and to strengthen and enforce the segregation laws separating whites from nonwhites and Jews. Like the National Party before it, the new Reunited National Party continued to be the main opposition party in South Africa and the strongest contender for power against Smuts and his United Party. And as before, it simply became known as the National Party in the political rhetoric of South Africa.

Smuts was deeply concerned about these developments and foresaw the possibility of a coup. In July 1940, he wrote to an old friend in Britain, M. C. Gillett, saying:

> *The German victories are putting great heart into my Opposition. They are holding meetings all over the country in favour of a separate peace. The Allies are finished, they say, and Smuts will be finished in a couple of months and thereafter they will seize power and proclaim secession and a republic. There will be a new constitution modelled on that of Italy or Portugal and an alliance with Nazi Germany."*

After the Mers el Kebir incident the French government

A South African war poster stressed unity. Note that all individuals in the drawing are white.

If an Invasion Came to South Africa

Our "Parashots" must wear Uniform

By Lt.-Colonel H. F. Trew

Lt.-Colonel H. F. Trew is well known in South Africa as a police officer, soldier and writer. Not long ago he predicted in The Week-End Argus that the Germans at a heavy cost would be able to turn the Maginot Line.

In this article he discusses modern war and what would happen if a mechanised army came to South Africa.

The Brutal Truth about Modern War

Hitler has Copied the War Methods of Japan

An article in a South African newspaper of June 1940 telling about the possibility of an Axis invasion by air.

broke diplomatic relations with London but did not do so with South Africa. This was welcomed in South Africa for two reasons; 1) it avoided another point of contention between the Smuts government and the hard-core Afrikaners and, 2) it provided the British Commonwealth with an avenue of communications to Vichy.

BRITISH CHILDREN TO SOUTH AFRICA

In the fall of 1940, several thousand children from England arrived in South Africa for temporary sanctuary after having been evacuated from British cities in the face of the ferocious German air blitz. Hard-core Afrikaners denounced the Smuts government's plan to harbor these children as a sinister plot to dilute the Afrikaner blood of the country and to open the door for European Jews. This proved to be wild and irresponsible rhetoric. When the blitz ended, the children were gradually returned to England as shipping accommodations could be found for them.

BASUTOLAND, BECHUANALAND AND SWAZILAND

These three British colonies in southern Africa were heavily influenced by South Africa both economically and politically. And, like South Africa, were at war with Germany and Italy. British Army recruiters found fertile ground in these colonies and thousands of young men signed up for service in the Pioneer (Engineer) forces of the British Army. After training, they were sent to all parts of the globe wherever the British Army needed them.

Basutoland was one of the poorest British colonies in Africa. Out of financial necessity, there were long-standing laws on the books requiring every young man to work for prescribed periods of time in the mines in order that the small colony would not be such a financial burden to Britain. The colony's only other export of note was livestock. With only two exports, the colony ran an annual deficit of two to one imports over exports. By joining the Pioneers the men of Basutoland fulfilled their work obligation, got to see other parts of the world, and avoided work in the mines.

Bechuanaland was also a poor colony, being mostly desert and sparsely settled. Its only exports were livestock and migrant laborers. When the British Army recruiters appeared offering enlistments, the men of Bechuanaland saw it as just another way to earn money by taking a job outside the country.

Swaziland was small, but a prosperous land, especially when compared with Basutoland and Bechuanaland. It was a semiautonomous protectorate ruled by Paramount Chief Sobhuza II with the British acting as advisers and administrators. Here Africans held more political power than in any other British colony in Africa. Poor blacks, which constituted the majority of the population, were discouraged from voting by a poll tax of 1.15 pounds per each male resident and 1.10 for his wife, or wives, up to a maximum of 4.40 pounds.

The soil was fertile, irrigation was well-developed, and there was iron, asbestos, and tin mining. Most of these assets, though, were in the hands of the whites, and the blacks were often underemployed or unemployed. For them, service in the British Army was a welcome means of steady employment.

Altogether, some 35,000 men from Basutoland, Bechuanaland and Swaziland volunteered for service in the British armed forces during the war.

SOUTHERN RHODESIA, NORTHERN RHODESIA AND NYASALAND

Despite their similar names, the Rhodesias were quite different from each other. Southern Rhodesia was, by far, more advanced than its northern neighbor. Southern Rhodesia had a population of 1.1 million (1938) with a European population of 50,000 and was a self-governing colony. It was a crossroads for south-central Africa in that the Cape Town-to-Cairo railroad ran north and south through the colony, and several railroads ran east and west hauling primarily ores from the mines in Northern Rhodesia and the Belgian Congo to seaports in Portuguese Mozambique and South Africa. Southern Rhodesia produced several type of ores itself, including gold, along with tobacco and a wide variety of food stuffs.

There were political forces at work to unite Southern Rhodesia with Northern Rhodesia, or with South Africa, or a union of all three. Segregation was formalized and rigidly practiced in Southern Rhodesia, and the blacks had been confined to well-defined reservations since 1902 and were required to carry identification cards. Yet many black lived outside the reservations because they worked on plantations, in the mines, and in the white society in general.

All white male citizens of Southern Rhodesia were subject to military conscription and could be sent outside the colony. The government offered financial incentives for men willing to take pilot training.

IAN SMITH

One of those who took advantage of the Southern Rhodesian government's incentive offer was Ian Smith. He became a fighter pilot and emerged from the war as one of Africa's great war heros. Smith fought in North Africa, was shot down, badly wounded, and spent several months in a Cairo hospital where his face was reconstructed with plastic surgery. He went back into action in Italy, was shot down again, and rescued by Italian Partisans. He fought then, as a Partisan, throughout the remainder of the war. By the time Major Smith returned to Southern Rhodesia, his exploits were well-known and he was hailed as a war hero. From this background he went into politics and rose to become Southern Rhodesia's Prime Minister.

Since the onset of the war the Southern Rhodesian armed forces were rapidly increased, and it was planned that military units would go to Egypt, British East Africa, and Britain.

Northern Rhodesia was a British protectorate with a population of 1.4 million including only 13,846 Europeans (1938) who lived mostly in guarded settlements called "blocks," which were usually close to a railroad and/or their places of employment. The colony's richest assets were, by far, its mines which produced ores of copper, cobalt, vanadium, and gold. Railroads ran from the northwest, servicing the mining areas of the Belgian Congo, to the southeast where they connected with the railroads in Southern Rhodesia. A new paved road, completed in the late 1930s, connected Northern Rhodesia's capital of Lusaka with Southern Rhodesia's capital, Salisbury. Other roads in Northern Rhodesia were mostly gravel or dirt, and some were impassible during the rainy season. With the coming of war, Northern Rhodesia's minerals were in great demand and some mines began working around the clock. Workers were imported by the thousands from neighboring colonies to meet the production demands in the mines.

Northern Rhodesia had a small prewar defense force which, with the coming of the war, rapidly increased. The King's African Rifles (KAR) also actively recruited in the colony.

The small colony of Nyasaland was, like Northern Rhodesia, a British protectorate with a population of 1.6 million (1938) making it more densely populated than either of the Rhodesias. This was the traditional homeland of the Bantu people who made up the largest segment of the population. Because of its dense population there were environmental problems such as water pollution, deforestation, over-farming, and diseases. This was not an area that attracted whites and the white population, a little over 2000, consisted mostly of colonial administrators, missionaries, and traders. Unlike its neighbors, Nyasaland had no native reserves or pass laws (the carrying of identification papers).

The coming of the war made little impact on Nyasaland, except that the KAR became more active in the colony seeking recruits, as did the mining companies seeking workers. During the war it was estimated that up to 40% of the working male population of Nyasaland went abroad as soldiers or workers. Traditionally some 20% of the male population was abroad.

Nyasaland's economy was based on agriculture, but most of what was produced was consumed locally. The colony did manage, though, to export tea and tobacco.

URANIUM

When Belgium was overrun by the Germans in May 1940, one of the assets the Germans acquired was the Union Miniere Company of Oolen, Belgium, a suburb of Brussels. This company was the world's only major refiner of uranium ore which was shipped to it from the Shinkolobwe mine near Elizabethville, Belgian Congo. The Germans acquired thousands of tons of uranium ore, but very little refined uranium metal. The metal had been shipped, in the last months of 1939, to Britain and the United States where independent researchers were experimenting with the ability of the uranium atom to be split by neutron bombardment and thereby release a tremendous amount of energy—a source of energy that might be used in an exceptionally powerful bomb.

German scientists, of course, knew of the atom-splitting potential of uranium but were slow to react to this potential, because Hitler had no interest in committing the time and national resources on such research. Therefore, most of the Oolen ore remained untouched and a serious German atomic bomb program never came into being.

The French had a small amount of uranium on hand and sent it to Algeria for safekeeping just before the nation surrendered in June.

In the Congo, production at the uranium mine ceased in May with the mine having lost its only major customer, the Union Miniere Company in Belgium.

THE BELGIAN CONGO

With the fall of Belgium in May 1940, the political situation in Belgium became chaotic and it was reflected in the Belgian Congo. The troubles began on May 25 when King Leopold III, commander-in-chief of the Belgian armed forces, suddenly surrendered the Belgian Army to the Germans, creating a large gap in the Allies front. He did this on his own without the approval of, or even consulting, the elected government of Prime Minister Hubert Pierlot. This was the tragic result of a prewar power struggle between Leopold and the various democratically elected governments of Belgium in which no understanding had ever been reached as to what to do in the face of a military disaster. It was not uncommon for both the King and the government to act unilaterally on various issues. Upon surrendering Leopold declared himself a prisoner of war of the Germans and returned to his palace at Laeken near Brussels. He vowed not to leave Belgium, taking his precedent from his father, King Albert, who during World War I, similarly vowed not to leave the country. This action immediately polarized the Belgian people and, of course, brought condemnations from Leopold's allies, Britain and France. Meanwhile, the Pierlot government fled to France and ultimately to London. In Belgium, about half of the general population approved of Leopold's actions, as did the political right wing and Cardinal J. E. Van Roey, spokesmen for the powerful Roman Catholic Church. The remainder of the Belgian population supported Pierlot. On May 27 the Pierlot government announced that Leopold, because of his captivity, was no longer able to act as the constitutional head of the Belgian government. This declaration was confirmed on May 31 by the Belgian Parliament, then meeting at Limoges, France. Leopold declared the actions of the Pierlot government traitorous and that, hereafter, he would assume the powers of government in Belgium. This was short-lived, however, because Hitler decreed that Leopold must stay out of politics. With this, all contact between Leopold and the Pierlot government ceased.

In the Belgian Congo the turmoil in Belgium caused some confusion at first but, in time, most of the colonial officials professed their loyalty to the Pierlot government and expressed their determination to continue the war. Ties with that government, though, were nevertheless weakened because the government-in-exile no longer had enough funds or other resources to contribute to the support of the Congo. On the contrary, it was now the taxes collected in the Congo that began to support the Pierlot government.

The weeks of political turmoil brought an economic slowdown in the Congo at first but this did not last long. The many things that the Congo produced were eagerly bought up by the Allies and other countries, especially the United State. Mining in the southern part of the country began to boom and provide good revenues for the colony which was then shared with the government-in-exile. Throughout the war, revenues from the Congo amounted to about 85% of the total revenue the Belgian government-in-exile received.

Virtually all of the ores produced in the southern Congo were shipped across the British territories of Northern and Southern Rhodesia and into South Africa, Portuguese Mozambique, or Angola. This dictated that the Congo's relationship with the British would remain close. To this end the Belgian government-in-exile charged its Minister of Colonies, M. de Vleeschauwer, to work with the British and collaborate activities in the Congo with those of the British. The British responded favorably by sending a military mission to Leopoldville, the capital of the Belgian Congo, to assist in the defense of the colony.

In the Belgian Congo itself, the Governor-General, M. Ryckmans, was given authority by the Belgian government-in-exile to increase the native army, the Force Publique, beyond it peacetime strength of 15,000 men to 23,000. Once trained, a small force would be sent to fight the Italians in East Africa and another small body of men sent to North Africa to act as guards.

Recruiting of Congo natives by the other Allied nations was not permitted inside the Congo, but the colonial administration made no effort to stop those natives who chose to leave the country in order to join one or the other of the Allied forces. This was something of a sacrifice for the Congo because there was a general labor shortage, especially in the mines. Nevertheless, quite a few Congolese crossed into the Rhodesians and joined the armed forces of those colonies.

As for the labor shortage the colonial government offered incentives to gain workers and, in some instances, drafted laborers. This was facilitated by a Depression-era make-work program already in place that required every able-bodied man in the Congo to work at least sixty days a year on some public project. This was increased to 120 days a year in 1940, and the work projects emphasized were roads, railroads, war-related facilities, collecting wild rubber, and the planting and harvesting of cash crops.

The smaller Belgian colonies of Rwanda and Urundi, on the eastern edge of the Congo, remained under the administration at Leopoldville and became a part of the Allied war effort to the limits of their abilities. A fairly large number of natives from those colonies crossed over into British East Africa and joined the British armed forces there.

PORTUGUESE AFRICA

Portugal and her colonial empire had been economically sound for about twelve years—during the worst of the Depression—and the country's Premier and dictator, Antonio Salazar, wanted to keep it that way. Most of all, he wanted to stay out of the war, and toward this end he followed a strict line of neutrality, but well edged with pragmatism. Beginning in 1940, he doubled the size of Portugal's 40,000–man army and sent many of the new soldiers to the colonies, especially the Azores and Cape Verde Islands. This was a warning to both the Allies and Axis to keep their hands off these strategic islands. To help finance this military expansion, a temporary defense tax was imposed on all the colonies.

To increase solidarity with her colonies, a large colonial congress was held in Lisbon in July 1940 with delegates from all Portuguese colonies. The topics of discussion, of course, centered on mutual efforts to maintain Portugal's neutrality, security, and well being in time of war. The problems of each colony were addressed by the congress and matters of economic interest, such as public health, anthropology, and other social issues were stressed.

During the early years of the war the Portuguese colonies prospered in varying degrees. Mozambique, though, became by far the most prosperous colony. Over the years it had become an economic satellite of South Africa, and since the economy was booming in that country the economy in Mozambique tagged along. Almost everything the colony produced was readily purchased by South Africa or others. Mozambique's ports were very busy exporting raw materials and ores from all over southern Africa. The colony was so prosperous that Lisbon saw fit to impose, for the first time, an income tax on the colony's residents.

The Portuguese had traditionally discouraged Mozambique natives from leaving the colony, but with the manpower shortages that developed in South Africa and the Rhodesians, especially in the mines, this policy was waved. In fact, some natives were conscripted as export laborers. Thousands of Mozambique natives, therefore, went to work outside of their home colony and, as expected, sent a large portion of their earnings home.

The Portuguese expected no military problems in Mozambique so the standing colonial army of 2400 men was not substantially increased.

Portugal's other African colonies, Angola, Portuguese Guinea, Sao Tomas and Principe Islands were prospering too, but none compared with Mozambique.

SPANISH AFRICA

The Spanish colonies in Africa were a constant source of concern for the Allies during the early years of the war. Axis agents were allowed to operate freely in those colonies, and the information they gathered was sent on to Germany and

Italy. Meteorological information was also passed on regularly to the Axis nations.

The Spanish colonies were unable to contribute much food and raw materials to the Axis because of the British blockade, but the seaports in the colonies were safe havens for Axis ships and submarines. Quite understandably, though, the Axis navies did not make much use of the Spanish colonial ports, because the Allies also had agents in the Spanish ports who could readily spot an Axis vessel when it arrived. When this happened, word was promptly passed on the Allied military authorities with the end result being that Allied ships and planes would gather in international waters off the coast awaiting the Axis vessel's departure.

Spain had air connections with all of its colonies through the state-owned Iberia Airlines, and this provided an easy route for Axis agents to come and go in Africa. The airline hired many German pilots who would, on occasions, deviate from their scheduled routes and overfly shipping lanes looking for Allies ships. The Allies put diplomatic pressure on Madrid to stop this behavior and were eventually successful.

AMERICA AND AFRICA

Historically, the United States had little military interest in Africa, viewing it as being completely within the European sphere of influence and no real threat to American security. And, the United States had no territorial claims in Africa. Commercially though, Africa was another matter. Nearly every colony in Africa was an American trading partner. America bought minerals, food stuffs, spices, lumber, animal skins, and dozens of other products from the dark continent, and the Africans, in return, bought Ford automobiles, Singer sewing machines, Standard Oil petroleum products, American cigarettes, American canned and processed food, and many other items.

At the outbreak of the war the United States had diplomatic relations with the three independent countries in Africa, Liberia, Egypt, and South Africa, and consulates in most of the major cities and ports of the various colonies. Some consulates, however, such as the one in Dakar, had been closed during the 1930s to save money.

AFRICAN MINERALS TO AMERICA

The rich mineral belt that runs from the southern Belgian Congo, through the Rhodesias and into South Africa was absolutely vital to America's war economy. Certain segments of the United States economy were based on the availability of the minerals provided by this remote section of the globe. Cobalt was a good example. This metal is absolutely essential to any industrialized society as an alloying agent for high–strength and heat–resistant metals. The mineral belt in southern Belgian Congo and Northern Rhodesia was the world's leading producer of cobalt and without a steady supply of cobalt America could not have become the great producer of war materials that it did. Cobalt was so essential that the U.S. government bought cobalt on the open market and stockpiled it for commercial users. The government also funded efforts to locate new sources of cobalt.

Near the end of the war, when the Germans developed the lead in the production and use of jet aircraft this effort was greatly hampered because the Germans lacked enough cobalt to properly make the turbine blades used in the jet engines. As a result, the German jet engines had a life of only a few dozen hours before they had to be torn down and new blades installed. The Allies, with plenty of cobalt, had no such problems.

AMERICAN OIL TO AFRICA

In all of Africa there were no significant sources of oil, and almost all petroleum products had to be imported. The Americans had only recently captured a large part of the African oil market with their development of the oil fields on the Persian Gulf side of Saudi Arabia and on the Persian Gulf island of Bahrain. In 1938–39, the Americans had developed these fields to the point where they were significant producers of oil and began shipping oil, in large quantities, to East Africa and southern Africa. American oil shipments to West and North Africa still primarily came from the United States.

The oil shipped to East Africa and southern Africa had a price advantage over oil that had previously been shipped by the British and other suppliers through the Suez Canal because there was a seventeen cent per barrel tariff on oil passing through the Canal. American oil went from the Saudi Arabian and Bahrainian fields directly to the African seaports. The British, who had been instrumental in developing the oil fields in Iraq and Iran, shipped their oil by pipeline to Palestine and then had to transport the oil through the Suez Canal to East Africa and southern Africa. This put the Americans and British in direct competition with each other, with the Americans having the price advantage. Fortunately, with the world economy expanding rapidly, there were customers–a–plenty for both the Americans and British, so the loss of the East African and southern African oil trade by the British was of no great consequence to the long–standing, and friendly, American and British political relationship.

After the defeat of France in June 1940, the United States continued diplomatic relations with the Petain government, which meant that American consulates in the French colonial Africa remained in operation as well. After the diplomatic rupture between France and Britain following the Mers el Kebir incident of early July 1940, the American consulates became an important listening post and avenue of communications for the British. America's neighbor, Canada, also maintained diplomatic relations with Petain's government, as did South Africa, providing a second and third avenue of contact for the British.

American trade with Africa increased significantly beginning in the late 1930s and was quite brisk by 1940. Both the British and French colonies did considerable business with the United States in both the commercial and military fields. The American Neutrality Law of 1935, which had forbad American manufacturers to sell war supplies to belligerent nations, had been modified in 1937, and again in 1939, to allow both France and Britain to buy war supplies in America, so long as they paid for them in hard currency and transported the supplies themselves out of the United States. This was known as the "Cash and Carry" program. When France surrendered and slipped into the Axis orbit, the "Cash and Carry" process was abruptly halted with France. It continued, more active than ever, though, with the British. Some of the war items previously ordered by the French were sold to the British for use in their African colonies.

MORE AMERICAN SHIPS GOING TO AFRICA

On June 11, 1940, one day after Italy declared war, President Roosevelt activated a provision in the American neutrality laws forbidding American ships from putting in at ports on the North African coast, in Italian and British East Africa, and in British and French Somaliland. This meant that American ships sailing between North America and the Indian Ocean would no longer use the Mediterranean-Suez Canal-Red Sea route, but would go around southern Africa. Those ships would thus make greater use of the African port for provisions and trading.

After France fell, the Americans honored the British blockade of the French colonies, but continued to carry on some trade with those colonies as permitted within the parameters of the blockade. This had a positive effect of drawing the colonial French administrators closer to the U.S. The trade that remained with the U.S. was now of great value to the French, and they saw the Americans as a sort of mediator between themselves and the British. Out of necessity, and to the advantage of both parties, dealing between the Americans and the colonial French with regards to trade became more direct—thus bypassing Vichy. This type of business dealings had a basis in international law in times of national emergencies. Vichy understood this and let it happen because the Petain government, too, looked upon the Americans as a possible mediator with the British, as well as a much-needed trading partner.

One area of trade with the French that hurt the Americans, however, was in the trade of mica, a natural ceramic material used in electrical and high-heat applications. Mica came from Madagascar and was America's prime source for that material. Mica was one of the many items the British would not permit to pass through their blockade. As a result, the U.S. had to find other sources.

AMERICANS CONCERNED ABOUT THE FRENCH FLEET

The Americans, like the British, were greatly concerned that the powerful French fleet should not fall into the hands of the Axis. The Americans repeatedly pressed Vichy on this issue, asking that the ships be sent to neutral ports, or perhaps to French colonial ports, where they would be relatively safe from an Axis takeover. The French gave the Americans the same answers they gave the British, which was that the French were on top of the matter and would scuttle their own ships rather than let them be taken over by anyone. This was not a satisfying answer in Washington, and the Americans continued to press the issue. As a show of their concern on this issue, the Americans appointed retired Admiral William Leahy as Ambassador to Vichy, a man very knowledgeable on naval affairs. Leahy had instructions to remind the French repeatedly that if the French ships fell into the hands of the Axis, the American government would treat it as a threat to American security and as an issue that could badly damage American-French relations. Actually, the French were in agreement with the Americans in that ships in French colonial ports were relatively safe from an Axis takeover, and made no major effort to bring those ships back to France. Similarly, they made no major effort to transfer ships from France to the colonies for fear of violating the terms of the armistices and provoking the Axis.

On July 19, 1940, President Roosevelt signed a bill in Washington that provided for a gigantic increase in the United States Navy. It was called "The Two-Ocean Navy Expansion Act." This meant that in time, there would be many more American warships sailing in the North and South Atlantic—an action that would affect Africa.

GERMANY'S ATTITUDE TOWARD AFRICA

From Berlin's point of view, Africa was one vast enemy territory capable of producing limitless supplies of raw materials, food, and man power for Germany's enemies. And, there was little the Germans could do about it. Their land army could not penetrate the area and the Luftwaffe's best bombers could only penetrate the northern rim of the continent. The German Navy, using submarines and raiders,

„Wir kämpfen das Kultur, Jimmy."
„Ja – aber was ist Kultur eigenlich?"

A German anti–African poster from World War II shows two barefooted African askaris. The German caption read: "We're fighting for culture, Jimmy." and the other replies, "But what is culture?"

could bring the war into the area's coastal waters, but the greater part of Africa was militarily untouchable by the Germans.

There was another weapon the Germans could use, however, against this distant enemy—propaganda. This was done by short wave radio broadcasts and the dissemination of literature and rumors through neutral sources, and groups, and individuals in Africa sympathetic to Germany's cause. Powerful short wave radio stations operated from Berlin and Stuttgart to spread the propaganda into all of Africa and the Middle East. The Italians, too, had a powerful radio station at Bari, Italy broadcasting Italian propaganda to the same audiences.

Most of the German propaganda was directed toward two general audiences: the Arab peoples of Africa and the Middle East, and the black people of sub-Saharan Africa. Propaganda themes to the Arabs were different than those to the blacks. To the Arabs, the theme was that Germany was their friend and would help them cast out the British and French usurpers of their lands. There were seldom, if ever, any racial overtones in the German propaganda suggesting that the Arabs were a lesser people.

To the blacks of Africa, however, racial attacks were the norm, with the theme that the British and French were attempting to despoil the blood of all Europeans by bringing blacks into Europe to become a permanent part of European society. The Germans preached that it was best that the blacks remain in place and await the time when a victorious and benevolent Germany could return to Africa and bring to the African people the blessing of culture and modern-day technology.

Much of this propaganda, both to the Arabs and blacks, was also for home consumption because it boosted the morale of the German population. This was nothing new in Germany. German society had long been sympathetic toward the Arab world and racist toward blacks. This latter attitude was seen in anti-African propaganda from World War I which had been based, primarily, on race.

Hitler still harbored the hope that Germany might regain all, or part, of her African empire. But, as he told Serrano Suner, a Spanish diplomat and Franco's brother-in-law, he did not see Africa as a land for future German settlement. Africa, the Fuhrer said, would be treated as an economic asset that would be exploited for what it could provide in the way of raw materials and food for the German people.

WHAT TO DO WITH DE GAULLE

By late June it had become clear in London that no Frenchman of a higher rank or higher name recondition than Charles de Gaulle was likely to step forward to lead the crusade to keep France in the war. The British were stuck with this relatively unknown one-star general who had served only a little more than one week in the French government as Undersecretary of War. Furthermore, only a handful of French political and military leaders had come forward to pledge themselves to de Gaulle and his fledgling Free French movement. For the most part, the rank and file of the French armed forces had, likewise, ignored his call to arms. And, out of all the colonies in the vast French Empire, none had pledged their loyalty to de Gaulle. De Gaulle's Free French

An anti–African German propaganda poster from World War I shows a black African soldier in a French Army uniform couching like an animal. The rabbit in the lower left suggests that the Africans breed like rabbits.

movement at this stage was little more than a name only, its entire military value hardly less than an army division. But, the Free French movement had a propaganda value and it provided a haven for those Frenchmen who were still undecided or might have a change of heart later on.

The British decided to go with what they had and promote de Gaulle and his movement for whatever value it might produce. On June 23, 1940, with the British government's approval, de Gaulle announced that he had formed a French National Committee to direct his movement. This was an organization which, under the right conditions, could be converted into a provisional government or a government-in-exile. This event was widely publicized by British propagandists with the added story line, which was mostly fictional, that many Frenchmen throughout the French Empire welcomed it and were just waiting for the right opportunity to declare for de Gaulle.

On June 28, 1940, with much fanfare, London announced that it formally recognized the French National Committee as the leader of all free Frenchmen everywhere and as an Ally.

In the weeks that followed, only a trickle of men came forward to join de Gaulle and his movement. But, the message from London had not fallen on deaf ears, and as time passed and millions of Frenchmen began to realize what the defeat of France really meant and that it was permanent, minds did began to change.

Then, on July 20, 1940, the first French colony threw off the Vichy yoke and declared for de Gaulle. It was the New Hebrides Island Group in the Pacific, and its decision to join de Gaulle had been accomplished by popular plebescite. Considering the size of the French Empire, the New Hebrides was but a crumb, but it was a beginning and it further showed that a majority of inhabitants of a French colony, when allowed to express their free will, chose de Gaulle.

By the beginning of August, de Gaulle's Free French began to look like a fighting force. Twenty-eight French warships, including a depot battleship, had been acquired by the Free French and were all manned with French crews—albeit skeleton crews in some cases. The Free French Air Force had grown to one bomber flight and one fighter flight, and the army had at least one brigade for each arm, a headquarters staff and service units. All told, the Free French fighting force numbered some 6,000 men, with more men coming in daily.

Chapter 7

THE FRENCH CIVIL WAR IN AFRICA (AUGUST 1940–JANUARY 1941)

THE VICHY FRENCH VS. THE FREE FRENCH

For the first two months of its existence, de Gaulle's Free French movement had not attracted any part of the French Empire in Africa to its cause. All that changed on August 26, 1940, when there came a startling announcement from Felix Eboue, the Governor of the colony of Chad in French Equatorial Africa, that he and his colony would support the Free French.

Eboue's announcement from his colonial capital of Fort Lamy was not a unilateral spur-of-the-moment action. Eboue had secretly contacted the British on July 4 (the day after Mers el Kebir), asking that a British representative come to see him in Fort Lamy. A British representative was sent, and Eboue expressed his desire to join de Gaulle and turn Chad over to the Free French. The British, in turn, offered to help him all they could. On July 8 Eboue sent a letter to de Gaulle via the British authorities in Lagos, Nigeria expressing his wishes in writing. De Gaulle responded and sent representatives to Nigeria to make contact with Eboue. This led to a series of meetings between Eboue, de Gaulle's representatives, and the British on a plan of action. The overall plan was to acquire all of French Equatorial Africa for the free French, with Eboue's announcement from Chad being the first phase of the operation. That announcement was timed for the day after the attack on Mers el Kebir in hopes that it would be the spark that would induce other French colonial administrators to break with the Petain government and join the Free French.

Chad was the northernmost colony in the federation of French Equatorial Africa, mostly desert and very poor. Its leaders and people, though, harbored strong pro-Free French sympathies, so it was believed that the Free French takeover in Chad would go quickly and peacefully. Acquisition of French Cameroons, Chad's neighbor to the south, would be next.

FELIX EBOUE

Felix Eboue was a mulatto born in French Guiana, South America and educated in France. As a young man he joined the French colonial service and was posted to French Equatorial Africa. He travelled extensively, learned several local languages and many of the native customs. He was an adroit and hard-working civil servant and moved up steadily in the colonial service.

At the time of his defection from Vichy, and all through his association with the Free French, Eboue maintained that his actions were motivated by national pride and honor. But, one has to wonder if race might not have been a significant factor in Eboue's action. Eboue was the only man of color to hold such a high position in French Africa. By August 1940, it might well have become clear to Eboue that the Petain government in Vichy was very much the vassal of Germany and that, sooner or later, Germany's racial policies would be imposed on Vichy. If this came about, Eboue would have no future. By joining the Free French, though, he would have a future and the potential of becoming a hero on the Allied side.

Chad was the second French colony to announce for the Free French. The first had been the New Hebrides Island Group in the Pacific on July 20, 1940. Chad was a land-locked colony which bordered two sister colonies, Ubangui-Chari and French Cameroons to the south, British-controlled

Nigeria and the French West African colony of Niger on the west, Italian-controlled Libya on the north, and the Anglo/Egyptian Sudan on the east. Fort Lamy was on the western edge of the colony on the Nigerian border, so Eboue and his little group had easy contact with the British and, if things went wrong, an easy escape route into Nigeria.

Chad was a poor colony, mostly desert but its location was strategic in that it bordered Libya. Militarily, this gave the British defending Egypt an opportunity to threaten the Italian's southern flank. At the time of Eboue's announcement, Chad's small defense force was stationed along the Libyan border on a war footing where it had been since before the armistices. The Chad force was too small and poorly equipped to be much of a threat to the Italians at this time, but that would soon change.

Fortunately Eboue's political position in Chad was strong. His second-in-command, Secretary-General Laurentie, the commander of French troops in Chad, Colonel Marchand, and a majority of the white residents supported Eboue's action. Furthermore, Chad's main trading partner was Nigeria, and both the Nigerians and Chadians feared that their common border might be closed by Vichy. This would have been economically devastating to Chad.

Immediately upon hearing the news of Eboue's announcement, de Gaulle, as planned, phoned Fort Lamy from London, personally thanking Eboue for his action and promising to do all he could to support Eboue and his people. Then de Gaulle officially announced Chad's adherence to the Free French cause and the British broadcasted the event around the world. It was an Allied victory and a much needed one at that.

THE DOMINOS FALL IN FRENCH EQUATORIAL AFRICA

The Free French were prepared to strike in French Cameroons immediately after Eboue made his announcement. A group of approximately thirty Free French soldiers under Colonel Philippe LeClerc had assembled secretly in the small seaport of Victoria, French Cameroons, forty miles east of Douala, the colony's main seaport and largest city. Soon after Eboue made his announcement, LeClerc and his men left Victoria in native canoes and arrived at Douala after dark on August 27. They occupied the Palais du Gouvernment, the city's main public building, without a struggle and the Vichy authorities fled at once to Youande, the colony's capital, 130 miles inland to the east. LeClerc and his men convinced two companies of soldiers from the Douala garrison to join the Free French and then, with a force now of about 100 armed men, marched on to Youande. They arrived on August 28 and under a flag of truce convinced the colonial governor to declare for the Free French. With this, French Cameroons became the third French colony to join de Gaulle.

Philippe LeClerc as a general. LeClerc was a colonel at the time of his exploits in Equatorial Africa.

Since French Cameroons bordered Chad on the north, British Nigeria on the west, and the Atlantic Ocean on the south, the new Free French stronghold in Africa had an outlet to the sea and a friendly British border to the west. Suddenly, Eboue and Chad were not so remote.

Meanwhile, another Free French force struck at Brazzaville, the capital of the French Equatorial Africa federation and the colonial capital of the colony of Middle Congo. This small band of Free French, under Commandant Delange, marched on the Governor-General's residence and captured Governor-General Louis Husson and the residence without a struggle. Husson protested the takeover and would not agree to join the Free French, but did agree to resign. With that, word was flashed across the Congo River to Leopoldville, Belgian Congo where one of de Gaulle's top aides, General Egard de Larminat, was waiting. Larminat and a few associates crossed the river and, with de Gaulle's warrant in hand, announced that he was the new Free French High Commissioner of all French Equatorial Africa. Since Brazzaville was also the capital of the Middle Congo that colony, too, joined the Free French. Upon hearing of the Free French takeover in Brazzaville, Governor Pierre de Saint-Mart of the colony of Ubangui-Chari telegraphed from his colonial capital of Banqui on August 28 that he and his staff would also join the Free French. That put four of the federation's five colonies under Free French control. The acquisition of Gabon, the fifth and last colony in French Equatorial Africa, would not be so easy.

On August 29, Governor Georges-Pierre Masson of Gabon wired Brazzaville from Libreville, Gabon's capital, that he too would accept Free French authority. But, the French naval commander at Libreville had other ideas. He mustered a small force of sailors from his naval force, which consisted of a sloop, a submarine, and several smaller vessels, and marched on Masson's headquarters. At the barrel of a gun, Masson was forced to send a second telegram to Brazzaville rescinding the first and announcing that Gabon would remain loyal to Vichy. There the matter stood, neither side being strong enough to attack the other and both calling frantically for reinforcements.

The Vichy authorities at Dakar responded quickly to the crisis in Gabon and sent Air Force General Marcel Tetu to

Libreville with a force of French bombers and the announcement that additional reinforcements were on the way. Tetu arrived at Libreville with the title of Governor-General of all French Equatorial Africa and orders to recover the colonies and oust the Gaullists. A short time later, a second Vichy submarine arrived at Libreville from Dakar along with a French freighter carrying a detachment of Senegalese soldiers and some war supplies. The balance of power in Equatorial Africa was quickly shifting in favor of Vichy.

Vichy ordered the newly arrived forces in Gabon not to attack the Gaullists just yet, because more reinforcements were on the way. A large naval force consisting of a squadron of three (later six) French warships under Admiral Jean Bourrague was to be dispatched from Toulon, France with a contingent of regular French Army troops. The French plan, with the approval of both the German and Italian Armistice Commissions, was for this force to make an amphibious assault on Pointe Noire, Middle Congo, which was in the hands of the Free French, and from there march on to Brazzaville, some 200 miles inland, and crush the Free French revolt. The two cities, Pointe Noire and Brazzaville, were linked by a railroad and a good all-weather road. Also to be sent were two French Air Force fighter groups and transport planes. The departure date was set for September 1.

Upon reviewing Vichy's military plans, Hitler intervened and insisted that only African ground forces would be used in the operation. He also warned that if Vichy was not successful, Germany reserved the right to intervene on its own.

Meanwhile, the British responded to the situation in Equatorial Africa by sending the cruiser HMS "Delhi" to Pointe Noire to help protect that vital port and assist in the British blockade that now included only Gabon.

In London, General de Gaulle had much grander plans but, he would need British help and need it fast. He, therefore, went directly to Churchill.

THE TIME IS NOW

In London, de Gaulle and Churchill conferred and a hasty decision was made. Considering the favorable developments in French Equatorial Africa and the ease with which the various colonies there sided with de Gaulle, it was believed that French West Africa might, too, be ready to fall into de Gaulle's lap, and de Gaulle had a plan. Churchill listened enthusiastically to the plan and gave his approval. It called for a joint British and Free French expeditionary force to be sent to Dakar and there, under a threat to attack, induce the French authorities to join the Free French as their neighbors had done in Equatorial Africa.

The expeditionary force was quickly assembled and consisted of two British battleships, an aircraft carrier, five cruisers, sixteen destroyers, five corvettes (three of which were Free French), and six British transports. Aboard the transports were 4,000 British troops and 2,400 Free French troops, most of them veterans of the Norwegian campaign. The force set off on August 31 from Scapa Flow and Liverpool bound for Dakar. Aboard, and ready to play a significant role in the operation, was de Gaulle himself. It was hoped that, once de Gaulle and the combined force appeared off Dakar, the local officials would welcome a chance to get back into the war and accept de Gaulle as their leader. If there was indecision within the Dakar leadership or outright refusal, then the 6,400 Allied soldiers would be landed and the issue settled by force.

If this operation was successful, the benefits would be enormous. The remainder of French West Africa would, almost certainly, follow suit and maybe even the other French colonies, such as Madagascar, French Somaliland, and the French West Indies. It was not expected that the French North African colonies would quickly announce for de Gaulle because of the lingering hatred for him and the British that existed there following the recent Mers el Kebir incident. But the presence of the Free French in Dakar and French West Africa would certainly be an influence on future developments in North Africa. With Dakar as a base of operations and a temporary capital for the Free French, de Gaulle could build up a significant army which would be very useful in either East Africa or North Africa or both. Furthermore, Dakar could become an important Allied air and naval base for antisubmarine activities in the central and southern Atlantic.

The Dakar force departed from England under a strict veil of secrecy, and neither the Germans nor the leaders in Vichy had any inkling of its existence.

MORE FRENCH COLONIES DECLARE FOR FREE FRENCH

Encouraged by the Free French success in Equatorial Africa several more French colonies declared for de Gaulle. They were the Pacific island of Tahiti on September 2 by plebiscite, the French Establishments in India on September 9 and New Caledonia Island in the Pacific on September 20 by plebiscite along with the island of Noumea.

Previously, on August 27, the British media had announced that the British government promised that any French colony declaring for the Allies would have the British blockade lifted immediately and would receive economic assistance. Also, the British government promised it would do all it could to maintain economic stability within those colonies and assist in fostering increased trade between those colonies and the other Allied nations. This was a significant promise, because the British blockade, which was steadily increasing in strength, was beginning to hurt some of the French colonies economically. Those French colonies that declared for the Allies did, in fact, experience a rapid resumption of trade once the blockade was lifted.

In the West Indies, the United States, with Britain's approval and cooperation, made a special arrangement with the French-owned islands there. There were several French warships in the islands that concerned both the Americans and the British, so the Americans offered a deal to the French West Indies colonial authorities that the islands would not be subjected to the British blockade and that normal trade relations with the United States, the number one trading partner for most of the islands, would continue unaltered if the authorities would guarantee to immobilize their warships. The matter was referred to Vichy, and the Petain government agreed to accept it. The arrangement was therefore put into effect with the Americans closely monitoring the French ships thereafter. All of the French West Indies islands, though, remained loyal to Vichy.

PETAIN TAKES STEPS TO HALT THE EROSION OF HIS EMPIRE

To halt the erosion of its empire, Petain demanded, and received, statements of continuing loyalty from the top authorities in all of the other French colonies. Vichy also spread false stories, broadcast over Paris and Dakar radio, that the Free French in Equatorial Africa were burning and pillaging native villages, summarily executing Vichy officials, and had even killed a high-level Catholic clergyman, Monseigneur Tardy.

On September 4, Petain relieved General Maxime Weygand from his duties as Minister of Defense in his government and appointed him High Commissioner of French North Africa. Weygand was one of the most respected generals in France, and it was Petain's hope that Weygand's presence in North Africa, along with the political and military power the office of High Commissioner commanded, would solidify Vichy's control over French North Africa. This move had the desired effect. French North Africa remained a faithful Vichy stronghold and the Free French found few supporters there.

WAR LOOMS BETWEEN VICHY AND BRITAIN AGAIN

In Vichy, pro-Axis Premier Pierre Laval was eager to use the crisis in French Equatorial Africa as an excuse for France to declare war on Britain. He had also sought a declaration of war at the time of the Mers el Kebir attack, but had been overruled by Petain. Petain, as before, rejected a declaration of war on this occasion but did agree to threaten the British with war. He sent word to the British through Madrid that British interference in French Equatorial Africa would not be tolerated and could possibly lead to a declaration of war on Britain.

The crisis in Equatorial Africa threatened to escalate matters further when the Spanish, on their own, warned Britain that if they interfered in French colonial matters Madrid might permit Axis forces to cross Spanish territory and march into French Morocco to protect that strategic protectorate from an Allied invasion.

The Churchill government, not wanting this to happen, made a conciliatory reply through Madrid that they had no intention of encouraging the Gaullist movement in French Morocco, and further offered to permit an increase in the shipment of humanitarian supplies to French North Africa, including French Morocco, through the British blockade. The British asked Madrid to pass this information on to Vichy.

CONFRONTATION AT SEA

Vichy's naval force of three cruisers and three destroyers destined for French Equatorial Africa left Toulon on September 9. French resistance sources reported the departure to London but, due to an administrative mistake and the lack of available ships, the British were unable to intercept the ships en route. The French force arrive safely on the first leg of their journey at Dakar on the night of September 14/15.

The leaders in Vichy had become suspicious on their own volition that, inspired by their success in Equatorial Africa, the British and Free French might soon threaten Dakar.

Debarking at Dakar from the newly arrived ships were several units of French Marines and several naval gun crews who had been sent to man Dakar's coastal defense guns. Those guns were previously manned by native troops who were not as well-trained as the Frenchmen. With the arrival of the French Marines, Dakar had become a well-armed and heavily defended city. And, because of this sudden turn of events, the British soon come to believe that Vichy had learned of the pending attack on Dakar. This, however, was not true. The French had no knowledge of the Allied force approaching Dakar and proceeded with their plans to send their six warships on to Equatorial Africa.

The Allied force, destined to attack Dakar, sailed past Dakar, as planned well out to sea, and put in at Freetown, Sierra Leone, 600 miles south of Dakar, to refuel and resupply. It was from Freetown that the attack on Dakar would be launched. While at Freetown, the British and Free French learned of the six French warships having just anchored at Dakar. This was disturbing news to the British and Free French because they believed that the six ships had been sent to defend that port and that the Vichy French had learned of the pending attack.

From the city of Dakar the British and Free French were getting confusing intelligence reports. Some reports stated that the action in Equatorial Africa had caused Free French sentiments to surface once again while other reports stated that the Dakar authorities were as determined as ever to oppose the Free French.

At this critical time the United States chose to reopen its consulate at Dakar and soon began passing information to the British and Free French, but it was of little value because it was no more accurate than what was already being received. Despite these new developments, the British and Free French decided to proceed as planned with the attack on Dakar.

On September 18 the Vichy French naval force left Dakar for Point Noire, Equatorial Africa and each of the three French cruisers had eighty Senegalese infantrymen aboard in compliance with Hitler's demand that only black troops be used in Equatorial Africa. The force planned to refuel at sea on September 22. The British at Freetown learned of the departure of the six ships but made no effort to intercept them.

On September 19, purely by chance, the HMS Delhi patrolling in the company of the cruiser HMS "Cornwall," encountered the Vichy refueling tanker "Tarn" and its escort the French cruiser "Primauguet" at sea 640 miles from Gabon and 1000 miles ahead of the approaching Vichy fleet. The British cruisers ordered the two French ships to turn about and return to Dakar under escort from the Cornwall. The French captains complied but, of course, radioed Dakar for instructions. Dakar consulted Vichy and it was concluded from this and other information Vichy received that a British attack on Dakar was very likely, although they were still unaware of the Allied force at Freetown. Out of caution, Vichy ordered both the Pointe Noire naval force and the refueling ships to return to Dakar to help defend the city in case of an attack. On the return trip, the French cruiser, "Glorie" developed engine trouble and fell behind. Likewise, the French destroyer "Ingerfield" of the Pointe Noire force and the cruiser Primauguet of the refueling unit developed engine troubles but were able to keep up with their companion ships while the Glorie could not. Informed of this, Vichy ordered the trouble-plagued Ingerfield and Primauguet to sail on to Casablanca rather than risking them in battle at Dakar.

The Pointe Noire force, now down to four ships, reached Dakar on September 20. All thought of proceeding on to Gabon was now postponed until further notice.

Meanwhile, the Vichy government had asked the Germans, through the German Armistice Commission in Wiesbaden, to release more French ships and several French air units to reinforce Dakar. The Germans, seeing no urgency, took their time reviewing the request and decided to send a German naval team to Dakar to inspect the situation before making a decision. That team left Europe on September 22 by air and arrived that evening at Casablanca with plans to travel on to Dakar the next day.

While these events were playing out, the Allied force, commanded by Admiral Sir John Cunningham, left Freetown on September 21. The lead ships soon encountered the French cruiser Glorie struggling northward with its engine problems. The British ordered the Glorie to proceed on to Casablanca and not to stop at Dakar. The Glorie relayed this information to Vichy which approved of Glorie's going on to Casablanca. And still, in spite of the Glorie having been intercepted, the French remained unaware that Dakar was about to be attacked.

On the 22nd a Spanish newspaper reported that de Gaulle had left Britain for some unknown destination possibly Morocco. This information made the French now more suspicious than ever that something might soon happen in West Africa.

At 5:00 a.m. on September 23 the Allied force reached Dakar. As planned, the British ships stayed out of sight over the horizon and the Free French ships approached the harbor. Unfortunately, it was very foggy along the coast line so the Vichy French ashore could not see the Free French ships arrive. Thus, the psychological effect of a surprise attack was lost to the Allies. The Dakar French soon learned of the Free French ships, though, by other means.

Word of those ships being off Dakar was flashed to Germany and Hitler personally ordered the German naval team to remain in Casablanca pending developments at Dakar. As for the French request for ships and planes, he immediately approved the release of planes but no more ships.

At 6:10 am, Free French aircraft flew over the city, dropping leaflets telling of de Gaulle's arrival and asking the French civilians to support the takeover of Dakar by the Free French. The planes were fired upon from the ground. It was an ominous beginning. At about 7:00 a.m., de Gaulle went on the radio, using the Dakar radio band, asking the French authorities to negotiate a settlement with him regarding Dakar. De Gaulle told the Dakar authorities that he was backed by a powerful British naval force and "numerous British troops" but that the British would not intervene if all went well. Minutes later a commercial air liner landed at Ouakam Airfield, Dakar's main airport, and several armed Free French officers and men emerged and took the airport director captive. At the same time two small Free French motor boats entered the harbor under a white flag bearing additional Free French officers and several seamen. The boats docked and the officer in charge asked to speak with Admiral Landrian, the port's naval commander. While the Free Frenchmen awaited a reply, they became suspicious that all was not well and pulled away from the docks in their boats. It was a good decision, because they were soon fired upon from shore. With this, the Free French boats sped out of the harbor.

This, then, was the French reply. It had come directly from High Commissioner Pierre Boisson. He not only ordered the action in the harbor but that the Free French officers and men at the airport be arrested.

For the British and Free French, this was a great disappointment, but they had planned for such an eventuality. Next the British ships came up over the horizon, and de

Gaulle went on the radio a second time at 8:07 a.m., warning the Dakar authorities that if they did not negotiate "...the enormous Allied forces which follow me will enter into action and the consequences will be serious." There was no reply from shore.

Meanwhile, the British ships joined forces with the Free French ships, but it was still foggy and they could not be seen from shore.

As the British ships were coming up two Free French sloops entered the harbor and sped toward the anchored battleship Richelieu intent on putting a boarding party on the Richelieu in an attempt to convince the ship's captain and crew to side with the Free French. It was hoped that this would change the minds of the French authorities ashore. Before the sloops could even get close to the battleship, though, they were fired upon by the Richelieu's guns. The sloops quickly turned around and dashed out of the harbor.

De Gaulle then went on the radio a third time, at 10:20 a.m., with a stern warning that if the Dakar authorities did not negotiate with him the British would "...take over responsibility for the matter."

The British ships had been discovered by now, and when a patch of fog thinned the French gave their reply to de Gaulle's third radio message. It was a barrage of fire from the French shore batteries. The British ships held their fire at first, but then, two French submarines were seen approaching on the surface and the British had no alternative but to protect themselves and fire at the subs. One of the submarines, the "Persee," was sunk and the other, the "Ajax" was disabled by depth charges and later captured by the Allies. The cruiser HMS "Cumberland" was hit by a shell from a shore battery and withdrew out of range.

Then, the Richelieu opened up on the Allied fleet with her big guns. For 34 minutes the guns of both sides fired away at each other until the Allied fleet withdrew out of range. Planes from the Ark Royal attacked the French ships and shore batteries and were met by defending French fighter planes and antiaircraft fire. Four British planes were lost. When the guns stopped firing, amazingly, no major damage had been done to the ships of either side.

There was then a lull in the fighting for the rest of the morning. Around noon, the British ships moved in again and began firing at the French ships in the harbor, and planes from the Ark Royal made a second raid on the town. The French ships, which were now maneuvering inside the harbor making them harder to hit, fired back. Again no major damage was suffered by either side although several French freighters inside the harbor were damaged.

Again the British pulled back but a short while later a third air attack was made on the city by planes from the Ark Royal. This time two British planes were lost.

The Allies then sailed up the coast fifteen miles where it was planned to put a Free French ground force ashore at the Bay of Rufisque. This force would land and attempt to enter Dakar from the landward side. It was after 5:00 p.m. when the landing boats were ready to assault the beach. As they approached, they were greeted by a withering barrage of small arms and artillery fire from a large number of French and Senegalese troops well dug in on the shore. At that point Admiral Cunningham called off the landing, over de Gaulle's objection, and ordered the boats to return to the fleet. This proved to be a sound decision because Boisson had some 25,000 French troops at his command and such a small force would have been easily overwhelmed.

The Allied force then sailed off over the horizon and the ships circled about all night as almost everyone aboard got some rest.

On the morning of September 24, just after midnight, the Allied ships approached Dakar, and at 1:00 a.m. Admiral Cunningham radioed to Boisson ordering him to turn over Dakar to the Free French by 6:00 a.m. or suffer the consequences. Boisson radioed back saying "France has entrusted me with Dakar. I will defend Dakar to the end!"

At 6:00 a.m., the British ships began bombarding the French gun emplacements and the ships in the harbor. The French guns again replied. The Allied ships soon broke off contact but returned that afternoon and once again bombarded the Dakar targets. And again the French fired back. Meanwhile, far to the north, the French took retaliatory action and, on September 24, bombed Gibraltar. They returned on the 25th and bombed a second time. These raids damaged the ship repair facilities, which were of great importance to the British fleet in the western Mediterranean.

On the morning of September 25, the Allied ships attacked Dakar again, but during this round of fighting the British battleship HMS "Resolution" was hit amidships with a torpedo from a French submarine and seriously damaged. Then a near miss from one of the big shells of the Richelieu damaged the British battleship "Barham." The British, seeing that the expedition was now a failure, broke off contact for the last time and ordered their ships to return to Freetown. They arrived there on September 27 and 28. The British had several ships damaged, but none were sunk. Six carrier aircraft had also been lost.

The battleship Resolution did not go to Freetown. Instead, it headed across the Atlantic to the United States where it would be repaired in an American ship yard because there were no dry docks at Freetown. The only dry dock on the west coast of Africa was at Dakar.

Back at Dakar the French were licking their wounds, too. About 200 military personnel and civilians had been killed and about 300 wounded. Two French submarines and one large destroyer had been lost during the battle, several ships had been damaged, and some of their shore batteries were knocked out. But, all in all, Dakar was still a powerful bastion, and all of West Africa was still firmly in the Vichy camp.

THE CONSEQUENCES OF DAKAR

The consequences of the Allied failure at Dakar were far reaching. The British, and especially Churchill who had to face an angry and questioning House of Commons, was bitterly disappointed and tended to place the blame on de Gaulle. De Gaulle, likewise, tended to blame the British. Churchill, in his anger, ordered the British naval blockade of French West Africa, and Dakar in particular, strengthened. He also began to reevaluate, altogether, his relationship with de Gaulle and the Free French. Within a short while, British propaganda directed toward Africa changed from one of asking the French to support de Gaulle to one of asking the French to abandon Vichy independently, with or without de Gaulle.

The British in West Africa also changed their minds with regard to de Gaulle. The governor of Sierra Leone urged London to terminate any further significant military cooperation with de Gaulle because Sierra Leone, which was bordered by Vichy-controlled French Guinea on the north, was vulnerable to an attack. Such an attack, he argued, would obviously be directed against Freetown, the only major British naval base between Gibraltar and South Africa.

From Gold Coast came word that the colonial authorities there no longer trusted de Gaulle nor Vichy.

A Vichy poster touting the Dakar victory shows the British, egged on by the International Jews, dangling de Gaulle as bait before the defenders of Dakar. The French caption is a play on words. It says "With that 'de Gaulle,' you will not catch anything, gentlemen!" The French word for fishing pole is "gaule" (one l).

The Germans were impressed with the defense of Dakar and the loyalty of French West Africa to Vichy. Hitler was especially pleased. Admiral Raeder urged Hitler to encourage Vichy to retaliate by sending French troops to invade and occupy Sierra Leone, capture Freetown, and then allow the German Navy to establish a base there. Hitler had no interest in pressing the French further, at least for now. He even ordered the German naval team in Casablanca to return to Germany for fear of upsetting the French at Dakar. Hitler had much greater things on his mind than Dakar and West Africa, because the very next day he ordered his generals to prepare for the invasion of the Soviet Union.

At Vichy, Petain was elated with the events at Dakar, and flush with victory, took the opportunity to present a formal request to the Germans that they promise not to occupy any French colony during the duration of the armistice, or as a result of any future peace treaty. The Germans did not reply, but Petain had made his point.

Petain's ardently pro-Axis Premier, Pierre Laval, went further and suggested again that France use the Dakar attack as justification for a declaration of war on Britain in return for a German/French peace treaty and German guarantees on the French Empire. Petain and others at Vichy had their doubts about this approach, but Hitler agreed to discuss the issue so the doubters decided to bide their time to see what developed.

On October 11, Petain made a public statement saying that "France must free herself from all so-called traditional friendships and enmities." This was seen as another step by the Vichy government toward the Axis camp.

On October 16, Vichy took another step to satisfy her Axis friends. Petain issued a decree forbidding the manufacture of any war materials, including guns, warships, and explosives anywhere in France or the French colonies. This concession had been called for by the armistices, but Vichy had been slow to implement it. Ironically, Petain's decree was welcomed by both the British and Free French.

From Washington came word that President Roosevelt was very disappointed by the failure at Dakar and felt that it was a mistake to have carried it out in the first place. Since the operation had been suggested by de Gaulle, Roosevelt questioned de Gaulle's judgement. Roosevelt, believing as did the British that Vichy had forewarning of the attack, also expressed his concern for security measures at de Gaulle's headquarters in London, saying that the Free French should not be trusted with top-secret information. These unkind words from Roosevelt gave Churchill even more reason to be concerned about de Gaulle.

ON TO EQUATORIAL AFRICA

Following the Dakar fiasco, it was decided that de Gaulle should go on to his newly acquired domain in Equatorial Africa and solidify his position there.

One good result of the Dakar operation was that the Vichy forces were foiled in their attempt to reinforce Gabon. With the forces de Gaulle had accumulated for Dakar and those he could gather in Equatorial Africa, the Free French now had a good chance of taking Gabon by force. There was another factor to all this, too. It was that de Gaulle best not show his face in London for awhile.

Therefore, on October 3, 1940, the combined British and Free French naval force, less the two British battleships Resolution and Barham, left Freetown for Douala, French Cameroons where de Gaulle would stage his forces for an attack on Gabon.

De Gaulle arrived at Douala on October 9, and received a tremendous welcome from the city's population. This visibly lifted his spirits. He soon met with the Free French leaders there and on October 12 ordered that military plans be made for the attack on Gabon. These plans included asking London for military support. After reviewing the request, Churchill ordered that no British ground or air units should be involved in the conquest of Gabon, but that the existing blockade could be significantly strengthened to prevent reinforcements from reaching the Vichy forces in Gabon. To this end, he ordered the cruisers "Devonshire" and Delhi into Gabon's waters as part of the blockading force.

From Douala, de Gaulle went off to tour his new domain, leaving General Egard de Larminat in charge of military operations. From Youande, de Gaulle flew first to Chad and was nearly killed during the journey. The Potez 540 aircraft in which he and his aides were flying developed engine trouble and had to make a harrowing forced landing in a swamp. Fortunately, no one was injured.

At Fort Lamy, de Gaulle conferred with Eboue and his staff and found them dedicated to the Free French cause and eager to fight. De Gaulle told them that one day soon he would like to see the Free French invade and conquer much of southern Libya. Eboue was very supportive of this idea.

From Fort Lamy, de Gaulle went on to the desert outpost of Faya deep in the Sahara. French troops had been stationed at such outposts ever since Italy declared war on France in June 1940. Again, he found the men loyal and eager to fight, but woefully under-equipped.

The Free French cause was widely publicized in neutral America. This poster asks Americans to join the "Free France Forever" movement in America. Note the uniform shown is that of France's colonial army.

DE GAULLE MAKES BRAZZAVILLE THE CAPITAL OF FREE FRANCE

De Gaulle then went on to Brazzaville arriving there on October 24. There he met with the prominent Free French officials who had gathered in Brazzaville at his request. He then crossed the Congo River and met with Governor-General Pierre Rychmans in Leopoldville, Belgian Congo on October 27. Rychmans expressed his willingness to cooperate with the Free French to keep central Africa supportive of the Allies.

De Gaulle remained in Brazzaville for several days setting up a national political administration called the "Council of Defense of the French Empire." De Gaulle described the Council as a body that was to function like a government on behalf of France until such time that France was liberated and free elections could be held. De Gaulle also issued a manifesto and two ordinances proclaiming that a true French government no longer existed, that millions of Frenchmen all over the world were longing to be freed from Vichy's control, and that he, himself, was the sole supreme authority in the French Empire. The manifesto read in part, "...all parts of the Empire freed from control of the enemy (will be administered) on the basis of French legislation enacted before June 23, 1940, for so long as it shall remain impossible to form a French government and a representation of the French people of a normal character independent of the enemy."

De Gaulle seriously considered moving his operational headquarters from London to Brazzaville, but the British objected to this and de Gaulle acquiesced.

General de Larminat, a member of the Council, was confirmed as the Free French High Commissioner of Equatorial Africa, and Felix Eboue, also a member of the Council, was promoted to Governor-General of French Equatorial Africa and given a special task described as "issuing directives for the Administration thus creating the basis for a Free French colonial doctrine." This was the beginning of a formal Free French declaration on the future of the French Empire.

London, now disenchanted with de Gaulle, was very slow to recognize the authority of de Gaulle's new Defense Council, and did not do so until January 1941.

While at Brazzaville, de Gaulle communicated with Governor-General Sir Bernard Bourdillon of neighboring Nigeria and asked him to end all trade with the Vichy territories on his northern and western borders. With London's approval, Bourdillon agreed to end all trade that had any military significance and much, but not all, of the commercial trade. De Gaulle was satisfied. This meant that increased trade with Free French-controlled Equatorial Africa would be expected to replace that terminated with the Vichy colonies.

One of the main duties of de Gaulle's new Council was to build up the Free French Army, and it was a foregone conclusion that that army would be comprised mostly of Africans. Once established, the new Free French army would be used to strike at the enemy in any part of the French Empire.

It was planned that after the conquest of Gabon, Colonel LeClerc would go to Chad to build up a Free French force there that would eventually undertake the invasion of southern Libya. Plans worked out in Brazzaville called for the Free French to conquer and hold the Fezzan, the lower one-third of Libya. This was mostly desert, but with several important oasis communities and trans-Saharan caravan trails. The main objectives were twofold; to threaten the Italians militarily from the south, and to hold the area until the end of the war and use it as a bargaining chip in future peace talks to counter Italian claims on French territory.

Also worked out in Brazzaville were plans for a mixed Free French brigade and a bomber group to go to East Africa. There they would aid the British in the conquest of Italian East Africa, and hopefully bring French Somaliland, and possibly even Madagascar, into the Free French camp.

VICHY OFFERS A DEAL

At Vichy's initiative, representatives from Vichy and Britain began meeting secretly in Madrid on October 1, 1940. Metropolitan France was experiencing shortages of many things, including food, so Vichy wanted the British to allow shipments of food and other nonmilitary items from various locations in the French Empire through the blockade. On September 17 Vichy had been forced to instigate food rationing in unoccupied France mainly because of the British blockade. In exchange for these concessions, Vichy was willing to guarantee that none of the items received would go to the Germans or Italians. The main Vichy representative, Paul Baudouin, hinted that if the Germans or Italians seized any of the cargos it would be grounds for Vichy to move closer to the Allies or even reenter the war. The British were less than enthusiastic about the proposals, but agreed to talk.

The Madrid talks were soon discovered by the Germans, and pressure was put on Vichy to end them. Vichy delayed, but eventually succumbed to German pressures and ended the talks in early November without anything being accomplished.

THE STRUGGLE FOR GABON

While de Gaulle was touring Equatorial Africa, the Free French made two military incursions into Gabon. General de Larminat sent a force of French Congolese troops from Middle Congo down the Ogowe River. They were able to penetrate deep into Gabon before being stopped by a superior Vichy force at Lambarene, only about 100 miles southeast of Libreville. Another small Free French force, under General Legentilhomme, advanced south from French Cameroons and reached Mitzic, over 100 miles inside Gabon and 140 miles east of Libreville. Gabon's capital was now threatened from two directions. Meanwhile, a war of leaflets began with both sides dropping propaganda leaflets and a few bombs on the other.

Vichy's forces at Libreville were formidable by African standards, consisting of four battalions of troops, a force of hastily mobilized colonists, some artillery, four modern bombers, the navy sloop "Bougainville," and the submarine "Poncelet." They were commanded by French Air Force General Marcel Tetu, who had orders directly from Petain to fight to defend the colony.

The Free French forces in the interior of Gabon pressed on, and on October 27, the day de Gaulle met with Governor-General Rychmans in Leopoldville, Mitzic fell to the Free French attackers. They then began to march overland toward Libreville. On November 5 the Vichy garrison at Lambarene surrendered and the Free French force resumed its march on Libreville.

Meanwhile, the British were actively patrolling the waters off Gabon to prevent any reinforcements reaching Tetu's forces by sea. Several Free French vessels had also joined in the blockade force. For political reasons, the British vessels were under orders not to participate in the forthcoming attack on Libreville. That attack was to be an all-French affair.

On the night of November 8, 1940, a Free French force from Douala, commanded by Colonel LeClerc, invaded Gabon by landing on the coast just north of Libreville. LeClerc's force consisted of a battalion of French Legionnaires and a mixed battalion of French native troops and colonists from the Cameroons.

That same evening, the Vichy submarine Poncelet sailed out to sea and soon encountered the British blockade ships. Poncelet fired a torpedo at a British sloop and hit it, but the torpedo failed to explode. The sloop struck back with a depth charge attack, damaging the sub and forcing it to the surface, whereupon its crew promptly surrendered. While the sub's crew was being transferred to the British vessels, the sub's captain secretly remained aboard, set charges, scuttled the submarine and, bravely, went down with his submarine.

The next day, November 9, LeClerc's forces advanced on Libreville and were met with a determined defense by Tetu's forces. Several Free French Lysanders and British-made

Blenheims arrived from Douala and bombed targets in Libreville and in the harbor, damaging the Vichy sloop Bougainville.

Soon afterwards, two Free French vessels entered the harbor and approached the Bougainville, sending messages of friendship to its captain and crew. These were ignored and the Bougainville opened fire on the approaching ships. The two Free French vessels returned fire and succeeded in setting the Bougainville aflame.

Native Free French soldiers. Black soldiers in the service of colonial armies were called "askaris" by both sides. "Askaris" in the service of the French were often referred to as "Senegalese" even though they were not necessarily from the French colony of Senegal.

Meanwhile, LeClerc's troops had fought their way into the city center and the Free French Legionnaires broke the last Vichy resistance at the airport. With this, Tetu surrendered.

There remained one Vichy stronghold left in Gabon, that of the fortress town of Port-Gentil, eighty miles south of Libreville at the mouth of the Ogowe River. After two days of negotiations, Port-Gentil's commander agreed to surrender without bloodshed.

Back at Libreville, former Governor Masson, who had first sided with the Free French and then reneged under pressure, had been taken captive and placed aboard the Free French sloop "Savorgna de Brazza." Now a victim of deep despair, Masson hanged himself. Other than Masson, the conquest of Gabon had cost a total of twenty lives on both sides. The wounded were taken to the same hospital and placed in beds, side-by-side.

General Tetu was taken captive, but rather than being sent to prison was entrusted, under his word of honor, to a local monastery run by the Fathers of the Holy Spirit. There he remained until 1943 when he joined the Free French.

As for the other Vichy fighting men captured by the Free French, they posed a dilemma. The Free French were in no position to hold large numbers of prisoners of war. Not being a government, their right to hold POWs was questionable under the edicts of the Geneva Convention; in addition they had no arrangements with neutral countries to monitor POW camps as called for by the Convention. Then too, the Free French did not want to commit the manpower and resources to holding POWs. Yet, the Free French had to keep some POWs as bargaining chips in future prisoner exchanges with Vichy, who held Free French POWs. Therefore, a plan evolved whereby the Free French screened each individual captured to see if they were willing to join the Free French; if not, most of them were released and returned to Vichy territory. They were well-treated while in Free French hands because it was believed that they would return home without harboring ill feelings toward them, and spread the message that being captured by the Free French was not all that bad.

On November 15 de Gaulle arrived in Libreville and was warmly welcomed by the populace. On the 17th he left for London making stops at Lagos, Freetown, Bathurst and Gibraltar. With his military victory in Gabon, his efforts to build a Free French fighting force, a provisional government, and his friendly contact with the Belgians in the Belgian Congo, de Gaulle had refurbished his tarnished image with the British. Upon arriving in London, de Gaulle sweetened his return by announcing that he now had a Free French fighting force of 30,000 men, twenty warships, 1,000 aviators, and sixty merchant ships.

A month after his return, de Gaulle received a pleasant surprise in that Anthony Eden, a widely respected political figure and ardent supporter of the Free French, became British Foreign Minister.

VICHY'S PLAN TO RECAPTURE EQUATORIAL AFRICA

Vichy could do little to save Equatorial Africa, but they could announce to the world, for propaganda purposes, that they would, one day soon, take it back. There were two possible military options open to Vichy in attacking Equatorial Africa, one by sea and one by land. By sea, Vichy forces would have to confront the powerful British blockade and make a successful amphibious landing on a hostile shore. By land, they would have to cross hundreds of miles of trackless desert. The most viable land route to Chad was from Naimey, the capital of Niger on the Niger River, along a road that paralleled the northern border of Nigeria to Zinder and then 300 miles across open county to Lake Chad on the border of Chad. This was a long and difficult march of over 700 miles with a very tenuous supply line. For any military operation, whether by sea or by land, Vichy would need sizeable numbers of men and equipment and Germany and Italy's permission to mobilize them.

Nevertheless, Vichy went through the motions of planning the invasion of Equatorial Africa. French General Charles Huntziger was assigned, in late November 1940, to work with German General Walter Warlimont to come up with a plan. Their choice was an attack by land via the Naimey-Zinder-Lake Chad route. Huntziger claimed that in order to build a large enough force for the undertaking, large amounts of military hardware and aircraft would need to be released by the Germans along with a sizeable number French prisoners of war from German POW camps. The Germans, however, argued that it could be done with less.

Details of the agreed-to plan were to include the sending of some 3,000 French troops to Dakar and then on to Naimey. If the British intervened, the French might retaliate by occupying Gambia, bomb targets in northern Nigeria and Gibraltar, and/or conduct air and naval attacks on Freetown. Also, the seaport of Takoradi, Gold Coast might be bombed because American aircraft, newly purchased by the British, were being assembled there. In Vichy, Premier Laval put pressure on the Germans to agree to make a statement at the time of the attack to the effect that the French Empire in Africa would remain intact after the war. This, of course, was an effort to thwart Italian and Spanish claims against French territory. Also at this time, Vichy upped its propaganda campaign against the Free French along with their continuing statements that the lost colonies would soon be recovered.

A tentative target date for the attack on Equatorial Africa was set for the spring of 1941. Planning went slowly, and neither side appeared to take the project seriously. Then, on December 13, 1940, Premier Laval, who had heartily backed the recovery of Equatorial Africa, was suddenly dismissed and arrested in a power struggle at Vichy. During this time, the 3,000 French troops arrived at Dakar where they were ordered to remain, awaiting further orders. The plan to attack Equatorial Africa, however, fell into limbo.

Laval's replacement, Admiral Jean Francois Darlan, was lukewarm toward the venture but allowed the planning to proceed. Darlan's approach toward French Africa was to take a more defensive stand than had been the policy of Laval. With Britain still holding out against Germany and Italy and showing no signs of capitulating, Darlan felt it prudent to avoid further confrontations with the British. Then, in early 1941, General Huntziger was suddenly killed in a plane crash and with this, Vichy lost interest and the plan to invade Equatorial Africa was shelved never to be revived.

THE VICHY FRENCH IN AFRICA COURT THE AMERICANS

Although President Roosevelt personally had little confidence in de Gaulle, he let various branches of the American government, and especially the American media, heap praise and admiration on the Free French leader and his organization. But the true facts were known to the Vichy leaders, some of whom believed that the Americans were still their secret friends. Among those Frenchmen were the two top leaders in French Africa, High Commissioner Weygand in North Africa and High Commissioner Boisson in West Africa. Both had ample lines of communications with the Americans because the American consulates continued to function in both North Africa and West Africa, and the American diplomats there were, generally, on friendly terms with the French leaders. Another American diplomat, Robert Murphy, the chief counsel at the American embassy in Vichy, had, with Vichy's blessing, free reign of French Africa and ready access to any of the top people. Murphy met several times with High Commissioner Weygand in North Africa, who secretly confided to Murphy that he might welcome an Allied invasion of North Africa in strength, and would do what he could to facilitate it. Weygand also told Murphy that he believed the United States would emerge from the war as the world's strongest power. Weygand discussed with Murphy some of France's most pressing problems, including the ongoing shortage of food, especially for the native population. He and Murphy would later be instrumental in creating a plan whereby American food would be shipped to French North Africa.

In West Africa, Murphy was in contact with High Commissioner Boisson at Dakar and met with him just before Christmas, 1940. Boisson made the surprising remarks to Murphy that, despite the attack on Dakar, he was still pro-

British and very much anti-German. Boisson stressed that if he had not stood up to the British and Free French the way he did, the Germans would have lost confidence in Vichy altogether and probably would have occupied unoccupied France and possibly Gibraltar. This was prophetic, because two years later when American and British forces invaded North Africa against relatively light French opposition, the Germans did occupy unoccupied France and Tunisia. Boisson went on to tell Murphy that the "self control" demonstrated by the French by not retaliating too strongly against the British was a clear sign that the French were sympathetic to the Allied cause. Boisson also assured Murphy that, reports to the contrary, German submarines were not using Dakar. Boisson admitted, however, that he had no love for de Gaulle, thinking him an opportunist and a renegade. During the course of the conversations, Boisson echoed Weygand's words that food was badly needed in French Africa and he would welcome American aid in this respect.

After a series of intense and closely spaced meetings with Weygand and Boisson, Murphy travelled to Washington in early January 1941 and met personally with President Roosevelt to report on what he had learned in French Africa. Murphy told the President that it was his belief that the French were in firm control in North and West Africa and would resist, even with force, any German attempt to establish themselves there. Murphy further reported that the French leaders in Africa feared that such an attempt by the Germans to gain concessions in French Africa might happen as early as the spring of 1941.

This information was shared with the British, and Churchill was impressed enough to send a secret message to Petain offering to send a strong British force to French North Africa if he, Petain, was willing to resume the war. Petain did not reply.

It was at this time that the British and Americans made a blunder. They allowed word to circulate in the media on Weygand's pro-Allied sympathies. Some reports speculated that Weygand was on the verge of breaking with Vichy. This compromised Weygand's relationship with Petain and doomed his future as High Commissioner in North Africa. But Petain played this to his advantage. He did not relieve Weygand of his position until German pressure became insurmountable. At that point, he used Weygand's removal to get something he wanted from the Germans. This game went on for months, and Weygand survived until November 1941.

NATIVES IN FRENCH COLONIES SUFFERING

By the end of 1940, the steadily increasing British blockade of the French colonies was beginning to have its effect. Export commodities of all sorts began to fill warehouses in the French colonies unable to be exported. As prices for such commodities fell, it was the native producers who were hit the hardest. Also, popular imports such as tea, vegetable oil, cotton cloth, sugar, and other items became scarce, and prices of these items rose. This, of course, is what the British wanted, because these conditions can bring on popular unrest, black markets, and even strikes. All the while, British and Free French propaganda made it known in the Vichy colonies that the economies in the neighboring British and Free French territories were robust and prosperous. The Allies wanted the natives to suffer, but not so much so that they starved or became destitute. The Allies certainly did not want things to deteriorate to the point where thousands of destitute natives began fleeing into Allied territory where they would become refugees for whom care was needed. Thus, the Allies were able to manipulate, to a great degree, the economic conditions in the French colonies through their blockade.

Actually, in Free French colonies, the economic conditions were not as robust as British and Free French propaganda claimed. Equatorial Africa had not been a self-supporting colonial federation before the Free French took over and it still was not afterwards. Through a secret agreement with de Gaulle, the British promised to buy palm oil, palm kernels, ground nuts, sesame seeds, and other products from Equatorial Africa at the same high prices they paid their own colonies. In return the Free French agreed not to sell these commodities to anyone else without British approval.

HITLER MEETS WITH VICHY LEADERS, FRANCO AND MUSSOLINI: AFRICA DISCUSSED

While de Gaulle was in Brazzaville setting up his fledgling government, Hitler journeyed through France to the Spanish border and then travelled on to Italy in his private train. He first met with Vichy Premier Laval at the resort town of Montoire in occupied France on October 22. Then he met with Generalissimo Franco on the French/Spanish border at Hendaye on October 23, then with Petain at Montoire on the 24th and, finally, with Mussolini in Florence on October 28. At all of these meetings Africa was discussed, but no major new decisions regarding Africa were made. With the French, Hitler restated his position that the final disposition on the French Empire would have to wait until after the war. With Franco, who was having second thoughts about joining the Axis now that Britain appeared to be holding her own, Hitler stated that he could not support Spanish claims in Africa, as long as Spain remained a nonbelligerent. With Mussolini, the big news for Hitler was that Italy, just that morning, had declared war on Greece and that Italian troops were invading that country from Italian-controlled Albania. This revelation was a complete surprise to Hitler, and it upset him considerably. He only learned the news en route to Florence through the Italian newspapers. Mussolini had not had the courtesy of telling him beforehand. This monumental event overshadowed all others at the meeting, but Hitler was able to keep his composure and conduct business in a rational manner. As for Africa, where the Italians had made some progress against the British in Egypt, Hitler urged Mussolini to press his advantage. As for Mussolini's demands in Africa, Hitler promised he would sign no peace treaty with France until those demands had been met. He called them "very modest."

HITLER DISCUSSES AFRICA WITH THE RUSSIANS

Two weeks later, on November 12–14, Hitler met with his other "Ally," the Soviet Union. The uneasy treaty of friendship between Germany and the Soviet Union of August 1939 was still in effect, but both sides had grown suspicious of each other more than ever. Nevertheless, Soviet Foreign Minister Vyacheslav Molotov came to Berlin to confer with Hitler and others, primarily on the Italian/Greek war in the Balkans. The Soviets, and the Czarists before them, had long considered the Balkans within the Russian sphere of influence and had considerable interest there. In these conversations, the subject of Africa was secondary but it was discussed when the Germans and Soviets defined their respective areas for future expansion. Hitler claimed that Germany's main area of expansion would be into the "central Africa region" and Italy was to be allotted north and northwest Africa. The Soviet's area of expansion was to be "in the direction of the Indian Ocean" and Japan was given the areas "south of the home islands and Manchukuo (Manchuria)."

All of this was a farce. As Hitler conversed politely with Molotov, his generals were actively planning the invasion and conquest of the Soviet Union which was to be launched within six months. Germany's true area of expansion was to be deep into the Soviet Union, not central Africa. Hitler knew full well that, with the invasion and conquest of the Soviet Union, he had every intention of putting Molotov and his Moscow comrades before a firing squad if he could get his hands on them.

Chapter 8
ALL AFRICA
(AUGUST 1940–JANUARY 1941)
THE OTHER CONFLICTS IN AFRICA

As the first episodes of the French civil war played out in West and Equatorial Africa, other events of major importance were happening on the dark continent.

ITALIANS INVADE EGYPT

By midsummer 1940, it had become apparent to Mussolini that Britain was not going to surrender quickly as France had done and that his goals in Africa would not be won without the use of force. Hitler was of the same opinion and urged Mussolini to attack from Libya and conquer Egypt and the Suez Canal as soon as possible. With the Suez Canal in Axis, hands the British fleet in the eastern Mediterranean would be forced to retreat into the Red Sea and eventually into the Indian Ocean, and the Italians could establish sea communications with their East African Empire. Later, a land link could be established by driving up the Nile River, through southern Egypt, The Sudan and into Abyssinia. Accordingly, Il Duce gathered his generals and began making plans to invade Egypt. A target date was set for early September 1940.

Before Mussolini committed himself to large-scale warfare in Africa, he wanted one more assurance from Hitler that Germany would support Italy's territorial gains once victory was achieved. To this end, Mussolini met with German Foreign Minister Joachim von Ribbentrop in Munich on June 19. At this meeting Mussolini restated Italy's territorial and economic goals in Africa, and von Ribbentrop, who spoke for Hitler, assured him that he had Germany's full support.

On July 7, Mussolini's Foreign Minister and son-in-law, Galeazzo Ciano, went to Berlin, restated Italy's demands, and heard from Hitler, himself, that Italy had Germany's full support. With these assurances, Mussolini was ready to fight.

On August 28, 1940, Italian planes bombed Port Said for the first time. This was the major British naval base at the northern end of the Suez Canal.

On September 9, the Italians made a diversionary attack by bombing Tel Aviv, Palestine to draw British attention away from their pending invasion. Then on September 11, five divisions of Italian troops, including the 1st and 2nd Libyan Divisions, under the command of Field Marshal Rodolfo Graziani, crossed the Egyptian border in force. The infantrymen and some 200 tanks advanced very slowly against light British resistance and took the Egyptian town of Sollum on the Mediterranean coast five miles beyond the border.

The defending British force, consisting of the 7th Armoured Division and the 4th Indian Division, fought

This photo, taken on September 12, 1940, shows the Libyan troops advancing into Egypt toward Sollum. Included in the Italian force of 220,000 men were 80,000 Libyans.

delaying actions as planned and then withdrew to their major defense line at Marsa Matruh.

On September 13, the Egyptian government declared a state of emergency, but refused, much to the dismay of the British, to declare war on Italy.

The Italian drive sped up somewhat after Sollum and on September 16, the Italians occupied the port town of Sidi Barrani, fifty miles inside Egypt, again against very light opposition. They were still seventy miles east of the British line at Marse Matruh. At Sidi Barrani, the Italians erected a victory monument and began digging in, a clear sign that their offensive was halted.

Several problems plagued the Italians, including a shortage of gasoline and spare parts for trucks. This was due, in part, to poor planning and to the British Navy's interdiction of Italian convoys crossing the Mediterranean.

On the afternoon of September 17, aircraft from the British carrier "Illustrious" made a very successful attack on Italian ships in the harbor at Benghazi, Libya. The destroyer "Borea" and two freighters were sunk. During the raid, the British aircraft laid mines in the approaches to the harbor and that night the Italian destroyer "Aquilone" and two patrol vessels hit the mines and sank.

On September 22, Mussolini spoke to the Italian people telling them that the war would not be a short one but that it would be good for Italy because only through a long war could Italy gain all she was due.

That same day, Egypt's Foreign Minister announced from Cairo that the Egyptian government would make good its previous pledges and defend its soil, and that the Egyptian Army would join with the British to expel the Italians. Martial law was declared throughout Egypt, but the government still refused to declare war on Italy. The next day the German government warned the Egyptians that, for their own good, they should break all ties with the British and not resist the Axis. The Egyptians, however, were committed.

The RAF in Egypt had been slow to react to the Italian invasion because they were still working feverishly to build up their strength. It was not until September 25 that the RAF made a serious attack on the Italians, which was the bombing of the Italian positions at Sidi Barrani and the bombing of Tobruk, Libya, the Italian's main port of supply.

The previous day a large British convoy docked at Port Said carrying 150 new modern British tanks. The convoy had left Britain on August 22 and sailed around the Cape of Good Hope. These tanks gave Wavell a slight advantage in the number of tanks over Graziani. Sending this number of tanks from England was quite a commitment for Churchill, because England was facing a possible cross-channel invasion by the Germans. Churchill gambled, though, that they would do more good in North Africa.

It was also at this time that the British and Free French debacle at Dakar was playing itself out.

On September 28, the British submarine "Pandora" sank the Italian freighter "Famiglia" off Benghazi. Then, as a part of the British buildup in North Africa the British Navy began, on September 29, a "sweep" of the eastern and central Mediterranean in preparation for an eastbound convoy that would leave Malta for Suez. This resulted in the British ships sinking one Italian destroyer, the "Arigliere," and two Torpedo boats on the night of October 11–12 as they tried to attack the convoy.

The Italians inadvertently contributed to the British cleansing of the eastern Mediterranean when, on October 6, the Italian sub "Tricero" accidently torpedoed and sank one of its own, the Italian sub "Gemma," off the Egyptian coast.

Meanwhile, in Egypt, there was a lull in the fighting with the Italians showing no signs of preparing for another advance. Mussolini pressed Graziani to attack but the latter, now knowing of the British superiority in tanks, used that as an excuse to delay. Graziani asked Mussolini for more tanks, but Mussolini did not have them to send. As a result, the Italian high command lapsed into a period of indecision.

The British welcomed the delay but the Germans did not. On October 4, 1940, Hitler and Mussolini met again at the Brenner Pass and Hitler pressured Mussolini to renew his drive into Egypt. He even offered to send some German forces to assist in the drive. Mussolini accepted the offer but, upon returning home, his top military leaders opposed it so he later told Hitler that he had changed his mind and would not accept the Fuhrer's offer at this time.

ITALY INVADES GREECE— EFFECTS NORTH AFRICA

On October 28, 1940, Italian forces suddenly, and without warning, invaded Greece from Italian-controlled Albania. This surprising news was received with mixed emotions by the British. For North Africa, it meant that the bulk of Italy's ground and air forces would be committed now to operations against Greece and not Egypt, thereby giving the British still more time to build their forces there. On the other hand, Greece was a British ally and would, most likely, need British help in the form of ground troops and air support. If this came to pass, some of those reinforcements would have to come from Egypt. In any case, the British could expect the lull in the ground fighting in North Africa to continue—which it did.

Two days after the Italians invaded Greece the Italian Air Force made a show of force in North Africa by bombing Cairo for the first time. This was intended to show the British that the Italian forces in North Africa were still formidable.

DECISION IN KHARTOUM

By coincidence, South African Prime Minister Smuts and British Secretary of State for War, Anthony Eden, were meeting in Khartoum, The Sudan on October 28, the day the Italians attacked Greece. The purpose of the meeting had been to discuss plans and preparations for the forthcoming British attack on Italian East Africa. The attack on Greece, quite understandably, dominated the agenda and made everyone's prearrangements for the meeting rather useless. Both Smuts and Eden could see that British forces might soon be needed in Greece and that some of them would have to come from Africa. It was therefore hastily agreed that a full-scale attack on Italian East Africa had to be postponed until the situation in Greece was clarified. It was further agreed that some limited military actions could be taken in East Africa by recapturing Gallabat and Kassala, both of which were inside The Sudan and had been taken by the Italians earlier. These operations were scheduled for November. Subsequently, the attacks on Gallabat and Kassala were approved by Wavell and passed on to General Sir William Platt, British commander in The Sudan, to execute.

South African troops in Kenya cheering Prime Minister Smuts during a speech.

Eden and Smuts also agreed that an attack on Kismayu, Italian Somaliland might be undertaken in January if all went well at Gallabat and Kassala. Kismayu was seen as a threat to the main British supply port of Mombasa, Kenya.

SMUTS NARROWLY ESCAPES DEATH

After the Khartoum meeting, Prime Minister Smuts departed for northern Kenya to visit the SAAF units stationed there. Early on the morning of October 31, Smuts and his party were on their way to Nanyuki to visit the 11th SAAF squadron. They were flying in two South African German-made Junker 86 bombers and escorted by two Hurricanes. En route the formation passed over the SAAF airfield at Archer's Post. Suddenly they were attacked by a squadron of SAAF Fury fighter planes that had risen from that airfield. There had been a communications foul-up, and the Archer's Post airfield had not been informed of Smuts' flight, but had been advised that an Italian air raid, that morning, was very possible. Smuts' planes, therefore, were thought to be enemy bombers. The Fury pilots saw the Hurricanes near the bombers but thought they were joining in the attack. The first Fury pilot to attack the bombers saw the South African markings on the Junkers at the last moment and broke off the attack without firing his guns. The next Fury pilot, though, did not see the markings and fired on the lead plane. Bullets went through the fuselage damaging some radio equipment but did not hit any one or any vital part of the plane. Moments after he had fired the second Fury pilot saw the markings and broke off his attack. From that point on no more shots were fired. Smuts' planes landed safely, but the Prime Minister was visibly shaken. He ordered that henceforth during the trip half of his staff was to fly in one plane and half in the other.

While in Kenya, Smuts wired Churchill suggesting that the Allied forces already there were sufficient to begin the attack into Italian Somaliland. He offered to send a second South African infantry brigade to Kenya as soon as sea transportation could be arranged. Churchill was aware that the 1st South African Division, a very powerful unit, was in training in South Africa and scheduled to go to Kenya after the first of the year. Both men knew that it was very possible to ship at least one brigade before that.

Churchill agreed and Smuts, upon his return, set in motion plans to transfer the 3rd Union Brigade to Kenya as soon as possible.

BRITISH NOT READY IN KENYA

General Sir Alan Cunningham, British commander in Kenya, was still reluctant to launch a major attack into Italian Somaliland because of the weather—the rainy season did not end until spring—plus he wanted still more troops. Specifically, he requested use of the two newly-formed West African Brigades, which were still in training, sent to him to further strengthen his force. Wavell tended to agree with Cunningham so Churchill backed down and accepted another delay in East Africa.

BRITISH ATTACK AT SEA

While the British were not yet strong enough to attack the Italians on the ground in Egypt, their eastern Mediterranean fleet was formidable and was able to carry the war to the enemy at sea.

On November 4, the British sub "Tetrarch" operating off Tripoli, sank an Italian freighter, then a second one on the 5th.

On the night of November 11/12, the British carried out one of the most successful naval operation of the war and certainly the greatest British naval victory in the war to date. On that night, planes from the British aircraft carrier Illustrious made a surprise attack on the Italian warships anchored in the Italian naval base at Taranto in the heel of Italy. British torpedo planes came in low over the harbor in several waves and launched their deadly "fish" into the anchored warships. The Italian antiaircraft defenses were slow to react for the first crucial minutes of the attack giving the British planes time to get close to the ships and score hit after hit on the Italian ships. When it was over, the Italian battleship "Conte de Cavour" was laying at the bottom of the harbor; a second battleship, "Caio Duilio," had been badly damaged and beached, and a third battleship, one of the newest in the Italian Navy, "Littorio," was badly damaged with three torpedo hits. With three of their battleships out of action the number of battleships in the Italian Navy was cut in half. It was a severe blow to Italy's ability to now control the Mediterranean, and it meant that North Africa-bound convoys would be all the more vulnerable to British attack. For the British, the brilliant attack cost them only two aircraft.

Five weeks later, on December 13, the Italians got a measure of revenge when the Italian submarine "Neghelli" sank the British light cruiser "Coventry" off the Egyptian coast and again on December 20 when the Italian sub "Serpente" torpedoed the British destroyer "Hyperion" 24 miles east of Cap Bon, Tunisia.

On January 10, 1941, the Italians scored again when the British destroyer "Gallant" hit a mine 120 miles west of Malta and sank.

But the Italians were taking their licks too. Between January 7 and 30, British submarines sank five Italian freighters making their way to Libya.

GERMANY THREATENS IN THE WEST. SETS NEW GOALS IN AFRICA.

While the Italians were, at least in theory, settling matters in the eastern Mediterranean, in Egypt, and in Greece, the Germans acted in the western Mediterranean. The Axis goal there was to occupy or neutralize the British bastion of Gibraltar, close the western entrance of the Mediterranean to the Allies, and establish a German presence in Morocco and down the Atlantic coast. This would be the forerunner to a deeper German leap into Africa at a later date.

In Berlin, German planners had been working for some time on Germany's ultimate goals in Africa. When the glorious day arrived that Britain was defeated and the Mediterranean secured, the Nazi planners saw no reason to remain tied to the previously stated demands for the return of Germany's former colonial empire. They would be in a position to take more. Furthermore, by seeking expansion in Africa—whether it happened or not—the Nazis had a convenient cover to convince their erstwhile Ally, the Soviet Union, that Germany had satisfied its need to expand eastward and was now looking to Africa for the final phase of its conquests.

THE BIELFELD PLAN

An outline of German goals had been made in late May 1940 by H. Claudius, private secretary to German Foreign Minister von Ribbentrop. That outline was approved by Hitler and passed on to a team of experts in the German Foreign Ministry, headed by H. Bielfeld, to work out the details. On November 6, 1940, Bielfeld's team presented their proposal to the Chancellory as to what the ultimate German goals in Africa should be. Fundamentally, Germany was to acquire its long-sought goal of establishing "Mittel Afrika" but on a much grander scale. Bielfeld's plan called for the following African colonies to come under direct Germany control: Togo, Dahomey, Gold Coast, Nigeria, southern Niger, southern Chad as far north as 15 degrees north latitude, The Cameroons, French Equatorial Africa, Belgian Congo, Rwanda-Urundi, Tanganyika, Uganda, Kenya, Northern Rhodesia, Southern Rhodesia, Nyasaland, and South West Africa.

Furthermore, Bielfeld's plan called for German naval and air bases to be established around the African continent at Dakar, Conakry, Freetown, Duala, Pointe-Noire, Boma, Zanzibar, Dar es Salaam, Mombasa-Kilindi, and Diego Suarez. German bases would be acquired on the islands surrounding Africa at Fernando Poo, Sao Tomas, St. Helena, Ascension, Pemba, the Comores, the Seychelles, and Mauritius.

Much of this could be accomplished before the end of hostilities by German advances overland through the Spanish and Vichy-controlled colonies in Africa. The remainder would be acquired at the peace table.

Bielfeld's plan went on to stress that in the postwar era, the resources and markets of a German-dominated Africa should be shared with an Axis-dominated Europe for the good of the entire Eurafrican region. All this would, of course, be operated by European monopolies under German control.

As for the African people, Nazi racial theory had already established that they were peasants by nature and inferior to whites in general and especially inferior to Aryan whites. Because of this natural order of things, Bielfeld declared that Africans would become permanent colonial subjects, and with time and proper racial management, would come to accept their lot. Industrial areas and the larger cities in German-dominated Africa would be basically all-white with the blacks living in preserves at the outskirts of town, commuting to and from their work places. Furthermore, the black work force could be shifted about from preserve to preserve to satisfy changing labor needs. All blacks, sixteen years and older, would be required to work and carry on their person a work record-book (Arbeitsbuch), as was already being done in occupied Europe.

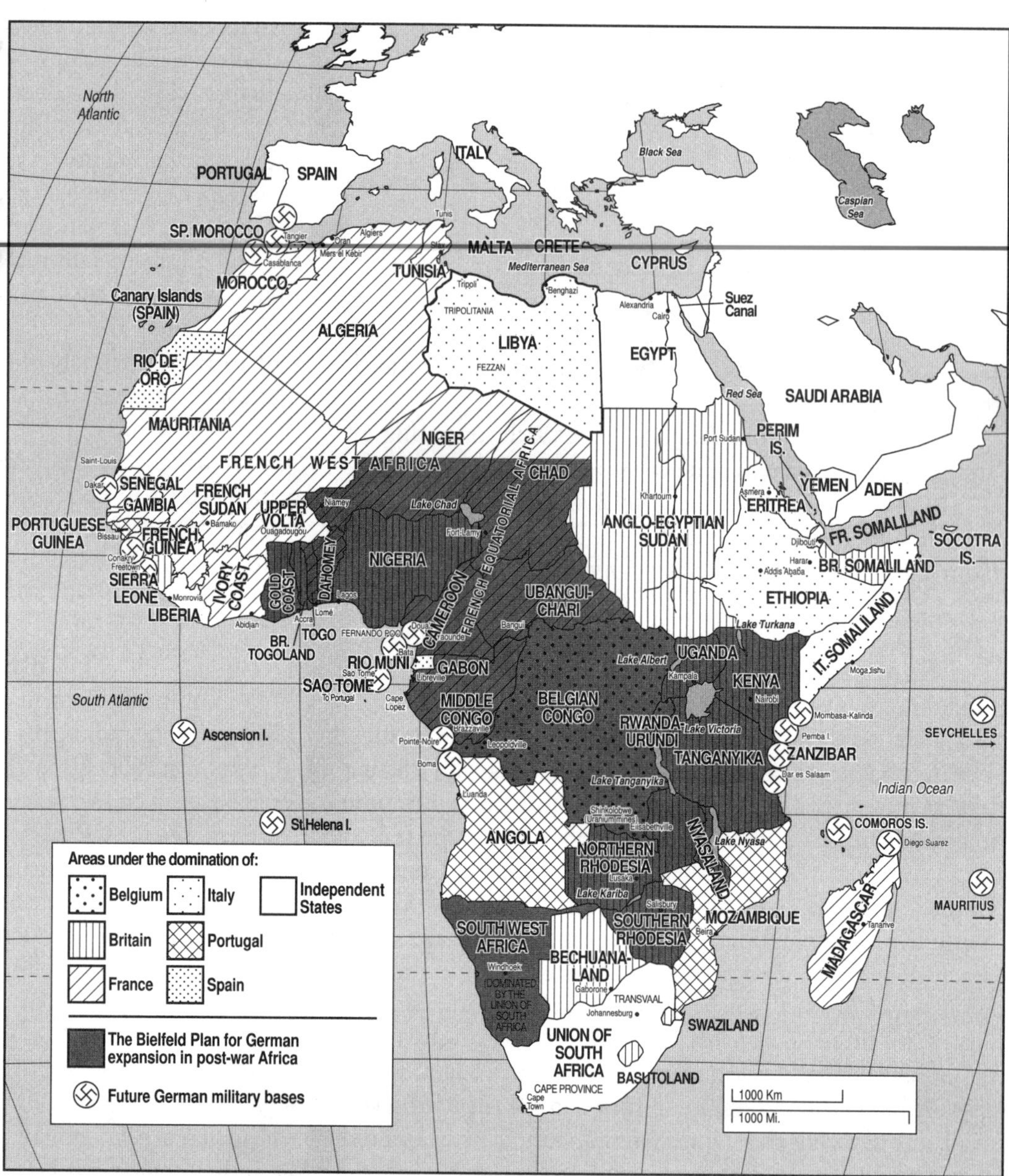

The Bielfeld plan for German expansion in postwar Africa.

Furthermore, and according to the Bielfeld Plan, the need was seen to preserve the purity of the white race in a German-dominated Africa. To this end, a bill was introduced into the Reichstag in September 1940 to amend the Nuremburg racial laws. The amendment stipulated that it would be a criminal offense for blacks to engage in sexual intercourse with whites, and that guilty blacks would be sentenced to harsh punishments, including death. Whites, on the other hand, would be fined or transferred to another location.

The Arab people of Africa, considered whites, would fall into social and economic categories well above the blacks but below the Europeans. And, of course, there would be no Jews in a German-dominated Africa.

Bielfeld's plan was coordinated with the other branches of the Nazi government in Berlin and each, in turn, submitted its own report to the Fuhrer on the role it would play in the future German-dominated Africa.

OKW (Obercommando der Wehrmacht—Supreme Command of the German Armed Forces) was already working on a plan to establish a colonial Wehrmacht command which would answer directly to OKW in Berlin. Training programs had already been created in all branches of the military services for officers who were to serve in the colonies. Likewise, the SS had established a colonial command structure in which the Waffen SS (SS Armed Forces) would play a major role.

Even the German police were preparing for the return to the colonies, and had established two training schools for future colonial police administrators. They were located at Oranienburg and Vienna. Graduates were sent for field training to Rome and North Africa to work with Italian police, who had considerable experience in the field of colonial police work.

Finally, Bielfeld suggested a slogan be adapted to express the ultimate aim of this great scheme: "Eurafrica for the Europeans."

All this, of course, presupposed the eventual defeat of Britain and the elimination of the Free French and the other lesser Allies. To bring the Bielfeld Plan to fruition, it was imperative to gain Spain's cooperation. Franco, it must be remembered, told Hitler at Hendaye in late October that Spain was not ready to enter the war. But Hitler and many of his advisers were of the opinion that once a German victory became certain, Spain would join in the fray and cooperate with Germany in order to gain some of the spoils of war.

To this end, and with Bielfeld's report being a large part of the equation, Hitler issued Directive #18 on November 12, 1940, ordering that political steps be taken to gain Spain's future cooperation for German troops to march through Spain, conquer Gibraltar, and advance into Morocco. This was known as "Operation Felix." To keep Franco well informed, and stroke his ego at the same time, Hitler sent one of his top military men, and one of the best-informed men in Germany, Admiral Wilhelm Canaris, to Madrid as Germany's special envoy to Spain. Canaris was head of the Abwehr (German Armed Forced Intelligence Organization) and spoke fluent Spanish.

The Germans could foresee, of course, that "Operation Felix" would very likely provoke a British reaction against Spain, directed at the Spanish-controlled Atlantic islands. Directive #18, therefore, called for joint German and Spanish military efforts to protect those islands.

As for Gibraltar, the capture of "The Rock" would be primarily a German military undertaking with minimal Spanish cooperation. Later, after the final German victory, Gibraltar would be returned to Spain.

Concurrently with the attack on Gibraltar, other German forces would move into southern Spain and Spanish Morocco where German bases would be established on both sides of the Strait of Gibraltar. Then, with Vichy's cooperation, German forces would move into French Morocco and establish strong naval and air bases down the Atlantic coast as far as Dakar.

In preparation of the assault on Gibraltar, a selected force of German mountain troops was ordered to begin training in the Alps at Jura and a group of fifty German military officers was ordered to Spain to coordinate military activities with the Spaniards. The German Navy was ordered to prepare plans to occupy and defend the Canary Islands, the Cape Verde Islands, and possibly the Portuguese-controlled Azores.

Portugal, of course, had to be considered and Hitler asked the German Navy to study Portugal's likely reaction to "Operation Felix." The Navy soon reported that Portugal wanted desperately to remain neutral and that it was in Germany's best interest that she remain so. Any German threat to Portugal might provoke a British reaction to occupy the Azores and/or Angola and possibly the Cape Verde Islands. It was best then not to threaten Portugal in any way.

The main threat to Portugal's neutrality, as the Germans saw it, would come from a British invasion of Spain through Portugal, which was possible, but not likely. Hitler suggested that at the time Germany occupied the Cape Verde Islands, which would represent Germany's greatest threat to the British position in the central Atlantic, that three German divisions might be sent to the Spanish/Portuguese border to discourage a British invasion via Portugal as well as keep the Portuguese quiescent.

HITLER'S TIMETABLE FOR VICTORY

By late November 1940, Hitler felt he had a timetable that would bring about a total Axis victory and the end of the war. That timetable was:

1. December 1940–January 1941: Activate "Operation Felix" and close the western entrance to the Mediterranean. If the Spaniards refused to cooperate, the entrance could still be closed temporarily by German air and naval forces carrying out a prolonged siege of Gibraltar.
2. By late March 1941: Send the Italians sufficient military aid to defeat the Allies in the Balkans and in Libya so that they could regain the initiative there and advance on the Suez Canal from the west.
3. Early May 1941: Invade the Soviet Union and conquer it by the end of the year.
4. Winter 1941–42: From the Caucasus, or through Turkey, or both, German troops would invade the Middle East, secure the Persian Gulf oil fields and drive on Suez from the east to secure a linkup with the Italians somewhere in Egypt. With both entrances to the Mediterranean Sea in Axis hands, the British Navy would flee the area and the remaining British strongholds, such as Malta and Cyprus, could be dealt with at the convenience of the Axis powers.
5. After consolidating their gains in North Africa, the Axis allies would begin to carry out the Bielfeld Plan. German and Italian forces would drive up the Nile Valley, march through The Sudan and make land contact with Italian East Africa. The Italian Navy would take control of the Red Sea, land Axis troops in Yemen, and invade and conquer Aden. The British-held island of Perim would be put under siege until it was starved into surrendering.
6. Following this, German troops, possibly with Italian forces in support and operating from Italian East Africa, would invade Kenya, Uganda, recapture the former German colonies of Tanganyika, Rwanda and Urundi and advance westward into the Belgian Congo and southward into the Rhodesias. Meanwhile, from French West Africa, German troops would invade the British colonies there, recapture the lost German colonies of Togo and Cameroon, and retake French Equatorial Africa from the Free French. From French Equatorial Africa, German troops would invade the Belgian Congo from the east

and eventually link up, somewhere within the Belgian Congo, with the western force driving in from Kenya.
7. Proclaim the German Reich reconstituted and whole and sue for peace.

BRITISH COUNTERATTACK IN NORTH AFRICA

In the Balkans, the Italian invasion of Greece turned into a disaster for the Italians. In early November 1940, the Greeks received significant help from the British when the RAF began flying combat missions in Greece to support the Greek ground troops, and in mid-November the Greeks launched a powerful counterattack. It was extremely successful and decimated some of the Italian Army's best divisions, thus halting the Italian advance. The Greeks pressed their attacks and by early December the Italians were forced to retreat back into Albania with Greek forces in close pursuit. Rome had no choice but to send in massive reinforcements to halt the Greek advance and save Albania.

For the British in Egypt the victories in the Balkans were a most welcome turn of events. It meant that there would be virtually no Italian reinforcements available now for North Africa and that the British, whose forces had been steadily increasing, had the initiative. They could count on the fact that the Italian troops in North Africa were demoralized by the events in Greece and that their strength would steadily decline if they were forced to do battle with little or no hope of receiving reinforcements.

Taking into account all of these factors, General Sir Archibald Wavell decided to go on the offensive and invade Libya. He chose General Sir Richard O'Connor as field commander. Wavell's plan and choice of commander had Churchill's full approval. During the third week in November the Royal Air Force (RAF) began a series of heavy air attacks on Italian ports, supply dumps, and lines of communication. Targets at Benghazi, Berka and Benina in Libya werehit. On November 24, the Italian Air Force struck back and bombed the British naval base at Alexandria, Egypt.

A DECISION IN BERLIN AND AN ATTACK IN EGYPT

On December 8, 1940, Mussolini was forced to swallow a bitter pill and ask Hitler for military help in the Balkans. The Fuhrer, who was deep into the planning stages of the forthcoming attack on the Soviet Union, had little choice but to agree. He could not risk having his strongest ally tottering on the verge of defeat and strong enemy forces in the Balkans on his right flank, when the greater part of the German armed forces plunged into the Soviet Union.

That same day Hitler received more distressing news. Admiral Canaris reported from Madrid that, due to the Italian setbacks in the Balkans and North Africa, Franco was more determined than ever to keep Spain neutral. This meant that "Operation Felix," the German march through Spain and into Morocco, was not likely to happen soon. The Fuhrer's grandiose plans for Africa were falling apart.

Some of the 38,000 Italian soldiers captured during their retreat from Egypt. Columns of Italian POWs would become a common sight in Africa in the months to come.

On the morning of December 9, the British attacked the Italian defenses in Egypt. Tanks of the 7th Armoured Division, recently formed in Egypt, and the Indian 4th Division smashed into the Italian line at Sidi Barrani, taking the Italian defenders completely by surprise. A hole was opened in the Italian line and within two hours the British tanks had encircled the main Italian camp at Nibeiwa. In the encirclement, one of the Italian commanders, General Maletti, was killed while still in his pajamas. The Italian defenses crumbled and they began a disorderly retreat to their reserve defenses at Sollum and Sidi Omar. In the four-day retreat that followed, four Italian divisions were destroyed, some 38,000 Italian troops captured (including four generals). Also captured were 73 Italian tanks, 237 artillery pieces, and over 1,000 trucks. British Army losses were 624 dead.

Overhead the RAF had gained air superiority and off the coast the British Navy actively patrolled the central Mediterranean preventing any reinforcements getting to the Italians by sea.

On December 11, the British Navy shelled the Italian defense at Sollum to soften them up as the British pressed forward. Some Italian units regained their cohesiveness in the Sidi Omar and Fort Capuzzo areas and put up stubborn defenses. But, in every case, the British prevailed, and by December 17 the Italian forces were retreating en masse back into Libya and to their next defense line at Bardia.

On December 19, 1940, Field Marshal Pietro Badoglio, the Italian Chief of Staff, resigned in disgrace. He was replaced by General Count Ugo Cavallero, who favored asking the Germans immediately for military assistance.

HITLER TRIES TO FORCE FRANCO'S HAND

Despite Franco's reticence, Hitler still hoped to close off the western Mediterranean to the British and establish German forces in Morocco. This would be of great help to the Italians in the eastern Mediterranean.

On December 12, Hitler, without warning, informed Franco that a German attack on Gibraltar would begin on January 10, 1941. Franco was shocked and angry that he had not been consulted. He vehemently refused to cooperate with such an attack, citing that the British would most certainly take countermeasures against the Canary Islands. Hitler's bluff did not work. He was forced to back down and accept the fact that without Franco's cooperation, a German initiative in the western Mediterranean would not likely succeed. There was no German attack on Gibraltar nor did they march into Morocco.

BRITISH RESUME THEIR ATTACK IN LIBYA

After a brief lull the British resumed their attack in North Africa. The Italian defenses at Bardia were pounded for two days, January 1 and 2, 1941, by the RAF and the British Navy. On January 3, the British Army resumed its ground attack, now led by the 6th Australian Division which had arrived and replaced the 4th Indian Division. The latter had been withdrawn, rested, and replenished and was to be sent off to southern Sudan in December, where it would take part in the coming British offensive against Italian East Africa.

The Australians, like the Indians before them, succeeded in breaking through the Italian defenses and took 8,000 Italian POWs the first day. They resumed their attack on January 4, and on the 5th captured Bardia. Another 40,000 Italian POWs were taken along with 129 tanks, 462 artillery pieces, and 700 trucks. The remnants of the Italian force retreated to Tobruk. Graziani's forces in Libya were now about half of what they had been in December. Wavell was in a position to press his advantage and possibly occupy all of Libya.

Wavell's Australians pursued Graziani's retreating force to the outskirts of Tobruk and paused to regroup and bring up supplies.

Meanwhile, Wavell's headquarters received word from London that German intervention in the Balkans was imminent and the British would have to send significant military aid to Greece to meet the threat. Some of that aid would come from Wavell's forces in North Africa. To this end, Wavell and Air Marshall Sir Arthur Longmore were ordered to go to Athens and discuss Greece's military needs with Greek Premier Joannes Metaxas and the Greek military Commander-in-Chief General Alexander Papagos. This they did on January 14/15, 1941. The grateful Greeks accepted whatever the British could offer but insisted that British forces delay coming to Greece for fear of provoking the situation, because German forces had not, as yet, appeared in Albania. It was known that German forces were in Bulgaria, Greece's neighbor to the north, and that the German government was approaching Yugoslavia to allow the passage of German forces through that country into Albania.

In the meantime, Wavell's troops in North Africa were still his to use against the Italians in Libya, but this was only temporary.

GERMANS IN THE MEDITERRANEAN. IMMEDIATE RESULTS FOR NORTH AFRICA

On January 10, 1941, a new development occurred in the Mediterranean when German aircraft, flying out of Sicily, attacked a strong British Naval force escorting a convoy from Gibraltar to Malta. This was the first appearance of German aircraft in the Mediterranean. The convoy was escorted by some of the most valuable British ships in the Mediterranean. The German planes were able to score several hits on the British aircraft carrier Illustrious making her unusable. She had to withdraw from the Mediterranean and was eventually sent to the United States for repairs. Also, the British cruiser "Southampton" and a destroyer were sunk, and the British cruiser "Gloucester," was damaged by the German air attacks. The Convoy got through to Malta but the British battle fleet had been substantially reduced. On January 16, the German planes damaged the Australian cruiser "Perth" at Malta putting her out of action. On January 30, German planes crossed the Mediterranean to the North African shore and sank the British minesweeper "Huntley" only thirty miles west of Marsa Matruh, Egypt. The end result of the arrival of the German planes in the Mediterranean and the subsequent losses to the British fleet was that Italian convoys could now get through more easily to reinforce the Italian troops in Libya battling Wavell's forces.

Furthermore, German aircraft began operating out of the Italian-owned Dodecanese Islands in the Aegean Sea. These planes posed a threat to the entire eastern Mediterranean, including Egypt and the Suez Canal.

Clearly, the balance of power in the Mediterranean was changing and the British initiative in North Africa was being challenged.

Furthermore, and unknown to the British, Hitler made the decision to send German forces to Libya in an effort to prevent an Axis defeat there. For this task, he had selected the well-equipped and experienced 15th Armored Division under the command of General Irwin Rommel. Hitler had only to convince Mussolini to bury some more of his pride and accept the German troops in North Africa. Hitler did this when he and Mussolini met at Berchtesgaden on January 19/20, 1941. At the meeting, Hitler increased Rommel's force to two divisions and set an arrival date in Libya of early April 1941.

EAST AFRICA

The British made no secret of the buildup of their forces all around Italian East Africa. It was a secret, however, as to how, when, and where those forces would be utilized. All indications pointed to a British invasion of the Italian colonies in the near future and the Italians were well aware of it, but there was little they could do. Without the possibility of receiving significant reinforcements, they could not hope to mount a preemptive strike nor do anything effective to stop the British buildup. Their only option was to wait and hope that the Italian forces in Egypt would be successful and that a secure land or water link for supplies could be established across The Sudan or down the Red Sea. The Italian invasion of Egypt in September gave the Italians in East Africa hope, but those hopes were dashed by the British offensive into Libya in December and January. The Italian setback in the Balkans was yet another blow to the East African Italians, and by January 1941, the morale of both the troops and settlers was at an all-time low.

THE BRITISH PLAN FOR EAST AFRICA

The British were, by no means, unanimous on the decision to invade Italian East Africa. Some leaders in London advised that it might be best to simply let the Italians in East Africa wither on the vine. They argued that if the invasion failed and the British forces were defeated, the way would be clear for the Italians to march north through The Sudan and threaten Egypt and the Suez Canal from the south. This argument did not prevail, however, and the British devised a plan to invade the Italian colonies from both the north and the south in a giant pincers movement. This would be very similar to the tactic the Italians used in 1935–36 to conquer Ethiopia.

Most of the British units used would be from colonial and Commonwealth forces and a target date was set for January 1941. This date, as stated above, was postponed in late October by Smuts and Eden at Khartoum as a result of the Italian invasion of Greece.

On December 2, 1940, General Wavell met with his East African commanders, General Sir William Platt who had commanded in The Sudan since 1939, and recently promoted General Sir Alan Cunningham, who commanded in Kenya. The purpose was to determine the time and tactics for the forthcoming invasion of Italian East Africa. Because of Italy's difficulties in both Greece and North Africa, and the rapid buildup of Allied forces in East Africa, Wavell, Platt, and Cunningham agreed that the original launch date of January 1941 could be met. It was decided that Platt's forces would launch the initial attack, in force, at Kassala and advance into Eritrea. At the same time, Cunningham would use a mobile force to create a diversionary attack into southern Abyssinia from Kenya. Cunningham's force would also take Moyale, on the border, advance along the line Kolbio-Dif and then halt. Then, in May or June, after the seasonal rains had ended in the south, Cunningham would launch a major attack into southern Italian Somaliland from Kenya with Kismayu as the first major objective. Soon afterwards, Platt's forces would turn south from Eritrea and invade northern Abyssinia. From then on, the giant pincer operation from the south and north would continue until they met somewhere inside Abyssinia.

"RIBBON WARFARE"

The type of warfare the British intended to conduct was called "ribbon warfare" because most of the planned advanced would follow existing roads and trails with the main force being strung out in long columns like a ribbon. The British columns would have one strong unit in the lead, usually with armored cars, and the rest of the force would follow closely behind ready to deploy quickly to the flanks when the enemy was encountered. This tactic was dictated by the terrain of East Africa which was mountainous in many places and desert-like in others and crisscrossed by ridges, wet and dry rivers, and gullies. In many area, too, the flat lands were strewn with large boulders and rocks or heavy underbrush. This made the operation of wheeled vehicles difficult to impossible in many places. Tanks might operate in some of these places, but the British forces in East Africa had few tanks.

"Ribbon warfare" gives an advantage to the defender because he can predict the directions from which the enemy will approach and probably attack. The defender, therefore, can pick points of ambush and defensive positions where wheeled vehicles cannot easily operate off the road. This, in turn, forces the attackers to attack on foot without the close support of armored cars and wheeled artillery pieces. The Italians would take advantage of this time-and-again.

In contrast, the warfare in North Africa was considerably different. There the Mediterranean coastal plain was relatively flat, sandy, and hard from Suez to the Tunisian border with few rivers and almost no mountains. This was tank country and in North Africa it was a "tank war" not a "ribbon war."

MILITARY ACTIONS IN EAST AFRICA IN LATE 1940

Soon after Italy went to war in June 1940, Italian forces crossed into both Kenya and The Sudan and occupied several border towns. By late 1940, they still held those towns. In early September 1940, they had penetrated even deeper into northern Kenya to occupy the village of Buna, twenty miles south of Moyale. The King's African Rifles (KAR) had held the town but voluntarily evacuated it because the roads leading to it from the south made it very difficult to bring up supplies. When the KAR moved out, the Italians simply moved in.

During these months there were cross-border skirmishes all around the periphery of Italian East Africa. Much of the action was in Kenya where the British had organized several bands of exiled Somalis into raiding parties who specialized in raiding into Italian Somaliland from Kenya and harassing the Bande units that the Italians used to patrol the border.

One of the bigger cross-border raids came on September 18/19, 1940, when newly-arrived Gold Coast units, serving with the KAR and assisted by the SAAF, raided Italian positions at El Wak on the Kenya/Italian Somaliland border. The Gold Coasters killed fifty of the enemy, captured 120 more, and then withdrew.

The RAF and SAAF were also active during the latter months of 1940, raiding targets throughout Italian East Africa. Almost daily, one or more targets were attacked. The Italian Air Force responded, but not as frequently, by attacking targets in Kenya, The Sudan, and Aden. Italian planes also attacked Allied convoys sailing up and down the Red Sea and in the Gulf of Aden.

In early October 1940, the British began an intensive campaign to drop propaganda leaflets all over Italian East Africa. They were written in Italian, Amharic, Arabic, and Somali and gave the war news in general and told the people about the Italian military weaknesses and the British strengths. The Ethiopians were told that Haile Selassie was alive and well and preparing to return with a new British-equipped Army. A typical line in the pamphlets read "Why should you die for the Italians? We bring you a message from your brother soldiers who have already deserted—They want you to know that they have been well-treated, and have been given hot meals, cigarettes and dry warm housing."

The leaflet campaign was very effective. Many native soldiers deserted and made their way into Kenya and The Sudan. With them came stories of shortages of food and clothing and some units riddled with disease. This information was fed back to the people in leaflets dropped later. The leaflet program proved to be so successful that the British kept it up all through the coming campaign in 1941.

During this time the Italian Air Force made one very ambitious attempt to bomb the oil facilities on the British Protectorate of Bahrain Island, over 800 miles to the north, in the Persian Gulf. The Italian navigators did a poor job, however, and the Italian planes bombed oil facilities not only on Bahrain but also in neutral Saudi Arabia.

On the night of October 18, 1940, the British added a new dimension to the war in East Africa by bombing at night. The first target was Mogadishu, the capital of Italian Somaliland. The Italian Air Force had no night fighters in its inventory so they could not respond effectively against such attacks. Most of the planes in the Italian Air Force were relics of the First East African War of 1935–36.

In late October, an Italian ground force of 1,500 men crossed the border into The Sudan and advanced along the eastern shore of the Blue Nile toward Rosieres some fifty miles beyond the border. As they approached Rosieres units of the Sudan Defense Force met them and attempted to block their advance. RAF and SAAF aircraft went on the attack and succeeded in destroying much of the Italians' supply column, which forced the invaders to halt their advance. After the British planes departed, Italian planes appeared, bombed Rosieres and gave the invading force some air cover as they slowly withdrew back into Abyssinia.

THE BUILDUP OF BRITISH FORCES IN EAST AFRICA

The buildup of British forces in East Africa was more rapid in Kenya than elsewhere. By August 1940, Churchill thought there were too many British troops in Kenya, and considered moving some of them to Egypt and other locations, but this did not happen and the British forces in Kenya continued to grow.

The forces in Kenya consisted of the 11th (KAR) and 12th (KAR) infantry divisions, each consisting of one East African and one West African Brigade, and the 1st South African Infantry Brigade which had arrived in July. These troops were stationed in a defense line in northern Kenya, some miles away from the border in positions that could be easily defended and adequately supplied, considering the primitive state of the roads in that part of the country. Also operating in northern Kenya was a large contingent of road-builders, mainly black Pioneers, from South Africa. They worked vigorously to improve the road system in northern Kenya in preparation for the coming attack on the Italians.

To the rear were several mobile units serving as reserves. Front line units were also brought back to the rear from time to time for rest and recuperation (R & R) and served as ready reserves. Beyond the British front in northern Kenya and the border were mine fields and tank traps. This no-man's-land was actively patrolled by small KAR and South African units trekking back and forth to the border. There were also in the area several British-formed, highly mobile Somali Irregular Companies comprised of Somali refugees and dissidents who worked closely with the KAR. These units were equipped with small arms and roamed the area at will and reported any irregularities.

The British–made Hawker Hurricane fighter, at 300 mph top speed, with good maneuverability and eight machine guns was one of the best fighters planes in the war.

The Italians, at times, sent Bande units into the Kenyan no-man's-land to skirmish with the patrols and Somali Irregulars in an effort to prevent the British from acquiring complete dominance there.

Meanwhile in Kenya, other local units were being formed and trained by the British and upon completion of their training were sent to the north and placed in the defense line. The British found plenty of recruits for these units among Kenyan natives as well as Ethiopian and Somali refugees and deserters. The large Turkana Tribe, which had traditionally been very loyal to the British, was one of the most reliable sources for manpower.

In South Africa, the 1st South African Division was in training and scheduled to arrive in Kenya in January 1941.

In late October 1940, the 3rd SAAF Squadron arrived in Kenya from South Africa with nine new British-made Hurricane fighter planes. This brought the total Hurricane count in Kenya to sixteen. The Hurricane was one of the most modern fighter planes of the day and the Italians had nothing in East Africa to match it.

These sixteen planes tipped the balance of air power in the region very substantially in favor of the SAAF. The Hurricanes went to work at once and in almost every encounter succeeded in shooting down Italian planes. The Italian Air Force in East Africa was, therefore, forced to go on the defensive. The appearance of the Hurricanes was not the only reason for this. By now the Italian Air Force had used up about half its supply of aviation fuel. They began adding alcohol to the fuel, but the fuel mixture did not work well in the Italians' newer engines, so planes with those engines had to continue using pure aviation fuel. The mixture worked satisfactorily in the older engines so the Italians received some benefit from the practice.

All sixteen of the Hurricanes operated with the SAAF in Kenya and therefore freed up some of the older SAAF planes and crews to be sent to The Sudan to work with the RAF there.

From London came pressures on General Cunningham to use his growing forces in Kenya to begin, at least, a modest advance into southern Italian Somaliland in the direction of Kismayu. Cunningham objected on several accounts saying that he was not quite ready for such an attack and that the rainy season, which lasted through November and December, would make movement very difficult, especially in the area between the Juba and Tana Rivers in Italian Somaliland where there were virtually no roads. Cunningham wanted to wait until after the first of the year, as planned. It was his argument that would prevail.

The Duke of Aosta, Viceroy of Italian East Africa and Commander-in-Chief of the Italian armed forces, watched the British buildup carefully and concluded that the British would strike first in the north into Eritrea and northern Abyssinia. As a result, he stationed more than half of his force in the north. This, of course, weakened his defenses in the south and was a considerable risk because if he was wrong and the British struck in the south it would take him at least ten days to transfer significant numbers of troops from the north to the south.

BRITISH LIMITED ATTACK FROM THE SUDAN ON GALLABAT

When the decision was made in Khartoum by Smuts and Eden on October 28 to postpone the general attack on Italian East Africa in favor of a more limited campaign, the British forces in The Sudan were ready. They had been planning for a large-scale attack and now they were called upon to carry out a much more limited operation.

In late October, units of the RAF and SAAF moved to forward fields in southern Sudan and began intensive bombing of airfields, fuel storage facilities, railroads, bridges, army facilities, troop concentrations, and other targets in the northern part of Italian East Africa. Eritrea, the Italian's most-developed colony, was heaviest hit. The objective was to weaken the Italians prior to the planned attack on Gallabat and Kassala, the gateways to northern Italian East Africa. Gallabat was on the road to Addis Ababa, the capital of Abyssinia, and Kassala was on the road to Asmara, the capital of Eritrea.

The Italians could see the attacks coming and began sending more ground troops to both areas. The British saw this move and changed their air objective to interdict the Italian truck convoys. This was very successful. On October 31 and November 1, British planes decimated several large truck convoys. Within the next few days, news of the destruction of the truck convoys was spread all over Italian East Africa by leaflets.

The Italians, though, were able to get two infantry battalions and half of a machine-gun battalion to Metemma, the town on the Italian side of the border opposite Gallabat. Most of the Italian troops were dependable Eritrean regulars.

Men of the 1st Essex regiment at Metemma.

overhead, the slow but nimble bi-planes fought each other in twisting and turning aerial dog fights. It was a scene right out of World War I. But it was all too much for the British. The men of the Garwahl Rifles withdrew to the safety of the elephant grass.

Meanwhile, word came from the south that the 1st Essex attack at Metemma started four hours late because the British troops had been slowed by the rough and rocky terrain. When it did begin, the 1st Essex came under wilting defensive fire from the Eritrean defenders and retreated in disorder. At both Gallabat and Metemma it was a victory for the Italians. Slim gathered the remnants of his force and withdrew around noon to the surrounding hills, in part, because the soil in the valley was too hard and rocky for the troops to dig in. In the air neither side was able to gain superiority, meaning that the ground troops on both sides were vulnerable to air attacks.

The Eritreans at Gallabat, though, had taken losses and were ordered to retreat to Metemma. That afternoon the Garwahl Rifles walked into Gallabat unopposed and occupied the town and its strong point, the old Gallabat stone fort. The Indians had suffered 42 dead and 125 wounded.

The next morning the battle resumed with the Italians bombing Gallabat. Since there was virtually no cover in the city for the British troops, the bulk of them abandoned the city during the air attacks for better cover some three miles away. A small contingent remained in the stone fort. The air attacks subsided and the British troops re-occupied Gallabat. Much to the surprise of the British, the Italians did not launch a ground attack following the air raids.

With this the battle of Gallabat ended. It was a draw; the British retook Gallabat, but the Italians held Metemma. The Italian radio, however, announced that the battle of Gallabat was a complete Italian victory.

There was a ripple effect to the Battle of Gallabat in that Ethiopian guerrillas, encouraged by the British attacks, became more active in northern Ethiopia and carried out more raids, especially targeting Italian police stations and barracks.

The Battle of Gallabat was unique in another way, in that the Italian Air Force never again committed so many aircraft in East Africa to one battle. This all but forfeited control of the skies to the RAF and the SAAF.

The garrison force holding Gallabat was also Eritrean.

The British force at Gallabat, under General William Slim, consisted of the 7000–man 10th Indian Brigade comprised of the 4/10 Baluchis (Indian), 3/10 Garwahl Rifles (Indian), the 1st Essex (British), a field artillery regiment, and the British 4th Tank Regiment with twelve tanks recently transferred to The Sudan from Egypt. For air cover the RAF provided six British bombers along with six British, six South African, and four Rhodesian bi-wing fighter planes. The Italian Air Force had about forty aircraft in the area, most of them bi-wing Fiat CR–42s.

The British attack on Gallabat began at dawn on November 6, 1940. It was the first British attack of any significance in Sub-Saharan Africa. The Garwahl Rifles had been assigned to take Gallabat while the 1st Essex was to bypass Gallabat and attack Metemma. The Baluchis were held in reserve. The Garwahl Rifles had the advantage of excellent cover at Gallabat because the town was nearly surrounded by eight-foot high elephant grass. By moving quietly through the elephant grass, the Indian troops were able to get close to the town without being noticed.

When the Garwahl Rifles came out of the elephant grass accompanied by the British tanks, disaster struck. Four of the tanks were put out of action almost at once as they crossed an undiscovered mine field and others broke down trying to maneuver over the rocky landscape. Eventually only three tanks remained on the attack. Furthermore, the RAF air cover was much weaker than planned and the Italian planes were quick to take to the air and attack the British planes. As the Garwahl Rifles tried to advance on Gallabat across open ground they were met with a withering enemy fire from the Eritreans. And

In the area around Gallabat, the war reverted once again to patrolling and cross-border skirmishes. Both the Italian and British Air Forces were less active than before. The Italians needed to conserve fuel, planes, and pilots, and the British needed more pilots and were short of spare parts because the Balkan campaign now had top priority. Furthermore, the seasonal rains began in mid-November hampering movement for everyone.

BRITISH LIMITED ATTACK FROM THE SUDAN ON KASSALA

The second limited attack on the northern front, at Kassala, the result of the Eden–Smuts meeting in Khartoum in late October, had been scheduled and took place at the same time as the attack on Gallabat.

The first phase of the attack began in early November when "Skinner's Horse" battalion under Colonel Frank Messervy, was sent to the Kassala area with the mission to first secure Tehamiyan Wells in the area. Skinner's Horse had long ago forsaken their four-legged mounts and had been equipped with American-made Chevrolet trucks which mounted machine guns and antitank rifles, and, which pulled eighteen-pounder artillery pieces. On their way to their objectives, Messervy's force encountered a sizeable camel caravan under the direction of a detachment of Eritrean troops. Messervy's men attacked and the Eritreans retreated to a rocky defensive position and called for reinforcements. Italian planes soon appeared and dropped bombs on both the British and their own troops. Under cover of the air support, many of the Eritreans attempted to escape to Kassala but lost twelve dead and 263 captured which was most of their force. After the remnants of the caravan had reached Kassala the Italian airplanes returned to attack Messervy's force. They had complete control of the air because British planes failed to appear. All available British aircraft were engaged at Gallabat.

The British force eventually withdrew to the nearby hills and set up defensive positions.

The Italian command rightfully recognized the attacks at Gallabat and Kassala as preliminaries for a much larger offensive and now concentrated their attention on their northern border. The Italian Air Force responded by bombing Khartoum, several bridges across the Nile, and RAF airfields in order to deter a large-scale attack.

Both sides would have a long wait, though. Further British action would not come until after the first of the year. Furthermore, the attacks at Gallabat and Kassala had been disappointments to the British. Neither had succeeded as planned. The British realized that the Italians would be tougher opponents than they first thought.

BRITISH STRENGTH IN EAST AFRICA GROWS STRONGER

The British strength in East Africa continued to grow at a rapid pace. On December 5, 1940, another SAAF air unit, the 14th Squadron, arrived in Kenya flying three American-made, two engine Martin Maryland bombers. These planes, like the Hurricanes, were modern-day aircraft and new to the region. They had been built for France, but were sold to South Africa after France's surrender, and they outclassed anything the Italians had in the way of bombers in East Africa. The Martins had a range of 1,000 miles and could fly high and fast with speeds that allowed them to get away from most of the Italian fighter planes that might attempt to pursue them. The SAAF did not use them right away as bombers, however. They were equipped with aerial cameras and used for air reconnaissance all over Italian East Africa. One plane

The Martin Maryland twin–engine bomber with SAAF markings.

was soon damaged in an accident, but the remaining two gave the British much-needed intelligence information on Italian military facilities, airfields, supply dumps, troop concentrations and movements, and other vital information needed by the British before they launched their attacks. And additional Martin Marylands were on their way to Kenya.

During December, one of the most modern and powerful units in all of Africa, the 1st South African Division, arrived in Kenya and were sent immediately to the western flank of the British defense line in the north. From there they would lead the forthcoming diversionary attack into southern Abyssinia when the British offensive in the south began. During late December, the 1st South Africans, the KAR, and other units stationed in the north moved forward, occupying most of the no-man's-land between their old defense line and the Abyssinian border. This was a deliberate move to make the Italians think that the initial British thrust into Italian East Africa might come from the south.

In the north, the veteran 4th Indian Division arrived at Port Sudan from the North African front over the three-day period of December 15–17. The Italians in East Africa knew of the transfer and feared this division because of its successes in North Africa. As a countermeasure, Italian aircraft were sent to attack the troop ships and docks at Port Sudan as the Indian troops were off-loading and in a vulnerable position. The British had foreseen this possibility and transferred some of the SAAF's Hurricane fighters to the Port Sudan area to guard against such attacks. When the Italian air attacks came the Hurricanes were ready along with the other RAF planes and, together, they successfully blunted the Italian effort. No serious damage was done to the 4th Indians as they disembarked. The 4th Indians then moved south and took up a position along the southern border of The Sudan. They would lead the attack into Eritrea via Kassala.

The arrival of the 4th Indian Division was soon followed by that of the 5th Indian Division. They too were sent directly to the southern border.

Also arriving in The Sudan in December was a Free French force from French Equatorial Africa under the command of Colonel Monclar. It consisted of a half brigade of French Foreign Legionnaires, a battalion of Senegalese from Chad, a company of French Marines, a tank company, an artillery company, and some service personnel. There were already a few Free French units in The Sudan, the biggest of which was a squadron from the Free French Air Force flying out-of-date Saphis with the RAF. A handful of Free French soldiers from Tunisia and some service personnel were also on hand.

The newly-arrived Free French force was put under British command and sent south to the border. They would participate in the advance into Eritrea and, it was hoped, reach French Somaliland where they would induce that colony, one way or the other, to abandon the Vichy government and join the Free French.

Yet another force arrived in The Sudan under the command of an enterprising young officer, Captain Orde Wingate. Wingate was a specialist in guerilla and unconventional warfare, and his unit had had experience in Palestine. His force consisted of a few like-minded Britishers who craved the excitement of this type of warfare, over 1,000 Ethiopians, and several hundred Sudanese. Wingate had been personally chosen by Anthony Eden for this theater of operation and was given the mission of working behind the Italian lines with the many Ethiopian guerilla units known to be operating there. Wingate's unit was known as the "Gideon Force," and he had a secret account of one million pounds with which to accomplish his mission. Bribery was one of his unconventional weapons.

The "Gideon Force" would also work closely with Haile Selassie's Army which by now had grown to two battalions of Ethiopians, an Operations Center, and four patrol companies. They were equipped with small arms, mortars, anti-tank rifles, and camels to carry the ammunition and other supplies. Selassie was also supplied with a large quantity of silver dollars specially minted in Bombay. They would be used, in the traditional Ethiopian way, to purchase the support and loyalty of local war lords and clan chiefs. Selassie and Wingate's forces would enter Ethiopia at Kurmuk, a border town about sixty miles south of Gallabat and on one of the roads that lead to Addis Ababa.

Thus, the British plan of attack in the north was set. The Allies would advance in three columns from Kassala, Gallabat, and Kurmuk. The Kassala attack would come first in mid-January and be the main British thrust into Italian East Africa via Eritrea. The Kurmuk attack would soon follow and carry Haile Selassie in a straight line toward Addis Ababa. The Gallabat would come last and be primarily a diversionary attack.

THE BBC AT WAR

The British enlisted the aid of the African service of the British Broadcasting Company (BBC) to set up powerful transmitters and broadcast news to the Allied soldiers in the coming conflict, as well as propaganda to the Italians and their askaris. The radio broadcasts were to work hand-in-glove with the on-going leaflet dropping program already in place. The general themes of the broadcasts were that the Allies had come to liberate Ethiopia and that the many men of color fighting on the Allied side eagerly sought victory. The men of color fighting for the Italians were urged to do what they could to hinder the Italian war effort and help the Allied forces in this noble undertaking. The British observed, early on, that the broadcasts had a positive effect on the Allied soldiers and, as the advance progressed into Italian East Africa, they learned that it had a similar positive effect on many of the enemy soldiers.

The implications in both the radio and leaflet campaigns were that men of color were capable of liberating their own. This, of course, smacked of decolonization, and the British were careful not to emphasize this theme any more than necessary.

A TRAINING EXERCISE

In the south, General Cunningham decided to launch another attack on the border the town of El Wak. This would be primarily a training exercise to give some of his troops actual combat experiences. The town, half of which was in each country, was held by a small Italian border force and was considered to be a relatively easy-to-take objective. He chose the 12th KAR Division for the attack using three of its elements, the 1st South African Brigade, the 24th Gold Coast Brigade, and the 1st South African Light Tank Company. Units of the SAAF would provide air support. Two KAR companies were included in the force and would guard the landing field, which would be occupied on the Kenyan side of the border during the first stages of the attack.

This was an overwhelming force—some 8,000 men—for such a small objective, but Cunningham wanted to make the most of the exercise for training purposes.

On the night of December 15/16, the 12th KAR units were trucked to the El Wak area under cover of darkness. At dawn the SAAF attacked the Italian positions centered around an old stone fort. Much of the fort and town on the Italian side were destroyed. When the tanks and infantry attacked, they were met with only light resistance from the Italian defenders. The defenders were, however, able to hold out for most of the day. By dusk, though, the defenders ran out of ammunition and capitulated. Some fled into the surrounding bush but most surrendered. The British counted 44 prisoners, including 21 Italian officers and enlisted men, and 13 artillery pieces. During the day the Italian Air Force did not appear. The men of the 12th KAR occupied the fort and town and set up camp all around the town. Later that evening three Italian Caproni 133 bombers attacked the tent camp. The British had learned of the attack from one of the POWs, so SAAF Hartbeestes fighters were on hand when the Italian planes arrived. The Hartbeestes attacked and shot down one of the Capronis which crash-landed outside the town. The Italian crew appeared to have survived and in a gentlemanly gesture the SAAF planes flew over the downed aircraft and dropped a first aid kit and cigarettes for the downed airmen. The Italian crew burned the plane and were last seen walking off to the east. The other two Capronis were chased off before they could do much damage.

Soldiers of the 12th KAR went to the site of the downed plane and discovered that two Italians remained, the wounded copilot and a crewman who had volunteered to stay with him. The British added them to their collection of POWs.

On December 17 and 18, the British began to withdraw from El Wak leaving a small force in control of the town. On the 18th the Italians bombed El Wak again, but by then almost everyone had departed. The attack did little damage.

Then, to the great surprise of the British, the Italians withdrew all their forces between the border and the Juba River—obviously a result of the El Wak attack. The Juba River was known to be the Italian's primary line of defense in southern Italian Somaliland. By abandoning this huge area, at places up to 100 miles wide, the Italians handed the British an important strategic victory. The area was mostly a trackless desert, which would have been difficult for an army to cross against a determined opponent. Only Bande units were left to roam the area, watching for further British movements.

Needless to say, the British were delighted with the results of their "training exercise" which also proved to be a great morale booster for the troops involved.

At this same time, more good news came from North Africa telling of the Italian retreat in Libya. December 1940 was a very good month for the British in Africa.

THE SEA WAR AROUND AFRICA

The waters around Africa remained a battleground with both German and Italian submarines attempting to interdict British and Allied sea traffic carrying men and supplies to North and East Africa. The Italians in East Africa made a commendable effort by sending their submarines on patrols fourteen times into the Red Sea and the Indian Ocean between September 1940 and February 1941. All this effort, though, resulted in no kills.

The German raider Atlantis which was operating in the Indian Ocean had much better luck. On September 9, 1940, she sank the Australian freighter "Athelking" out of Australia, bound for British East Africa. The next day she sank another Allied ship, the "Benarty," not far from where the Athelking went down. The Atlantis then moved into the southeastern part of the Indian Ocean and on September 19 sank the "Commissaire Ramel." This was a former French ship being operated by the Australians. From all three ships the Atlantis collected prisoners of war. Now her below-deck cells were full with 260 prisoners of war and she had a problem as to what to do with them.

During October, the Atlantis captured only one ship, the Yugoslav tramp steamer "Durmitor" but the German captain used this ship to solve his POW problem. He put a German prize crew aboard the Durmitor and sent her off to the nearest friendly port which was Mogadishu, Italian Somaliland. There the prisoners and the ship were interned by the Italians. The Italians also acquired the Durmitor's cargo—salt.

On September 12, 1940, the raider Penguin sank the

British freighter "Benavon" and captured its crew off the coast of Madagascar. The Benavon was out of Singapore for London with a cargo of hemp and rubber.

On September 26, the raider Thor, operating in the South Atlantic, captured the Norwegian whaler "Kosmos" returning from the Antarctic hunting grounds, with 17,662 tons of valuable whale oil. The Thor's captain wanted to send this prize on to Germany but the Kosmos was low on fuel and could not make it. Reluctantly, he sank the ship with its cargo still aboard.

In the Atlantic, the Italian submarine "Cappellini" torpedoed and sank the Belgian steam ship "Kabalo" on October 15 just south of the Azores.

On the other side of the continent, at this same time, the Italian Navy and Air Force from East Africa were attacking a British convoy in the Red Sea over a three day period, October 19–21. The convoy was heading for Egypt. The Italian Air Force struck first and bombed the convoy from a high altitude but failed to do any damage. Four Italian destroyers from Eritrea then attacked but were driven off by the convoy's escort force which consisted of a light cruiser, a destroyer, and five smaller warships. In the maneuvering that took place, the Italian destroyer "Francisco Nuelo" ran aground on the afternoon of October 21 on Hamil Island just off the Eritrean coast. The next morning the British destroyer "Kimberley" attacked the grounded ship but was soon damaged by Italian shore batteries and driven off. The Francisco Nuelo was too hard aground to recover and was abandoned.

On November 11, the Atlantis, still operating in the Indian Ocean, captured the British merchantman "Automedon" after a brief attack which killed the Automedon's captain. A German boarding party went aboard the Automedon and discovered a locked strong box which contained top secret British documents about the defenses of Singapore, several code books of codes used at Singapore, and six million newly-printed Straits dollars. At that time the Atlantis had in its possession a captured Norwegian tanker, the "Ole Jacob," carrying 10,000 tons of aviation fuel, which the Atlantis had captured in the Bay of Bengal on November 8. The Ole Jacob was manned by a German crew and following the Atlantis. Realizing the importance of the documents, the Atlantis's captain decided to send the Norwegian tanker on to Tokyo carrying the secret documents. He also put aboard the Ole Jacob all of his prisoners of war. The Atlantis's captain kept the six million Straits dollars, though, and then sank the Automedon. The Norwegian tanker reached Tokyo on December 4 and it and the prisoners were interned by the neutral Japanese government. The secret documents and code books were taken to the German Embassy in Tokyo and, after being examined, and with Berlin's approval, handed over to the Japanese. When the Japanese invaded Malaya a year later the information on Singapore's defenses was of great value to the attackers.

In mid-November 1940, the Germans found a weakness in the Allies' seagoing transportation system. The Germans noted that Allied ships sailing southward out of Freetown, Sierra Leone often sailed alone. North of Freetown most ships sailed in convoys. The German Naval Command therefore dispatched submarine U-65 to work the waters south of Freetown off the coasts of Liberia and Ivory Coast. Upon arrival, U-65 found an abundance of easy targets and succeeded in sinking four Allied ships in four days. The Allies, reacting to this sudden carnage, sent out emergency orders ordering all ships in the area to remain in port until the submarine could be sunk or driven off, or convoys made available. Almost overnight targets for the U-65 dried up and she sailed off to work another part of the ocean. But she had accomplished her mission. She had sunk four Allied vessels and disrupted Allied supply lines in a vital area of the Atlantic for weeks.

The sea war then shifted to the waters off South Africa. There, on November 17 the raider Penguin captured and sank the British freighter "Nowshera" out of Durban with a cargo of zinc ore, wool, and wheat for England. Three days later, on November 20, the Penguin captured the British refrigerator ship "Maimoa" out of Durban for England with cargos of meat, eggs, butter, lard, grain, and piece goods. The Penguin's captain took the British crew aboard his ship as prisoners and put a German prize crew on the Maimoa intending to sent her and her valuable cargo back to Germany. The next day Penguin encountered a second British refrigerator ship, the "Port Brisbane," also out of Durban with a similar cargo. The Port Brisbane just before surrendering, gave out the international distress signal "RRR" and her location indicated she was being attacked by an enemy raider. This act doomed both British ships. The German captain, realizing that his location was now known, had to sail out of the area for safer waters, and soon. He quickly hauled the Port Brisbane's crew aboard as prisoners, retrieved his prize crew from the Maimoa, and sank both ships. He then headed off to safely in the vast emptiness of the South Atlantic. Following the Penguin into the South Atlantic was the Norwegian freighter "Storstad" which the Penguin had captured in September. She was being sailed by a German crew and being used to hold some of the prisoners of war.

On November 30, the Penguin was once again off the coast of South Africa and encountered yet another British refrigerator ship, the "Port Wellington" a sister ship to the Port Brisbane. Penguin captured the British ship, which did not give out the "RRR" signal, took the crew as prisoners and sank the ship. Now with 405 prisoners of war on his hands the German captain transferred all of them to the "Storstad" and sent her off to the German-controlled coast of France. En route the Storstad encountered the German raider Atlantis and her supply ship "Nordmark" and transferred much of her diesel fuel to those ships along with items of her original cargo that the Atlantis and Nordmark could use. She then sailed on and made it safely to Gironde, France with all her prisoners aboard.

THE BRITISH MAKE IT TOUGH FOR THE FRENCH IN WEST AFRICA

By the end of November 1940, the British had been able to accumulate enough ships to enforce the blockade of French West Africa and stop, altogether, the French sea trade between her West African colonies and Unoccupied France. This was a blow to both French locations. Would-be cargos piled up on the docks and in the warehouses of West Africa and prices fell on many items, while in France the already bad food shortage became worse. It was to the advantage of the British, though, not to let conditions in the African colonies, or in Unoccupied France, deteriorate so far that the French would be forced to ask the Axis Powers to provide the necessities of life. This would result in counter demands by the Axis powers and drive the Vichy French one step closer to Germany and Italy. There was also the possibility that food riots and other acts of popular unrest might erupt in the French lands, which would give the Germans and Italians an excuse to intervene and take control of more French territory. To prevent this, an unofficial three-party arrangement was worked out between London, Vichy, and Washington, DC under which American ships would be allowed through the British blockade to bring just enough food, medicines, consumer goods, and humanitarian supplies to the French to meet their minimal needs. This would assure that virtually everything delivered would be consumed by the French and little or none of it would reach the Axis nations. The cargos carried by the American ships would be determined by the British and inspected by British agents at their ports of departure. The ship's captain would then be given "Navicerts," documents that, in case the American ship was stopped at sea by a blockading ship, would prove that the ship's cargo had been inspected and that the ship could sail on to the French port of destination.

As might be expected, having the Americans feeding the Vichy French was a controversial subject in both London and Washington, but the argument of having the Vichy French dependent on the Americans rather than the Axis powers prevailed. The opponents of the program, nevertheless, delayed a formal agreement which was not signed until February 1941. That agreement became known as the "Murphy/Weygand Agreement." In practice, only a very few ships were sent to the French and those ships went only to French Morocco rather than risk the dangerous war conditions that prevailed in the Mediterranean. It was up to the French in North Africa to get what they could of the American supplies across the Mediterranean to Unoccupied France.

On November 13, the Americans made Vichy an unusual offer. They offered to buy the French battleships Richelieu anchored at Dakar and the Jean Bart anchored at Casablanca with the promise that the ships would not be used during the war. This action was taken on rumors reaching Washington that the ships would be moved to Toulon, France. The Vichy government rejected the offer but, once again, gave assurances that the ships would not be used against the British or fall into the hands of the Axis Powers. Washington replied on November 18 saying that the offer to buy the ships still stood and was expanded to include any other warship in the French inventory. Vichy replied again on the 21st, saying that there was no intention of moving the two battleships and that if those ships were to be moved, Washington would be given prior notice.

In January 1941, the French tested the British resolve again by sending a convoy from West Africa to southern France laden with food and raw materials. The convoy did not make it. It was met by British warships in the Strait of Gibraltar and turned back. The British blockade still was not perfect though. This convoy was stopped but individual French ships and an occasional small convoy would get through.

U-65 RETURNS

In late December, the German submarine U-65 returned to the waters off Sierra Leone and Liberia where the British had again relaxed their defense. U-65 quickly repeated her success of the previous month by sinking two Allied ships in four days. U-65 then moved to the waters off Dakar and sank three ships in seven days. As the U-65 departed for home, the Italian submarine "Capallini" arrived and sank the British cargo ship "Shakespeare" off Dakar on January 5 and the British freighter "Eumaeus" on January 14 off Sierra Leone.

With so many Allied ships being sunk off the coast of French West Africa, the Allies were concerned that the submarines might be operating out of Vichy-controlled Dakar. Formal inquiries were made of the French but they denied any and all allegations. Intelligence information was gathered by agents at Dakar and as far as could be determined the French were telling the truth. Postwar records confirmed this. The Axis submarines were coming down from Europe.

During December 1940, the first two of six British corvettes arrived on permanent station at Freetown to act as convoy escorts. These were small, fast, rough-riding but very efficient submarine killers. They were loaded to the gunwales with depth charges, deck guns, sonar, and other antisubmarine devices. The remaining four vessels arrived in early 1941, and their presence began to make the waters off this part of West Africa much safer for Allied ships and much more dangerous for Axis submarines.

THE AIR AND LAND ROUTES ACROSS AFRICA

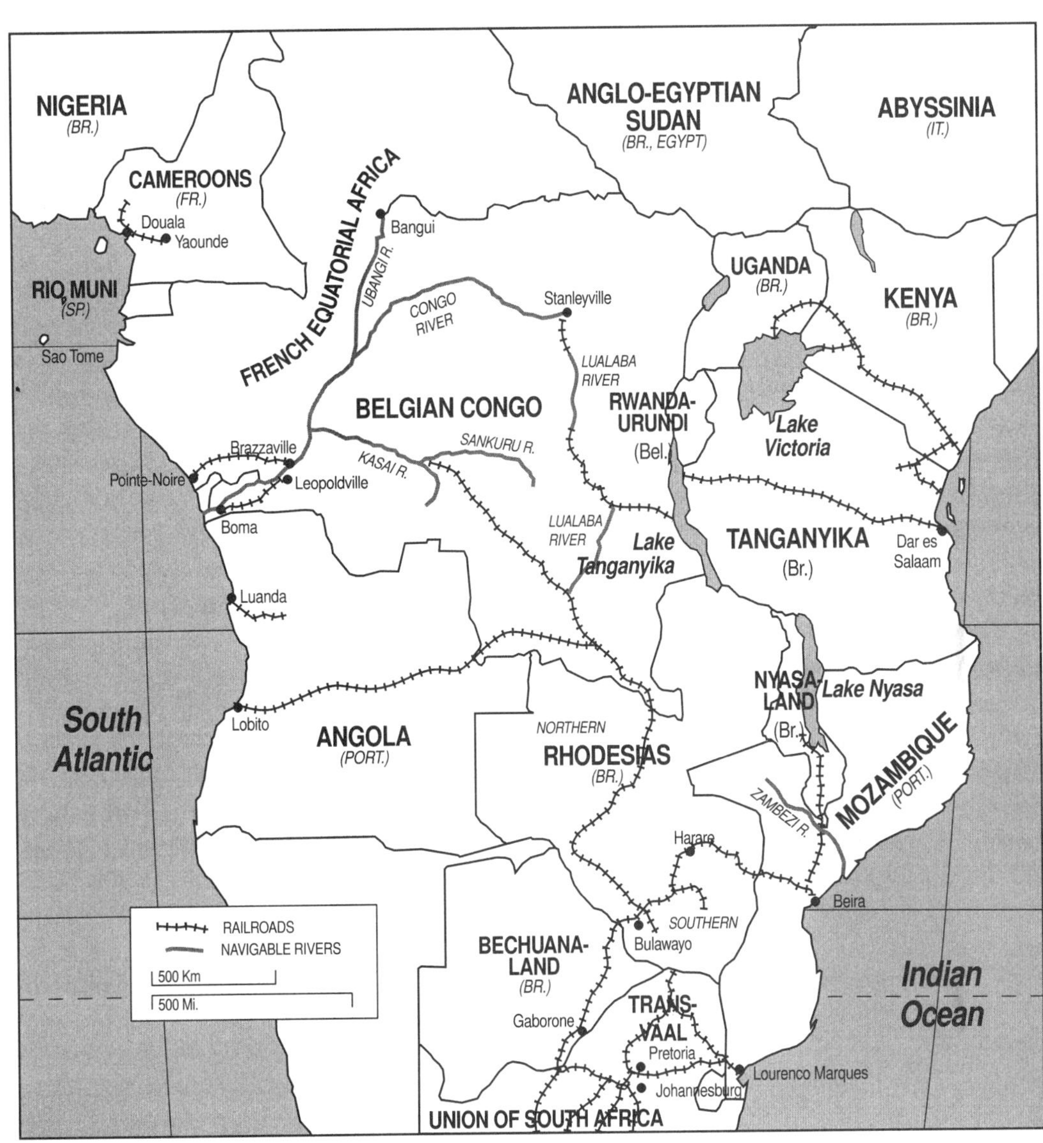

The existing land routes across central Africa in 1940.

When the Mediterranean became a war zone, the regular Allied air routes across that body of water and along the North African coast became dangerous. Land routes across North Africa were closed immediately with Libya's entry into the war. The Allies, therefore, were forced to find alternative routes to get from the Atlantic Ocean across Africa to the Indian Ocean and northward to Egypt and the Middle East. The geography of Africa dictated that those routes be sought across central Africa. Air routes already existed across central Africa, but the airfields and their supporting facilities were not adequate for military purposes.

As for land routes across central Africa, the picture was bleak. There were no railroads or all-weather roads immediately south of the Sahara Desert that spanned the African continent from the Atlantic to the Indian Ocean. There were, however, two land routes consisting of railroads and/or river and lake transportation. The northernmost route began at the mouth of the Congo River and ended at Dar es Salaam on the Indian Ocean. This was a slow and arduous route because it consisted of a combination of rail, river steamer, and lake ferry travel that required numerous off-loading and reloading of cargo. It was impractical for large-scale military traffic.

Further south, there was a rail line that stretched from Lobito, Angola on the Atlantic to either Beira or Lourenco Marques in Mozambique on the Indian Ocean. This route was too far south to be of much practical use. Furthermore, it began and ended in Portuguese territory and it was very unlikely that the Portuguese government, which was trying to steer a policy of strict neutrality, would permit the Allies to use their portions of the rail lines and their ports for large-scale military traffic. Furthermore, this transcontinental rail line had been built primarily to haul ores from the mining areas of Northern Rhodesia and southern Belgian Congo. With the war on, this mining region was booming and the railroads that served it were working at near capacity and could not accommodate much more traffic.

So, the answer was simple—and disappointing for the Allies. There were no feasible land routes across central Africa, and what air routes there were would need a major overhaul before they could be used. Therefore, in the late summer of 1940, the British began the massive undertaking of improving the existing airfields and facilities stretching from British West Africa to The Sudan and building new ones.

Air routes, though, were a different matter. In the 1930s Britain's Imperial Airways had established commercial air routes across central Africa to service British colonies in both

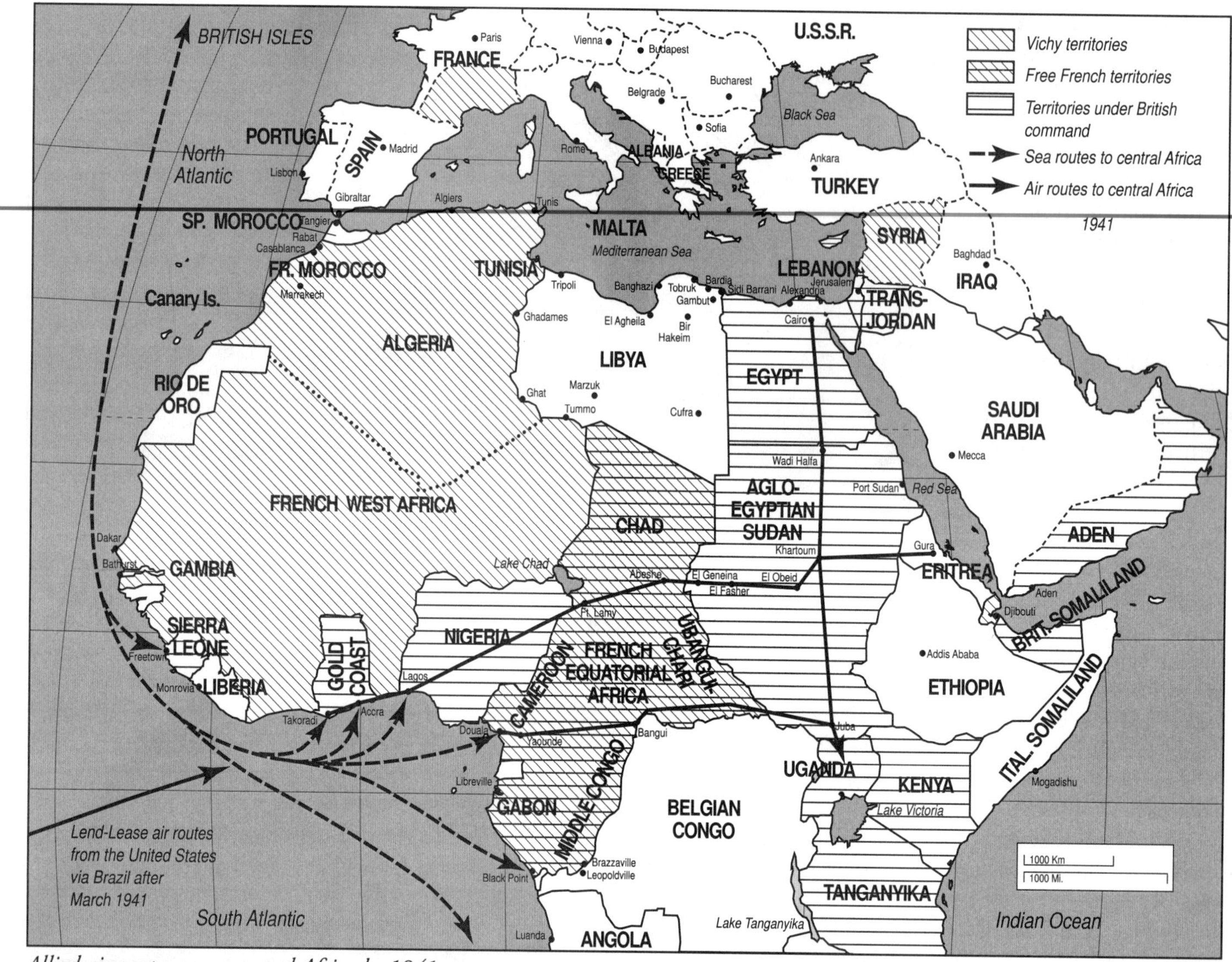

Allied air routes across central Africa by 1941.

West and East Africa. Airfields were built at Bathurst, Gambia; Freetown, Sierra Leone; Takoradi and Accra, Gold Coast; Lagos and several other locations in Nigeria; Fort Lamy, French Equatorial Africa, and at El Geneina, El Fasher and El Obeid, Sudan. From The Sudan they connected with other existing air routes north to Egypt and south into British East Africa. When Britain went to war in September 1939, the British government took control of all British commercial air routes, including those in Africa, and the emphasis quickly shifted from one of commercial use to one of military use.

With the entry of Italy into the war in June 1940 and the closing of the Mediterranean, the central African air route became vitally important to the Allies. The British military took an active hand in improving conditions at most of the existing airfields so that they could handle more air traffic, larger aircraft, do more aircraft maintenance, offer more fuel storage and warehousing, provide accommodation for personnel, and the like.

British use of the west-to-east air route across central Africa was disrupted in late June 1940, when France fell and French Equatorial Africa became Vichy territory. But it opened again when the Free French gained control of that area in August and September. With French Equatorial Africa on the Allied side, a second air route was opened up from the seaport of Duala, Gabon, across French Equatorial Africa to Juba, Sudan.

Takoradi Airfield, in the Gold Coast, became a very large and important facility when an aircraft assembly plant was built there. Disassembled aircraft and aircraft components were brought to Takoradi by sea, assembled into fighters and bombers at the plant, flight tested, and sent on to the battle fronts in East and North Africa. By the fall of 1940, a steady flow of modern Hurricane fighters and Blenheim bombers was coming from the Takoradi plant and being flown on to the war zones.

In late 1940, some American-made planes began arriving at Takoradi for assembly, having been purchased in the

United States and transported on British ships. This was the period known as "Cash and Carry," when American neutrality laws had been modified to allow belligerent nations, primarily Britain, to purchase war materials in the United States so long as the materials were paid for in cash and transported by the purchaser.

During late 1940, the British took over the Italian aircraft maintenance center at Gura, Eritrea to service Allied planes for both North Africa and East Africa. The British were short of technicians so they brought in a mix of Czechs, Poles, Dutch, and Frenchmen. This system did not work very well because of language difficulties and shortages of parts. Churchill, therefore, asked Roosevelt for help and on November 19, 1941, the Gura facility was turned over to the Americans. The American takeover was top secret, because the United States was still neutral and this could be construed by the Axis Powers as a violation of neutrality. Three weeks later, though, the United States was at war and secrecy was no longer needed. The facility was contracted to America's Douglas Aircraft Company which sent in their own technicians and became the supplier of most of the spare parts. The Americans hired some of the former Italian technicians, after properly screening them, and many local people for the non-skilled jobs. Indian troops guarded the facility. The Americans paid their non-skilled workers about double what the British had paid them, which made the workers very pleased—but did not please the British.

Across the ocean, the United States government saw the importance of the air route across central Africa and a plan was devised to establish an air route from North America to West Africa which would connect with the existing British routes there. For political reasons it was best that the new route from North America be established under the guise of neutrality. Therefore, the American government contracted the civilian air line, Pan-American Airways (Pan-Am), to explore routes and pick airfield sites along the proposed route. Pan-Am was the premier American international air carrier at the time, and had considerable experience building air facilities and acquiring air rights in foreign countries. During 1940, the Pan-Am people, working closely with Army Air Corps personnel, explored the routes, picked airfield sites, and made arrangements with foreign governments. The Federal Aviation Administration (FAA) and Army Air Corps eventually agreed upon a route and Pan-American Airways was contracted by the Federal government to make it a working reality. The program was called the Airport Development Program (ADP) and was funded by the American government. Subsequently, Pan-Am went to work in late 1940 developing a series of operating and emergency airfields, using some existing ones and building news ones, that reached from the southern part of the United States to West Africa. Airfields were acquired in Cuba, Haiti, Dominican Republic, Puerto Rico, Venezuela, Brazil with the African terminus located at Monrovia, Liberia. All of the countries involved were neutral nations at the time. The target date for the opening of the new air route was set for the spring of 1941.

PAN-AMERICAN AIRWAYS ALREADY FLYING TRANS-ATLANTIC

Pan-Am already had an existing trans-Atlantic route that had been established in 1937. It operated three days a week from New York City to Lisbon, Portugal and returned via Bolama, Portuguese Guinea (Africa); Port of Spain, Trinidad (South America); San Juan, Puerto Rico; Miami, Florida, and back to New York City. There was also an auxiliary Pan-Am base at Bathurst, Gambia but Pan-Am had to abandon it in September 1939 because the Johnson Act of that year forbad American commercial aircraft from flying into and out of the territories of belligerent nations.

On their trans-Atlantic route, Pan-Am used its famous "Clipper" sea planes that did not require airfields because they landed on water.

U. S. Army Air Corps personnel continued to work closely with Pan-Am in the construction of the air route and had a secondary mission. This was to find and recommend one or more air routes beyond West Africa all the way to India. The route chosen eventually became known as the "Cannonball Route" and was activated after the United States entered the war in December 1941.

VICHY-CONTROLLED AFRICA

Hard times had come to Vichy-controlled colonies in Africa due primarily to the intensification of the British blockade. The whites and acculturated blacks were hardest hit. The bulk of the natives suffered less because they had little to begin with and could make do, to a degree, by living off the land and their small holdings. An active black market thrived in Vichy colonies, and there was considerable smuggling of consumer goods into Vichy-controlled territory from adjoining British colonies.

In early November 1940, a call came from Governor General Jean Decoux of French Indo-China (Viet Nam) for military reinforcements to counter a Japanese threat to that colony in Southeast Asia. Vichy responded by ordering the dispatch of four battalions of Senegalese troops from French Somaliland to Indo-China. The troops departed Djibouti in mid-November, but their ship was intercepted by vessels of the British blockade and forced to return to Djibouti. Vichy

Palm oil was a major export of French Equatorial Africa and an important food supplement for the Allies. Here natives prepare a shipment for England.

asked the Americans to intercede but Washington refused to take action. In the months that followed the Japanese made serious inroads into French Indo-China and then used it, during December 1941, as a base of operations to launch their military offensive into Southeast Asia.

On January 27, 1941, the Vichy government issued a decree that brought it one step closer to being a fascist-like state. On that date the Vichy government required all French military officers to take a personal oath of loyalty to Petain, France's Head of State. Such oaths had been required of German officers to Hitler and of Italian officers to Mussolini. The penalties for violating the oath to Petain ranged from fines, to reduction or loss of pensions, to imprisonment. This action was directed, to a large extent, toward the officers in the colonies where distance from Vichy made the opportunity to deal with the Allies, or to defect, the greatest. Virtually every French military officer in Vichy-controlled Africa took the oath.

FREE FRENCH-CONTROLLED AFRICA

Economic conditions were much better in Free French-controlled colonies because these areas could still conduct international trade. Consumer and manufactured goods were in short supply, but this was also common in many other parts of the world. The Free French areas exported about all they could produce, usually at good prices, and there was nearly full employment.

One item in great demand from Africa was wild natural rubber. There were no rubber plantations anywhere in French Africa, but natives were able to roam the forests and accumulate quantities of wild rubber large enough to sell. This was often dangerous work because of wild animals and diseases.

In November 1940, while he was still in Equatorial Africa, de Gaulle promoted Felix Eboue Governor-General of all Equatorial Africa. Eboue had been the former governor of Chad and the first colonial governor in Africa to declare for the Free French.

In military matters, the first Free French expeditionary force was formed in late 1940 and sent off to fight with the British in East Africa. In Chad another military expedition was put together by General Leclerc to invade southern Libya. Small and mobile Sudanese Defence Forces, under British command, had already been penetrating southeastern Libya from southern Egypt and northern Sudan, attacking Italian lines of communication and oasis garrisons.

BELGIAN CONGO DECLARES WAR ON ITALY

On November 26, 1940, the administration of the Belgian Congo declared war on Italy. This was, of course, with the full approval of the Belgian government-in-exile in London. Heretofore, Belgium and her colonies had been at war only with Germany. This was primarily a political move meant to assure Belgium a seat at the postwar peace conference with Italy. It looked fairly certain to the Belgians that the Allies would be victorious in the coming invasion of Italian East Africa and they wanted to be a part of it. To back up their declaration of war, the Congo Administration organized a small military force to be sent to East Africa to serve under the British.

THE DUKE OF AOSTA'S WIFE

The wife of the Duke of Aosta, the Commander-in-Chief of Italian forces in East Africa, was a Belgian. She was Princess Marie Jose, daughter of the King of Belgium.

Back in Belgium several right-wing political groups and would-be collaborators were vying with each other for the attention and support of the Germans. One of the leading contenders in this race, and the one that would eventually come out on top, was Rexist Organization headed by Leon Degrelle. Degrelle proposed to the Germans that he and his organization be allowed to raise a corps of Belgian aviators and enough Belgian officers to command a regiment of colonial soldiers for the time when the Germans invaded the Belgian Congo. These fighters would need to be equipped by the Germans and would fight under German command. The Germans were not impressed and completely ignored Degrelle's suggestion.

Another interesting thing happened with regard to the Belgian Congo during October and November 1940. A Belgian businessman and mining executive, Edgar Sengier, then living in the United States, purchased all of the above-ground uranium ore that still remained at the Shinkolobwe uranium mine in Katanga Province. The mine had been closed since May 1940, when its only customer, the Union Miniere Company in Belgium, was taken over by the Germans. The ore, some 1,250 tons, was shipped across Portuguese Angola to the port of Lobito and then on to the United States where it was stored in a warehouse on Staten Island, New York. Sengier had a hunch that the ore would become extremely valuable.

Mrs. Jan Christian Smuts, wife of South Africa's Prime Minister, is shown operating a sewing machine in a war plant during the war. She was one of thousands of South African women who worked in war plants.

SOUTH AFRICA

Despite the fact that South African ground and air units were serving with distinction in East Africa, there was still considerable tension at home over the nature of the war. South Africa did not have conscription so this very controversial activity was avoided, but a large number of South Africans who had voluntarily joined the country's armed forces differed greatly with the government's war policies and had little qualms about speaking out against those policies. It was, in many ways, the same atmosphere that prevailed in South Africa in 1914 before the deadly riots of that year. There was one exception, however, people were more restrained and there were no calls from any responsible leader to take action in the streets.

The Smuts government received numerous reports of the rebellion within the nation's security forces. One such report stated that pro-Nazism was rife in the ranks of the Army and that 80% of the officers were against the war. Another report stated that most of the South African police were against the war.

Still, the system functioned. Men accepted the military training requirements given them and then went about their duties as soldiers and policemen.

To strengthen the loyalties of the individual servicemen to the nation, and hopefully bypass some of the internal differences, Smuts asked the men of the South African armed forces to take a special voluntary oath of loyalty to the nation. This was done in the latter part of 1940. Most servicemen realized the need for national unity in these critical times, so the majority of servicemen took the oath. The one outstanding exception, though, was in some of the hard-core Afrikaner areas, where only about 25% of the personnel took the oath.

Despite politics, the business of building an army proceeded. Regiments with colorful names such as "The Duke of Edinburgh's Own Rifles," "The Royal Natal Carbineers," and the "1st Transvaal Scottish" were in training, along with tank and artillery units and a much-expanded Pioneer (engineer) force utilizing many black troops. Many of the white troops were given special training in highly mobile bush warfare, where they could be expected to be cutoff from all ground support for up to a month and supplied only by air. It was the Army's intent to use these specially trained men in the forthcoming struggle in East Africa, so they trained in terrain and under conditions they could expect to find there.

The South Africans, though, proved to be a disappointment to Charles de Gaulle and his Free French. The South African government continued to maintain diplomatic relations with Vichy rather than switch its recognition to de Gaulle's Committee of Liberation in Brazzaville. The Smuts government thought it more important to keep a line of communications open in Axis-dominated Europe than opt for a line of communications to a relatively unimportant center like Brazzaville.

The Free French did not allow political problems, though, to interfere with trade with South Africa. Many items were traded back and forth including armored cars which would later become very important to the Free French war effort in Libya.

In November 1940, the openly pro-Nazi Grey Shirts organization, led by Louis Weichardt, changed its name to more accurately reflect its Nazi-like political philosophy. The new name was the "South African National Socialist (Nazi) Union." Weichardt announced that his organization supported the fascist-like, anti-Semitic Oswald Pirow wing of the National Party.

But the National Party was no longer good enough for former Prime Minister J. B. M. Hertzog, who had joined it after his ouster by Smuts in September 1939. Hertzog was, by now, a bitter man and had become an outspoken opponent of the war and of Prime Minister Smuts. Hertzog had come to favor South Africa becoming an independent state free of the British Commonwealth with a neo-fascist government. He concluded that the National Party was no longer far enough to the political right to suit his beliefs so he resigned his membership in order to preach his extreme political doctrines as an independent.

GOLD TO NEW YORK

Quite understandably, much of Britain's gold supply was produced in South Africa. Due to the fragile political situation there, London thought it best to remove much of that gold to the safety of the American banks. Washington was happy to oblige, and in early January 1941, the U. S. cruiser "Louisville" arrived at Simonstown, South Africa to fetch the gold. The Louisville departed Simonstown on the 6th with $148 million in gold and arrived safely in New York City on January 22.

Chapter 9

THE SECOND EAST AFRICAN WAR (JANUARY–JULY 1941)

FASCISM'S FIRST MAJOR DEFEAT

Well before the British launched their long-anticipated offensive in East Africa, the Duke of Aosta, Commander-in-Chief of Italian forces there, had developed a pessimistic outlook regarding his situation. He had concluded that any hope of receiving meaningful reinforcements from Italy was very remote due to the serious military setbacks of the Italian forces in North Africa. He also believed the British force confronting him on his northern border alone was in the neighborhood of 60,000 troops. This was a gross overestimate. Furthermore, at Gallabat on the Sudanese border, where a British attack could be expected, his troops were suffering from an outbreak of malaria. Aosta, therefore, had to make the hard decision that in East Africa he would have to go on the defensive and hold out for as long as possible, in hopes that the situation in Libya would reverse itself and that Italian forces would eventually conquer Egypt and march southward to his aid.

As part of his defensive strategy, he decided to give up the border posts of Kassala and the Gallabat/Metemma area and withdraw to more easily defended positions inside Eritrea and northern Abyssinia. Accordingly, on January 17, 1941, Italian troops began to withdraw from Kassala to Agordat, over 100 miles inside Eritrea and from the Gallabat/Metemma areas to Gondar, 75 miles inside Abyssinia.

By abandoning the Kassala area they also abandoned the airfield at the border town of Tessenei, which had long been the terminus for aircraft flying in from Libya. The loss of the airfield made it all the more difficult for reinforcements to reach Italian East Africa.

THE FIRST BRITISH MOVEMENTS

The first British movements that indicated a major offensive was underway came in the south on January 24, 1941, when three large forces, under General Alan Cunningham began moving out of their encampments at Bura and Garissa, about eighty miles inside Kenya, toward the border with Italian Somaliland. This force consisted of the 11th and 12th King's African Rifles (KAR) Divisions and 1st South African

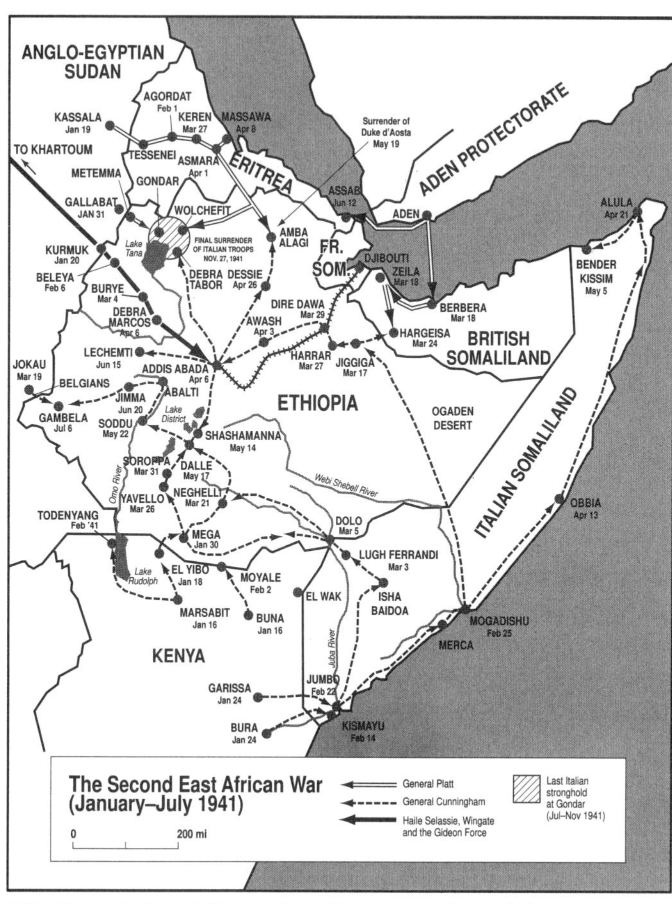

The Second East African War (January-July 1941)

THE 11TH AND 12TH (KAR) DIVISIONS

These KAR Divisions were typical of all the KAR divisions used by the British throughout the war, in that they comprised an interesting mix of humanity from many parts of the British Empire. The 11th (KAR) Division consisted of two brigades; the 22nd KAR Brigade was comprised primarily of soldiers from the various British East African colonies, but it also had an Indian artillery battery, and the 23rd (Nigerian) Brigade was comprised primarily of Nigerians. Other units attached to the 11th (KAR) Division consisted of a KAR armored car regiment; a South African light tank company, five field artillery batteries, an antitank battery, an antiaircraft battery, a Pioneer unit with two field companies, a Kenyan ambulance unit, a field hygiene unit, an ordnance field park, and a KAR machine gun section.

The 12th (KAR) Division consisted of three brigades; the 21st KAR Brigade with two KAR regiments and a Northern Rhodesian regiment, a Gold Coast field company, and a Zanzibari ambulance unit; the 24th (Gold Coast) Brigade comprised of all Gold Coast personnel and included three regiments, a light artillery battery, and an ambulance unit; and the 25th KAR Brigade comprised of two KAR regiments, a mountain artillery battery, an armored car unit, a South African field company, an Ugandan ambulance unit, a signals unit. Other units attached to the division consisted of a KAR armored car unit, a machine gun section, a hygiene section, an ordnance park, four South African artillery batteries, four antiaircraft sections, and a field company.

Brigade (not to be confused with the 1st South African Division which was also stationed in the area).

According to the British plan, Cunningham's force was to invade southern Italian Somaliland and occupy the enemy seaport of Kismayu 110 miles beyond the border. They would then advance another twenty miles beyond Kismayu and force a crossing of the Juba River near its mouth to establish a staging area for the next phase of the invasion, an advance on Mogadishu, the colonial capital. From the Kenyan border the British columns had to travel across hostile desert terrain with the only roads being dirt tracks. Once Kismayu was taken it would become their main supply port.

On February 2, the British aircraft carrier Formidable, passing up the east coast of Italian Somaliland on its way to the Mediterranean, sent some of its planes to bomb Mogadishu far in advance of Cunningham's troops. Thinking they were helping Cunningham they were, in fact, causing more harm than good. The British bombs did not hit any significant military targets but, instead, killed a number of civilians. The British planes also dropped magnetic mines into the harbor. This was a useless undertaking because most of the Italian warships were operating out of Eritrean ports and there was no military-related sea traffic of any consequence at Mogadishu. Furthermore, when the British finally reached Mogadishu weeks later, they had to remove those mines before British supply ships could use the harbor.

A column of Indian troops serving in Eritrea.

ACTION ON THE NORTHERN FRONT

Just prior to Cunningham's southern forces moving out, General Platt's northern forces in The Sudan moved out on January 19, 1941, on undefended Kassala and occupied the town that same day. Platt's forces then continued eastward into Eritrea. Platt's forces consisted of the 4th and 5th Indian Divisions and the Sudan Defense Force.

The opposing Italian force in the north, under General Frusci, consisted of 17,000 troops with light tanks and artillery units. They were just completing their withdrawal to Agordat when Platt's troops moved on Kassala.

HAILE SELASSIE RETURNS TO ETHIOPIA

On January 20, Haile Selassie's reconstituted Ethiopian Army, in the company of Wingate's Gideon Force, crossed the Abyssinian border at Kurmuk 200 miles southwest of Gallabat. Kurmuk had been occupied by the Italians in June 1940, but it was subsequently abandoned. The road from Kurmuk was the shortest of several in the area that led eastward to the capital, Addis Ababa. The Emperor's army had virtually no motorized equipment and depended on mules and camels for transportation. The Ethiopians were very vulnerable to air attacks, so before the advance began the RAF bombed all of the Italian airfields in range of their advance and then provided air cover during the advance.

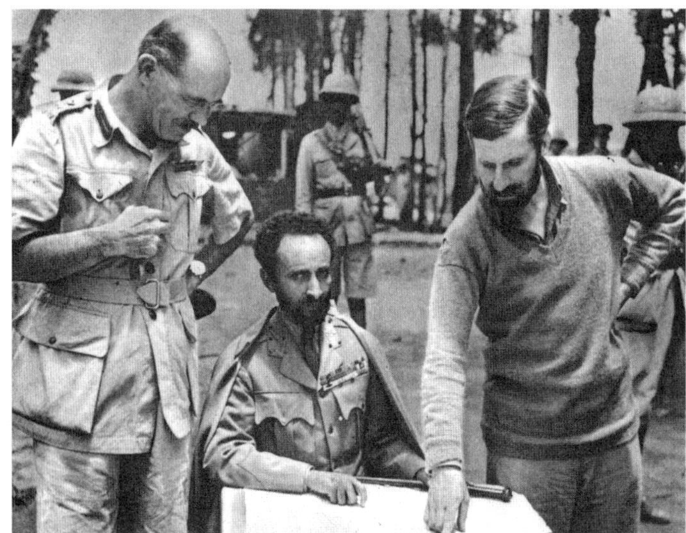

Emperor Haile Selassie, center, confers with Major Orde Wingate, right, and Brigadier Sandford, left.

Upon crossing the border, the Emperor participated in a brief ceremony in which he raised the Ethiopian flag once again on Ethiopian soil.

Selassie's force then advanced about fifty miles into Ethiopia and on February 6, occupied the town of Belaya, the main center in the Gojjam highlands. There the Emperor and his army halted and Selassie set up headquarters in a cave. The British had supplied Selassie with a radio transmitter and a printing press, and upon his arrival at Belaya, his headquarters began spreading the word of the Emperor's return via the on-going British leaflet-dropping campaign. Soon, delegations of tribesmen, clansmen, and guerrilla organizations from all over the kingdom began to arrive to pledge their loyalty to their returned Emperor.

At this point, Wingate's Gideon Force suffered a setback of sorts when a large number of his Ethiopians abandoned him to join the local guerrillas.

The defending Italian force in the area, under Vice Governor-General Guglielmo Nasi, was comprised of many Ethiopian conscripts and considerably outnumbered the Emperor's force. The Italian force was spread very thinly, though, and plagued by desertions. Nasi's force would prove to be not much of an impediment to the Emperor's advance.

SLAVES

Some of the Ethiopian chieftains who supported the Emperor and fought the Italians in East Africa had slaves. It is an uncomfortable thought for the Western mind to realize that during World War II there were slaves fighting on the Allied side.

The Ethiopian Army was not powerful enough to conduct a sustained offensive against the Italians, so it was planned that the Emperor and his army would establish themselves in the Gojjam highlands and from there liberate as much of the surrounding countryside as possible in a piecemeal fashion. The Gojjam highlands was one of the better agricultural areas of Ethiopia so the army was expected to sustain itself as much as it could off of the assets of the region. The mere presence of Selassie and his army in the Gojjam area would force the Italians to make an effort to contain their expansion, and in so doing draw Italian troops away from the other fronts. The more area Selassie's army liberated the better because news of this would provide excellent propaganda all over Abyssinia.

The arms and supplies necessary to keep the Ethiopian Army a fighting force continued to flow in from The Sudan, and the RAF flew in emergency supplies and important personnel.

In the weeks and months that followed, many individual Ethiopians and small groups of men made their way to Belaya eager to join the Emperor's army and fight the Italians. With Wingate's help, the new volunteers were organized into small military units and sent out into the surrounding area to secure still more territory for the Emperor, as well as to establish a defensive perimeter around their growing domain.

IN THE SOUTH

Meanwhile, in the south, all three of Cunningham's forces began their march, in three parallel columns, toward Kismayu. The 11th (KAR) was on the south, the 12th (KAR) was in the center and the 1st South African Brigade was on the north. This advance, together with Platt's advance into Eritrea, was the beginning of a giant pincer movement which would force the Italians to fight on two fronts. The plan was very similar to that used by the Italians to defeat Ethiopia during the First East African War (1935-36).

All across Italian East Africa, the RAF and SAAF attacked ground targets, especially near the fronts. They flew from bases in Kenya, The Sudan, Aden and the aircraft carrier "Formidable" still operating offshore in the Indian Ocean. The Italian Air Force, which had more aircraft than the British, challenged the intruders on many occasions and shot down some of the British planes but, overall, the British clearly had the upper hand because of their more modern and higher quality aircraft.

A THIRD FRONT

In northern Kenya, the bulk of the 1st South African Division moved out from its defensive position at dawn on January 16. They began an advance toward the southern Abyssinia border across desert terrain as desolate, if not more so, than that on the Kismayu front 200 miles to the southeast. The main South African force advanced from Marsabit toward the border town of El Yibo while the smaller force made a feint from Buna toward Moyale. This operation was the beginning of the planned diversionary attack into southern Abyssinia. From the air, the SAAF bombed suspected enemy positions in the path of the ground advance.

The South Africans quickly crossed the no-man's-land, and on January 18 occupied El Yibo on the Kenyan side of the border. El Yibo was not defended by the Italians because it was the domain of the Shifta bandits who had controlled the border area for years. All that time, neither the British nor the Italians had been able to pacify them. The Shifta had no loyalty to either side. When they saw the size and capabilities of the South Africans, however, they let them pass without incident.

From El Yibo, the South Africans moved into Abyssinia and followed a road eastward to Mega, occupying that town on January 30 against a small Italian force, most of which was captured. The Italian force defending Moyale to the southeast was now threatened from the west as well as from the south. Seeing this, the Moyale force abandoned the town and retreated deeper into Abyssinia. The British force from Buna then entered Moyale from the south and secured the city.

ANGRY TRIBESMEN STOP BRITISH COLUMN

As part of the diversionary attack into southern Abyssinia, the 25th KAR Brigade was to march up the western shore of Lake Rudolph in the three corners area of Kenya, The Sudan, and Abyssinia. They were then to round the north end of the lake, and made an incursion into southern Abyssinia. However, when the KAR men reached the village of Todenyang on the northwestern shore of the lake they were confronted by a large and hostile band of well-armed Merille tribesmen who would not let them pass. The Merilles, a warlike tribe, were not pro-Italian, but were angry with the British who had recently struck a deal with their traditional enemy, the Turkana tribe, and supplied them with arms and money. Cunningham dispatched several planes of the SAAF to the area, and they attacked the chief's camp in hopes of dispersing the tribesmen. It did not work. The Merille held their ground and the planes returned peppered with bullet holes. The Merille were good marksmen. Cunningham then concluded that it was a waste of resources to do battle with the Merille and ordered the KAR force to halt and go on the defensive. Soon, a British negotiating team arrived and eventually made a deal with the Merille similar to that which had been made with the Turkana. By then, however, the diversionary attack to the east was coming to an end and the Lake Rudolph advance was no longer needed. The 25th KAR was brought back and put in reserve for the 1st South African Division.

FIVE FRONTS

In the north, on January 31, the 9th Indian Brigade entered the undefended Gallabat/Metemma area and occupied both towns. The road beyond led to Gondar, one of the strongest Italian positions in all of East Africa. It was not intended that this force march on to Gondar and challenge the strong forces there, rather they were to establish a stationary front, pose a constant threat to Gondar and draw away Italians troops from other fronts. The 9th Indians advanced beyond the towns, but soon ran into an exceptionally large mine field and were ordered to halt. There they would remain until May.

With the attack at Gallabat/Metemma, Italian East Africa had been invaded on five fronts; at Kassala, Gallabat/Metemma, and Kurmuk in the north and at Kismayu and the Mega/Moyale area in the south. Only the advance at Gallabat/Metemma had been stopped.

There was hard fighting, though, in the north at Agordat, Eritrea where the Italians made a stand against the 5th Indian Division. After two days of fighting, the Indians succeeded in taking the town of Barentu on the Italian's left flank, threatening to envelope the Italian positions from the rear. To prevent this, the Italians withdrew to Keren, which was the strongest defense line in northern Eritrea. The 5th Indians occupied Agordat on February 1.

Keren, 45 miles northwest of the colonial capital, Asmara, was a natural fortress area where the flat plains suddenly gave way to sharp mountain peaks and a narrow pass through the mountains. From the peaks, the defenders could see for miles and bring fire to bear on anything that moved in front of them. The narrow pass through the mountains was ideal for ambushes and a potential death trap for any force that tried to make its way through. On top of all this, the Keren defenses were commanded by General Nicolangelo Carmineo, one of the most capable Italian officers in East Africa.

BRITISH STOPPED AT KEREN

On February 3, upon seeing the defenses at Keren Platt, Platt decided to attack at once, hoping that the Italian defenders might not yet be ready. He was wrong. For the next nine days, men of both the 4th and 5th Indian Divisions attacked at Keren but were repulsed on every occasion. Italian counterattacks failed to gain ground, but served to wear down Platt's forces. On February 12 Platt called an end to the attacks, realizing that he needed a stronger force to dislodge the Italians.

Platt could console himself, though, in knowing that by reaching Keren he had conquered about one-third of Eritrea.

On February 23, Platt received some of the reinforcements he had hoped for in the form of another Free French brigade which had been in reserve in Egypt. It consisted of four

CHURCHILL CRITICAL OF AFRICAN DIVISIONS

Despite the victory handed him by his African troops, Prime Minister Churchill remained critical of the makeup of the African colonial divisions. In a memo to the Secretary of State for War dated February 17, 1941 (three days after Kismayu fell), on the subject of what constitutes an army division, Churchill began by writing, "The term `division' must not become a stumbling block. A division is a tactical unit of all arms for use in its integrity against the enemy... for administrative purposes a divisional command may be bestowed upon a number of troops equal to a division, who have special duties assigned to them (and) this should not mislead us." Churchill goes on to write, "The African Colonial divisions ought not surely to be called divisions at all. No one contemplates them standing in the line against a European army. They comprise a large body of West and East African riflemen organized into battalions, and here and there, largely for administrative purposes, in brigades." He continues to say that after the defeat of the Italians in East Africa, "...these African `divisions' will be distributed in small posts and garrisons, with a number of mobile columns comprising armored cars, etc. The idea of their being supplied with divisional and corps artillery, together with a share of the line of communication troops on the British scale, is not sensible. They cannot be used as far north as Libya on account of the cold... They are, indeed, only miscellaneous units of the African Defence Force."

Churchill seemed not to be too well informed as to just who was fighting in East Africa. In a memo to Director of Military Operations he asks, "Are there any British battalions in East Africa?"

In 1943, Churchill apparently changed his mind about the value of the African divisions because he authorized their use in Burma against a formidable Japanese opponent.

Senegalese battalions, one Chad battalion, the 13th Demi-battalion of the French Foreign Legion (which included many Germans and Italians), and several companies of African-born Frenchmen. They joined the other Free French forces, which had arrived in December 1940, and were attached to the 4th Indian Division which held the left flank of the line at Keren. During March, three modern, British-made, Free French Blenheim bombers, flown by Free French crews, arrived from Equatorial Africa and were attached to the SAAF in Eritrea. This was followed by the arrival of two Free French sloops, the "Savorgnan de Brazza" and the "Commandante Duboc" which were placed under the command of the British Navy and operated in the Red Sea.

Late that month, General de Gaulle came to Eritrea to review his Free French forces there.

BRITISH VICTORIES IN THE SOUTH

In the south, the British forces faced much lighter opposition than in the north. This was understandable because Aosta had anticipated the strongest British attack would come in the north and had stationed over half of his forces there.

Advancing out of the trackless desert beyond the Kenyan border, the 11th (KAR) Division approached the seaport of Kismayu encountering very light opposition. As they neared the city, the British aircraft carrier HMS Hermes sent planes to bombard Italian defenses and the big gun of the cruiser HMS "Shropshire" also pounded the Italian defenders. The Italian tanker "Pensilvania" attempted to escape from Kismayu harbor but was fired upon and damaged by the Shropshire. The Pensilvania's captain then beached his vessel to keep it from sinking.

The KAR men entered the city on February 14, and much to their amazement were hailed as liberators by the black populace. This was especially surprising because these people had lived for more than two generations under Italian rule. There were virtually no white people in town. Most of them, being Italians, had fled in haste, leaving a significant amount of military supplies behind and many personal belongings. This phenomenon would happen in other town in Italian Somaliland in the coming weeks.

The 12th (KAR) Division and 1st South African Brigade had marched parallel to the 11th across the desert and crossed the Juba River further upstream. From there the 12th (KAR) turned north and, with the river on their left flank for protection, advanced northward toward southern Abyssinia. This was now a sixth front opened against the Italians in East Africa. The 1st South African Brigade moved southward and joined the 11th (KAR) for its advance on Mogadishu. After Kismayu was secured, the 11th (KAR) and South Africans advanced together to the Juba River and crossed it at Jumbo with little difficulty. The much-touted Italian Juba Defense Line was not nearly the obstacle the British thought it would be. It was lightly manned, and the troops were short of food and other supplies. In many places there were no defenses at all.

From Jumbo there was a good coastal road that led to Mogadishu that facilitated the British advance. Mogadishu was 225 miles away.

About this time, General Wavell came to Kenya to confer with Cunningham and was delighted with what he discovered. He was assured by Cunningham that Mogadishu could be taken soon, before the seasonal rains began, rather

Part of the Italian ammunition captured by the British at Mogadishu.

than after the rains in May, as had been planned.

In the Italian camp, Aosta had to blame someone for the defeat in the south and the loss of Kismayu and the failure of the Juba River Defense Line, so he fired the area commander, General Pesenti, and replaced him with General Di Lauro. This made little difference. The Italian forces in the south were simply too weak and demoralized to mount an effective defense.

As the 11th (KAR) and South Africans advanced up the coast, they found only light opposition offered by some "Black Shirt" units. They too were demoralized and quickly retreated under fire. The Allied advance continued and the port cities of Brava, Merka were occupied without opposition. At 5:00 a.m. on February 25, the lead Allied unit, the 23rd (Nigerian) Brigade, a motorized unit, entered Mogadishu unopposed. The Italians had decided not to fight for the city and declared it an open city. This was the first enemy colonial capital to fall to the British and a much-needed victory for the Allies. The capture of Mogadishu was hailed as a great achievement throughout the Allied camp.

The Allied advance on Mogadishu was so swift—it covered the 225 miles in three days—that not all of the Italian troops were able to get out of their way, and an additional 20,000 POWs were added to the British POW rosters. At one point, the Italians were surrendering so fast that the British told them they would have to go away and come back later to be processed. At Mogadishu, the British also captured 350,000 gallons of gasoline, food rations for 10,000 men for six months, and weapons of every kind. Furthermore, a prisoner of war camp was liberated, which held 200 British seamen, as well as an internment camp with 287 civilians, of which 197 were British citizens.

The capture of the food rations was most fortunate because the British found that the civilian population in and around Mogadishu was badly in need of food. For weeks, the local farmers had refused to deliver food to the city in an act of rebellion against the Italians. The captured food was quickly distributed to the populace.

When the Italians withdrew from Mogadishu, they showed no signs of planning a defense outside the city. Rather, they moved quickly up the "Strada Imperiale," one of the few paved roads in Italian East Africa, that led northward into Abyssinia. It soon became obvious to the British that the Italians were abandoning all of Italian Somaliland. The British were therefore obliged to send a small force up the coast of Italian Somaliland to secure the remaining 60% of the colony. It was a long journey up the coast to the famous Horn of Africa and the Gulf of Aden—some 900 miles—and the British force did not reach its last objective, the port of Bender Cassim on the Gulf of Aden, until early May.

The Italians retreating from Mogadishu did not intend to stop until they reached their next major defense line in the Harrar Plateau, over 600 miles north of Mogadishu and well inside Abyssinia. Between them and their goal was the barren and waterless Ogaden Desert. Once the Italians reached the Harrar defenses they were only 275 miles east of Addis Ababa.

At Mogadishu, the British did not set out in hot pursuit of the Italians. They took time to rest their troops and bring up supplies. On March 1, the main British force finally left

At regular intervals along the "Strada Imperiale" Mussolini had placed busts of himself. As the British passed, this was the fate of most of them.

Mogadishu following in the wake of the Italian retreat up the Strada Imperiale. In the lead again was the motorized 23rd Nigerian Brigade of the 11th (KAR) Division travelling on Italian gasoline.

Once again, the advance was rapid. The Italians put up a sizeable delaying action at Dagabur about 100 miles in front of their defense line in the Harrar Plateau, but this was quickly dispersed by the superior British force, and the British advance resumed. On March 10, they reached the Italian defense line in the Harrar Plateau at Jiggiga. There the British force halted to reconnoiter the situation and bring up supplies again.

In London, Churchill was very pleased with the rapid advance from Mogadishu and commented that "these were fine operations." And it looked so easy he considered taking the 1st South African Division, which was now on a very minor front in southern Abyssinia, from East Africa altogether and using it elsewhere.

WHO'S IN CHARGE NOW?

The British forces marching on the Harrar Plateau were somewhat weakened because many men had to stay behind to secure the conquered areas. The conquest had been so rapid that the British had not yet formed the body of individuals who would comprise the formal military government of occupation for the conquered Italian territories. Therefore, individuals and small groups of men had to be taken from the forces at hand to form an occupation regime. Some of the immediate problems they faced were that in parts of Mogadishu and in other towns, law and order had broken down and there was considerable looting by the populace, so soldiers had to be used to restore order until a police force could be organized. Furthermore, Mogadishu harbor had to be cleared of wreckage and especially the magnetic mines dropped four weeks earlier by planes from the Formidable. This was dangerous and slow work. Sailors from the British warships and the newly-released British POWs were pressed into service here.

In addition, there were tens of thousands of POWs that needed guarding and care. This involved still more manpower.

1st SOUTH AFRICAN DIVISION WITHDRAWN AND SENT ELSEWHERE

In the Mega/Moyale area of southern Abyssinia, the diversionary attack carried out by the 1st South African Division had ended and in late February it was replaced by the 25th KAR Brigade. The 1st South Africans were withdrawn, given rest, and then sent to Mombasa for departure to the Middle East.

In South Africa, Prime Minister Smuts was not happy to see his best unit depart. He wanted to keep it in East Africa and let that opinion be known in London. Churchill's private and rather crude retort was that war matters in Africa should be left "to the settlers" to resolve, implying that Dominion troops were to be used for more important things.

Another Fascist monument toppled from its pedestal. The Fascists counted the years in Roman numbers starting from their rise to power in 1922. The date at the base of the monument, eighteen, indicated that the monument was raised in 1940.

SOUTHERN ABYSSINIA

While the 11th (KAR) Division and 1st South African Brigade carried out the Mogadishu operation, the 12th (KAR) Division advanced up the Juba River Valley toward southern Abyssinia. Here again, the Italians offered only token resistance except on one occasion when they launched a spirited counterattack. The 24th Gold Coast Brigade took the brunt of the attack, but held their positions while suffering heavy casualties. The Italian attack was broken and the bulk of the Italian force continued their retreat leaving their wounded behind for the British to care for. Morale was very low and some Italian units simply fell apart—their askaris ran off into the bush and their Italian officers retreated on their own to the north. The 12th (KAR) advanced so fast that some small Italian units were bypassed but they usually surrendered when they ran out of food and water.

ITALIAN OFFICER'S DIARY

An Italian officer's diary was found during the 12th (KAR's) advance and an entry dated February 22 showed the decrepit conditions of the Italian fighting units. The diary read, "I am put in charge of 190 askaris. The following day they have shrunk to 130 and then after that to eighty. They got away during the night, either to the British lines or into the bush..."

At Bardera, the 12th (KAR) force turned east on February 28 on the road that led to Isha Baidoa on the main highway leading north out of Mogadishu. They occupied Isha Baidoa and turned north again, advancing up a good highway that led to Lugh Ferrandi. They occupied that town on March 3. Then, on March 5 they crossed the border from Italian Somaliland into southern Abyssinia and took the border town of Dolo.

At Dolo, the 12th (KAR) was joined by the 25th KAR Brigade coming in from the Mega area to the west. They joined forces and continued the advance northward. As the British force moved beyond Dolo they encountered some of the Ethiopian guerrillas that had held out in the mountains since the Italian conquest of 1935/36.

These freedom fighters greeted the men of the KAR warmly and showed their eagerness to help. Since the Ethiopian guerrillas operated primarily behind Italian lines, their aid could be of great value. However, there was a problem. There was no way to communicate with them because none of the guerilla unit had modern radio transmitters and receivers. The British had a quick answer. They brought in 200 carrier pigeons, their keepers, lofts, and food and assigned them to work with the guerrillas. From then on the guerrillas could communicate with the British by carrier pigeon.

From Dolo, the 12th (KAR) advanced to the northwest along the Ganale Dorya River, a tributary of the Juba River, toward the town of Neghelli. The Italians chose not to fight for Neghelli and withdrew. On March 21, Gold Coast troops occupied the town, followed by the 1st South African Brigade. From Neghelli, the 12th (KAR) force took a road to the west to Mega and then north to advance on the town of Yavello. They were then in an area of Abyssinia known as the Lake District. The Italians abandoned Yavello but made a stand a few miles beyond at the village of Soroppa, their force stiffened by "Carabinieri" units. The British forces launched a frontal attack on the Italian positions on March 31, with the support of an artillery bombardment and air cover by planes of the SAAF. It was too much for the Italians, and they retreated under fire, but not before several hundred surrendered to the British.

DIAMOND FIELDS ADVERTISER. KIMBERLEY, THURSDAY, MARCH 6, 1941

THERE'S GOING TO BE A NICE BIG SPLASH !

In South Africa, victory in East Africa looked like a certainty. This cartoon appeared in the Diamond Field Advertiser of Kimberley on March 6, 1941, with the caption "There's going to be a nice big splash." The animal shown is a springbok, a local antelope, whose name was used as a nickname for the South African armed forces.

After Soroppa, the British force halted because the seasonal rains had begun making further advances extremely difficult over the primitive, and sometimes nonexistent, roads. Furthermore, rivers became a major problem because there were very few bridges, and most of those that existed would not stand up under military traffic. Also, it was all but impossible for infantry to cross the rain-swollen rivers without boats—an item the 12th (KAR) did not have in their possession.

About this time trouble developed to the rear of the 12th (KAR) when the Boran people and a group of Somalis—traditional enemies—began fighting each other. Some of the KAR troops were detached from the front and sent to the rear to quell the disturbance. Also, during the rainy season, Cunningham took the opportunity to restructure the 11th and 12th (KAR) Divisions. Various units were moved about and the 11th (KAR) Division, in the Jiggiga area of eastern Abyssinia, became comprised of the 1st South African Brigade, the 22nd KAR Brigade, and the 23rd Nigerian Brigade. The 12th (KAR) Division remained in the south and was comprised of the 21st KAR Brigade, the 25th KAR Brigade, and the 24th Gold Coast Brigade.

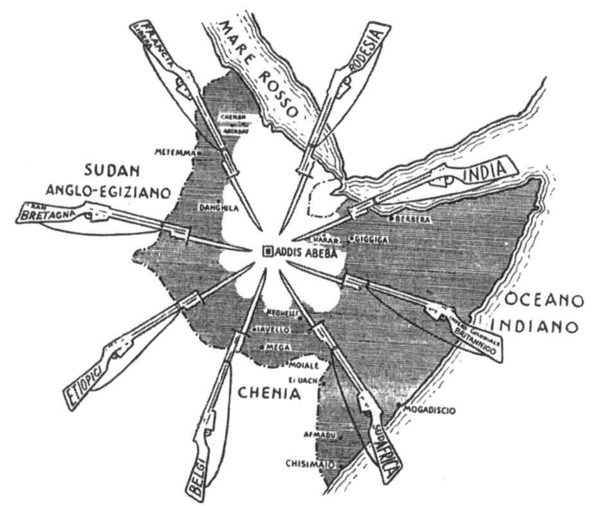

A leaflet directed at the askaris serving the Italians showing the array of Allied forces against them. Other leaflets read, "Why continue a hopeless struggle? Who will cultivate your fields? Who will educate your children? Why all die uselessly? Your surrender today is an honorable thing."

BACK IN MOGADISHU

The British were anxious to move more troops and supplies out of Mogadishu to support the advance of the 11th (KAR), but there were delays. The need to bring law and order to the city and clear the harbor were the main problems. When the harbor was made serviceable again, British warships began to dock and off-load reinforcements and supplies. The nearby port of Merca, thirty miles southwest of Mogadishu, was also used. The British ships in the area were all warships and had no way to carry or off-load vehicles larger than motorcycles, so larger vehicles were driven up from bases in Kenya some 800 miles away. This took time and added to the delay.

As for the Italian POWs, several large camps were provided for some of them in Italian Somaliland and others were shipped off to Kenya, the Middle East, India, South Africa, and Australia. Again, this took time and manpower.

In London, the British government addressed the newly acquired problem of administering conquered enemy territory. On March 26, 1941, the India Office and Colonial Office jointly announced the formation of the "Occupied Enemy Territories Administration (OETA)." The first concern of the "Standing Committee" was, of course, East Africa and they began to tackle the problem at once. Within weeks, capable and experienced administrators from all over the empire began arriving at Mogadishu to relieve the military troops for combat duty. One of the first things the new administrators did was to begin organizing a 1,500–man police force comprised of specially-selected Somali volunteers. As the policemen were trained, they were able to relieve soldiers.

IN THE NORTH

The RAF, operating from newly-acquired airfields inside Eritrea, had succeeded in gaining air superiority in the Keren area by the end of February 1941. This was an important step in any further British attempt to assault the strong Keren defenses. Also, Platt had received some Matilda "I" tanks and the 9th Indian Brigade as reinforcements. The 9th had participated in the failed advance from the Gallabat/Metemma area in January, and had been withdrawn and sent to the Keren area. The Gallabat/Metemma front had been put on hold by the British for the time being.

On March 15, Platt launched a major attack on the Keren defenses with all of his forces participating. This time his troops were able to make small gains into the Keren defenses but there were still hard battles ahead.

HAILE SELASSIE MOVES CLOSER TO ADDIS ABABA

In northwestern Ethiopia, Haile Selassie's army, working closely with Wingate's Gideon Force, had advanced down the road to Addis Ababa and on March 4 took the small town of Burye. This enabled the Emperor to move his headquarters forward to that town. He was then only 175 miles from his former capital and was the closest of any of the Allied columns. This news was, of course, spread all over Ethiopia by radio and leaflets.

On March 4, the Italians counterattacked, hoping to retake Burye. They had with them as allies a force of local Ethiopians who had long been enemies of Haile Selassie and did not want to see him return. Selassie's and Wingate's men held their positions and the Italian attack was repulsed. The Italians then retreated to their next defenses at the town of Debra Marcos only 110 miles northwest of Addis Ababa.

FROM FOUR DIRECTIONS

The third week in March 1941 was a difficult time for the Italians in East Africa because the British launched four attacks from four different directions within seven days. On March 15, the British renewed their attack at Keren in Eritrea, on March 16, a British amphibious force from Aden landed in Italian-occupied British Somaliland, on the 17th Cunningham's forces attacked the Italian defenses on the Harrar Plateau at Jiggiga, and on March 19 a KAR unit, in the company of the Belgian Congo Expeditionary Force from the Belgian Congo, invaded western Abyssinia from The Sudan.

At Keren, General Platt's reinforced 4th and 5th Indian Divisions continued their determined frontal assaults on the Italian defenses. The British, knowing a frontal attack would be costly, had considered a flanking attack, but the difficulty of the terrain ruled out much chance of success. Now, though, Platt had air superiority and that made virtually all of the Italian defense positions vulnerable from the air as well as the Italian supply columns in the rear. The British attacks lasted for three days with the British making only small gains. Those three days cost the British 3,000 casualties. Then there was a lull in the fighting. On March 20, the Italians counterattacked in strength and regained some ground with the Italian Air Force providing support for the attackers. The RAF planes rose to the challenge and a series of air battles developed over the battlefield.

In London, the British high command was worried about events at Keren and searched the area for possible reinforcements. But the Italian attacks that followed were much less intense and finally ceased altogether with no further gains.

On March 25, Platt's Indians attacked once more and after two more days of hard fighting finally broke through the main Italian defenses. The Italians began to retreat in disorder and Platt's men followed in close pursuit. The Italians were unable to make another stand and the town of Keren fell on March 27. All signs indicated that the Italians were now totally defeated in Eritrea. The British pressed their advantage and marched on to the capital, Asmara, and occupied it on April 1. There a POW camp was discovered and several hundred British POWs were freed. Then the 4th Indian Division turned toward the Red Sea and quickly covered the sixty miles to Massawa, Eritrea's main seaport. That city fell on April 8. Free French units played a major role in the capture of this important city. In the rapid advance, the British acquired another 10,000 POWs. British casualties rose to 4,000, making the battles at Keren the most costly, so far, of the East African campaign.

The remnants of the Italian force retreated into northern Abyssinia heading for their next defense line, a natural fortress area in the mountains around the town of Amba Alagi on the main Asmara-Addis Ababa road. Here, they would make another stand.

Churchill was elated by the victories in Eritrea and the capture of a second Axis colonial capital city. He sent his hardiest congratulations to Platt and the men of the 4th and 5th Indian Divisions.

The second of the four attacks, on March 16, occurred at Berbera, the capital and main seaport of the British colony of British Somaliland, which had been conquered by the Italians in August 1940. Two fresh Indian battalions plus Adenese and Somali units, called the "G (R) Force," were transported on two British cruisers, two destroyers, and several smaller ship from Aden and landed at Berbera. They quickly captured the city against very light opposition. Once ashore they immediately advanced westward along the coast toward the port city of Zeila which they took on March 18. They then turned inland to threaten the Italian left flank at Jiggiga on the Harrar Plateau in Abyssinia. On March 24, they occupied the town of Hargeisa, British Somaliland and were only 85 miles east of Jiggiga with a good road ahead of them leading to Jiggiga. By then, though, the Italians had withdrawn from Jiggiga, so the G (R) Force was ordered to halt at Hargeisa. The Italian force which confronted them at Hargeisa, the 70th Colonial Brigade, was now trapped between the G (R) Force and the British troops at Jiggiga. They attempted to retreat across open country north of Jiggiga to reach Diredawa, but in the process the Italian force completely disintegrated. Only the Italian officers made it to Diredawa on muleback. Their askaris had all disappeared.

A unit of Cunningham's 11th (KAR) Division then marched eastward from Jiggiga, linked up with the G (R) Force at Hargeisa, and, thus opened a line of communication and supply to the ports of Zeila and Berbera. Soon afterwards, Zeila and Berbera became the new ports of supply for Cunningham's forces. Heretofore, his supplies had to come overland from Mogadishu over 600 miles to the south.

The third of the four attacks took place at Jiggiga, when General Cunningham's KAR troops attacked Italian positions there. The Italians, seeing the threat to their left flank by the G (R) Force evacuated Jiggiga and were in this process when the KAR troops attacked. The Italians made a hasty retreat to their next defense line at Marda Pass, a natural defensive position where the road leads up from a grassy plain into a small mountain range. It was very similar geography to that of Keren.

Here the Italians had built fortifications in the late 1930s against a possible British invasion from British Somaliland. The Marda Pass defenses had gun emplacements, trenches, tank traps, tunnels, mine fields, and barbed wire obstacles. Cunningham's troops, of course, were aware of the fortifications and, after a delay of more than a day to resupply, moved forward approaching the Italian defenses with caution. Small units of the 23rd Nigerian Brigade were sent forward to scout the defenses and were soon fired upon and withdrew. The next day, Italian radio announced that the British had launched a major assault on the Marda Pass defenses and were repulsed. This was, of course, Italian propaganda for home consumption, but the British had learned by now that it was a good omen in that it gave the Italians an opportunity to retreat without losing too much prestige. Chancing that this might be the case, Cunningham ordered an immediate assault on the defense line for the next morning, March 21. The task was assigned to the 23rd Nigerians who were given considerable artillery support. The Nigerians attacked but failed to make much headway. The battle lasted all day. At dusk, however, the Italians withdrew blowing up many of the defensive positions before departing. By the next morning the defense line was empty and the Nigerians moved forward to secure it. Cunningham quickly sent his South Africans of the Royal Natal Carbineers through the defenses to pursue the retreating Italians. Using a flanking movement, the South Africans surprised the retreating Italians before they could get organized at their next defense line, Babile Pass on the Lyh River. The Italians quickly abandoned the Babile Pass defenses and retreated again toward the Bisidimo River, six miles from Harrar. On the morning of March 25, the 25th Nigerians attacked with strong artillery support and the Italian defenses quickly crumbled. The Italians declared Harrar an open city and the Nigerians quickly marched in and secured the town. The Nigerians moved into Harrar so rapidly that they caught the Italians in the process of beginning their retreat and not prepared to fight. Many of the Italian troops surrendered peacefully and, once again, abandoned sizeable quantities of supplies, especially ammunition. The surviving Italian forces retreated in good order to Diredawa where the British believed they would to make yet another stand. Since the area between Harrar and Diredawa was rugged, the Italians had many opportunities to create road blocks and they did so. They demolished bridges, blew down sections of cliff faces to cover the road, piled trees and rocks on the roadway and laid mines. These attempts delayed the British advance but did not stop it.

The British did not know it but after the losses at Harrar the Italians had only two brigades now in front of Addis Ababa.

At this moment, March 25, Cunningham's troops had been on the march constantly from Mogadishu for thirty days and had covered 1,054 miles.

About this time, orders came from Middle East Command in Cairo to Cunningham telling him that his South African artillery units would be withdrawn from East Africa and brought to Libya in the very near future. Rommel and his Afrika Corps had landed in North Africa and the British urgently needed reinforcements because some of their units had been withdrawn from North Africa and sent to Greece. Therefore, Cunningham was to accelerate the East African campaign and hopefully complete it before the South African artillery units were taken.

To this end the Italians cooperated nicely. They marched on through Diredawa without making a stand. The Transvaal Scottish were the first to enter the city on March 29 arriving just in time to prevent it from being looted. At Diredawa they discovered an ugly scene. One of the Italian colonial units had deserted en mass but not before killing seven of their Italian officers. Also at Diredawa was another POW camp, which was promptly liberated.

By taking Diredawa, the British cut the rail line between Addis Ababa and Djibouti in French Somaliland. And Addis Ababa was only 170 miles to the west.

The Italians withdrew now to the town of Awash on the west bank of the Awash River, twenty miles from Diredawa.

A temporary bridge constructed by British Pioneer (Engineer) units on the road to Addis Ababa.

As they retreated they blew up sections of the railroad and the all-weather road that paralleled it. Again the British expected their enemy to make a stand at Awash. This time they were right. The Awash River ran through a deep narrow canyon and was an excellent natural defensive position. Defenders on the far side of the canyon could cover every square inch of the canyon with deadly close-range fire. The Italians blew up both the railroad and highway bridges that spanned the canyon and dug in for another defense. At this point they were defending the capital of Abyssinia, Addis Ababa, which was only ninety miles to their rear.

Along the western ridge of the canyon the Italians had accumulated the remnants of several units totalling about 4,000 Italians and 2,000 Eritreans. Within this mix of defenders were policemen from Addis Ababa, Black Shirts, Carabinieri, airmen, engineers, and Shoan Bande units.

Cunningham knew the Italians were in serious trouble and were concerned about the 20,000 Italian civilians in Addis Ababa and the maintenance of law and order there. He therefore sent word to the Italians that if they would surrender the city, British forces would advance swiftly and secure it in an orderly transfer of power. The Italians did not reply. Meanwhile, the British continued their advance toward Awash.

On April 2, the lead British element, the 22nd KAR Brigade, reached the Awash River canyon and halted in front of the formidable natural obstacles with the Italian defenders in view on the western bank. The British plan of attack was to strike quickly and at the Italian's right flank. At about 7:00 a.m. on April 3 a company of KAR troops crossed the Awash River at a ford about six miles south of the blown railroad bridge. They had good artillery and small arms support from the east ridge. A second and third company followed and together they succeeded in reaching the top of the west-

The Addis Ababa-Djibouti Railroad bridge across the Awash River destroyed by the retreating Italians.

ern ridge. As they began to roll up the Italian line, the Italians broke and ran. Other British troops crossed the river and that day the town of Awash was occupied. Some 500 Italian askaris and seventy officers were captured.

The South African and East African Pioneers began work immediately on a temporary road bridge across the Awash which was completed on April 4. On April 5, the main body of the British force crossed and began to march on Addis Ababa with the 22nd KAR Brigade in the lead. The Awash had been the last natural defensive position in front of the capital.

The fourth of the four attacks against the Italians came on March 19, 1941, when KAR troops and the Belgian Congo Expeditionary Force entered western Abyssinia at the Sudanese border town of Jokau and marched up the Subai River in the direction of the town of Gambela sixty miles distant. Jokau had been occupied by the Italians in June 1940 and recaptured by the Sudanese Defence Force on February 25, 1941. Now, the only opposition encountered by the Congolese force was a 400-man Bande unit which was quickly dispersed. On March 21, as the Allied force approached the outskirts of Gambela, they ran into a strong line of defense established by a number of Bande units. The Congolese were sent forward to assault the defenses but were forced back. The next day the KAR unit circled around to the north and attacked the Bande defenses on their right flank. The Bande troops were taken completely by surprise and quickly withdrew. Soon afterwards the Congolese advanced forward and occupied the town. The KAR and Congolese then dug in at Gambela, their mission accomplished. Their value now was to draw away Italian troops from other fronts.

APRIL 1941: A BRITISH VICTORY AT HAND

During the month of April 1941, the British moved considerably closer to closing the 1,200-mile pincers movement that had begun in January at Kassala, Sudan in the north and Bura, Kenya in the south. As of April 1, though, large areas of Italian East Africa still remained in Italian hands, including Addis Ababa and the country's rich heartland around it and to the north. Also, areas of southern and western Abyssinia were, as yet, unconquered. Aosta's ground forces had been strengthened to a degree because the Italian Air Force had lost so many planes by now that it had a surplus of personnel. Therefore, some Italian airmen were pressed into the infantry.

British forces, on the other hand, were weakened due to attrition and having units called away. With the situation worsening in North Africa Wavell was becoming desperate for reinforcements of any kind. With the Italian Air Force all but defeated in East Africa, he ordered several RAF and SAAF air units, during the first week of April, to depart from Eritrea and Abyssinia for Egypt. Platt and Cunningham would have to conclude the East African campaign with what air units remained.

IN ERITREA

In Eritrea, Platt's 4th Indian Division, with the Free French unit in the lead, had captured the seaport of Massawa on April 6. Platt, however, had received disturbing news. On March 27, Wavell informed him that he would soon call away the main elements of his force, the 4th and 5th Indian Divisions, to Egypt and that Platt should wrap up the East African affair as soon as possible. The 4th Indian would be called.

On the other hand, Platt received a surprise when a local Eritrean chieftain, Ras Seyum, rode into Asmara and offered the services of his 7,000-man force to the British.

AT ADDIS ABABA

The Italians knew now that Addis Ababa could not be held. On April 3 and 4 the Duke of Aosta began dispersed his remaining forces in three directions into mountain redoubts with orders to hold out as long as possible. On April 5, a very successful air raid on the Addis Ababa Airport by the SAAF destroyed or damaged all thirty the Aosta's remaining aircraft in the area.

Now, for Aosta, it was no longer a matter of saving the East African colonial empire, but one of holding out in the mountain redoubts as long as possible in order to tie down as many Allied troops as possible. There was a glimmer of hope, though. General Irwin Rommel and his powerful Afrika Corps, together with the Italian forces in North Africa, were beginning to push the British back toward Egypt. If the Germans and Italians could conquer Egypt, they might yet march up the Nile Valley to save the situation in East Africa. And, it was remembered throughout the Axis world that on March 16, Hitler had predicted that the war would be won for the Axis by the end of the year. Aosta's troops, therefore, had a reason to hold out as long as possible. Also, the weather was with the Italians. The seasonal rains would begin again in late May or early June. This would hurt the British more than the Italians at this stage of the campaign and insure that the East African war would drag on for many more months, keeping sizeable numbers of British forces engaged in East Africa.

The first of the three mountain redoubts was Amba Alagi, 240 miles north of Addis Ababa astride the northern section of the Strada Imperiale. Amba Alagi was already occupied by many of the troops retreating from Eritrea. Aosta would go to Amba Alagi and command that stronghold himself.

The second redoubt was the Lake Tana/Gondar area, 230 miles northwest of Addis Ababa. This was another natural fortress area. The third redoubt was the mountainous Omo River area in the southern lakes district, about 100 miles southwest of Addis Ababa and would be commanded by General Pietro Gazzera, Aosta's second in command.

On April 5, civilians began evacuating Addis Ababa because law and order was beginning to break down. That evening the city's Chief of Police, General Mambrini, went to the village of Acachi, a few miles east of Addis Ababa and made contact with the leading elements of the British column as they approached. Mambrini pleaded with the British to march into the city at once to maintain order. The British were sympathetic to Mambrini's plea but could not react that fast. During the night, though, most of the British forces came up and early on the morning of April 6, they entered Addis Ababa with Mambrini leading the way.

The South Africans were the first to enter the city. This was a political concession to Prime Minister Smuts who was having political difficulties at home and badly needed a victory. Following closely behind were the KAR troops.

THE VATICAN RADIO CONTINUES

Soon after their conquest of Ethiopia in 1936, the Italians allowed the Vatican to install a radio station at Addis Ababa to broadcast religious messages, along with a generous dose of pro-Italian propaganda, to the Christian population. When the British arrived they found the station still in operation under the direction of Vatican personnel. The British allowed the station to continue operating but with close oversight and censorship.

After securing Addis Ababa, Cunningham sent the 1st South African Brigade north following the Italian troops as they retreated to Amba Alagi. He had yet to close the pincers by meeting Platt's troops in the north and this was the logical direction to proceed. Besides, Cunningham learned that the Duke of Aosta was accompanying the troops moving to Amba Alagi. The capture of Aosta was a top priority for the British.

KAR units nearing Addis Ababa.

As the British troops moved north several Ethiopian guerilla units joined them and were assigned to guard the flanks of the advancing force, cut the enemy's lines of communication, and contain isolated enemy garrisons. The British kept the guerrillas supplied with arms, ammunition, food, and money by air drop.

PROBLEMS IN ADDIS ABABA

Back in Addis Ababa, a city with a prewar population of 130,000, the civilian situation was very tense. The British had very few people they could spare to maintain order in the city as well as guard the many POWs that had been accumulated. The Italian police, with police Chief Mambrini's cooperation, were put under British command and ordered to do their best to help out.

In London, Churchill knew of the situation in Addis Ababa and expected trouble. On April 4, he wrote President Roosevelt telling of the possibility that the white civilian population might have to be placed in concentration camps for their own protection. Churchill wrote:

> *"We have no means of discharging such a task (law and order in Addis Ababa) until the organized fighting ends... Every ounce of transport we possess is sustaining our troops in their long advance. Results might be a lamentable breakdown, whole burden of which would be cast on us, like the concentration camps in the old South African (Boer) War."*

WEST OF ADDIS ABABA

West of Addis Ababa, Haile Selassie's and Wingate's forces attacked the Italian defenders at Debra Marcos on April 6, the same day Cunningham's forces occupied Addis Ababa. The Italians at Debra Marcos put up a token defense but then surrendered. Selassie and Wingate found they had 4500 POWs on their hands. The Emperor was now only 150 miles from his capital, but there was still a sizeable Italian force in front of him.

That force now became a threat to Addis Ababa if they chose to attack the city from the west. Cunningham saw this threat and had to post some of his forces just to the west of Addis Ababa to protect the city from that force, which Cunningham estimated at 40,000 strong. But, like the other Italian forces, this force was demoralized and short of almost everything. They did, however, have some 200 antiquated artillery pieces and several armored trucks serving as armored cars, and, they were capable of attacking Addis Ababa if they chose to do so. Cunningham believed an attack was not likely. He would be proven right.

ITALIANS STAND AT DESSIE

On April 17, the lead elements of the 1st South African Brigade reached the Combolcia Pass about ten miles south of Dessie. There the Italians had strewn the highway with wrecked vehicles, making it impossible to pass. As more British troops came up to remove the vehicles, they came under sudden and heavy fire from both sides of the highway. It was a clever ambush and the South Africans had blindly walked into it. After taking heavy casualties the South Africans withdrew. The Italians were well entrenched, so a British frontal assault was out of the question. The only alternative was to reduce the Italian positions one at a time with artillery, air support, and ground attacks across the rugged terrain. This took the British forces five days to accomplish making it the longest, and one of the bloodiest, battles of the entire campaign.

On April 22, the last of the Italian strongholds was taken and the Italian defense collapsed. Many Italian troops surrendered but others fled to the north. The way to Dessie was now open but the South Africans did not rush into the city. They had to regroup their forces, clear the wrecked vehicles, and guard against another ambush along this mountainous stretch of road. Therefore, the South Africans inched their way toward Dessie and entered the city on April 26.

As a result of the battle for Dessie the South Africans captured 6,000 Italian troops, 52 artillery pieces, 236 machine guns, and 240 trucks and other vehicles.

On April 29, the Italian forces reached Amba Alagi and began digging in to defend that area.

At this time, no British force was organized to pursue the Italians retreating into the Lake Tana/Gondar region. That force would be dealt with at a later date.

SAAF UNITS OFF TO EGYPT

In mid-April Wavell called the 1st and 2nd SAAF Squadrons to Egypt to help stop Rommel. With the rainy season coming in East Africa, the aircraft would be of more value up north. A week later the 14th SAAF Squadron, flying the valuable Martin Maryland bombers, went off to Egypt along with the 12th SAAF Squadron and the 60th SAAF (photographic) Squadron.

INTO THE LAKE DISTRICT

It was at this time that Cunningham sent the 11th (KAR) Division south out of Addis Ababa to pursue the Italians fleeing to the Omo River area in the lake district. The 11th (KAR), though, had suffered considerable attrition during its long march from Kenya and had to be reinforced. To this end several fresh units from South Africa, on their way to Egypt, were assigned temporarily to the 11th. These were the 2nd South African Brigade, the 1st Natal Mounted Rifles, and a field force battalion of replacements. The units were on loan only until May 27.

As for the 11th (KAR's) mission, it was very important to the security of Addis Ababa because if the Italians could establish themselves on the Omo River line, only 100 or so miles from Addis Ababa, they were close enough to attack the capital and/or its supply lines if they chose to do so. The other two Italian mountain strongholds were further from the capital and no threat to it.

Therefore, the first mission of the 11th (KAR) Division was to place itself between the Omo River line and Addis Ababa. This mission would be accomplished when the 11th (KAR) reached the town of Shashamanna 115 miles south of Addis Ababa. After reaching Shashamanna they were to march on the short distance to Dalle and there link up with the 12th (KAR) moving up from the south.

The operation began during the third week in April, with the reinforced 11th (KAR) Division moving out of Addis Ababa, heading south along the road to Shashamanna. The 22nd KAR Brigade was in the lead, the road was good, and the opposition almost nonexistent. They quickly took the town of Bocoggi and on April 24 occupied Pointi Machi. Several days ahead of them, now, were the fleeing Italians units.

During the first week in May, enough Italian forces accumulated in the Shashamanna–Lake Margherita–Soddu area to be in a position to block the advance of the 11th (KAR).

In southern Abyssinia, a Gold Coast battalion was brought in from Mogadishu to strengthen the 12th (KAR) Division which was now ordered to continue its advance northward into the lake district. Their advance was slowed, however, because it was now raining heavily. With the 11th (KAR) moving south out of Addis Ababa and the 12th (KAR) moving north the Italians would be caught in yet another pincers movement. Plans called for the two British forces to meet at Dalle, just south of Shashamanna.

As the British moved deeper into the lake district from both the north and south, they encountered more Ethiopian guerrillas, some of whom had been holding out since the Italian conquest of 1935/36. As a result of their presence, a typical guerrilla-type war had already evolved in parts of the lake district whereby the guerrillas held the countryside and the

Italians held the towns, and during the daylight hours the Italians held and used the roads, but at night they became the domain of the guerrillas. The British, of course, supplied the guerrillas with additional arms and ammunition, but that caused an unexpected problem. Some individuals and small groups took advantage of the situation to attack rivals and murder collaborators. Some Italian prisoners were also mistreated and a few were killed. The British had to take steps to corral their unruly allies.

On May 10, a detachment of 12th (KAR) advancing out of Neghelli, to the east of the main force, attacked and captured the town of Wardara after a week-long, off-and-on, rain-delayed battle with the Italian defenders. Wardara was on yet another road that led to the Dalle area from the east. With the capture of Wardara, the Italians in the lake district were now being threatened from three directions.

In the northern part of the lake district, the Italians put up a strong rear-guard action just north of Shashamanna which had to be overcome by a determined and successful attack by the 1st Natal Mounted Rifles. The next day, May 14, the 11th (KAR) took Shashamanna, their first main objective. Some 800 Italian POWs were taken along with two artillery pieces and nine light tanks.

All three of the Italian forces in front of the three-pronged British pincer arms, comprising the remnants of seven Italian divisions, now came together at Dalle and turned westward toward Soddu and the Omo River defense line which was being constructed by General Gazzera's forces.

On May 17, the 11th (KAR) Division's 22nd KAR Brigade took Dalle and immediately turned westward in pursuit of the retreating Italians. Neither of the units of the 12th (KAR) Division, coming up from the south and east, had yet reached Dalle, their advances being plagued by rain and mud.

The Italian force thus eluded the British pincers and made it safely to the Omo River defenses.

The town of Abalti, on the Jimma-Addis Ababa road, was the northern anchor of the defense line and Soddu was the southern anchor. Smaller Italian forces were positioned east of the river to await and delay the British.

BACK AT AMBA ALAGI

On the northern front, Cunningham's South Africans were approaching Amba Alagi from the south while General Platt's 5th Indian Division moved down from Eritrea in the north. It was the Indians who made first contact with the Italians in their stronghold on April 29. At that point they halted, awaiting the pincers to close.

THE AXIS POWERS WIN IN GREECE

By the end of April 1941, the Axis forces in Greece had succeeded in defeating the combined Greek and British forces there. The badly-mauled British units began evacuating Greece on April 28. It was a bitter defeat for the Allies, but it had its positive side in that more British forces would now be available for North Africa. This, in turn, lessened the pressure on the British to pull units out of East Africa.

HAILE SELASSIE RETURNS TO ADDIS ABABA

In late April and early May, the Italian forces opposing Haile Selassie's army disintegrated with many of the troops marching south to the Omo River area. A force of 4,500 troops was left behind to hold Debra Marcos but they were demoralized, short of everything, and no real threat to the Allied force. Selassie was able to bypass the Debra Marcos force and march on to Addis Ababa. That great day came on May 5 when the Emperor, his army, and the British forces under Wingate entered the city in a triumphal parade. It had been five years to the day since the Italians had entered the city with their triumphal parade. Wingate was in the parade riding a white horse and leading his irregulars. The Emperor raised the Ethiopian flag over his palace and proclaimed that the nation of Ethiopia existed once more. The word "Abyssinia," the Italian name for the country, faded into history.

Churchill sent his congratulations to the Emperor saying "It is with deep pleasure that the British nation and Empire have learned of Your Imperial Majesty's welcome home. Your Majesty was the first of the lawful sovereigns to be driven from his throne and country by the Fascist-Nazi criminals and you are the first to return in triumph."

WINGATE—A HERO DEMOTED

Back in England, Colonel Orde Wingate had become a celebrity. The remarkable exploits of his Gideon Force were widely reported in the British press and he became the hero of the hour. Having the public's ear, Wingate heaped praise on the Ethiopians saying, "The value of the Ethiopian help to us in that campaign was greater than we ever admitted. It shortened the war by many months."

But Wingate went too far. While still in the public's eye he criticized some of his superior officers in East Africa calling them "military apes." For this grievous breach of military protocol, he was summoned to Middle East Headquarters in Cairo and demoted to major. Soon afterwards, while still in Cairo, he caught malaria. The fall from grace was so devastating to Wingate that on July 4, 1941, racked with fever from the malaria, he attempted suicide by slitting his throat in two places. Quick action by others saved his life.

Selassie's new government was a government in name only, however. The British insisted that as long as there were hostilities in the land and British troops were engaged with the enemy, the British military commanders should rule. Selassie had little choice but to accept the situation.

MAY–JUNE 1941: THE BEGINNING OF THE END IN EAST AFRICA

In the north, Cunningham's troops made contact with the enemy at Amba Alagi on May 1. Now the Italians were forced to defend their stronghold on two fronts. On May 3, both Cunningham's and Platt's troops attacked the stronghold at the same time. The Italians were well-entrenched and repulsed both attacks. Amba Alagi would be a tough nut to crack. On May 4, Platt's Indians circled around to the west and, under a heavy supporting artillery barrage, succeeded in capturing and holding three strategic mountain peaks. On May 6, a British force attacked again and was driven back. Several attacks were launched on May 9, and again the Italians prevailed. British attacks continued for the next seven days, but as the Italians began to run low on ammunition, food, and water they gave way. The Italians, by now, also had a large number of wounded on hand and inadequate medical supplies. On May 18, troops of the 5th Indian Division broke into the stronghold and captured the town of Amba Alagi. This threatened the integrity of the entire Italian defenses. Finally, with the fall of Amba Alagi, the Duke of Aosta announced that he would surrender. The surrender did not apply to other Italian troops holding out elsewhere in East Africa.

On May 19, a formal surrender ceremony was held at Amba Alagi and the Duke and some 7,000 of his troops became prisoners of war. With this, the supreme Italian command in East Africa passed to General Gazzera, commander of the forces on the Omo River front.

Immediately following the victory at Amba Alagi, Cunningham's 1st South African Brigade were called away to Egypt and within days embarked for the north at the port of Massawa. A short time later Platt's 5th Indian Division was also transferred to Egypt.

ONE DOWN, TWO TO GO

With the demise of the Amba Alagi stronghold only two Italian redoubts now held out in East Africa, that in the lake district along the Omo River in the south and that in the Lake Tana/Gondar region in the north. The British decided to attack both at the same time. As the British ground forces maneuvered for their attacks, the British Navy took action to resolve still another problem that remained in Eritrea—Assab.

THE CAPTURE OF ASSAB

In Eritrea, the port of Assab, at the eastern end of the Eritrean coast, had been bypassed by the British when they moved into northern Abyssinia. Assab was an Italian naval base and posed a threat to Allied shipping in the Red Sea. But, without renewed supplies of fuel, food, and other necessities, the Italian ships and planes were of little value. In early June, therefore, the Italians abandoned Assab and dispersed into the bush. British naval personnel, assisted by several ships from the Royal Indian Navy, then occupied the port on June 12, 1941. An Indian unit arrived a few days later from Aden to relieve the British sailors and to carry out the occupation duties.

BACK IN ABYSSINIA

When the 11th (KAR) Division reached Dalle, the 12th (KAR) Division was still miles away to the south having been delayed by heavy rain and mud. It was raining on the 11th (KAR) too but not as heavily. They did not wait, however. They turned westward in pursuit of the fleeing Italians.

On May 18, the Italians made a stand at the village of Colito, a few miles east of Soddu. At dawn on May 19, the 1st Nigerian Regiment attacked the Colito defense hitting the Italian's flank. The Italians, after firing a few shots, broke and ran and retreated to Soddu. A KAR unit then occupied Colito.

The Italians did not stop to defend Soddu, rather they retreated to the west bank of the Omo River, to make their stand there.

On May 22, the 11th (KAR's) Nigerians occupied Soddu unopposed. The capture of Soddu did not result in the breaching of the Omo River defense line, because Soddu was on the east bank of the river and the defense line was on the west bank.

After the capture of Soddu, the 2nd South Africa Brigade was pulled from the 11th (KAR) Division and sent to Berbera for transfer to Egypt as planned. They were replaced by a KAR battalion brought in from Mogadishu and a Nigerian battalion from Addis Ababa.

The Omo River defense line was a strong natural barrier. The river ran through a small canyon with steep cliffs on either side, and the river plain was a dense, mosquito-plagued jungle. And, because of the rains, the river was swollen and still rising. The three roads leading into the valley had been heavily mined and were within range of Italian artillery. There was yet another problem. The British were now short of bridging materials, having already built some seventy emergency bridges during their advances. Bridging material was on its way to the 11th (KAR) but had not yet arrived. Meanwhile, the 11th (KAR's) commander decided to put men on the other shore as soon as possible. The mined roads were cleared and on the night of June 2 a battalion of KAR troops was put across the river in assault boats. Once ashore, they were discovered by the Italians and were pinned down by artillery. They remained there for three days.

On June 5, two KAR companies and two Nigerian companies established a second bridgehead and were promptly attacked by Italian Black Shirt units but, with fire and support from the east bank, the KAR men and Nigerians were able to drive them off. Later that day, the Nigerians established a third bridgehead.

All three bridgeheads had to sustain themselves for five more days with whatever supplies could be brought over the river by boat, because the bridging material had not yet arrived. Despite their precarious situation, the Nigerians were able to advance some 2,000 yards up the river.

On June 10, the bridging material arrived and a pontoon bridge was promptly constructed under the protective cover of the guns of the British artillery units from the east bank. By nightfall the tanks and armored cars of the 11th (KAR) were across the river. They linked up with the bridgeheads, and together they began rolling up the Italian defense line heading north toward Abalti. That town was soon taken without a fight, and the Italian's Omo River defense line was no more. Another 3,900 Italian POWs were acquired.

From Abalti, the 11th (KAR) men turned westward and followed the road toward Jimma with the remnants of the Omo River defense line fleeing before them. The fall of Jimma was imminent. This was confirmed when the remaining flyable Italian aircraft at Jimma departed en mass for Gondar in the north. Cunningham feared that Gazzera's forces might try to march northward and join the defenders in the Lake Tana/Gondar region, so to prevent this he sent a sizeable force westward out of Addis Ababa to occupy the road junction at Lechemti seventy miles north of Jimma. This would block Gazzera's escape route to the Lake Tana/Gondar region.

As the 11th (KAR) approached Jimma, more Italian askaris surrendered or deserted. The remaining Italian force passed through Jimma without stopping and continued to retreat to the west. They would make no attempt to reach the Lake Tana/Gondar stronghold in the north. General Gazzera, his headquarters staff, and the Jimma garrison joined the westward retreat. On June 20, Jimma fell to the KAR troops unopposed.

During the next week, Ethiopian guerrillas occupied the nearby towns of Gore, Bonga, and Yubdo while Nigerian troops of the KAR occupied Ghimbi.

TROUBLE IN JIMMA

The area around Jimma had been strong guerrilla country ever since the end of the first East African war in 1936. When it fell into British hands, some 12,000 Ethiopian guerrillas descended on the city to celebrate and seek revenge by looting and killing collaborators. Cunningham was appalled at the behavior of his allies and ordered the 22nd KAR regiment to remain in Jimma to restore order. He also had another problem. In the preceding days, his rapidly advancing force had captured another 15,000 Italian troops and they need guarding. This task was also assigned to the 22nd KAR regiment at Jimma, which meant that the 22nd was lost to him as a combat force. But, the Italians were showing few signs of offering strong resistance, so Cunningham gambled that the units he had left in his striking force could continue the pursuit successfully.

There was yet another problem at Jimma. Before the Italians fled they left a large portion of the colony's gold bullion in the care of the local Roman Catholic bishop who promised to guard it as best he could. The British soon learned of the hidden gold and a detachment of KAR men were sent to fetch it. The gold was hidden in the church's basement. Upon entering the church, the KAR men were confronted by the angry bishop who threatened to excommunicate any one in the detachment who was a Roman Catholic if they took the gold. Since several of the officers and men were Roman Catholics, they backed off. A second detachment was then formed of non-Catholics and they succeeded in retrieving the gold.

GAZZERA SURRENDERS

Gazzera's force, now down to 5,000 askaris and 300 Italian officers, including nine generals, retreated to Dembidollo in the Gore region for one last stand. They could retreat no further because there they encountered the Belgian Congo Expeditionary Force that had invaded western Abyssinia in March and had been manning a static defense line at nearby Gambela ever since. The Congolese were itching for a fight and this was their chance. As Gazzera's column approached, the Congolese went on the attack. Fortunately for the Allied forces the weather improved and the SAAF began bombing the retreating Italians several times a day. With the Congolese advancing on them from the west, SAAF constantly planes overhead, and the KAR troops closing in from the east, the Italians were trapped. Furthermore, it began raining heavily again.

Gazzera could see that his position was hopeless and, on July 3, radioed the Allied command in Addis Ababa that he was ready to surrender all the remaining Italian forces in his area. Arrangements were made and on July 6, the Belgian Congolese commander, Major General Gilliaert, accepted Gazzera's surrender at Gambela.

Hearing of the surrender at Gambela, several smaller Italian units than had been bypassed by the British advance, surrendered. This included a 600–man force at Kretei.

TWO DOWN, ONE TO GO

Now, only the Lake Tana/Gondar stronghold remained. This area, like that of Amba Alagi, was an ancient nature fortress area where armies had made last stands in years past. Leading away from the northern and eastern shores of the lake is a gentle sloping plain that ends in all directions in a semicircle of sharp mountain peaks. With an attack across the lake unlikely, holding the mountain passes and the peaks became paramount for the Italians.

At the southern end of, and inside, the semicircle of mountains is the town of Debra Tabor. This is an excellent staging area for troops. Soldiers guarding the mountain passes beyond Debra Tabor had the luxury of returning the short distance to Debra Tabor from time to time to sleep in a bed and eat hot meals.

The British, fully aware of the importance of Debra Tabor, bombed the city repeatedly to make it as unpleasant as possible for the Italians.

The Gondar defenses were even more formidable because the Italians had long planned that the Gondar region might someday be needed as a mountain redoubt and had stocked it with large amounts of food, water, and other supplies. They had also prepared many defensive positions in the mountains and ambush sites along the roads and passes leading over the mountains.

In early April, one of Platt's Sudanese units attacked the Italians twice at the town of Wolchefit, on the road leading into the mountains northeast of Gondar. Both times the Sudanese were beaten back. At the end of June, the Sudanese tried again. This time they had Ethiopian guerrillas operating behind the Italian lines. But, again, the Italians held. By this time the spring rains had come and conditions were rapidly worsening for both sides.

The British tried again by attacking from the southeast at Debra Tabor in early July. This attack was coordinated with an attack from the west by units operating out of the Gallabat/Metemma area. Again, the Italians held on both fronts.

By now the rains were making many of the roads impassible and the British were having trouble bringing up supplies. Besides, their forces were much in need of rest and there were thousands of POWs to guard and care for. Therefore, the British command decided to call off the final offensive against Gondar until the rains stopped in October. The British, therefore, established defensive positions around Gondar and settled down to wait out the rains. The Nigerian and Gold Coast troops were sent home and a large part of Cunningham's forces were shipped off to Egypt where the situation was still critical. Also going to Egypt was Cunningham himself, where he was to command the British 7th Army. Major General H. E. deR. Wetherall took over Cunningham's responsibilities at Gondar.

There were still a force of about 600 Italians and some Bande units holding out on the border with French Somaliland, but they were cut off from supplies and were harassed by the local Danakil tribesmen. In early July, they surrendered to the British.

The Free French Expeditionary Force from Equatorial Africa, along with some British troops, was placed around the border of the Vichy-controlled French Somaliland to establish a land blockade of that colony. The British Navy, of course, maintained the blockade at sea. The only communication the French colony now had with other parts of the French empire was by air and an occasional submarine that ran the blockade to Madagascar.

CHURCHILL TOOK PITY ON THE BABIES

With the tightening of the blockade around French Somaliland Churchill displayed a measure of pity for the babies in the French colony and, on June 11, sent the following memo to General Ismay, Chief of Staff of the War Cabinet:

"Our policy is the strictest possible blockade of Djibouti. The fairest terms have been offered to these people. Nothing must be done to mitigate the severity of the blockade. It might however be possible to arrange that if a return were furnished of the number of newborn babies and young children a very limited amount of nourishment might be allowed to pass into the town under the most strict restrictions and surveillance... no supplies of any kind are to move into the town without my approving the arrangements first."

With the collapse of the Italians in the south, all of the SAAF air units there were now sent to the north and put under the command of the RAF. As weather permitted, the SAAF and RAF planes raided targets in the Gondar region to wear down the Italians as much as possible and keep them on the defensive.

The 12th (KAR) Division was brought in from the lake district and assigned the task of guarding the approaches to Gondar until plans for the new attack in the fall materialized. They were soon joined by Haile Selassie's Ethiopian Army and many of the Ethiopian guerrillas. All in all, the British forces around Gondar amounted to some 15,000 men.

During the lull the Italians were active, too. Rome radio praised the Gondar defenders for holding off the attackers in June and July and held them up to the world as the finest the Italian Army had to offer. The defenders also used their time to mine the passes, build more defensive positions, ambush sites and make other improvements. By fall, the Italian's fighting spirit was again high and they were prepared.

MAJOR CHANGES IN EAST AFRICA

With the war all but won in East Africa, London saw the opportunity to use the resources there for the benefit of the Allies. First and foremost, of course, was the removal of combat units for service elsewhere, especially in North Africa. This process had already begun when, on June 4, 1941,

Churchill wrote a lengthy letter to Wavell setting the parameters for reorganizing East Africa. Churchill wrote, "All future British Indian divisions will go in at Basra (Iraq where an Iraqi rebellion had occurred in May and Iraq was still an unstable theater of operations), and I hope that Eritrea, Abyssinia, Kenya, and the Somalilands can be left to native African forces… and armed white police."

Since some industry had been developed in Eritrea by the Italians, Churchill now saw that industrial capacity benefiting the Allies. His letter to Wavell stated that "military workshops" should be installed in Eritrea at Massawa and Asmara as well as Port Sudan, The Sudan, and Djibouti, French Somaliland—"when we get it."

It had earlier been agreed that, with the end of hostilities in East Africa, Middle East Command in Cairo would be relieved of the burden of command for East Africa and a new East African Command established. This was accomplished during the summer of 1941 when the new Command's headquarters was located in Nairobi. General Platt was appointed Commander-in-Chief East Africa and had responsibility for everything in East Africa from Eritrea to the Zambesi River, which was the southern border of Northern Rhodesia.

Chapter 10
THE WAR IN THE NORTH AND RELATED ISSUES (JANUARY-AUGUST 1941)
THE APEX OF HOSTILITIES IN AFRICA

Between January and May 1941, two wars raged in Africa, one in East Africa and the other in North Africa. This period of time marked the apex of armed conflict on the African continent during World War II. The war in East Africa all but ended in May, while the war in North Africa continued until May 1943.

During the first months of 1941, prospects of an Allied victory in both East Africa and North Africa were bright, but by March the Germans had come on the scene in North Africa and the outcome there became very much in doubt.

JANUARY-MARCH 1941: A TIME OF ALLIED VICTORIES IN AFRICA

On January 19, 1941, as the British offensive in East Africa was getting underway, Hitler and Mussolini were meeting at Hitler's mountain home at Berchtesgaden. In the preceding weeks the Italians had suffered major military setbacks in both the Balkans and North Africa. In the Balkans, Greek troops had pushed Mussolini's best army units out of Greece altogether and back into Italian-controlled Albania where they were forced to go on the defensive. Mussolini's plans for conquering Greece were in shambles.

In North Africa, the two British Divisions there, the 6th Australians and British 7th Armoured, known as the 8th Corps, had pushed the Italians out of Egypt and advanced into Libya and encircled the major Libyan port-city of Tobruk.

Offshore the British Navy was getting the upper hand in the Mediterranean Sea over the Italian Navy while the RAF, time-and-again, out-fought the Italian Air Force in both the Balkans and Africa.

Quite understandably, Hitler was upset with these reversals because, unbeknownst to Mussolini, he was planning to attack the Soviet Union in May and did not want to have powerful British and Greek forces on his southern flank when that attack began.

At the Berchtesgaden meeting, Hitler was quite insistent that Mussolini accept German military help in both the Balkans and North Africa. Hitler believed that with adequate German reinforcements the Axis Powers could win in both places. Mussolini had to bury his pride and agree that such help was needed. It was agreed that two German divisions would be sent as soon as possible to North Africa and the additional German forces would be sent to the Balkans beginning in April.

That help in North Africa could not come too soon, because two days later, Australian troops broke through the Italian defenses at Tobruk and on the next day, January 22, occupied the city. Italian losses were tremendous. The Australians captured 25,000 prisoners and 87 tanks at a cost of only 400 casualties. Furthermore, the Italians were forced to scuttle the cruiser San Giorgio at Tobruk.

LIBYAN LOYALTIES

As the British invaded Libya they found, much to their surprise, that hundreds of Libyans came forward and offered to serve in the British forces. Some were accepted, but most were not.

Within forty-eight hours the British cleared Tobruk harbor of mines and wreckage and began using it as their main base of supply for their ground forces.

With Tobruk secured, the British juggernaut rolled on to the west. The British force now split in two with the 6th Australians following the Libyan coast and the 7th Armoured, under General Sir Richard O'Connor, cutting across the open desert of Libya's "bulge." The mission of the 7th Armoured was to reach the coast of the Gulf of Sidra south of the major Italian port of Benghazi as soon as possible and, hopefully, trap the entire Italian 10th Army at Benghazi. The terrain in this part of Libya, Cyrenaica Province, was flat and hard, so armored cars led the 7th Armoured's march across the barren desert driving at near highway speeds and meeting virtually no Italian opposition. The British tanks and motorized infantry, which were much slower, kept up as best they could.

On January 23, O'Connor's armored cars discovered an Italian force, equipped with tanks, defending Mechili, 100 miles west of Tobruk and 45 miles southwest of Derna. There the armored car spearhead halted until the British tanks came up. On January 27, the British attacked the Mechili defenses, in what was to become the first sizeable tank battle of the North African campaign. The British, using their "Matilda" tanks which proved to be superior to those of the Italians, soon prevailed. The Italians lost eight tanks and one was captured while the British lost one "Matilda" and six lighter tanks. The Italians abandoned Mechili, and the race across the Cyrenaican bulge resumed.

Meanwhile, on the coast, the Australians took the coastal city of Derna on January 30, 90 miles beyond Tobruk, and continued their advance toward Benghazi.

On February 5, O'Connor's armored cars reached the Gulf of Sidra at the town of Beda Fomm and cut the road leading out of Benghazi just in time to stop the Italian retreat. The entire Italian 10th Army was trapped. The Italians had hoped to reach a new defense line at El Agheila on the southern coast of the Gulf of Sidra where they had planned to make a determined stand. Now, that plan was foiled.

On the coast, the Australians were rapidly approaching Benghazi from the east. On February 6, the Italians gathered most of their strength at Beda Fomm and attempted to break out of the trap—but the 7th Armoured held the line. That day the 7th Armoured was able to get another force to the rear of the Italian force south of Benghazi, cutting off the Italian's retreat back to that city. Later that day the Australians took Benghazi and marched on to link up with O'Connor's forces.

On February 7, the Italians tried again to break out at Beda Fomm, but the 7th Armoured held again while the British column south of Benghazi and the Australians smashed into their rear. In the process the entire Italian 10th Army was decimated. The Italian troops abandoned their tanks and vehicles and surrendered by the thousands. In the next few days the British and Australians gathered in 130,000 Italian prisoners, 380 tanks, 1000 artillery pieces, and 241 aircraft. British loses were 500 dead, 1,373 wounded and 55 missing. It was a glorious victory of the Allies.

As the Australians mopped up in the Benghazi/Beda Fomm area, O'Connor's 7th Armoured charged ahead another 100 miles and occupied El Agheila on the southern shore of the Gulf of Sidra on February 9. At this point half of Libya had been conquered except for a few isolated oases in the south. Also at this point, London called a halt to the British advance and withdrew some of the British units in North Africa for service in Greece. Furthermore, an anti-British rebellion was beginning in Iraq and the possibility was arising that German forces might soon appear in both Iraq and Vichy-controlled Lebanon and Syria. These actions would threaten the peace of the whole Levant and possible require additional British troops there. Some of the troops would have to come from North Africa.

In anticipation of this, the 6th Australians and 7th Armoured Divisions were withdrawn, returned to Alexandria, Egypt, given rest and rehabilitation and eventually sent off to Greece in March. In their place at El Agheila came the 9th Australian Division, an Indian brigade and thc 2nd British Armoured Division minus one armored brigade, which had been sent to Greece. All of these units were inexperienced in desert warfare and were so short of tanks that some of the captured Italian tanks had to be repainted with British markings and put into service. Their mission was to hold the line at El Agheila until stronger forces returned.

The RAF units in North Africa suffered a fate worse than the ground forces in that all but one squadron of fighter planes was withdrawn for service in Greece.

At sea, however, the British still held the upper hand. British submarines were sinking Italian cargo ships with regularity. Six ships went down off Libya between February 11 and 25, but two of the British subs were damaged in the attacks and had to be withdrawn from service.

In the eastern Mediterranean, which by now had been secured by the British Navy, the first British convoy of troops from North Africa left Alexandria harbor for Greece on March 4. In all, four divisions would leave North Africa in what the British called "Operation Lustre." Their troop ships were escorted by a strong contingent of warships from the British Navy consisting of four cruisers and four destroyers. The British wanted to make sure these men got to their destination. They were too precious to lose at sea.

ENTER ROMMEL

While the Italians were suffering the pangs of defeat in Libya Hitler, on February 6, appointed General Irwin Rom-

The First German tank in Africa being off-loaded from an Italian freighter at Tripoli on February 12, 1941.

mel, a hero of the conquest of France and an exceptionally talented tank commander, to command the German forces that were to be sent to North Africa. Two days later, in typical German efficiency, the first German unit, the 5th Panzer Regiment left Naples for Libya by sea. It landed at Tripoli, the capital of Libya, on February 12. That same day Rommel arrived by plane to take command.

Also on February 12, German planes from Sicily made their first air attack on the British installations at Benghazi. This was the first appearance of the Luftwaffe in Africa. This bombing campaign intensified and the depleted RAF forces remaining in North Africa were unable to stop it. As a result the British were forced to abandon Benghazi as a supply port and fall back on Tobruk, 200 miles to the east.

Over the next few weeks, the rest of Rommel's force arrived in Libya and was given the designation "Afrika Korps." The Afrika Korps began with two divisions, the 15th Panzer Division and the 5th Light Division, and later grew into three divisions; the 15th Panzer Division, the 21st Panzer Division (originally the 5th Light Division which was upgraded), and the 90th Light Division. The Italians, at the time of Rommel's arrival, had six divisions in Libya, and Rommel technically served under the Italian command. Recognizing Rommel's skills in commanding armored units, the Italians placed their one remaining armored division, the "Ariete" Division under his command. Therefore, by commanding all of the armored units in North Africa, which were the primary offensive weapon of the conflict, Rommel, in effect, directed the campaign from then on.

Rommel and the Italians had plenty of time to build up their forces and make plans. The two weakened British divisions holding the line at El Agheila were not about to go

Rommel's tanks moving up to the front in Libya.

on the offensive. In late February, Rommel, systematically and at his own pace, moved his units eastward in preparation for an attack on El Agheila. At this point, he had only the German 5th Light Division and the Italian divisions with which to work. His second major unit, the 15th Panzer Division, was still in the process of arriving at Tripoli.

On February 27, German advance units made several probing attacks against the British lines at El Agheila to test the British strength and then withdrew. This was the first clash between German and British troops on African soil. Rommel, then, was ready to attack, but Hitler ordered him to wait. Developments in the Balkans were coming to a head and large-scale German forces would soon be engaged in Albania and Greece. The Fuhrer wanted to see the more important Balkans operation well underway and nearing a successful conclusion before he committed any more resources to North Africa. It was Rommel's immediate mission to hold the line against any British advance and await developments in the Balkans. For the next five weeks there would be a pause in the ground war in North Africa as the Balkan war developed.

During this period, command of the Italian forces changed hands in North Africa. General Graziani, seeing that his tenure there was about to end due to the tremendous setbacks, had asked Mussolini, on February 8, to replace him. Marshal Italo Garibaldi was chosen as Graziani's replacement and the change of command took place on March 21.

The sea war off North Africa continued to be a duel between Italian merchant ships and Allied submarines. On March 9 and 10, the British sub "Utmost" sank three Italian merchantmen off the coast of Tunisia and western Libya. Then, on March 19, the British sub "Truant" sank another Italian freighter off Tripoli and on the 20th the Greek submarine "Triton" sank an Italian freighter off Tunisia.

THE SEA WAR IN THE MEDITERRANEAN WAS TERRIBLE

The naval actions reported here are related to activities in Africa and are but a small percentage of the total naval actions that took place in the Mediterranean theater of operations. During the war, over 500 vessels were sunk in the Mediterranean and hundreds more damaged.

During the third week of March, Berlin gave Rommel permission to take the offensive. He was ready. On March 24, German and Italian forces launched an attack, planned by Rommel, on the British defenses at El Agheila. It was a resounding success in that the weak British forces there were quickly overrun and forced into a rapid withdrawal. With this the war in North Africa entered a dramatic new phase.

GERMAN PEOPLE PREPARED FOR ADVENTURES IN AFRICA

Back in Germany, Dr. Joseph Goebbels' propaganda machine went into high gear to prepare the German people for Germany's new role in Africa. This renewed propaganda campaign fit in with their long-standing colonial claims in Africa and the long-held belief by many of them that Germany should have its rightful place, politically and economically, in Africa. Emphasis on Africa also continued the deception toward the Soviet Union that Germany's expansionist desires were to the south and not to the east.

Along with the press and media campaigns regarding Africa came two German movies that dramatized Germany's interests in Africa. The first movie, "Carl Peters," released in late March 1941, fictionalized the real-life career of Carl Peters, an early colonial administrator who was responsible for Germany's acquisition of her African territories in the late 1800s. Peters was played by Hans Albers, one of Germany's most popular leading men. In the movie his character comes across as a benevolent colonial administrator who always helps the natives and has a constant struggle with short-sighted politicians and bureaucrats in Berlin to convince them of the importance of the German colonies. British colonial administrators are portrayed as being cruel exploiters of the natives and the continent's resources. In real life, Peters was eventually dismissed by the Berlin officials on the grounds that he was cruel to natives. In the movie, this is glossed over by the explanation that Peters was framed when a black bishop, in the pay of the British, gave false testimony against him.

The second movie, released soon after Carl Peters, was "Ohm Kruger" (Uncle Kruger) and was sympathetic to the Boers of the Boer War (1899-1902) in South Africa. The Dutch/Germanic Boers were the forbearers of the current-day Afrikaners and the Germans had always sided with the Boer's side of the war. Stephanus Johannes Paulus Kruger, the real-life President of the independent state of Transvaal, is portrayed as a benevolent, Hitler-like, authoritarian, peace-loving patriarch who loves his people more than life itself but is forced into a war by the evil British. The arch-villain is the conniving, neo-criminal, power-lusting Cecil Rhodes. Unlike Hitler, Kruger was in real-life and in the movie, was the father of many children and a devoted family man. The Boers are seen in the movie as hard-working, God-fearing "volk" who are trying to carve out a living space for themselves in the African wilderness and living in complete harmony with nature and the natives.

But beneath their rich farmland of Transvaal is gold, and the British, especially Rhodes, covets that gold. The British missionaries are Rhodes' clever tools who teach the natives the white-man's religion while, at the same time, inciting them to take up arms against the Boers, whom, the missionaries claim, have stolen their land. In one famous scene from the movie the natives are seen assembled in church singing "Onward Christian Soldiers" while the British pastor passes among them handing out rifles. The natives revolt against the Boers, and the British use that as an excuse to intervene.

Winston Churchill appears in the movie as the commander of a notorious British concentration camp where Boer women and children are incarcerated and treated most inhumanely. Queen Victoria is portrayed as a pathetic character who is Kruger's true friend but is senile, overweight, and a Scotch-drinking alcoholic. She is surrounded by conspiring British politicians in London, such as Kitchener and Chamberlain, who foil her honest efforts to make peace. Her son, the Prince of Wales, is shown to be a womanizing playboy. In one scene, the Queen and Kruger are seen sitting together telling each other how they both suffer from rheumatism.

Near the end of the movie is a ghastly scene in the concentration camp where Churchill's men are about to hang Kruger's beloved son, Jan. The inmates, mostly women and children, revolt against the British guards with sticks and rocks and are mercilessly gunned down. The scene fades showing a field of dead women and children with a lone baby crying in the distance and Jan's lifeless body hanging from a tree.

In the final, scene Kruger is seen in a Swiss hotel where he has been living in exile. He is blind and in failing health. He writes to Victoria, who is on her death bed. Upon receiving Kruger's letter, she sees a vision in which the British nation is punished for its crimes at some time in the future, by a nation much stronger than Kruger's Transvaal.

Dr. Goebbels saw to it that Ohm Kruger gained its rightful place in the world of German arts by having it win Germany's "Best Picture of the Year" award for 1941.

JEWS TO MADAGASCAR—AGAIN

Yet another ploy to direct the attention of the German people, and the leaders in Moscow, to Germany's interests in Africa occurred on April 28, 1941, when the Nazi-controlled World News Service repeated a story from an Italian newspaper that it was rumored that there was a secret clause in the German/French armistice which provided the island of Madagascar as the new homeland for Europe's Jews after the war. There was no such agreement, but the rumor served the Nazi's purpose at the time.

In Vichy, Marshal Petain was aware of the continuing Axis interest in Madagascar and concluded that it was best to send a new governor to the island that was absolutely loyal to him. That man was Armand Annet, a reliable bureaucrat with considerable experience in government service. Annet arrive in April 1941, and within a few days posters were put up in all the major cities, and especially in Tananarive, the capital, reminding civil servants that their jobs and pensions depended on their continued loyalty to Vichy. If, indeed, Madagascar was ever to be given to the Jews, Petain wanted to be in firm control there and in a position to bargain it away in return for substantial concessions from Germany.

FREE FRENCH ATTACK LIBYA FROM THE SOUTH

Almost from the beginning of the Free French occupation of Equatorial Africa, de Gaulle had planned to invade southern Libya from Chad where the two colonies shared a common border. That border was deep in the Sahara Desert and a very forbidding place to live, let alone conduct military maneuvers and fight. Dirt roads had to be built to the border, supply depots built, desert-worthy vehicles obtained, men trained, and supplies of all kinds accumulated for easy transport. Once the Free French forces plunged into the Sahara Desert the problem of supply would be difficult.

General Leclerc planned and organized the campaign which would be commanded by General Georges Catroux. It would be highly motorized and consist mostly of African troops—over 80%—under the command of French officers. All of the necessary preparations were made during the latter months of 1940, and by the end of December Catroux's force was ready to attack. The timing was good because the British had attacked from Egypt and were rapidly pushing the Italians back into Libya.

In early January 1941, Catroux's force crossed the border into Libya where a caravan trail led northward to the Fezzan area in southwestern Libya where a number of oases existed. Their advance, led by Marmon-Herrington armored cars, went as planned and on January 28 the Free French took the oasis of Murzak, one of the largest in the area.

At Murzak, the Free French were only about 480 miles due south of the Libyan capital of Tripoli and a threat to the Italian's southern flank with a good road ahead of them that led northward to the coast.

Soon after Catroux's column began its advance on Murzak, a second, and smaller, Free French force

Marmon-Herrington armored cars, bearing de Gaulle's Cross of Lorraine symbol and purchased from South Africa, led the advance into southern Libya.

accompanied by a British Long-Range Defense Group moved out of northeastern Chad, across open desert, to the oasis of Cufra in southeastern Libya. It took this force eleven days of hard driving to reach their objective. Once they reached Cufra they surrounded the oasis and harassed the defenders with small-arms fire while Free French aircraft flew in from Chad to make bombing raids.

At Cufra the Italians had an airfield used as a refuelling stop for planes flying to and from Italian East Africa. There was also a supply depot for material destined for East Africa. The Italians had several small motorized units in the Cufra area which contested the Allied advance but, after several skirmishes, the Allies beat off the Italian attacks and succeeded in occupying the oasis on March 1, 1941. They captured 64 Italians and 352 Libyans. By occupying Cufra's airfield Axis air communications to the Duke of Aosta's forces in East Africa all but ended. Furthermore, this area had, at one time, belonged to the Anglo-Egyptian Sudan and both the British and Egyptians had claims on it.

Back at Murzak, Leclerc's force took off once again across 375 miles of open desert in a northwesterly direction to occupy the Libyan town of Ghadames in the three-corners area of Libya, Algeria, and Tunisia. Here they were in a position to threaten both Tripoli, 300 miles to the northeast, and the port of Gabes in Vichy-controlled Tunisia 260 miles due north. From Ghadames, good roads led to both locations.

IN FREE FRENCH-CONTROLLED EQUATORIAL AFRICA

While Leclerc's troops were marching into southern Libya, other events of note were happening in French Equatorial Africa.

Part of the cache of Italian weapons captured by the Free French and British at Cufra. These had been destined for the Duke of Aosta's forces in East Africa.

On January 6, 1941, the British formally recognized the Free French Council of Defense of the French Empire based in Brazzaville. This established de Gaulle's organization as an equal ally and gave British support to both the political and war aims of the Free French. Henceforth, the British armed forces and Free French armed forces would act in mutual support of each other and the British would cooperate with the Free French on economic and political matters. This recognition was also an important first step in recognizing de Gaulle's organization as the future provisional government of France. For de Gaulle and his Council, it was their greatest political triumph to date.

The United States, which still had diplomatic relations with Vichy, could not extend similar recognition to the Free French but could deal with the Free French on matters of trade. Therefore, soon after the British action was taken, the United States sent a trade commission to Brazzaville. That trade commission wanted to purchase chromium, nickel, lead and tin ores as well as butyl and other items necessary to America's war industry. In return, the Free French were offered a wide variety of consumer goods and some military supplies from the United States.

In military matters, the Free French armed forces needed officers so in late February 1941, an army cadet school was established at Camp Colonna d'Orana. Also the Institut Pasteur established a research facility in Brazzaville to do research on sleeping sickness, a disease that plagued civilian and military personnel alike.

In London, Churchill had kind words for the Free French and de Gaulle. In a memo on general issues concerning the war, dated February 23, 1941, addressed to Sir A. Cadogan, Permanent Foreign Under-Secretary, the Prime Minister said, "All of this goes to show that we should continue to give increasing support to General de Gaulle. I cannot believe that the French nation will give their loyalty to anyone who reaches the Head of the State (Petain) because he is thought well of by the Germans."

OF MEN AND CATTLE

In consolidating their hold on Equatorial Africa, the Free French removed all individuals from the civil administration and the armed forces who remained loyal to Petain. These people were then rounded up and unceremoniously dumped into Vichy-controlled West Africa with little more than the clothes on their backs. There, they became the wards of the West African administration who had to rush food, water, transportation, and other necessities of life to the new arrivals to keep them from starving.

In Dakar, High Commissioner Boisson was so angry that he called an immediate halt to the unofficial cattle trade that was going on between French West Africa and the British and Free French colonies. This was a mistake. Soon there developed a surplus of cattle in West Africa and those involved in the cattle business there began complaining to Dakar. To solve this problem Boisson ordered the colonial administration to buy up the cattle, slaughter them and, store the meat in a large frozen food warehouse in Dakar—the only such facility in all of West Africa. The warehouse soon filled and the slaughter of cattle had to be halted causing, once again, a surplus of cattle in the hands of the producers. By this time a shortage of various consumer goods, the other equation of the cattle trade, developed in West Africa along with increased black market activities. Boisson, eventually, had to quietly allow the cattle trade to resume for the good of the West African economy.

OTHER EVENTS IN FREE FRENCH-CONTROLLED AFRICA

De Gaulle was, quite naturally, anxious to increase his contribution to the Allied war effort and thereby increase his status in the alliance. To this end, his subordinates in Equatorial Africa were ordered to take measures to induce the African population to produce more food and other items needed by the Allies. Special emphasis was placed on the production of gold and the gathering of wild rubber. In addition, the Brazzaville government confirmed to the mulatto population that the decree of September 15, 1936, under which they were granted government-assisted educational opportunities and improved living conditions, was still valid and would be implemented.

For the benefit of all the people, measures were also taken to control certain diseases which were spreading due to the general migration of people within the colonial federation.

FREE FRENCH SERVING IN FOUR THEATERS

By the summer of 1941, Free French forces in Africa had risen to over 50,000 men. Most of this number was comprised of colonial troops but their loyalty to de Gaulle was unwavering. After organizing and training his growing army, de Gaulle committed the men to four theaters of war with the approval and cooperation of the British. The force under General Catroux, as we have seen, advanced into Libya from Chad while a second force had been sent to fight in East Africa. A third force was sent to Egypt and was integrated into the British forces there while a fourth force went to Palestine and was stationed, along with British troops and other Free French forces, on the border of Vichy-controlled Lebanon and Syria.

IN VICHY-CONTROLLED AFRICA

Grim and unsettling—those words describe the situation throughout Vichy-controlled Africa during the first months of 1941. On the domestic scene, shortages of all kinds plagued the colonial administrators and depressed the colonial economies. On the political scene there was no end to the war in sight. The British not only had survived the terrible air blitz of the fall and winter of 1940 but were winning victories in East Africa, North Africa, and Greece. There were many in Vichy-controlled Africa who began to wonder if France might not have made a mistake in surrendering, prematurely, to the Axis powers.

Also the Vichy French saw themselves being drawn deeper into Hitler's web. The Germans, intent on sending German troops to help the Italians in North Africa, wanted those troops and their supplies to flow from Sicily, across the narrowest part of the Mediterranean Sea, to Vichy-controlled Tunisia. This would give them as little exposure as possible to the Royal Navy and RAF as they crossed the open water in the Italian convoys. Technically, under the terms of the armistice, the Germans had to get Vichy's permission to allow German troops to land in, and pass through, Tunisia. Petain, upon first hearing of this, expressed his strong opposition. But Hitler was not to be denied. On February 10, Hitler presented his formal demand to the Vichy government for passage through Tunisia, coupled with two other demands; that Pierre Laval, the very pro-German Premier who had recently been discharged be reinstated; and that the German Navy be allowed to operate out of Vichy-controlled Mediterranean ports in France and North Africa. Following on the heels of this demand came yet another demand from Berlin on February 13: that the not-so-secret talks taking place in Madrid between Vichy and the British over blockade issues be ended at once. In these talks, the Vichy government had indicated that it was willing to make concessions to the British in exchange for a loosening of the blockade.

The old Marshal, though, had a few bargaining chips of his own. His subordinates in North Africa had actively negotiated with the Americans on the prospect of obtaining food from the United States. Hitler knew of this and could see that if he forced an end to these negotiations, Vichy would then demand food from Germany. Also, General Weygand, the High-Commissioner of French North Africa, was known to bitterly oppose any form of German presence in French North Africa and had negotiated, again not-so-secretly, with the British on what could be done if the Germans forced their hand with regards to the North African ports. Petain, quite understandably, let these talks proceed because they strengthened his hand against Hitler. The implication here was that if Hitler forced his hand to get German troops into French North Africa, Weygand was in a powerful position to denounce that action, declare for the British, and allow British troops to enter French North Africa to save it from the Germans.

Churchill was fully aware of the predicament Petain was in with regard to North Africa and on February 2 wrote to General Sir Hastings Ismay, Chief of Staff of the War Cabinet saying, "One must consider that at any moment Weygand might move our way..." and that the British must be prepared to act quickly in French North Africa. Furthermore, with the British in French North Africa, Libya could then be attacked from the west.

In Vichy, Petain felt strong enough to deny Hitler some of his demands. He steadfastly refused to allow German troops to land and pass through Tunisia or for the German Navy to use French Mediterranean ports. He did, however, reinstate Laval and terminate the Madrid talks which, unbeknownst to Hitler, were approaching a deadlock anyway. Hitler, under the circumstances, felt it was best to take what he could get and not risk provoking an anti-Vichy rebellion in French North Africa led by its High Commissioner, Weygand.

In Berlin, of course, Weygand was now seen as an enemy of the Reich and the Germans began to put pressure on Vichy to dismiss him. Petain could see that Weygand's dismissal was inevitable, but he would, through various means, delay it as long as possible.

The breakdown of the Madrid talks had its consequences, too. The British, now with more men and ships, began intercepting French ships for the first time, sailing in the Mediterranean between unoccupied France and French North Africa ports. In retaliation, Vichy announced that it would arm some of its merchant ships and asked the Germans to permit the release of French warships to escort French convoys across the Mediterranean. Hitler denied the Vichy request, reasoning that it was best to keep the British Navy busy chasing French ships rather than Italian ships and that it was to his benefit that the French be subjected to a little punishment—a punishment he might later rescind in exchange for more concessions. Thus, an undeclared sea war erupted again between Britain and Vichy, this time in the Mediterranean—all to Hitler's delight.

For many an African native living in Vichy colonial territory, their lives were adversely effected by the political wrangling between Vichy, Berlin, and London. Therefore, they simply took matters into their own hands—or more specifically—their own feet. They simply walked across the border into British or Free French territory where jobs were plentiful and there were few shortages. The Vichy authorities did little to stop this exodus because there was little they could have done even if they tried. And secretly, many of the French administrators were happy to see their colonial subjects leave because that meant fewer mouths for them to feed.

Another problem for Vichy colonial administrators was the money system. Because of the economic problems in Vichy-controlled Africa, the French colonial franc fell drastically in value and became very unstable. In West Africa this problem was partially resolved by using the British West African pound as a medium of exchange this was relatively easy to come by thanks to the unofficial trade with the British West African colonies. The people in French North Africa, Madagascar, and French Somaliland had no similar trading arrangements and had to live with the difficult monetary situation.

AMERICA SENDS FOOD AND SPIES

During February 1941, negotiations between the United States and Vichy concerning the matter of America sending food to French North Africa came to fruition. On February 7, the British had somewhat reluctantly agreed to issue navicerts to certain American vessels so they could pass through the British naval blockade and deliver food and other humanitarian supplies to French North African ports. The British insisted that American inspectors should operate in French North Africa to insure that none of the food went to the Axis nations. Petain readily agreed to this because closer ties with the United States provided a much-needed counterbalance for Vichy with regards to Germany.

Details for the food shipments called for a wide variety of food and nonmilitary items to be shipped from the United States to French North Africa and French West Africa, which would be paid for from French funds previously frozen in the United States. Thirteen American inspectors, with the titles of Vice-Consuls, would be permitted to roam freely throughout French North and West Africa, insuring that all of the food and other items were consumed locally. The Vice-Consuls were all men with experience in French North Africa. Four of them had served in the French Foreign Legion and one had graduated from the French military academy at St. Cyr. It was also an unwritten understanding that the Vice-Consuls would gather military and political information and feed it back to Washington, and that much of it would, in all probability, be passed on to London. In other words, the thirteen American Vice-Consuls would be spies. Murphy was appointed to oversee the food distribution program and was given the title of United States High Commissioner for French North Africa. This was a rank equal to that of General Weygand's, which afforded Murphy ready access to Weygand. Murphy also retained his position as counselor to the U.S. Embassy in Vichy.

Petain turned a blind eye to this situation because the Murphy/Weygand Agreement strengthened his political position vis-a-vis the Germans and helped solve the food shortage problem in Africa, which was one of his more pressing concerns.

Berlin knew what was going on and, not surprisingly, formally objected to the food-from-America program. But, the Germans did little about it not wanting to complicate the delicate relationship with Vichy, especially at this time, when there were more pressing problems in Libya, the Balkans, and East Africa.

Churchill, on the other hand, was not convinced that sending American food to French North and West Africa was the right thing to do and hoped to find, in the near future, a way to control it and, if possible, stop it altogether. In a note to Sir A. Cadogan, Permanent Foreign Under Secretary, dated February 23, Churchill wrote "We should reason patiently with Washington against giving any food to unoccupied France or North Africa" and Churchill went on to instruct Cadogan, "For this purpose all the unsatisfactory feeling about the Vichy-Weygand scene should be in the hands of our Ambassador in Washington."

Because of all the controversy created by the Murphy/Weygand Agreement, Vichy felt the need to restate publicly its overall policy of neutrality. Several officials spoke out on this issue including Weygand who, on March 4, stated publicly once again that the French would defend their African possessions against any invader with all their military means available. This was one of the ploys taken by Petain to strengthen Weygand's position in North Africa and prolong his tenure there.

THE TIT FOR TAT CONTINUES

To counter the presence of the American Vice Consuls in North Africa and to get a better hold on conditions there, the Germans informed Vichy that they were going to implement the clause in the armistice agreement that allowed Germany to send armistice commissions to North Africa. Heretofore, the Italians had established armistice commissions in French North Africa and the Germans had relied on information gathered by them. Now this would change. Soon, German armistice commissions appeared in Casablanca, Dakar, and other major cities in French Africa. It was an unofficial understanding that they, too, were spies.

Vichy then took a step asserting its independence by announcing, on March 15, 1941, that the Trans-Saharan Railroad between Algeria and Dakar would be completed. Construction of this railroad had begun before the war but progress was very slow due to lack of funding from Paris. Now, for Vichy, the completion of the railroad would provide a badly-needed strengthening of the empire by making it possible for both military and commercial products to flow back and forth between North and West Africa by rail. This would circumvent the British naval blockade at sea and strengthen military and economic ties between North and West Africa. Furthermore, the surplus of food and other items that had piled up in West Africa could be relieved. Renewed construction on the railroad did not happen quickly, however. Vichy had trouble finding funds, and it was not until early September 1941 that construction resumed.

The British, quite understandably, were not happy with the proposed railroad but could do little to stop it. The Germans saw both good and bad in it. The bad aspect was that it would strengthen Vichy both economically and politically vis-a-vis the armistice, but the good was that it would provide the Germans with another safe land route into sub-Saharan Africa when it came time for Germany to recover her lost colonies and acquire African Atlantic ports.

The United States also took note of developments at Dakar and on April 24, Secretary of the Navy, Frank Knox, informed the American public on the dangers of an enemy presence there. Knox said:

> *"Too few of us realize, and still fewer acknowledge, the disaster to American hemispheric safety if Germany, already the conqueror of France, should establish herself at Dakar. From there, with her surface ships, submarines, and long-range bombers, a victorious Germany could substantially cut us off from all commerce with South America and make the Monroe Doctrine a scrap of paper."*

As another sop to the Germans, Petain appointed a violently anti-Semite, former Assemblyman Xavier Vallat, to the newly-created governmental post of "Commissioner-General for the Jewish Question." This was a clear indication that Vichy would soon adopt some Nazi-style anti-Semitic legislation. The legislation would, primarily, affect Metropolitan France, but there would be some ramifications in the colonies.

Still another concession to Germany was made on April 19, when Vichy withdrew from the League of Nations.

Three days later, the first two American cargo ships arrived in French North African ports carrying grain under the Murphy/Weygand Agreement.

AMERICA'S VIEW OF THE WAR—LEND-LEASE

In the United States, the government and the American people were intensely watching the war developments. The American view of the war was the broad picture and not of any one theater in particular with the exception of the air blitz of England during the latter half of 1940. Americans were very sympathetic toward the British and became increasingly supportive of that nation, often ignoring their own neutrality laws.

Beginning in October 1940, American eyes turned toward the Balkans where the Greeks were scoring victory after victory over the Italians, and to the Mediterranean where dramatic sea battles were taking place. Then, as British victories mounted in North Africa, beginning in December 1940, American interests turned to that theater of war. As for the war in East Africa, that conflict was seen as something of a side show that the British were winning with ease against an isolated, weak, and demoralized enemy. That war received much less attention in the American media than those in North Africa and the Balkans.

The Lion of Judah Rides Again

The Detroit News • Tuesday • January 21, 1941

A somewhat uncomplimentary cartoon published in the Detroit News on January 21, 1941, showing Haile Selassie's return to Ethiopia in the wake of the British lion.

In February 1941, British Prime Minister Churchill, who was in frequent contact with President Roosevelt, secretly informed the President that Britain was running out of money with which to buy war materials from America. America's neutrality laws had previously been amended to allow Britain and her allies to purchase American-made war materials so long as they paid for them in cash and provided their own outbound transportation. This was known as the "Cash and Carry" program. Now, Britain was running out of cash and the flow of American-made war supplies to the Allied powers was in jeopardy. Roosevelt then concocted the idea of loaning war supplies to Britain and her allies for the duration of the war on the promise that those supplies would be returned after the war. Roosevelt, a good judge of the tenor of the American people, thought the time was right for such a program and presented the plan directly to the American people in one of his famous evening radio addresses known as "Fireside Chats." In his typical folksy and charismatic way, he likened the lending of war materials to Britain to a situation where a man loans his neighbor a length of garden hose to put out a house fire with the understanding that the garden hose would be returned afterwards. Roosevelt termed this neighborly gesture as "Lend-Lease." Roosevelt's idea started an instant and heated debate all over America concerning America's overall role in the world crisis. It was clear that the neutrality laws would have to be amended once again and there was sizeable opposition in Congress against that from the still-powerful isolationist faction. There was also a faction in Congress that had long called for the liberation of all colonial lands worldwide at the earliest possible moment, who argued that strengthening Britain would strengthen colonialism. These critics, and others, were quick to bring up British oppression of the Irish, Indians, and even the Boers in South Africa.

Careful scrutiny of the Lend-Lease program revealed that it was not a lending program at all but an outright giveaway program, because a large part of the so-called loaned material would be lost in the war and another large part would be so battle-worn and out-of-date that it would not be worth taking back.

For the better part of a month the Lend-Lease issue was hotly debated throughout the land in both the media and in Congress. But Roosevelt had guessed right—the timing for such a plan was at hand and it gained momentum.

AXIS VICTORIES IN NORTH AFRICA (MARCH–JUNE 1941)

Rommel's attack of March 24 on the British lines at El Agheila was so overwhelming that the British had to retreat hastily to the east. This was a devastating blow to the British because El Agheila had been their first line of defense. The El Agheila defenders retreated forty miles to a secondary defense line at Mersa Brega and the Axis troops followed cautiously. After carefully studying the British defenses, Rommel sent his tanks on the attack again on April 2, and the British line quickly gave way again. The British again retreated rapidly, abandoning fifty armored cars and thirty light tanks. Rommel's tactics and tanks had broken the backs of the British defenses and the road now lay open for many miles to the east. Rommel then divided his force in two. The main force, consisting of the bulk of the German and Italian tanks, cut across the bulge of Cyrenaica, just as the British had done two months earlier, and headed for the coast and Derna where the British planned their next stand. A second force, led by the Italian Brescia Division, moved up the coast and occupied Benghazi, which fell on April 4. On April 5, the main force took the town of Msus, one third of the way across the bulge of Cyrenaica. The Axis forces moved rapidly, and just two days later they took Mechili, 45 miles south of Derna.

APRIL 6, 1941: A DISASTROUS DAY FOR THE ALLIES

On April 6, the British suffered a serious blow in Libya when the British field commander, General O'Connor, and six other generals were surprised by a fast-moving advanced German patrol and taken captive. O'Connor and his party had been on an inspection tour of the front and became lost in a blinding sandstorm. This left the British forces in Libya temporarily leaderless.

On that same day, another war developed in the Balkans. Germany, Italy, Hungary, and Bulgaria simultaneously invaded Yugoslavia from several directions. At the same time, German troops invaded eastern Greece through Bulgaria. For the British in North Africa this was a disaster of the first magnitude, because it meant that all British military help possible would now be needed in the Balkans and that the British forces in North Africa would have to try to stop Rommel with the forces on hand and with little prospect of receiving significant reinforcements.

ROMMEL SURGES ON

After capturing Mechili, Rommel's tanks turned toward Derna from the south while the Brescia Division approached Derna along the coastal road from the west. The British had had very little time to prepare the Derna defenses and had to abandon them. They withdrew again to their next defense line, Tobruk, which was already being manned by the 9th Australian Division. The British were able to scrape up another Australian brigade and some tanks, and rush them to Tobruk by sea. The 2nd Armoured Division, 9th Australian Division, and 3rd Indian Brigade, which had withdrawn all the way from El Agheila were, by now, badly battered and in no condition to defend Tobruk. It was up to the newly-arrived Australian brigade to hold Tobruk.

Rommel reached the Tobruk defenses on April 11 and his troops launched an immediate attack. By now, though, the Axis troops were fatigued and experiencing shortages of supplies. The attack failed.

On April 13, 1941, Rommel received orders from Berlin to bypass Tobruk and drive on eastward into Egypt as far as possible. His ultimate objective was to be the Suez Canal which was much more important than Tobruk.

On the 14th, Rommel made one more attack on the Tobruk perimeter, but it failed too. He decided not to try again until the newly-arrived 15th Panzer Division, which had just left Tripoli, came up to reinforce him.

In London, Churchill was very concerned about the situation in Egypt and wired his friend, President Roosevelt, with assurances that the British would not abandon North Africa, but that they badly needed supplies. He asked if the Americans could help now under the Lend-Lease program.

Then, on April 16, the Allies scored an important victory at sea. An eight-ship Italian convoy carrying 3000 German troops was attacked by four British destroyers and all eight ships were sunk. Only 1250 of the troops were rescued. The British lost one destroyer. And that was not all. The entire month of April was a bad one for the Axis at sea. In addition to the convoy lost on April 16 British subs sank another four Italian, two German, and one Vichy French merchantmen in the waters off Libya during April, and three more German merchantmen were sunk by British subs on May 1.

The actions at sea forced Rommel to view Tobruk as a threat to his rear because the British Navy ruled the waters off Libya and could easily bring in reinforcements to Tobruk and attack him from behind. So, to relieve this threat, he ordered the newly-arrived 15th Panzer Division into the siege line around the seaport and prepared to attack the city. This would be the first engagement of the 15th Panzers in North Africa. This action left Rommel with only his tired, supply-short 5th Light Division and Italian Divisions to face the British in Egypt.

The next day Rommel was reminded of the British Navy's presence when British warships bombarded Axis positions behind his lines at Fort Capuzzo.

On April 20, the 15th Panzer Division attacked the Australian defenses at Tobruk and gained some ground but were unable to break through. The Australians had good support from the RAF, which pounded the Axis troops from the air while the Royal Navy, using its big guns, pounded the Axis troops from offshore.

The next day, British warships bombarded Tripoli concentrating on ships in the harbor and the dock areas. One Axis cargo ship was sunk but the off-loading of supplies from other ships continued almost uninterrupted.

As for Berlin's order for Rommel to march on to the Suez Canal, that undertaking would not be accomplished any time soon.

AXIS VICTORY IN THE BALKANS

In the Balkans, the Axis had successfully defeated the Greek and British forces and on April 21 the Greek government signed a German-dictated armistice and the fighting ended. On April 23, the Greeks formally surrendered and on the 24th the British evacuated their troops, some 40,000 in number. Some of those troops were sent on to the island of Crete with the remained returning to Egypt. After a period of rest and reorganization they would be able to fight again—this time against Rommel.

ROMMEL ENTERS EGYPT

Rommel's advanced units crossed into Egypt and on April 25, attacked the new British defense line at Halfaya Pass, just beyond the Egyptian border. But, once again, Rommel's advance was so swift that the British did not have time to adequately prepare the defenses and were forced to withdraw to their next line of defense at Mersa Matruh. At Mersa Matruh the story was different. Here defenses had been prepared in late 1940 against the Italians and were still in good condition. The British quickly moved in and made additions and refinements. The Mersa Matruh line would be a strong defense line, and both Rommel and Hitler knew it. What Hitler and Rommel did not know, however, was that the British defenders were now down to about 25,000 men, the remnants of British, Australian, Indian and South African units. Also, they had very few operable tanks. The Axis forces greatly outnumbered the British in both men and tanks at this time but, on the other hand, their most fresh unit, the 15th Panzer Division, was tied up at Tobruk and those at the front in Egypt were battle-worn. At this stage of the battle, numbers were secondary to the fighting condition of the troops. With neither side capable of taking the initiative in Egypt, the fighting now slowed to a standstill.

The war in Egypt and Libya.

Back in Germany the people were not told this. They knew only that Rommel had resoundingly beaten the British in North Africa and invaded Egypt. The German state-controlled media praised Rommel and his Afrika Korps repeatedly and Rommel had become a national hero. He also had acquired a new and complimentary title, "The Desert Fox."

KING FAROUK'S CONTACTS WITH THE GERMANS

King Farouk of Egypt was fully aware that if the Axis forces pushed the British out of Egypt, his country would fall into the Italian sphere of influence and that the Italians, in all likelihood, would simply step into the shoes of the British and maintain the oppressive controls over Egypt. Farouk and other Egyptian leaders came to believe, though, that if they could develop strong ties to Germany those ties would be a counterbalance to Italy's influence and, in the long run, beneficial to Egypt.

Egyptian contacts with Berlin had been maintained for years, some of them secret and some of them public. Now, with the Germans at the Egyptian border, Farouk wanted those ties strengthened. For this purpose he chose his father-in-law, Zulficar-pasha, an Iranian, as his primary contact. Zulficar-pasha had met with German representatives in the past and was well-known in Berlin to be a spokesman for Farouk.

During April 1941, Farouk sent his father-in-law to Tehran, Iran to meet with Germany's Ambassador to Iran with a very specific message for Hitler. The message was that King Farouk hoped for a German victory over Britain and that German troops would soon liberate Egypt. The message continued that Farouk saw the German troops as liberators and the Italians as oppressors. Zulficar-pasha told the Ambassador that Farouk would facilitate the German occupation of Egypt when he was able, but at the moment his hands were tied by the British.

On April 30, German Foreign Minister von Ribbentrop replied to the Egyptians through Tehran, stating that Germany's fight was not against Egypt nor any other Arab country and that Germany wanted to see the British ousted from all the Arab lands. Ribbentrop also stated that Germany had no territorial claims against Egypt or any other Arab land and that both Hitler and Mussolini desired the independence of Egypt and the entire Arab world.

Upon close examination of von Ribbentrop's reply, it can easily be seen that Ribbentrop offered nothing of substance. Reference to the independence of Egypt was relatively meaningless because the British, even now, regarded Egypt as independent. It was not the theoretical independence of Egypt that mattered, it was the treaties that Egypt had been forced to sign and the presence of foreign troops in the land that served as the real power in the land of the Nile and the Suez Canal.

It is inconceivable to think that Germany, after the final Axis victory, would take any substantial measures to favor the Egyptians at the expense of the Italians. On the contrary they would, in all likelihood, favor the Italians and cooperate with Rome in forcing Farouk to cooperate with the Italians. In this respect, the Germans had an ace in the hole in the person of the ex-Khedive of Egypt, Abbas Hilmi II, who had been dethroned by the British in 1914. Abbas Hilmi resided in occupied Europe and had close ties with the Germans. From the German point of view, if Farouk ever proved to be uncooperative, Abbas Hilmi could be looked upon as a possible replacement for Farouk himself. All in all, Farouk's belief that he could prevent Egypt from becoming anything but a vassal state after an Axis victory seemed quite naive.

ROMMEL AT THE FRONT

On April 30 and May 1, Axis forces attacked the British defenses at Tobruk again, and again were repulsed—a great disappointment for Rommel.

With his troops at Tobruk now in need of rest and resupply, a lull fell over this front, too. And herein lay a problem. Supplies from Germany were beginning to diminish, not only because of the British actions at sea, but also because, unbeknownst to Rommel, the deadline for the attack on the Soviet Union was nearing and the needs of the German forces there had been given top priority.

The war in North Africa now became one of supply and it was a contest Rommel was not winning. For the British, their great problem of supply, that of furnishing the needs of the troops in the Balkans, was over and supplies and reinforcements were, once again, arriving in Egypt. A part of those resources would go immediately to help the Australians at Tobruk.

On the night of May 5/6, 1941, two British destroyers slipped into Tobruk harbor and brought the Australian defenders their first major shipment of much-needed supplies since the city came under siege. This first delivery went smoothly and the process was continued. Supplies were brought in and the wounded and POWs taken out.

During these weeks the sea war in the Mediterranean heated up because during the third week of May the Germans and Italians invaded the Greek island of Crete, 230 miles directly north of the Libyan/Egyptian border. The land assault came in the form of a massive parachute attack which required large elements of the powerful Luftwaffe, while at the same time, the bulk of the Italian Navy was called out to blockade the island and keep Allied reinforcements from reaching the Crete defenders. The British, now, were forced to commit the bulk of their naval, air, and some land resources, to the defense of Crete. All this was, once again, at the expense of their forces in North Africa. With both sides heavily committed at Crete the war in North Africa now became of secondary importance. But still it continued as both sides spared what ships and planes they could for North Africa. What followed was a seesaw air and sea battle along the North African coast.

On May 7, German planes attacked the British ships in the harbor at Tobruk and sank the British minesweeper "Stoke."

On May 10, elements of the British Navy struck at Rommel's supply system once again by bombarding ground targets at Benghazi.

On May 12, the Luftwaffe sank the British gunboat "Ladybird" off the eastern Libyan coast.

On May 20, the British sub "Urge" sank an Italian cargo ship and a tanker approaching Tripoli.

On May 25, German planes sank the British sloop "Grimsby" forty miles north of Tobruk.

On May 30, the British sub "Triumph" sank an Italian armed merchant cruiser in Benghazi harbor and that same day the British sub "Utmost" sank a German freighter approaching Benghazi.

During early June, the war in Crete ended with an Axis victory, but the sea war in the eastern Mediterranean continued. During that month the Luftwaffe sank a British antiaircraft cruiser, a destroyer, a gunboat and a sloop in the waters of eastern Libya and western Egypt, while British subs sank six Italian and one German merchantmen.

During July, the Luftwaffe sank another British destroyer and the Italians sank the British sub "Cachalot" and the British destroyer "Nestor." British subs, though, sank six Italian merchantmen, two Italian minesweepers, and the Italian light cruiser "Giuseppe Garibaldi." After mid-July the Luftwaffe was withdrawn from the Mediterranean because the invasion of the Soviet Union was under way and those air units were needed elsewhere.

During August British subs quickly regained their advantage over the Italian Navy and sank another nine Axis merchantmen in Libyan and Tunisian waters. No warships were lost on either side.

In North African, most of the British troops that were able to escape from Crete were taken to Egypt and added to the British forces there.

BACK TO THE GROUND WAR

On May 12, a British convoy reached Alexandria and delivered 238 badly-needed tanks and 43 Hurricane fighters. This convoy, code named "Tiger," was most unique because it was the first British convoy in months to travel the length of the Mediterranean from Gibraltar to Alexandria. It took almost every Allied warship in the Mediterranean to get the convoy through but it made it with the loss of only one transport which hit a mine. Running the convoy through the Mediterranean was Churchill's idea to show the world that the Mediterranean had not yet become an Axis lake.

Unfortunately, upon arrival at Alexandria many of the tanks needed repairs before they were battle-worthy and this took time—time that the newly-organized tank crews could have used for training.

On May 15, some of those tanks and their half-trained crews went into action as the British struck out from their Mersa Matruh defenses and attacked Axis positions in the Halfaya Pass area. The British succeeded in retaking Halfaya Pass and moved on to take Sollum and Capuzzo. The attack, though, was weak and had no sustaining power. The next day Rommel's forces counterattacked and recaptured Capuzzo and Sollum but not Halfaya Pass.

Also that day, Berlin saw Rommel's dilemma and ordered that the 15th Panzer Division be moved into the line in Egypt and the siege of Tobruk turned over to the Italians. Within the week, the 15th Panzers were in Egypt and ready for front line action. On May 27, Rommel used his new-found strength to attack the British and succeeded in forcing them out of the Halfaya Pass area and back to their defenses at Mersa Matruh. At Halfaya Pass, the Axis forces dug in forming their own defense line.

A British "Matilda" tank which broke down in battle being retrieved for repair by a recovery vehicle.

With both sides now operating from defensive positions, a lull settled over the North African battlefield. Both sides needed rest, supplies, and reinforcements. During this time elements of the veteran 4th Indian Division arrived in Egypt from East Africa and 7th Armoured Division returned to the front after having been rested at Alexandria. Both units were rushed to the front to strengthen the Mersa Matruh line. The Axis forces were not so lucky. Only a small number of reinforcements arrived and not nearly enough supplies.

In London, Churchill had come to believe that Rommel's force was much weaker than it actually was and that Wavell's force was stronger than it actually was. Therefore, a plan for a major British offensive, called "Operation Battleaxe," was designed to push the Axis forces

Men of the 4th Indian Division in a foxhole facing the Halfaya escarpment. They are observing a shellburst to their left.

out of Egypt, relieve Tobruk, and recover much of Cyrenaica. Wavell was reluctant to implement Operation Battleaxe but Churchill insisted. Therefore, on June 15, the British moved out, once again, to attack the Axis defenses at Halfaya Pass. But, with the 15th Panzers now in the line, the Germans were too strong. After two days of hard fighting and losing 91 tanks, Wavell was forced to call off the attack and retreat back to Mersa Matruh. The British tanks still had mechanical problems and had proven to be very susceptible to the German 88 mm antitank guns. The Germans lost only twelve tanks.

Churchill finally realized that his forces in Egypt had to be much stronger than they were to break through Rommel's defenses. Rommel, on the other hand, was still plagued with shortages and too weak to go on the offensive. As a result, another lull fell over the North African battle fields. This one would be much longer, lasting until September.

Churchill had to find a scapegoat for the failure of Battleaxe so he blamed Wavell and on July 5 removed him from command and replaced him with General Sir Claude Auchinleck. Wavell was sent off to India as the British Commander-in-Chief there.

REVOLT IN IRAQ EFFECTS AFRICA

As it was becoming clear that the Germans would intervene in both the Balkans and North Africa, a mini-war unexpectedly erupted in Iraq which soon involved much of the Middle East. Iraq was, technically, an ally of the British—but a most troublesome one.

Iraq had been a part of the pre-World War I Ottoman Empire and in 1919 was recognized by the League of Nations as a separate political entity. It was placed under a British mandate designed to bring independence to Iraq at the earliest possible moment. That mandate progressed rapidly and in the 1930s Iraq gained its independence. The British, however, had managed to secure for themselves favorable military and economic agreements that allowed them to remain in the country with strong military forces and become a dominant factor in Iraq's rapidly expanding oil industry. As World War II progressed, the British had built up their military strength in Iraq to protect their oil interests and to serve as a deterrent against an incursion into the area by either Turkey or the Soviet Union, both of whom had favorable relations with Germany in the early stages of the war. The British military force was also intended to keep the Iraqis quiescent. This was not to be the case, however.

Within the Iraqi government and military there were powerful factions that resented the continued presence of the British and made no secret about the fact that they would work toward the ousting of the British by any means available.

On April 3, 1941, the worst of all scenarios happened from the British point of view. An anti-British military clique pulled off a coup d'etat in Baghdad and came to power. The new government was headed by Rashid Ali Gailani, an ardent anti-British and pro-Axis politician, who had been in contact with German, Italian, and Vichy French agents for some time. Gailani had secretly acquired assurances of military help from all three. The first stage of that help would be the arrival of German and Italian aircraft flying in from Vichy-controlled Syria, Iraq's neighbor to the west.

Now in power, Gailani began making demands on the British to withdraw from Iraq and threatened to use force if they did not comply. The British had no intention of complying. To enforce their position, on April 19, the British landed the 8th and 10th Indian Divisions at Iraq's main port of Basra and marched north toward Baghdad. These troops had previously been destined for Malaya in the Far East. Already there were a sizeable number of British troops inside Iraq at the large British air base at Habbaniyah west of Baghdad, along with the Jordanian Arab Legion, stationed in the Basra area.

During the first week in May, the Indian and Iraqi troops clashed at several places and on May 12 German fighter planes, with German pilots, appeared at an Iraqi-controlled air base at Mosul in northern Iraq. Within two days some fifty German fighter planes were in action supporting Iraqi ground troops against the advancing Indians. These planes had come from Europe via Syria. On May 17, Italian aircraft arrived in Syria and joined the fighting in Iraq. In retaliation RAF planes bombed French airfields in Syria.

WORLD REACTION TO THE WAR IN IRAQ

In London, the British government sent a warning through neutral sources to Vichy on May 22, to immediately cease collaboration with the Germans and Iraqis or face the possibility that British forces might attack Syria or any other Vichy-controlled part of the French Empire. This message went unanswered.

In Washington, the Roosevelt administration received an urgent request from London to stop food shipments to the Vichy French in North Africa—an arrangement the British had not supported from the start. To back up their request, the British claimed that a reliable report had been received by their embassy in Lisbon that 60,000 Germans were amassing in Spain and that the Vichy French might allow them to move into French North Africa. American intelligence sources had no information to support this rumor and the Americans suspected it might be a British ploy to shut off the food shipments. Rather than embarrass the British the Americans accepted the claim at face value and delayed, but did not end, the shipments.

In Berlin, the attack on the Soviet Union was just weeks away and Hitler could spare no more than a token force to help the Iraqis. But he believed that if the Iraqi's could hold on for two months, German troops would, by then, be in the Soviet Caucasus region and able to advance south to aid the Iraqis with strong ground forces. Hitler also saw in the Iraqi situation a chance to draw Vichy deeper into collaborating with the Axis. He convinced the Vichy French that Germany would commit sizeable forces to Iraq, but did not tell them how or when. He led the Vichy French to believe that a large part of those forces would come by sea and have to pass through Lebanon and Syria by land to reach Iraq.

THE HIGH-POINT OF VICHY COLLABORATION WITH THE AXIS

In Vichy it looked to Petain and his government that World War II was almost over and would end in a complete victory for the Axis. The recent Axis victory in the Balkans and the pending defeat of the British in Egypt gave testimony to that fact. The Vichy government, therefore, concluded that it would be best for France to collaborate fully with Germany during these final days of the war and become an active partner in the final push toward victory. This would put Vichy in a position to expect significant concessions thereafter. The chief proponents for this view in Vichy were Premier Laval and Admiral Jean Francois Darlan, the number two man in the Vichy government under Petain who held the offices of Vice-Premier and was Commander-in-Chief of the French Navy. Petain went along with it.

About this time Vichy announced, once again, that it would retake the areas in Africa that had gone over to the Free French. In Paris, Vichy and German representatives met on May 27, 1941, to work out a formal agreement for Vichy's increased military collaboration with Germany which, of course, was already under way. The result of these meeting was the creation of the "Paris Protocol," a formal agreement which gave the Germans virtually all the concessions they had been asking for. Specifically, in Syria and Lebanon, the Vichy French gave the Germans permission to use airfields, port facilities, roads and railroads to transport men and materials to Iraq. Vichy also agreed to immediately turn over to the Iraqis a large amount of the French military stores already in Lebanon and Syria.

In yet another concession, the Vichy French authorized the Germans to use the ports in Tunisia, Algeria and French Morocco for naval and air operations, and to use Dakar for submarine operations. This put Germany in a position to lay siege to Gibraltar and effectively close the western entrance to the Mediterranean, as well as interdict Britain's maritime lifeline into the South Atlantic. By granting these very significant concessions, Vichy came close to becoming a cobelligerent ally of Germany.

PLANNED USE FOR DAKAR AND OTHER CONCESSIONS

The Paris Protocol called for the Germans to begin using Dakar in two stages starting in July, 1941. In stage one, German supply ships servicing submarines at sea would be allowed to use the port. Later, German submarines could use the port directly. At some unspecified time in the future it was agreed that other German warships and aircraft could also use Dakar. In return, Vichy would be allowed to increase and deploy her armed forces beyond the armistice limitations as circumstances allowed.

In further concessions, Vichy agreed to send certain supplies from French North Africa, through Tunisia, to the Axis forces fighting in North Africa, and the French would help transport those supplies.

In return for Vichy's cooperation, the Germans made a reduction of 300 millions francs per day in their occupation charges, eased travel across the demarcation line between occupied and unoccupied France, released all older French POWs who had served in World War I and made several other minor concessions.

The Paris Protocol was supposed to be secret but the signs of Vichy's political moves toward the Axis Powers became so apparent that its contents were soon accurately deduced by others. The existence of the Paris Protocol was announced publicly in both Germany and France but few details were given. In Germany, it was hailed as a "new era" in German/French relations and from Vichy came talk of a pending peace treaty.

As the Paris talks were underway, the Americans could see as clearly as anyone that the Germans would, very likely, put pressure on the Vichy French for a military base at Dakar. On the same day the Paris Protocol was signed President Roosevelt went on radio in another of his Fireside Chats and warned Vichy that a German presence at Dakar was a direct threat to American interests.

The Paris Protocol was, by no means, welcomed unanimously by all the Vichy leaders. In North Africa, High Commissioner Weygand strongly opposed the protocol as did High Commissioner Boisson at Dakar.

Unfortunately for Vichy and Berlin the Paris Protocol came too late to help Iraq. On May 30, the Indian troops, after marching up from Basra, reached the outskirts of Baghdad and the Gailani government abandoned the city and fled to Iran. The next day an armistice was signed, British troops entered the city, and on June 4 a pro-British government was restored in Baghdad. This ended most of the hostilities in Iraq. Rebellious Iraqi units held out in various parts of the country and it would take several weeks of mopping up operations before the two Indian divisions could completely pacify the country.

BRITISH REACTION TO THE PARIS PROTOCOL

As the details of the Paris Protocol became known in London, the British had no other option but to carry out the warning they made to Vichy on May 22 and use military action against some part of the French Empire. The logical place to strike, the British concluded, was against Lebanon and Syria (the Levant) which bordered British-controlled Palestine and Trans-Jordan. It was Lebanon and Syria that the Vichy government had put most at risk by allowing the Germans and Italians to use those territories to transport arms and men to Iraq. Furthermore, conquest of Lebanon and Syria would put Allied troops on the southern border of neutral Turkey to serve as a deterrent to any Turkish accommodation with the Axis.

Once again, as with the recent situation in the Balkans, the British had to search deeply for troops. Fortunately, the war in East Africa was winding down and some of the British troops there could be sent immediately to Palestine and Trans-Jordan.

Vichy could see that the British were likely to strike in the Levant, so on June 3, the Petain government renewed its pledge to strongly resist any invasion of Lebanon and Syria and that it would have German help in doing so. The former was true, but the latter was a myth. With the invasion of the Soviet Union only days away, Hitler could not risk sending any significant military help to the Levant. This was made obvious when, on the very next day, Germany withdrew all of the remaining Luftwaffe units from Syria. The Vichy French would have to defend Lebanon and Syria on their own.

PETAIN REFUSED TO RATIFY PARIS PROTOCOL

By late May, it was becoming apparent to Petain and others at Vichy that the Paris Protocol had been a mistake. And, fortunately, for Petain there was still a way out. Since the agreement had been made by his subordinates, Laval and Darlan, it was not valid until, and unless, Petain ratified it. On June 3, Petain met with his Council of Ministers to discuss the situation. High Commissioners Weygand of North Africa and Boisson of West Africa were in attendance. These two gentlemen took the lead in denouncing the agreement and were supported by some of Petain's ministers. After several hours of heated debate it was agreed that Petain should not ratify the agreement, but neither should he reject it outright. To accomplish this and save face, it was decided to use the old political trick of demanding more concessions, concessions the Germans would not accept, and drag out the negotiations indefinitely while the main conditions of the agreement went unfulfilled. Those additional concessions should be, the French leaders agreed, adjustments beneficial to Vichy concerning the territorial boundaries between occupied and unoccupied France.

When Hitler learned of Vichy's action he was very angry with Petain and his government and could see immediately what the Vichy French were up to. But, with the invasion of the Soviet Union only days away, he had no time to address this issue. Rather, the Germans asked for a delay in negotiations which, in their view, meant a delay until after the Soviet Union was defeated.

The Petain government had anticipated Hitler's displeasure and on June 14 made yet another concession to Hitler on one of his favorite subjects—the Jews. On that date, Vichy expanded its anti-Semitic law of October 3, 1940, to exclude Jews in unoccupied France from practically all fields of cultural and economic activities. Furthermore, the October 1940 law, which had applied mainly to unoccupied metropolitan France, was expanded with this action to include all of the colonies.

Then, on June 22, the Germans invaded the Soviet Union. At that moment Petain and his associates understood why the Germans wanted to delay negotiations on the Paris Protocol. For Vichy this was a most welcome development and they pursued it no further. Neither did the Germans pursue the issue and the Paris Protocol fell into a political limbo with no more of its conditions implemented by either side.

THE ALLIED INVASION OF LEBANON AND SYRIA

Fortunately for the British, they already had significant forces in Palestine and Trans-Jordan and were able to react rather quickly. On June 8, they invaded the Vichy-controlled colonies. The largest force available to the British command, under General Sir Henry Maitland Wilson, was the 55,000-man Free French component which consisted primarily of French Foreign Legionnaires, Senegalese infantrymen, Moroccan Spahis, Tunisians, Algerians, several battalions of Equatorial Africans, and a force of 100 Circassian (Syrian) cavalrymen who had fled Syria earlier and joined the Free French in Palestine. Vichy propagandists used this mix of nationalities in exaggerated claims that de Gaulle's forces were made up of Negroes and Jews.

The main British forces were the 7th Australian and the 4th Indian Division sent to Palestine from Egypt.

The Vichy forces in the Levant, numbering only 39,000, were commanded by General Fernand Dentz, an ardent Vichy Loyalist. Some 18,000 of his troops were colonials; Syrians, Lebanese, Moroccans, Senegalese, and Foreign Legionnaires. In addition, Vichy had made plans to send several large Senegalese units to the Levant but were unable to get them through the British blockade. By various means only a few hundred reinforcements were able to make it to the Levant and most of them arrived too late to make a difference.

The British opened the attack during the darkness hours of June 8 and advanced into southern Lebanon. There they were met with strong resistance from the Vichy forces well entrenched along the Litani River. All hopes that the French in the Levant would abandon Vichy and join de Gaulle vanished.

The Allied forces were able to advance quickly along the coast, though, and on June 9 occupied Tyre, Lebanon. The same day a British column advancing out of Trans-Jordan took Dera'a, Syria. On the 10th, Vichy resistance along the Litani River collapsed. Allied forces then moved northward at a rapid pace and by June 12 were only a dozen miles from Damascus, the capital of Syria. There, the Vichy French were well entrenched again. On June 16, a Vichy counterattack resulted in the recapture of El Quneitra and three days later another Vichy counterattack succeeded in retaking the town of Mezze. The next day the Allied force renewed their attacks and threw the enemy back to their starting point in heavy fighting. On June 21, the Allied attack resumed and the Australians and Free French succeeded in capturing Damascus.

Also that day, units of the 8th and 10th Indian Divisions invaded eastern Syria from Iraq following an oil pipeline and its service road leading to Palmyra.

At Vichy, the Petain government had obtained German permission to send strong reinforcements to Syria, especially French Air Force units.

Then, on June 22, came the startling news that Germany had invaded the Soviet Union. This was a shock and surprise to everyone in the Levant but it had little effect on the military situation of either side with the exception that on the Vichy side rumors circulated that the Germans would soon be sending reinforcements from Greece. This was not to happen. More reliable news came from Vichy, namely, that strong French Air Force reinforcements were on their way to the Levant. This news served to bolster the morale of the Vichy troops which was demonstrated when a small force of only 150 Vichyite French Legionnaires stopped a force of 3500 Indians advancing from Iraq. This victory was only temporary, though. The Indians attacked the next day and drove the Legionnaires back to their last defense line in front of Palmyra.

On July 3, the Indians attacked the Palmyra defenses, broke through, and occupied the city.

In Lebanon the Australians had, by July 9, succeeded in surrounding Beirut, the capital. This spelled the end for the Vichy troops in the Levant. On July 10, Dentz asked for a truce. The British and Free French agreed and two days later an armistice was signed at Acre in northern Palestine. Terms of the armistice placed Lebanon and Syria under joint British and Free French control and allowed those Vichy troops, who refused to join the Free French, to leave rather than be incarcerated. Out of the original 39,000 Vichy troops, 5668 declared for de Gaulle. A large percentage of them were Africans.

De Gaulle was not happy with the results of the war in the Levant. He had hoped more French troops would join his cause and he was not happy sharing political power with the British. He felt that since Syria and Lebanon had been French mandates, their control should have been turned over to him. In an unofficial show of protest he left London for another tour of his African territories. One of the messages he took with him to his subordinates was to be wary of British intentions and promises.

With the end of hostilities in the Levant the British now had troops to use elsewhere and the most logical place to send them was to North Africa.

In Vichy, the Petain government's foreign policy was now in shambles. Obviously, the end of World War II was not at hand and Vichy now needed to back away from its strong commitment toward Germany and hopefully return to a more neutral stance. Therefore, concessions were also in order to the Allies while, at the same time, a show of continuing cooperation with Germany had be demonstrated. Fortunately for Vichy, Hitler, seeing the controversy that arose over the possible German use of French North African and West African bases—especially Dakar—had concluded that it was not worthwhile at the moment to pursue these issues. He passed word to Petain that Germany would not exercise its options on the French ports in the near future for "political" reasons. Hitler did not want to put any more of the French Empire at risk at a time when he was fully committed in the Soviet Union and could not effectively help Vichy defend its territory.

This was welcome news in Vichy and on August 4, for the benefit of the Allies, Vichy announced that German forces would not be permitted to occupy French bases in North and West Africa. There was one exception, though. In early June, soon after the Paris Protocol was signed, Vichy allowed the Axis Powers to send food, clothing and other nonmilitary supplies through the port of Bizerte in northern Tunisia. No troops, war supplies or ammunition was allowed. This arrangement would continue.

On August 12, for the benefit of the Axis Powers, Vichy made the general statement that the Petain government would continue to cooperate fully with Germany and Italy under the terms of the June 1940 armistice agreements. That same day, Petain did the Germans another favor by appointing Admiral Darlan as Minister of War in his cabinet. This made Darlan the supreme commander of the French Army, Navy and Air Force in both unoccupied Metropolitan France and the Empire. It also put all of the High Commissioners in the French colonies directly under Darlan on all military matters and was further seen as a move by Vichy to put tighter controls on Weygand and Boisson, both of whom had spoken out strongly against the Paris Protocol at the June 3 meeting in Vichy.

On August 23, Petain gave the Germans yet another sop by decreeing a renewed crackdown on anti-Nazi activity in unoccupied France.

The Polish 1st Carpathian Brigade departing Alexandria for Tobruk.

HITLER WRITES TO MUSSOLINI

On June 21, 1941, the eve of the German attack on the Soviet Union, Hitler wrote a letter to Mussolini explaining his decision for the attack. Anticipating a quick victory, Hitler told Mussolini that he saw no need for Italy to send troops to the Soviet Union. Hitler wanted the Italians to maintain the status quo in the Mediterranean area until the Soviet Union was defeated. Furthermore, Hitler told Mussolini rather curtly, "An attack on Egypt is out of the question altogether..." This was agreeable to Mussolini. He had no intention of attacking deeper into Egypt.

BACK IN NORTH AFRICA

In North Africa the Axis took advantage of the ground war lull to reorganize and resupply their forces. As part of these changes, the Italian High Command in Rome, on July 12, replaced General Garibaldi with General Ettore Bastico. Bastico, like Garibaldi before him, was technically Rommel's commander. Also, the Italians gave up using Libyans in combat troops because they were just too unreliable. Henceforth, Libyans would be used only as service troops.

As the Germans slowly received replacements and supplies, Rommel's force grew to the strength of three divisions and was redesignated "Panzer Group Africa." The 5th Light Division was renamed the 21st Panzer Division and became an armored division equal to the 15th Panzer Division. A new infantry division was also formed.

While there was little ground action in North Africa during July and August, it was quite different in the air. The RAF repeatedly bombed Tripoli and Benghazi as well as ports in Italy and Sicily from which supplies reached Rommel. The Italian Air Force, along with German and Italian long-range artillery, pounded Tobruk time and again. One of the main targets in Tobruk was the water supply system. The Axis bombs and artillery shells did considerable damage in this respect, and at one time the water ration to the troops inside Tobruk dropped to a pint a day.

On July 14, there was a new development in the North African air war when German bombers, operating out to the newly-captured island of Crete, bombed Port Said at the northern end of the Suez Canal. This demonstrated that the Germans had yet one more location from which they could strike at North Africa by air. But, this advantage was short-lived because the Luftwaffe was in the process of being withdrawn from the Mediterranean.

As for Tobruk, the Australian government had been asking London to relieve the Australian troops there who were in need of rest and recuperation. London agreed and during the nights of August 12 to 18, 1941, some 5,000 Australians were removed by destroyers and mine sweepers, and the 6,000-man Polish 1st Carpathian Brigade under General S. Kopansik, which was fighting under British command, moved in.

HITLER WORRIED—MAY LOSE NORTH AFRICA

By late August 1941, after only two months of combat in the Soviet Union, Hitler could see that his timetable of conquering the Soviet Union by the end of the year would probably not be met. To prepare his top advisers for such an eventuality he allowed a top secret memorandum, dated August 28, 1941, to circulate among selected individuals detailing his thoughts on the subject.

Also mentioned in the secret memorandum were Hitler's thoughts on North Africa. Hitler said that he expected the United States to significantly aid the British there while Germany was still involved in the Soviet Union, and that there was a chance that all of North Africa might be lost before Germany could extricate herself from the Soviet Union. As it turned out, Hitler was right.

Chapter 11
ELSEWHERE IN AFRICA (JANUARY–AUGUST 1941)
STILL MORE CONFLICTS IN AFRICA

THE SEA WAR IN THE INDIAN OCEAN

As the new year of 1941 blossomed, German raiders were still operating in the Indian Ocean. One of them was the Atlantis which, in late January, was operating off the Seychelles Islands, just north of Madagascar disguised as a Norwegian freighter. On the evening of January 23, she spotted the British freighter "Mandasor" out of Calcutta for England with a cargo of pig iron. The Atlantis tried to stalk the Mandasor through the night but lost her. The next morning the German raider launched her small float plane which soon located the Mandasor and strafed and bombed her. The Mandasor fired back at the plane without hitting it while at the same time sent out the QQQ distress signal. The Atlantis quickly closed in and fired at the British ship at close range, hitting her several times and causing her to begin sinking. All but six of the Mandasor's crew got off the ship safely into lifeboats and the captain of the Atlantis wanted to take them prisoner. To assist in this effort the Atlantis' float plane landed on the water near the survivors but, in landing, damaged one of its pontoons and began to sink. The German pilots were then rescued by the British seamen in the lifeboats. The Atlantis eventually came up and took all aboard.

Knowing that his location was now known due to the QQQ signal, the Atlantis' captain turned the ship northward and sped into the Arabian Sea.

There, Atlantis found another victim on January 31. She was the British cargo ship "Speybank" out of Indo-China for New York with cargos of manganese ore, carpets, tea and shellac. The Speybank and her crew were captured, a German crew put aboard, and the ship sent out to a remote part of the Indian Ocean to await a future linkup with the Atlantis. Two days later the same fate befell the Norwegian tanker "Ketty Broevig." She too was sent out into the Indian Ocean to join the Speybank and await further action.

IN THE ATLANTIC

During the early months of 1941, the Germans had two battleships roaming the Atlantic Ocean. The "Admiral Scheer" made the first sortie from Germany in early November 1940. She promptly decimated an Allied convoy, and then disappeared from Allied view. The second German battleship, "Admiral Hipper," left Brest, France on February 1, headed south, and on the 12th encountered an unescorted England-bound convoy east of the Azores coming up from Freetown. The convoy immediately scattered as the Admiral Hipper approached, but the giant ship, with her fast speed and long-range guns, was able to chase down and sink seven of the convoy's nineteen ships. Knowing that her position was known, the Admiral Hipper returned promptly to the safety of Brest, France to wait and strike again.

The Admiral Scheer, with which the British had lost contact, reappeared in the South Atlantic in late December operating in the waters midway between the west coast of Africa and the east coast of South America. This was an area of the ocean out of range of Allied aircraft and coastal patrols operating from either continent. Here the Admiral Scheer took several lone vessels and, in late January 1941, disappeared again.

ANOTHER GERMAN BATTLESHIP IN THE INDIAN OCEAN

After leaving the South Atlantic the Admiral Scheer sailed unnoticed around the southern tip of Africa and entered the Indian Ocean. This was the second German battleship to have entered the Indian Ocean during the war, the first being the Graf Spee in late 1939.

The German warships already operating in the Indian Ocean and further east, the raiders Atlantis, Komet, and Penguin, knew the Admiral Scheer was coming. Only the Atlantis, however, was close enough to cooperate with the battleship. There were no German subs in the Indian Ocean at the time.

On February 11, the Admiral Scheer met with the Atlantis and three other ships in a quiet and remote location at sea. This would be the largest accumulation of German ships in the Indian Ocean during the war. The other three ships were the captured British freighter Speybank, the captured Norwegian tanker Ketty Broevig, and the German supply ship "Tannenfels" operating out of Kismayu, Italian Somaliland. The purpose of the mid-ocean meeting, which lasted for several days, was to resupply both the Atlantis and the Admiral Scheer and to plan future naval operations in the Indian Ocean. The ship captains agreed that four of the ships would work together as a team to attack Allied shipping in the water north of Madagascar. The fifth ship, the Speybank, was sent on to Europe. The Allies knew nothing of this rendezvous and had not yet discovered that the Admiral Scheer was in the Indian Ocean.

The plan went well at first when the two warships succeeded in capturing the British merchant ship "British Advocate," which was taken as a prize and sent on, successfully, to Europe. Then, for the next week the Germans found nothing. On February 25, the German warships met again at sea to revise their strategy. At this meeting it was decided that the ships would split up into three groups, each patrolling adjacent areas of the western Indian Ocean off Africa. The Admiral Scheer and Atlantis would each act separately while the captured Norwegian tanker Ketty Broevig was to serve as the third search ship along with the German freighter "Coburg" which had just fled Massawa, Eritrea in the face of the British advance on that port. The Ketty Broevig and Coburg would act as a two-ship search team and call in the warships if a target was spotted. It was also planned that the ships would meet for a third time in a week or so. This third meeting, though, was not to be. On February 25, an SAAF reconnaissance plane spotted the Admiral Scheer and two British cruisers, operating just east of Madagascar, were dispatched at once to pursue her. Within days the British were able to bring in five more cruisers and an aircraft carrier to add to the search. SAAF land-based air coverage was also intensified. The Admiral Scheer's captain soon learned that a sizeable British task force was searching for him and decided to leave the Indian Ocean as quickly as possible rather than risk a confrontation. At one point a British cruiser came up behind the German battleship and a high-speed chase ensued. Luckily for the Germans, however, foul weather set in and the Admiral Scheer was able to elude her pursuer. She then rounded the southern tip of Africa, out of range of land-based aircraft, and made it to the relative safety of the South Atlantic.

Meanwhile, British cruisers encountered the Ketty Broevig and Coburg capturing both of them and their German crews.

ACTION IN THE RED SEA

Ever since Italy entered the war in June 1940, naval action in the Red Sea had been relatively quiet compared to the other waters around Africa, despite the fact that Italian destroyers and submarines were in an excellent location at Massawa and Assab, Eritrea to intercept Allied convoys and warships sailing up and down the full length of the Red Sea going to and from Egypt. For reasons of their own the Italians chose not to aggressively challenge that traffic.

Such was the case in late February 1941, when the British aircraft carrier Formidable entered the Red Sea heading for the Mediterranean. German aircraft, though, dropped mines in the Suez Canal and the Formidable was ordered to wait in the Red Sea until those mines could be cleared. This, however, opened up an opportunity for General Platt, Commander of the Allied forces in Eritrea, to seek help from the Royal Navy. The Royal Navy cooperated and on February 21, and again on March 1, planes from the Formidable bombed targets in Massawa in preparation for Platt's advance on that seaport.

Also during this time, in the Indian Ocean, the Italian cargo ship "Leonardo de Vinci" fled Mogadishu, Italian Somaliland hoping to reach Diego Suarez in Vichy-controlled Madagascar. She did not make it. The Italian ship was intercepted by a British cruiser and sunk. Also, the Italian freighter "Ramb I" fled Massawa into the Indian Ocean hoping to make it safely to an Axis port in Europe. But luck was not with the Ramb I either. On February 27, the New Zealand cruiser "Leander" located her off the Maldive Islands and sank her. The other Italian merchant ships at Massawa fared no better. As the British forces approached the port in March they were all scuttled.

Submarines, though, were too valuable to scuttle, so between March 1 and 4, four Italian subs "Perla," "Archimede," "Guiglielmotti" and "Ferrarris" fled Massawa and struck out for the 16,000 mile journey home. They planned to sail down the Red Sea, around the southern tip of Africa and back to Europe. On the first leg of their journey they rendezvoused with Atlantis and her supply hip "Normark," were given fuel and other supplies, and sent on their way. They had been ordered by Rome not to attack Allied shipping en route. Getting home safely was the first priority. Luck was with the Italians. All four subs made it safely to the German naval base at Bordeaux, France.

An Italian sloop which left Massawa at the same time made it safely to Japan.

With the departure of the four Italian submarines there would be no more Axis submarine activity in the Red Sea or the Indian Ocean until November 1941.

The departure of the Italian subs did not end the threat of Italian naval action in the Red Sea. The Italians still had five destroyers and some smaller warships based at Massawa.

It was very unlikely that these ships could make it back to Europe safely around South Africa, so Rome ordered the five destroyers to make a last attack against the British base at Port Sudan and then scuttle themselves. That attack started on April 1, when all five destroyers departed Massawa for Port Sudan. One destroyer, the "Leone," hit an uncharted rock that afternoon, punctured its hull, and began flooding. After fires started the Leone was abandoned. The other four destroyers approached Port Sudan on April 3, and were met by Port Sudan's defending aircraft, and aircraft flown in from the carrier "Eagle" which was awaiting passage through the Suez Canal. In the battle that followed, one of the destroyers was sunk and two damaged but still able to sail under their own power. The three survivors escaped and, as ordered, were later scuttled by their crews off the coast of neutral Saudi Arabia. The crews were thus interned by the Saudis.

As General Platt's forces approached Massawa on April 8, the Italians scuttled the remaining ships in the harbor which included ten Italian and six German merchant ships, the Italian ocean liner "Columbo" and the minelayer "Ostia."

As British warships patrolled Massawa offshore, a brave and determined Motor Torpedo Boat (MTB) crew charged out of the harbor and sent a torpedo into the British light cruiser "Capetown." The MTB was then blown out of the water by the other British ships. The Capetown remained afloat under her own power but was out of action for several months. Thus ended the Italian naval threat in the Red Sea.

On April 11, President Roosevelt declared that the Red Sea and the Gulf of Aden were no longer combat zones and were open, once again, to American shipping. This allowed American ships carrying Lend-Lease materials to sail right up to the British docks in Egypt.

On May 13, to counter the American move, Berlin declared the northern end of the Red Sea a combat zone because their bombers could reach this area. Washington took no heed of Berlin's move. It was American law, not German law, that applied to American ships.

SUBMARINES AND POLITICS

Because Germany was negotiating with Vichy for the use of Atlantic ports in North and West Africa, Hitler thought it advantageous to show the flag in the waters off the African coast to impress the French that the Germans could hold their own in that area of the Atlantic. That same show of force would also impress the Spanish from whom he also hoped to gain concessions. Therefore, in late February, Hitler ordered Admiral Doenitz, Commander of the German Submarine Fleet, to sent enough German vessels into the area to amply demonstrate Germany's sea power.

German and Italian subs had worked the area before and were continuing to do so, but in recent months Axis activities there had slacked off. Now though, with Hitler's order, the west coast of Africa was to become a very active battleground.

HIGH-POINT OF THE GERMAN SURFACE FLEET

November 1940 to late May 1941 proved to be the high-point of action for the German surface fleet. During this time most of the Germany Navy's submarines and disguised raiders were at sea along with most of their big ships. Germany's battleships Admiral Scheer, "Gneisenau" and "Schornhorst" each made one sortie into the Atlantic during this time with the Admiral Scheer being the only one of the three to penetrate the South Atlantic and Indian Oceans. Gneisenau and Schornhorst did approach the west coast of Africa and, for a short time, caused the Allies a serious problem north of the Cape Verde Islands. The battleship Admiral Hipper made two sorties, both in the North Atlantic.

Then in May 1941, the battleship "Bismarck" and cruiser "Prinz Eugen" sortied together into the North Atlantic and the Bismarck was sunk by the British. With this loss, and the German naval losses suffered during the invasion of Norway in April 1940, Hitler concluded that his conventional surface fleet was no match for that of the British. From then on, for the remainder of the war, he kept his capital ships, for the most part, in port.

His submarines and raiders, though, were worked as hard as ever. The Allies, of course, were not aware of this decision concerning Germany's big ship and were constantly on the alert, especially throughout the remainder of 1941, for these ships to venture forth at any time.

Hitler did not plan to leave his surface fleet idle throughout the war. His plan was, after the defeat of the Soviet Union, to build more and larger surface vessels, including up to eight aircraft carriers. With these new vessels he would then challenge the British and Americans for control of the Atlantic and use his enlarged navy to protect Germany's new colonial empire.

SUBMARINES, RAIDERS AND BATTLESHIPS OFF WEST AFRICA

As already related, there were three ships lost to Axis subs off West Africa during early January 1941. Following that, there was a pause of almost two months in African waters, except on February 10 when the German sub U-37 ventured south of Gibraltar and torpedoed and sank the British freighter "Brandenberg" just north of Madeira. The

The innocent-looking German raider "Kormoran." She was equipped with six 5.9" guns, four torpedo tubes, and two scout planes. She sank or captured eleven Allied vessels before being sunk herself in Australian waters in November 1941.

Brandenberg was part of a small convoy coming up from Freetown.

The pause ended in early March when three German subs, U-105, U-106, and U-124 invaded West African waters again. On March 8, U-105 and U-124, working together, discovered the lightly guarded Freetown-to-England convoy, SL-67, about 300 miles off the Mauritanian coast. Both subs maneuvered for attacks. U-105 was the first to strike by torpedoing and sinking the British cargo ship "Harmodius." Two hours later U-124 fired a spread of torpedoes into the convoy and sank four ships; all British cargo ships, "Nardana," "Hindpool," "Tielbank," and "Lahore." U-105 and U-124 then withdrew for their own safety.

Three days later, on March 11, U-106 found her first victim, the British freighter "Memnon" sailing alone in the same area where the other two German subs had attacked convoy SL-67. The Memnon, an easy target, was torpedoed and sunk.

The next day the German disguised raider "Kormoran" joined in the naval warfare off West Africa by attacking and sinking the empty British tanker "Agnita." The Agnita had just delivered oil to Freetown and was on its return trip to Venezuela for more. The Germans captured the Agnita's crew of 38 British and Chinese seamen.

Then on March 16, a most unique sea battle took place off Mauritania in which German battleships and subs cooperated in attacking a British convoy. On that date the German battleships Gneisenau and Schornhorst suddenly appeared in West African waters. They had been operating together in the North Atlantic since early February raiding British shipping and had slipped into West African waters unnoticed. The two fast and modern warships soon made contact with the northbound Freetown-to-England convoy SL-68 protected by the old British battleship "Malaya" and three corvettes. The Malaya moved out to challenge the approaching enemy but the two German ships, which were much faster than the old British warhorse, maneuvered to stay out of range of her big guns yet keep her a good distance from the convoy. Meanwhile the German submarines U-105 and U-106 went to work and attacked the now lightly-defended convoy. U-106 struck first, torpedoing and sinking the Dutch merchantman "Almkerk." That was at 4:36 on the afternoon of March 16. The German subs were unable to make any more attacks before nightfall, but all night long the cat and mouse game continued, and it continued for the next five days and nights. As the German battleships kept the Malaya at bay the two subs attacked the convoy repeatedly as it sailed along the Mauritanian coast. The British, in a desperate effort to protect the ships of the convoy, called in some of the ships in the area which were enforcing the naval blockade against French West Africa to act as temporary convoy escorts. In addition, aircraft too, were called in from Bathurst. But this all took time and some of the ships summoned were not necessarily equipped to fight submarines and the airplanes did not fly at night. The German subs took full advantage of the situation. Acting like a pair of hungry wolves, they would make an attack, then retreat and attack again from another direction. The sub commanders preferred to strike at night when it was more difficult for the convoy escorts to see them and when the British airplanes were grounded. Over the five days and nights the Germans took a heavy toll, sinking seven ships of the convoy and damaging the Malaya with one torpedo strike.

After this, the subs battleships and subs broke off contact with the convoy and went their separate ways.

The Vichy French, taking advantage of the reduced British blockade, dispatched a French freighter out of Port Etienne, Mauritania in hopes that it could break through the blockade and carry its cargo to France. It did not work. British patrol-torpedo (PT) boats intercepted the French ship and chased it back to Port Etienne.

CHURCHILL TAKES NOTE OF SL-68'S PLIGHT

In London, Prime Minister Churchill, who prided himself as something of an expert on naval affairs, took note of the losses to convoy SL-68 and concluded that destroyers, not battleships, were needed in this area as convoy escorts. On March 21, 1941, he wrote to the First Lord of the Admiralty:

> *"The spectacle of this big convoy (SL-68) now coming up from Sierra Leone having one or two ships sunk every day by a trailing U-boat, and now the battleship escort herself being torpedoed, is most painful. Nothing can be more like `asking for it' than to have a battleship escort waddling along with a six-and-a-half-knot convoy without any effective antisubmarine escort (other than the three corvettes). The Sierra Leone convoys will have to have destroyers with them."*

On March 25, the raider Kormoran struck again off Freetown. Her victim was another empty British tanker returning to Venezuela, the "Canadolite." The tanker was captured intact along with her crews. She was a brand new German-made vessel, made just before the war for a British shipping firm by Germany's Krupp Works. For this reason the Kormoran's captain decided not to sink her, but to send her on to Europe with a German crew and the Kormoran's accumulation of prisoners. The Canadolite successfully eluded the British blockade and made it safely to Gironde, France. Meanwhile, the Kormoran headed south along the African coast.

Kormoran was not the only German raider working the area. The raider Thor was working the waters off the Cape Verde Islands, disguised as a Yugoslav cargo ship. On March 25, she spotted the British passenger ship "Britannia" and was able to get close enough to make an attack. The Britannia was a fast ship and was armed. She also had some 500 passengers aboard. Her captain decided to run and fight as well as radio the RRR alarm because he knew there were British warships in the area. The Thor's captain heard the RRR alarm and knew that there were British warships about. But he decided to take up the pursuit. A running sea battle then began. The Thor, was slightly faster than the Britannia and slowly closed the gap. The Thor's gunners were able to score several hits on the British ship, but she kept running. All the while radio signals flashed back to the Britannia from British warships announcing they were on the way to her rescue. The Thor picked up the coded message but could not understand them although the Germans could deduce what they might be, and knew that time was of the essence.

Finally the Britannia was so battered that her captain stopped his ship and ordered it abandoned. The German's held their fire and waited anxiously as the passengers and crew piled into lifeboats. When the passengers were all off the ship the Thor moved in to finish off the ship with gunfire. When it was clear that the British ship was sinking Thor steamed out of the area at top speed. But her day was not over yet. Within a few hours she encountered the Swedish ship "Trolleholm" under charter to the British carrying coal from Newcastle, England to Port Said, Egypt via the South African route. The Germans captured the ship, scuttled her with demolition charges and sped away out of the area with the Trolleholm's crew below in her prison cells.

The German submarine U-124, which had not been involved in the attack on convoy SL-68, was now the only German sub working the West African coast and on April 4 torpedoed and sank the British merchant ship "Marlene" 100 miles off the coast of Liberia. Three days later, U-124 torpedoed and sank the British steamer "Portadoc" 200 miles off Freetown.

U-124 continued its successful string of kills throughout April and was joined by two newcomers, U-107 and U-103, and the raiders Thor, Kormoran and Penguin. Their cumulative toll for April was fifteen Allied merchant ships. The only losses to the Germans was some shell damage done to Thor in a running battle with an armed British merchantman. Thor had to retire to France for repairs.

THE "ZAMZAM" INCIDENT

On the night of April 15/16, 1941, the neutral Egyptian passenger ship Zamzam was sailing in the Central Atlantic out of New York with 340 passengers and a mixed cargo for South Africa and Egypt. One hundred and thirty eight of the passengers were Americans. She had a British captain and an Egyptian crew. Virtually all of the passengers were civilians; international travellers, European refugees, missionaries, wives of RAF servicemen going to join their husbands in Egypt, six North Carolina tobacco men on their way to buy tobacco in Southern Rhodesia, 24 volunteer ambulance drivers on their way to join the Free French, and one Life Magazine photographer.

Late on the evening of the 15, the Zamzam picked up a distress signal from a nearby Norwegian vessel being attacked by a disguised German raider. The Zamzam's captain ordered his ship to change course to avoid the area and ordered the ship blacked out. This was a serious mistake because neutral ships almost always sailed well-lighted at night as part of their identity as neutrals.

Soon after midnight, the Atlantis, which was also blacked out, encountered the Zamzam and began to stalk her. From her profile the Germans believed that the Zamzam was an armed British merchantman. Just before dawn the Atlantis closed in and fired on the Zamzam without warning. The Egyptian ship was hit several times, stopped and began sinking. On board the passengers panicked. Mercifully, the Germans stopped firing when they discovered the Zamzam's true identity. More mercifully yet, the Zamzam stopped sinking an stabilized. This allowed most of the passengers and crew to get off the Zamzam into lifeboats with most of their luggage. The survivors, and their luggage, were then taken aboard the Atlantis and the sick and wounded treated in Atlantis' sick bay. A German demolitions team then went aboard the Zamzam, examined the cargo and then set charges which sank the ship.

All the while the Life Magazine photographer, David Sherman, was secretly taking photographs of the action.

On April 17, the German blockade runner "Dresden" was summoned by Berlin to rendezvous with the Atlantis at sea and take as many of the civilian passengers as she could from the ship. The Dresden then went her way and by a very circuitous route arrived safely at Saint Jean-de-Luz, France on May 21.

At this point no one but the Germans knew that the Zamzam had been lost. When she did not arrive at her destinations the British Admiralty announced, on May 20, that the ship had probably been sunk by enemy action and that all aboard had most likely perished. This was dreadful news in the United States but it was short-lived. The next day the Germans announced that the Zamzam had, indeed, been sunk but that most of the passengers were safe in France and would be released. Here again, Hitler wanted to avoid confrontation with the Americans. The Germans claimed, though, that the sinking of the Zamzam was justifiable because it was carrying contraband, namely railroad rails, to the British forces in North Africa.

Eventually, the civilians were released by the Germans, including the photographer, Sherman, and returned to the United States via Lisbon. Sherman had been able to conceal his photographs from the Germans and upon returning home they were published in Life Magazine. This caused a sensational uproar of ill will in the United States against the Germans.

The Zamzam story, however, did not end there. Later investigations showed that the order to black out the Zamzam had come directly from the British Admiralty, and that the British ship captain had obeyed the order. It could clearly be deduced then, that the Admiralty certainly knew of the presence of the German raider in the area and that the two ships might encounter each other and that the blacked out ship might be mistaken for an Allied ship. This caused an anti-British backlash in the United States because the British action was seen as a sinister ploy to draw America into the war. After all, it had been the sinking of the passenger ship "Lusitania" in 1917 that drew America into World War I.

There was yet another facet to the Zamzam story. Thanks to Sherman, the British Navy now had accurate photographs of the Atlantis.

AMERICAN NAVY IN CENTRAL ATLANTIC

Ever since the beginning of the war, the United States had proclaimed a Pan-American Security Zone out into Atlantic waters in which, Washington insisted, American warships could act in defense of the United States and the Western Hemisphere. Among the defensive measures taken within the Zone was the self-proclaimed right of American warships to follow and track suspected belligerent nation's ships and to radio, in the clear, their location and direction of travel. This was a very one-sided arrangement, though. Ships of the Axis nations were followed and their locations revealed, while ships of the Allied nations were not. Then too, as the war progressed the eastern boundary of the security zone was moved steadily eastward. On April 11, President Roosevelt extended the eastern boundary of the zone to the 26th west meridian which ran through the middle of the Azores Island group and to within 200 miles west of the Cape Verde Island group. This placed more than half of the North Atlantic within the zone and in the Central Atlantic allowed American warships to patrol to within 750 miles of Dakar. A joke circulating Washington at the time stated that ultimately the eastern boundary of the Pan-American Security Zone would be the west bank of the Rhine River.

REALLY? THE CAPE VERDE ISLANDS?

America's isolationists pounced on Roosevelt's decision to extend the Pan-American Security Zone as another example of his secret agenda to drag America into the war.

On May 29, Charles Lindbergh, American's aviation hero and a leader in the isolationist movement, addressed a rally in Philadelphia saying, "Our own President says that the safety of America lies in controlling the Cape Verde Islands off the coast of Africa." The audience responded with boos and catcalls. Lindbergh went on to say, "Even Hitler never made such a statement like that" and the audience cheered.

Having defined their security zone, the Americans now had to come up with enough ships to patrol it. The first priority for American ships was the North Atlantic part of the zone but as more and more ships came rolling down the ways at American shipyards, other parts of the zone were covered. In mid-April, in preparation for patrolling the Central and South Atlantic, Washington announced that a "South Atlantic Force" would soon be available to patrol that part of the zone bounded by Trinidad–Cape San Roque, Brazil–Cape Verde Islands. That force would consist of four old cruisers "Memphis," "Cincinnati," "Omaha," "Milwaukee" and fifteen destroyers and would be based at Recife, Brazil. Brazil was a neutral nation, but much like the neutral United States, was very concerned about Western Hemisphere security and was willing to take significant steps toward that end.

Another reason for the extension of the Pan-American Security Zone was that more and more American vessels were now sailing down the west coast of Africa and around South Africa, delivering Lend-Lease goods to the British in Egypt and the Middle East. Those ships would, of course, benefit for a longer portion of their voyage thanks to the presence of American warships due to the increased size of the zone. To identify themselves as neutral ships both inside the zone and out, all American ships had large American flags painted on both sides of the hull which were brightly lighted at night to ward off Axis submarine attacks. This, of course, was no guarantee that attacks would not occur.

Unbeknownst to the Americans, their ships were quite safe because Hitler had ordered that his submarines take extra precautions not to attack American ships anywhere. With German troops involved in the Balkans, North Africa, and Iraq and soon to be very deeply involved in the Soviet Union, Hitler did not want to provoke the Americans anymore than he already had.

AMERICAN SHIPS— GERMAN SUBMARINES

Theoretically, under German law, American ships carrying Lend-Lease materials to the Allies were fair game for German submarines. This had been decreed by Berlin early in the war when the German government defined its naval blockade of Allied territories. That decree declared that ships of any nation, neutral or not, known to be carrying contraband, or even suspected of doing so, to the Allies could be intercepted by German naval and air forces. On January 30, 1941, Berlin had repeated the warning and stated specifically that neutral ships delivering war supplies to British ports would be torpedoed.

A short time later, however, Hitler secretly negated part of the decree by ordering that American ships not be attacked. Ships of other neutral nations, though, were not exempted and attacks continued on them.

On April 24, the American South Atlantic Force left Newport News, Virginia to carry out its assigned task.

IN THE INDIAN OCEAN

With the demise of the Italian Navy in East Africa, the only Axis warships operating in the Indian Ocean were the German raiders.

On April 25, the raider Penguin, in the company of one of her captured ships, the Norwegian whaler "Adjutant," captured and sank the British freighter "Empire Light" out of Madras, India bound for Durban with a cargo of ore and hides. Then on May 7, Penguin intercepted the British tanker "British Emperor." The British ship's captain chose to run rather than surrender, all the while sending out the RRR alarm. Nearby was the British cruiser Cornwall which heard the alarm and sped to the area at top speed. As the chase ensued the Penguin's guns fired away at the tanker, hitting her several times, causing fires to break out and eventually forcing her to stop. The British crew abandoned their ship as it began to sink. The Penguin and her captive, knowing that their location had now been revealed, parted company and sped out of the area. The Penguin took on the disguise of a Norwegian ship.

About 4:00 p.m. the Cornwall's spotter plane located the Penguin off the Seychelles Islands and the Cornwall raced to the scene. As the Cornwall approached the Penguin, still flying the Norwegian flag, the Penguin gave out the Allied alarm, RRR, as if it were an Allied ship thinking it was about to be attacked. This confused the Cornwall's captain and he closed in to take a closer look. When he got to within the range of Penguin's guns, the German ship dropped its disguise, raised the German ensign and fired on the Cornwall. That fire was accurate, hitting the Cornwall and damaging her steering mechanism. The Cornwall's crew reacted quickly and fired back at the Penguin. The British were able to quickly repair the damage done to their steering mechanism. For ten minutes the two ships fired away at each other. Then, at 5:26 p.m. the Penguin suddenly blew up, tossing men and metal high into the air and quickly sank. One of Cornwall's 8-inch shells had hit Penguin's store of 130 mines. The Cornwall was able to rescue sixty German crewmen and 22 British and Indian seamen who were prisoners aboard the Penquin. The rest of the Penguin's crew, numbering 292 including her captain, and 155 captive Allied seamen perished.

This was the first of the German raiders to be sunk. She had, in her short career, accounted for the loss of 32 Allied ships.

The captured Norwegian whaler, "Adjutant," was not involved in the battle and was soon acquired by the raider Thor which was also operating in the Indian Ocean.

The raider Kormoran was also operating in the Indian Ocean and on June 26, sank the empty Yugoslav cargo ship "Velebit" out of Bombay, India for Mombasa, Kenya. Nine of the Velebit's crewmen were captured by the Kormoran.

BACK IN WEST AFRICAN WATERS

April had been a bad month for the Allies in West African waters, but May was to be even worse. During May, six German and one Italian submarines sank thirty Allied vessels off the West African coast. One submarine, U-103, accounted for nine of the thirty. Furthermore, the raider Atlantis was working in the South Atlantic and sinking additional Allied ships.

On May 21, 1941, the Germans demonstrated their great displeasure with the Lend-Lease Act recently enacted by the United States, by sinking an American ship which, ironically, was not carrying Lend-Lease goods. The unfortunate ship was the "Robin Moor" out of New York bound for South Africa with passengers and commercial cargo. The ship was in the mid-Atlantic between West Africa and South America and had just passed out of the Pan-American Security Zone. The Robin Moor, now in international waters, was stopped about 10:00

a.m. in the morning by the German sub U-69, which was operating on the surface. The German sub commander ordered the American crew to abandon the ship because he intended to sink it. The American crew complied, and all 38 crewmen and eight passengers made it safely into four lifeboats. The German sub then sank the Robin Moor with a combination of torpedoes and gunfire. This appeared to be a violation of Hitler's decree that American ships not be attacked. But since the American ship was attacked - in a merciful way that cost no lives - and considering that the German crew could not possibly have mistaken the ship for an Allied vessel in broad daylight, the order to sink the ship could only have come from the highest source in Germany. After the Robin Moor went down, the sub came in among the lifeboats and gave the survivors four tins of bread and two tins of butter. The German captain apologized that he could not give them more food, but did promise to radio their location as soon as he was out of the area. It was doubtful that he did this, because for five days the lifeboats drifted aimlessly across the ocean. During a storm, one of the boats separated from the others. Soon afterwards, the survivors in the three lifeboats were rescued by a British ship and eventually taken to Cape Town. The fourth lifeboat drifted for thirteen more days and its survivors were eventually rescued off the coast of Brazil.

Thus, the sinking of the Robin Moor was a message to Washington of Germany's displeasure and that American ships, at any moment, could become the subject of German attacks.

Six days later, President Roosevelt publicly condemned the sinking of the Robin Moor as "ruthless" and a breach of international law. He demanded compensation from Germany for the loss of the ship. He also declared an unlimited national emergency in the United States and stated that the American government would protect its interests in the Atlantic Ocean even beyond the already defined security zones.

After sinking the Robin Moor U-69 went on to lay mines off Takoradi, Gold Coast and Lagos, Nigeria.

During June, the British increased their antisubmarine patrols considerably with noticeable effect and the presence of American ships patrolling the Central Atlantic certainly helped. The main British effort was the introduction of more aircraft flying antisubmarine patrols out of Freetown and Bathurst, and the arrival of several World War I-era American-made destroyers recently acquired from the Americans. The British Navy acquired fifty such vessels in exchange for British permission which allowed the Americans to occupy several British bases in the Western Hemisphere. The Americans also gave the British Navy ten Coast Guard cutters under Lend-Lease, and some of them were sent to Freetown.

The Germans and Italians were soon to experience the increased British strength. During June, the Germans sent eight subs into West African Waters and the Italians sent two with high hopes of continuing the carnage. But, the submarine captains soon discovered that there were more patrol planes overhead, forcing them to keep submerged, and more destroyers to chase them away from convoys. Together, they still managed to sink nineteen vessels but at increased risk. Clearly, by this score the Axis Powers were having to exert a greater effort while obtaining a lesser result.

In the South Atlantic, the raider Atlantis was still running loose and not greatly threatened by the increased Allied security measures. But, on the other hand, Atlantis was not finding many victims due to the increased use of convoys. She sank only one ship in May and two in June.

During June and July, very few German subs ventured down to, and beyond, the Equator for several reasons. In June, the British had captured a German submarine in the North Atlantic and aboard found secret documents revealing the locations of all of the German supply ships at sea in the Atlantic which were refuelling and resupplying submarines. The British Navy swooped down on these supply ships quickly and sank most of them. One of the supply ships, the "Egerland," was sunk in African waters just south of the Cape Verde Islands on June 6 by two British cruisers. Furthermore, through diplomatic efforts, the British were able to induce the Spaniards to close their ports in the Canary Islands, in addition to their other African ports, to German subs and supply ships effective July 16, 1941. Therefore, German subs going to West African waters could only patrol for a relatively short time before they had to return to the Atlantic coast of France for fuel and supplies. Occasionally a submarine was able to refuel from a passing German supply ship en route to somewhere else.

The British/Spanish agreement did not cover ports in Spain where German subs could still put in for fuel and supplies. There was a German supply ship, the "Thalia," anchored at Cadiz, Spain and another, the "Dessel," at Vigo. At these ports a departing German sub, heading south, could top-off its tanks or a returning sub could put in during an emergency.

Unfortunately for the Allies, the Spanish violated the agreement repeatedly and German vessels continued to use the Canary Islands as a source of fuel and supplies.

After losing their easy access to the Canary Islands, the Germans asked Vichy if their subs could refuel at Dakar. Vichy, not wanting to give the Allies another reason to threaten that strategic port, refused the German request.

Still another factor in the reduction of German subs in the south was the attack on the Soviet Union which occurred on June 22. The German Navy needed a part of its sub fleet now to do battle with the Soviet Navy and the Allied convoys that were beginning to bring military aid to the Soviets.

July saw even more intensive Allied air coverage over West African waters and a strengthening of convoy escorts. In response, only four German and four Italian subs patrolled West African waters that month taking twelve Allied ships.

Up to now, no Axis sub had been sunk or damaged in West African waters, but Doenitz could see that those waters were becoming more dangerous for this U-boats. In August, he sent only one sub into the area and it sank one ship. Likewise, the Italians sent only one of their subs into the area and it sank only one ship.

By the end of August 1941, the Allies could rightfully claim that they were winning the battle for control of West Africa's waters.

MORE AIR ROUTES TO AND THROUGH AFRICA

As might be expected, air activity intensified throughout Africa as the war progressed. The initiation of Lend-Lease by the Americans in March 1941 assured that activity would increase significantly, because Lend-Lease materials were badly needed by the British in Egypt and logistics dictated that a part of that material be sent by air. The most direct air route to Egypt, avoiding the dangerous Mediterranean area, was that which already existed; United States–Brazil–West Africa–East Africa–Egypt.

Quite naturally, as air traffic increased over the trans-African air route, new facilities had to be built and existing ones enlarged. This would become an on-going process for the rest of the war with the Americans the primary builders.

Of all the weapons of war that might be transported via the trans-African air route, none was more suited than airplanes themselves. Rather than ship completely assembled aircraft via slow-moving freighters and taking up considerable space aboard ship, it was faster and more economical to ship aircraft components via ship to the already-existing aircraft assembly center at Takoradi, Gold Coast, assembled them there and then ferry them on to their final destinations. The British, who badly needed aircraft in North Africa and the Middle East, were eager to work with the Americans on the "Takoradi Route," as it had become known.

Soon after the Lend-Lease bill was enacted, American General Harold "Hap" Arnold, Commander of the Army Air Forces, dispatched several survey teams of AAF people to Africa to meet with the British and explore the existing route to see what improvements needed to be made. Arnold's teams went as far east as India, gathering information and picking sites. To the American, the new air route became known as the Cannonball Route.

Churchill, himself, was most appreciative of Arnold's work and on May 11, 1941, sent Arnold a personal note in which he stated:

> *"I am much obliged for the information reported by your observer in Egypt. The Air Ministry tells me that we have recently sent out to Takoradi the best officers we can find... and (we) welcome your offer of American experts."*

The Americans were to work under British supervision, and the British had promised to provide living space and tools for them at Takoradi. Thus Churchill further reported to Arnold:

> *"In the climate of tropical West Africa no man can work as hard or as long as at home. We should like to work three shifts, and are planning to use ships for additional living quarters... and M.A.P. (Ministry of Aircraft Production) is being pressed to provide tools and equipment."*

Churchill went on to tell Arnold of the immediate need for transport aircraft and concluded his note by asking:

> *"Can your promised deliveries of American transport aircraft to Africa be accelerated?"*

Arnold's reply was that it could even though the American Air Forces (AAF) were desperately short of pilots.

Negotiations then began between Arnold's representatives, the British, and the commercial air carrier Atlantic Airways, Ltd. for delivery of twenty American-made transport planes to Africa as soon as possible. Atlantic Airways was jointly owned by Pan-American Airways, Inc. and British Overseas Airways Corporation (BOAC). BOAC was the largest British commercial air carrier in Africa, and was continuing to function as such. Agreement was reached on May 29 whereby Arnold's AAF would provide twenty planes under the Lend-Lease program, Atlantic Airways would provide the pilots, and the British would provided the navigators and pay all expenses.

In June 1941, the Americans made another advancement with regards to military air transportation by creating the "Air Transport Command" (ATC) within the AAF. But, for now, Pan-American Airways was the mainstay of the operation and the men of the ATC were instructed to learn from them.

Also in June, the AAF contracted with another American commercial air carrier, Eastern Air Lines, to establish an air route from Natal, Brazil to Ascension Island (where a new airfield was being planned) and then on to Accra, Gold Coast. Eastern was flying the new Curtiss C-46 transports which did not have the range to fly the 1,850 miles directly from Brazil to West Africa, but could fly the 1,400 miles from Brazil to Ascension and a second 1,400 miles to Accra. This route was used mainly to fly men and materials. It could also effectively service the assembly center at Takoradi because it was only 110 miles west of Accra.

On June 21, the first ten transports took off from Miami and flew to Trinidad and then on to Belem, Brazil. There the crews were unexpectedly arrested by the Brazilian authorities on a technicality. Ownership of the planes had been transferred to the British in Miami and thus became the property of a belligerent. Brazil, being neutral, had previously approved the transit of American-owned planes - America being another neutral - across her territory but not those of a belligerent. When the British-owned planes arrived that violated Brazil's neutrality laws, and theoretically, they were subject to internment for the duration of the war. Frantic negotiations began and it was finally concluded, after three days, that ownership of the ten planes would be transferred back to the Americans there in Brazil and then transferred again to the British once they reached Africa. This satisfied the Brazilians. The planes flew on to Natal, Brazil then across the Atlantic to Bathurst, Gambia. Seven of the remaining planes followed in late July and the last three in early September. All of the following planes remained American-owned until they reached Africa.

BATHURST UNTENABLE

Bathurst was the capital of the small British colony of Gambia which was surrounded on three sides by Vichy-controlled territory. Defending Gambia was militarily untenable because it was so small that it could be overrun by the Vichy French at any time. Therefore, as the trans-African air route system was being established, Bathurst was one of the least-used and least-important links. Freetown, in Sierra Leone, was more secure and therefore more preferred.

FREETOWN STRENGTHENED— POLISH OFFICERS—ITALIAN ARMS

During the time of the Paris Protocol, Churchill could see that the colony of Sierra Leone and its vital port, Freetown, were vulnerable to attack by the Vichy French. A new native brigade was being formed in Sierra Leone called the "Shadow Brigade," but it was short of white officers, NCOs, and equipment. Furthermore, even when activated, it and the other existing forces in Sierra Leone would not be enough to withstand a determined attack. Therefore, Churchill put pressure on his Chief of Staff, General Ismay, to find troops to defend Sierra Leone. In the discussions that followed it was agreed that the West African Brigade, currently engaged in Italian East Africa, could soon be released and sent to Sierra Leone. As for white officers, NCOs, and equipment for the new Shadow Brigade it was discovered that the Free Polish legions under General Wladyslaw Sikorski had a surplus of officers and he was willing to release up to 400 men to serve in the Brigade. As for equipment, it was decided they would equip the new brigade with captured Italian weapons from East Africa. During the late summer of 1941, these things were done and the security of Sierra Leone was thereby improved.

ATTACK ON THE SOVIET UNION AFFECTS AFRICA

On June 22, the day after the first of the twenty American transports left for Africa, the Germans invaded the Soviet Union. Two days later, President Roosevelt made a public statement that the United States would send significant amounts of military aid to the Soviets. A check of the map shows that one of the ways by which that aid would be sent was across or around Africa, through the Middle East, and into the southern part of the Soviet Union. Thus, all of a sudden, the existing air route across Africa and the sea routes around it increased in importance.

400 BOMBERS

The next significant shipment of American aircraft to the British was to be 400 Glenn Martin medium bombers purchased by the British before Lend-Lease. Here again, the Americans and the British turned to civilians to do the job.

The Pan-American Clippers were the most modern trans-oceanic aircraft of their day.

THE LAST "CLIPPER"

In July 1941, Boeing Aircraft Company of Seattle, Washington, delivered its last Clipper to Pan-American Airways. It was to have been used for flights between the United States, South America, and South Africa. To highlight Pan-Am's new interests in Africa the plane was christened the "Cape Town Clipper." Flying to South Africa, a belligerent, caused a political problem though. As a privately owned aircraft, American neutrality laws forbad it to fly into any belligerent nation. To resolve this, the American government purchased the Cape Town Clipper and leased it back to Pan-American Airways for one dollar a year. Now, being a government-owned plane, it could fly into any Allied territory receiving Lend-Lease under the provisions of that law.

Pan-American Airways, Inc. was approached by the American government again, and it was agreed to set up three subsidiary companies to ferry the Martins as well as any additional Lend-Lease aircraft from the United States to Africa and points beyond. The first of the three new companies, Pan-American Air Ferries, Inc., was to deliver the planes from Miami to Khartoum, where British air crews would take over. Later this was extended for American crews to fly the planes to Cairo and as far east as Tehran, Iran. The second company, Pan-American Airways-Africa, Ltd., was established to take over the existing British air transport system across Africa and coordinate the former British system with that of Pan-American Air Ferries, Inc. This would free up British airmen and aircraft for other duties. Pan-American Airways Company, the third subsidiary, was to use one of Pan-American's famous "Clippers," which was recently withdrawn from service in the Pacific and purchased by the American government. The Clipper was leased back to Pan-American Airways Company to ferry air crews back to America and various maintenance and administrative personnel from America to West Africa. Up to 68 passengers could be accommodated each way on the Clipper.

DE GAULLE WANTED AMERICAN AIR BASES IN EQUATORIAL AFRICA

In Equatorial Africa, General de Gaulle wanted the Americans to come into his realm to provide his Free French government and his military forces with a much-needed air link to the outside world. De Gaulle had another motive, too. Since his Free French were not yet receiving Lend-Lease, he saw this as a first step in cooperating with the Americans toward that end.

In July, de Gaulle's organization in America made special arrangements with America's National Broadcasting Company (NBC) to allow him to address the American public directly by radio. That broadcast took place in America on the evening of July 14, 1941. De Gaulle spoke in English, from Brazzaville, and appealed to the American people and the American government to provide substantial military and economic aid, under the new Lend-Lease program, to his Free French movement. President Roosevelt did not welcome de Gaulle's address because the pesky Frenchman was, in effect, going over his head. This was but one more example that would sour the personal relationship between the two Allied leaders.

The Americans were receptive, though, to de Gaulle's offer of air bases, and several sites were selected in Equatorial Africa to be a part of the Cannonball Route. Also, Pan-American Airways asked for, and de Gaulle granted, the right to establish commercial air facilities in the Free French-controlled New Hebrides Islands and New Calidonia Island in the South Pacific. These air facilities would improve America's air links with Australia and New Zealand. Both parties agreed that, for the moment, the South Pacific routes would be strictly commercial but could be used for military purposes if necessary.

In August 1941, the first American mission arrived in Chad to set up air facilities at Fort Lamy.

On August 17, 1941, Roosevelt officially announced to the American public that the United States was involved in ferrying Lend-Lease aircraft from America to British forces in North Africa and the Middle East. In neutral America, this was still a controversial issue. For the interventionists, it was seen as the right thing to do. For the isolationists, it was seen as another step toward disaster.

THE ATLANTIC CHARTER

Between August 9 and 12, 1941, President Roosevelt and Prime Minister Winston Churchill met at Placentia Bay, Newfoundland and drafted what came to be known as the "Atlantic Charter." This was a document intended to spur the Allies on to victory and, as is stated in the first paragraph of the Charter, to bring about "...a better future for the world."

The Charter outlined eight principles which Britain and the United States hoped to bring about after the war. The first three principles dealt with freedom and politics. The Charter read:

> *"First, their countries (Britain and the United States) seek no aggrandizement, territorial or other.*
>
> *"Second, their countries (Britain and the United States) desire to see no territorial changes that do not accord with the freely expressed wishes of the people concerned.*
>
> *Third, they (Britain and the United States) respect the right of all peoples to choose the form of government under which they will live; and they wish to see sovereign rights and self-government restored to those who have been forcibly deprived of them."*

The other five principles dealt with social, economic, and labor matters.

For colonial people all over the world, and especially for the nationalist organizations that represented them, the first three principles of the Charter were a bombshell. Here, the leader of the world's largest colonial empire speaks of no "territorial aggrandizements," "the freely expressed wishes of the people concerned," and "the right of all peoples..."—ALL PEOPLES—"...to choose the form of government under which they will live..." For those who wished to shake off colonial rule, the Atlantic Charter sounded like a dream come true. Here was the world's largest colonial master, Great Brit-

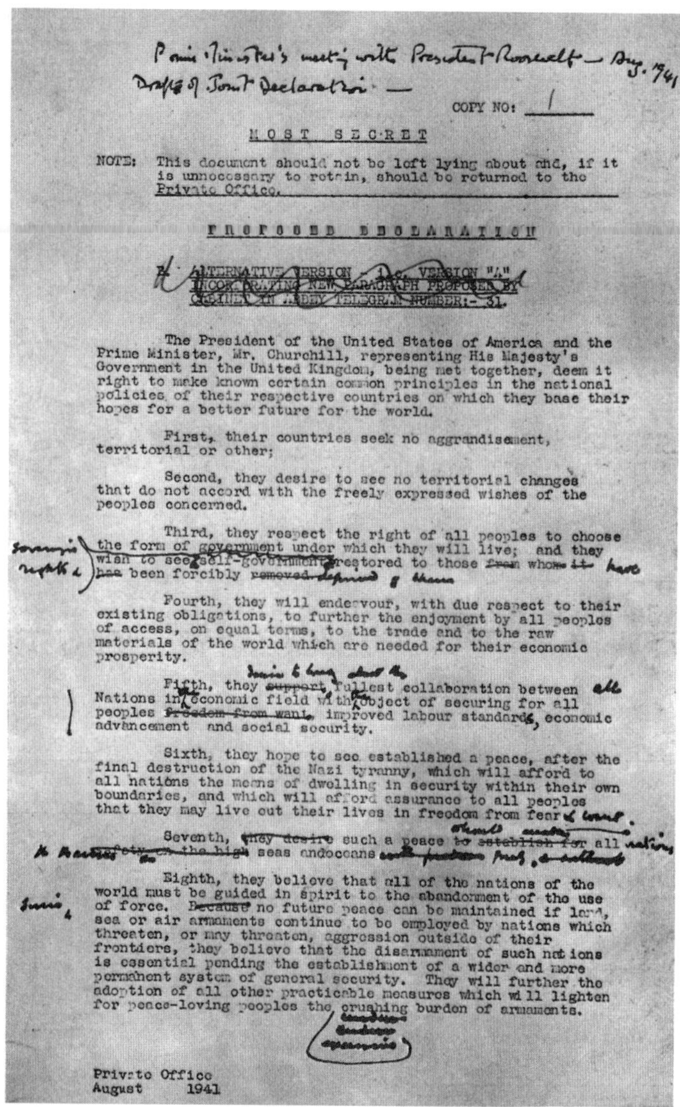

Prime Minister's meeting with President Roosevelt — Aug. 1941
Drafts of Joint Declaration —

COPY NO: 1

MOST SECRET

NOTE: This document should not be left lying about and, if it is unnecessary to retain, should be returned to the Private Office.

PROPOSED DECLARATION

ALTERNATIVE VERSION - i.e. VERSION "A" INCORPORATING NEW PARAGRAPH PROPOSED BY CABINET IN ABBEY TELEGRAM NUMBER:- 31.

The President of the United States of America and the Prime Minister, Mr. Churchill, representing His Majesty's Government in the United Kingdom, being met together, deem it right to make known certain common principles in the national policies of their respective countries on which they base their hopes for a better future for the world.

First, their countries seek no aggrandisement, territorial or other;

Second, they desire to see no territorial changes that do not accord with the freely expressed wishes of the peoples concerned.

Third, they respect the right of all peoples to choose the form of government under which they will live; and they wish to see self-government restored to those from whom it has been forcibly removed.

Fourth, they will endeavour, with due respect to their existing obligations, to further the enjoyment by all peoples of access, on equal terms, to the trade and to the raw materials of the world which are needed for their economic prosperity.

Fifth, they support fullest collaboration between Nations in economic field with object of securing for all peoples freedom from want, improved labour standards, economic advancement and social security.

Sixth, they hope to see established a peace, after the final destruction of the Nazi tyranny, which will afford to all nations the means of dwelling in security within their own boundaries, and which will afford assurance to all peoples that they may live out their lives in freedom from fear.

Seventh, they desire such a peace to establish for all safety on the high seas and oceans.

Eighth, they believe that all of the nations of the world must be guided in spirit to the abandonment of the use of force. Because no future peace can be maintained if land, sea or air armaments continue to be employed by nations which threaten, or may threaten, aggression outside of their frontiers, they believe that the disarmament of such nations is essential pending the establishment of a wider and more permanent system of general security. They will further the adoption of all other practicable measures which will lighten for peace-loving peoples the crushing burden of armaments.

Private Office
August 1941

The final draft of the Atlantic Charter.

ain, admitting that the era of decolonization and political self-determination was at hand. And furthermore, these ideas were being stated in agreement with the United States, a country that had long called for decolonization. With the publication of the Atlantic Charter the hopes and aspirations of colonial peoples soared all around the world. From this moment, on the Atlantic Charter would become a tool used by nationalist leaders and organizations everywhere to promote their goals.

When it became clear that colonial nationalists were using the verbiage in the Charter for their own purposes, Churchill felt the need to make several public statements explaining that the guarantees in the Charter applied to the restoration of independence to the nations overrun by the enemy and did not apply to the colonies of the British Empire. Then, when pressured, Churchill could fall back on the fact that the Atlantic Charter was only a joint declaration and not a binding international agreement. But this backsliding was too late. The words were there for all to see and the leaders of nationalist organizations would use them time and again.

Furthermore, there were those in the United States who supported the concept that the Atlantic Charter was, indeed, a document for decolonization. One such individual who spoke in this vein was Sumner Welles, the Under Secretary of State. He not only was one of Roosevelt's closest advisors, but he had been a member of the American delegation at Placentia Bay. Welles later would say, "... the right and determination by peoples is not limited by divine warrant, nor by the Atlantic Charter, to the white race." On another occasion he said, "The war must assure the sovereign equality of people throughout the world. The age of imperialism is dead." These words were most unwelcome to those in foreign lands who held the reigns of colonial power.

SPANISH AND PORTUGUESE AFRICA

In Spanish and Portuguese West Africa, and especially in the island groups of the Azores, Canaries, and Cape Verdes, Axis submarines, supply ships, and blockade runners occasionally visited the neutral ports there to obtain fuel and other supplies. One of the most frequented ports was Las Palmas in the Spanish-owned Canary Islands, but ports in the Portuguese-owned Cape Verde Islands were also used. The Portuguese-owned Azores were the least used of the three island groups. This activity was perfectly legal under international law so long as the vessel in question departed within the time limit allotted. This was not hard to comply with because the Axis vessels wanted to stay as short a time as possible. In every port there were Allied agents who reported the vessel's presence as soon as it arrived. The captains of those vessels knew this and, quite naturally, wanted to conclude their business quickly and depart before an Allied warship could be summoned to the area to intercept them as they sailed out of the harbor.

The Portuguese and Spanish knew this and knew that the Germans and Italians did not want to waste time haggling over prices. Therefore, the Spanish and Portuguese usually got top prices for whatever items they had ready to deliver on short notice. Since Axis money was of less value outside of Axis-controlled areas, the Spanish and Portuguese vendors usually demanded that the items purchased be paid for in American dollars, or British pounds, their own national currencies.

The British were very concerned about the Axis vessels using the island ports, especially with regards to the Portuguese Cape Verde Islands. These islands allowed the German vessels to refuel and then penetrate deep into the South Atlantic. As Axis submarine activity increased along the west coast of Africa, the British drew up a plan to invade the Cape Verde Island, called "Operation Brisk," and Churchill came very close to implementing it. In a memo to the First Lord of the Admiralty and the First Sea Lord dated March 22, 1941, Churchill stated:

"The evidences of German infiltration into the Cape Verde Islands, and the probability that they are being used to refuel U-boats, make it necessary to carry out "Operation Brisk" at the earliest date. Once we have got possession we must make a good refuelling base there (for ourselves), and expel the enemy's U-boat tenders from the islands... As many flying-boats as can be spared, up to six, should be employed in the Freetown area, and will also work from the islands when captured. Pray let me have your thought on the above, together with all possible means of carrying it out."

British resources at this time were stretched to the limit, and the invasion of the Cape Verde Islands did not progress beyond the planning stage.

On May 25, after the sinking of the Robin Moor (May 21), President Roosevelt warned the Axis Powers that any attempt by them to occupy either the Azores or Cape Verde Islands would be considered a threat to the security of the United State. To put that threat in perspective, Roosevelt pointed out to the American people that the Cape Verde Islands were only seven hours flying time from South America and that the islands were at the narrowest point in the Atlantic Ocean - the choke point as it were - where Axis vessels could most easily cut off international north-south shipping lanes.

To enforce his word, Roosevelt publicly ordered additional U.S. warships transferred from the Pacific to the Atlantic to strengthen the American Neutrality Patrol within the Pan-American Security Zone. Secretly, Roosevelt ordered the United States armed forces to prepare a plan for a quick occupation of the Azores, should such action become necessary.

Thus, in the early summer of 1941, the Americans had military plans available to invade the Azores while the British had similar plans to invade the Cape Verde Islands, both Portuguese possessions.

The Portuguese, of course, were deeply concerned about the public pronouncements and subsequent rumors concerning their island possessions. After Roosevelt's public statements of May 25, Lisbon asked Washington for clarification of America's intentions. Secretary of State Hull responded saying that the United States had no aggressive intentions against Portuguese territory, but yet retained the right to take measures in self-defense. This ambiguous reply did not satisfy the Portuguese. In the weeks that followed, the Portuguese sent another large contingent of army forces to the Azores, a process of military buildup in the islands that had been developing since January.

Then, on June 20, 1941, the German submarine U-123 accidently torpedoed and sank the Portuguese freighter "Ganda" off the west coast of Africa. The Portuguese, as would be expected, protested to Berlin. In the negotiations that followed, the Portuguese, who currently were very angry with the British, agreed to allow a false report to be made public that the Ganda had been sunk by a British submarine which was known to be in the area at the time. The Germans were more than happy to cooperate in this deception and even went to the extent of falsifying their own records of the sinking. London, of course, denied that it had been their submarine that sank the Ganda and refused to negotiate on the matter of compensation. It was there that the issue rested. But Lisbon's hand was politically strengthened by its claim against the British, and Lisbon's actions had demonstrated that an Allied attack on any Portuguese possession might drive Portugal into the Axis camp.

PORTUGUESE NOT TOO ANGRY

The Portuguese, who had been longtime political friends and trading partners with the British, were not angry enough that it effected trade. Trade between the two nations continued to be brisk and increased by 20% during 1941 over 1940. The British counted heavily on Portugal for wine and fish products, and the Portuguese imported large amounts of rice from the various British colonies.

On July 7, the Portuguese received another warning of sorts when American forces landed in Iceland and took over the occupation of that island from the British. This was proof that the Americans were ready and able to occupy Atlantic islands if their interests demanded it.

Also during July, the British, after a lengthy diplomatic effort, were able to get the Spanish to agree to close their ports in the Canary Islands, including Las Palmas, to Axis submarines. This, coupled with the destruction that month of the German supply ships, severely curtailed Axis submarine activities in the Central and South Atlantic.

Back in Germany, Admiral Raeder was worried that the British activity off West Africa portended an Allied invasion of one or more of the Spanish and/or Portuguese island groups. Hitler could not disagree. Therefore, tentative plans were made for German troops to advance through Spain, Spanish Morocco, and into Vichy-controlled French Morocco as a countermeasure. This was made know to the Allies in hopes that it would serve as a deterrent.

Back in Washington, the Roosevelt Administration modified its plan to occupy the Azores, to make such an action one of mutual cooperation rather than one of aggression. In this respect, the United States enlisted the help of Brazil to participate in a friendly occupation of the Azores should it become necessary. The inclusion of Brazil was seen as a friendly gesture toward the Portuguese. Brazil, a Portuguese-speaking nation, had friendly ties to Portugal and, at the same time, a mutual concern with the United States for the security of the Western Hemisphere.

On July 21, Roosevelt sent a personal letter to Portuguese Prime Minister Antonio Salazar, stating that the United

States and Brazil were ready to aid Portugal in jointly defending the Azores if such action was requested by Lisbon. Salazar replied that his government would accept military supplies from the United States if such supplies were not available from Britain, but as for foreign troops defending the Azores, Salazar said that they would not be needed.

When Roosevelt and Churchill met at Placentia Bay, Newfoundland in August, the subject of the West African island groups was discussed. It was agreed that the British diplomatic action of July had neutralized the Spanish Canary Islands for the time being, but that the Portuguese Azores and Cape Verde Islands remained problems. The existing British and American military plans to occupy the island groups were discussed and coordinated. It was secretly agreed that if the invasion of one group of islands became necessary, the other group should be invaded too and at the same time. In the case of the Azores, the British agreed to the inclusion of Brazil in the occupation of that island group.

THE YACHT, THE SPANIARDS, AND THE BOXER

On July 22, 1941, a sleek sailing yacht, flying the American flag, sailed into the harbor of Villa Cisneros on the southern shore of the Spanish colony of Rio de Oro. The vessel identified itself as the American racing yacht "Kyloe" which was participating in a transocean sporting activity. When the vessel docked the Spaniards were surprised to discover that the captain and crew were all Germans. The German captain went immediately to the local German Consulate, turned the ownership of the vessel over to the Consul General, and he and his crew then left by plane for Madrid. From Madrid they flew on to Germany.

The Kyloe was, indeed, a fast sailing yacht, but it had not been on a sporting adventure. The vessel was owned by the German Navy and had been specially fitted out to look like an American racing yacht. It had left Paimpol, France in May, skirted the coast of Brazil, then sailed across the South Atlantic, and deposited a very special passenger at the coastal village of Groenriviermond, South Africa, 225 miles north of Cape Town. It then sailed on to Villa Cisneros, the first Spanish port with regular air connections to Europe.

The passenger deposited in South Africa was Robey Liebbrant, a well-known Olympic boxer of Afrikaner descent and a man known to be very anti-British. Liebbrant had been caught in Europe when the war started and wanted to go home. He was eventually contacted by the Germans and agreed to return to his homeland and become a part of the pro-Axis Afrikaner movement there. When he arrived he had suitcases full of money and explosives.

Liebbrant had no need to conceal his return. He was a South African citizen of some renown, and the Smuts government was most reluctant to touch him despite the questionable method of his return. Liebbrant was, of course, welcomed by the hard-core Afrikaners, and soon made contact with van Rensburg, leader of the OB. But the two men took a dislike to each other from the start. Liebbrant was too radical for van Rensburg and van Rensburg was too moderate for Liebbrant. At one of their first meetings, the hot-tempered boxer threatened to beat up van Rensburg on the spot and had to be physically restrained by some of van Rensburg's "stormtroopers."

After this, Liebbrant took the few followers he had accumulated and formed his own Nazi-like political party, the "National Socialist Rebel Party of South Africa" (NSRP) with himself as its "Fuhrer." The NSRP remained small and attracted only the most radical elements of the Afrikaner right wing.

As time would show, Liebbrant and his followers were not above taking violent action.

SOUTH AFRICA (JANUARY–AUGUST 1941)

Having been at war for over a year, the Union of South Africa was, by now, operating on a wartime footing. Industry had converted almost entirely to war work and the nation's armed forces were steadily growing. Much of the South African industrial effort was devoted to the manufacture of munitions for their own forces and Allied forces.

Unlike so many nations at war, South Africa was lucky in that there were virtually no shortages. With the sea lanes open, international trade was brisk and the nation, as usual, was able to continue drawing much of its needs from its neighbors in sub-Saharan Africa. South Africa's immediate neighbors, too, were experiencing good economic times because the booming economy spilled over into those areas.

The Smuts government, wanting to take full advantage of the economic situation, sent trade missions to the British West African colonies, Free French-controlled Equatorial Africa, the Belgian Congo, and Angola to explore business opportunities for the war effort as well as for the post war era. Smuts, himself, even spoke of building a modern highway from Johannesburg to Asmara, Eritrea so that South Africa could better tap the East African markets. In London, these activities were not necessarily appreciated because they were not in step with British wartime and post war planning.

South Africa's good economy made it an ideal place to send POWs from East and North Africa. POW camps sprang up all over the country with a very large one at Johannesburg. The POWs were employed in the local economy within the guidelines of the Geneva Convention and, in that respect, helped ease the shortage of male workers.

South African politics, though, was as rough and tumble as ever. The majority of the people still supported Smuts, his United Party, and the war effort, but that majority was not great and tended to grow and shrink with the fortunes and misfortunes of the Allied war effort.

Bitter feelings were, as always, just below the surface. On February 2 a large anti-British riot broke out in Johannesburg and Smuts was obliged to call out the army to restore order.

In late March, the Federal Council of the National Party, Smuts' main opposition party, called once again for the breaking of ties with Britain and the establishment of a republic. Nationalist zealots, associated with the Ox Wagon Sentinels (OB), even went so far as to draft and publish a proposed constitution for the hoped-for republic. This was at the time when Rommel began his offensive against British positions in Libya, forcing the British into a rapid retreat.

It was also at this time that the leader of the National Party, Daniel Malan, gave a speech at Stellenbosch, telling his audience that if his party came to power he would make peace with Germany "tomorrow" and sever all ties with the British Commonwealth.

With the prospect of a British defeat in North Africa, the National Party unilaterally claimed that a wartime emergency existed within South Africa and voted its leader, Daniel Malan, dictatorial powers within the party. In true fascist-like manner, Malan then took unto himself a title, "Volkileier." This title did not mean "leader" in the same sense as "Duce" and "Fuhrer"; it had more of a paternalistic meaning. When it was suggested to Malan that he take the title of "leader," he rejected the idea on the grounds that he did not want total dictatorial power, and that all factions of the Afrikaner community might not accept him as their leader. Malan knew his people well—the Afrikaners had a long history of coming together and then splitting apart. They even had an Afrikaner word for this phenomenon, "Broedertwis" (brotherly conflict).

At this point, in time the Afrikaners were as politically united as they had ever been in that the two major political factions in the country, the National Party and the OB, were cooperating with each other. The OB, the more radical of the two groups, was constantly in trouble with the Smuts administration and there were rumors that Smuts might have to take measures to restrain, or even forcefully dissolve, the OB. Malan, in support of his political ally, threatened that if that happened he and the National Party would support a policy of civil disobedience. With this threat hanging over his head, Smuts did not act directly against the OB. Although he did, through an executive order, require all government employees to resign from the organization.

With regard to other matters in South Africa, on March 30 the American cruiser "Vincennes" arrived at Simonstown to pick up another load of British gold. She then proceeded to New York City arriving there on April 16. The gold was taken temporarily to several American banks and eventually sent on to Fort Knox, Kentucky.

On April 5, 1941, the Smuts government received a political boost when it was announced that South African troops had been the first to enter Addis Ababa—in South African-made armored cars no less—and that the South African flag had been hoisted over the Emperor's palace. Behind the scenes, this had been arranged by Churchill through General Cunningham in East Africa just for this specific purpose. What the South Africans did not know was that their flag remained over the palace just long enough to be photographed. Then it was replaced with the Ethiopian flag.

Congratulations and expressions of praise were forthcoming from London on the fine job the South Africans were doing in East Africa. In early May 1941, Churchill saw to it that his old friend, Smuts, was promoted to the rank of Honorary Marshall in the British Army. His promotion became official on his 71st birthday, May 24. Smuts was the first South African to hold that rank.

By the end of May, the British had stopped Rommel's advance in North Africa, and political fortunes once again began to favor the Smuts Administration in South Africa.

With the war in East Africa winding down, London asked the Smuts government to send the 1st South African Division, currently in East Africa, and the newly formed 2nd South African Division, still in South Africa, to North Africa and the Middle East. Smuts readily agreed, and in a rare display of unity, so did Malan. Some South African Air Force units were ready to depart at once and did so within days. In June, the 2nd South African Division, under Major General I.P. de Villiers, departed for Egypt. With time, the South African forces north of the Sahara would amount to some 100,000 men.

With the departure of the 2nd South African Division, the South African government began building the 3rd South African Division with the understanding that it would remain in South Africa permanently for home defense.

Also in late June, Britain aligned herself militarily and politically with the Soviet Union, which had been attacked on June 22. This gave the hard-core right-wingers in South Africa another devil in the closet - Bolshevism. New cries arose from the far right claiming that the British Empire was in danger of going Communist.

Then, during July 1941, South Africa became the temporary home of the Greek government-in-exile. The Greek monarch, King George II, and his government had fled to Cairo when Greece was conquered in April and May. But now, with Cairo threatened by Rommel, the Greeks moved to South Africa. Later, when Cairo became secure again, the Greek government-in-exile returned to Cairo.

Also in July, militant members of boxer Robey Liebbrant's National Socialist Rebel Party broke into a steel mill in Pretoria, injured two elderly watchmen, and stole a large quantity of explosives. Smuts was outraged and ordered the national police to crack down on the NSRP. A few days later, the police cornered Liebbrant and his gang near Warmbaths and a confusing and poorly orchestrated shoot-out occurred in which Liebbrant escaped. Mountains of criticism came down upon the South African police which, everyone knew, was riddled with Afrikaners sympathetic to Liebbrant and his cohorts. Smuts could do little to correct the situation. It was inconceivable that the national police could be anything other than an integrated organization open to Afrikaners and English-speakers alike. It was one of the problems with which Smuts, and everyone else in the country, had to endure.

Then, on August 28, came a very special broadcast from Berlin over Radio Zeesen, the German propaganda station directed to South Africa's Afrikaners. Berlin praised the President of the Ox-Wagon Guard, van Rensburg, and identified him as the Berlin-designated leader of the Afrikaner community. This praise of Rensburg at the expense of Malan proved to be a grievous mistake on the part of the Germans. Van Rensburg was now seen by many as a puppet of Berlin, and a man with whom Malan, always seen as a loyal South African, could no longer work. This action by Berlin sparked the end of the National Party/OB alliance. Before the summer was out, the Nationalists and the OB experienced "Broedertwis" once again. Each organization then went its own political way, and as time would reveal, the split became permanent and bitter.

Former Prime Minister General Hertzog, who had previously resigned his seat in Parliament in an earlier protest, went with the OB. Hertzog declared that after a German victory the only form of government that Hitler would tolerate in South Africa would be a national socialist (Nazi) form of government in accordance with Afrikaner traditions. Hertzog still had a voice in South African politics, but fewer and fewer people were taking him seriously.

The Smuts government was delighted with the latest "Broedertwis" and was considerably strengthened as a result.

Malan, too, was a winner of sorts in that he had rid himself of the embarrassing Hertzog and other right wing radicals. Furthermore, he had shown foresight by not proclaiming himself "leader" of all of the Afrikaners. By showing such moderation he gained some respect among Smuts' supporters and the English-speakers, and was seen as a man who did not have an all-consuming ambition to become South Africa's dictator. By Berlin's own proclamation, Malan was not viewed as a tool of the Germans—van Rensburg now took on that role.

WHERE IS THE GOLD?

On the same day as the fateful Radio Zeesen broadcast from Berlin, Churchill was thinking of another matter - gold. He sent a memo that day to the Chancellor of the Exchequer asking: "How much gold have we actually got left in this island or under our control in South Africa? Don't be alarmed: I am not going to ask you for anything."

THE BELGIAN CONGO

This important colony, firmly in the Allied camp, was experiencing a robust economy during 1941, especially in the mining areas of the south. The colony's main contribution to the Allied war effort continued to be in the supplying of raw materials. A wide variety of minerals and ores flowed from the Congo's mines to the Allies.

In January 1941, the Belgian government-in-exile in London negotiated an agreement with the British that tied the Congo franc to the British pound at the ratio of 176 francs to the pound. This made the Congo franc as acceptable as the British pound anywhere in the world. In addition, the Belgians had agreed to let Britain have first choice at purchasing any and all war-related materials produced in the Congo. This meant that other nations, including the Allied nations, had to negotiate with the British for a share of the Congo's resources.

As for gold, the Congo's entire production was sold, by agreement, to the Bank of England, who paid for it in pound sterling.

As we have seen, the Congo sent a small military expeditionary force to East Africa that participated in the successful Allied conquest of western Ethiopia.

On the darker side of the economy, much of the native population was in flux. Many natives left their tribal villages and went to nearby towns hoping to find war work. But there was very little war work in the Congo's towns and cities. The great majority of that work was in the mining areas in the south. But there, the newly-formed unions dictated who worked and who did not work. A great number of frustrated workers accumulated in the towns and mining areas and became prey for nationalists, revolutionaries, and corrupt officials. This resulted in periodic eruptions of riots and strikes. One strike, in the mining area, was particularly bad and the colonial army had to be called in to restore order. Before that could be accomplished, some seventy people were killed.

MADAGASCAR AND JEWS

In Germany, at Hitler's headquarters, the old idea of sending Europe's Jews to Madagascar just would not go away. In July 1941, Hitler told the visiting Foreign Minister of Croatia that plans were still under consideration to send the Jews to Madagascar or Siberia. Hitler's mention of Siberia was a new development in His thinking toward the Jews because now, with the Soviet Union being conquered, the option of sending the Jews to the far end of the Eurasian continent was certainly a possibility.

Chapter 12
ALL OVER THE CONTINENT (SEPTEMBER-DECEMBER 1941)
ISSUES APLENTY

URANIUM ORE, $1.60 A POUND

In the United States the top-secret "Manhattan Project," the program designed to develop the atomic bomb, had just gotten underway. General Leslie Groves, who was to oversee the program for the U.S. Army, received his assignment on September 17, 1941. One of his first concerns was to acquire a large quantity of uranium ore. He soon discovered that the only large quantity of the ore in the United States was in a warehouse on Staten Island, New York and was owned by a Belgian businessman, Edgar Sengier. It consisted of 1,250 tons of ore stored in 2,000 steel drums and had come from the Shinkolobwe Mine in the Belgian Congo, which produced the richest uranium ore in the world. Groves and an aide contacted Sengier immediately and agreed to buy the entire lot of ore at $1.60 per pound, the lowest market price at the time. A short time later, the ore was shipped to a newly-built secret facility in Tennessee called the Clinton Engineer Works (Oak Ridge).

Ironically, in occupied Belgium, the Germans had a similar supply of ore from the same mine but did nothing with it throughout the war.

When word of the sale in New York reached the Belgian Congo and the owners of the Shinkolobwe Mine, which had been closed since May 1940, production was immediately resumed.

THE SITUATION IN NORTH AFRICA

During September and the first half of October 1941, there was relative quiet on the North African front. The Axis and British forces were entrenched facing each other at the Halfaya Pass on the Egyptian border, and both sides were building their strength for the battles that would surely resume. In this respect the British were building faster and stronger than the Axis forces. New units and thousands of tons of war equipment were pouring into Egypt to reinforce General Auckinleck's army. Furthermore, Churchill was pressing Wavell to attack as soon as possible in North Africa because the Soviets were calling upon the Western Allies to open a second front and Churchill wanted to be able to show Stalin that the Western Allies were cooperating.

On the Axis side, Rommel was under no particular pressure from Hitler to attack. Hitler had his hands full in the east. And, Rommel's supply picture was not good. The RAF, operating from several points in North Africa and Malta, was bombing the Italian shipping ports in Sicily, southern Italy and Libya almost daily. On the water, the Royal Navy continued to maintain its dominance in the Mediterranean, making it very difficult for the Italian Navy to get men and supplies across to North Africa. One notable British success occurred on September 18, when the British sub "Upholder" torpedoed and sank two of Italy's largest troop ships, the "Neptunia" and "Oceania." Many Axis soldiers and hundreds of tons of equipment were lost at sea.

Rommel was very concerned about his vulnerable seaborne supply route and sent an urgent appeal to Berlin asking for German submarines to come to the Mediterranean to help protect the Italian convoys. Hitler agreed and twenty U-boats were subsequently ordered to proceed to patrol the waters between Italy and North Africa. The first wave of six U-boats passed Gibraltar successfully on September 24.

On September 27, the British lost the services of one of their major warships in the Mediterranean, the battleship

"Nelson," when she was damaged by a torpedo dropped by an Italian torpedo bomber. The Nelson was escorting a Malta-bound convoy at the time.

During the night of November 8/9, a seven-ship Italian convoy was completely destroyed by a British naval force 200 miles east of Malta. The attacking force was the British Task Force "K," operating out of Malta and consisted of two cruisers and two destroyers. They also sank one of the convoy's escorts. An Italian covering force of heavy cruisers and destroyers, patrolling nearby, was unable to intervene in time to save the convoy.

At this point, the Axis supply problem became critical. Only about 40% of the supplies sent from Italy were making it to North Africa. The Axis forces used, on average, 70,000 tons of supplies a month and during September only 30,000 tons arrived.

On November 19 warships of the Royal Navy decimated two more Italian convoys crossing the Mediterranean. This time the British were aided by "Ultra," the name given to the recent breaking of a heavily-used secret German naval code.

Furthermore, the war in the Soviet Union was falling behind Hitler's timetable and proving to be more costly in men and equipment than expected. This made it even more difficult for Rommel to get his share of reinforcements and supplies from Germany.

THE "BLACK CODE"

The British had "Ultra" but the Italians had the "Black Code." The latter was the name of a secret American diplomatic code used in Cairo to send messages to Washington. During September 1941, Italian secret agents were able to obtain a copy of the code and thereby read the American diplomatic messages. Of most interest to the Italians were the messages sent by the U.S. Military Attache at the Embassy, Colonel Fellers. Fellers often explained, in great detail, British plans of attack in North Africa and the whereabouts of British troops. This was of considerable help to the Axis forces in North Africa until June 1942, when the Americans changed the code.

At Tobruk, which was still in British hands but surrounded on three sides by Axis forces, Auckinleck moved in the newly-arrived British 70th Division, commanded by General Scobie, and moved out the last of the Australians. Remaining in place in was the Polish Carpathian Brigade.

By the middle of November, Auckinleck was ready to strike out from Halfaya Pass. He had seven divisions at his command in the newly formed British Eighth Army comprised of two corps, the XIII and XXX Corps. Within the Eighth Army were combat troops from Britain, Australia, New Zealand, South Africa, India, Greece, the Free French, and Poland, as well as Pioneer troops from a number of British colonies. The field commander of the Eighth Army was General Alan Cunningham who had recently arrived from Kenya. The British had 748 tanks and large numbers of aircraft, as well as the support of the Royal Navy offshore. Among the aircraft were the first of several Lend Lease American-made B-17 bombers, which had been put to use bombing the Axis supply lines. In December, the RAF received four American-made B-24 heavy bombers. Both planes were new to the North African theater. More would follow and contribute significantly to the strength of the RAF.

In the Middle East, two more British Armies had been formed, the Ninth Army in Palestine and the Tenth Army in Iraq and Iran. If necessary, Auckinleck could draw from these armies for North Africa.

The Axis Powers had three German divisions, Seven Italian divisions, and 395 tanks, but were still short of some supplies, especially gasoline and diesel fuel.

THE BRITISH STRIKE

The name for the new British offensive was "Operation Crusader." It was originally scheduled to be launched on November 11, but the 1st South African Division, which had just come up from East Africa, was not yet ready. Therefore the launch date was postponed for a week.

HAPPY BIRTHDAY IRWIN

November 17 was Irwin Rommel's birthday and a party was planned for him by this staff at his desert headquarters. The British learned of this and sent a small mobile raiding party to dash across the desert and hopefully capture him at the party. The British raiders crashed the party but Rommel was not there.

On November 18 Auckinleck launched Operation Crusader at 6:00 a.m. from his positions at Halfaya Pass. He attacked south of the pass, bypassing its defenders and those at Fort Capuzzo and Bardia. The German ground troops were taken by surprise and Rommel was not at his headquarters. He was in Rome consulting with his German superiors and the Italians on a planned attack on Tobruk he had scheduled for November 21. He had already gathered some of his forces in the Sidi Rezegh area 25 miles east of Tobruk, leaving the center of his line at Halfaya Pass weakened. It was there that the British struck. Upon hearing of the British offensive Rommel left Rome immediately and reached the front on the evening of November 18.

Not all of the opening attacks of Operation Crusader were successful, but the main effort by the British XXX

Corps, which had most of the tanks, was very successful. The XXX Corps was able to smash through the weakened Axis lines and advance rapidly against only flank opposition to a point about sixty miles inside Libya. Just east of Sidi Rezegh, the XXX Corps encountered the Germans frantically building a defensive line east of the town. These were the troops Rommel had hoped to use to attack Tobruk. Now they had to turn about and defend their rear while at the same time maintain the siege lines abound Tobruk.

The Axis forces were in trouble. They had accumulated only enough supplies to sustain the limited operation against Tobruk. Now they would have to spend those resources fending off a major offensive. Unless a miracle happened, the Axis forces could not withstand a prolonged campaign in Cyrenaica.

It was at Sidi Rezegh that the hard fighting began. It would last four days and become the largest land battle yet in North Africa. For the British, though, a major problem was beginning to develop—the mechanical reliability of their tanks. In the first two days of action they lost forty tanks, mostly due to mechanical problems. The Axis forces lost less than ten.

The battles around Sidi Rezegh were extremely fluid, where the front lines were often indistinguishable. On one of the nights during the confusing battle Rommel and his staff were caught behind the British front and did not know it. They spent that night in thc desert not too far from the British command post.

The quality of Rommel's tanks was proving to be an advantage although tank losses were heavy on both sides. By November 22, the Axis forces were able to even the score. They could count 170 operable tanks while the British were now down to 150.

On November 23 the fighting was extremely hard once again. The South African 5th Brigade was virtually annihilated in a counterattack by the German 21st Panzers and Italian forces near Sidi Rezegh. The South Africans suffered 3,400 killed or captured. With this, the British attack all but stalled. Axis losses, too, were heavy. In only 24 hours, they had lost seventy of their 170 tanks and the New Zealanders captured Rommel's headquarters along with most of his communications equipment. Furthermore, German infantry casualties were extremely heavy. The Germans gave this dreadful day, Sunday November 23, a name -"Totensonntag" (the Sunday of the dead).

Then on November 24, Auckinleck, knowing he still had superior numbers, ordered his forces to attack all along the line hoping to be able to break through at some point and force the Axis forces into a general retreat. "Attack and pursue. All out. Everywhere" was his command. By coincidence, Rommel ordered an attack that same day and the two forces met head on. It was Rommel's attack that prevailed and the British were forced to retreat all the way back to the Egyptian border. General Cunningham wanted to retreat further, but Auckinleck would not allow it and flew to Cunningham's headquarters to enforce his order and work with Cunningham to save the situation.

Rommel, too, had his problems. His tanks were running out of fuel, and the RAF had gained control of the air and were harassing his ground troops at every turn. The Luftwaffe was of little help to him because it consisted now of only one air unit, Fliegerkorps XIII operating out of Sicily, and it had recently been assigned to concentrate on convoy protection. Furthermore, the New Zealanders and a small British force, left behind at Side Rezegh during the British retreat, were close to breaking through the Axis siege lines at Tobruk and linking up with the Tobruk garrison. If and when these two forces combined it would placed a powerful and united British force in Rommel's rear. Rommel, though, believing that the British were virtually out of tanks and, ignoring the threat to his rear, ordered an attack on November 24. That attack threw the British back toward the border and continued on for two more days. The British, now holding Fort Capuzzo and Sidi Azeiz, held out doggedly, forcing the Germans to expend a considerable amount of their resources. Then, on November 26, Rommel realized that he had guessed wrong and that the British force to his rear still had a sizeable force of tanks and appeared to be preparing to attack him on the Egyptian border from the west. He, therefore, ended his attack on the border and turned about to face the danger from the rear.

That same day Wavell concluded that Cunningham had to be removed and replaced him with Lieutenant General Neil Ritchie.

Early on the morning of November 27, in a very determined attack, the New Zealanders captured Sidi Rezegh at Rommel's rear. Then, they broke through the Axis siege lines at Tobruk and linked up with the defending garrison. Later that day, Rommel's tanks attacked the British tank force, building in the Sidi Rezegh area, with everything they had. Once again, this sparked a week of hard and confused fighting around Tobruk which exhausted both sides. After this, another temporarily lull fell over the battlefield.

That lull was of little value to the Axis forces, who were now at a decided disadvantage on several counts. Many of their senior officers had been killed or wounded, and supplies were coming through only at a trickle. Virtually no new tanks were available to Rommel because of the demand at the Eastern Front, but he had some spare parts for his tanks and others could be cannibalized. Therefore, the Germans began a crash program to repair damaged tanks. This was modestly successful. By mid-December, Rommel's tank inventory rose from 180 to 250.

The British, on the other hand, were getting generous supplies of new tanks, men, and most everything else they needed.

IN THE MEDITERRANEAN

During September, Allied subs scored some successes off the North African coast. On September 7, the Dutch sub "O-21" sank the Italian cargo ship "Ernesto" off Bizerte, Tunisia. That same day, the British sub "Thunderbolt" sank the Italian merchantman "Sirena" fifty miles west of Benghazi. During the rest of the month British subs sank seven more Italian merchantmen off the Libyan coast.

During October, British subs sank another five Italian cargo ships off Libya and one off Tunisia.

Meanwhile, despite their losses in the Mediterranean, the Axis was becoming more successful in getting convoys through to North Africa. In November, two more Luftwaffe air units were sent to the Mediterranean from the Eastern Front, Fliegerkorps II and Luftflotte 2, to participate in convoy protection.

The British Task Force "K" out of Malta continued its efforts to intercept the Axis convoys, but they now found them better protected and the Axis ship captains had improved their skills at avoiding the British attackers. The British did succeed, however, in badly damaging two Italian cruisers during this time.

On November 4, the Italian sub "Dandolo" accidently torpedoed and damaged a neutral Vichy tanker off Spanish Morocco. Then, on the 8th Dandolo accidently torpedoed and sank a Spanish freighter in the same area. By now the German subs were going into action. The first submarine action, though, amounted to a loss.

On November 16, U-433 was sunk east of Gibraltar by the British patrol vessel "Marigold" using depth charges and artillery fire. Six Germans were killed and 42 taken prisoner.

Then, on November 25, the German sub U-331 scored a major victory against the British when she torpedoed and sank the British battleship "Barham," one of the most powerful British ships in the Mediterranean. The old battleship rolled over and exploded. Over 860 sailors were lost. The Barham, which was a part of task force "K" out of Malta, was in the process of attacking an Axis convoy out of Greece bound for Benghazi. Before she was sunk the Barham and her companion ships had succeeded in sinking two of the convoy's freighters.

The old British battleship "Barham" explodes in the Mediterranean after being hit by four torpedoes from German sub U-331.

On November 27, U-559 sank the Australian patrol vessel "Parramatta" off eastern Libya.

On November 28, the Allies struck back by sinking U-95 off Algiers. She was sent to the bottom by another sub, the Dutch O-21, which used a torpedo. Twelve Germans perished, and 35 were taken prisoner.

The appearance of the German subs and the increased strength of the Luftwaffe in the Mediterranean, combined with the increasing skills of the Italian sea captains, portended trouble for the British Navy. The British Navy suffered a setback because twelve days earlier the aircraft carrier "Ark Royal," on its way to the Mediterranean, was torpedoed and badly damaged outside Gibraltar by U-81. The damage was so extensive that the Ark Royal could not be saved. In just two weeks, the British had lost the use of two major warships in the Mediterranean area—and it would not be the end.

BACK IN LIBYA

In southeastern Libya, a column of the Sudanese Defence Force advanced out of southern Egypt during November and captured the important oasis of Jalo from its Italian garrison. The Sudanese then remained to permanently occupy the oasis along with several others in the area.

In the north, during the first days of December, Rommel made repeated attempts to reinvest Tobruk but without success. On December 5, he made the hard decision to withdraw to the west and give up much of Cyrenaica.

DECEMBER 1–13, 1941: A DYNAMIC TWO WEEKS

Aside from the bloody battles going on in North Africa there were other major events happening in the world at this time—all of which would have their effect on Africa.

On December 1, the Japanese Leaders made the irreversible decision to go to war against the United States. That same day German tanks reached a point outside Moscow nine miles from the Kremlin. The weather in the Moscow area dropped to -38 degrees Centigrade and the German troops were exhausted, depleted in numbers, and freezing. Some German battalions were down to fewer than 100 men. On December 6, the Soviets launched a major counterattack at Moscow that would through the Germans back and end the German offensive in the Soviet Union for 1941.

That same day in Washington, Roosevelt approved secret research funds for an atomic bomb.

On December 7, 1941, Japan attacked Pearl Harbor and declared war on the United States. America was in the war.

In North Africa on December 7, the Axis forces began a fighting withdrawal from the Tobruk area to new defenses to the west at the town of Gazala. On December 8, the British Eighth Army reestablished contact with the Tobruk garrison. The 242-day siege of Tobruk had ended. The defenders of Tobruk had been sustained all that time by the British Navy, which lost 25 small ships, including two destroyers—another blow to the strength of the British Navy in the Mediterranean.

That same day, December 8, the British took Sidi Rezegh which had been bypassed by the British in their pursuit of the Axis forces retreating toward Gazala.

On December 11, Germany and Japan, living up to treaty agreements, declared war on the United States. The United States reciprocated. The United States was now a belligerent in the European and African theaters of war.

On December 13, British forces broke through the Axis defenses at Gazala in heavy fighting. The Germans and Italians attempted, with some success, to contain the breakthrough. But two days later, Rommel, now running very low on supplies, decided to give up all of Cyrenaica. The Axis forces began an orderly retreat toward the old defense line at El Agheila.

AT SEA AGAIN

On December 2, the German sub U-562 sank a British freighter off Spanish Morocco. On the 13th U-453 accidently sank a Spanish tanker off Algeria and on the same day U-431 sank a British tanker off the Egyptian coast.

The Italian Navy, too, was suffering. Earlier, on December 13, two Italian cruisers, serving as tankers trying to get much-needed fuel to North Africa, were sunk off Cape Bon by one Dutch and two British destroyers. Also that day, another Italian convoy left Italy escorted by the main ships of the Italian Navy. Within hours, two troop ships were torpedoed and sunk by British subs, and the next day the battleship "Vittorio Veneto" was damaged by another British torpedo. Later that day the convoy turned back to Italy.

On December 15, the German sub U-557 sank the British cruiser "Galatea" off Alexandria. The next day the Germans lost U-557 of Tobruk when it was accidently rammed by an Italian torpedo boat. All 43 members of the sub's crew perished.

On the 16th a very unusual sea battle occurred. Another heavily-escorted Italian convoy heading for North Africa and a heavily-escorted British convoy out of Alexandria bound for Malta accidently met at sea. The respective escort vessels fired a few salvos at each other but neither side pursued an attack. Rather, they were both anxious to disengage and protect their cargo ships.

December 19, was a very bad day for the British Navy in the Mediterranean. In the early morning hours the warships that had escorted the Alexandria-to-Malta convoy were returning to Alexandria and stumbled into a huge Italian mine field. The British cruiser "Neptune" was lost when she struck four Axis mines and sank rapidly with only one survivor. A British destroyer was also lost in the same mine field and two other cruisers suffered damage before they could extricate themselves from the dangerous waters.

That evening about 7:00 p.m., three Italian midget submarines, launched from the mother sub "Scire" offshore, penetrated the harbor at Alexandria, the home base for the British fleet in the eastern Mediterranean. The crews of the midget subs were able to attach magnetic mines to four ships, the British battleships "Valiant" and "Queen Elizabeth," the British destroyer "Jervis" and the Norwegian tanker "Sagona." When the mines exploded they sent the two battleships to the bottom of the harbor and badly damaged the Jervis and the Sagona. The battleships were refloated months later but they were of no more help to Auckinleck and Operation Crusader.

During the rest of December, German subs sank four Allied merchantmen and the British corvette "Salvia" at various locations along the North African coast. The British were winning the war on the land but not necessarily at sea.

But the Axis was taking its losses, too. On December 22, an Italian cargo ship, along with a German merchantman, blundered into a newly-laid Italian mine field northeast of Tripoli and were sunk.

In late December, the Germans lost two subs within five days. The first was U-79, sunk December 23, off of eastern Libya by two British destroyers. The 44-man crew was rescued. The second sub lost was U-75, sunk on December 28, off of western Egypt by the British destroyer "Kipling." Fourteen Germans perished and thirty were taken prisoner.

ON TO EL AGHEILA AGAIN

From Gazala the Axis forces were in retreat across western Cyrenaica with the British in pursuit in two columns, one along the coast and the other across the Cyrenaican bulge. It was a repeat of O'Connor's offensive of November-December 1940. Derna, Mechili, and Benghazi fell in short order, but on December 28, the Axis forces made a determined stand at Agedabia, temporarily stopping the British drive. By now, the British had lost many tanks and were short of many supply items due to their rapid advance. And unfortunately, the supply picture for the Allies in North Africa had changed suddenly due to Japan's entry into the war. With Japanese forces marching into Southeast Asia, British troops and supplies destined for North Africa were now being diverted to the Far East to protect Malaya, Borneo, Singapore, Burma, and the other British possessions there. Furthermore, Australia and New Zealand were now threatened by the Japanese and those governments were pleading with London to release their respective forces in Africa and return them home. This was a request London could not deny for long.

The Axis troops withdrew in an orderly fashion to their old defenses at El Agheila, arriving there on December 31. The British followed at a safe distance.

Once again a long pause developed in the fighting as both sides licked their wounds and brought up reinforcements and supplies. For the British the advance to El Agheila was hailed as a victory because it was the first major land victory over the Germans thus far in the war. And a victory it was, because the Axis forces lost some 38,000 men—men they would find hard to replace. Rommel, quite understandably, appealed to Hitler for more men while, at the same time, Auckinleck appealed to Churchill for more tanks.

Back on the Egyptian frontier the British mopped up. The bypassed 7,000-man Axis garrison at Bardia fell to British and South African troops in early January, as did the remaining German defenders at Halfaya Pass.

END OF THE FIGHTING IN EAST AFRICA

In East Africa the annual rainy season (May to October) was coming to an end and it was time, once again, to make war. The fighting that remained would be small in comparison to that which had gone on before. Only one large Italian force still held out in the mountain and lake-protected Gondar enclave, but the Italian troops were demoralized and short of many supplies and their African askaris were on the verge of desertion.

On the Allied side, most of the best-equipped Allied units were gone, shipped off to North Africa. The Allied troops that were left were virtually all Africans, but hopes were high, supplies adequate, and morale good. They could sense that final victory over the Italians was near.

Also, American Lend-Lease was beginning to reach the Allies in East Africa. A good example of this was the arrival of twenty American-made Curtiss Mohawk IV fighter planes for the SAAF. These were not quite the equal of the venerable Hurricanes, but they were better than any of the aircraft the Italians still possessed.

During the last week of September 1941, before the British offensive against Gondar had really gotten underway, the British received a welcome surprise. At the town of Wolchefit north of Gondar, the Italians had built a strong defensive position. Wolchefit was an advanced Italian defensive position on the flat lands just outside the ring of mountains protecting the Gondar plain.

The British forces in that area, under Brigadier C.C. Fowkes, consisted of the 25th and 26th KAR Brigades, a KAR armored car unit, the British Argyll and Sutherland Highlanders Brigades, a Gold Coast unit, a Sudanese battalion, a Belgian Congo unit, an Ethiopian Army battalion, several artillery batteries, and various support units, most of them Ethiopian. Fowkes could also count on RAF and SAAF air support and the Ethiopian guerrillas.

In preparation for a future attack on Wolchefit, the British made several probing attacks on the Italian positions to test their strength. The Wolchefit defenses were being bombed now as the weather improved and the Ethiopian guerrillas were also harassing the Wolchefit defenses in the rear and on the flanks.

MONEY FROM THE SKY

The Ethiopian guerrillas had been recognized by the British as a regular ally and the men were to be paid. In preparation for the coming attack on Wolchefit, and to keep the guerrillas engaged, the British had air-dropped 100,000 Marie Theresa thalers into the guerrilla camp in order to inspire their efforts against the Italians. These efforts paid off because supplies from Gondar to Wolchefit were cut off much of the time, and the defenders at Wolchefit were short of many things, especially food. This was due mostly to guerrilla raids. It was becoming common in the Wolchefit area for the Italian troops to trade arms and ammunition with the locals in exchange for food.

The King's African Rifles accord the honors of war to the Wolchefit garrison as they march into captivity.

Then, on September 27, troops of the 25th KAR Brigade, recently brought in from the Lake Rudolf area, made a routine probing attack against Wolchefit. The Italian commander took the opportunity to declare that it was a major attack, one which his troops could not withstand, and suddenly surrendered. The KAR troops rushed in to take Wolchefit and then advanced to the edge of the mountains surrounding Gondar. It was a major development for the British. Seventy one Italian officers, 1,560 Italian troops, and 1,300 askaris were captured.

TROUBLE IN FRENCH SOMALILAND

When the Paris Protocol was written in late May 1941, and the Vichy French began their intense collaboration with the Axis Powers, it had reverberations throughout the French Empire. Not only did the Vichy French allow German and Italian airplanes to use Syrian airfields to participate in the war in Iraq, but they also allowed the Italian aircraft to start using the airfield at Djibouti, the capital of French Somaliland, to supply Italian forces in East Africa. The British, of course, knew of this new development but, at the time, did nothing about it for several reasons. First of all, the Italian air traffic was very light, consisting usually of only one transport plane at a time. The Italians made no effort to fly in significant numbers of war planes. Secondly, during the summer of 1941, East Africa was being gleaned by the British for all available manpower to be sent to Egypt and the British did not want to create a new set of problems in East Africa by confronting the Vichy supporters at Djibouti. The French had six well-trained and loyal Senegalese battalions in the colony and the British knew they would fight if ordered to do so. Furthermore, the French had built concrete defensive positions all around their border with the former Italian colonies, and these were a deterrent to military action.

By September, however, the situation had changed. British strength in East Africa had stabilized and was on the rise again. On September 23, orders came down from Wavell's headquarters in Shepheard's Hotel in Cairo that Italian aircraft in French air space, or on the airfield at Djibouti, were to be attacked. RAF planes from Aden and SAAF and Free French planes from East Africa began overflying Djibouti and French air space watching for Italian aircraft. The recently-arrived Curtiss Mohawks participated in these patrols. On October 5, an SAAF Curtiss Mohawk made the first attack on a transport plane on the ground at the Djibouti airfield and destroyed it. Vichy, of course, protested the attack and claimed that the destroyed plane belonged to the Red Cross and was flying wounded out of Gondar. Nevertheless, the Italians called a halt to their air activities in French Somaliland knowing that their transports were defenseless in the face of the British fighter planes. It was another small victory for the British.

BACK AT GONDAR

The sudden fall of Wolchefit caused the British to scrap their plans for attacking Gondar from the south and concentrate on the Wolchefit area as their main area of attack. On October 8, British units probed the Italian defenses in the northern mountains in force and succeeded in gaining some ground on the flanks of the Italian defenders. It was still raining making large-scale operations difficult. The British, therefore, carried out a series of small attacks on the Italian positions as the weather permitted, and again, some ground was gained.

Meanwhile, the British carried out a diversionary operation on the southern front toward the town of Debra Tabor. This "attack" was done mostly with phony radio signals and troop movements, to make the Italians believe an attack was being prepared from that direction. This force, under Lieutenant Colonel R. G. I. Collins, consisted of one KAR regiment, a Gold Coast artillery battery, field company of South African sappers, and a battalion of East African Pioneers.

The rains lasted longer than usual this season at Gondar, not stopping until the first week of November.

Finally, on November 13, the British launched their offensive against Gondar. The first attack was a diversionary attack in the Debra Tabor area by Collins' force of KAR troops, supported by Ethiopian guerrillas operating against the Italian's flanks and rear. The Italian defenses proved to be strong and the next night the KAR troops withdrew. On November 25, the KAR troops attacked a second time in the same area only with a larger force and again with guerrilla support. At the same time another diversionary attack was made by Sudanese units attacking Italian defenses in the mountains west of Gondar at Celga.

Another British attack at Kulkabar, southeast of Gondar city, was met by strong opposition from three Italian battalions. The British commander called upon the Sudanese to make another diversionary attack on the Italian flank, and then attacked the Italian center. During the course of the battle, all three Italian battalion commanders were killed and the Italian resistance collapsed. The KAR troops overran the enemy positions and by 3:00 p.m. occupied the town of Kulkabar. Taken prisoner were 1,648 Italians and 775 of their askaris. The remnants of the Italian force withdrew to another defense line at Azozo only ten miles south of Gondar.

Now for a second time, with the sudden success at Kulkabar, the emphasis of the British attack shifted back to the south. The British rushed every unit they could to the south opposite the Azozo defenses. At 5:00 a.m. on November 27, with good artillery and air support, a large force of KAR troops made a frontal assault on the Italian defense at Azozo. Fighting was heavy and casualties high on both sides. By noon, however, the KAR men had driven a deep wedge into the Italian defenses threatening to split those defenses

Downtown Gondar in late 1941.

KAR troops entering Gondar.

in two. By 3:00 p.m. General Nasi, the Italian Commander, could see that the battle for Gondar was lost and sent emissaries to the British under a flag of truce to ask for armistice terms. Before the emissaries returned, however, a Kenyan armored car unit, supported by Ethiopian guerrillas, surged into Gondar city and captured General Nasi in his headquarters. Nasi promptly surrendered. Word of this spread quickly and the Italian troops all along the line surrendered en masse. Some of the Italian troops burned their supplies and inside Gondar city looters took advantage of the situation. British forces rushed into the town to stop the looting and prevent the further burning of supplies. The next day, November 28, letters signed by General Nasi were air-dropped by British planes on the Italian garrisons at Celga, in the west, and Gorgora, on the shore of Lake Tana, ordering them to surrender. They immediately complied. With this, the battle in East Africa ended. Another 11,500 Italian troops and 12,000 native troops became British prisoners of war. Some of them were retained in the area for a while to help clear mine fields.

On December 6, the Ethiopian Crown Prince, who had participated in the capture of Gondar, ceremoniously raised the Ethiopian flag over Fasilides Castle in Gondar city in the name of the Emperor.

NEAR MUTINY OF THE 25th KAR

With the end of hostilities in East Africa, all British units, with the exception of the 25th KAR Brigade, were sent home for much-needed rest and relaxation. The 25th, however, was sent to Gura and told that they were to be shipped overseas. With this a near mutiny broke out within the ranks of the unit as the men demanded that they too be sent home. Furthermore, many of the KAR men claimed that they were told upon enlisting that they would not be sent to fight outside of Africa; if they were to be sent overseas they demanded an increase in pay. The British authorities, seeing that serious trouble was brewing, acquiesced and sent the men of the 25th home on leave.

ALLIED ADMINISTRATION OF EAST AFRICA

The conquest of Italian East Africa created three new political entities, the occupied enemy territories of Eritrea and Italian Somaliland, the liberated Kingdom of Ethiopia, and the liberated colony of British Somaliland. The British were obliged by the traditions of war to administer the conquered territories while returning Ethiopia to its Emperor and government. Administration of the Italian territories, therefore, passed to the Occupied Enemy Territories Administration (OETA), which had been established in March, 1941.

There were still major problems in the war-torn area, though, and the British saw the need to keep strong controls over the entire region for several reasons. First of all, the Ethiopian economy and infrastructure was in shambles and

General Nasi, center, and two of his top aides, General Poli, left, and Colonel Ricard, right, at Massawa on their way to a British prisoner of war camp.

some of the old tribal and clan rivalries had surfaced to threaten the security of certain areas of the country. Also, Haile Selassie's government had very little money and had to reestablish the country's tax collecting system.

Secondly, French Somaliland still posed a threat to the whole area, as did the advent of war with Japan. Any threat from Japan was primarily from the sea, but it was one that had to be addressed. Then too, there were questions of territorial boundaries that existed before the British conquest which came to the fore again. The main territorial boundary disputes were between Eritrea and Ethiopia in the north, and Italian Somaliland and Ethiopia in the Ogaden Desert region in the east. Also there were thousands of Italian POWs and civilian refugees in Ethiopia and the conquered areas that had to be sustained and dealt with.

The British War Cabinet in London had decreed early on that the future of Italian East Africa would not be decided until the end of the war. Therefore, British forces would have to remain in the area for an undetermined length of time as an occupation force.

To facilitate their administration, the OETA decreed that Italian law would be retained, as much as possible for the time being, and that the present judges and magistrates could stay on if they wished. It was also decided that English would be the official language of the occupation and that English lessons would be made available for locally hired employees.

The OETA also began, at that time, to accumulate administrators from all over the empire to send to East Africa.

Lord Rennell Ofrodd, a stern and experienced administrator, was appointed military governor of occupied Italian Somaliland and would rule from Mogadishu for the next six years.

As early as January 1941, the British decided that occupied Italian Somaliland and the whole of the disputed Ogaden Desert region would be administered as one unit from Mogadishu. It was the same structure the Italians had used. This, of course, did not please Haile Selassie because it portended that favored treatment would be given to Italian Somaliland in any future territorial settlement regarding the Ogaden.

In occupied Italian Somaliland, the Italian-trained policemen were found to be unreliable and were interned as POWs for the duration of the war. British-trained policemen from Tanganyika, Uganda, and Nyasaland were brought in to replace them, along with local Somalis who were already in British service and deemed reliable. Some of those reliable Somalis were guards trained by the British to watch over the thousands of Italian POWs that accumulated during the conquest. These new guardians of the peace were armed with captured Italian weapons.

The first order of business for the police in Italian Somaliland was to disarm the population. There were caches of abandoned Italian weapons all over the country and many of the Bande units were still armed and roamed about at will. Furthermore, Somalis had long taken pride in owning weapons and resisted giving them up. Somali nationalism had surfaced and it was rumored that some of the fringe elements of Somali society were hoarding weapons and planning jihad (holy war) against the new occupier in hopes of bringing about an independent Somaliland.

The program of collecting weapons was pursued aggressively by the British authorities, and by August 1941 the police had accumulated 14,000 Italian rifles and six million rounds of ammunition from the populace. This activity, in general, and the way in which it was carried out, made the police very unpopular. The police would conduct "sweeps" and search through individual's homes and personal possessions without warning, often in a destructive manner. In addition, the police would carry out collective punishment on those who would not cooperate. To disarm the nomadic tribes in the Ogaden Desert the British placed machine guns at wells and water holes and required those seeking water to submit to searches before they could draw water. Many of the nomadic tribesmen were of Ethiopian stock and resented being harassed in this manner by authorities from Mogadishu.

Then, there was the problem of script. As the conquest of Italian East Africa had progressed, British forces requisitioned camels, goats, and sheep, and paid for them in military script (promissory note). The holders of the script then had to find some British agency that would honor it. The practice of requisitioning live stock and paying in script continued long after hostilities had ended in Italian Somaliland and was very unpopular.

As the occupation got under way, the British closed many Italian-owned businesses in Somaliland. throwing thousands of local people out of work. Other business enterprises were taken over by the British or their supporters, and the workers were paid the same low wages the Italians had paid. Furthermore, the British confiscated and removed Italian-owned agricultural equipment, thereby causing a food shortage. On the other hand, the British tried to maintain the profitable plantation system and when enough workers could not be found they resorted to forced labor. Some of the plantations had to be abandoned due to the lack of labor and fuel. As if this were not enough, the British raised taxes on many items and imposed the first income tax in the history of the colony.

By the end of 1941, the Somalis had come to hate the British as they had hated the Italians.

ERITREA—?

In Eritrea the British occupation was similar to that of Italian Somaliland, but the people of Eritrea were more westernized and more cooperative than the Somalis. Eritrea was also more industrialized and had a stronger economy than Italian Somaliland so unemployment and displacement were not so commonplace. Nevertheless, the Eritreans came to resent the British occupation as they had resented the Italian occupation. Answering their needs, more and more, in both Italian Somaliland and Eritrea were the fledgling nationalist organizations who were slowly and laboriously coming to the fore.

As for Eritrea's future the British had no idea what would happen to the colony and admitted as much. It was almost certain that the colony would not be returned to Italy but beyond that, its future was anyone's guess. Ethiopia claimed the entire colony because it had been an integral part of Ethiopia until the Italians conquered it in the 1880s. There had also been talk that Eritrea might be considered as a future homeland for the Jews. Furthermore, there was some consideration by colonial sources in London that part of Eritrea might be attached to The Sudan. Also from London came the idea of uniting Eritrea, or its remnants, with the Ethiopian province of Tigrai and creating a "Greater Tigrai" under an Anglo-Ethiopian trusteeship. Yet another possibility saw Eritrea as a mandated territory under the guidance of some advanced nation which would lead it toward independence, as had been the case with those areas mandated after World War I by the League of Nations—that is if the new world organization was given the authority to issue mandates. All things considered, the future of Eritrea would be one of the major questions of Africa which would remain until after the war. Meantime, it would be occupied enemy territory.

In November 1941, the British decided to remove some 34,000 Italian civilians from the former Italian East Africa. With the help of the Red Cross, this was begun in December. The British had asked the Vichy French in French Somaliland to cooperate in this humanitarian effort by sending the refugees up the Addis Ababa/Djibouti Railroad to the port of Djibouti for embarkation. The port was virtually unused at this time. Vichy refused, however, because it would mean that British ships would have to be allowed to come and go at Djibouti, which would be a considerable security risk. Therefore, the British were forced to evacuate the Italians through the ports of Zeila and Berbera in British Somaliland. Unfortunately, these were the main ports of supply for the British forces in East Africa and were working to capacity, so, a rapid departure of the refugees could not be expected. To manage this slow process, a series of staging camps were set up, one each at Zeila and Berbera, one across the strait at Aden, and two along the route from Addis Ababa. The refugees were moved progressively from camp to camp as shipping became available for them at the two ports.

The women, children, elderly, and infirm were returned to Italy via neutral sources, while the men of military and/or working age were sent to internment camps outside of the former Italian colonies. In most cases, the men were then employed, within the guidelines of the Geneva Convention, in the economies of the host countries.

Managing the relocation of these people was assigned to the KAR and some 10,000 soldiers were committed to carry it out. So many KAR units were needed for this operation, plus the guarding of POWs, that the British raised several Arab units in Kenya for coastal defense service at Mombasa (a traditional preserve of the KAR). That, in turn, freed up KAR troops to handle the refugees.

Some Italian men eluded the relocation program or escaped from custody and remained at large in East Africa. They made no organized effort to arm themselves or carry out guerrilla operations, but the British viewed them as security risks and took measures to apprehend them whenever possible.

The overall relocation program went slowly; shipping and accommodations at the other end were constant problems, so the program was not completed until November 1942.

RING AROUND DJIBOUTI

French Somaliland posed a very special problem and the British intended to isolate it from the rest of the world as much as possible. A 25 mile wide military corridor, with land taken from Eritrea, Ethiopia, and British Somaliland, was placed around the French colony and heavily patrolled. Free French units participated in this operation and were stationed on the western border blocking the coastal road from Djibouti into Eritrea. A Free French sloop also joined in the ongoing naval blockade of the colony. Also patrolling the corridor were the Somali guards originally trained to guard POWs, but who were assigned to this duty as the POWs were gradually taken away. Some Allied authorities hoped that the French colonial leaders in French Somaliland would renounce the Petain government and join the Allies in order to rid themselves of the blockade. In this regard, leaflets were periodically dropped over Djibouti, urging the French to renounce Vichy, rid themselves of the blockade, and take part in the new war-related prosperity that was surging throughout Africa. At one point the British offered the French a month of free food and supplies if they would renounce Vichy. Another time they offered to evacuate French women and children to Madagascar. These efforts were to no avail. The French colonial leaders remained loyal to Vichy. Furthermore, circumstances began to favor the French.

After the entry of Japan into the war, most of the British vessels enforcing the naval blockade at French Somaliland were called away, as were some of the ground troops patrolling the corridor. As the British blockade weakened the French could once again get adequate supplies from the smugglers and blockade runners. The Yemenis had become very adept at this business, sailing their small supply-laden boats across the Red Sea and through the British blockade. Arab traders from Aden and Eritrea also joined in the lucrative trade. The smuggling of livestock was especially brisk.

Another source of supply for those in French Somaliland was by submarines which occasionally ran back and forth between Djibouti and Madagascar. In this manner, the French were able to get some items the Arabs could not supply.

The British knew of these activities but could do little stop them, especially after December 1941. What they also knew, from spies inside French Somaliland, was that arms and ammunition were now getting through to make the French colony an increased military threat to the region. The British knew, too, that there was an acute shortage of fuel in the colony.

"GREATER SOMALIA"

In London, the colonialists in the various government colonial offices could see the possibility of acquiring another major British colony in East Africa because of the conquest of Italian East Africa. After all, the British reasoned, who better could administer the area than themselves. A look at the map showed that British Somaliland and possibly French Somaliland could be added to Italian Somaliland to comprise a "Greater Somalia." Further speculation on the part of the British colonial planners indicated that the Ogaden and other parts of Ethiopia might become a part of the new colony as well as parts of eastern Eritrea. The plans to create Greater Somalia were not formalized because such decisions could only be made after the war and with Britain's allies. The plans were shelved but not forgotten. Word of British interests in Greater Somalia were hard to keep secret, and rumors circulated in East Africa as to Britain's intentions.

ETHIOPIA IN POLITICAL LIMBO

Haile Selassie had been sitting on his throne since May, but by the end of the year the British government had not yet concluded the necessary diplomatic measures that entitled him to take over control of his country from the British military authorities. This was quite understandable during the first months of the Emperor's return. He had to restructure his government, impose his authority over all sections of the country, rebuild his army and police, collect taxes, and do many other necessary things. Only after these things had been accomplished could Selassie hope to manage his country effectively.

In September 1941, in an effort to raise money, Selassie's government signed an agreement with the American-owned Sinclair Oil Corporation, giving that company a fifty-year concession to explore for oil and develop the country's oil industry. Other international commercial deals were also being pursued by the Ethiopians.

Furthermore, as a victor in the East African war, Selassie rightfully believed that he should share in the spoils. High on his list of priorities was an outlet to the sea. This could be accomplished by the acquisition of eastern Eritrea and the seaport of Asab, or the acquisition of all or part of British Somaliland and one on more of its seaports. Also of interest to Selassie was control, or even partial control, of the French-owned rail line between Addis Ababa and Djibouti. Due to the blockade the rail line was not in use, causing Ethiopia an economic hardship as well as the French. Selassie let it be known to the British that if military action was taken against the Vichy supporters in French Somaliland the Ethiopian Army and the country's resources would be at their command. This was with the understanding that after the conquest of the French colony Ethiopia would have a say in the ownership and operation of the rail line and ready access to the port of Djibouti.

Also of great importance to Selassie, was the acquisition of the Ogaden region to which Ethiopia had a long-standing claim. The Ogaden was not the only area of Ethiopia still under British occupation. There was, of course, the Ethiopian portion of the 25 mile corridor around French Somaliland and, under British insistence, the Haud region and several smaller regions, all in northern Ethiopia, known as the Reserved Areas. The British claimed that these areas needed to be under British military control for war-related reasons. The Ethiopians where not all that convinced. They, too, had heard rumors of Greater Somalia and feared that the British might, after the war, try to detach some or all of those occupied areas from Ethiopia and add them to their colonial empire.

All of these interests and fears of the Ethiopians were known to the British and were taken under consideration, but without formal diplomatic relations they could go no further. To this end, then, by the end of 1941, the Ethiopian government was pressing the British hard to reestablish normal diplomatic ties.

SAUDI ARABIA MOVED CLOSER TO THE ALLIES

With the Red Sea and the Gulf of Aden under Allied control, King Abd el-Aziz Ibn Saud and the government of neutral Saudi Arabia moved closer to the Allies. This was a significant development in the Middle East because the Saudis, during the 1930s, openly courted the Germans and Italians as a counterbalance to the British who had significant political and military influence in the region as well as major oil interests in the Persian Gulf area. Furthermore, the Saudis, in the early days of their independence following World War I, had been financially dependent upon, and politically beholden to, the British and wanted this relationship to end. This was gradually changing in favor of the Saudis, because during the 1930s Ibn Saud's oil revenues began to make him and his country self-supporting. With regards to their vast oil reserves, the Saudis had turned to the Americans—not to the British, nor the Germans, nor the Italians, nor the French—to develop this great resource on Saudi Arabia's Persian Gulf coast. The Americans were seen as a neutral party in the turbulent politics of the Middle East.

During the First East African War, the Saudis had shown their friendship toward the Italians, and displeasure with the British and French, by refusing to abide by the economic sanctions imposed against Italy by the League of Nations. Throughout the war the Saudis supplied the Italians with food and raw materials, and allowed Rome to send an Italian Air Force mission to its government. That mission remained until February 1939 when Saudi policy again reverted to strict neutrality.

As World War II developed, Saudi Arabia maintained a policy of strict neutrality and permitted no belligerents to use Saudi territory. But now the door was open wider for the Allies and, with American cooperation, Saudi Arabia's oil as well as her other resources were readily available for the Allies to purchase. Allied use of Saudi territory was, however, still strictly forbidden.

FRENCH AFRICA

On September 23, 1941, de Gaulle created the "Free French National Council" in London with himself as its president. He also formed a "cabinet" and announced that at the proper time the Council would serve as the provisional government of France. There were no plans for the Council to move to Brazzaville.

In Brazzaville, though, Governor-General Felix Eboue called a meeting in early October of leading local politicians, judges, and businessmen which, for the record, established the new and liberal tone toward colonial matters that had been shown by the Free French from its inception. The Free French had learned that by showing fairness to colonial peoples, they reciprocated by supporting the Free French cause. This wartime measure could only lead to a new colonial relationship between France and her colonies in the postwar era if the Free French emerged victorious.

At the conference Eboue, who was a mulatto, spoke as a Frenchman saying:

> *"To attempt to make, or remake, a (colonial) society in our own image or even according to our habits of thinking, would court certain failure. The native has a way of behaving, laws, and a homeland which are not ours. We cannot make him happy by applying the principles of the French Revolution... nor the Napoleonic Code... nor by replacing his chiefs with our officials..."*

The liberal pronouncements of this meeting were of great interest to those in Africa and elsewhere in the French Empire that held nationalistic ideals. The message was clear to every native within the French Empire; to support the Free French now, and after the war your lives will be improved.

For some, they would not have to wait until the end of the war. In July, the Free French had proclaimed Syria an independent nation and before the year was out they also gave Lebanon its independence.

To promote this new colonialism, the Free French established a very powerful radio station in Brazzaville to broadcast their messages around the world and especially into Vichy-controlled territories.

During October, the Free French increased their presence in North Africa when the "Alsace" fighter group and the "Lorraine" bomber group began operating with the RAF. Also, several Free French sloops and trawlers arrived to take part in convoy operations.

On November 11, 1941, de Gaulle got what he wanted from America—Lend-Lease. Roosevelt said at the time, "The defense of the territories rallying to Free France was vital for the defense of the United States." Along with Lend-Lease came the first formal political contacts. In Washington, Adrien Tixier, former Director of the Free French International Labor Office, was appointed de Gaulle's representative to the U.S. government, and in London the American Embassy established formal contacts with de Gaulle's headquarters.

On December 8, 1941, the day after the Japanese attack on Pearl Harbor, Free France declared war on Japan. This meant that Equatorial Africa and the other Free French territories around the world also went to war against Japan.

In Vichy-controlled Africa, economic conditions were still as bad as they had been at the beginning of the year. To add to these difficulties, the millet harvest in Niger was poor in 1941, which portended a shortage of that basic food staple for the natives.

At this same time, the Vichy supporters in North Africa had a new problem to worry about. During the fall of 1941, British reconnaissance planes began making regular flights over the Atlantic coast of French Morocco. It was obvious that they were photographing harbors, airfields, roads, bridges, and landing beaches. The natural response by the French was that this activity indicated possible Allied attacks on, or possibly an invasion of, French Morocco.

In Algeria, the Vichy leaders there had to contend with a new wave of nationalism. With the Germans smashing into the Soviet Union and Rommel's forces pressing the British hard in Egypt, the Germans looked stronger than ever while the French, having lost Syria and Lebanon, looked ever weaker. The proclamation in July of Syrian independence by the Free French also had its effect. In August 1941, a well-known pro-Vichy Algerian publicist named Zenati, writing in a local newspaper, admitted that an estimated 80% of the

Algerian people were now pro-German and saw Germany as a potential liberator of Algeria. This was surprising because the German propaganda broadcasts to Algeria and other Arab lands almost never stressed outright Arab independence. The same could be said about Italian propaganda broadcasts to the Arabs. Rather, they spoke in general terms of the liberalization of oppressive colonial conditions, and that Germany would help the Arab people shake off the oppression of the British and French. What was not said but was certainly implied, given the thinking in both Berlin and Rome, was that the existing colonial structure would be assumed by the Axis Powers and that the native population would be better off under their new masters as opposed to their old masters.

In Algeria, the idea of a plebescite on the country's future circulated within the native population. Such a plebescite, it was generally believed, would allow the Algerian people a chance to vote on their future relationship with France and possibly even on Algerian independence. The Vichy supporters in control of Algeria, maintaining the old fiction that Algeria was an integral part of France, had no option but to clamp down on the plebescite rumors. Governmental clampdowns were not new in Algeria. Earlier in the year, the Vichy authorities were forced to disarm a group of militants associated with the Algerian People's Party (PPA). Vichy had deemed this group to be a threat to internal security.

In early August, Petain felt the need to gain still a firmer hand in North Africa and appointed his most trusted associate, Admiral Darlan, to manage future political policy there under Vichy's direction. High Commissioner General Weygand, who formerly had that authority, would now report to Darlan. This was a sop to the Germans who trusted Darlan but not Weygand.

A BOOST TO NATIONALISM

On September 24, elaborate ceremonies were held in Washington and London for fifteen Allied nations which formally adhered to the Atlantic Charter. Those nations included all the dominions of the British Empire, the European governments-in-exile and the Soviet Union. For the nationalists in Africa and elsewhere around the world this was yet another indication that the advanced nations of the world supported the rights of self-determination for all people and that the era of decolonization was another step closer.

EGYPT SUPPORTS THE ALLIES—SOMEWHAT

On December 9, 1941, the Egyptian government, under pressure from the British and Americans, broke diplomatic relations with Japan but refused to declare war. Six days later, on the 15th, under pressure this time from Britain and the Soviet Union, Egypt broke diplomatic relations with both Hungary and Romania. Britain and the British Commonwealth nations had declared war on both of those nations on December 6, and both had been at war with the Soviet Union since the summer. But again, Egypt refused to declare war.

THE WEYGAND CONTROVERSY

On November 20, Hitler finally got his way on one issue in North Africa. High Commissioner Weygand was dismissed after persistent German pressure on Vichy. Petain, in a show of independence and defiance, eliminated the post of High Commissioner that Weygand had held and returned the High Commissioner's political powers back to the three colonial governor-generals of French Morocco, Algeria, and Tunisia. He did, however, keep the military command unified and placed it under General Alphonse Juin, whom he knew was loyal to Vichy. This weakened, somewhat, the chain of command in North Africa in the event of an emergency such as an Allied invasion.

Weygand's dismissal had repercussions in Washington, who saw in him the one man in French North Africa that could facilitate an Allied landing. As a show of Washington's displeasure, Roosevelt ordered an immediate halt to the flow of American food to French North Africa under the Murphy/Weygand agreement.

Churchill felt differently about ceasing food supplies to North Africa and on November 30, 1941, wrote to his Foreign Secretary to make his feeling known in Washington. Churchill wrote:

> *"I think it most important that the United States should continue their relations with Vichy and their supplies to North Africa and any other contacts unostentatiously for the present. It would be a great mistake to lose any contacts before we know the result of the battle in Libya and its reactions. There is always time to break, but it is more difficult to renew contacts."*

The Germans, quite understandably, were annoyed about Petain's show of defiance and weakening of the defense command of French North Africa. In an attempt to work this out, Petain received a summons from Berlin to meet with Hermann Goering, Germany's number two Nazi, at Saint-Florentine, France on December 1. The timing was bad for the Germans, because it was becoming obvious that their forces in the Soviet Union would not likely be taking Moscow in the face of very determined Soviet opposition, and that the costly war there would go on for at least another year.

At the meeting, Goering, as expected, demanded that the French do more to protect their colonies, especially North Africa. Petain was ready for Goering's demands, and he knew that the Germans were in a weak bargaining position at the moment. The old Marshal responded that he was willing to do as the Germans asked, but produced a list of demands that more of the French armed forces be freed from their restrictions of the armistice, and that Germany supply those forces with certain military items and fuel. When Petain handed Goering the list he refused to take it. Petain then, unceremoniously, stuffed it into one of Goering's pockets. The two men parted company visibly irritated. It was obvious to both that the detente of the Paris Protocol, seven months earlier, was dead.

News of the Saint-Florentine meeting were well received in London and Washington as Petain knew they would be. Then, on December 7, the Americans suddenly entered the war, and on December 11, Germany and Italy declared war on the United States. These events strengthened Petain's hand even more, because now the major Axis Powers had another very powerful enemy and a whole host of smaller enemies in the nations that declared war on Germany and Italy in the following days.

To cover himself with the Germans Petain went on radio on December 12 to confirm that his regime would remain neutral in the newly expanded war, and they would defend the French Empire with all the military means at its disposal against any enemy. He also gave reassurances that the French Fleet would not be allowed to fall into the hands of any foreign power.

That same day, the Americans carried out a very unfriendly act against Vichy by requisitioning all Vichy ships in American ports. Washington used America's entry into the European war as justification for this act, but it was clear that the Americans did not fully trust Vichy promises regarding their fleet. Vichy, of course, protested but took no further action—a sign that Petain understood.

While the Weygand controversy was going on, the American diplomat, Robert Murphy, who still had a free hand in French North Africa, discovered that Admiral Darlan had permitted the shipment, from French North Africa into Libya, of several trucks and some gasoline and food which went to Rommel. When Washington complained of this to Vichy, Petain immediately ordered all such shipments stopped.

The American freighter "Lehigh" sinking off Freetown. She was the tenth American merchantman sunk so far in the war by German subs. She was also the first to be clearly photographed while sinking. Note the large American flag on the hull.

Roosevelt, now convinced that Petain was distancing himself from the Axis Powers as best he could, authorized the resumption of American food shipments to French North Africa. Churchill welcomed the news.

THE "SHOOT ON SIGHT" ORDER

On September 11, 1941, in direct response to the German sinking of the American destroyer Greer (September 4), President Roosevelt issued to the U.S. Navy what became known as the "Shoot on Sight" order. It authorized American ships, operating inside the Pan-American Security Zone, to shoot first when encountering ships of the Axis nations. To justify this, Roosevelt told the American people, "It is the Nazi design to abolish the freedom of the seas and to acquire absolute control and domination of the seas for themselves."

Then on September 16, Washington announced that American warships would begin escorting Britain-bound convoys carrying Lend-Lease goods as far east as the 26th west meridian, the eastern limit of the Security Zone. And on the 26th, the U.S. Naval Command ordered all American warships to follow, and sink if possible, any German or Italian commercial vessel or warship found within the Security Zone. On November 7, Germany retaliated by announcing that its U-boats had been ordered to attack any and all armed vessels, neutral or not. For all practical purposes the Unites States Navy was at war with Germany and Italy inside the Security Zone.

SEA WAR OFF WEST AFRICA

The submarine war off West Africa dropped off in August, picked up again in September, then began to diminish again as the year wore on. The tragic tallies were as follows.

During August 1941, an Italian submarine sank one Allied tanker. During September, Italian subs sank no ships but German subs sank nine merchant ships.

For October, German subs sank five Allied ships including another the empty American cargo ship, "Lehigh" on October 19. She was 75 miles west of Freetown at the time on her way to pick up African manganese ore. All 39 crewmen were rescued by passing ships. The British destroyer "Cossack" was also torpedoed and sunk northwest of Casablanca.

During November, German subs sank two ships and the British light cruiser "Dunedin" on November 24 with the loss of over 300 seamen.

In December, German subs sank two ships, including the American freighter "Sagadahoc," on December 3, when the United States was still neutral.

In other naval action in West African waters, the Americans made available to the British three escort groups of warships, which would be based at Freetown and used in the British convoy system between Freetown and Gibraltar. This was yet another serious provocation by the Americans because these convoys almost never sailed within the Pan-American Security Zone. Also, Washington knew that the American ships would be subject to attacks as a result of Berlin's announcement of November 7.

On October 4, the British got their first submarine kill in the waters off West Africa. The victim was U-111 which was located operating off the Canary Islands and sunk by the British trawler "Lady Shirley." The British ship damaged the sub with depth charges, forcing her to the surface where she finished her off with gunfire. Eight of the German crew were killed and 44 captured.

On November 6, the German blockade runner "Odenwald," masquerading as an American ship inside the American Security Zone and carrying rubber from the Far East to Germany, was captured in the South Atlantic by the American cruiser "Omaha" and the destroyer "Somers." This was the first action by American warships taken under Roosevelt's Shoot on Sight order.

In Washington, Congress modified America's neutrality laws once again to allow American merchant ships to be armed while travelling in war zones. With this, America's neutrality laws with regards to naval operations were virtually meaningless.

At this time, the Americans made still another provocative move at sea. An American convoy, WS-124 (Winston's Special), the first of its kind, was used to transport 20,000 Canadian troops to British possessions halfway around the world. American justification for this was that the troops were being transported from one non-war zone to another non-war zone. The convoy's route was Halifax–Trinidad–Cape Town–Bombay–Singapore–San Francisco. Most of the Canadian troops would be put ashore at Bombay and Singapore.

On November 22, the German raider Atlantis met her end off the West African coast. She had just returned from the South Pacific where she had gone to "hide" after the Zamzam incident. The Atlantis was caught in the act of refuelling the German sub U-126 when the British cruiser Devonshire, guided by information from Ultra, came upon the scene. U-126 was able to dive quickly and get away. Her captain, however, was not aboard. He was on the Atlantis having breakfast with the Atlantis' captain. To make matters worse, the Atlantis had one of her engines down for repair. The Atlantis promptly took on one of her disguises but it did not fool the British. They now had accurate photographs of the Atlantis from the Zamzam incident. The German ship was quickly identified and the Devonshire opened fire without hesitation. It was not much of a fight with the Devonshire's 8" guns against the Atlantis' 5.9" guns. The Atlantis sank slowly enough for most of her crew to get off into lifeboats. After Devonshire departed, U-126 returned to the scene and took as many survivors as she could aboard and towed the rest in their lifeboats. This was day 622 for the Atlantis being at sea without entering a port.

"Atlantis" survivors crowd the deck of U-126 after their ship was sunk.

The German supply ship "Python," which was not far away, was diverted to pick up the Atlantis survivors from U-126.

Then on December 1, the Python, herself, was spotted by the British cruiser Dorsetshire, a sister-ship to the Devonshire while refuelling two submarines. Again, Ultra had helped the British find the enemy. The subs dived out of sight, but the Python was left to face the monster warship. Knowing that a fight was useless the crew of the Python scuttled their vessel and got off safely along with the Atlantis survivors into very crowded lifeboats. There were 360 survivors in all. The two German subs returned to the area and took aboard as many survivors as they could but one of the subs, as ordered by Doenitz, had to tow the balance of the survivors in ten lifeboats and five rubber dinghies until two more German subs and four Italian subs could be brought to help. Even with that, some of the survivors had to be towed back to France in their open boats.

The loss of the Python ended Admiral Doenitz's plan to send a number of submarines into the South Atlantic, all of which would have been resupplied by the Python.

As might be expected, conditions for German submarines off West Africa were becoming more risky. The Germans were suddenly awakened to this when they lost the second and third submarines for the year in West African waters during month of December. They were U-208 which was sunk 100 miles north of Casablanca and U-131 which was sunk east of Madeira. Despite these losses, 1941 had been a good year for the Axis submarines off West Africa.

THE FRENCH TAKE ADVANTAGE

Along the northwest coast of Africa, the British had difficulty maintaining their sea blockade of French West and North Africa because of the continuing naval actions at sea. The Vichy French, therefore, took advantage of the situation

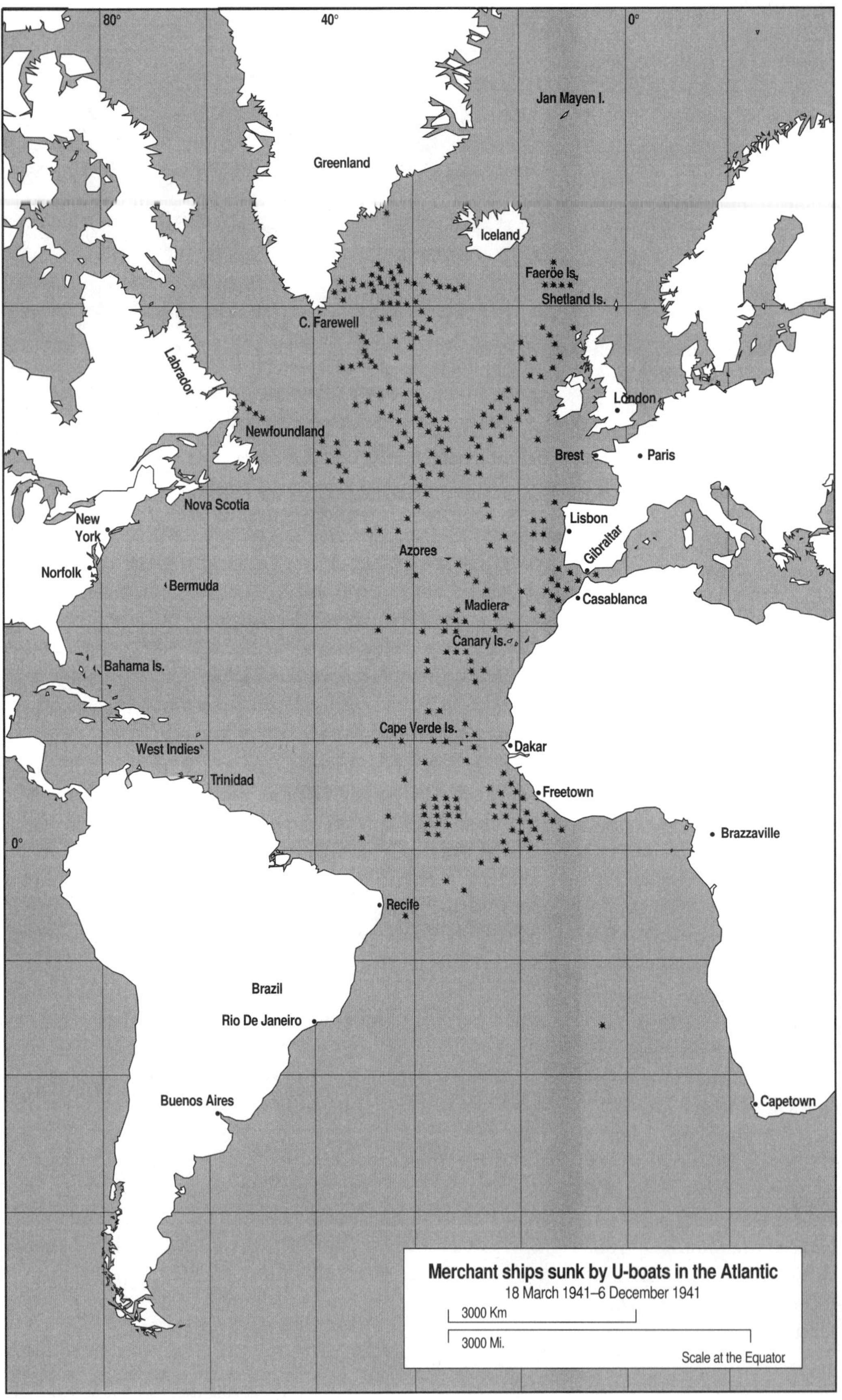

Merchant ships sunk by Axis submarines in the Atlantic from March 18 to December 6, 1941.

and was able to run a number of ships back and forth along the coastline from Dakar to Metropolitan France. In two years, the British were only able to stop four Vichy ships along this sea route.

BRAZIL TAKES ACTION IN THE SOUTH ATLANTIC

Brazil, cooperating with the United States with regards to the Pan-American Security Zone, granted permission for American warships to operate out of Brazilian Atlantic ports. The first American ships to take advantage of this were the destroyer "Greene" and the seaplane tender "Thrush" which began operating out of Natal on December 10.

The next day, December 11, Germany and Italy declared war on the United States. Brazil immediately broke diplomatic relations with both Axis countries and opened her Atlantic coastal facilities to all branches of the United States armed forces. Soon, additional American warships were operating out of Brazilian harbors and "Catalina" long-range flying boats (PBYs) were operating from Brazilian bases, with new bases were being built by the Americans on Brazilian soil. With the PBYs operating out of Brazil and similar long-range aircraft operating out of Freetown, Sierra Leone, the 1,850 mile gap in the Central Atlantic Ocean was now mostly covered by Allied air patrols. This was the first time Allied air coverage spanned across the Atlantic. Furthermore, the Brazilian Navy, still neutral, began tracking and reporting Axis vessels within the Pan-American Security Zone.

DAKAR AGAIN

With Japan in the war, Admiral Raeder, Commander of the German Navy, presented a plan to Hitler to utilize his idle surface fleet in the waters of the South Atlantic and the Indian Ocean, where Allied naval defenses were weaker than in the North Atlantic. Raeder's plan called for Germany's large ships to leave Europe, go to a halfway point, refuel, and then sail around South Africa, cross the Indian Ocean, and refuel again at a Japanese base somewhere in the Far East. All the while the ships would be raiding Allied commerce going out and returning. As for the halfway station Raeder recommended Dakar. Hitler, however, was not interested. His overriding concern was still the Soviet Union and Raeder's plan was rejected.

SEA WAR IN THE INDIAN OCEAN AND RED SEA

During this period there were no Axis submarines in the Indian Ocean, but there were other naval actions of interest.

On September 7, 1941, the American freighter "Steel Seafarer" was attacked and sunk by German aircraft in the northern part of the Red Sea. There was no loss of life. On September 23, the German raider Kormoran captured the empty Greek ship "Stamagios G. Embricos" out of Mombasa bound for Colombo, Ceylon. The entire ship's crew was taken prisoner and the ship sunk. This was victim number twelve for the Kormoran.

On October 27, a Vichy convoy of five merchant ships with an escort of one sloop and a submarine was discovered and reported by a Dutch cargo ship sixty miles south of Fort Dauphine, Madagascar. The convoy was heading around the Cape. Theoretically, Vichy-controlled Madagascar was under the British blockade, but the blockade was so weak the French all but ignored it. Now, things had changed. A flotilla of six small warships of the South African Navy set out from Durban to intercept the convoy, and were assisted by aircraft of the SAAF. On the evening of November 1, the South Africans located the convoy and tracked it through the night. The French knew they had been located but scornfully sailed through the night with all lights ablaze, as was the custom for ships of neutral nations. Meanwhile the South Africans called in the British cruiser Devonshire which was nearby. The Devonshire arrived on the evening of October 3, and, with the South African ships, tracked the convoy through a second night. At dawn on November 4, the Frenchmen knew that they could expect to be attacked at any moment. Therefore, they unexpectedly stopped the convoy in mid-ocean and the crews abandoned the ships, while scuttling charges were exploded aboard all of the ships. Small fires began on the ships, but most went out and none of the vessels sank. After awhile, the French crews re-boarded their ships, and, all but the French submarine surrendered to the South Africans. Four of the French ships could still travel under their own power while the other two had to be towed. The ships were taken to East London and Port Elizabeth. When tallied, the total tonnage of the convoy was 40,000 tons, the largest war prize yet taken by the Allies in the Indian Ocean.

Vichy then ordered two of the French submarines stationed at Madagascar, the "Leheros" and "Le Glorieux" to attack Allied shipping in retaliation for the loss of the convoy. On November 15, the Le Glorieux attacked an Allied ship without success, but on November 17, Leheros torpedoed and sank the Norwegian cargo ship "Thode Fageland" 35 miles east of East London. With this, the Vichy subs were withdrawn. Vichy also suspended all sea traffic south of Dakar. This further isolated Madagascar and the French possessions in the Far East from Metropolitan France and French West and North Africa. Now, only an occasional Vichy submarine or blockade runner would attempt to travel south of Dakar.

On December 10, 1941 the British lost two capital ships, the battleship "Prince of Wales" and cruiser "Repulse" to Japanese aircraft off the north coast of Malaya. They had been on a mission to disrupt a Japanese invasion then in progress in Malaya. These ships had been part of the Royal Navy's Indian Ocean Fleet stationed at Colombo, Ceylon. Their loss affected Africa, in that the principle British force standing between the African east coast and the Japanese was weakened by the loss of those ships.

LET'S DIVIDE EURASIA!

Soon after their attack on Pearl Harbor, the Japanese suggested to the Germans and Italians that they establish a dividing line between their respective spheres of interest on the Eurasian continent. Tokyo suggested that line be the 70th east meridian which ran along the west coast of India. The Germans and Italians agreed and after some negotiations it was decided that the 70th meridian would be used to divide the Indian Ocean, but on land, existing political boundaries would be used. This agreement, formalized on January 18, 1942, put all of India, Afghanistan, and most of Soviet Siberia into the Japanese sphere. All of Africa, the Middle East and Arabian Peninsula would belong to the European Axis Powers. Also at this time, the German Navy let it be known that it would be receptive to the idea of Japan establishing military bases on the Island of Madagascar, which was in the German and Italian sphere of interest. This suggestion was warmly received in Tokyo.

MORE AIR ROUTES

During the latter part of 1941, air traffic across the Cannonball Route of central Africa increased significantly, as more airfields were built and more aircraft became available. The air routes operated by the British and Americans dominated air travel in Africa, but in October the Free French made a contribution when they opened regular air service, for both military and commercial purposes, from Brazzaville to Cairo and Syria.

Heretofore, the bulk of British and American air service across Africa was for miliary purposes, but in late October 1941, Pan-American Airways, with the blessing of the American government, established regular commercial air service from the United States to Khartoum. In November, that service was extended to Cairo and Basra, Iraq.

On November 7, the United States formally extended Lend-Lease to the Soviet Union (although some Lend-Lease goods had actually been sent to the Soviet Union as early as August 1941). This meant that some American-made aircraft, destined for the Soviet Union under the Lend-Lease program, would now be flying across Africa.

By the end of the year, the Pan-Am commercial routes were extended to Leopoldville, Belgian Congo; Asmara, Eritrea; India; Burma; and China. Pan-American commercial operations in Africa were controlled from its own base of operations at Accra, Gold Coast which had been established in October.

British Overseas Airways Company (BOAC), which already had established commercial routes throughout Africa, expanded some of its routes from Africa into the Middle East.

The American-dominated military air routes from the Western Hemisphere to West Africa were expanded during the latter part of 1941 into four distinct and direct routes. Using Natal, Brazil as the hub, American military personnel, supplies, Lend-Lease aircraft, etc. flew either from Natal to Bathurst; Natal to Freetown; Natal to Fisherman's Lake, Liberia; or Natal to Takoradi.

American-made pipes to be used somewhere in Africa under the Lend-Lease program.

During November 1941, yet another trans-Atlantic air route was established when the American air carrier Eastern Air Lines followed Pan-American's lead and contracted with the U.S. government for a military air route. It would be inaugurated during 1942, and would be from Natal to Ascension Island to Accra.

Then, on December 7, 1941, when the United States was attacked by Japan, the American government suddenly stopped sending all Lend-Lease aircraft abroad, pending a review of America's own war needs. This lasted several weeks, after which the ferrying of Lend-Lease aircraft resumed.

On December 12, the day after Germany and Italy declared war on the United States, the U. S. Navy established the "Naval Air Transport Service" (NATS). The U.S. Navy could see that it was about to take on a worldwide commitment and it needed such a service to transport its own men and supplies. Some of those planes would soon be flying the African routes.

When Brazil broke diplomatic relations with Italy in December 1941, it terminated the operating license of the Italian airline, LATI, to operate within its borders. LATI's overseas route from Natal to Dakar to Italy also ended. Heretofore, it had been one of the holes in the British blockade.

IN SOUTH AFRICA

On September 24, 1941 South Africa, along with fourteen other governments, formally adhered to the Atlantic Charter. This was a show of solidarity among the Allies. At the same time, it was an encouragement to the small and heavily-oppressed nationalist groups that existed in that country.

With the final elimination of the Italians in East Africa, the Smuts administration received a boost in its popularity. Photographs of the Union flag flying over the former Italian headquarters at Gondar, the same one that had flown over the Imperial Palace in Addis Ababa, were widely published. Many of the South Africa troops came home for well-earned furloughs, but were soon sent off again to North Africa. There the activities of the South African troops were traced regularly and in great detail in the local newspapers. When the 5th South African Brigade was badly mauled by Rommel's forces in late November, it was sad news for all South Africans.

In December, South Africa acquired a host of new enemies. On December 6, 1941, for political reasons in Europe, South Africa and the other British Commonwealth nations declared war on Finland, Romania and Hungary, because those nations were at war with the Soviet Union. Then, on December 7, just minutes before the Japanese attack on Pearl Harbor, the Japanese government declared war on Britain and the Commonwealth nations, including South Africa. The next day, South Africa along with the other Commonwealth nations, declared war on Japan. Then, incredibly, on December 13, Germany's ally, Bulgaria, declared war on the United States, Britain, and all of the British Commonwealth nations including South Africa. War with Bulgaria seemed so ludicrous that the South Africa Parliament had to debate the issue before deciding what to do. Not until January 2, 1942, was the issue settled, when the Smuts government decided to declare war on Bulgaria. Finally on January 23, Thailand declared war on the United States, Britain, and the British Commonwealth nations. Once again the South African government debated and then reciprocated. Within a month, South Africa had acquired six new enemies.

And then, there was the enemy within. On December 14, boxer Robey Liebbrant and his South African Nazis blew up several sections of rail line outside of Pretoria. Liebbrant and his gang had been hunted men ever since they raided a steel mill in July, but had remained at large because there were many people in South Africa who were sympathetic to their cause and would give them refuge. The South African police could only redouble their effort to catch these local terrorists. Unknown to Liebbrant, an informant had infiltrated his organization and learned that he was planning a massive sabotage campaign to begin on January 20, 1942. Working closely with the informant, the police lured Liebbrant and his closest associates into a trap at a road block on December 24 and captured Liebbrant and his aides alive. Most of the other members of the gang were rounded up in the next few weeks, along with much of their arms and explosives. This decimated Liebbrant's organization and it quickly fell apart. Liebbrant was sentenced to death for treason, but his sentence was later commuted to life imprisonment by Prime Minister Smuts, because Liebbrant had served under him honorably in the Boer War.

News of Germany's failure to subdue the Soviet Union in December and the new war in the Pacific brought mixed feelings to the South Africans. It tended to widen the gulf between those who supported the war and those who did not.

ELSEWHERE

Rastenburg, East Prussia (Hitler's eastern headquarters) October 4: It was lunch time. As he frequently did, Hitler was dining with a group of his closest aides and, as usual, dominating the table talk. On this occasion he spoke of the future. He told his captive audience that within fifty years there would be five million Germans farming the vast reaches of European Russia, feeding most of Europe. The Belgian Congo, which would also be in German hands, would be Germany's main source for tea and coffee. He spoke of areas of his empire-to-be that would provide Germany with oysters, crabs, and caviar.

Soviet Union: With the entry of the Soviet Union into the war, some items produced in Africa were now made available to that country as war aid. Items of note were coffee from East Africa, oilseed from West Africa, and industrial diamonds from South Africa.

Sierra Leone: A petty problem here grew so out of proportion that Churchill, himself, saw the need to intercede. It concerned the allowance each of the newly-arrived Polish officers was to receive for his tropical uniform. On November 29, Churchill wrote to General Ismay, Chief of Staff of the War Cabinet, about this problem and informed him that more Polish officers were being sought for West Africa:

> *"I am dissatisfied with the way in which this project for Polish officers in West Africa, in which I took a personal interest, has been followed up. It was evidently necessary that a proper outfit allowance should be paid to the Polish officers proceeding to these tropical regions. Yet all these months have passed haggling about it. First five pounds is offered, then finally fifteen pounds… On other papers I have directed that two hundred more Polish officers are to be invited to present themselves for examination (for service in West Africa). A weekly report is to be supplied to me personally of the progress made both in West Africa and at home."*

Spain: In Spain the Madrid government was raising a division of volunteers to fight with the German Army in the Soviet Union. It was to be called the "Blue Division" and serve as a repayment, in part, for Germany's substantial help given to Franco's Nationalist forces during the Spanish Civil War (1936-39). Recruiting was conducted throughout the Spanish Empire, and a sizeable number of Africans volunteered for service. By late 1941, the first elements of the "Blue Division" were on their way to the German front, north of Moscow, including a contingent of "Africanistas."

THE "ARCADIA CONFERENCE"

With the United States in the war, Churchill was most anxious to meet with Roosevelt and the American military leaders to plan future strategy. Roosevelt wanted this too. So, on December 13, Churchill set sail for America on the British battleship "Duke of York" to meet with Roosevelt in Washington. He arrived on December 22, and met with the Americans for several days thereafter in what became known as the "Arcadia Conference."

Among the many items discussed was an Allied invasion of French North Africa at Casablanca. A second invasion at Dakar, code named "Operation Black," was also discussed. This would have been an all-American affair commanded by General Joseph Stilwell. Stilwell was flown in from California for discussions on the plan. Operation Black was eventually dropped, but the joint invasion of French North Africa was given much attention.

Several long-range decisions came out of the conference, namely that the two Allies would direct the bulk of their resources to defeating Germany first and later Japan. Furthermore, four major offensives were planned, one of which would be in North Africa. They were:

- "Operation Sledgehammer": An invasion somewhere in Europe in 1942 to relieve military pressure on the Soviet Union.
- "Operation Roundup": The cross-channel invasion of Europe in 1943.
- "Operation Gymnast": An Anglo-American invasion of French North Africa sometime after May 1942.
- "Operation Bolero": A massive U.S. and British military buildup to pursue final victory in western Europe.

The Americans were not thoroughly convinced of the necessity of Operation Gymnast and argued for an early invasion of the European continent. The British, especially Churchill, thought Gymnast a very important first step because it would clear the Mediterranean and reestablish the shortest sea link between west and east. It would also expose, what he called, the "soft underbelly" of Europe for Operation Sledgehammer. This was an issue that the two allies would have to work out.

Chapter 13

WAR AND MORE WAR IN AFRICA (JANUARY–SEPTEMBER 1942)

SEESAW BATTLES IN NORTH AFRICA AND AN ALLIED VICTORY IN MADAGASCAR

ROMMEL, ROMMEL, ROMMEL

As 1942 began, the British were, once again, halfway across Libya at El Agheila with high hopes of driving on to Tripoli and conquering all on that colony. Indeed, these were the orders from London. Both London and the British Middle East Command at Cairo believed that their Axis adversaries had been badly beaten and were in no condition to go on the offensive. All the British needed now were reinforcements and a little time to get ready to renew the attack. But Rommel did not give them that time. Rommel and his Italian allies quickly gathered together what resources they had and, on January 21, went on the attack. The timely arrival of a complete convoy from Italy on January 7 with new German tanks, fuel, ammunition, replacements, spare parts and the like made this possible. Then, on January 19, two German transports brought another 45 new tanks to North Africa. This brought the German tank strength up to 139 along with the existing 89 Italian tanks. Furthermore, during December and January, the Vichy French in North Africa had supplied the Axis forces in Libya with approximately 5,500 tons of gasoline and aviation fuel.

On the British side of the line, the inexperienced British 1st Armored Division had 150 tanks but they were widely dispersed along the El Agheila front in defensive positions. The British had additional tanks, but these were at various locations in the rear.

When the Axis forces attacked on January 21, the British were taken by complete surprise. It was from this point on, for the next seven months, that Rommel would display his remarkable leadership skills which would make him the legendary military leader that history has recorded. With great skill, daring, and much luck, outnumbered by his enemy most of the time and troubled by constant supply problems, he would force the British 8th Army back into Egypt and come close to winning the war in North Africa for the Axis.

These things were in the future. For the moment, it was the counterattack at El Agheila that mattered. With three columns and strong air support, the Axis forces smashed through the British defenses at El Agheila with relative ease.

The British defenders withdrew hastily to Agedabia, a distance of eighty miles. But Rommel's tanks followed close on the heels of the retreating British and took Agedabia, the next day, before the British could get organized and even before some of the British forces arrived. The British then fled to Msus, 100 miles to the east, but it was the same story. Rommel's tanks gave them no time to stop and set up defensive positions. In the rout, the British 1st Armoured Division (one of the best British units), which had just arrived from England two weeks earlier, lost 96 tanks, 38 artillery pieces, and 190 trucks.

From Msus, the main Axis force gave up the rapid pursuit of the fleeing British and turned back to the coast, and on January 28, took Benghazi, a much-needed supply port, from the 4th Indian Division. After securing Benghazi, the Axis forces advanced along the coastal road following the retreating Indians. The British rushed in troops from Tobruk and elsewhere, and were able to establish a defense line that extended from Gazala, on the coast, to Bir Hacheim, about 100 miles to the south. While the Gazala-Bir Hacheim line was being built, the British also rejuvenated their defenses around Tobruk. Their plan was to hold Tobruk at all costs, even if the Gazala-Bir Hacheim line failed, and use Tobruk as a threat to Rommel's rear, once again, as it had been used so effectively in November 1941.

On February 3, the Axis forces took Derna and moved on to make contact with the British defenders at Gazala. There they stopped on February 4. For the next six weeks, there was a lull in the ground fighting as both sides prepared for the next phase of the battle.

THE WAR AT SEA

Just as on land, the battle at sea was still undetermined. On January 12 U-77 sank the British destroyer "Kimberly" near Tobruk. Then on the 17th U-133 sank a second British destroyer, the "Gurkha," off the western coast of Egypt. During the month, British subs sank three Italian merchantmen off western Libya.

During February the British suffered another setback when, on February 12, all three ships of a three-ship convoy out of Alexandria bound for Malta were sunk by German submarines. Three days later, the British temporarily halted all shipping in the Mediterranean. This meant that the British ground forces could no longer count on the British Navy providing them with artillery support and supplies along the coast, and Axis supply ships from Europe were more likely to get through with supplies and reinforcements for Rommel.

During February, British subs sank three more Italian freighters in the waters off Tunisia and western Libya.

Then, on February 17, Auchinleck was ordered by London to release two of his seven divisions for service in the Far East against the Japanese. Later, this was changed to one division, the British 70th Division. This was in addition to the Australian divisions already scheduled to leave.

During late February, bad weather hampered activities on both sides, especially in the air.

On March 11, U-565 sank the British light cruiser "Naiad" off western Egypt. Three days later, the Italian sub "Mocenigo" accidently sank a small Vichy sailing vessel off Algeria. On March 17 U-83 sank a British cargo ship off of western Egypt and on

March 20 U-652 torpedoed and sank the British destroyer escort "Heythorp." Nine days later, she sank the British destroyer "Jaguar" and the British tanker "Slavol." During March, British subs sank three more Italian merchant ships off Tunisia as they approached Tripoli.

On March 20, the British broke the lull in the North African ground war by attacking the Axis positions at Derna. This was a diversionary attack to draw away Axis attention, and hopefully air power, from the Mediterranean, while another convoy tried to make it through to Malta after the disastrous loss of the three-ship convoy in February. The attack did draw off some Axis aircraft and the convoy made it safely to Malta.

On April 6, the Italian sub "Aradam" sank the British destroyer "Havock" off Tunisia and the next day, U-453 attacked another British Malta-bound convoy off Alexandria and sank the British freighter "Somersetshire." Other ships of the convoy succeeded in getting through.

British subs managed to sink five Italian merchantmen, an Italian tug, and an Italian landing craft during April.

Throughout April, German and Italian subs roamed the Mediterranean almost at will. During that time, along the North African coast, German subs sank four British ships, five Egyptian ships, one Norwegian ship, and one French ship, while the Italian sub, "Corallo," accidently sank two Turkish ships off the coast of Tunisia.

During the month of April, more Axis supply ships arrived from Europe, and the Axis ground forces in North Africa received 99% of the supplies sent to them—some 150,000 tons. Rommel's supply situation was about as good at this point as it had ever been.

All the while another long lull was occurring in the ground war in North Africa and was broken only by skirmishes and air raids.

The next action of significance occurred again at sea when, on May 2, two British destroyers and an RAF Catalina flying boat teamed up to sink the German sub U-74 just east of Cartegena, Spain. All 47 crewmen perished. Then on May 11, German aircraft, flying out of Crete, sank three British destroyers as they tried to attack an Axis convoy bound for Libya.

During May, the German subs continued their dominance in the eastern Mediterranean by sinking one British cargo ship, two Greek ships and a Norwegian ship. Italian subs sank no ships during May. While it was the Germans that dominated most of the eastern Mediterranean, it was the British subs that dominated the waters off Libya. During May they sank nine Italian merchant ships and the Italian destroyer "Pessagno."

On May 28, the Germans lost another sub, U-568, to a British destroyer and two destroyer escorts off Tobruk. All 47 members of the sub's crew were rescued.

On June 2, the Germans lost another sub. U-652 had to be scuttled by her crew off eastern Libya after having been damaged by depth charges from a British plane. The 46 crew members were rescued by U-81, which was unsuccessfully attacked by the British sub "Turbulent" during the rescue operation. The next day the British trawler "Crocker" was sunk by an unknown cause off western Egypt. On June 7, the Italian sub made another mistake by sinking the neutral Turkish sailing vessel "Hady M'hammed" off Tunisia. On June 15, the British sub "Umbra" sank the Italian cruiser "Trento" off Benghazi.

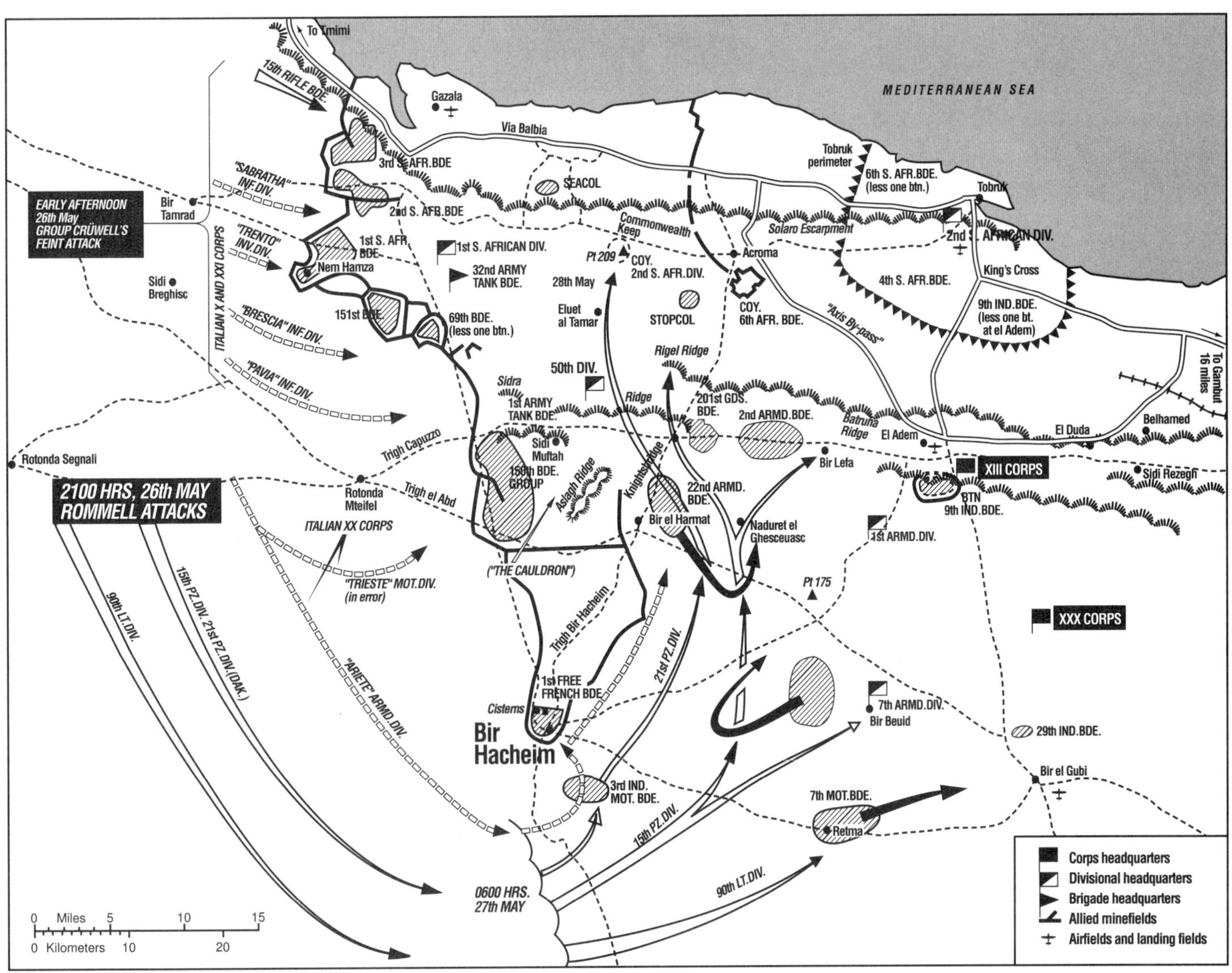

Rommel's attack on the Gazala-Bir Hacheim line, May 26, 1942.

On June 16, U-205 sank the British light cruiser "Hermione" off Alexandria, and five days later the Italian sub "Alagi" accidently sank an Italian destroyer, the "A. Usodimare" off Tunisia. On June 23, the British sub "Thrasher" sank an Italian freighter off Benghazi and on the 27th sank the Italian sloop "Diana" off western Libya. The next day, U-97 sank a British and Greek merchantman off Port Said and on June 30, U-372 sank the British submarine tender "Medway" off Alexandria. Clearly, the war in the Mediterranean was just as undecided as the war on the land.

ROMMEL ATTACKS AGAIN

By late May, Rommel's forces were ready again to take the offensive. On May 26, Axis forces launched a major offensive against the British Gazala-Bir Hacheim line. The German offensive, labelled "Operation Venezia" had as its objective the recapture of Tobruk and, if possible, an advance to the Egyptian border. A second offensive, "Operation Aida," was being planned which would take the Axis forces all the way to the Nile Delta.

Operation Venezia began with Italian infantry making a feint attack at the center of the British line, while all of the Axis tanks, German and Italian, swung far to the south hoping to outflank Bir Hacheim and come in behind the British defenses. It was a daring move by Rommel. He now had 560 tanks, with 77 more in reserve, while the Allies had 849. Rommel also had an advantage in air power with 704 planes compared to the British force's 320.

Some of the British armored units were now equipped with American-made "Grant" tanks which gave them a capability they did not have before, namely a large caliber gun that could fire a high explosive shell at antitank gun positions.

Seven days of hard fighting ensued, with the British finally stopping Rommel's end run around Bir Hacheim but at a heavy cost. Two British brigades were decimated. Finally on June 1, Rommel halted his offensive to regroup. On June 5,

Colonial antiaircraft gunners serving in the Free French Brigade.

the British counterattacked but quickly lost two more infantry brigades and four artillery regiments. They then halted.

On June 10, Rommel attacked again at Bir Hacheim, this time directly into positions held by 1st Free French Division and a battalion of 1,000 Palestinian Jews. The Free French had only recently arrived in North Africa and this was their first experience operating with the British.

A RAMSHACKLE UNIT

The 1st Free French Division, under General Marie-Pierre Koenig, was a ramshackle unit made up of an interesting mix of humanity. Within its ranks were Frenchmen from Metropolitan France, African-born Frenchmen, Moroccans, Algerians, Tunisians, Foreign Legionnaires (which included some Germans, Italians and Americans), Ubanghis from Equatorial Africa, Pacific Islanders, and a unit of British antiaircraft gunners.

In five days of very hard fighting at Bir Hacheim, the Free Frenchmen and the Jews put up one of the most heroic defenses in the annals of World War II. Finally on June 10, after suffering many casualties and cut off from reinforcements, the Free Frenchmen and Jews gave way and retreated. The Axis forces swung around Bir Hacheim and headed for Tobruk. A British tank force attempted to stop the onslaught at a desert location known as "Knightsbridge," but was badly beaten and lost many tanks. The Axis forces appeared to be unstoppable.

"BLACK SATURDAY"

After Rommel's forces circled north from Bir Hacheim, the battle spread over a broad front as Axis troops came in behind the Gazala-Bir Hacheim line and pushed toward Tobruk and the sea. The British forces tried desperately to stop them and still hold the north end of Gazala-Bir Hacheim line. Then the British made a terrible mistake. Despite Ultra information on Rommel's defenses, they sent their main force of 300 tanks against what they believed was the Axis front. In reality it was a clever trap—an ambush—in which the entire force was caught in the cross fire of the powerful German 88mm artillery pieces. For the British tank men it was Armageddon. Only seventy tanks survived. This was on June 13, the day the British would call "Black Saturday." Fortunately other British forces were able to hold the line, but now, with their tank force decimated, the British were on the defensive. On June 15, the 1st South African Division and the 50th British Division were ordered to abandon the northern sector of the Gazala-Bir Hacheim line and withdraw to the east.

The British were trying desperately to build up, once again, the defenses around Tobruk, but supplies were not getting through. Between June 10 and 16, German subs sank six ships trying to get supplies through to Tobruk. On June 16, a whole convoy was forced to turn back for fear of the German subs. The next day, Axis forces reached the sea east of Tobruk, encircling that stronghold once again. They also captured Gambut airfield, Tobruk's main airfield. Inside the Tobruk ring were the 2nd South African Division, the British 201st Guards Brigade, the 11th Indian Infantry Brigade, and the 32nd British Tank Brigade. South African General Klopper was in command.

Rommel wanted no strong enemy force to the rear this time as he had in November so he mustered all of his forces and, on June 20, launched an all-out attack on the city. The fighting was constant and deadly for 48 hours. A weak British relief attack failed, and on the afternoon of June 21, the Tobruk garrison surrendered. All of the British units inside the Tobruk ring, including the 2nd South African Division, were destroyed as fighting forces. Some 33,000 British troops became POWs and the Axis forces acquired 2,000 tons of fuel, 5,000 tons of rations and 2,000 vehicles. Included as German captives were several thousand askaris who were members of the British Pioneer forces.

The British, South Africans, and Indians surrendering at Tobruk.

SPIRIT OF THE "PARIS PROTOCOL" REVIVED

On the evening of June 21, after news of the fall of Tobruk had been received at Vichy, Pierre Laval, who was once again Prime Minister, went on French radio and boldly stated that Germany would win the war. Although he did not say it in so many words, Laval's message was clear; France must be prepared to collaborate with the New Order in Europe, as it had been at the time of the Paris Protocol in May 1941.

With only weakened British forces now opposing him to the east, Rommel sent his fastest unit, the 90th Light Division, in pursuit. Within 24 hours they had crossed the Egyptian border and, once again, were approaching Sidi Barrani, 100 miles inside Egypt.

Into Berlin and Rome came messages of congratulations from Tokyo on the capture of Tobruk and suggestions that a linkup between the European Axis nations and the Japanese might now be seriously considered. The Germans were not too enthusiastic about such talk and diplomatically told the Japanese that there were many more victories to be won before plans for a linkup could be seriously considered.

In Cairo, the Egyptian government remained defiantly silent with regard to the events happening on its western border. This was the third Axis invasion of Egypt in two years and still the Egyptian government did not declare war on Germany or Italy.

General Auchinleck now lost confidence in Ritchie, especially after the disastrous ambush of Black Saturday, and had him removed from field command of the British 8th Army on June 25. Auchinleck, himself, flew to the front and took command.

On the other side of the line, Germany acquired a new field marshal, Irwin Rommel. His promotion came through directly from Hitler on June 26.

In Washington, Roosevelt and Churchill were meeting once again and the fall of Tobruk was tragic news to them. Roosevelt, wanting desperately to do what he could to help, promised Churchill that 300 new American-made "Sherman" tanks and 100 self-propelled artillery pieces would be sent off to North Africa as soon as possible.

Meanwhile, Rommel's tanks surged on, past Sidi Barrani, to Mersa Matruh, 175 miles to the east. There they were stopped, but not for long, by a huge mine field and a strengthened British defense line defended by the X Corps. On June 26, the Axis troops forced their way through the mine field, swung around the southern end of the British defense line, and by the evening of the 27th had the bulk of the X Corps encircled with their backs to the sea. The next day, however, the British defenders broke out of the Mersa Matruh trap and headed rapidly to the east and the next defense line at El Alamein 115 miles away. The breakout was costly. Some 8000 British troops were captured. Rommel's tanks again followed in hot pursuit and on June 29 reached a point fifteen miles from El Alamein. At this point they were only 95 miles from the huge British military base at Alexandria, and the deepest yet that Axis forces had penetrated into Egypt. But the Axis forces were, by now, exhausted, badly depleted, and in need of rest.

EL ALAMEIN AN EXCELLENT DEFENSIVE POSITION

El Alamein was an excellent natural defensive position because forty miles south of the Mediterranean coast was the Qattara Depression. This is a natural below-sea-level desert basin with steep cliffs all along its northern edge which are impassible, at most places, for tanks. Therefore, the southern end-around flanking movements that typified the fighting in North Africa would not work here. The British had only a forty mile-long front to defend and knew that the Axis forces would have to make costly frontal assaults to penetrate it.

A thousand miles to the rear, Mussolini arrived at Tripoli. He had flown in from Rome with his new white marshal's uniform and favorite white horse in preparation for his triumphal entry into Cairo. In the Axis scheme of things, Egypt was to become an Italian protectorate with the Italians virtually stepping into the shoes of the British. Then, after the linkup in the Middle East of the Axis forces from North Africa with Axis forces coming down from the north, the next Axis campaign would be into southern Egypt, up the Nile, to conquer the remainder of Egypt, The Sudan, and reconquer Italian East Africa. Indeed, Hitler saw the same possibility. On June 30, he issued a directive that planning should begin for the linkup in the Middle East with Axis forces which would march down from Bulgaria, through Turkey (with or without Turkey's permission) and into the Levant to meet Rommel's North Africa force somewhere in Palestine. That directive was issued the day Rommel's forces reached the British defenses at El Alamein.

At this time Axis planes intensified their bombing of Alexandria and some of the British warships left for safer harbors to the east such as Port Said, Haifa and Beirut. Port facilities at Alexandria were prepared for demolition if necessary.

In their euphoria, however, neither Mussolini nor Hitler could see that Rommel's forces were not capable of going on. His forces were literally worn out, and he had only 55 German and 70 Italian operable tanks left. Yet, if—and it was a big "if"—his forces could punch through the El Alamein defenses British resistance in Egypt might come down like a house of cards. From Rommel's point of view it was worth a try. So, on July 1, he sent all 55 of his tanks forward into the British defenses in hopes of effecting a breakthrough. It did not work. The British defenses held. In a crucial battle at a defensive point known as Deir el-Shein, the 1st South African Division stopped the German 90th Light Division in its tracks, and the 18th Indian Infantry Brigade blocked the rest of the Afrika Korps. No one knew it at the time, but this was the deepest penetration the Axis forces would make into Egypt, and it cost Rommel eighteen of his 55 German tanks. Furthermore, Rommel lost, at this time, one of his primary sources of intelligence when the American embassy in Cairo changed its Black Code, the diplomatic code that the Axis had been reading.

As the battle at Deir el-Shein raged on July 1, Axis planes bombed Haifa, Palestine in preparation for the linkup that would never come about. The next day, July 2, the British mustered enough of a force to counterattack around Rommel's southern flank and forced his whole line to retreat a short distance. On July 3, the Ariete Division, Rommel's best Italian armored division, attacked positions held by the New Zealanders and it became a disaster for the Italians. All but five of Ariete's tanks were put out of action. On July 4, the 9th Australian Division arrived in Egypt and were rushed to the front. On the other side of the line Rommel could not count on similar reinforcements. He knew the time had come to halt his offensive. The British counterattacked one more time and it cost him another German tank. Rommel was now facing a serious shortage of ammunition. Therefore, he withdrew his German forces, placed Italian troops on the front and began to rebuild. Auchinleck, too, decided it was time to rebuild and began to do likewise on his side of the line.

THE AMERICAN AIR FORCE IN EGYPT

While the bloody battles were being fought in Libya and Egypt, the American Air Forces (AAF) was moving onto airfields in Egypt with new B-24 heavy bombers. These magnificent airplanes could carry large bomb loads for long distances and were capable of penetrating deep into the Balkans and the Middle East. Their first target was the Ploesti oil fields of Romania, the main source of petroleum for all of the European Axis Powers. The first B-24 raid on Ploesti came on June 12. It was costly, but did substantial damage. Other raids would follow.

In another development regarding American aircraft, unassembled P-40 fighter planes were now being received at Massawa, Eritrea by freighter and sent to the American-operated aircraft maintenance facility at Gura, Eritrea. There they were assembled and most of them sent on to Egypt.

The Egyptian government was less than pleased with the presence of the AAF on Egyptian soil, believing that it gave the Axis Powers yet another reason to attack targets in Egypt. But, the Anglo/Egyptian military treaties permitted Britain's allies to operate in Egypt and there was little the Egyptian government could do about it.

TROUBLE IN CAIRO

To his rear Auchinleck had other problems to deal with—in Cairo. As Rommel's forces moved deeper into Egypt, anti-British nationalists became emboldened. Egyptian college students openly demonstrated in favor of the Germans and the secret anti-British clique in the Egyptian Army made plans to support Rommel's drive on the city. Within this group was a future President of Egypt, Anwar Sadat. To add to the problem, many of the openly pro-British Egyptians fled the city for Palestine. The trains to Palestine were jammed.

On Wednesday, July 1, the day of Rommel's attack, the British embassy staff in Cairo began burning many of their secret papers. The smoke and ash coming from the embassy was very noticeable and the locals dubbed it "Ash Wednesday." From the Finnish embassy in Cairo (Finland was a German Ally fighting the Soviet Union) came reports that, in the opinion of their observers on the scene, 80% of the Egyptian people were anti-British. This is not surprising considering what had happened in Cairo in February.

EGYPT THE PAWN

In early February 1942, twenty-two year old King Farouk had sensed that it was very possible that the Axis forces might conquer Egypt and, at that time, took the unilateral action of dismissing the Prime Minister the British had forced upon him, Hassan Sabry. Farouk then appointed his own trusted advisor, Ali Maher, in Sabry's place. This was the second time Maher had been appointed Prime Minister by the King so far in the war. Maher had been hastily recalled from his ambassadorial post in Washington where he had been exiled the year before then the British had maneuvered Sabry into the Premiership. Farouk's motive was that Maher, who was absolutely loyal to him, would be more acceptable to the Axis Powers and reflect Farouk's well-known pro-Axis and anti-British sentiments.

The British saw this move as a neo-rebellion by the King and his entourage and would have none of it. On February 4, they took firm action. British Ambassador Lampson called upon the King while at the same time British troops and tanks surrounded the palace. Lampson demanded that Farouk dismiss Maher and appoint Mustafa al-Nahas, head of the Wafdist Party, as Prime Minister. If he did not Lampson made it clear that he, the King, would be removed. Under the circumstances Farouk complied. Al-Nahas, from the British viewpoint, was something of a fair compromise. He had, only recently, made anti-British statements, but he was a popular politician and commanded the respect of the people. The British now gambled that by maneuvering al-Nahas into the Premiership, he would become more supportive of them and that the Egyptian people would follow his lead and continue their tacit support of the British war effort, or at the least, not hinder it. This, as it turned out, was a major miscalculation by the British. The Egyptian people and most of their leaders deeply resented the strong-arm tactics used by the British. Pictures of British troops and tanks surrounding the King's palace appeared all over Egypt and the people were humiliated. In the near term, and for the remainder of the war, it would cause major consequences for the British. This was the second time during the course of the war that the British had forced Farouk to appoint a Prime Minister of their choice under threats of a forced abdication.

Farouk soon came to realize that he had won a victory of sorts over the British. As it became apparent that the Egyptian people and their leaders were turning against the British he became the hub around which all Egyptian politics now began to revolve.

The British soon realized this too, but the die was cast and they had to live with it. As long as Farouk remained on the throne, the British knew they would have their problems in Egypt, but to force his removal, with the attitude of the people building against them, was now unthinkable because of the political destabilization that might follow.

Ironically, the Axis Powers, too, wanted to see Farouk remain on the throne, but their fear was that the British might try to kidnap him as Axis forces approached Cairo. Therefore, German agents made contact with Farouk and offered him plans whereby he could be whisked to safety, on short notice, to Rommel's headquarters or to German-occupied Crete in the event a British kidnapping became imminent. Farouk thanked the Germans but rejected the offers, saying he planned to go into hiding if the British made any attempts against his person.

In yet another effort to strengthen Farouk's hand, the Axis propagandists refrained from attacking the British-installed al-Nahas government. The Axis Powers, of course, wanted a stable Egyptian government in place, able to keep order, when they marched into Cairo.

On July 3, 1942, Germany and Italy issued a joint statement on the coming occupation of Egypt. It read:

> *"At the time when their victorious armed forces are marching forward across Egypt, the Axis states reaffirm their decided intention to respect and ensure the independence and sovereignty of Egypt. The armed forces of the Axis are entering Egypt not as into an enemy land, but for the purpose of expelling the English from Egyptian territory and in order to continue military operation against England and to liberate the Near East from British rule.*
>
> *The policies of the Axis powers are guided by the principle: Egypt for the Egyptians."*

Here again the above declaration was not all it might appear to be. Upon close examination it did not refer to "complete independence and full sovereignty" as did a similar declaration earlier in the year with regard to Iraq. Nor did it refer to the aspirations of most Egyptian leaders to extend Egyptian control over The Sudan.

In reality, there was little the Egyptians could do to help themselves. One way or the other, Egypt would remain a pawn of the great powers.

On the day the joint statement was made by the Axis Powers, Rommel had some unusual visitors at his field headquarters. They were members of the secret, underground "Egyptian Liberation Movement" who had come to offer their services to Rommel once he reached Cairo.

The Egyptian nationalists, and others of the same ilk, were playing a complex, and rather naive political game hoping to use Germany as a counterbalance to Italy's intentions for Egypt. The Egyptian nationalists knew, of course, that the Axis plans called for Egypt to become an Italian protectorate, but they still held out hope that Germany could, somehow, prevent this from happening or, perhaps, lessen Italy's control.

In the political atmosphere of the times, and considering the plans that both Germany and Italy had for building empires, the Egyptian nationalists were chasing an impossible

FAROUK AS A CALIPH

In the Moslem world, a "caliph" is an individual who is recognized as the successor to Mohammed himself, and has full religious and political powers assigned to him according to the Koran. Very few men have been recognized as caliphs, but King Farouk hoped to be one of them. It was obvious that the British would never recognize Farouk in such a manner, but there were indications that the Axis Powers might. This was yet another reason why Farouk was drawn toward the Axis camp. One problem would have to be reckoned with, though. Several years earlier Mussolini had proclaimed himself "Protector of Islam." At this point in time it was not clear just how a Protector of Islam differed from a caliph.

Years later, in May 1952, Faruok proclaimed himself a caliph and took the title El Sayed. Two months later he was overthrown by a military coup and forced to leave the country.

dream. Egypt's strategic location in North Africa and the presence of the Suez Canal predetermined in the minds of the Axis leaders, as it had in the minds of the Allied leaders, that this vital part of the globe could not be left in the hands of the politically unstable and militarily weak Egyptians.

AXIS PLANS FOR OCCUPIED EGYPT

Up to now the Germans and Italians had given little attention to the details of occupying Egypt, but now, in early July, they addressed that issue in a series of negotiations conducted between officials in Berlin and Rome. It was agreed that generally, Italy would take charge of the civil administration of the country while the Germans would control the military occupation, at least in the early stages.

For the civil administration, a "Delegato Politico" (Political Delegate) would be appointed and the Germans would appoint a high-ranking German military officer as liaison to work with him. Count Serafino Mazzolini, Italy's last ambassador to Egypt, was selected as the "Delegato Politico."

Then after the final Axis victory, and when the Italians would be in control of most of the Middle East and East Africa, the occupation of Egypt would become a great opportunity for Rome to prove to the Arab populations of the world that Italy could be a benevolent master and would create an economically vibrant, culturally secure, and peaceful land for the Arab people. In this manner, Mussolini would make good his claim to be the Protector of Islam.

King Farouk would remain on the throne and the country would be considered independent. Ali Maher would become premier again, and almost all of the existing governmental structure would remain intact. Egypt, though, would be obligated to sign a number of treaties with Italy, much on the order of those which she had signed with the British, to insure that the Italians would have the final say in almost all matters of importance.

As for the Suez Canal, the Italians would take complete control of it and operate it much like the British had done.

On July 3, 1942, the Italian government, with the approval of the Germans, formed an economic organization which would be the backbone of Italian rule in Egypt, the "Cassa Mediterranea di Credito par l'Egitto." The "Cassa Mediterranea" would have the authority to issue script in the initial stages of the occupation with a value of 72.5 lire and 9.5 Reichmarks respectively to the Egyptian pound. Script would be redeemable at some undetermined future date.

As for the issue of war booty in Egypt, which included anything of value including Egypt's great store of antiquities, the Germans and Italians could not come to an agreement. The Germans proposed that such booty should belong to the country whose troops captured it. This gave the Germans an advantage because their military units were more mobile than the Italian's units and in any race to gobble up tombs and temples the Germans would win. The Italians objected to this and proposed that Germany should be the recipient of all war booty in the Soviet Union, where Italian troops were also fighting, but that Italy be the recipient of all booty found in Egypt. Berlin objected to this, and the issue remained unresolved.

One of the first problems the Italians could see was that occupied Egypt would need a large and steady supply of food. In Greece, which was now under Italian occupation, terrible food shortages had developed and the Arab world was well aware of it. Rome did not want this to happen in Egypt. In this regard the Italians turned to the Germans for help in obtaining food. Lengthy negotiations followed, but the end result was that Hitler rejected the concept of Germany sending food to Egypt to make the Italians look good. The Italians would have to build the Arab "paradise" in Egypt on their own.

As for Egypt feeding itself, this was unlikely. Thousands of acres of cotton-growing land had already been converted to the growing of food, and it was not enough. To put more cotton land into food productions would reduce one of Egypt's main cash crops and possibly cause serious problems in the country's economy. Here the problem rested—to be dealt with after Egypt was conquered.

THE AUSTRALIANS AND ULTRA

At El Alamein, Auchinleck had two new powerful weapons, the newly-arrived, well-equipped, and well-trained Australian 9th Division and increasingly reliable intelligence information from London as the result of Ultra. Ultra told him that Rommel had gone on the defensive at El Alamein and, as he had done before, put the Italian infantry divisions in the front lines in order to withdraw his armored divisions to the rear for rest and refitting. Auchinleck, thus, saw an opportunity. On July 10, he sent the 9th Australians, with all the air and artillery support he could muster, smashing into the Italian defenses. The battle lasted for two days and the Italian Sabrath Division, guarding the northern end of the front, was completely routed. Rommel had to throw his exhausted armored units into the breach to hold the line. Elsewhere the line held, but the Italian losses were high.

On July 15, Auchinleck struck again, this time in the south. In another two-day battle the British routed both the Italian Brescia and Pavia Divisions, and once again the Germans had to rush forward to plug the hole. A lull then fell over the battlefield.

Back in Tripoli, Mussolini finally gave up waiting for Cairo to fall and flew back to Italy on July 20. Besides, he was suffering from a nasty case of dysentery which he picked up in Tripoli.

On July 21, Auchinleck struck at the Axis defenses again with tanks and infantry, but the attack collapsed in confusion.

Then on the night of July 26, Auchinleck tried a night

Churchill meets in Cairo with his leading military men in Africa and the Middle East. Left to right, standing: General Arthur W.T. Tedder (RAF); General Alan F. Brooke, Chief of Imperial General Staff; Admiral Sir Henry Harwood, Commander of the Royal Navy in the Mediterranean; Baron Richard G. Casey, British Minister of State Resident in the Middle East. Seated left to right: Smuts, Churchill, Auchinleck, Wavell.

attack at the northern end of the line. But in the darkness the armor and infantrymen became confused and disoriented, and that attack, too, fell apart. With this the British commander decided to call off his attacks and await reinforcements, which he knew were coming. He was also awaiting a new field commander, Lieutenant General W.H.E. Gott.

Auchinleck was fairly secure in knowing by now that the Axis forces were weak and exhausted, and their drive on Alexandria and Cairo had been stopped. This series of battles would go down in the history books as the "First Battle of El Alamein." In October, there would be the "Second" battle.

THE AIR WAR CONTINUES

While the ground armies rested and rebuilt after the "First Battle of El Alamein," air operations continued to be very active on both sides. The Allies continued their steady air campaign against the Axis supply lines and on August 1, Axis planes bombed British installations in the Cairo area. Two weeks later more American bombers arrived and joined in the attacks on the Axis supply lines and bombed Axis positions on the El Alamein front.

During the summer, the RAF in North Africa received model II D Hurricane fighters equipped with two 40 mm cannons. These planes were specially built as tank destroyers. Furthermore, the RAF in North Africa was receiving model "VB" Spitfire fighter planes that were better in air-to-air combat than any fighter the Germans or Italians had in the region.

The Allies also had a third and forth air force adding their weight to the air campaign; they were the SAAF and the Australian Air Force. With this increased air strength the Allies were able to gain air superiority over North Africa during August and September.

BACK AT EL ALAMEIN

On August 2, Rommel became very ill and asked to be relieved of command. Hitler refused. The Desert Fox had to carry on as best he could, even from his sick bed.

On August 5, Prime Minister Churchill, on his way to Moscow, paid a secret and hasty visit to the El Alamein front with a host of dignitaries and photographers. After he was safely back at Cairo, his visit was announced and the photographs published. The message was clear. The El Alamein front was so strong that the British Prime Minister could visit it safely and mix with the men in the trenches. Churchill was impressed with the troops in the field, but not so with Auchinleck. That evening he wired Clement Attlee, Secretary of State for the Dominions in London that a replacement for Auchinleck must be found.

On August 7, tragedy struck the British command when General Gott was killed in a plane crash the day after his appointment. The post was then given to Lt. General Bernard Montgomery. As for Auchinleck, Churchill selected General Sir Harold Alexander to be his replacement. Auchinleck would be reassigned to command the Iraq-Iranian sector of the Middle East.

Churchill talks to British tank crews telling them of the American-made Sherman tanks that are being shipped to them.

THE SEA WAR IN THE MEDITERRANEAN CONTINUES

In the Mediterranean, the contest for control of the sea proceeded as before, still with neither side becoming dominant. The British continued to batter the Axis convoys, and the German and Italian subs continued to do likewise to the British. During July, an Italian sub sank one Allied merchant ship and German subs sank three, while British subs sank one German and two Italian merchant ships.

August was a bad month for the British Navy off the North African coast. On August 11 and 12, Axis subs and German aircraft successfully attacked a British convoy off the coast of Algeria and northern Tunisia, sinking several ships. On August 11, U-73 sank the small British aircraft carrier Eagle off Algiers and on the 12th, the Italian sub "Axum" sank two British light cruisers, the "Nigeria" and "Cairo," off eastern Algeria and a British cargo ship in the same area. Later that day, the Italian sub "Alagi" took yet another British light cruiser, the "Kenya," and another merchantman of northern Tunisia. Still that day, from the same convoy, the Italian sub "Dessie" sank two cargo ships while "Bronzo" sank another. German aircraft assisted in some of the sinkings. To round out the successful month, German subs sank a Canadian merchantman on August 17 off Cairo and a British cargo ship nine days later off Port Said.

On August 4, though, the Germans lost sub U-372 off Palestine to a force of British ships and aircraft. During the rest of the month, British subs sank eleven Italian and two German merchant ships and, on the 5th, off the coast of Tunisia, the Italian destroyer "Strale."

THE FIRST GUIDED MISSILE

On August 13, 1942, the Italians flew an unmanned, radio-controlled, bomb-laden SM 79 bomber from Sicily to the coast of Algeria with the hopes of crashing it into an Allied ship. The plane was guided by a companion plane sending it radio signals. The bomber fell short of its mark, but this unique approach of attacking the enemy represented the first use of a guided missile in the war.

During September, surprisingly, there was no significant action along the North African coast by either German or Italian subs. There was, however, Axis sub action in other parts of the Mediterranean. The British subs, though, kept up their attacks on the Axis African-bound convoys. During the month, they sank one German and six Italian merchant ships, a French blockade runner, and an Italian minesweeper.

BACK AT THE FRONT

On August 15, Auchinleck relinquished command of the British 8th Army to Alexander and his new field commander, General Montgomery. The latter had arrived on August 12. One of Montgomery's first moves was to bring up two divisions, the 44th Division and the 10th Armoured Division, from the Delta area and place them in the line at El Alamein.

On August 30, Rommel made a sudden and surprisingly strong attack on the southern end of the British defense line. His plan was to smash a hole in the British line and then rush through three highly mobile divisions all the way to the Nile River, bypassing Alexandria. They would occupy Cairo from the south and move on to cut the Suez Canal at Ismailia, and then march north to Port Said on the Mediterranean coast. This would close the Suez Canal to the Allies and provide a staging area for an Axis advance into Palestine.

CAIRO, AN OPEN CITY?

King Farouk and most of the other Egyptian leaders had long pleaded with the British that if the Axis Powers appeared poised to occupy Cairo that the British declare it an open city to spare it the destruction of war. The British remained noncommittal. Cairo might yet become a battle ground.

It was a desperate plan. Rommel had counted on receiving six shiploads of fuel and ammunition for this offensive. Only two of them got through. To reach the Suez Canal he would have to capture British fuel supplies along the way in order to keep going.

From Rommel's point of view this was an all-out effort to win the final battle for Egypt. He told his associates, "The decision to attack today is the most serious I have taken in my life. Either we reach the Suez Canal now, or else... ." But the British were strong—very strong. They stopped the drive in four days of very hard fighting and inflicted heavy losses on the Axis forces. Furthermore, Rommel was now even more short of fuel, because another tanker bringing the much-needed gasoline and diesel fuel to Tobruk was sunk by a British submarine as it entered the harbor. With the loss of this fuel Rommel had to postpone plans for another attack he had hoped to make later in September.

On September 2, Rommel ordered a staged withdrawal in the south, but held on to about five miles of newly-won terrain. He expected a British counterattack, but it did not happen. Instead, the British attacked piecemeal over the next three days and failed each time. On September 6, Montgomery called off the attacks realizing that the enemy was still very strong. He began planning for an all-out effort which now appeared to be his only option. In the meantime, the RAF and other Allied air forces were ordered to intensify their attacks on the Axis positions and soften them as much as possible for the coming offensive.

Before launching an all-out offensive, Montgomery tried one more approach. On the night of September 13/14, with heavy covering support from the Royal Navy, British Commandos made an amphibious hit and run attack at Tobruk, which was now Rommel's primary port of supply. It was an utter failure and the surviving troops that landed had to be taken off the beaches. Two British destroyers were sunk in the operation. A similar operation took place against Barce, 200 miles west of Tobruk, which was more successful in that several Axis aircraft were destroyed. At the same time, Montgomery tried a long-range, 500 mile, over-the-desert attack on Benghazi from Cufra Oasis in southeastern Libya, which was held by the Free French. This too failed. Despite the series of failed British attacks, Montgomery was praised in the British media for having stopped Rommel and saving Cairo. Montgomery's popularity rose rapidly with Churchill, the troops, and the British public.

AXIS PINCERS AND ALLIED PINCERS

Even though the Axis forces in Egypt were stalled, the Axis planners still hoped to conduct a giant pincers movement in the Middle East. This called for the Axis forces in Egypt to regain the initiative, drive on through Egypt and into Palestine, Trans-Jordan and Syria forming one arm of the pincers, while a powerful Axis force, forming the second arm, drove down from the Caucasus region or Turkey into Iran and Iraq for an eventual linkup.

Even though the southern arm of the pincers was stalled at El Alamein, the northern arm was still viable. During July, Axis forces had driven into the Caucasus and were advancing toward the Iranian border. At this point, they were 1,800 miles away from Rommel's forces. The advance through Turkey was still on the table, but Axis fortunes in the Soviet Union would have to improve considerably before enough troops could be found for this operation.

The other pincers being planned for the region, the Allied pincers, which was discussed at the Arcadia Conference in December 1941, was progressing as planned. This undertaking called for the invasion of French Morocco and Algeria, and a drive eastward into Tunisia and Libya in conjunction with a westward advance by the British 8th Army out of Egypt. The name of this undertaking had been changed from Operation Gymnast to "Operation Torch." On September 20, a target date had been set for the invasion; November 8. Three objectives were established by the Allied Joint Chiefs of Staff and were given to the planners at Norfolk House in London, who were planning the details of "Operation Torch."

Gymnast had included the possibility of an invasion of Dakar, but the Americans decided against it and the British agreed. Soviet Premier Joseph Stalin also thought little of the value of invading Dakar. When told of the pending Allied plans Stalin said of Dakar, "Dakar is all right, but where can you go from there?"

British and American forces were being gathered in England for the invasion of Algeria, and a large American force was gathering in the New York City and Chesapeake Bay areas of the United States for the invasion of French Morocco. Since the Americans had little experience fighting in desert conditions, the American contingent had gone through extensive training in the desert areas of southern California and western Arizona. American General Dwight D. Eisenhower had been assigned to command Operation Torch.

AXIS CONVOY TROUBLES

During September, Allied air power in the Mediterranean increased significantly with aircraft flying from both Egypt and Malta. This and the on-going attacks by the British Navy proved very detrimental to the Axis forces in North Africa. In repeated Allied air and naval attacks throughout the month, only one-third of the Axis cargo ships got through to North Africa. The Italians lost so many cargo vessels that by the end of September their merchant fleet was only one-third the strength it had been when Italy entered the war in June 1940.

To make matter worse, a large portion of the supplies that did get through were given to the weaker Italian units because of political arrangements between Rome and Berlin.

MONTGOMERY'S PLAN OF ATTACK

On September 14, Montgomery finalized his plan of attack on the El Alamein front, called "Operation Lightfoot," and submitted it to London. It called for two major and simultaneous attacks, a lesser one and a greater one. The lesser one would come in the south using one armored division and one infantry division of the 8th Corps, while the larger attack in the north would use two armored divisions of 30th Corps to clear a path through the extensive Axismine fields and open a hole in the Axis lines. Through that hole would then charge the two armored divisions of the 10th Corps and, hopefully, cut the Axis supply lines in the rear. After that, the course of the battle would be determined by the initial results. To avoid the terrible heat of the daylight hours the attack would begin at night under a full moon. Late October was set for the launch date.

When Churchill saw the Lightfoot plan he approved it but asked that the launch date be moved up to the end of September. He was in political trouble in the Parliament and needed a victory to strengthen his position. Both Alexander and Montgomery talked him out of it and the late October date was retained.

On September 23, Rommel, who was still ill and suffering from high blood pressure and a liver ailment, left for

Europe to seek medical treatment. He had also scheduled personal interviews with both Mussolini and Hitler to ask for more men and supplies. Only Hitler promised to help but, as circumstances turned out, he was unable to do so. Left in charge in North Africa was Rommel's deputy, General George Stumme.

On September 30, the British launched a probing attack in the south to test the Axis defenses there using two brigades of the 44th Division. The attack was repulsed with heavy losses, proving that the Axis defenses were strong. With this, in addition to new intelligence information indicating that the Axis mine fields were more extensive than first thought, Montgomery changed his attack plans. In the main effort in the north, both the 10th and 30th Corps would attack together rather than one at a time.

JAPAN THREATENS FROM THE EAST

The entry of Japan into the war in December 1941, brought a new threat to Africa from the Indian Ocean. As Japanese forces surged into Southeast Asia conquering Malaya, the Dutch East Indies, and Burma, they acquired a position on the eastern rim of the Indian Ocean which changed the balance of power there. As early as January 15, the Japanese submarine I-165 sank the first ship, the Indian freighter "Jalarajan," in the Indian Ocean off the coast of Sumatra. From that point on, the Japanese subs moved rapidly westward and within days were sinking ships in the area of the southern tip of India and waters off the large British Island colony of Ceylon. The Japanese subs remained active in the area during February and March, sinking about a dozen more Allied ships.

In late February Tokyo informed Berlin and Rome that they intended to acquire military bases on both Ceylon and Madagascar. To do so on Ceylon meant a military invasion, whereas bases on Madagascar might be acquired through negotiations with the Vichy French in a similar manner in which bases had been acquired a year earlier from Vichy in French Indo-China (Viet Nam, Laos, Cambodia). All this news was received with mixed feelings in Berlin, even though the German naval leaders had, in December, welcomed the concept of Japanese bases on Madagascar. The German naval leaders, however, did not speak for the German government, and there were those close to Hitler who were opposed to this move by Japan. Most certainly, Japan was violating the gentlemen's agreement of January 18, 1942—an agreement that the Japanese had suggested—dividing their respective spheres of influence in the Indian Ocean by the 70th east Meridian. Ceylon was within the Japanese sphere but Madagascar was as far west as the 45th east Meridian. Critics in Berlin felt that Japan had designs on other parts of Africa and/or possibly the Middle East, especially in the oil-rich Persian Gulf area. On the other hand, proponents of the Japanese plan argued that the presence of Japanese submarines, surface vessels, and aircraft in Madagascar would aid Germany, in that the Japanese would be in a position to interdict Allied sea traffic coming up from the southern tip of Africa supplying both North Africa and the Middle East. Furthermore, German vessels operating in the Indian Ocean could also make use of the Japanese-operated Madagascar bases. The proponents for cooperating with Japan pointed out that it was very unlikely that the European Axis Powers and Japan would be able to establish a land linkup across the vast and rugged terrain of central Asia; a linkup by sea was very possible if and when the European Axis Powers reached the northern coast of the Indian Ocean via the Persian Gulf, the Arabian Peninsula, or East Africa. Hitler contemplated both arguments and decided to take a wait-and-see attitude. In the meantime the Japanese would have their way.

During February 1942 Japanese propagandists directed their attention to the Indian Ocean area, stating that Japan had every intention of expanding its influence into that area. Much of the propaganda was directed toward India, urging the Indians to sever their ties with Britain and join Japan in the new order she was establishing in Southeast Asia. That new order, which the Japanese called "The Greater East Asia Co-prosperity Sphere," called for lands like India, Burma, Ceylon, the Dutch East Indies, and other former colonies to break away from their old colonial masters, become independent with the help of Japan, and cooperate with Japan in setting up an East Asian economic bloc which would be beneficial to all concerned. This message of independence had an effect in every land into which it was broadcast, including areas in Africa, even though the Japanese propagandists did not, necessarily, target Africa.

Behind the scenes the Japanese government asked the German government for its approval and support in establishing military bases on Madagascar, provided the Vichy French would agree. Hitler finally concluded that a Japanese presence on Madagascar would be beneficial to Germany, so he approved the Japanese plans. He did not, however, offer political or military support.

Also at this time, the Japanese naval leaders asked their counterparts in the German Navy for up-to-date maps and other information they might have on Ceylon. This, of course, would facilitate a Japanese invasion of the island. The Germans complied and sent what they had.

In the United States, President Roosevelt alerted the American people to the dangers building in the Indian Ocean when he went on radio on the evening of February 23, 1941, in another of his Fireside Chats. Roosevelt said that it was very possible that Japan might "...immediately extend her conquests... toward India, and through the Indian Ocean to

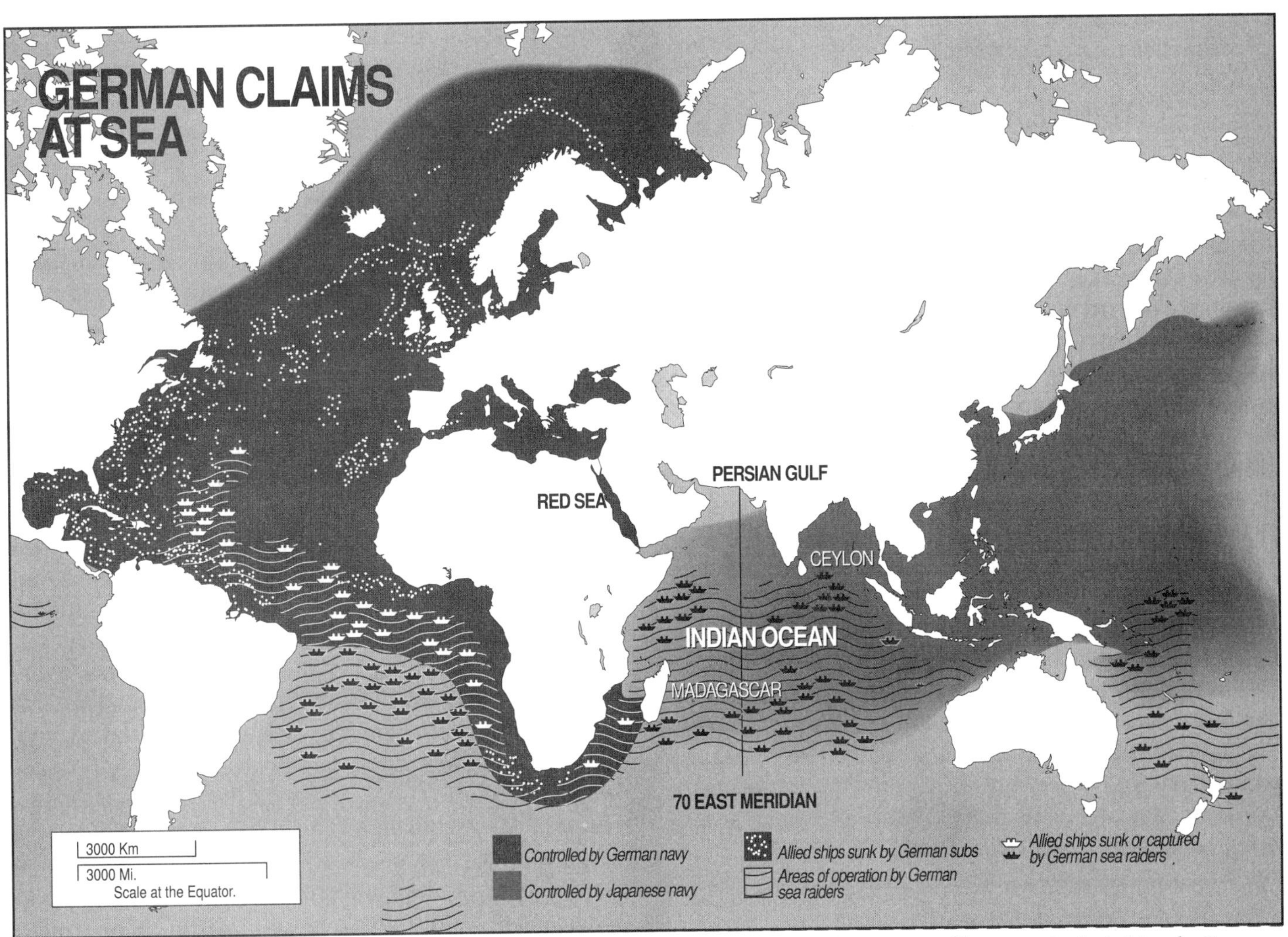

This map, published in the German picture magazine Signal in early 1943, shows the Axis division of the Indian Ocean. The northern part of the Indian Ocean was to come under Japanese control while the central portion, shown by the wavy lines and little ships, was under joint German and Japanese control. Note that the Red Sea and Persian Gulf are not included in the Japanese area. The little ships represent an exaggerated number of German raiders, supply vessels, and blockade runners in the Indian Ocean. The small white dots in the Atlantic represent Allied ships already sunk by the German Navy. This was not exaggerated.

Africa, to the Near East and try to join forces with Germany and Italy." Roosevelt went on to warn about possible disaster in North and West Africa, saying, "...if we were to stop sending munitions to the British and the Soviets in the Mediterranean, in the Persian Gulf, and the Red Sea (via the Indian Ocean) we would be helping the Nazis to overrun Turkey, Syria, Iraq, Persia (Iraq), Egypt, and the Suez Canal, the whole coast of North Africa itself... and the whole coast of West Africa, putting Germany within easy striking distance of South America."

A GERMAN/JAPANESE LINKUP

In early March 1942, Admiral Raeder, Commander of the German Navy, presented Hitler with an ambitious plan to link up with the Japanese by sea. Raeder's plan presupposed the conquest of the Suez Canal and the Middle East, whereby Germany would have access to the Red Sea and the Persian Gulf. The plan called for the German Navy to establish powerful units in these areas and, together with the Japanese, gain control of the waters of the northern part of the Indian Ocean. This would allow sea trade to be carried on with the Japanese in a mutually beneficial arrangement. Hitler studied the plan and filed it away for future reference. As with most everything else in Germany, Raeder's plan depended on the military outcome in the Soviet Union. A short time later, in early March, Raeder again asked Hitler to put pressure on Vichy to allow the establishment of Japanese bases on Madagascar. So far this had not been done. Despite his commitment to cooperate with Japan, Hitler was still taking a wait-and-see attitude toward Madagascar.

Japan's interests in the Indian Ocean were not kept secret from the German public. On the contrary, it was a powerful propaganda tool to show the cooperation enjoyed between Germany and her Japanese ally.

JAPANESE LEADERS DISAGREE OVER FURTHER EXPANSION

Unbeknownst to the rest of the world, there was a controversy going on within the Japanese high command over whether or not to invade Ceylon and extend Japanese influence to Madagascar as opposed to using those military resources elsewhere. The invasion of Ceylon and the acquisition of bases on Madagascar had not been in the original Japanese plans of conquest. But, the conquest of Southeast Asia had gone so smoothly that the Japanese naval leaders now promoted the idea that the parameters of the original plan could, and should, be expanded. The Japanese Army leaders had interests elsewhere, mainly in Siberia in the event that the Soviet Union collapsed, and argued against expansion in the Indian Ocean. The Army leaders had the upper hand on this issue because without army troops there could be no invasion of Ceylon.

The Japanese naval leaders, nevertheless, decided to proceed on their own and hopefully destroy the British Navy in the Indian Ocean in the same manner in which they had destroyed the American Navy in the Pacific. This would protect the western perimeter of the newly-won empire, just as the destruction of the American Navy had protected the eastern perimeter. The bulk of the British Navy's Indian Ocean fleet was based at Ceylon, therefore, that island was the next target for the Japanese Navy.

In late March, a naval task force of four battleships, five aircraft carriers, three cruisers, and nine destroyers was assembled and set sail for the Indian Ocean. Their first objective was to attack the large British naval base at Colombo, Ceylon's capital and largest city.

ALLIED ACTIONS IN THE INDIAN OCEAN

On March 10, 1942, all Allied forces fighting in the Dutch East Indies surrendered to the Japanese. Remnants of the Dutch East Indies colonial fleet escaped to the west and reached Mombasa, Kenya safely. Several of the ships were turned over to the Royal East African Navy (REAN) for local use. They included several harbor craft and two minesweepers, which were subsequently manned by Kenyan crews.

Allied air defenses out of East Africa were getting stronger thanks to the arrival of several dozen American-made "Catalina" flying boats through Lend-Lease. These long-range aircraft, piloted mostly by British Commonwealth crews, including many Canadians, carried bombs and depth charges and were perfectly capable of sinking enemy submarines. Their presence in the region made the heavily-travelled waters of East Africa and the Mozambique Channel considerably safer for Allied shipping.

CEYLON ATTACKED

The British had intelligence information that a powerful Japanese fleet was about to attack Ceylon and, on April 4, sent their main battle force, stationed at Colombo, to sea in an effort to intercept the Japanese fleet. They found nothing and returned to Colombo during the night.

The next morning at dawn, 127 planes from the Japanese carriers "Akagi" and "Kaga" attacked the British base in an attack very similar to that which they had carried out at Pearl Harbor. Many of the Japanese airmen and sailors, including the Japanese commanders, Admiral Nobutaki Kondo (ships) and Admiral Chuichi Nagumo (aircraft), had participated in the Pearl Harbor attack.

The British were not well prepared and the island's small air force, with its obsolescent aircraft, was no match for the fast and modern Japanese planes. The cruisers Dorsetshire and Cornwall were caught by surprise at sea in the process of returning to base and rapidly sunk by the Japanese torpedo and dive bombers. A British merchant cruiser was also sunk at Colombo and extensive damaged was done to the port's facilities. The pitifully small Ceylonese Defense Force was rushed to the beaches in the Colombo area fully expecting an invasion, but it did not come. The Japanese fleet withdrew, refuelled at sea, and went on the hunt for commercial shipping off the coast of southern India and in the Bay of Bengal. This was an area of heavy sea traffic and the British had virtually no naval or air defenses in the area capable of dealing with such a powerful Japanese force. In addition to Nagumo's force a second Japanese task force consisting of the carrier "Ryujo" and six cruisers under Admiral Takeo Kurita was, at the same time, operating in the Bay of Bengal and also attacking Allied shipping. Together the two Japanese task forces sank 22 merchant vessels and a sloop of the Royal Indian Navy.

On April 9, Nagumo's fleet returned to Ceylon and attacked the other British base on the island at Trincomalee on the north side of the island. Again it was another Pearl Harbor-like attack and a disaster for the British. The aircraft carrier "Hermes" and Australian destroyer "Vampire" were caught at sea unprepared and sunk by the Japanese planes. The British hospital ship "Vita" was travelling with the "Hermes" and "Vampire" but was not attacked.

The Japanese planes went on to attack the Trincomalee naval base, sinking a corvette, two tankers, and damaging some of Trincomalee's port facilities. Again, the British on the island expected an invasion but it did not come. Instead, the Japanese fleet withdrew and disappeared into the vastness of the Indian Ocean.

News of the carnage wrought by the Japanese fleet at Ceylon spread throughout the Indian Ocean basin, and war jitters developed on every shore including Africa. The great fear was that the powerful Japanese fleet would now strike other places.

The British, after losing four warships at Ceylon, withdrew their remaining warships from the area, leaving the island virtually undefended. The British ships sailed for the safety of Addu Atoll in the Maldive Islands, 500 miles southeast of Ceylon, where a new and secret British naval and air base was being constructed. They then moved on to Mombasa, Kenya while still other ships headed for the Persian Gulf. The British Indian Ocean Fleet was still a formidable force consisting of three aircraft carriers, five old battleships, six British cruisers, two Dutch cruisers, fifteen destroyers and many smaller vessels, but the British wanted to avoid an all-out confrontation with the Japanese.

The Japanese fleet did not strike again in the Indian Ocean. It returned to Southeast Asia to assist in landings on New Guinea. There were, however, plans for the navy to return to the Indian Ocean and strike again. Madagascar was to be one of their objectives.

The political message of the events at Ceylon were not lost on the many nationalist groups in Africa, India, the Middle East and Southeast Asia. Here the British Navy, the most powerful navy in the world, had been defeated and scattered by the navy of a non-European nation and had withdrawn from the battle leaving their colonial subjects at the mercy of the attackers. The message was clear; the Europeans were not invincible and Britain was incapable of adequately defending its far-flung empire.

On April 15, Churchill expressed his alarm at events in the Indian Ocean, saying in a communique:

> *"Until we are able to fight a fleet action (in the Indian Ocean) there is no reason why the Japanese should not become the dominant factor in the Western Indian Ocean. This would result in the collapse of our whole position in the Middle East, not only because of the interruption of our convoys to the Middle East and India, but also because of the interruption of the (oil) supplies from Abadan (Iran) without which we cannot maintain our position either at sea or on land in the Indian Ocean area."*

THE DOOLITTLE RAIDERS BRING A RESPITE TO THE INDIAN OCEAN

Half a world away, on April 18, an American bomber force, commanded by General Jimmy Doolittle, came out of the emptiness of the western Pacific and bombed Tokyo and other cities in Japan. Damage was slight but the Japanese were startled that the Americans could pull off such a feat. The Japanese leaders in Tokyo concluded that if it could happen once, it could happen again. They also correctly deduced that the staging area for the American bombers had to have been the Hawaiian Islands. After careful consideration, the Japanese leaders made the decision that the Hawaiian Islands had to be invaded and conquered in order for Japan's eastern frontier to be secure. The conquest of the Hawaiian Islands would force the American warships and aircraft back to the North American mainland.

The invasion of Hawaii had not been within the original plans of conquest for the Japanese, but it had always been an option and plans had been prepared. Now, that option would be exercised. The Japanese plan called for the invasion and occupation of the Hawaiian Islands in three stages; 1) the occupation of Midway Island at the extreme western end of the island chain for use as an initial staging base, 2) the invasion of the big island of Hawaii to use as a larger staging area from which American defenses on Oahu would be militarily reduced and, 3) the invasion of Oahu and the remainder of the islands. It was hoped that, after receiving enough punishment from the Japanese forces, the Americans might abandon Hawaii as the British had abandoned Ceylon.

To conquer the Hawaiian Islands, the bulk of the Japanese fleet had to be used. Therefore, the ships that had participated in the Indian Ocean raids were recalled to Japan, resupplied, and added to the task force that would attack Hawaii. Future plans regarding the Indian Ocean area were put on hold.

In late April, Tokyo informed Berlin that Japan's primary objectives were now in the Pacific and not in the Indian Ocean. On May 2, and again on May 15, Tokyo informed Berlin further that an invasion of Ceylon was no longer being considered at this time. And accordingly, Japanese interests in Madagascar had waned.

ALLIED SHIPPING HALTED IN THE INDIAN OCEAN

The Allies had no way of knowing that the Japanese Navy had withdrawn from the Indian Ocean, and had to take steps to protect their interests in that vital part of the world. Besides, Japanese subs were still active in the Indian Ocean and had begun attacking Allied shipping off the west coast of India. As yet, though, no Japanese sub had been reported in East African waters.

The first step the British felt obliged to take was to stop virtually all commercial shipping in the Indian Ocean until convoys could be organized and aerial and naval defenses improved. As for the latter, the new British naval and air base at Addu Atoll in the Maldive Islands would be an important part. Two other air bases already existed in the island chain, and together they would provide a barrier to further Japanese advancement toward Africa. Also, aircraft and small ships, some of them Lend-Lease from America, were arriving weekly in East Africa and in British and Free French-held islands in the western Indian Ocean. It would not take long for Allied shipping to resume in these waters in convoys.

THE BRITISH CONCERN FOR MADAGASCAR

Even before the Japanese attacks on Ceylon, the British could see that Vichy-controlled Madagascar was vulnerable to attack by the Japanese. Their greatest fear was that Vichy would allow the Japanese to establish military bases on the island as they had allowed the Japanese to do in French Indo-china. Indeed, during February, Vichy hinted at this by announcing that it would not hesitate to ask the Japanese to help defend the island if it were attacked by the Allies. The British could see, too, that Japanese bases on Madagascar would be used by German submarines, raiders, and blockade runners.

Furthermore, reports were already being received by the British that Japanese subs were being refuelled and resupplied by the French at their naval base at Diego Suarez on the northern tip of the island, and that a Japanese military mission was on the island negotiating with the French for the use of the island's ports. These reports were false, but the British had no way of knowing it at the time.

Taking all of this into account, Churchill and his War Cabinet decided during March to preempt any Japanese moves toward Madagascar, and to occupy Diego Suarez as soon as possible, and the rest of the island at a later date, if and when it became necessary.

VICHY'S POSITION ON MADAGASCAR

In mid-April, the very pro-Axis Pierre Laval had again become premier of France at Vichy and promptly formed a new government that was more collaborationist than the one before. Soon afterwards, Laval ordered that all known de Gaulle sympathizers throughout the French Empire, including Madagascar, be arrested and imprisoned. He also decreed other measures of cooperation with the Axis Powers.

The end result of all this was that the Allies could see that Laval would, in all likelihood, give the Japanese and Germans anything they wanted with regard to Madagascar.

In the early months of 1942, the British did not have the military resources to occupy the 1,000 mile-long by 400 mile-wide island, but they did have enough strength, to occupy the seaport of Diego Suarez. That port had one of the best natural harbors in the world and was strategically located so that Allied planes and ships could give meaningful protection to Allied shipping throughout the western Indian Ocean. Furthermore, Diego Suarez would be relatively safe from a counterattack by the French since it was isolated from the rest of Madagascar; there were no roads connecting it with the more heavily populated areas of the island to the south. The only land connection with the south were tortuous foot trails that wound over mountains and through jungles.

The British believed that the Vichy forces on the island were relatively large and would probably resist an invasion. The majority of the French force, British intelligence had revealed, was made up of well-trained Senegalese troops from French West Africa who were very loyal to their French officers. A smaller contingent of the force comprised local Malagaches who were believed to be less reliable and aggressive than the Senegalese. The Malagache people, in general, were known to be peace-loving and non-aggressive.

Malagache troops doing morning calisthenics at the palace in Tananarive, the island's capital.

The British also knew that the French troops were armed adequately with small arms but lacked heavy equipment, armored vehicles, artillery, and many other items.

Furthermore, there was a modest French air force on the island and some submarines and small warships in the various ports.

British information on French troop strength was not all that accurate. The French had only 8,000 troops on the island, a relatively small force for such a large land mass, and two-thirds of them were Malagaches with the remaining one-third being Senegalese. Most of the Malagache troops were conscripts.

BRITISH OCCUPY DIEGO SUAREZ, MADAGASCAR

The date for the attack on Diego Suarez was set for May 5. This action would be carried out solely by British Army troops and ships of the Royal Navy. De Gaulle's Free French were not informed of the planned operation and not invited to participate because the British believed the Vichy French on the island would offer less resistance to an all-British force. This belief was based on their experiences at Dakar and in Syria. Furthermore, the Governor General of Madagascar, Armand Annet, was known to personally hate de Gaulle and be very loyal to Vichy. De Gaulle was very angry when eventually told of the operation, but could do nothing about it.

Governor General Armand Annet of Madagascar. He hated de Gaulle and was very loyal to Vichy.

In late March, the British troops left England for Madagascar in preparation for the attack on Diego Suarez now known as "Operation Ironclad." The landing force consisted of the British 29th Independent Brigade (which was trained in amphibious landings), the 13th and 15th Infantry Brigades of the British 5th Division (which were on their way to India), the British Number 5 Commando unit, and a detachment of Royal Marines. The total invasion force consisted of 13,000 men. Once Diego Suarez was secured, the British troops would be withdrawn and replaced by African troops as soon as possible.

Vichy intelligence had reported that British action against Madagascar was very likely, so Petain turned to the Japanese for help. He asked them to do what they could to defend the island. Although Japanese interest in the island was diminished, Tokyo agreed to study the situation.

The Ironclad force arrived at Durban during the third week in April, refuelled and resupplied and on April 25 a slow convoy left Durban heading for Diego Suarez. It was followed by a fast convoy that left on April 28. Escorting the convoys were the battleship "Ramilles," the British cruiser Hermione, the Dutch cruiser "Van Heemskerk," the aircraft carrier Illustrious, five assault ships, nine troop transports, and eleven destroyers, minesweepers and corvettes. The Illustrious had sailed to Durban directly from the United States where she had undergone repairs of damaged suffered in combat at Malta in January, 1941. Aboard were new American-made Grumman "Wildcat" fighters along with the antiquated, but still useful "Swordfish" bi-wing torpedo bombers. Most of the other ships had sailed from England and had been a part of the British Home Fleet until American ships arrived to replace them. En route the naval force had picked up some additional ships at Freetown. Due to an acute shortage of landing craft, assault ships, and troop transports, those vessels were to be withdrawn from the operation as soon as possible and sent on to Burma where the British were planning a landing at Akyab. Vice Admiral E. N. Syfret commanded the naval force, while Major General R. G. Sturges commanded the ground troops.

On the other side of the continent, the British blockade was strengthened at Dakar to prevent the French from sending reinforcements to Madagascar.

The two Diego Suarez-bound convoys came together on May 4 in the Mozambique Channel off Cape Amber. The day before, a second aircraft carrier, the "Indomitable," and two destroyers which had escaped from Ceylon, joined Syfret's force.

A second British naval force formed around a third aircraft carrier, "Formidable" took up a position east of Diego Suarez to guard against any interference from the Japanese.

From Mombasa, Kenya, several squadrons of planes from the SAAF stood ready to provide additional air support during the operation. The SAAF had already photographed the Diego Suarez area extensively from the air in preparation for the invasion. Those photographs were turned over to the British Navy. For the British Navy the invasion of Diego Suarez was a new and major undertaking because it represented the largest gathering of British amphibious forces since the Dardanelles Campaign of World War I.

Just after the British invasion force left Durban, it was spotted by the small reconnaissance plane from the Japanese sub I-30 which was operating in the area. This information was flashed to Tokyo, and the Japanese naval leaders correctly deduced that the British ships were headed for Diego Suarez. I-30 and four other Japanese subs working the western Indian Ocean were ordered to concentrate in the Diego Suarez area but, throughout the landing operation, they were unable to attack the British ships. Furthermore, the warning of the approaching British force never reached the Vichy commanders on Madagascar.

On the morning of May 5, at 4:30 a.m., the British forces landed on the Madagascar coast northwest of Diego Suarez, which was less heavily defended than the harbor entrance on the east coast. The French garrison on the northwest coast was taken completely by surprise. Six French officers and ninety Malagache troops were captured while still in bed. At 5:00 a.m. British aircraft flew over Diego Suarez and dropped leaflets demanding the surrender of the French garrison. The planes then attacked ships and installations in the harbor area sunk the French submarine "Beveziers," damaged a cargo ship and left a French sloop beached and burning.

The French commander at Diego Suarez, in response to the leaflets, went on local radio and announced that the French would fight as they had said they would all along.

After securing their beachhead, the British landing party marched inland toward Diego Suarez with the Commandos in the lead.

French officers and their askaris at Diego Suarez marching past a British guard of honor on their was to a POW camp.

As the British troops streamed ashore on Madagascar, London radio announced the invasion and assured the French people that Britain had no designs for acquiring Madagascar as a part of their empire and that Madagascar would remain French. London radio gave the primary reason for the invasion as the Japanese threat to the island.

Also during these first hours of the invasion, the British received some political help from the United States. As the invasion was underway, Washington sent an urgent message to Vichy stating that the American government approved of the British operation on Madagascar and warned the Vichy government not to resist the landing. It was of little value. The defenders of the island had long-standing orders to resist any invader, and they obeyed them.

The British tried the diplomatic approach at Diego Suarez a second time. As his ground force approached Diego Suarez, General Sturges sent a captured French officer ahead of the force with a message to the base commander to surrender and avoid bloodshed. The French commander refused and, from the officer and other sources, now had a good idea of the strength of the British force and the direction from which it was approaching.

Later that morning, the British lost their first ship, the corvette "Auricula," which struck a mine off the northwest coast of the island and later sank.

Meanwhile, to the east of Diego Suarez, a naval force built around the carrier Illustrious, had circled around the peninsula and approached the eastern shore, feinting a second amphibious landing. Illustrious's aircraft were launched and dropped dummy paratroopers along the eastern shore to draw away French troops from the west. Planes from both the Illustrious and Indomitable attacked the French airfield five miles south of the harbor; they destroyed most of the French aircraft on the ground.

Late in the day on May 5, the British advance on Diego Suarez was stopped by a strong French defense line backed up by artillery. The British could not reply in kind because their artillery had not yet been off-loaded from the landing ships. The next afternoon, the British artillery arrived and a renewed ground attack, supported by that artillery and aircraft, broke through the French defenses about 3:00 p.m. The British resumed their drive on the port.

That evening, just after dark, the British destroyer "Anthony" boldly sailed into Diego Suarez Harbor, pulled up to a wharf at Antsirene, the smaller seaport two miles across the harbor from Diego Suarez, and off-loaded a force of fifty British Marines. The French were taken by complete surprise and had no available forces to oppose them. The Marines quickly seized the French naval depot at Antsirene and its commander, then went on to capture the French artillery commanded at this command post. They also freed some fifty British POWs in a small POW camp in the area.

On the morning of May 7, the western force entered Diego Suarez against very light opposition and occupied parts of the town. That afternoon, at 3:00, the French commander surrendered the city. British losses were less than 100 dead and about 300 wounded. French losses were 650 dead and wounded.

On the eastern shore two harbor forts still held out. That afternoon, the British warships assembled offshore and bombarded the forts. Both forts promptly surrendered and the land battle for Diego Suarez ended.

During the afternoon of May 7, the French submarine "Heros," one of three French subs that were at sea when the attack began, attacked a British transport on the west side of the peninsula. Planes from the Illustrious quickly arrived on the scene and sank the Heros with depth charges.

On May 8, the Vichy submarine "Monge," which had been at sea, arrived off Madagascar and made an unsuccessful attack on the carrier Indomitable. Minutes later the sub was located by Indomitable's escorts and sunk. This was the third French submarine lost at Diego Suarez.

On May 13, the British troop transports and assault ships left Diego Suarez for Burma with the men of the British 5th Division. The 29th Independent Brigade and Commandos remained at Diego Suarez.

On May 29, an unidentified aircraft flew over Diego Suarez and was shot down and crashed at sea. The British feared it was a Japanese reconnaissance plane portending a Japanese attack from the east. The battleship Ramilles and several escorts were dispatched to investigate while British aircraft searched far out to sea. They found nothing. But the Japanese were planning an attack, one that could not be seen on the surface of the water.

The plane that overflew Diego Suarez and went down was, in fact, a Japanese reconnaissance plane from the submarine I-10. This sub was one of three Japanese submarines offshore, the others being I-16 and I-20. Together they were planning an attack on Diego Suarez harbor. I-20 carried a two-man, two-torpedo midget submarine which would be used in the attack. On the night of May 30, the midget submarine entered Diego Suarez Harbor undetected and managed to fire both torpedoes at the battleship Ramilles at close range. One torpedo hit the battleship, but the other hit the tanker "British Loyalty," which was leaving the harbor with a load of fuel oil and other cargo and sailed inadvertently into the path of the second torpedo. The Ramilles was badly damaged and the tanker burst into flames and sank quickly to the bottom of the harbor.

The Japanese midget sub then developed mechanical problems while trying to escape, so its two crewmen beached her inside the harbor and fled inland to hide and hope for a rescue. The beached submarine was soon discovered as were the presence of the crewmen. A fifteen-man Commando unit was sent immediately to capture the crewmen but the two Japanese sailors, armed with only a pistol and a sword, chose to fight rather than surrender. They were eventually killed by the Commandos but not before they killed one of the Commandos and wounded four others.

The next day, May 31, the reconnaissance plane from the Japanese sub I-10 overflew Diego Suarez unnoticed and reported on the damage done. The plane made a second fly-over on June 1, and that flight, too, went unnoticed by the British.

The attack by the Japanese midget sub was given wide publicity by the British and used as justification for the claim that the reason for the invasion of Diego Suarez, in the first place, was the threat from the Japanese.

The Ramilles was able to sail under her own power to Durban and then on to Plymouth, England where she was laid up for repairs for a lengthy period. She would not see action again until June 1944. The tanker British Loyalty was eventually raised, repaired, and put back into service, only to be sunk again in March 1944, by the German sub U-183 at the British naval base at Addu Atoll in the Maldive Islands.

Again, the British believed that the subs that attacked Diego Suarez had been refuelled by the French on the island, but this was not true. Actually, the Japanese subs were being supplied by two Japanese supply ships operating in the central Indian Ocean. In retaliation for the supposed refuelling by the French, bombers from the SAAF "Sugarcane" wing, which had moved onto the airfield at Diego Suarez, bombed several of Madagascar's seaports.

With the departure of the British aircraft carriers, Allied air operations at Diego Suarez were turned over to the SAAF. By now that air force as fairly well equipped. It was flying British-made "Beauforts," American-made "Marylands" and "Lodestars" and German-made Junker JU-52s.

All of the other British troops eventually left Diego Suarez, except the 29th Independent Brigade, and a brigade of KAR troops was brought in from British East Africa to serve as occupation troops.

MADAGASCAR AND POLITICS

The conquest of Diego Suarez was not undertaken purely for military purposes; there were considerable political questions involved, one the most important being that the British sorely needed a victory somewhere. In North Africa, the British 8th Army was in retreat as were the Soviets on the eastern front. Furthermore, the British had, in the preceding months, lost Hong Kong, Malaya, Singapore, Burma, and the other British possessions there to the Japanese while India, Ceylon, Australia, and New Zealand were still being threatened.

Another political consideration was that the loss of Diego Suarez would be a serious blow to the prestige of Vichy's newly appointed Premier, Pierre Laval.

Not surprisingly, when Diego Suarez was secured the British media hailed it as a great victory and a great blow to Vichy and the Japanese.

NEGOTIATIONS WITH TANANARIVE

With Diego Suarez firmly in their hands, the British began negotiations with French Governor General Annet in Tananarive, Madagascar's capital, for the surrender of the remainder of the island. Annet was firm in his loyalty to

Vichy and refused all offers. With this, the British weighed their options on whether or not to invade the remainder of Madagascar. From South Africa, Prime Minister Smuts, who favored the invasion, offered to supply a South African Army brigade for the effort. Churchill welcomed the offer and told Smuts that the brigade would be utilized if another invasion was decided upon. For the moment, though, the invasion of the rest of the island would not go forward.

From Vichy's perspective, the fact that the Free French had been excluded from the invasion provided fuel for Petain's propagandists. Vichy began broadcasting that the exclusion of the Free French was proof that the British intended to take over segments of the French Empire for themselves. The British responded by announcing again that they had no intention of annexing Madagascar to their empire, and that the Free French would eventually be given a role in administering the conquered area of Madagascar and in the liberation of the rest of the island. De Gaulle confirmed this by making similar public statements of his own.

At Diego Suarez, the low-level Vichy officials were asked to remain on their jobs, but they refused fearing that they would lose their pensions. Most of them indicated, though, that they would remain if "forced" to do so by the British. The British obliged.

OTHER ACTIONS IN THE INDIAN OCEAN

As the struggle for Diego Suarez was going on, the Japanese sub I-30 was working the Gulf of Aden area without much success. On May 7, she sent her float plane, undetected, over the British naval base at Aden to discover what ships were in the harbor. The next day, her plane flew further to the west and inspected the harbor at Djibouti. Again it was undetected. The results were disappointing. No major ships were in either harbor. I-30 then sailed down the coast and on May 19, sent her plane over Dar-es-Salaam—again undetected—and again finding no major ships in the harbor.

Also at this time, both German and Japanese disguised raiders were at work in the Indian Ocean preying on unsuspecting Allied ships. Two of the Japanese raiders, the "Aikoku Maru" and "Hodoku Maru" were operating off the east coast of Madagascar and on May 10, the Allied freighter "Genota" was sunk by one of the Japanese raiders. That same day the German raider Thor captured the Allied ocean liner "Nanking" in the eastern Indian Ocean and sent her, and her, passengers and crewmen off to internment in Japanese-held Southeast Asia. On June 5, the Japanese raiders struck again off Madagascar sinking the steamer "Elsia."

JAPANESE RECONSIDER CEYLON AND MADAGASCAR

As Rommel's forces pushed the British back in North Africa and other Axis forces plunged deeper into the Caucasus region of the Soviet Union, Tokyo revived the prospects for an east-west linkup in the Indian Ocean. On or about May 21, Tokyo informed Berlin that if the Germans took either the Suez Canal or moved south of the Caucasus into the Middle East, then Japan would reconsider occupying Ceylon. Along with this commitment came the understanding that Japanese interest in Madagascar would also be renewed.

JAPANESE SEND SUBMARINES TO HELP ROMMEL AND VICHY-HELD MADAGASCAR

During the first days of June 1942, the Japanese Navy sent the three subs that had attacked Diego Suarez, I-10, I-16, and I-20, along with a fourth sub, I-18, to patrol the eastern coast in Africa and the heavily-travelled Mozambique Channel. They were supplied at sea by two Japanese auxiliary cruisers that stayed close by in less-travelled waters. During the thirty days of June, the four subs sank sixteen Allied ships, all sailing alone along the east coast of Africa. Most of the Allied ships were carrying supplies to Egypt and the Middle East, but some were carrying supplies to India and Ceylon. None of the Japanese submarines were lost. This sudden carnage off the coast of East Africa startled the Allies, who had to accept the fact that their antisubmarine defenses there were not as good as they thought them to be. Quick action was needed and one of the first things the British did was to pull the 209th Air Squadron from Ceylon, where it was almost as badly needed, and send it to Mombasa to patrol East African coastal waters. The 209th was one of the best patrol units in the area because it had Canadian crews flying the long-range and well-armed Catalina flying boats.

What the Allies needed most urgently in the western Indian Ocean were escort vessels to expand their convoy system all along the African east coast. But this was impossible at this time, because neither the British nor the Americans could supply the escort vessels needed. With the new war in the Pacific, the on-going war in the North Atlantic, and the great effort being exerted by the Allies to get supplies to the Soviet Union via the Arctic route, Allied escort vessels were in very short supply world wide. The Allied commanders in the Indian Ocean area had to do what they could to combat the Japanese by other means.

The British still remained ignorant of the two Japanese auxiliary cruisers that were supplying the Japanese subs, and continued to believe that the subs were being supplied at ports on Vichy-held Madagascar. This became one of the most important factors in the British decision to eventually occupy the remainder of the island.

Fearing a possible re-invasion of the Diego Suarez area by the Japanese—with Vichy support—the British brought in a strong South African unit, the 7th South African Brigade armed with artillery and armored cars. The presence of the 7th Brigade at Diego Suarez was kept secret as long as possible.

On July 1, Lieutenant General Sir William Platt, the veteran commander of the second East African War and now Commander-in-Chief of East Africa, was put in direct command of future operations on Madagascar. London had decreed that henceforth the conquest of Madagascar would be primarily an African affair.

While the Japanese submarines were having a field day along the east coast of Africa, the German raider Thor was doing its dirty work in the central Indian Ocean. On June 16, Thor sank the Dutch tanker "Olivia" and three days later the raider captured another Allied ship, the Norwegian tanker "Herborg" and sent her, her captured crew, and a full load of oil off to Japan.

THE COMOROS ISLANDS

The Comoros Islands, long a part of the French Empire, are a small group of islands at the north end of the Mozambique Channel and were under Vichy's control. The main island was Mayotte, which held the islands' largest town and seaport, Dzaudzi. At Dzaudzi there was a small harbor, an airfield, and a radio station. In the hands of the Allies these islands could provide a very strategic location to monitor and protect oceangoing traffic through the Mozambique Channel. The island's governor and his staff were known to be very pro-Vichy, but it was believed that the fifteen or so other Europeans in the islands were, generally, pro-Allied. There were no French armed forces on the island, only a forty-man native police force. It was also known that the islands' important facilities had been mined, and that the administrator had orders to blow them up if and when an invader set foot on the islands.

During June 1942, the British decided that these islands should be taken and a plan to occupy them, called "Operation Throat," was drawn up. The operation was carried out beginning on June 30, when two British destroyers "Dauntless" and "Active" departed for the islands with a force of thirty British Commandos, a company of well-armed KAR troops from the 5th KAR Regiment, and a detachment of Royal Marines. The British troops were landed on Mayotte Island at 3:00 a.m. on the morning of July 2 at Choa Bay, an undefended and isolated beach. They promptly marched on to occupy the radio station without incident. The Commandos and KAR men then surrounded the police barracks and captured most of the policemen while still in bed. At the same time, the Royal Marines secured the airfield. Both operations went off without incident. The town of Dzaudzi was easily occupied and the governor, too, was captured in his bed. The Chief of Police and two others French officials managed to flee in a car, but were later caught. By noon, it was all over. No one had been killed or wounded and none of the important installation blown up. Within a few days, British Navy patrol vessels and RAF seaplanes were operating out of Mayotte's harbor and land-based planes of the SAAF were operating from the airfield. Their primary mission was to conduct antisubmarine patrols.

THE BATTLE OF MIDWAY STYMIES JAPANESE PLANS IN THE INDIAN OCEAN

Between June 4 and 6, the Battle of Midway was fought in the central Pacific off the Hawaiian island of Midway. A large Japanese naval force was intent on occupying Midway as the first step in the occupation of the entire Hawaiian Island chain. The American Navy, somewhat revived after the disaster of Pearl Harbor, was just as determined to prevent the landing. In an epoch three-day battle at sea, the Americans prevailed by sinking all four aircraft carriers accompanying the invasion fleet. Without air support the invasion could not go forward and the Japanese were forced to withdraw. It was not only a major victory for the Americans but the turning point in the Pacific war. With only seven aircraft carriers left now to defend their newly-won empire and prospects for acquiring additional carriers almost nil, the Japanese Navy was forced to go on the defensive. This meant that expanding into new areas, such as the Indian Ocean, had to be postponed indefinitely. The occupation of Ceylon and Madagascar were no longer options for the Japanese.

Furthermore, the Japanese leaders could expect the American Navy to steadily increase in strength owing to the production capacity of the United States, and expect them also to counterattack in considerable strength in the central and western Pacific. Because of this, the Japanese Navy now had to concentrate on defending its Pacific frontier and withdraw naval units from other areas to do so. One of those areas from which warships were drawn was the Bay of Bengal in the northeastern part of the Indian Ocean. That left only Japanese submarines and raiders operating in the Indian Ocean. The eastern coast of India was no longer threatened and, worst of all for the Japanese, the southern coast of newly-conquered Burma was exposed and virtually undefended. This opened new military opportunities for the Allies in the eastern Indian Ocean.

JAPANESE SUBMARINES CONTINUE TO MENACE THE INDIAN OCEAN

As long as the Allied defenses remained weak in the Indian Ocean the Japanese saw no reason to drastically scale back submarine operations there. Furthermore, on June 27, the Germans had informed the Japanese that continued Japanese submarine action in the western Indian Ocean against Allied supply lines would facilitate their planned advance into the Middle East, and they encouraged the Japanese to keep up their submarine activities there. The Japanese obliged and continued their submarine patrols off the coast of East Africa. During July, the four submarines went on to sink seven more Allied ships. During August, however, the four subs were withdrawn and no Allied ships were sunk in the western Indian Ocean that month. Berlin took note of this downturn in activity along the African east coast and, on August 11, again urged Japan to continue attacking Allied shipping. Tokyo replied that it would do what it could and repeated, once again, that when the Germans captured the Suez Canal or moved south out of the Caucasus, Japan would occupy Ceylon. Tokyo, of course, knew that a Japanese invasion of Ceylon was out of the question, and they appeared to be placating the Germans or attempting to deceive them into thinking that the Japanese armed forces were stronger than they actually were.

In August and September, the Japanese did manage to send one sub, I-29, to work the waters north of Madagascar. On August 19, I-29's float plane flew over the Seychelles to gather data on Allied ships at anchor there, and during the rest of August and September, I-29 managed to sink four Allied ships in the area. In October more Japanese subs would return and it would get worse for the Allies—much worse.

While the Japanese submarines were working the coast of East Africa, the German raider Thor was prowling the Indian Ocean east of Madagascar. On July 4, she captured the Norwegian tanker "Madrono" and, like the others, sent her, her crew and cargo of oil off to Japan. Then, on July 20, Thor sank the armed British freighter "Indus" but was damaged when the Indus fought back. Thor was then ordered by Berlin to go to Yokohama, Japan for repairs.

HITLER DISCUSSES MADAGASCAR AND JEWS AGAIN

On July 24, 1942, Hitler mentioned once again to his aides that it might be a good idea to send Europe's Jews to Madagascar. The Fuhrer seemed to be fascinated by this idea because he mentioned it so often.

MADAGASCAR MUST BE CONQUERED

By mid-July, the Allies were more than ever convinced that the Japanese submarines operating off the coast of East Africa were being supplied at Vichy ports on Madagascar. Prime Minister Smuts was a firm believer of this and became a leading advocate for the conquest of the rest of Madagascar. London, still in need of forces in North Africa, could offer Smuts no significant numbers of British troops, but gave their approval for the operation if the Africans felt they could carry the major portion of the load themselves. Smuts felt they could do so and informed London. On July 19, Churchill gave his approval for the occupation of the remainder of Madagascar. Therefore, planning began for the invasion using primarily South African and KAR troops. The operation was dubbed "Stream Line Jane." The only British unit of any size to be used in the operation was the amphibious-trained 29th Independent Brigade which was still at Diego Suarez. The invasion was scheduled to begin in early September and was to be completed during October before the return of the seasonal rains. Once again, because the terrain of Madagascar was so rugged, it would be "ribbon warfare" with the British troops invading southern Madagascar following the existing roads.

In late August, the 29th Independent Brigade was sent to Kenya for field and amphibious exercises and to gain experience working with the KAR troops. As a cover, rumors were intentionally circulated that the 29th would be sent to India after its training.

The Allied plans called for southern Madagascar to be invaded on both the west and east coasts with two forces driving, simultaneously, on the capital, Tananarive. The SAAF was put to work photographing the planned landing sites at Majunga, on the island's west coast, and Tamatave, on the east coast as well as the roads over which the advances would take place.

Chapter 14
ELSEWHERE IN AFRICA (JANUARY–SEPTEMBER 1942)
AFTER THREE YEARS OF WAR

While the battles were raging in North Africa and on the island of Madagascar, there were other wartime activities of importance on the continent of Africa. Men were continuing to die in Africa's surrounding waters, the Vichy French were still a serious concern for the Allies, and the politics of Egypt and South Africa were still in flux.

On February 22, 1942, the British Empire, including all of the British colonies and Commonwealth territories in Africa, acquired another enemy. This was the Provisional government of India. It was a political organization, with its own small all-Indian army, created by the Japanese. This Army was attached to the Japanese Army in Burma and remained there on the eastern border of India. Neither the Provisional government of India nor its army were significant threats to Africa.

THE SEA WAR OFF AFRICA'S ATLANTIC COAST

During January 1942, Admiral Doenitz began sending his submarines to the western hemisphere, especially to the coast of the eastern United States. The Americans were almost totally unprepared for enemy submarine actions and the German submarines found an abundance of easy targets. The only country in the western hemisphere that had any real measure of antisubmarine defenses was Canada, which had been at war for three years and had developed a small navy of destroyers, corvettes, and other craft capable of doing coastal patrols and convoy escort duties.

With the increase in submarine activity in the western hemisphere there was a corresponding decrease in submarine activity along the west coast of Africa, where Allied antisubmarine efforts had been increased during the latter part of 1941.

During January and February 1942, there were no Allied ships sunk off West Africa by German submarines. Only the Italian sub "Barbarigo" was successful in the area on January 23 when she torpedoed and accidentally sank the Spanish passenger ship "Navemar" northeast of Madeira. Fortunately, the Navemar was carrying no passengers. She was returning to Spain after a voyage to New York where she had delivered a group of Jewish refugees.

On January 15, another German submarine, U–93, was sunk by the Allies 600 miles off the coast of French Morocco. Then on February 2, another German submarine, U–581, was sunk west of the Azores. These were the fourth and fifth German subs sunk in West African waters so far in the war. The loss of two German subs in January and February with a corresponding loss of no Allied ships was an indication to Doenitz that he could best use his subs in other parts of the world.

In March 1942, the German Navy introduced the first of ten new Type XIV supply submarines, dubbed "Milch Cows" (Milk Cows), which were capable of staying at sea for a long time and supplying operating submarines at sea. These were large, slow, and not very maneuverable submarines that replaced the submarine supply ships that had, by now, become too vulnerable to Allied detection. The Milch Cows carried fuel, replacement crews, food, clothing, spare parts, and many other items and did not take part in attacking enemy shipping. They supplied operating subs working in the western hemisphere, the South Atlantic, and the Indian Ocean, thereby extending their operating range.

For a while both the supply ships and the Milch Cows operated, but by late 1942 all of the supply ships had been sunk. Two of the last supply ships were sunk in African waters; the "Esso Hamburg" was sunk June 4, 1942, in the mid-ocean gap between West Africa and South America and the "Babitonga" was sunk June 21, 1942, south of the Cape Verde Islands.

One of the first Milch Cow submarines was sent into the South Atlantic in March 1942, along with the operating subs U–68 and U–505. And, once again, they were successful in sinking Allied ships off the coast of West Africa. They did, however, avoid the waters north of Freetown to Gibraltar, which were heavily patrolled by the Allies. The waters south of Freetown were another matter.

U–68 took the first victim on March 3, when she torpedoed and sank the British cargo ship "Helenus" off the coast of Liberia. U–505 then torpedoed and sank the British freighter "Benmohr" on March 5, and the Norwegian tanker "Sydhav" on the 6th in the same area. Two days later U–68 sank the British steamer "Baluchistan" with a combination of torpedoes and gunfire in the Gulf of Guinea off the coast of Ivory Coast. During March U–505 left for other waters but U–68 remained and sank another five ships, all in the Gulf of Guinea.

SOME VICHY SHIPS SEIZED, SOME NOT

Vichy ships sailing around Africa were a constant concern for the British who did not have the wherewithal to stop and inspect each and every ship. Some

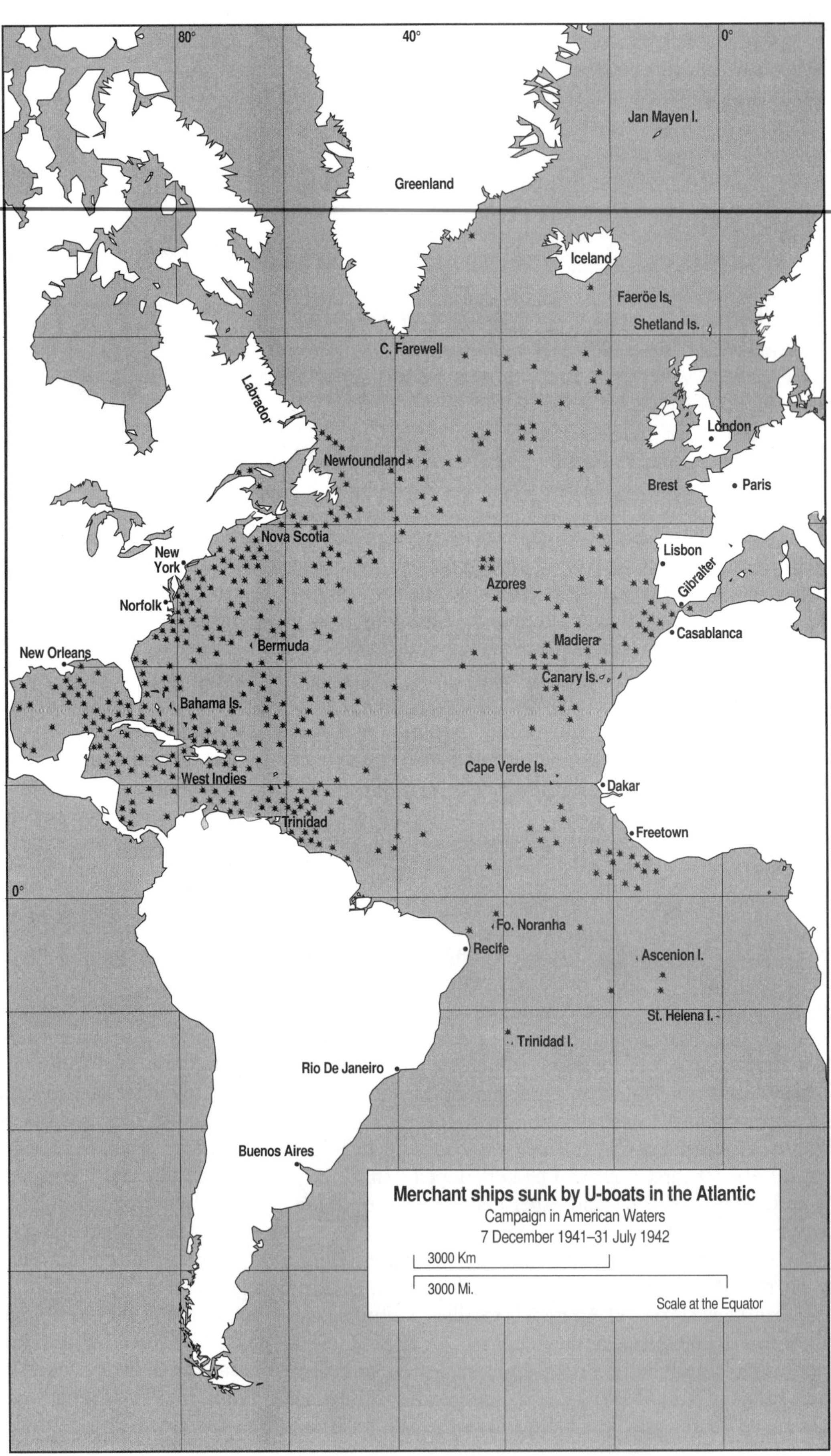

Allied merchant ships sunk in the Atlantic Ocean from December 7, 1941 through July 31, 1942. Clearly, the emphasis of the German U-boat command was on the Western Hemisphere and not Africa.

THE MILCH COWS WERE SLAUGHTERED

The Germany Navy built ten Milch Cow submarines, and by the end of 1943 all had been sunk. When they were on the surface of the water supplying operating submarines, the two vessels together were very vulnerable to radar detection and attacks because they were both virtually dead in the water. When attacked the faster operating submarine could get away safely, but the lumbering Milch Cow was so slow that her enemies could pursue her until she was destroyed. This was especially so after the use of sonar (underwater detecting device) became commonplace for the Allies. While they operated, though, the Milch Cows were of great value to the operating submarines.

Vichy ships were allowed to pass through the British blockade while others were turned back or confiscated. Most confiscations took place in South African waters targeting ships going to and from Madagascar. Between December 1941 and April 1942, the British seized six Vichy ships as they rounded the Cape. Each seizure brought bitter protests from Vichy. Finally, during April, Vichy decided that their ships sailing the Cape routes would be armed in the future. If necessary, the Vichy French would fight their way through the British blockade.

MORE ACTION IN THE ATLANTIC

During April U–505, returned to the Gulf of Guinea and sank two more Allied ships. Axis subs could now penetrate this far south again, thanks to the new Milch Cows. On April 9th U–117 laid a string of mines off Casablanca, French Morocco and the next night, U–455 laid a second string of mines in nearby waters. Before they were discovered and swept, the mines sank one ship and damaged two others.

On April 21, the German raider Michel captured the American tanker "Connecticut" in the South Atlantic on her way to Cape Town. Michel was a new German raider on the scene. This was her second success. Michel picked up the survivors from the Connecticut and eventually took them to Japan.

On May 10, the American aircraft carrier "Ranger" appeared off the West African coast, not to hunt submarines, but to deliver aircraft. She had brought 68 American-made P–40 fighter planes from Quonset Point, RI and when the ship was within range of Accra, Gold Coast, American pilots flew the P–40s from the carrier's deck to Accra's airport. From there they flew across the Cannonball Route to points east.

Then there was a lull in naval activity in African waters until late May. At that time U–159 appeared in the waters south of the Azores and sank two Allied ships. Then another lull followed until the Italian sub "Da Vinci" appeared and sank a Panamanian vessel off Liberia on June 2. Da Vinci struck again on the 7th, sinking the British merchant ship "Chile." Da Vinci sank two more Allied ships in June in the same general area before departing.

On June 6, a unique drama took place in the waters off South West Africa when the raider "Michel" encountered the American Liberty ship "George Clymer" drifting helplessly with engine troubles. Michel launched one of her two torpedo boats which approached the George Clymer and demanded the ship's surrender. The American captain refused and the torpedo boat then fired two torpedoes into the American ship. The George Clymer sent out a distress signal and appeared not to be sinking. The distress signal was picked up in Cape Town and a message was returned in English saying that a merchant cruiser was being sent to pick up survivors. The Michel picked up the message and decided to wait in the area and attack the merchant cruiser as she approached the stricken American ship. The Michel sailed off over the horizon, turned around and took on the disguise of another British ship coming, on its own, to assist the George Clymer. The merchant cruiser "Alcantara," dispatched by the British, was a fast ship and arrived sooner than the Germans had anticipated. She rescued the American crew and attempted to sink the derelict American ship but failed. The Alcantara then sailed off to Cape Town leaving the George Clymer adrift. By the time the Michel returned there was nothing in sight except for the drifting George Clymer.

On June 13, another German raider "Stier," operating in the South Atlantic, sank the British freighter "Lylepark" out of New York with war supplies for South Africa.

In July German submarine activity picked up again in African waters when three subs, U–116, U–201, and U–582 teamed up to patrol the area west of the Canary Islands. Between July 12 and 15, they sank six Allied ships. U–201 and U–582 then headed south and teamed up with U–130 and U–752 in the waters off West Africa between Dakar and Liberia. This deadly foursome sank eight more Allied ships before the month was out.

On July 16, the raider Michel struck again. The victim this time was the American armed merchant ship "William F. Humphrey" off the coast of French Equatorial Africa. The American ship tried to fight off her attacker with her deck gun, but the Michel's firepower was much greater and succeeded in setting the American ship ablaze from stem to stern with artillery fire and torpedoes. Six of the ship's crew were killed, 29 taken prisoner by the Michel and eleven escaped in a lifeboat. They were picked up later by a passing Norwegian ship and taken to Freetown.

The Germans lost two more subs in West African waters during July, U–136 west of Madeira Island on the 11th and U–213 midway between the Azores and Madeira on the 31st.

These were losses number six and seven in West African waters. Worldwide, July 1942 was not a good month for the German submarine service. They lost eleven subs that month.

On July 19, the American carrier Ranger was back in West African waters with another load of P–40 fighter planes. This time 72 planes were flown from her deck to Accra and all went on, across Africa, to Burma.

During August, five German subs, U–109, U–130, U–506, U–572, and U–752, worked the waters off West Africa south of Freetown and took ten Allied ships, while another group of five subs, U–156, U–214, U–406, U–516, and U–566, worked the waters around the Azores and sank nine Allied ships.

Also during August, two German raiders were operating in the South Atlantic. On August 9, Stier sank the empty British cargo ship "Dalhousie" out of Cape Town for Trinidad. Two days later Michel sank the British freighter "Arabistan" out of Cape Town bound for Trinidad.

The month of September saw five more German subs, U–68, U–109, U–125, U–156, and U–506, working the Gulf of Guinea again and sinking fourteen ships. To the north U–107 braved the heavily patrolled waters along the coast of French Morocco and took two ships while U–109 broke out of the Gulf of Guinea and sank an Allied ship northwest of the Cape Verde Islands.

The German raider Michel took another Allied ship on September 10. She was the American merchant ship "American Leader" out of Colombo, Ceylon via Cape Town bound for Newport News, Virginia with a cargo of nature rubber and petroleum products. The American Leader was sunk 800 miles west of Cape Town with 39 survivors who were taken aboard the Michel. They stayed with the raider until she reached Singapore and were then turned over to the Japanese as POWs.

THE "LACONIA" INCIDENT

It was after sunset on September 12, 1942, off the coast of Liberia that the German sub U–156 spotted the British passenger ship Laconia sailing alone in a southerly direction. She was an easy target. U–156, operating on the surface of the water, approached the ship and fired two torpedoes. Both hit their mark and the Laconia stopped, listed to one side; slowly sinking. All the while her radio operator was sending out a distress signal. U–156 stayed in the area to make sure the ship would sink. Her plan was to then sail on to the waters off South Africa where she and several other subs were heading to attack Allied shipping there.

Aboard the Laconia there was panic. She was loaded with 2,732 passengers and many of them went into the water hanging on to ship's debris for lack of space in the lifeboats. U–156 moved closer to the Laconia for a better look. It was then that the submarine's captain, Lt. Commander Werner Hartenstein, discovered that some of the men in the water were Italians. He pulled several of them aboard and discovered that the Laconia was carrying 1,800 Italian POWs from the North African campaign and that hundreds had already been killed because the torpedoes flooded the prison cells below deck. Hartenstein also learned that aboard were 160 Polish guards and some 800 Britishers including eighty women and children. Hartenstein had a very hard decision to make; to stay in the area and try to help save survivors knowing that the Laconia's distress signal would soon bring enemy planes and vessels, or sail off leaving the passengers to their fate. Hartenstein radioed Admiral Raeder in Germany detailing the situation. Raeder, with Hitler's approval, promptly radioed back for Hartenstein to save as many passengers as he could and that other German subs and an Italian sub were on their way to help. Furthermore, Raeder informed the French naval commander at Dakar of the situation and asked him to send help.

Hartenstein then drew in the lifeboats around his submarine and picking up survivors in the water packing them inside the sub, on its deck, and evenly distributing them in the lifeboats. Meanwhile the sub's radio operator send out uncoded messages on several wave bands asking ships in the area, even Allied ships, to come to the rescue with the promise that they would not be attacked if the sub was not attacked. In the distance the Laconia finally went under ninety minutes after being torpedoed.

All night long and into the morning hours, U–156 searched for survivors, but no ships had yet come to help, although the French at Dakar had replied that they were sending ships. Two British merchant ships also heard the message and signaled that they were on their way to the scene.

It was not until the 14th that the first vessel arrived. She was the German sub U–506 and took on 132 survivors from U–156 and helped the other survivors in the lifeboats. It was two more days until the next vessel, U–507, arrived to help out. By now some 400 people were aboard the subs, with the crowded lifeboats strung out in long lines behind each submarine being towed and traveling slowly on the surface to the northwest in the direction of the approaching French ships.

About noon, an American B–24 bomber from Ascension Island appeared overhead and began circling the area. Hartenstein draped a Red Cross flag over his unmanned forward gun while his signalman, using a flashing light, flashed to the plane that a rescue operation was underway. A British seaman was then given the light and he flashed the plane again in English. With this, the plane flew away. Hartenstein presumed that the messages had been understood. It had not. The American airmen did not understand the flashing messages. The air crew, of course, reported what they had seen to their commander at Ascension. The base commander at Ascension, who had only partial information of what was going on at the scene, correctly deduced that a rescue operation was under way but presumed that the German subs were rescuing only the Italians POWs and that the bulk of the survivors in the lifeboats were British and other Allied personnel. Based on this he ordered the plane to return and attack the subs. It did so a half hour later dropping three depth charges. One lifeboat was wrecked and U–156's periscope and signal antenna were damaged. With this Hartenstein ordered those survivors on deck into the remaining lifeboats and submerged. Unattended, the lifeboats drifted apart.

Because of the antenna damage Hartenstein could not contact Raeder until the sub surfaced again and the damaged antenna was repaired. It was late on the evening of the 16th when Hartenstein reached Raeder by radio and reported what had happened. Raeder was very angry with the Americans for their action but ordered U–506 and U–507 to continue their rescue efforts. Meanwhile U–156 was ordered back to France because of the periscope damage and her load of survivors.

By dawn on September 17, there was still no rescue vessel in sight. At noon four American bombers from Ascension Island arrived and attacked U–506 which quickly dived and escaped undamaged. After the American bombers left she surfaced and resumed aiding those in the lifeboats.

Later that day, the French cruiser "Gloire" and two sloops arrived from French West Africa followed shortly by the Italian submarine "Cappellini." Together they were able to take all of the survivors and the German subs then departed. The French ships searched the area for several more days and found four more lifeboats crowded with survivors. By now, 1,091 people had been rescued, but four lifeboats were still unaccounted. They were eventually discovered four days later, but by then 99 of the 119 aboard had died of exposure and/or their injuries.

Back in Germany, Hitler and Raeder reviewed the Laconia situation and concluded that such rescue attempts should not be attempted in the future. Therefore, Admiral Doenitz, Commander of the German submarine fleet issued such orders to all subs at sea. This became known as the "Laconia Order."

After the war Doenitz was accused of war crimes at Nuremberg and the Laconia Order was used as evidence against him. He was eventually acquitted, however. If Germany had won the war it might have been the American commander at Ascension Island that was accused of war crimes.

A SECOND DRAMA AT SEA

Only days after the Laconia Incident another sea drama unfolded in the South Atlantic. On the morning of September 27, the armed American Liberty Ship "Stephen Hopkins," out of Cape Town bound for Paramaribo, Dutch Guiana, was attacked by the German raider Stier in the waters off South West Africa. Accompanying the Stier was the armed German blockade runner "Tannenfels." Both German ships fired on the Stephen Hopkins with artillery and machine gunfire. The American ship began to run while her rear deck gunners fired back repeatedly at the German ships. Their fire was accurate and Stier was hit several times. Her steering mechanism was damaged and she began running in a circle. Also, an American shell hit her oil pumps and her engines overheated and seized up, bringing the ship to a near stop. As the gun battle raged, all of the American gunners were killed and their places taken by volunteers. Their fire, too, was accurate and the Stier was hit several more times. The American ship, though, was hit repeatedly. She slowed to one knot and began to sink. One brave seaman, Cadet Midshipman Edwin O'Hara, manned the gun until the last minute firing the ship's last five rounds. All five rounds hit the Stier but O'Hara was killed seconds later by return fire. By now both ships were dead in the water and sinking within sight of each other. The Tannenfels rescued all but three of the Stier's crew while the fifteen survivors of the Stephen Hopkins' original crew of 42 piled into the only undamaged lifeboat. Thirty-one days later the Americans, emaciated but alive, reached safety at a Brazilian fishing village. The Stephen Hopkins was Stier's fifth and last victim.

JAPANESE SHIPS PENETRATE THE BRITISH BLOCKADE

The British blockade was so large and so far-flung that it had many holes. Blockade runners could sail across great expanses of water via seldom-traveled routes and then race through one or more of the weak spots in the blockade to reach their destination. The Japanese became very good at this, and during the first half of 1942 a total of nine Japanese blockade runners made it safely from the Far East to German-controlled ports in Europe. These ships brought badly-needed raw materials to the Germans, especially rubber, and returned with manufactured items such as prototypes of newly developed German weapons and machine tools.

CAPE WATERS BECOME SAFER

By mid–1942, the waters off South Africa had become much safer for Allied shipping. The South African Navy was steadily acquiring more patrol vessels and the SAAF more aircraft. A great help in this respect was the arrival of a quantity of American-made B–34 "Ventura" bombers. These were four-engine planes with a range of 1660 miles and could carry bombs and depth charges. When the wars in Madagascar were concluded, many of the South African vessels and aircraft used there returned home and were assigned to antisubmarine patrols.

EVENTS IN FRENCH AFRICA

By 1942, it had become unpleasant living anywhere in Vichy territory. There were shortages of all kinds and repressive decrees coming from Vichy that made demands on the people diminishing their civil rights. One such measure that was adopted in early 1942 was the forced recruitment of French citizens to go to Germany as workers in German war industry. Under an agreement between Vichy and Germany the recruitment of workers would result in the Germans release of some French POWs from the 1940 campaign. Individuals who did not want to go to Germany searched for alternatives and found opportunities in West Africa by volunteering for work on the railroad being built across the Sahara Desert from Algeria to Senegal.

Furthermore, in French North Africa there was a mini industrial boom under way due to the shortages. The new job opportunities created also attracted Frenchmen who might otherwise be sent to Germany. Many of these jobs required skilled workers.

The new enterprises produced goods mainly for local consumption.

In Algeria, where a lot of fruit was grown, there was an expansion in industries making jams and jellies, dried fruit, and alcohol. Soap was made from olive oil. Sugar beets, which grew well in Algeria, were produced in large quantities to make sugar formerly imported from sugar cane-producing areas. The abundance of Algerian wool brought about an increase in textile manufacturing, and Algeria's coal mines, which produced a low grade of coal, were worked around the clock because there was virtually no imported coal to be found.

It was a similar situation in Tunisia. There was an increase in textile manufacturing, while paper, twine, and sacks were made from local alfalfa grass. The lignite mines at El Oudiane and Oum Douil increased production to provide fuel, a substitute for coal, for Tunisia's power industry and electric railroads.

In French Morocco, there were increases in the production of textiles, alcohol, oil refining, chemicals, shoes, paper, and frozen foods. The fishing industry also expanded.

The people in French West Africa, French Somaliland, and Madagascar were less fortunate, because those lands did not have the industrial base from which to rapidly build new industries. Those people, Frenchmen and native alike, had to live with the shortages.

During February, another problem developed for the Vichy French in North Africa when the Vichy government suddenly ordered the battleship Dunquerque moved from the French naval base at Mers el Kebir to the French naval base at Toulon France. The Dunquerque was one of France's newest and most powerful battleships. She was built in 1937 and carried eight thirteen-inch guns. This move brought to the fore once again for the Allies the question of the future of the still-powerful French Navy. There were renewed fears in the Allied camp that Vichy might be on the verge of turning this ship, and possibly others, over to the Axis Powers. The French reply was that the Dunquerque, which had been damaged in the British attack on Mers el Kebir during July 1940, was simply being sent to Toulon for final repairs. Allied intelligence reports from France soon confirmed this. Actually, it turned out to be a benefit for the Allies in that the Dunquerque was no longer in a position to oppose the Allied invasion of Algeria that came in November 1942.

During March, there was an invasion scare in French Morocco and on the 15th Vichy suddenly ordered all British subjects living in the coastal cities to move inland, lest they aid the British if a landing occurred.

The Vichy French were holding many British citizens throughout the French Empire because the British were holding Frenchmen throughout their empire. The British started this process soon after the fall of France in July 1940 in order to keep Frenchmen of military age from returning to Vichy France. At the time there were many French soldiers, some of them African, in England who had been evacuated from Dunkirk. The British hoped, that with time, many of the young Frenchmen would join the Free French. In the meantime they, and many other able-bodied French civilians, resided in British territory as guests of the crown.

FRENCH NORTH AFRICAN FOOD TO THE GERMANS

By 1942, there was a general food shortage throughout Europe. It was worse in some areas than others and since Germany controlled so much of Europe it fell upon the Germans to find and distribute enough food to feed the millions of people under their control.

French North Africa had long been a provider of food for France and this practice continued during the war because the British blockade in the Western Mediterranean was very weak. French ships were able to sail back and forth between North Africa and southern France almost at will. Unfortunately, because of the food shortages in French North Africa, the amount of food shipped to Europe was greatly reduced from prewar levels. The main food items that were shipped, however, were lamb, vegetables, fruits, olive oil and grain. Most of the food was shipped to Marseille, which was still under Vichy control. But now, because of the general food shortage in Europe, the Germans put pressure on Vichy to share much of the imports from French North Africa with them. In some cases the Germans took up to 70% of the imports. This forced Vichy to put pressure on the food producers in North Africa to send still more food to France. This, in turn, aggravated the food shortages in North Africa and gave the Arab nationalists yet another propaganda weapon to use against their colonial rulers.

THE NATIVES GOT RESTLESS

In southern Senegal members of the Joola tribe, led by a priestess named Aline Situe, rebelled against Vichy authority because those authorities had ordered the tribe to produce more rice than the tribal members felt they were capable of doing. The surplus, of course, was to be turned over to the authorities. In protest Joola tribesmen took over much of their local province and French troops had to be called in to restore order. In the fighting several tribe members were killed. The priestess was captured and exiled to Timbuktu, where she later died. Meanwhile the Joola farmers returned to their rice paddies, harboring bitter resentment against their colonial masters.

In Ivory Coast the 200,000–member Brong Tribe chose another method of defiance. They defected, en masse, to the British in neighboring Gold Coast.

Heretofore, the Brong had been very cooperative with the French over the years. In the early stages of the war, over 1,000 tribesmen had joined the French armed forces and some saw combat in France. Three of those men were sons of the head chief, Nana Kojo. One son was killed in action, a second son died when his ship was torpedoed, and the third son became a German POW. Furthermore, the Brong had contributed 500,000 francs and 112 pounds of gold to the French Red Cross along with 25 tons of cocoa to be made into chocolate for the French Army.

By early 1942, though, Chief Nana Kojo and the other elders of the tribe had become disillusioned and angry with Vichy rule because of the shortages of many staple items and the harsh decrees coming from Vichy. It was at that point that they decided to defect to Gold Coast. But moving 200,000 people all at once was a difficult undertaking. Chief Nana Kojo and his advisers were afraid that once the movement began the French would close the border and trap a large part of the tribe in Ivory Coast. But Nana Kojo and his advisers had a plan. The French were building a new road along the eastern border of Ivory Coast to strengthen their military defenses against the British in Gold Coast. Nana Kojo, in an apparent show of his traditional loyalty to the French, volunteered the services of the entire tribe to help build the road. The French accepted and, in February 1942, the entire tribe moved to the work sites along the border. When all was ready, Nana Kojo gave the word and late one night the entire tribe dashed across the border into Gold Coast. Once in Gold Coast, Nana Kojo contacted de Gaulle and offered the services of his tribe to the Free French.

FRENCH EXCHANGE OF PRISONERS FAILED

Because of the French schism each side acquired prisoners of war from the other with a high percentage of the prisoners being Africans. Attempts were made by both sides, from the earliest days, to exchange prisoners, but the Germans would not allow Vichy to participate. The burden of keeping prisoners was especially difficult in French West Africa because of the many shortages. The POW camps there were very poorly maintained, and the lack of food and hygiene contributed to the general misery of the prisoners and an increased incidence of disease. The International Red Cross verified these conditions and intervened with what little resources they had available in West Africa to help improve the camps.

Finally during March 1942, High Commissioner Boisson took matters into his own hands. Defying both Vichy and the Germans, he released 236 of his 808 French prisoners and allowed them make their way to British colonies in West Africa and to French Equatorial Africa. This was made known to the Free French and British with the hope that they would reciprocate. The Free French and British, however, did not respond in kind and Boisson stopped the unilateral release of prisoners. There the problem rested and was not resolved until months later when, after the Allied invasion of North Africa, French West Africa joined the Allies.

JEWS TO THE GHETTOS IN ALGERIA

On April 28, 1942, a harsh new anti-Semitic law enacted by Vichy, was implemented in Algeria. The law, first enacted on August 1, 1941, was enforced at that time only in Metropolitan France. It required all Jews to move into the Jewish ghettos. Furthermore, Jews were prohibited from buying or selling any businesses. This new decree applied only to Algeria because Algeria was considered to be an integral part of France and did not apply to Tunisia, French Morocco, or any of the other African colonies.

INVASION FEARS CONTINUE IN FRENCH NORTH AND WEST AFRICA

The Vichy leaders concluded that if an Allied invasion of French North Africa and/or French West Africa came it would come during the summer of 1942. The Germans concurred with this analysis. Accordingly, additional quantities of French arms were released by the Germans for use in the defense of the French territories in question. Under this arrangement, a newly-formed French armored unit was sent to Dakar and French armored units in North Africa received additional tanks and other supplies.

In return for this concession, the Vichy French leased to the Germans the neutral cargo ships which had been interned in French Mediterranean ports since the beginning of the war. These ships were promptly put to use transporting men and supplies to Rommel and the Italians in North Africa.

CIVILIANS EVACUATED FROM DAKAR

Because of the invasion scare and the general food shortage in French West Africa, Vichy decided to remove some of the French civilians from Dakar. During September 1942, a census was taken of such individuals and on November 3 the evacuation of 1,000 French families from Dakar to Metropolitan France began. This process was soon interrupted, however, by the Allied invasion of French North Africa on November 8.

THE FREE FRENCH IN AFRICA

As Rommel and the Axis forces pushed the British out of Libya and back into Egypt during the first months of 1942, the war in southern Libya continued much as before. The Free French units operating out of Chad and the occupied oases in southern Libya's Fezzan area regularly harassed the Italian forces there by raiding their oases and supply lines. During March the Italians succeeded in recapturing the oasis of Jola in southeastern Libya from the British-commanded Sudanese Defence Force unit that had captured that oasis in November 1941. The Sudanese attempted to recapture the oasis in September 1942 but without success.

These operations were too far from the main front in North Africa to have an effect on it, but they posed a constant threat to Rommel's southern flank and drew Italian forces away from the main front. No German forces were sent to the Fezzan. The Free French operations were led by General Philippe Leclerc and were so successful that, in April, de Gaulle appointed Leclerc Commander-in-Chief of all Free French forces in Africa. During May the last Italian stronghold was eliminated in the Fezzan and the Free French could operate there somewhat at will. Leclerc then ceased military operations in southern Libya and awaited developments on the North African front.

THE FREE FRENCH AND ALLIED POLITICS

On January 1, 1942, the Free French were forced to endure a diplomatic snub from their Allies when they were not invited to Washington, DC, along with 26 other nations, to sign the Declaration of the United Nations. This act set in motion the mechanics for the creation of that anxiously-awaited postwar organization. The Free French were not invited because many of the Allied nations, including the United States, did not yet recognize them as the political entity acting for the French people.

On March 2, 1942, the United States did its part to change this by extending formal recognition to the Free French as the sole political entity representing those people of French Equatorial Africa and the other parts of the French Empire that had joined their cause. Furthermore, the United States promised to cooperate with the Free French on all matters of defense of those territories. As a part of the agreement the United States established a consulate in Brazzaville.

Since the United States still had diplomatic relations with Vichy, seven days later that government registered a formal protest with the American government in Washington. The Americans ignored it. At this point Vichy would have been perfectly justified in breaking diplomatic relations with the United States for having politically recognized what Vichy considered to be an illegal rebel organization in control of French territory. But the Petain government chose otherwise because diplomatic relations with the Americans was one of the few political weapons the Vichyites had left as a counterbalance against the Axis Powers. America's diplomatic relations with Vichy thus continued but were now weakened as a result.

In the weeks that followed, the United States and the Brazzaville authorities reached an agreement whereby American aircraft could use the airfield at Pointe Noire in exchange for eight new commercial aircraft which would be used by the Free French to establish scheduled air service between Brazzaville and Damascus, Syria. In mid-September the first American troops arrived at Pointe Noire to operate the airfield.

DE GAULLE AND MADAGASCAR

The British invasion of the Diego Suarez area of Madagascar came as a complete surprise to de Gaulle and the Free French. Quite understandably de Gaulle was upset at not having been consulted or even informed of the operation before hand. The cut went deeper because as the invasion got underway, during the early morning hours of May 5, de Gaulle was roused out of bed by a phone call at 3:00 a.m. from a news journalist seeking his reactions to the event which he, at that moment and much to his embarrassment, knew nothing about.

Furthermore, he and his British ally had had many conversations over Madagascar but not a hint of the British plans had been given to him. Ever since the Japanese entered the war, de Gaulle had seen the pressing need to win over Madagascar for the Allies one way or the other. He had sent messages to this effect to Churchill and others in England and to Prime Minister Smuts in South Africa. In February, he had presented the British War Office with a plan of operation for conquering the island by force. That plan called for a blockade of Diego Suarez while a Free French brigade landed at Majunga, on the west side of the island, and, with British air support, marched on the capital Tananarive. Ironically, the latter part of the plan—the landing at Majunga and the march on Tananarive—was the plan of operation the British would take later in the year, but not with Free French help.

Further adding to de Gaulle's dismay with the British and the Americans as well, were the announcements from Britain and Washington that Madagascar would eventually be returned to French rule. Those announcements did not say "to Free French rule." This brought up many anguished questions in de Gaulle's mind, which he later related in his war memoirs "The Call to Honour." De Gaulle wrote then of this incident:

> *"But what did that mean (the return to France... that meanwhile Madagascar would be taken away from the French? To what power, other than Anglo-Saxon, would*

she be attached? What would be the participation of the French there during the war? What would be left of the French authority in the future?"

On May 5,, a message came from the British Foreign Minister, Anthony Eden, asking de Gaulle to come see him regarding Madagascar. De Gaulle, in a display of anger and independence, purposely put off the meeting until May 11.

That meeting, when it finally occurred, was very tense for both men because by then negotiations were underway between the British and Madagascar's governor General Annet to bring over the rest of the island to the Allied cause. Eden could not guarantee de Gaulle that some arrangement might be made whereby Annet would remain in power in Madagascar and that the Free French would be excluded altogether. Eden, of course, realized that this was not what de Gaulle wanted to hear and offered to make the public statement that, at some unspecified time in the future, the Free French National Committee would be given authority over Madagascar. De Gaulle agreed to this, and a statement by the British government was made to that effect on May 13. The next day de Gaulle went on the radio acknowledging the British pledge. After the broadcast he ordered General Leclerc in Equatorial Africa to prepare a Free French brigade to be ready to go to Madagascar on short notice.

A few days later, de Gaulle informed the British that he wished to send a liaison officer to Diego Suarez and had chosen Lieutenant Colonel Peckhoff, his current liaison officer with the South African government, for the job. However, obstacles were put in Peckhoff's way preventing him from leaving South Africa.

This was not the end of de Gaulle's suffering. Problems with the British had been mounting for some time. Events in Syria and French Somaliland had not gone de Gaulle's way and there were current reports that a British mission out of Gold Coast, directed by a Mr. Frank, was making mysterious contacts with unknown individuals in Niger, a part of Vichy-controlled West Africa. Also, de Gaulle's Free French missions in Bathurst and Freetown had recently been told, without explanation, that they would have to leave those important seaports. Furthermore, de Gaulle had expressed a wish to go to North Africa to review and congratulate the Free French forces fighting there, but the British refused his request. If that were not enough, de Gaulle sensed that he was being avoided by British ministers and top level military leaders. The American Admiral Ernest King, Commander-in-Chief of the American Atlantic Fleet, had recently spent several days in London and had not called on him. Most or all of these apparent slights were related to the fact that the British and Americans were deeply involved in the planning of "Operation Torch," the invasion of French North Africa, but de Gaulle had no way of knowing it. To him it appeared that the British and Americans might be conspiring against him in favor of some other French leader or, perhaps, to acquire for themselves some parts of the French Empire. If this were to be the case, de Gaulle's relationships with his Anglo-Saxon allies would have to be drastically altered. After careful consideration he sent a message to Churchill and Eden on June 6 which mounted to an ultimatum. The message was relayed through Charles Peake, the Foreign Office Diplomat attached to his headquarters. De Gaulle recorded this message in his book, The Call to Honour:

> *"If it should happen that in Madagascar, in Syria or elsewhere, France was forced, by the action of her allies, to lose any part whatsoever of what belongs to her, our direct cooperation with Great Britain and eventually with the United States would no longer have any justification."*

De Gaulle went on to say that if this came to pass he could have to leave London and reestablish his headquarters on French territory, possibly Damascus or Brazzaville, and fight on independently against the enemy.

De Gaulle informed Catroux and Larminat in Syria, and Eboue and Leclerc in Equatorial Africa of his actions and instructed them to confirm his intentions with their local British and American liaison personnel.

De Gaulle's threat brought a prompt response from Churchill, who asked him to come and see him on June 10. In an hour-long meeting Churchill tried to assure de Gaulle that he and Roosevelt were not conspiring with any other French leader nor had they designs on Madagascar or any other part of the French empire. Churchill tried to assure de Gaulle that the Free French were needed in the grand alliance, and he heaped praise on the Free French troops who had held out so bravely at Bir Hacheim. He further promised de Gaulle that, one day, they would march side-by-side to regain France itself. Churchill, of course, could not give de Gaulle any information about the coming landings in French North Africa, an action that de Gaulle would, almost certainly, take offense with when he learned that he had been excluded yet one more time. Churchill was fully aware that his relationship with de Gaulle and the Free French was now, and would be in the coming months, most tenuous.

Three days later, Foreign Secretary Eden met with de Gaulle and gave similar assurances as to British intentions not to acquire any part of the France Empire and that the Free French were an important part of the alliance. Eden gave de Gaulle some good news, that the way had been cleared for his man Peckhoff to proceed from South Africa to Diego Suarez as the Free French representative there.

De Gaulle later recorded that he believed Churchill and Eden were sincere and that, "...one day the Cross of Lorraine would fly over Madagascar." He also recorded, "I felt more clearly than ever that in the last resort England would not give up her alliance with us."

It was about this time that de Gaulle came to believe that the original name of his organization, the "Free French," had outlived its usefulness and that a more all-encompassing title should be used. On July 14, he officially changed the name of his organization from the "Free French" to the "Fighting French."

EAST AFRICA

By 1942, the British were in firm control of all of East Africa except for French Somaliland. The former Italian colonies were being administered as occupied territories and contributing, to some degree, to the Allied war effort.

On January 31, 1942, Britain and Ethiopia signed a treaty that reestablished diplomatic relations between the two countries and recognized Haile Selassie's regime as the legitimate government of that country. The treaty also defined Britain's presence in the country, which was substantial and on-going. Ethiopia was still rebuilding and far from being a self-supporting nation. Full law and order had not yet been established in some large cities, so in February the British, with the Emperor's acquiescence, declared those cities "British cantonments." This was a legal device that allowed the British military to rule under martial law until such time that the Ethiopians could provide an efficient peacekeeping force of their own. The British cantonments did not last long. By the end of the year all of the cities involved, with the exception of Diridawa, were returned to Ethiopian control.

In all actuality, Ethiopia was run by British advisors and administrators attached to Selassie's government in Addis Ababa. These people received their instructions from, and answered to, the Occupied Enemy Territory Administration (OETA) office in Nairobi, Kenya. Ethiopia was contributing virtually nothing to the Allied war effort and was really more of a liability than an asset. Since October 1935, when the Italians first invaded the country, Ethiopia had lost the following: 760,000 people killed; 525,000 dwellings destroyed; and fourteen million head of cattle perished.

In the disputed Ogaden Desert region the old problems of inter-clan fighting had resurfaced and the British had to send in KAR troops, Somali policemen, and other law enforcement units that they might have used elsewhere to bring order to that troubled area.

In Italian Somaliland the British dismantled many of the Italian-owned facilities and shipping them elsewhere. Mogadishu was hit the hardest. There an oil storage plant, an oilseed crushing plant, a power generating station, a salt works, seventy miles of railroad track, and five diesel locomotives were all confiscated and shipped out of the country. Many Somalis lost their jobs in the process. On the other hand the British armed forces took over Italian airfields and naval facilities and often improved or enlarged them, providing some new jobs.

The British East African colonies of Kenya, Uganda and Tanganyika, unlike Ethiopia and the former Italian colonies, were prospering very well. Markets were plentiful for their foodstuffs, sisal, minerals and services. Sisal was especially vital to the American war effort after the loss of alternate sources in Southeast Asia. The British were aware of this and put controls on the prices the farmers got for their sisal and then purchased all of the sisal production. They then doubled the price and sold it to the Americans. With the profits they bought war supplies, much of it from the United States.

East African men, both European and African, were steadily recruited for the KAR and other British armed forces. There was a general manpower shortage in British East Africa due to so many men being in the armed services and the robust economy. Fortunately, some of the British administrators and other skilled people who had been evacuated from Malaya and Singapore had been transferred to British East Africa and found ready employment there. Thousands of Italian POWs captured in East Africa had been scattered throughout British East Africa in POW camps and were widely used in agriculture, road building, transportation, and the like. Other newcomers to Kenya included approximately 100 Jewish refugees from Europe. This brought the colony's Jewish population to over 400.

Throughout East Africa, though, there was a shortage of skilled workers. This problem was addressed by the British Army, which set up a number of schools in Kenya to train Africans for both military and civilian needs, such as carpenters, masons, blacksmiths, electricians, motor mechanics, tailors, signalers, drivers, etc.

In other developments some 10,000 acres of land in the Athi highlands of Kenya, formerly used for grazing of domestic and wild animals, was converted into crop land. And throughout the colony during planting and harvesting seasons, there were not enough farm hands available so the local authorities had to resort to the conscription of local laborers, virtually all of them black, to meet the agricultural needs. This was very unpopular with the black citizens of the colony. Also resented by the blacks was the fact that white farmers often received better prices for their crops than black farmers. Such issues as these were not addressed during the war because many believed it was unpatriotic to do so. But, on the other hand, they were not forgotten and provided ammunition after the war for the emerging nationalist groups and others in East Africa interested in shaking off colonial rule.

About this time another of those fledgling nationalist groups was founded in The Sudan. It was known as "Ashiqqua" (National Unionist Party) and, like such groups elsewhere, claimed to speak for the black population. The Ashiqqua grew slowly during the war years and did not come into bloom until the postwar years.

Accra Airport was a modern facility by 1940s standards.

Another problem for the British in East Africa was an outbreak of bubonic plague during the early part of 1942. The British promptly took measures to eradicate it using men and resources that could better have been used elsewhere.

Another medical problem in East Africa was an on-going problems with tuberculosis. On March 3, 1942, the Duke of Aosta died of that disease in a Nairobi hospital while still a prisoner of war. He had commanded the Italian forces in Italian East Africa. Altogether, 1,190 Italian POWs perished from the same disease while in captivity in Kenya.

In Uganda, agricultural production was the backbone of the economy and virtually everything grown there was in great demand. A great deal of sugar cane and cotton were grown in Uganda, so two new sugar mills and a cotton gin were built. At Malago, the large hospital there expanded its medical school to train more African doctors and medical assistants. The bubonic plague also affected parts of Uganda.

In Tanganyika, sisal and rubber were plentiful. Some of the old German-owned rubber plantations, that had been long neglected or even abandoned, were put back into production and thousands of people were engaged in the gathering of wild rubber.

During the year, about 5,000 Polish refugees arrived in Tanganyika and were housed in camps built for them in the highlands. Also arriving during the year were some 500 Jewish refugees from Europe.

In Nyasaland, increased exports of dairy products, tobacco, and tea were noted and modern farming methods were introduced to help the small landholders to be more productive. A total of 94 Jewish refugee families from Cyprus were also settled in Nyasaland during the year.

Zanzibar, the world's leading exporter of cloves, had always been a food importer. That was slowly changing as more land was devoted to the growth of food for local consumption.

In British Somaliland, the Somaliland Camel Corps was called in to do battle with a plague of locusts that threatened crops.

American Army Air Corps Ferrying Command crews boarding a transport at Accra Airport for the return flight home.

Several thousand Jewish refugees from Europe had settled on Mauritius Island, and there was a significant increase in cottage industry while the island's exports of sugar and copra continued to flourish.

Throughout East Africa inflation and black marketeering were daily facts of life. Inflation was worse in some areas than others and in still other areas out paced wage increases. The black markets persisted throughout the war until the normal flow of imported goods was restored.

FRENCH SOMALILAND ISOLATED

All during the first months of 1942, French Somaliland remained isolated by the British blockade surrounding it on land and sea. When Diego Suarez, Madagascar fell to the British in May it was a blow to this small colony because it was from Diego Suarez that some of the items smuggled through the blockade originated. The three French submarines and some of the smaller vessels sunk at Diego Suarez had been used to smuggle supplies to Djibouti.

The British and Free French repeatedly dropped leaflets over Djibouti and sent radio broadcasts into the colony. But even though conditions were slowly worsening in the colony, its administrators remained absolutely loyal to Vichy.

AIR ROUTES

By the early months of 1942, the military air routes that stretched from the United States all the way to East Africa had become fairly well established. Two-engine and four-engine bombers were now taking that route regularly, as were a few single-engine planes that could make the approximately 1,900–mile crossing from Brazil to West Africa. Most single-engine planes were still being shipped unassembled, however, to Takoradi and there assembled for the flights eastward.

Two-engine planes, generally with shorter range than four-engine planes, flew from Natal, Brazil to either Hastings Field in Sierra Leone or Roberts Field in Liberia. The latter field had been built by Pan-American Airways in the 1930s. From there it was a series of short hops across the Cannonball Route to Khartoum, The Sudan in East Africa.

Most four-engine planes could make it from Natal to Accra, Gold Coast but often stopped at Hastings Field or Roberts Field for refueling.

At Khartoum the military air routes divided. Planes going to India flew Khartoum–Aden–Karachi or Khartoum–Cairo–Habbaniya, Iraq or Basra, Iraq–Karachi. Planes continuing on to China flew the India route and then on to Dinjan, India–Kunming, China. American military transports had begun flying from India into China over the "Hump" (Himalaya Mountains) in April 1942. This airlift would grow to become the largest of the war, and many of the planes used were flown to India via the Cannonball Route.

Lend-Lease planes going to the Soviet Union flew Khartoum–Cairo–Basra–Tehran, Iran where they were turned over to Soviet air crews.

The American Army Air Corps Ferrying Command was responsible for all of the many functions needed to get the military planes from place to place. That included scheduling, providing fuel, maintenance, lodging and food for the crews, weather reports, and many other services. In the early months of 1942, the Ferrying Command on the trans-Atlantic-Cannonball Route was, at first, understaffed and those who staffed it were newly-trained personnel. Other air routes to Europe and the Pacific had higher priority and absorbed the more experienced personnel. As a result there were delays, confusion, communication problems, duplication and other problems until the personnel acquired the necessary experience and skills to perform their jobs efficiently.

As 1942 progressed, more commercial airlines established routes across the Atlantic from Brazil. Some of them had scheduled service. In May 1942, American Export Airlines established a new route to Lisbon, Portugal. During the summer months American Export's planes, new Sikorsky VS–44 flying boats, flew a northern route from New York to Ireland to Lisbon. During the winter they flew New York–Port of Spain, Trinidad–Bermuda–Bathurst, Gambia–Lisbon.

During June 1942, Trans-World Airlines (TWA) joined the pack and established a temporary air route from Natal to Accra, Gold Coast. It was over these domestic routes that nonmilitary personnel and cargo flew. Passengers consisted of journalists, businessmen, Red Cross personnel, refugees, merchant seamen, etc. Military personnel also flew the commercial routes when military service was not available or filled. Space on these airplanes was seldom wasted. If a plane was not filled with passengers then cargo was taken aboard. Military and commercial cargoes were generally flown outbound while raw materials, such as crude rubber, mica, industrial diamonds, quartz crystals, and other high-value items came on the inbound flights.

When the commercial air liners crossed the Caribbean and the Atlantic, the passengers were frequently asked to take turns looking out of the windows for dark cigar-shaped shadows just under the surface of the water—submarines. During the course of the war several enemy submarines were located in this manner.

ALTERNATE AIR ROUTES EXPLORED

The Allied leaders where aware that the Cannonball Route could become subject to enemy attacks, especially if the Axis forces captured Cairo and began advancing up the Nile River and into The Sudan. Furthermore, with all of the military action planned against the Vichy French in 1942, in Madagascar and North Africa, the possibility existed that the Vichy French might retaliate by attacking Allied aircraft flying that route as well as the airfields along the route. As a precaution, a more southerly route was explored across Africa and the Indian Ocean to the Far East. American survey teams began in early 1942 to plot this alternative route. The plane they used was Pan-American Airway's "Capetown" Clipper, now leased to the American government, because it could land on water where no land airfields existed. The teams could then travel over land to inspect possible sites for new airfields. The new route would be, from west to east, Natal, Brazil–Ascension Island–Pointe Noire, Equatorial Africa–several possible locations in the Belgian Congo and Tanganyika and end at Mombasa, Kenya. From Mombasa it would cross the Indian Ocean on a line approximately parallel to the equator but about ten degrees south. It would hop to the island groups Seychelles–Coetivy–Chagos–Cocos and on to Port Hedland, Australia.

The airfield at Ascension Island.

From Mombasa or any of the island groups, routes could be extended to the north into the Middle East, the Soviet Union, India or China. This route was not without its dangers, however. With Japanese forces on the Dutch East Indies island of Sumatra the Cocos Islands were within range of Japanese ships and aircraft. Another Indian Ocean route was feasible for four-engine planes from Mombasa to Ceylon and then to points in India, and China.

There was also the possibility that the aircraft assembly center at Takoradi might be threatened, so plans went forward to establish a second assembly center at Port Elizabeth, South Africa if necessary. The assembled aircraft could then fly northward along the already-established Cape Town to Cairo air route and connect with either of the new proposed routes.

CHANGE OF NAMES

During June 1942, the name Army Air Corps was dropped by the United States military and replaced with the new title, United States Army Air Forces (USAAF or AAF). The name of the Air Corps Ferrying Command was also changed to the Air Transport Command (ATC).

"IF I DON'T MAKE ASCENSION MY WIFE WILL GET A PENSION"

During July 1942, the new airfield on Ascension Island became operative. It had been under construction since March. With this development certain single-engine planes could now be flown across the Atlantic and on to Africa, eliminating the long delays of having those planes sent by ship to Takoradi and then assembled. Since Ascension Island was just a speck in the South Atlantic the above saying evolved among the Air Transport Command (ATC) pilots flying the route. To prevent pilots missing the island, Ascension had an exceptionally powerful homing beam that pilots, even way off course, could pick up on their radios and follow to the island. Also, being a desert island, the weather was generally clear making the island easy to see during the daylight hours.

There was one major hazard at Ascension—birds—thousands of sea birds that had inhabited this cinder island for centuries. To make air operations safer, thousands of birds had to be killed and driven away and many of their nesting areas covered over to prevent them from laying eggs.

PARACHUTES

A favorite item of barter with the African natives were the American-made silk and nylon parachutes. Seldom before had the natives seen such fine cloth. Brightly-colored parachutes, used to identify items dropped, were the most popular.

SOUTH AFRICA

The early months of 1942 proved to be good times for the Smuts government in South Africa. The German defeat at Moscow and the successful Soviet counterattacks during the winter months tended to splinter Smuts's already splintered pro-Axis right wing opposition even more.

Nevertheless, in February Smuts received a communique from his embassy in Washington telling of a secret plot against South Africa ordered by Hitler himself. The communique stated that Hitler had ordered his followers in South Africa to stage a coup when Rommel succeeded in occupying all of northern Egypt. The report from Washington stated that all activities were being directed from the neighboring Portuguese colonies of Mozambique and Angola with the cooperation of bribed Portuguese officials. It claimed that arms, munitions, and short wave radio sets were being smuggled into South Africa and going to coup organizers in Johannesburg, Cape Town, and South West Africa. The last line of the secret report read, "If Rommel should succeed, Nazi supporters in South Africa are prepared to declare independence and establish connections with Japan."

Smuts, who felt his internal security forces had the situation well in hand and would have certainly learned of such an extensive plan on his own, wired back to his Washington delegation, "At present there is no reason for alarm as internal situation very well in hand. No danger to Union at present anticipated from movements in Angola or Mozambique."

The South African scene, though, was not all that peaceful. Between February and April there was a rash of sabotage carried out mostly by individuals and small groups usually associated with the OB. At Delmas, an attempt was made to blow up the local power station while phone lines were cut at many places in Transvaal and Orange Free State and phone poles were cut down. At Krugersdorf a bomb damaged the town's main electric cable, and at Johannesburg a bomb blew up in a post office killing one person. There was a surge in bank robberies throughout the country, which the authorities attributed to those causing the violence as a means of raising money for their activities.

In May an unsuccessful attempt was made to bomb the home of one of Smut's cabinet members, J. H. Hoefmeyr, an outspoken liberal. The bomb was placed and the fuse lit, but the fuse went out before it could detonate.

In June, van Rensburg, head of the OB, boasted to a few associates that OB members had been instrumental in getting information to the Germans about Allied shipping and that several ships had been sunk by German submarines as a result. Word of this reached Smuts, but he had no proof and did nothing about it.

Also Smuts did nothing when various OB members and other individuals spoke openly about their support of Germany and Italy and their hopes for an Axis victory. In most other countries around the world such talk in wartime would be labeled seditious or even treasonable—but not in South Africa.

During the year, though, Smuts was not entirely passive. He used his emergency wartime powers to intern several hundred suspected terrorists including two OB "generals." He could have acted much more harshly, but chose not to for fear of creating martyrs and risking a 1914-type rebellion.

GODFATHER SMUTS

During this time in 1942, the Greek Royal family was living in exile in South Africa and a new baby daughter, Princess Irene, was born to them. Prime Minister Smuts agreed to be the baby's Godfather. The ceremony was performed on May 29 in a Greek Orthodox church. Princess Katherine served as the Godmother.

ANOTHER DRAFT CONSTITUTION

During January 1941, Dr. Daniel Malan, leader of the National Party, introduced, once again, a bill in Parliament that would require the South African government to sever all ties with the British Commonwealth and become an independent republic. And again, the bill failed to pass. In conjunction with Malan's bill the National Party published a new draft constitution for the nation which indicated the direction they would take if and when it came to power. The draft constitution called for South Africa to terminate ties with the British Commonwealth and become a republic, and it was strikingly similar to the draft constitution published by the Ox Wagon Sentinels (OB) the year before. Both constitutions called for a "Christian-national" government, the use of both English and Afrikaans as official languages, the preservation of the white race and a guardianship of the white race, over the black race. Malan's constitution had a carefully-worded clause intended to keep Jews out of South Africa. It read, "(the Republic) shall be protected effectively against the capitalistic and parasitical exploitation of its people as well as against the undermining influences of its people as well as against undermining influences of hostile and unnatural elements." Another clause made it possible for the government to deport all the Jews already in the country at some unspecified date.

Other clauses in the constitution outlawed Communism, changed the national flag to that of the old Boer Republic, made the President of the Republic independent of the legislature, and authorized the President to allow the Prime Minister to rule by decree in times of national emergencies. There were still other clauses patterned after clauses in the German and Italian constitutions that would have turned South Africa into a neo-fascist state. Some of the redeeming facets of the draft constitution were that certain issues would be subject to a public referendum and there was no specific prohibition against opposition political parties.

BUSINESS WAS GOOD

While the politicians wrangled in the halls of government, the country's economy was booming. White unemployment was at new lows, wages were good, and there were few shortages. Employment opportunities for South Africa's blacks were also available. Manufacturing expanded considerably in South Africa, creating an increase in exports and a decrease in imports as South Africans made more of what they consumed. During 1942, factories in South African produced steel, aircraft, munitions, armored cars, uniforms, blankets, canned foods, cigarettes, and many other items. The provisioning of ships was also a very big industry.

The darkest cloud on the horizon was Rommel's new offensive in North Africa, which began in January and would not end until September. Many South African troops were fighting in North Africa with the British 8th Army and there were deep concerns for the boys at the front. Both the 1st and 2nd South African Divisions were serving in North Africa along with many SAAF personnel. Casualty reports flowed in from North Africa to the heartbreak of many South African families, and during the winter the SAAF had lost 65 aircraft.

South Africa's remoteness and strong economy made it a good place to send Axis POWs. POW camps sprang up all over the country with a very large one located at Johannesburg. The POWs were employed in the local economy within the guidelines of the Geneva Convention and the racial laws of the country, which helped to ease the manpower shortage of white males.

Not coming to South Africa, however, were European refugees. Since many of them were Jews, the Smuts government was resistant to allowing them into the country because of the internal political situation.

Certain South African businesses established a special relationship with French businesses in Free French-controlled Equatorial Africa. Farsighted French businessmen in Equatorial Africa could see the day coming when most, or all, of Vichy-controlled Africa, and even occupied France itself, would be liberated. At that point there would be a strong demand for all kinds of goods and commodities and it would be a seller's market. When that glorious day arrived the French businessmen wanted to be in a position to meet the new demands, especially for French industry. Therefore, the enterprising Frenchmen began stockpiling items in Equatorial Africa that they believed would be in high demand. A large percentage of those material, were bought from South Africa. Therefore, a steady stream of South African raw materials flowed northward to the Equatorial African ports of Duala and Pointe Noire for storage and future sale.

In another development concerning the French, the South African government broke off diplomatic relations with Vichy in April 1942. Vichy/South African relations had been deteriorating for several months because of Vichy's real and suspected aid to the Axis forces in North Africa and to the Japanese on Madagascar.

THE BOYS AT THE FRONT

Late May and the entire month of June were anxious months in South Africa because of the British setbacks in North Africa. There was great concern throughout the country for the men serving there.

Then, in late June, the worst happened. The bulk of the 2nd South African Division was captured when the Axis forces took Tobruk. Some elements of the 1st Division were captured too, but most of that unit retreated safely into Egypt. The South African people could console themselves in the fact that there was little bloodshed and that most of the men of the 2nd South Africans became prisoners. Someday—after the war—the men of the 2nd South African would come home again. A total of 10,727 South Africans, including 1,760 blacks and the division commander, General H. R. Klopper, were in Axis hands.

Reaction was swift by the South African government. Smuts called for 7000 volunteers to build up a new division and asked that more South African white women take jobs in industry to release men for military service. Meanwhile, the South African Army gathered together as many replacement troops as possible and sent them to North Africa. Most of them were placed in the 1st South African Division.

Coming the other way, from Cairo to South Africa, were some 4000 British women and children who had been evacuated in the face of the Axis advance. They arrived in Durban by ship and most of them were given temporary sanctuary there in private homes until more permanent places could be found for them elsewhere in the country. Among those arriving in South Africa was the wife of the British Ambassador to Egypt.

At the end of July there was more bad news from the north. The SAAF, which had been fighting constantly in the air over the battlefields, had lost ninety aircraft which represented over 60% of its strength. Clearly, the SAAF now needed time to rebuild.

As the El Alamein front stabilized, a patriotic group of citizens in South Africa began raising money for the war effort through a fund called the "Thank You General Smuts Fund." The fund's goal of 100,000 pounds was reached and given to Smuts in early September for him to use as he saw fit for the war effort.

Another significant South African contribution to the war effort was the "Scorpion." This was a land mine detonating device that South African engineers had been working on since early in the war. It consisted of a rotating drum with heavy loose chains attached to its periphery and mounted on the front of a British "Matilda" tank. The drum rotated rapidly, powered independently by two Ford V8 engines, throwing the chains out by centrifugal force. As the drum rotated the chains pounded the ground in front of the tank, detonating land mines. In this manner, tanks equipped with Scorpion devices could clear at path quickly through a mine field for themselves and other tanks as well as the infantry.

The Matilda-mounted Scorpion worked very well and was soon put to use in North Africa. The concept was picked up by the Soviets who used it on the Eastern front and by the Americans who used it at Normandy and later in France and Germany.

THE RHODESIAS AND NYASALAND

Both Northern and Southern Rhodesia developed rapidly during the war and the economies of both grew closer to that of South Africa. Nyasaland developed to some degree, but not on the same scale as the Rhodesias.

Southern Rhodesia, a self-governing colony of the British Commonwealth, was the most developed of the three when the war started. It had considerable mineral wealth, a good agricultural base, some manufacturing, over 1,600 miles of roads and over 1,300 miles of railroads. Here, as in South Africa, an all-white government ruled in much the same manner as the South African government. The white ruling class of Southern Rhodesia had long struggled with London to keep Southern Rhodesia from becoming a part of British East Africa, preferring instead to be associated with South Africa. The necessities of war served nicely to strengthen that bond and was actively promoted by Southern Rhodesia's Prime Minister Huggins, who established a close personal relationship with South Africa's Prime Minister Smuts and supported a future amalgamation of Southern Rhodesia with South Africa.

The Southern Rhodesian government had sent a considerable number of its young white men off to serve in the British armed forces, especially the RAF, and had raised both white and black military units on its own. The white units served primarily with the British 8th Army in North Africa while the black units, known as Rhodesian African Rifles, served in several other African theaters.

Like South Africa, Southern Rhodesia was enjoying a strong economy with few shortages. And, like South Africa, Southern Rhodesia practiced strict separation of the races. The tightening of the bonds forged by the war would continue in later years to the benefit of both countries.

Northern Rhodesia was still a British colonial dependency of the crown. Like Southern Rhodesia it was rich in mineral wealth, but being mostly desert it had a relatively weak agricultural base and very little manufacturing. The populations of both Northern and Southern were about the same, some 1.4 million people, but the percentage of whites in Northern Rhodesia was much less and a large number of them were employed in the mining industry and were not necessarily permanent residents.

As might be expected, Northern Rhodesia's mining industry was booming during the war and both black and white workers from other areas of Africa were recruited to work in that industry. This made the population of Northern Rhodesia even more transient. Because of geography Northern Rhodesia was tied economically to Southern Rhodesia and thereby to South Africa. Northern Rhodesia also had strong ties with its neighbor to the north, the Belgian Congo, because the bulk of that colony's mineral wealth was geographically adjacent to that of Northern Rhodesia's and both used the same rail systems across central Africa to export their respective minerals to the world markets.

Northern Rhodesia received a significant boost in its manufacturing industry when, during 1942, three munitions factories were built in the colony. Since munitions cartridges were made of copper-rich brass, that material was refined and alloyed from local ores and rolled into sheet metal for use in the munitions plants. Steel, which was used for the projectiles, was available from South Africa, thereby establishing one of the many economic bonds between the two countries.

Further improving Northern Rhodesia's economy was the construction of an all-weather road across Tanganyika connecting Northern Rhodesia with Kenya.

As for the natives, the Northern Rhodesian government set aside an additional 3.7 million acres of land at this time for a native preserve to relieve crowded conditions at the older reserves near Fort Jameson. Before the natives were moved onto the new land the government made an extensive survey to determine the best living and farming areas and also undertook measures to prevent soil erosion.

Nyasaland, like Northern Rhodesia, was tied geographically to Southern Rhodesia even though, in London, it was still regarded as a part of British East Africa. The necessities of wartime, however, worked against this theoretical grouping because thousands of Nyasalanders, from this poor and heavily-populated colony, went to the Rhodesias and South Africa to find work. Once there, they sent money and other necessities of life back to their families in Nyasaland.

BRITISH WEST AFRICA

During the spring of 1942, the British made a significant change in their administration of British West Africa by creating the wartime office of Resident Minister. This was a position designed to unify and coordinate all major political, economic, and military activities of the British West African colonies under one head for the benefit of the British war effort. Viscount Phillip Swinton was sent from London to fill the post and to establish a central headquarters in Achimota, Gold Coast. Assisting Swinton was a West African War Cabinet which consisted of the governors of the four colonies, Gambia, Sierra Leone, Gold Coast, and Nigeria along with representatives from the British Army, Navy, and RAF. A Secretariat was established that had branches that endeavored to streamline production and supply efforts to make them more efficient. Swinton also had the power to establish unified political and military policies with both the Vichy French and the Free French. Some problems developed within this arrangement, mainly from the four governors each of whom had conducted his own set of policies in this regard. The new arrangement under Swinton prevailed and eventually worked well.

Also stirring in British West Africa was native nationalism, especially in Nigeria. For several years a native newspaper chain, known as the "Nigerian Youth Movement" (NYM), had been operating under the direction of its founder, Nnamdi Azikiwe, a detribalized American-educated Ibo. The NYM was a moderate publication that stressed unity among Nigeria's hundred-plus tribes, along with urging the black people of Nigeria to take an interest in community and colonial affairs. In 1941, Azikiwe lost control of the NYM to a more aggressive individual, Obafemi Awolowo, who spoke out more forcefully on the subject of increased native rights and colonial autonomy. Azikiwe returned to Iboland and two years later founded another movement and publication known as the "National Council of Nigeria and the Cameroons" (NCNC). Azikiwe slowly became more aggressive in his editorials and more critical of British rule.

A third native organization surfaced in 1942, the "Nigerian Reconstruction Group," and it too agitated for more native rights and became critical of colonial rule.

LIBERIA

The small independent nation of Liberia in West Africa was one of the poorest lands in the world. During the 1930s it defaulted on its international loans and almost went bankrupt. Some world leaders at the time thought the country should be taken over by the League of Nations and run as a trusteeship. The United States government and the Firestone Rubber Company, which had large plantations in Liberia, prevented this from happening. With the coming of war, Liberia's economy picked up and the government of President William Barclay was able to begin repaying some of its loans. The export of rubber increased as did the export of palm kernels and oil, piassava, coffee, cocoa, ivory, and Kola nuts.

Liberia remained neutral in the war but, because of its strong political and economic ties with the Unites States, was very much supportive of the Allied cause. Under agreements with the Liberian government the Americans had, by 1942, built two airfields in Liberia as part of their air ferrying system. Also rivers and lakes in the country, especially the large Fisherman's Lake, were being used by the Americans and the Allies for seaplane operations. American and Allied naval operations in Liberia were nil because there were no harbors in the country capable of handling large ocean-going ships. Liberia's import/export trade was funneled through Freetown in neighboring Sierra Leone. Also, there were only about 250 miles of roads in the country and no railroads. The Americans began building roads in Liberia for their own military needs.

Around these new facilities whole villages sprang up as natives came to work for the Americans. Conditions were primitive in these new settlements, so the Americans were obligated to provide basic services such as clean water, electric power, dirt and gravel roads, hygiene, etc. Prostitution became rampant in the new villages and an epidemic of venereal disease soon followed. The Americans tried to suppress this activity by introducing sports programs and other activities, but they did little good. The best results were obtained by weekly medical inspections of all the women in the villages. In general, a wide variety of diseases existed throughout the country so the Americans established hospitals and aid stations to administer to the sick, they also undertook campaigns to eliminate malaria-carrying mosquitos and the tsetse fly menace.

Liberia had only a small, poorly-armed militia and no navy or air force. A visiting Life Magazine reporter commented that, "a hundred soldiers landed from a gun boat" could take over the country.

Between May and June 1942, a sizable force of American soldiers arrived in Liberia, under agreement with the Liberian government, to protect the country, primarily, from the Vichy French. Many of the American soldiers were black and were well-received by the population.

At the same time the Liberian government ordered the German consulate in Monrovia to close and the few German traders, who resided in the country, to leave.

BLACK AMERICAN SERVICEMEN EXPERIENCE RACIAL TROUBLE IN THE CONGO

The American government was very cautious about sending black American servicemen to certain parts of Africa for several reasons. The main reason was that the presence of black

WITCHCRAFT

During the war there was a significant increase in the belief of witchcraft and anti-witchcraft throughout black Africa, and it was especially widespread in Gold Coast. This phenomena was not wholly unexpected, because it had been documented in the past that periods of relative prosperity and foreign influence had brought witchcraft to the fore in African societies. The most noticeable aspect of this phenomena were the pilgrimages undertaken by believers to anti-witchcraft shrines, where one could implore the good spirits to protect them from the evil ones. The further distant the shrine, the more meaningful was the pilgrimage. In days of old the distances traveled were whatever the individual could manage on foot or by animal power. But, in the 1940s, with automobiles and other means of transportation available, pilgrimages were conducted over great distances.

From the white man's point of view these pilgrimages were a great waste of man-hours, fuel (which was often rationed), and other resources. Nevertheless, the strong belief in witchcraft and the pilgrimages continued throughout the war.

American soldiers might cause racial problems for the white colonial administrators and settlers. No American servicemen, black or white, were allowed to fraternized with the local natives because of problems with hygiene, prostitution, and personal safely. This meant that black American servicemen would be housed alongside white American servicemen, albeit in segregated quarters, but in living areas reserved for whites. The white colonial administrators and settlers in many parts of Africa objected to this, because it violated the strict dividing lines between blacks and whites. In late 1942, an incident happened at Matadi, Belgian Congo which was typical of what Washington feared would happen. At Matadi, a company of black American Army truck drivers was stationed in that community and created a racial backlash from the white citizenry. The report on the situation, written by the white company commander, Captain James V. Harding, tells the story. Harding wrote, "Racial restrictions are extreme, and no consideration is given our colored troops above that of the native Negro by the white population... There are no places where our (black) troops can go to be served food or drink... (and the) native villages are `off limits' to all Americans due to sanitary conditions and safety precautions... The conditions of the native population is exciting considerable comment among our (black) men who are rapidly becoming to feel that things they are fighting for are fallacy."

THE HAILEY COMMITTEE

The British were not blind to the aspirations of the various nationalist groups in Africa and elsewhere in the empire, and to the fact that the war had badly tarnished the British image as a colonial master able to control and defend its far-flung empire. Furthermore, there were those in Britain who had long been calling for decolonization. Some of the most outspoken proponents of decolonization were leaders of the main opposition party, the Labour Party. As a result, a lively debate had been going on in Britain for years over the future of the British Empire. That debate was accelerated during the war because of the rise of nationalism in all quarters of the empire and the dynamic, and often liberal-oriented, changes that were expected in the postwar era.

There was also the long-standing element of American foreign policy which called for decolonization at the earliest possible moment. This policy was known in every colonial land. The Atlantic Charter had its effect on the colonies and it was widely expected that the soon-to-be-created United Nations Organization would, like the old League of Nations, take an active role in colonial matters. It was becoming generally accepted that the United Nations Organization would, in all likelihood, act as a trustee over certain colonial areas in the postwar era with the ultimate goal being self-determination for the colonies in question.

To address all these issues and hopefully formulate a forward-looking policy, the British government turned to Lord Malcomb Hailey, a well-known expert on colonial matters and the author of the informative book on Africa entitled "African Survey." Lord Hailey, with official authorization, formed a committee to advise the government on future colonial matters. One of the first things the Hailey Committee did was to suggest that the word "trusteeship" be scraped in favor of "partnership" which clearly implied a greater participation of colonial peoples in their own affairs.

Clearly, the British government was moving away from its old colonial system and it was hoped that the Hailey Committee would show the way.

SPANISH AND PORTUGUESE AFRICA

For the first nine months of 1942 the status quo was the order of the day in the Spanish African colonies. Wartime conditions at sea and in the surrounding areas dictated much of the economic and political activities within those colonies. The Allies continued to be suspicious that Spain was aiding the Axis Powers whenever it was in her interests to do so. This belief was reinforced on March 2, when the American consul at Tenerife, in the Canary Islands, reported seeing a German submarine being refueled in Tenerife harbor. This was a direct violation of the Anglo-Spanish agreement of July 1941. Other reports of Spanish complicity with the Axis Powers trickled into the various Allied capitals during 1942.

Portuguese Mozambique was, by now, an acknowledged hotbed of Axis espionage activity. Many ships, both Allied and neutral, were putting into her ports to pick up the ores and other raw materials produced in the Belgian Congo, the Rhodesias, and elsewhere in southern Africa for export to world markets. The Axis agents in Mozambique dutifully reported to their spy masters on shipping activity in the ports as well as what they could learn about shipping traffic in the busy Mozambique Channel.

The colony was prospering thanks to the wartime activities and a new railroad was built in the Tete area to add to the colony's shipping capabilities. A large irrigation project was begun in the Limpopo River valley and plans were underway to bring in more Portuguese settlers.

In late January, 1,100 Portuguese troops left Lorenco Marques, the colonial capital, for Timor, a Portuguese island possession in the East Indies threatened now by the Japanese. Portugal was not at war with Japan but Timor was an important trading center and neither the Portuguese nor the Allies trusted Japanese intentions there.

Lorenco Marques had also become a transfer point for diplomats from the various belligerent nations being exchanged under international law. During the spring and summer of 1942, there was considerable activity in this respect with Axis diplomats and their families arriving from Allied nations and Allied diplomats and their families arriving from Axis nations and re-embarking on neutral ships, usually Portuguese or Swedish, for their home countries. Japanese ambassadors Nomura and Kurusu who, on December 7, 1941, presented U.S. Secretary of State Cordell Hull with Japan's declaration of war, passed through Lorenco Marques on their return to Japan.

In Portuguese Angola, the economy was also prospering as Allied and neutral ships came and went in Angolan ports, taking away the ores and raw material produced in the Allied colonies to the east. To further accommodate this traffic, the port facilities at Luanda were considerably improved.

In June, Portugal's Colonial Minister, Dr. Vieira Machado, made a tour of Angola, Mozambique, Belgian Congo and South Africa. This was seen as a friendly gesture by Portugal toward the Allies.

The Portuguese-owned Cape Verde Islands were not as fortunate as Mozambique and Angola. Those islands suffered a prolonged drought that began in 1941 and lasted well into 1942. Some estimates stated that up to 20,000 people perished. Still, though, the islands were a source for contract laborers and a large number of the islanders regularly went overseas, mostly to the Western Hemisphere, to take jobs.

With the introduction of Milch Cow supply submarines by the Germans in the Atlantic, the Allies soon discovered that the areas where the Milch Cows and operating submarines met were in areas outside of Allied air coverage but within air range of the Azores and Cape Verde Islands. Quite understandably the Allies now looked at these island groups more covetously than before. As a result, both the American and British governments put pressure on Lisbon to allow Allied aircraft to operate from their Atlantic islands. This put the Lisbon government in an awkward position. If the Portuguese government agreed to cooperate with the Allies they could expect some sort of retaliation from the Axis Powers, but if they refused the Allied requests the Allies might take the islands by force. Lisbon's response was to delay making a decision for as long as possible.

THE BELGIAN CONGO

With the loss of raw material sources in East Asia to the Japanese, the resources of the Belgian Congo became ever more important to the Allied cause. Tin was one of those important items and the British government contracted with the Belgian government-in-exile in London to purchase the colony's entire production. Other metals important to the Allied war effort were copper, radium, and various alloys for making steel. Palm nuts and lumber were also exported in large quantities from the Congo.

During August 1942, the top secret Manhattan District of the U. S. Army Engineer Corps came into being in New York City. This was the beginning of the "Manhattan Project" that would develop the first atomic bombs. Uranium was the material from which the bombs were to be made and the Belgian Congo was, at this time, the world's leading producer of uranium ore.

BRAZIL

For about a year, neutral Brazil had been cooperating with the Allies in enforcing the western hemisphere's Atlantic Security Zone. The Axis Powers had retaliated by sinking a number of Brazilian ships, claiming they were either carrying contraband to the Allies or sunk by mistake. Then in June, Hitler decided to punish Brazil further and on the 15th ordered Admiral Raeder to carry out a submarine blitz against Brazil off the Brazilian coast. Hitler knew full well that this action might force Brazil into a declaration of war on Germany.

On August 16, 1942, the German sub U–507 appeared off the coast of Brazil and promptly sank three Brazilian ships within hours of each other. In the sinking of one of the ships, the "Baependy," over 300 Brazilian soldiers were killed. The next day U–507 sank two more Brazilian cargo ships. Then, on August 19, U–507 sank yet another Brazilian cargo ship further south off the Brazilian coast. Some of the sinkings were within sight of shore.

The Brazilians were outraged by these actions and on August 22, Brazil declared war on Germany and Italy.

This changed the nature of the war in the South Atlantic because the Brazilians had a respectable navy with a large number of small vessels which were ideal for patrol work and convoy escort. In early September, British Admiral Pegram, commander of British naval forces in West Africa, flew to Recife, Brazil to confer with his Brazilian and American counterparts to establish procedures for patrolling the Atlantic narrows.

With Brazilian manpower and territory now available, the United States soon made arrangements to supply the Brazilians with more ships and planes. Some of them were equipped with radar and sonar. Also Brazilian service personnel were brought to the United States and given the latest training in antisubmarine defenses.

It was not long before Brazilian vessels were operating in both the South and North Atlantic, making life more hazardous for the German and Italian submariners and blockade runners. Within the first six months of being at war with Germany, the Brazilians sank five German submarines. By October 1943, the total rose to ten. Such was the result of Hitler's attempt to punish the Brazilians.

GERMANY

During January 1942, the German Foreign Ministry drew up yet another plan for the division of Africa after an Axis victory. This plan was basically the same as the Bielfeld Plan with some exceptions, one of which showed that South Africa was to be given a share of the spoils. It was presumed in Berlin that as Axis forces plunged deep into Africa, the Smuts government would fall, Malan and the National Party would come to power, disengage South Africa from Britain and the Allies and make peace. For this they would be rewarded.

Another change from the Bielfeld Plan was that Germany would give up its claim to the French half of Togo and it, along with Dahomey, would remain French. Gold Coast and Nigeria would remain British but Germany would claim Gambia and Sierra Leone. Germany would also lay claim to Spanish Guinea and Rio Muni with Spain receiving compensation elsewhere.

In February 1942, the British government took steps to counteract one of the major German propaganda themes directed repeatedly toward Britain's colonial subjects, that being that Britain was willing to "fight to the last dominion or colonial soldier." The British counteraction was to report on the casualties suffered so far in the war, up to mid–October 1941, by Britain and her empire. According to the report the United Kingdom had suffered 71.3% of the casualties while the dominions suffered 18.2%, India 5.5%, and all other colonies a total of 5%.

On March 8, 1942, a German newspaper published an article on some of the major construction projects that would be undertaken by Germany and her allies after the war to provide electrical power for Europe. One major project would be the tapping of, what the paper called, the "dormant water power resources" in the Congo. Furthermore, the article went on, various water power sources in the Mediterranean area would be tapped, including a dam that would be built across the Strait of Gibraltar to generate power from the changing of the tides.

BY THE YEAR 2000

On April 16, 1942, Heinrich Himmler, head of the SS, told a group of police chiefs at a luncheon meeting that he wanted to recover the good German racial stock from both Africa and the Americas, and he predicted that by the year 2000 the Germanic population of Greater Germany would be between 400 and 500 million.

THE UNITED STATES

In the United States a new activist group known as "The Council of African Affairs" (CAA) was gaining some notoriety. It was headed by the popular black singer Paul Robeson and Max Yergen, a prominent black YMCA official who had worked for years in Africa. The CAA called for the immediate independence of colonial lands in Africa and elsewhere. The organization published a monthly magazine, "New Africa," which was widely read, especially by the American black community.

The CAA was a politically leftist organization and was labeled by some as a neo-Communist organization.

On April 8, 1942, the CAA sponsored a rally in New York City at which the famous author, Pearl Buck, appeared. The main theme of the rally was African independence. Some 3,000 people attended.

On September 2, 1942, the CAA held another rally at the Manhattan Center in New York City called the "Free India Rally." Some 4,000 attended this rally. The CAA leaders also supported Soviet demands for an Allied second front in Europe.

The CAA had little influence on American politics, but its activities were noted in Africa by the various nationalist groups, and gave them encouragement.

During the summer of 1942, the American government leaders who were privy to the secrets of the Manhattan Project could see that backup sources for uranium were sorely needed. Total dependence upon the sources in the Belgian Congo was simply too risky. In this regard, mining operations were begun on a known deposit of uranium in Canada and Colorado.

On September 7, 1942, President Roosevelt held his third folksy Fireside Chat over American radio, talking to the American people. In that broadcast he dwelled at some length on the military situation in North Africa and praised the British Commonwealth troops; the South Africans, Australians, New Zealanders, and Indians for their fighting ability and successes against the Axis. He also said, in a more general way, "Certain vital military decision have been made. In due time you will know what these decisions are—and so will our enemies. I can say now that all of these decisions are directed toward taking the offensive." Roosevelt, in his own way, was telling the American people that the Allied invasion of French North Africa was at hand.

Chapter 15

FROM MADAGASCAR THROUGH "TORCH" (SEPTEMBER 1942–MAY 1943)

THE END OF THE FIGHTING IN AFRICA

During September 1942, the British and Americans were planning three amphibious operations and one ground offensive in Africa. The two largest amphibious operations would be the two simultaneous, but independent, invasions of Operation Torch, the invasion of French North Africa. They would consist of joint British and American landings on the Mediterranean coast of Algeria and the all-American landings on the Atlantic coast of French Morocco.

The third amphibious operation being planned was the invasion of southern Madagascar, designed to secure the remainder of that island for the Allies. The ground operation planned was the British attack at El Alamein with the objective to push Rommel and the Italians out of Egypt. It would be the invasion of Madagascar that occurred first.

THE INVASION OF SOUTHERN MADAGASCAR

The first military action against southern Madagascar occurred on September 9, 1942, when the 7th South African Brigade struck out from British-occupied Diego Suarez on the northern tip of the island and advanced on foot southward over the mountain and jungle trails that connected Diego Suarez with the rest of the island. This was the preliminary phase of "Operations Stream Line Jane," the British plan for the conquest of all of Madagascar. "Stream" would be the initial landing on the island's west coast at Majunga, "Line" would be the drive on Tananarive, the island's capital, and "Jane" would be a second amphibious landing on the east coast.

Before dawn, on September 10, 1942, the main British invasion force carried out "Stream" by landing at "Red Beach," several miles north of the small port city of Majunga at the mouth of the Betsiboka River. The assault was led by the amphibious-trained British 29th Independent Brigade out of Diego Suarez. It had arrived in a fifty-ship convoy bringing troops from both Mombasa, Kenya and Diego Suarez. Aircraft from the carrier Illustrious covered the landing.

The 29th did not advance immediately on Majunga, hoping that the Majunga garrison would move out of the town toward Red Beach. This they did and with the town now defenseless a small contingent of British commandos landed in Majunga's harbor, made a dash for the French headquarters, and took the French commander and his staff by surprise. The French commander then surrendered his garrison force and the city to the commandos. Losses for the British were five killed and seven wounded. As the sun came up, the French commander had breakfast with his captors, and the fight for Majunga went down in the British records as "The Battle Before Breakfast."

Once the port was secured General Platt, the overall operations commander, established his headquarters in the town and elements of the 22nd KAR Brigade were landed at Majunga harbor. They were to lead an advance along the Majunga–Tananarive Road which was to be as rapid as possible in order to secure as many bridges as possible intact.

The lead elements of the 22nd KAR landed first and departed, at once, down the Majunga–Tananarive Road. In the lead were South African-made Marmon-Herrington armored cars manned by South Africans. They met no French resistance and shortly after noon captured their first bridge across the Kamoro River. By 4:30 p.m. they took a second bridge, also intact. Six miles short of the Betsiboka River, however, the 22nd KAR ran into a roadblock consisting of large palm trees strewn across the road. Before the men of

KAR troops crossing the river at Andriba.

the 22nd KAR could clear the roadblock night fell and the advance halted. During the night, the Vichy forces destroyed the bridge across Betsiboka River. This was the largest bridge and deepest river on the Majunga–Tananarive Road.

Also on the 10th a second, smaller amphibious force consisting of commandos had landed at the port city of Morondave 230 miles south of Majunga on Madagascar's southwestern coast. This was a diversionary move designed to draw Vichy troops away from the advance in the north. The small French garrison at Morondave surrendered without a fight and the commandos advanced inland some thirty miles to the next town, Mahabo, where they set up defensive positions. They would remain there for the time being, posing a constant threat to the French left flank.

On September 11, before dawn, the men of the 22nd KAR and the South African armored cars resumed their march toward Tananarive. Again there was no French resistance. Supporting them overhead now were planes of the SAAF which had arrived that day at the Majunga airfield. This relieved the aircraft from the Illustrious. When the KAR men reached the Betsiboka River they discovered that the destroyed bridge was still passable. The main section of the bridge's roadbed had fallen intact and was only about three feet under water. Therefore, the troops and most vehicles could ford across the fallen road bed of the bridge. As the KAR men were crossing the bridge a lone French plane appeared and dropped six bombs. None of them caused any casualties or damage. A short time later a French rear-guard unit fired at the KAR men with small arms. A fire fight ensued and a charge by two platoons of KAR dislodged the French and forced them to withdraw. In the process six KAR men were wounded, ten French soldiers, mostly askaris, were killed, four wounded, and 37 captured.

By dark the KAR's armored cars and other vehicles were crossing the Betsiboka River.

On that same day, September 11, elements of the South African forces advancing southward out of Diego Suarez occupied the small port of Vohemar, sixty miles southeast of Diego Suarez on Madagascar's east coast. Two days later they captured the small island of Nossi Be off the northeast coast of the island. They then continued their advance over the trails in a southward direction. Their objective was to continue on the trail that led eventually to a junction with the Majunga–Tananarive Road at a point about fifty miles east of Majunga. This would clear the northwestern part of the island between Majunga and Diego Suarez of enemy troops.

In an effort to reduce the French opposition, London announced, as it had at the time of the invasion of Diego Suarez, that Madagascar would remain a part of the French empire and that the salaries and pensions of French military and administrative officials who cooperated with the British would be guaranteed. London also offered to quickly establish trade with the island in an effort to stimulate its economy. From Tananarive came an official rejection of the British offer but, as the invasion progressed and opportunities presented themselves, many of the individual French officials accepted the British offer.

On September 12, the 22nd KAR took the entire day to bring all of their vehicles, men, and supplies across the Betsiboka bridge.

On September 13, the KAR men resumed their advance and ran into more roadblocks but no substantial French resistance.

On the 14th, newly-arrived elements of the 22nd KAR took the lead along with the South African armored cars. Up to now the advance had been across relatively flat land, but ahead were high hills where ambushes and stronger resistance could be expected. The next day, as the lead KAR elements entered the hills they encountered more roadblocks and some light French rear guard action. When the KAR men fired back the rear guards quickly retreated. There were also more destroyed bridges. Most of the bridges, however, were small and of wooden construction across fordable streams. To "destroy" the bridges the French soldiers simply removed the wooden planks and hid them nearby. The KAR men quickly found the planks and replaced them, making the bridges serviceable again. Later in the day, September 15th, the KAR men took the town of Andriba, 95 miles northwest of Tananarive, without a fight.

Surprisingly, up to now no land mines, or artillery barrages, or large-scale air attacks had been encountered by the advancing forces. It appeared that the island's Governor, Armand Annet, might be playing a dual game; offering resistance in compliance with his oath of loyalty to Petain, but conducting defenses that spared as much bloodshed as possible. With a force of only 20,000 men, most of whom were poorly armed and demoralized, Annet knew his position was hopeless in the long run.

On September 16, the KAR men reached the Mamokamita River to find the bridge blown and unusable, a formidable roadblock, and a company of French Senegalese troops defending the position. The South African armored cars and a company of Nyasalanders, under a covering fire of mortars and light artillery, attacked the Senegalese and a sharp skirmish resulted. The Senegalese were overwhelmed by the superior British firepower and withdrew, but not before killing four KAR men, an officer, and wounding eight others.

The river was fordable so the KAR men were able to establish a bridgehead on the far side, giving the engineers cover to build a temporary bridge over the river during the night. The next morning the KAR advance resumed and that day they captured the airfield at the small town of Marotsipoy. SAAF aircraft soon moved forward to offer close air support.

Meanwhile in the north the men of the 7th South African Brigade were moving steadily southward from Diego Suarez, fighting more mosquitos than Frenchmen. It was finally decided, though, that the advance on Tananarive was going so well that the services of the 7th South Africans would not be needed. Therefore, they stopped at Miromandia, and the main force returned to Diego Suarez leaving a small defensive force at Miromandia. The 7th's engineers, though, proceeded southward along the trail out of Miromandia to make the trail passable in case it was needed in the future.

On September 17, word came from Tananarive that Governor Annet was willing to discuss armistice terms. The two sides met the next day, but Annet felt that the British terms were too harsh and rejected them. The meeting ended without agreement. On the 18th the British forces resumed their advance on Tananarive and reached a point sixty miles from the capital after having encountered 64 more roadblocks.

That was not the big news of the day, however. At Tamatave, on the east coast of the island, the British pulled off their third amphibious landing of the campaign at that small seaport. From Tamatave there was both a road and railroad leading to Tananarive.

The same assault ships that had participated in the Majunga landing were used here. They had sailed around the northern end of the island carrying the British 29th Independent Brigade. As at Majunga, the 29th spearheaded the invasion, with aircraft from the carrier Illustrious providing air protection. Unlike Majunga though, the lead landing boats of the 29th went in during daylight, about 7:30 am, displaying the white flag of truce, hoping the French would not fire on them. It did not work. The French responded by firing at the boats with machine gunfire. The landing boats then withdrew and a cruiser, a destroyer, and several other ships opened fire with their big guns on the French coastal defenses. The barrage lasted only three minutes before the French raised a white flag and surrendered. The British landing boats then went in again, splitting into two forces. One landed north of the city and the other to the south. As they marched on Tamatave from both directions, a British destroyer rushed into the harbor and landed more troops from the 29th and the 5th Commandos on the jetty. By this time the French had abandoned the town and the British occupied it without casualties.

Just by chance a train steamed into Tamatave minutes later. The British commandeered the train, turned it around, and set out with as many men and guns as it would hold to take the next objective in their path, the port city of Brickaville, 35 miles down the coast.

The train proceeded unopposed to a point two miles from Brickaville, where a bridge had been blown. The British troops dismounted from the train and attacked the city, taking the French garrison completely by surprise. A brief fire-fight ensued before the French surrendered. Later that evening, the British forces regrouped and, with the 5th Commandos in the lead, set out along the Brickaville-Tananarive road. Annet's eastern flank was now threatened.

To the west, the 22nd KAR resumed their march on September 19, but were slowed by blown bridges, roadblocks, and occasional rear-guard fire which, when fired upon, quickly ended. It was the same the next day. By that evening the KAR men were approaching the village of Mahitsy about thirty miles from Tananarive. There it was learned from local people that the French had dug in for a stand at the edge of the town. As they approached the Mahitsy defenses, which were defended by three French companies backed up with a relatively large artillery unit, the KAR men were fired on, and several French aircraft appeared and attacked the advancing troops. On September 21, the KAR troops mounted a frontal assault supported by their own artillery and SAAF planes. They captured some ground and several French artillery pieces, but the French held on. The next day KAR troops worked their way around the French defenses, threatening to encircle them. The French quickly withdrew losing 45 of their number as prisoners. Most of the French artillery was also captured, which represented half of the French artillery on the island.

With the fall of Mahitsy and Tananarive now threatened, the Malagache troops under French command began to lose heart and desert in ever increasing numbers.

On September 23, KAR troops approached the outskirts of Tananarive and were met with a stronger-than-usual rear guard force, but a less-than-determined defense. The superior British firepower soon overcame the defenders and the KAR men entered the city.

Annet, his government, and his remaining loyal troops had already abandoned the city and retreated to the south toward the town of Antsirabe. The British made no immediate attempt to pursue Annet and his entourage. Instead

A KAR soldier awarded a medal at Tananarive.

they secured the city and brought up their reserves and supplies.

As they entered Tananarive, the KAR troops were surprised by a tumultuous welcome given them by the local citizenry. It appeared that the citizens of the town were ecstatic at being liberated by black troops. The KAR men moved into the comfortable French barracks and the SAAF moved their planes forward to the Ivato Airport, the town's main airfield. On September 26, General Platt moved his headquarters from Majunga to Tananarive. The advance from Majunga had cost the British only one officer, and seven KAR were dead with 31 wounded.

While the KAR men were fighting their way into Tananarive, a report came on the 20th that a French force had been discovered north of Majunga and was in a position to attack the city, which was now the main port of supply for the KAR troops. That evening a force of KAR men in armored cars and trucks raced back to Majunga. On September 21, they started marching up the jungle and mountain trails north of the city, and on the next day made contact, at Antsohihy, with the 7th South African engineers working their way south. No French force was encountered. The report had been false.

The KAR troops returned to Tananarive and on September 24 a KAR unit marched east out of the capital to link up with the South Africans coming in from Brickaville. They met that day at Moramanga. Back in Tananarive the main KAR force conducted a victory parade.

The KAR troops returned from Moramanga to Tananarive and on September 26, the main body of the KAR 22nd Brigade set out on the road south in pursuit of Annet and his remaining forces. A railroad paralleled the road. British intelligence reported that the French still had fourteen companies of troops at their disposal. It was also the beginning of the rainy season and rains could be expected any day.

At Behenjy, a few miles south of Tananarive, a company of Malagache put up a token resistance and then disappeared into the bush. The advance was slowed by many roadblocks. In one stretch of 2.5 kilometers, the KAR men encountered 29 stone walls erected across the road. In another half-mile stretch, some 800 trees had been felled across the road. The French had hired many of the local people to help create the roadblocks, and when the KAR troops arrived they hired many of the same people to remove them.

On September 28, the KAR troops occupied the town of Ambatolampy, thirty miles south of Tananarive, without a fight but in heavy rain. There they liberated sixteen British civilians who had been interned by the French.

The KAR men pressed on, and on September 30, encountered a force of 600 Malagache at Gare de Sambaina, who put up a token resistance and then vanished during the night.

On October 2, KAR troops occupied the town of Antsirabe without resistance. So far the advance had covered only sixty miles in seven days. At Antsirabe the KAR force halted to bring up supplies and prepare for the next advance which, they believed, would meet heavy French resistance. At Antsirabe the railroad from Tananarive ended. It had not been damaged by the French over its entire length. The next day, SAAF planes moved to the airfield at Antsirabe.

KAR troops marching through Tananarive in a victory parade.

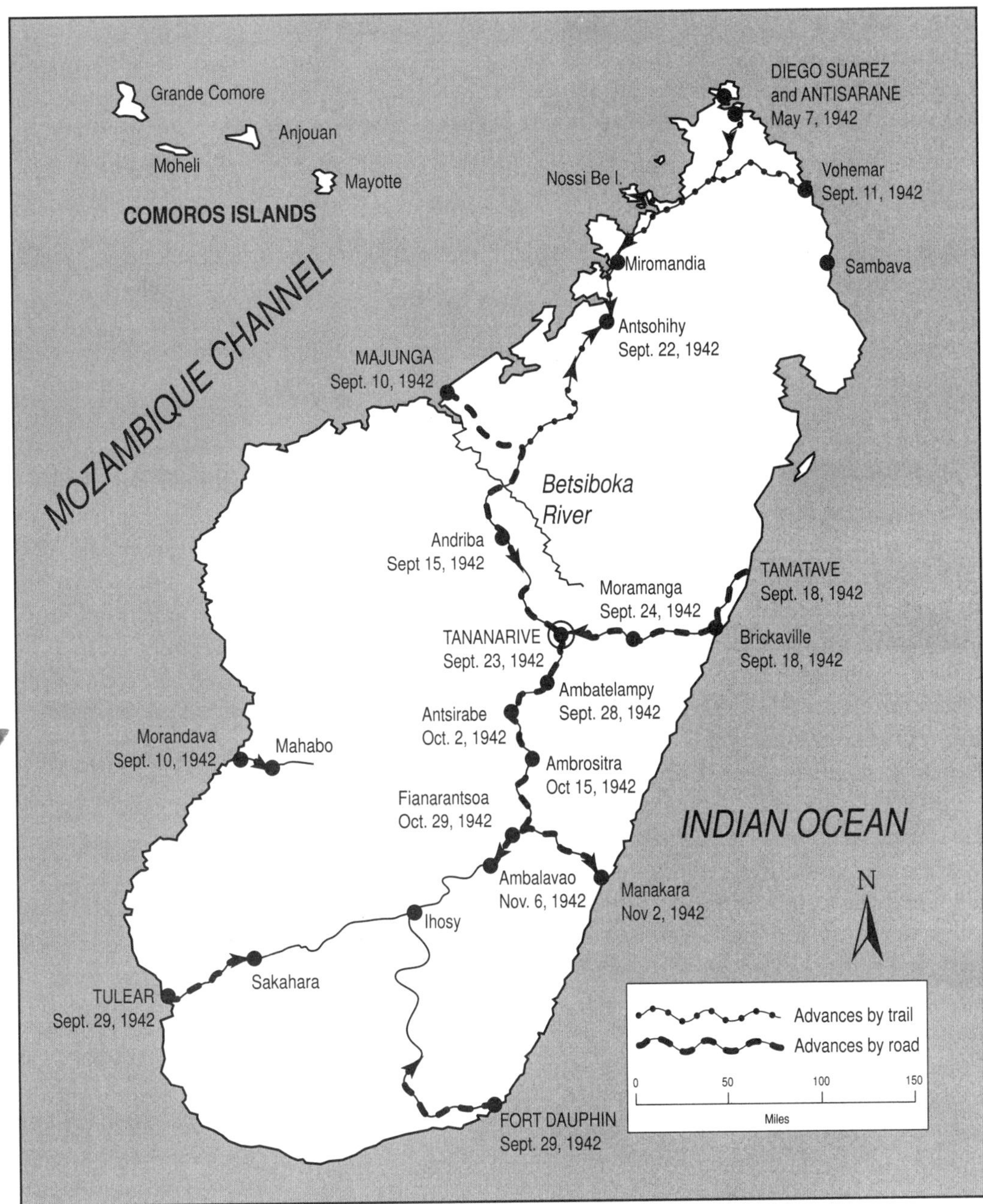

The Madagascar campaign, September–November 1942.

Meanwhile, South African forces carried out two more amphibious landings on the island. At Tulear, on the southwestern coast, the South African Pretoria Regiment occupied that port and then advanced inland to the town of Sakaraha and stopped. Tulear had an airfield and a seaplane base which now gave the Allies the opportunity to increase air coverage over the Mozambique Channel.

At Fort Dauphin, on the southeastern coast, another South African unit landed and advanced inland about fifty miles before halting. Neither force met resistance. Their presence was to threaten the French rear and prevent Annet and his troops from escaping by sea.

On October 9, the KAR resumed their march out of Antsirabe and promptly ran into a well-planned and executed ambush. It was a brief but intense fight. Four KAR men were killed and six wounded before the French broke off contact and retreated. The KAR resumed their advance and that evening occupied the town of Ikata. The next day the French put up another brief fight south of Ikata but caused no British casualties while losing thirty men as prisoners.

On October 11, General Platt turned over command of operations on Madagascar to General Smallwood and returned to his main headquarters at Nairobi, Kenya.

For the next three days the KAR advance was slowed by roadblocks, blown bridges and rain. On the 12th the French put up another brief rear guard action, which quickly dissipated.

On the 13th they made a more determined stand north of Ambositra, the largest city still in French hands. For three days the KAR and French exchanged artillery and small arms fire, but then the French withdrew and the KAR men occupied the city.

The KAR passed quickly through Ambositra but ran into another strong French defense south of the city. This battle lasted another three days before the French suddenly collapsed on the 19th and began surrendering in large numbers. The KAR troops took some 700 prisoners, including 192 French officers and NCOs. Also captured was the last of the French heavy artillery. With the losses at Ambositra the French had only eight companies of infantry left. The end was near. Still the going was tough for the KAR because of more roadblocks, blown bridges, rain, and occasional rear guard actions.

On October 29, the French put up another fairly strong fight north of Fianarantsoa, the old southern capital. It lasted several hours then ended as the French withdrew. That evening the KAR men occupied the town.

As the French were evacuating Fianarantsoa, planes of the Royal Navy, which were now cooperating with the SAAF in providing ground support for the KAR troops, strafed a French road convoy and nearly killed Governor Annet.

From Fianarantsoa, a small KAR force proceeded down the road eastward to the port of Manakara and occupied that town on November 2 without incident. This was the last port through which the French could escape by sea.

Still the French refused to surrender and the KAR advance resumed once more. For the next few days it was more of the same, roadblocks, blown bridges, rear guard actions, and rain. Late on the afternoon of November 4, as the KAR troops approached Ambalavao, where the paved road ended and turned into a trail, word was receive that the French military commander, General Guillemet, requested surrender terms on behalf of Governor Annet. Annet was now at Ihosy, fifty miles south, the last town of any size still in French hands. That town was also threatened from the west. The South African Pretoria Regiment, which had landed September 29 at Tulear and moved inland to Sakaraha, began advancing up the Sakaraha–Ihosy road toward Ihosy.

The KAR commanders quickly responded and on November 5, surrender terms were worked out. At one minute past midnight on November 6, the surrender documents were signed. The reason the documents were signed at this unusual hour was due to a French request. According to French Army regulations officers and men had to be engaged in a campaign for at least six months before they could be awarded medals and decorations. On November 6, the six months time limit was reached and the Frenchmen could get their rewards.

Thus ended the fighting in Madagascar. On November 8, the South African Pretoria Regiment occupied Ihosy, and during the next few days the SAAF planes dispersed to the various airfields around Madagascar and began active anti-submarine patrols over the Mozambique Channel and the western Indian Ocean.

From London came the announcement from the Fighting French National Committee on November 11 that the civil administration of Madagascar would be taken over by the Fighting French, and that General Legentilhomme would assume the office of High Commissioner for Madagascar. Control of the island was formally transferred to the Fighting French on January 8, 1943, with the understanding that Diego Suarez would continue to operate as a British naval base for the duration of the war.

The 7th South African Brigade returned to South Africa and the 27th Northern Rhodesian Brigade was brought in to occupy Diego Suarez. Previously, in late October the British 29th Independent Brigade had been withdrawn to Durban for rest due to a high incidence of malaria. The 22nd KAR Brigade remained as the primary occupation force in southern Madagascar until Fighting French forces could take over. In December, the 22nd was informed that, after the Fighting French took over, it would be sent to fight the Japanese in Burma. In preparation for that new assignment, the men of the 22nd KAR began jungle training there in Madagascar. The men of the 22nd had performed so well that a number of their sergeants were assigned to be platoon leaders, a position normally reserved for whites.

KAR men also guarded the several POW camps that were established in Madagascar to hold the French troops. Many of the Malagaches, and some of the Senegalese, offered to join the British, but were refused. As POWs they were used as laborers especially at Diego Suarez where they handled cargo and provisioned ships.

Later, when the Fighting French took over the island, the Malagache and Senegalese troops were released as POWs and many of them joined de Gaulle.

THE BRITISH TAKE THE OFFENSIVE IN EGYPT

On October 6, 1942, Montgomery's "Operation Lightfoot" began at El Alamein with large British forces moving toward the front with meticulous care, while probing attacks were carried out by small units. There was plenty of time, up to two weeks had been allotted for these initial phases.

JEWS PERSECUTED IN LIBYA

In Rome the mounting British threat to Libya was quite evident and since the German forces in North Africa would soon be called upon to make another major effort to help protect Italy's colony Mussolini thought it appropriate to make a political concession to Hitler. Therefore, on October 9, he decreed that all of Italy's anti-Semitic laws would, henceforth, be enforced to Libya.

The British forces now outnumbered the Axis forces with 195,000 men compared to the Axis's 105,000. The British also had 1029 tanks, including the new American-made Sherman tanks, compared to 490 for the Axis; 530 aircraft against 350; and 1,400 antitank guns compared to 744.

On October 20, the first major Allied military action began when the combined Allied air forces initiated a four-day aerial campaign against Axis aircraft, airfields, fuel dumps, repair facilities, etc. designed to gain air superiority before the ground attack began. Montgomery considered this essential.

ALLIED PREPARATIONS IN THE WEST

On October 22, 1650 miles to the west of El Alamein, an American submarine deposited a party of Americans on a beach near Algiers, Algeria under the cover of darkness. The party was headed by American General Mark Clark who had come to confer secretly with anti-Vichy French officials who were in positions to facilitate the coming Allied landings of Operation Torch. The top Frenchman at the meeting was General Charles Mast, Commander of the French Algerian Division. Mast assured Clark that his forces, which commanded a part of the front in Algeria, would obey orders from General Henri Giraud, a French general the Americans had selected to rally the North African French. Assurances were given to Mast and later announced over Allied radio, soon after the invasion began, that all of French North Africa would remain French. At the secret meeting, though, Mast admitted he could not give assurances as to what the French Navy would do.

About this same time the first ships, which were to participate in the landings, left Britain and America. Already en route were five American submarines which would patrol the intended landing areas along the Atlantic coast of Morocco and survey conditions there. When the invasion came it would be their mission to guide the troop ships to the correct beaches.

THE SECOND BATTLE OF EL ALAMEIN

In Egypt, during the night of October 22/23 and throughout the daylight hours of the 23rd, the British units continued moving into their assigned positions as quietly as possible. Then at 9:30 on the evening of the 23rd the desert stillness was suddenly broken by the report of over 1,000 British artillery pieces. For over twenty minutes this horrific barrage pounded the Axis defenses. The Axis forces did not reply in kind because they were under orders to conserve ammunition. The British barrage ended as suddenly as it began, and at 10:00 p.m. the British 30th Corps broke out of its positions, made its way through the miles-wide mine fields with the help of Scorpion-equipped Valentine and Sherman tanks, and smashed full force into the Axis defenses. British infantry followed the tanks and fierce battles erupted at several points. This was the beginning of "The Second Battle of El Alamein." Slowly, the British forces penetrated the Axis lines, paying for each foot in blood.

Prior to the attack at El Alamein, October 23 had been a very eventful day. Rommel was, once again, not at the front. He was in Europe and had left his deputy, General Stumme, in charge of the German forces in Egypt.

Also on the 23rd, at the western end of North Africa, Admiral Francois Darlan, former Vice Premier at Vichy and now commander of all Vichy armed forces, arrived in Rabat, Morocco. The Vichy French were now more suspicious than ever that an Allied invasion of French North Africa was likely, and Darlan had come to North Africa to confer with his subordinates on military plans to meet such an invasion. Darlan had a second reason for coming to North Africa. His son, an officer in the French Navy, had contracted polio and was in a hospital in Algiers. The Admiral planned to visit his son before returning to Vichy on November 10.

Also that day, on the other side of the Atlantic Ocean, the American troop convoys that were to carry out the landings in French Morocco left ports in the Chesapeake Bay and New York City areas. This would be the first time in American history that American troops would leave from American shores and land directly on enemy beaches. The ground troops aboard these ships, known as the "Western Task Force" or "Task Force 34," were under the command of General George S. Patton, Jr.

Later, on October 23, the RAF carried out very heavy air raids on Genoa and Turin, Italy, both debarkation ports for Axis reinforcements and supplies to North Africa.

Back at El Alamein, October 24 proved to be a second day of hard fighting with the British forces gaining more ground, but not as much as hoped. Later in the day the RAF bombed the Italian cities of Milan, Monza, and Novara.

Also on October 24, the German forces at El Alamein became temporarily leaderless. General Stumme was riding in the turret of an armored car when it was hit by a small shell. The shock caused Stumme to have a heart attack and fall out of the turret without the driver noticing. A short while later the driver realized Stumme was missing and a frantic search began to find him. Four hours later he was found sprawled on the desert, dead. General Ritter von Thoma, the next in command, promptly took over.

On the 25th, Rommel returned to North Africa and ordered a counterattack. It was beaten back. The British recovered quickly and continued to press their attack. At Tobruk, the Axis forces main supply port, Allied planes sank two Italian tankers, the "Proserpina" and "Luisiano," both loaded with fuel for tanks. This was a serious blow to the Axis forces. Once again fuel became a critical item for the German and Italian tanks.

The next day, the British made more small gains while the Allied air forces, which now dominated the air, made it difficult for the Axis forces to assemble any sizable number of tanks in one place, lest they become targets for concentrated air attacks. Notwithstanding, German tank losses had already been sizable. The German 15th Armored Division, which had taken much of the brunt of the British attack, was down from 119 serviceable tanks to 39.

Also that day, the first troops ships left England carrying the American and British troops that were to land in Algeria. This was known as the "Eastern Task Force." This force was soon spotted by the Germans, as it sailed south out of British waters and information was flashed to Berlin and Rome. Almost at once the Axis leaders began to speculate on its purpose. The Germans believed it might be another reinforcement for Malta or, perhaps, an invasion of Dakar. The Italians were closer to the mark. They believed it was an invasion fleet heading for French North Africa. Both agreed that the Vichy government should be informed of the British force and that the French should be on the alert.

The Germans, though, did not heed their own advice. At this time a Freetown-to-England convoy had been spotted further down the coast of West Africa, and the German submarines off Gibraltar, which might have intercepted the British task force, were sent to intercept that convoy.

During October 27 and 28, there was more hard fighting at El Alamein. Several Axis counterattacks were turned back with the Germans and Italians losing tanks on each occasion. By the end of the 28th, the Axis counted only 148 German and 187 Italian tanks still serviceable. The British still had over 800.

On October 29, Montgomery received information through Ultra about Axis troop positions at El Alamein and decided to change the focus of his attack from the north to the center, where the Axis line was held by the weaker Italian Trento and Bologna Divisions. On October 30/31, while Montgomery was repositioning his troops for the attack on the center, the 9th Australians, in a surprising success, broke through the Axis front in the north, turned toward the sea, and for a while trapped a large number of Germans and Italians in a pocket. Other German tanks, however, punched a hole in the Australian ring and relieved the trapped troops. This was a clear sign, though, that the Axis defenses were weakening.

RELATIVELY QUIET IN THE MEDITERRANEAN SEA

During October, for the second month in a row, German and Italian subs made no significant attacks on Allied shipping along the North African coast. British subs were busy, though, and sank six Italian and German merchant ships. And, on October 19, the British sub "Unbending" sank the Italian destroyer "Da Verazzano" off Tunisia. On October 30, the German sub U-559 was sunk by three British destroyers and two destroyer escorts off Port Said. On November 7, U. S. aircraft sank the Italian sub "Antonio Sciesa" off the coast of Libya.

THE YANKS ARE COMING

In the Atlantic, by October 28, the huge American task force which was to invade Morocco was in the central Atlantic heading on a bearing for Dakar. This was a feint to disguise the real target. Vichy French intelligence, however, had spotted the task force and as a precaution evacuated women and children from Dakar into the interior. Another fear the French had in both West Africa and French Morocco was that an Allied landing might spark a native uprising, so internal security measures were strengthened accordingly.

On November 2, the American task force suddenly changed course for Gibraltar. . . another feint.

On November 2, Montgomery launched his new attack, now called "Operation Supercharge," on the center of the Axis line. The first action was in the south where the British 44th Infantry Division and the Fighting French Brigade made feint attacks. The main attack, though, was led by the 2nd New Zealand Infantry Division and, with heavy artillery support, opened a hole in the line defended by the Italian Trento Division. Then, the British 9th Armoured Brigade poured through the hole in full force. Rommel rushed his 15th Panzer Division to plug the hole but by the end of the day the British had established a firm bridgehead on the west side of the huge Axis mine field, albeit, at a very high cost in men and tanks. The British poured in more forces and the next day there was very hard fighting in the Axis center. But British superior numbers and mastery of the air began to gain the upper hand. Rommel's tank force now dwindled to 32 tanks. Late that day some Axis units began to retreat. By nightfall, Rommel realized he could no longer hold the front and gave the order to withdraw. The Italian "Folgore" Parachute Division, the "Ariete" Armored Division, the "Littorio" Infantry Division and the "Trieste" Motorized Division were given the thankless jobs of holding the British as long as possible in order to give the other Axis forces time to organize and retreat. At 10:30 p.m. came a message from Hitler ordering Rommel to hold his ground. "It would not be the first time in history that the stronger will triumphed over the stronger enemy battalions," Hitler said. The die was cast, however. The Axis troops were already retreating. Hitler's order was too late.

The next morning, November 4, the British attacked again and, after a period of hard fighting by the Italians, the Axis center crumbled. In the process the Ariete, Littorio and Trieste Divisions were decimated. By nightfall, the Axis forces were in full but orderly retreat. The Folgor" Parachute Division courageously fought on until the 5th, holding out long enough to delay the British and give the other Axis units precious time to disengage. When the Italian paratroopers finally received the order to withdraw, they were down from 5,000 men to 32 officers and 262 other ranks.

This victory cost the British dearly. The 9th Armoured Corps suffered the worst with 75% casualties. But Montgomery had more tanks available, which were able to charge past their fallen comrades and penetrate deeply into the Axis rear.

From Cairo, Alexander's headquarters flashed the good news to London that the Axis forces "are now in full retreat."

November 5, was a glorious day for the Allies. Montgomery confirmed that his troops had forced the Axis forces into full retreat at El Alamein and had even penetrated the enemy's secondary defense line at Fuka. Montgomery announced that General Ritter von Thoma, Rommel's second in command, and nine other Axis generals had been captured along with 10,000 German and 20,000 Italian troops. Also, 450 Axis tanks and 1,000 artillery pieces had been destroyed or captured. All four German and all eight Italian divisions were badly mauled in the five days of fighting.

To add to the glory of the day, word was received from Madagascar that fighting had ended there and the Vichy French were negotiating surrender terms.

Still on November 5, General Dwight Eisenhower and his staff arrived secretly at Gibraltar to establish headquarters there from which he would direct the invasion of French North Africa. Offshore the first ships of the Eastern Task Force were beginning to pass through the Gibraltar Strait. Soon to join Eisenhower at Gibraltar was French General Henri Giraud, a hero of the battle for France in 1940. Giraud had been taken prisoner by the Germans, escaped and made his way to Gibraltar. Since Giraud had not been associated with either de Gaulle or Petain, the Allies hoped Giraud would be instrumental in rallying the North African French to the Allied side at the time of the landings.

The British victory in Egypt came just in time, because heavy rains occurred on November 6 and 7 hampering all operations. The rains gave the Germans and Italians an opportunity to put some distance between themselves and the pursuing British.

Meanwhile in Berlin, the Germans were aware of the Allied troop convoys leaving England and America and knew that a major Allied invasion was about to happen. German subs in the Atlantic and western Mediterranean were now ordered to intercept the Allied convoys and especially the troop transports. They made the effort but, for the most part, they could not get past the very strong escort force. Only one transport, the American "Thomas Stone," a part of the convoy out of England, was hit and damaged by a torpedo but did not sink. This happened in the Mediterranean just east of Gibraltar. The troops aboard were evacuated to landing craft in which they made the remainder of the voyage.

As the Allied convoys from England passed through the Strait of Gibraltar on November 6 and 7, they steamed parallel to the French North African coast. The Axis leaders had no idea where the Allied convoys were heading, so alerts went out throughout the western Mediterranean to prepare for a possible Allied invasion. Then, during the night of the 7/8th, the convoys made sharp right turns and headed for the shores of Algeria.

In the Atlantic, the American task force was off the coast of Morocco on a course for Gibraltar. It too turned sharply to the right and headed for the beaches of French Morocco.

ALLIES LAND IN FRENCH NORTH AFRICA

In a well-coordinated attack, Allied troops landed simultaneously on the morning of November 8 at two places in Algeria and three places in French Morocco. The primary objectives of this first stage of Operation Torch was to capture the port cities of Oran and Algiers in Algeria, and Casablanca in French Morocco. Once these ports were captured, their harbor facilities would be utilized to bring in large numbers of men and equipment. To minimize French resistance, leaflets were dropped on the major North African cities telling the populace that the Allies came as friends. In Vichy, Admiral William Leahy, the American Ambassador, delivered a letter from President Roosevelt to Petain. Roosevelt told Petain that the Allies had come in peace in North Africa to save those areas for France. Roosevelt's letter stated in part, "...Germany and Italy plan to invade and occupy French North Africa in order to implement their plan for the domination and conquest of the whole continent (of Africa)... ."

True to their word, though, the Vichy French ignored all of these last minute gestures and did what they said they would do all along—oppose any invader. The strongest French resistance came at Oran, but there was some resistance at all of the invasion sites. In Algeria, some of the soldiers in the French Army opposing the Allies were Algerians, and in Morocco, Moroccans fought the Americans.

At Casablanca, the Americans lost 242 landing craft due to enemy action, accidents, and the inexperience of the crews. The Americans, though, established a firm beachhead north of the city and began marching on it that day.

By nightfall on the 8th, the city of Algiers had been secured and the Allies had established strong beachheads at all other locations.

As the American and British troops landed, de Gaulle went on the radio from London to address the people throughout the French Empire telling them of the invasion. He asked for their support and for French forces not to resist. He further stated that "Our Algeria, our Morocco, our Tunisia are to be made the jumping-off ground for the liberation of France." De Gaulle and his Fighting French had not been invited to participate in the landings because of the very strong anti-de Gaulle feelings among most of the top French leaders in North Africa. Both Roosevelt and Churchill had agreed to this. De Gaulle resented this treatment, but had no option but to go along and cooperate. There were strong anti-British feelings in French North Africa too, so this is one reason why the Americans were given a leading role in the invasion and the appointment of an American, Eisenhower, as the top Allied commander. It was hoped that the Americans would have a moderating influence on the North African French.

At Vichy, the Petain government immediately broke diplomatic relations with the United States but, wisely, did not declare war on either Britain or the United States.

In Berlin and Rome, the Axis leaders now knew what the Allied were up to — a giant pincers from both east and west to force the Germans and Italians out of North Africa. For Hitler the news of the American and British invasion came at a very troubled time. He was just beginning to receive reports of tremendous losses suffered by his forces at Stalingrad. Nevertheless, the Germans were able to react within hours to the new developments in North Africa. From U-boat command in Paris, at about 6:30 am, came orders to fifteen subs in the area to converge on the invasion forces and attack the landing operations. This was of little value along the Atlantic coast of Morocco, because by the time the U-boats reached the landing areas the troops and equipment had been off-loaded and many of the ships had departed. In the Mediterranean it was a different story. German subs were close at hand and Axis aircraft from Sicily were able to attack the invasion fleet on the 9th. Despite the heavy Allied escort force, sub U–331 was able to torpedo and sink the American cargo ship "Leedstown" after she had been damaged by bombs and an air-launched torpedo. The American battleship "Massachusetts," two cruisers, two destroyers, and several smaller ships were also damaged in the Mediterranean by Axis aircraft.

Meanwhile, American and British ground forces pressed their attacks on November 9 to take other important North African ports, while forces loyal to Vichy continued to oppose them. The Axis aircraft made no effort to support the Vichy ground forces. Fighting was most intense at Oran, Algeria and at Port Lyautey, Morocco.

In Tunisia, the French took the defensive action of blocking the country's two main ports, Tunis and Bizerte, by sinking old vessels at their entrances, but the Allies made no attempt to invade Tunisia.

On the other side of North Africa, in Egypt, the rains had stopped and the British pursuit of the retreating Germans and Italians accelerated. The Axis forces made a stand at Halfaya Pass on the Egyptian–Libyan border but the British successfully attacked on the 10th forcing the enemy to withdraw into Libya.

In London, Churchill addressed the British people and made two of his more witty remarks for which he was famous. As for the happenings in North Africa he said, "This is not the end. It is not even the beginning of the end. But it is, perhaps, the end of the beginning." And, with regard to the future of the British Empire, he declared, "I have not become the King's First Minister to preside over the liquidation of the British Empire."

Also on November 9, General Mark Clark and French General Henri Girard flew from Gibraltar to Algiers. Giraud had agreed to take over the civil administration of the liberated French territories in North Africa and cooperate with the Allies. But, much to the dismay of both men, Giraud was given a very cool reception by the French North African leaders. Suddenly and unexpectedly Allied hopes for rallying the North African French to their cause were in jeopardy. Where would they find a leader to rally the men of France?

Meanwhile, that morning, Vichy Premier Laval gave in to strong German and Italian demands that Axis forces be allowed to enter Tunisia at once without opposition. Within hours the Germans and Italians began scraping up combat units all over Europe and rushing them to debarkation points in Italy and Sicily. Before the day was out, the first units, German airborne troops, began landing at El Aouina Airport near Tunis. Over the next few days, thousands of Axis troops streamed into Tunisia, many of them by air.

During the afternoon of November 10, the political situation in French North Africa changed suddenly for the better for the Allies. Admiral Darlan, who had been captured by the Allies in Algiers where he was visiting his son, agreed to cooperate with the invaders. Darlan had been in discussions with the Allies for two days before agreement was reached. One of Darlan's first actions, taken only minutes after agreement was reached, was to order all French forces in North Africa to cease fire, effective at 7:00 a.m. the next morning, November 11. Darlan promised that those Frenchmen who obeyed his order would not become prisoners of war, but could elect to fight on against the Germans and Italians and remain under French command. Darlan's order was almost universally accepted. Darlan had done what Giraud could not. Furthermore, Darlan's authority was strengthened because he had secretly been given authority by Petain, three days prior, to act as he saw fit in North Africa. Ironically, following Darlan's order, Petain announced from Vichy that he personally was taking command of all of the French armed forces and that his long-standing order to resist any invader still stood. This action was virtually meaningless, though, because it was obvious that Petain was acting under duress and there was no French resistance offered in Tunisia as Axis forces "invaded" that country.

The French North African military leaders ignored Petain's order and complied with Darlan's. Most of them appeared eager to do so. Before the day ended French resistance ended at Oran and Port Lyautey and Allied troops entered both cities. The French Navy, however, remained loyal to Petain and continued its attacks on the American ships off the coast of Morocco.

During the next few days events happened rapidly. On November 11, German and Italian forces suddenly, and without warning, occupied the remainder of Metropolitan France and the French island of Corsica, violating and ending the armistice agreements of 1940. Petain protested vigorously through diplomatic channels and over the radio, but took no military action against the Axis forces. There was one exception, though, at Toulon where the bulk of the French Navy was anchored. There French troops established a defense perimeter around the naval base and the fleet to protect it from the advancing Germans and Italians.

With the Axis Powers occupying southern France, including the town of Vichy, Petain's authority melted away.

In Morocco and Algeria Darlan now ruled and all French resistance ended at 7:00 a.m. on November 11 in accordance with Darlan's order. During the day Casablanca was occupied by the Americans, and the British made another amphibious landing, without French opposition, at Bougie, Algeria, 110 miles east of Algiers. This action was taken in order to get the bulk of the British First Army, under General Kenneth Anderson, closer to Tunisia to confront the strong Axis forces building up in the Tunis area. It was Anderson's mission to capture Tunis as soon as possible.

Off Algeria's Mediterranean and Morocco's Atlantic coasts, the sea battle continued to rage with the Allies taking substantial losses. Axis subs and aircraft took a high toll of British and American cargo ships, transports, and tankers, but also managed to sink the British destroyer "Martin" on November 10, the American fleet oiler "Winooski," the American destroyer "Hambleton" on the 11th and the British patrol craft "Stork," the British destroyer tender "Hecla," and the British destroyer "Marne" on the 12th. On November 12, the Allies sank their first German submarine, U–660, off Algeria. More ship and submarine sinkings occurred in the days that followed.

To the east, on the Egyptian/Libyan border, Montgomery's 8th Army occupied Bardia, Libya and ousted the last Axis troops from Egypt.

On November 12, the British 6th Commando unit carried out yet another amphibious operation in eastern Algeria at Bone, 260 miles east of Algiers. The purpose of this action was the same as at Bougie—to move Allied troops eastward for an attack into Tunisia. Along with the amphibious operation, a British paratroop battalion landed about twenty miles south of Bone and a force of two American Army parachute companies landed another 75 miles further to the south of them.

Also on the 12th, in Metropolitan France, German troops reached France's Mediterranean coast and occupied Marseilles. From Berlin came an announcement that German forces would make no attempt to capture the French warships at Toulon.

On November 13, Montgomery's forces reached Tobruk and a battle for that vital port loomed once again.

Admiral Darlan, General de Gaulle, General Giraud—the three contenders for power in North Africa after the Allied invasion.

In French North Africa, British troops from Bone had rapidly moved into Tunisia and reached the town of Takarka, eighty miles west of Tunis, the capital. So far, Axis resistance in Tunisia had been very light. In southern Tunisia Italian troops from Libya entered the Protectorate and took control of the prewar French-built Mareth Line. This was an African version of the famous Maginot Line built in the 1930s by the French to protect Tunisia from an Italian invasion. It would now be utilized by the Axis forces to defend Tunisia from a British invasion.

Small German units moved south out of Tunis to link up with the Italians, thereby occupying most of coastal Tunisia.

General Eisenhower and his staff left Gibraltar on November 13 and arrived in Algiers where he set up a new headquarters. He also met Admiral Darlan for the first time.

WHO WILL BE IN CHARGE?

By accepting Darlan's cooperation, the British and Americans had seriously complicated the French political picture. Darlan, who was heavily tainted by his association with Vichy and collaboration with the Axis Powers, was now in a position to become the commander of all the French military leaders in North Africa and possibly elsewhere. This put de Gaulle, still cooling his heels in London, into a political limbo. To complicate matters even further, the Allies still had General Giraud still waiting in the wings.

When Eisenhower and Darlan met on November 15 in Algiers, the big question on everyone's mind was, "who would emerge as the French leader in North Africa; Darlan, de Gaulle or Giraud?" As it turned out, a solution, of sorts, was worked out on November 16. From Eisenhower's point of view, it appeared that Darlan was the man who could do the most for the Allied cause at this point in time. With military matters of foremost importance and political matters secondary, Eisenhower agreed that Darlan would assume the title of "Protector" of French interest in North Africa and that Giraud, who was willing to cooperate with Darlan, would become commander of the French armed forces.

Not surprisingly, resounding condemnations of this arrangement came from both de Gaulle in London and Petain in Vichy. De Gaulle disassociated the Fighting French from both Darlan and Giraud, and Petain branded Darlan as a traitor and stripped him of all his Vichy posts and his French citizenship. Vichy also started vicious rumors about Darlan, one of which stated that he had been hoarding food all through the war.

There were critics, too, in London and Washington of this arrangement, but it was generally agreed by Churchill and Roosevelt that Eisenhower had made the right decision—for the moment.

ALONG THE MEDITERRANEAN COAST

With the invasion of French North Africa, the Axis subs now had numerous targets in the western Mediterranean and a mission to interdict the Allied seaborne supply lines. But they also faced more Allied antisubmarine defenses. That became most evident during the second and third week of November.

On November 12, U–660 was caught by two corvettes and sunk off Oran. On November 13, German and Italian subs and German aircraft combined to sink three British cargo ships and a Dutch destroyer, and the next day U–73 sank another British merchantman. That same day the Germans lost two more subs. U–595 was damaged and beached on the Algerian coast near Tenes after being attacked by RAF planes. The second sub, U–605, was sunk in the same area after being attacked by the same RAF planes. The next day, the Germans lost another sub, U–259 off Algiers, to RAF aircraft. On that day, though, November 15, the Italian sub "Ascianghi" sank a British minesweeper off Bone. Two days later another German sub was lost, the U–331, off Algiers to British planes from the aircraft carrier Formidable.

To the east the British subs were still concentrating on the Axis convoys heading for Libya and during November sank nine Italian cargo ships.

BACK TO THE GROUND FIGHTING

On November 16, another British paratroop force landed in eastern Algeria and moved rapidly into northern Tunisia, occupying the coastal city of Tabarka later that day. About 95 miles to the south the American paratroops had moved into the Tebessa area of Algeria and were approaching the Tunisian border.

Also on November 16, another battalion of American paratroopers was dropped in an area about thirty miles south of Tabarka. These were the first Americans in Tunisia. To the north, more British forces entered Tunisia from the Bone area as clashes were reported between French and German troops further south near Mateur. Those units were the French 19th Corps under General Georges Barre who had rallied on his own to fight the Germans. Included in Barre's force were some 7,000 Tunisian soldiers from the Tunisian Division of the French Army who had also rallied to the Allied cause.

Barre quickly made contact with the British to coordinate their respective activities. So far only the French and Germans had clashed in Tunisia, but not the British and Germans nor the American and Germans. The next day, though, it happened. Lead elements of the British 78th Infantry Division, heading for Tunis, clashed with a strong German force at a point seventy miles west of the city. This stopped the British drive on Tunis. To the south, the American paratroops entered Tunisia from the Tebessa area and quickly took the Gafsa airport.

On November 18, the Germans counterattacked against both the British and Barre's Frenchmen, but both of the Allies held their positions. Following that, the battlefields fell silent as the British paused to bring up more men and supplies. Recent rains in the area had made roads and airfields in Algeria muddy, but not so in Tunisia where roads and airfields were paved. For a few days, the Axis Powers enjoyed air superiority because their planes could take off and land while those of the Allies could not.

During this time, the Allies stabilized their lines in Tunisia. The British 1st Army under General Anderson, with the defected members of the Tunisian Division, occupied the northern sector of the front while the American 2nd Corps, under General Fredendall, took over the southern sector. In the middle sector, where a mountain range formed what was known as the western dorsal of Tunisia, was the French 19th Corps under General L. M. Koeltz. This force was the weakest of the three Allied forces and consisted at this time primarily of Moroccan and Algerian units of the French Army hastily sent eastward to Tunisia. Koeltz's force, however, was building rapidly as new French units were being reconstituted and rearmed all across North Africa.

VICHY SWINGS TO THE AXIS

In Vichy, now occupied by German troops, Petain gave all emergency powers to his Premier, Pierre Laval. This was done on November 19 and was permissible under the new fascist-inspired constitution which allowed the Premier to rule by decree.

But Laval's real authority was very much in question. Only those French leaders in occupied France and in Tunisia could be expected to follow his orders. As for the rest of the French empire, it was still anybody's guess as to what would happen.

In newly-occupied southern France was the powerful French fleet, anchored at Toulon. At any moment Laval could order the fleet to take action against the British and Americans, thus altering the balance of naval strength in the Mediterranean. Or if the French sailors and officers resisted his authority, he could give the Germans and Italians the authority to seize the ships. At this moment, all eyes were on the French fleet at Toulon.

IN LIBYA AND TUNISIA

In eastern Libya, Montgomery's 8th Army was advancing rapidly into that colony. The retreating Axis forces seemed unable to stop long enough to create an effective defense. Even at Tobruk they made no stand, and that vital and much-fought-over port fell to the British easily on November 13.

Montgomery's advance was, by now, taking on the image of an unstoppable juggernaut. On November 20, they took Benghazi with little effort. In three days the British advance had captured one-fourth of northern Libya. Rommel and his Italian allies pulled back to Agedabia where they had made previous stands, to await the next British assault. The British, however, were slow to follow the Axis withdrawal. They now needed time to regroup and bring up supplies after their rapid advance across eastern Libya.

Elsewhere, November 20 proved to be an action-packed 24 hours. In Tunisia, the Barre's French forces withdrew from Medjez el Bab giving up territory to the attacking Germans.

Turin was bombed again by the RAF in what was to be the most devastating air raid yet on an Italian city.

From Vichy, Laval announced that his policy would be one of close collaboration with Germany. He told the French people that the British and American were "tearing France limb from limb (and that) the Entente with Germany is the sole guarantee of peace in Europe."

In Algiers, Darlan went on the radio in a broadcast directed toward the French armed forces saying, "I confirm to you my previous order to fight at the side of the American and the Allied forces for defense and liberation of our territories... ." Darlan took care to use the word "Allies" and not to mention the British nor the Fighting French.

Still, on November 20, an emissary from de Gaulle, General Francois d'Astier de la Vigerie, arrived in Algiers and conferred with Darlan to explore the possibilities of de Gaulle and Darlan joining forces. Darlan, however, refused to consider the idea and the French leadership remained divided. Giraud, though, seemed more receptive to d'Astier's proposals and the two men remained in touch with each other. At this point, yet another Frenchman of note entered the picture; the Count of Paris. He offered to arbitrate the French political dilemma but Darlan declined the offer. The Count and d'Astier then joined forces and, with some local Fighting French supporters, began plotting a coup to remove Darlan and replace him with the Count of Paris.

At this point, the French leadership was at its greatest point of turmoil. Actually, it was Laval that said it right when he said that the Americans and British were tearing the French Empire "limb from limb."

With both Tobruk and Benghazi in British hands Rommel's main port of supply was now Tripoli. On November 21, American B–24 bombers hit that port city hard in a large-scale air raid.

A German propaganda cartoon emphasizing that the American and British were struggling over control of Africa.

The Allies in Tunisia were having supply problems. Only one antiquated rail line ran from Algiers to Tunisia and it was overburdened. Furthermore, heavy rains added to the Allies' supply problems. As a result the Allied forces in Tunisia were at a standstill.

STALINGRAD

In the Soviet Union on November 22, the Red Army had succeeded in encircling the entire German 6th Army and many smaller German, Romanian, and Italian units at Stalingrad. This meant that 270,000 Axis troops were trapped and the worst of the Russian winter was just beginning. No one knew it at the time but the greatest German defeat of the war was in its beginning stages. At Hitler's headquarters the possibilities of such a defeat were beginning to be recognized as each day passed, and all other matters, including the actions in Tunisia and Libya, now became of secondary importance. The Axis leaders in North Africa knew this and were well aware of the fact that they could not hope to match the ever-growing strength of the Allies in men and supplies.

FRENCH WEST AFRICA FOR THE ALLIES

In response to Darlan's order, High Commissioner Boisson at Dakar agreed to forsake Vichy and declare for the Allies. On November 23, Allied forces arrived at Dakar and occupied the port city without opposition. The colonial governors throughout French West Africa followed Boisson's lead, each declaring for the Allies, and this huge colonial holding became Allied territory within a matter of hours and without a shot fired. There remained, though, one glaring political issue. Boisson had declared for the Allies but not for de Gaulle and the Fighting French. This strengthened

Darlan's hand in Algiers. Laval's "limb from limb" statement was coming to pass.

ON TO TUNIS

With all of French Morocco and Algeria secured, and French West Africa having declared for the Allies, the American forces that had invaded Morocco under General George Patton now moved to the east and started to arrive in western Tunisia during the last week in November. They took up positions south of and adjacent to Koeltz's 19th French Corps. Eisenhower now had a plan. He believed the time was right to advance on Tunis and oust the Germans and Italians from northern Tunisia. Following that, Allied forces could move swiftly into western Libya, crush the Axis forces there, and win the war in North Africa before the end of the year. Therefore, Eisenhower ordered the British First Army, building rapidly west of Tunis, to advance on the city and occupy it.

On November 25, the British launched their attack toward Tunis and quickly recaptured Medjez el Bab. Heavy fighting ensued and on the 27th the British reached a point twenty miles west of Tunis. The British soon discovered that the German defenses in northern Tunisia were strong, and getting stronger, at other locations. Eisenhower's order to take Tunis would not be easy to carry out.

HITLER, VICHY, THE FRENCH ARMY AND THE FRENCH NAVY

November 27, 1942, was a day of disaster for Vichy. At dawn German and Italian troops began occupying the French naval base at Toulon. From Germany came word to Petain that Hitler, in his anger at what was happening in Tunisia, had ordered that the entire French Army be abolished. In his message to Petain, Hitler cited specifically the betrayal of General Barre and that he no longer trusted the French generals and admirals.

At Toulon, the base commander, Admiral Jean de Laborde, took swift and independent action as the German and Italian troops approached. He gave the order to scuttle every warship in the harbor. This was a grand act of defiance against the Germans and it was carried out with great efficiency. The captains of some vessels disobeyed Laborde's order and escaped to join the Allied. But, by the end of the day, the French fleet at Toulon was no longer a major factor in World War II. On this day, November 27, not only the French Army ceased to exist, but a major part of the French Navy was destroyed.

Sent to the bottom of Toulon harbor were three battleships, seven cruisers, eleven destroyers, two submarines, and 25 other warships. A few of the smaller ships were captured by the Germans and Italians and not scuttled. Four submarines were able to escape from the harbor and later joined the Allies.

On December 3, Germany and Italy announced that all French warships under their control, including those at Toulon, would be confiscated.

At German-controlled Bizerte, Tunisia there were a small number of French warships decommissioned and anchored in the harbor but no attempt was made to scuttle them. The Germans and Italians confiscated the French ships on December 8. Germany acquired two corvettes, and Italy acquired one corvette and three patrol-torpedo boats.

None of the French ships in the other harbors of French North Africa were scuttled, but neither had many of their crews yet responded to Darlan's call to join the Allies. As a result, only a few French ships were operating with the Allies in the waters off North Africa and along the Atlantic coast.

The Allies, of course, were trying to strengthen their naval blockade of Tunisia and both sides laid extensive mine fields, making the waters between Tunisia and Sicily one of the most heavily-mined areas of the world. Not surprisingly, many ships on both sides became victims of these mines.

In the air struggles over Tunisia and the central Mediterranean, the matter of air superiority had not yet been determined. The Allied air forces had two missions; try to help enforce the naval blockade of Tunisia while at the same time give support to the Allied ground troops. Similarly, the Axis air forces had two missions; help protect their convoys and ships at sea and support their ground troops. In this struggle, the Allies clearly had the advantage in that new aircraft were arriving steadily from the factories in America and Great Britain. Aircraft from the German factories were going to the eastern front. In Libya, though, the matter of air superiority had already been decided in favor of the Allies and was being maintained.

15 MILES FROM TUNIS

On November 28, the British forces reached a point fifteen miles from Tunis but had begun to meet stiff German resistance. The Axis forces had now grown to 15,000, men well-equipped with artillery and a growing number of tanks. Furthermore, to the south two British regiments were in danger of being surrounded due to several successful German counterattacks.

During the next two days, the British drive on Tunis stalled in the face of very strong German defensive action with the main battle raging near the German-held Ovenda Airfield.

On December 1 and 2, one of the large naval battle of this time erupted off the northern Tunisian coast between three Italian destroyers and two patrol-torpedo boats on the one hand and two British cruisers and four destroyers on the other. The end result was that the Italians lost a destroyer while one of the British cruisers was damaged. Control of the sea was still undecided.

During the first days of December, more French and American troops entered Tunisia. Working together, the two Allies occupied the Faid Pass south of Tunis threatening the German southern flank.

An American instructor demonstrates to French troops the workings of an American weapon. Note from the fez-like hats that many of the French soldiers are North Africans.

It was not enough, though, to prevent the Germans from counterattacking against the British on the 4th, and with heavy fighting, recapturing the small town of Tebourba.

The Allied ground offensive in Tunisia was noticeably in trouble, but it was a different story in the air and at sea. During the first days of December, four convoys left Italy for Tunisia and were attacked so heavily by Allied ships and aircraft that three of them turned back. The forth convoy, consisting of four freighters, did not make it. All four freighters were sunk along with an escort vessel. The British lost one destroyer in the attacks.

Also on the 4th American B–24 heavy bombers, operating out of French North Africa, bombed the port of Naples, Italy. This was the first attack by American planes on the Italian homeland.

With the Axis force in Tunisia desperate for manpower, the Petain government, under strong German pressure, decreed the conscription of 2000 Tunisian Jews for a labor battalion to serve the Axis forces. Later, in February 1943, a special war tax of ten million francs was levied on the Jewish population of Tunisia.

IN TUNISIA—POLITICS

The politics of Tunisia was much like that of Egypt. Both countries had once been independent, became protectorates of European powers, had sitting heads of state and shadow governments and sought to regain full independence.

Under Axis plans, Tunisia was to fall within the Italian sphere of influence after the final Axis victory, and in this scenario some Tunisians saw a better chance to attain their national identity. This was quite naive because the Italians had no intentions of advancing Tunisia toward independence once they took over.

A majority of the Tunisians saw World War II as a European war and few Tunisian young men wanted to militarily support either side. In 1939, the French Army was able to recruit and form a Tunisian Division, but France fell before it was tested in battle. That division remained in Tunisia and, under the conditions of the armistices, was allowed to continue functioning as a military force.

In June 1941, three infantry battalions and a cavalry squadron of the Tunisian Division were sent by Vichy to Syria to fight the British and Free French.

The nominal head-of-state in Tunisia was Bey Sidi Muhammad al-Moncef, who had recently ascended to the throne in June 1942; he was well-known for his nationalist sentiments and had already clashed with the French Governor-General Admiral Jean-Pierre Esteva over reform issues.

When the Germans and Italians invaded Tunisia in November 1942, the Bey took a wait-and-see attitude toward the new situation. Tunisia's leading nationalist, Habib Bourguiba, who was in jail in France for past nationalist activities, saw an opportunity developing for himself. Bourguiba saw, in the presence of the Germans and Italians in Tunisia, an opportunity to strengthen his nationalist cause while the French were out of the picture. In this respect Bourguiba was able to convince the Vichy government and the Italians that he would work with the Italians toward the future of Tunisia to become a cooperating entity within the Axis alliance. Bourguiba was then released from jail and went to Rome to establish a working relationship with the Italians. In Tunisia many of his jailed followers, mostly members of his outlawed nationalist Neo-Destour Party, were also released. With Axis approval, the Neo-Destour Party was allowed to reconstitute itself along with its several youth movements and newspapers. Furthermore, the city administration of Tunis was turned over to Bourguiba's followers in return for a promise that the Neo-Destour Party would help recruit Tunisian workers for the German and Italian armed services in Tunisia. This was a difficult undertaking because the Germans and Italians, upon arriving in Tunisia, had undertaken a program of requisitioning food, animals, vehicles, and other necessities from the populace, which had greatly angered the Tunisian people.

Having gained a measure of political power, hopes surged among the Tunisian intellectuals and masses that some sort of Tunisian autonomy might be attainable in the near future.

With this sentiment growing, the Tunisian politicians began playing up to the Germans, hoping to gain their favor at the expense of the Italians. One of the Neo-Destour Party's major newspapers, Al-Cha'ab (The People), became resolutely pro-German while ignoring the Italians. In Rome, Bourguiba cleverly supported the pro-German activities of his comrades in Tunisia by refusing to come out publicly in favor of the future Italian control of Tunisia. The Italians, frustrated by Bourguiba's lack of cooperation, turned to the

Bey for support. But he and the members of his older and more conservative Destour Party flatly refused to endorse Italy's program for the future of Tunisia. News that both the Bey and Bourguiba's nationalists were standing up against Italy showed that the country's two most powerful leaders were politically united with the end result that the Tunisian people now became more supportive of these leaders than ever before. Together, the Bey and Bourguiba had demonstrated that the Italians were incapable of bringing about a political solution in Tunisia and, at the same time, had gained some measure of support from Germany due to their ongoing pro-German propaganda.

It was a clever ruse, but time and circumstances were against the Tunisian nationalists. On May 7, 1942, British forces occupied Tunis and the entire political picture changed.

IN ALGIERS—POLITICS

Back in Algiers, Admiral Darlan had, with Allied approval, assumed the leadership of the newly-formed "Imperial Council of France" which was given both military and civil controls in North Africa. This was on November 17. Most of the members of the Council, with the notable exception of General Giraud, had been active supporters of Vichy. One of Darlan's first actions was to announce that, because of the German occupation of Vichy, Petain was a prisoner of the Germans and that he was no longer able to freely exercise power. Because of the void thus created Darlan claimed extraordinary powers for himself and his Council with regards to the entire French Empire.

From Washington, Roosevelt announced that the agreement with Darlan was acceptable but only temporary. This was a move to soothe de Gaulle's ruffled feathers. Darlan knew his tenure was temporary and made it known that he would resign whenever asked to do so by the Allies. He also commented that upon resignation he, his wife and son wanted to go Warm Springs, Georgia where his son could receive treatment for his polio. Warm Springs was where President Roosevelt went to treat his polio.

Darlan's eventual resignation was also on the minds of the British and Americans. They began secret talks among themselves on how Darlan's tenure could be terminated and who would replace him.

As for military aid to the French, the British and Americans had agreed to rebuild the French Army in North Africa to eight divisions equipped with modern weapons. A large percentage of men in these divisions would be North Africans. Later, when Allied forces entered Metropolitan France, the British and Americans agreed to rebuild three more divisions—primarily of Frenchmen. Also in North Africa the Allies agreed to equip seventeen French Air Squadrons with modern aircraft and give extensive aid to the French Navy.

Back in London, de Gaulle was steaming. Almost overnight his erstwhile Allies, Britain and the United States, had allowed a small group of former high-level Vichy officials, shamefully tainted by their collaboration with Germany and Italy, to take complete political control in French North Africa and set up a council in direct competition to his own. De Gaulle remained prudently silent on this issue until late November when he publicly announced that he and his Fighting French "...were taking no part whatsoever in, and assuming no responsibility for, negotiations in progress in North Africa with Vichy representatives."

From the Allied point of view it was most regrettable, but it was the most expedient way to get the French in North Africa to recommit themselves to the Allied cause. Because of the deep resentment that still lingered among the North African French against de Gaulle, it would have been very unlikely that de Gaulle could have rallied the French as Darlan had done. With the military situation paramount, the complex French political situation had to be pushed aside for the time being. It was hoped by the Allies that, eventually, Darlan and de Gaulle could reconcile and work together.

On December 17, Darlan again demonstrated his worth to the Allies. On that day he issued an order to all of the remaining French ships, most of which were in African ports, to join the Allies. The response was very positive. Most of the French crews complied with Darlan's order and the French ships soon began participated in the naval blockade of Tunisia.

Because of the political changes in Algeria, the Algerian nationalists saw an opportunity to make themselves heard. Ferhat Abbas, one of the leading Algerian nationalist, made a public statement on December 22, requesting that the "responsible authority" in Algiers agree to meet in conference with representatives of the Algerian people to discuss political reforms. This request was ignored by Darlan and the Allies, but it demonstrated to the Algerian people that the Algerian nationalist movement was active and able to speak out.

IN MOROCCO—POLITICS

In the Protectorate of French Morocco, the Sultan was looked upon by both the Allies and the Moroccan people as the nominal head of state and was relatively untarnished by any serious collaboration with the Vichy French or the Axis Powers. During the Vichy years he was able to steer a neutral coarse and, at times, even buck some of Vichy's policies. This was particularly true with regard to the anti-Semitic laws Vichy tried to impose on Morocco. Under the Protectorate agreement with France, the Sultan retained control of religious matters in the country and gave the Jews a measure of protection they did not enjoy in Algeria or Tunisia.

Nationalism, though, came alive in Morocco as it did elsewhere in Africa, and during 1943 two new nationalist-oriented organizations came into being. They were the "Istiqlal" (Independence) Party and the "Parti Communiste Marocain." Both organizations grew rapidly and would become major factors on the Moroccan political scene in the coming years.

THE TIDE TURNS IN THE MEDITERRANEAN SEA WAR

With so many more Allied warships and planes now in the western Mediterranean, those waters became very dangerous for Axis vessels of any type. Despite having lost five subs in three weeks off French North Africa in October and November, the Germans and Italians did not withdraw to safer waters but kept up the fight. On December 1, U–375 sank the British mine layer "Manxman" east of Oran. Then on December 2 and 4, British subs sank one Italian and two German freighters off Tunisia. On the 6th, a British sub sank the Italian sub "Porfido" off Tunisia. On the 9th, U–602 sank the British destroyer "Porcupine" off Spanish Morocco. And so it went throughout the rest of December. By the 31st, the Allies had lost another ten ships including the destroyer "Partridge" and the light cruiser "Argonaut." The Axis lost an additional 23 ships including two Italian destroyers "Aviere" and "Camicia Nera" and the Italian sub "Alagi."

During January 1943, the Allies lost seven ships including the British trawler "Jura" while the Axis lost 24 vessels including two minesweepers and the German sub U–224.

HARD FIGHTING IN THE TUNIS AREA

During the second week in December the Germans and Allies clashed repeatedly in Tunisia with neither side winning an advantage. The British, though, withdrew to better defensive positions at Medjez el Bab, their drive on Tunis now all but abandoned. Two German tank attacks, one each on December 10 and 11, failed to dislodge them, but British tank losses were substantial. Also, there was considerable air action with neither side having yet gained air superiority. Then too, rain caused difficulties for both sides.

At Algiers, three Italian mini-subs entered the harbor unnoticed and sank four Allied cargo ships. The war at sea was still undecided.

On December 18, Laval met with Hitler and it was agreed that a division of French and Tunisian volunteers would be raised in Tunisia by the Vichy authorities there to fight on the Axis side. The unit was to be known as the "African Falange." Not surprisingly, French and Tunisian enthusiasm for such an undertaking was very weak and the project floundered. Only 274 Frenchmen and 132 Tunisians responded to the call to arms. The Germans were more successful on their own in Tunisia. They formed an "Arab Legion" to serve in the German Army and attracted 1,200 volunteers.

Algerians working on German submarine pens on the Atlantic coast of France.

ALGERIANS SERVING THE AXIS

Prior to the Allied invasion of North Africa, Algeria had been a fairly good recruiting area for the Germans. After the fall of France, thousands of Algerians volunteered to work for the German occupation authorities in Metropolitan France. Some 18,000 of them were put to work building the West Wall defenses along the French Atlantic coast. About 200 Algerians were recruited to work in the "Milice," a Vichy-controlled anti-partisan force in France. When Germany invaded the Soviet Union in June 1941, another 200 Algerians volunteered for service in the Soviet Union to fight the atheistic Communists.

IN LIBYA

In Libya, Rommel and the Italian leaders agreed that they could not make a third stand at El Agheila. With the Allies maintaining air superiority, strong British ground forces building once again in front of them and most of their own reinforcements and supplies now going to Tunisia, they concluded that the line could not be held. Therefore, on December 13, the El Agheila line was abandoned and the Axis forces withdrew to the west. British and New Zealander troops followed close behind. On December 15, Montgomery, taking note that his enemy was weak and outnumbered, sent his New Zealanders far to the south to turn around the end of the Axis defense line and threaten the retreating Axis columns. This action hastened the Axis retreat lest parts of their column be cut off.

The British 8th Army reached Surt on December 21, over 300 miles west of El Agheila. Now, over half of northern Libya was in British hands, while the Fighting French from Chad consolidated their gains in the Fezzan and advanced northward to threaten the retreating Axis forces from the south. At Surt, the 8th Army halted for a day to rest and bring up supplies. On the 22nd the advance resumed but there were new signs that the Germans and Italians would make a stand at Buerat, 100 miles to the west. On the 23rd, the Libyan front received heavy rains which slowed operations on both sides. It was also raining hard in Tunisia, and Eisenhower decided to formally abandon the attack on Tunis until the rainy season subsided.

DARLAN ASSASSINATED

On December 24, Admiral Darlan was suddenly gunned down and killed by a young French student named Fernand Bonnier de la Ahmera, a monarchist and, so it was rumored, a supporter of de Gaulle. This tragic event dramatically and instantly altered the entire French political scene. General Giraud, serving as Darlan's deputy, assumed the post of High Commissioner of French North Africa on December 26. Giraud did not, however, assume the title of "Protector" given to Darlan by Eisenhower. This indicated that Giraud had somewhat less power than Darlan had had. Furthermore, it was becoming clear to those close to the French leaders that Giraud was not enthusiastic about playing a major political role. His primary interest was not political but commanding the military. Therefore, something a of political void developed in Algiers as Giraud demonstrated his weak political abilities and showed his distaste for politics. All of this was to play very nicely into the hands of Charles de Gaulle.

De la Ahmera was captured at the scene and, in one of the most controversial actions of Allied justice during the war, executed by firing squad two days later on December 26. At the time, de la Ahmera's quick demise benefited everyone on the Allied side. A lengthy trial in which de la Bonnier would be allowed to express his political views would have been a great embarrassment to Allied unity.

PREMONITION OF DEATH

Twenty-four hours before Darlan was assassinated he had lunched with a group of Allied naval officers and in the course of the table talk Darlan said, "You know, there are four plots in existence to assassinate me. Suppose one of those plots is successful. What will you Americans do then?"

BRITISH ADVANCE DEEPER INTO LIBYA—STALEMATE IN TUNISIA

The Axis forces in Libya had prepared a defensive line at Surt, but the British simply bypassed it to the south on December 25/26, forcing the Axis troops to retreat once again. They headed for yet another defensive line being built west of Buerat.

On December 29, British forces reached Buerat to find the town abandoned and no Axis defense line. They continued their pursuit of the retreating Axis forces, encountering only light rear guard actions.

To the south, the Fighting French units from Chad had crossed the Sahara Desert from the Fezzan and were now approaching Tripoli. They were closer to Tripoli than the British. Their only meaningful opposition was occasional attacks by Italian aircraft. At sea in the Mediterranean the Allies had finally gained the upper hand and were regularly decimating Axis convoys. During December, the Axis lost 110,000 out of 200,000 tons of supplies shipped to Tunisian ports and Tripoli.

In Libya, during the first days of January 1943, British forces made contact with the Axis defenses west of Buerat and halted again to rest and bring up supplies. For more than a week all was quiet on the Libyan front. At Buerat, Rommel received an order from Mussolini to hold that position to the last. It was an order Rommel would ignore.

In Tunisia, Axis and Allied forces battled each other daily in the areas west of Tunis with neither side gaining an advantage. For the Allies this was a great disappointment because there would be no rapid conquest of Tunis. And furthermore, it was becoming obvious that the fighting would increase in southern Tunisia if and when the Axis forces from Libya withdrew into that area.

On January 5, the American forces in Tunisia were organized into the U.S. 5th Army under the command of General Mark Clark to better prepare for the coming battle in southern Tunisia.

THE CASABLANCA CONFERENCE

On January 14, 1943, President Roosevelt, Prime Minister Churchill, Generals de Gaulle and Giraud, the British/American Combined Chiefs of Staff and other top Allied military leaders met secretly in a resort hotel in the Casablanca area. The meeting was not so secret, though. The Germans knew about it from the first day and even announced it over the radio.

The purpose of the meeting was multifaceted. First of all, by meeting in Casablanca the Allied leaders demonstrated there that French North Africa was now a secure region and firmly in the Allied camp.

More importantly, the Allied leaders met to plan the next phase of the war against the European Axis after all of North Africa was secured. After much discussion, it was decided that the next major military move would be the invasion of Sicily and Italy with an understanding that a cross-channel invasion of France would be carried out sometime in 1944. Issues in the Far East regarding Burma and China were also discussed.

As for the French political situation, and with Darlan out of the picture, the Allied leaders forced their wills on both de Gaulle and Giraud to cooperate with each other. It was para-

This photo of Generals de Gaulle (right) and Giraud (left) shaking hands in the presence of Churchill and Roosevelt at Casablanca was distributed widely throughout the French Empire to demonstrate the new unity in the French leadership.

mount for the Allied cause that the French leadership appear united even though there were deep divisions behind the scene. To accomplish this, the two Frenchmen were called to Casablanca and, under strong pressure from both Roosevelt and Churchill, instructed to form a new committee of liberation to which virtually any Frenchman could adhere for the struggle against the common enemy. The structuring of that committee was to be undertaken immediately.

UNCONDITIONAL SURRENDER

In a press conference during the meeting, Roosevelt startled everyone by announcing that the Allied war aim was the "unconditional surrender" of the Axis nations. Roosevelt made this comment without previous consultation with his British and French allies and thereby put them in an embarrassing position. Unconditional surrender, the complete and absolute defeat of the enemy nations, had never been discussed, let alone agreed to. Some believed then, and even today, that Roosevelt's statement was ill-spoken because it ruled out any chance of a negotiated peace. On the other hand, it demonstrated to the world that there would be no compromise with Fascism or Japanese Imperialism. Churchill, the French leaders and eventually other Allied leaders, had to go along with Roosevelt's statement, at least in giving it lip service, so as not to show disunity.

ROOSEVELT AND THE SULTAN

Before Roosevelt returned home, he held a dinner party for Sultan Mohammed V of Morocco. This was on January 22. The Sultan's government had been very supportive of the Allied cause and the President wanted to thank the Sultan for this and, at the same time, demonstrate a favorable gesture toward the Arab world. The two men had a very cordial and well-publicized meeting and conversed in French. Roosevelt promised Morocco postwar aid and hinted at the possibility of supporting Morocco's regaining its independence.

The meeting, though, was a diplomatic slight toward the French on two counts. In the first place, the French were not invited to the dinner party, and secondly, in the original protectorate agreement signed decades earlier between Morocco and France, the French were given authority to conduct all matters of foreign policy on behalf of Morocco, which included meetings with heads of state. Roosevelt's justification for circumventing the French could be explained in the fact that, at the time, there was a political void in the French leadership with Darlan's assassination and the de Gaulle-Giraud relationship still in flux. Those critical of Roosevelt's actions also pointed out that it was a less-than-friendly gesture toward de Gaulle, whom Roosevelt was known to dislike, as well as a blatant example of America's long-standing anticolonial foreign policy.

The meeting was also a diplomatic affront to Spain because the protectorate agreement between Morocco and Spain gave them control of Morocco's foreign policy activities with regard to Spanish Morocco. But, given Spain's pro-Axis stance, there was little tolerance in the American administration for Madrid's concerns. Furthermore, the meeting with the Sultan was a warning to Madrid that the United States was ready to deal independently with other parts of the Spanish Empire if it suited the Allied cause.

Throughout the remaining years of the war, and well into the postwar era, Sultan Mohammed demonstrated that he was a solid friend of the United States.

BACK AT THE FRONTS

On the day after the Casablanca Conference, a British attack on the Axis defenses west of Buerat, Libya succeeded with surprising ease. At this point, they were only 250 miles from Tripoli with the Tunisian border just beyond. The main British force continued their advance in two columns along the coastal road and around the southern end of the Buerat line. While Leclerc's Fighting French advanced from the south, three Allied columns converged on Tripoli.

In Tunisia, though, it was the Germans who gained the upper hand with the help of the new German Mark VI "Tiger" Tanks that had just been introduced to the battlefields. These tanks were superior to anything the Allies had, and when they were used they usually won the day for the Germans. Also in Tunisia, command of all of the Axis forces had been unified under the able German General Jurgen von Arnim.

Arnim used his superior armor at this time to move into southern Tunisia, thus lengthening the front. This move forced the Allies to stretch their front and temporarily go on the defensive.

In Libya, the British occupied Al Khums on January 19, and were then less than 150 miles from Tripoli and in contact with Leclerc's Fighting French advancing up from the Fezzan. The Axis forces offered virtually no opposition and by the 22nd the main British force was only seventeen miles from the colonial capital. The next day they occupied the city. The last Italian colonial capital in Africa was in Allied hands.

To the west in southern Tunisia, the American 1st Armored Division had gone on the offensive and pushed the Germans out of the Ousseltia Valley. These positions were then turned over to the French who had become responsible for a major portion of the Allied front in central Tunisia. By this time the French forces in North Africa had grown to some 300,000 men.

On January 25, the British forces moved west of Tripoli and became engaged in a five-day battle at Zwara, Libya. Finally, though, the Zwara defenses were overcome and the British moved into southern Tunisia on February 4.

Montgomery's advance from Egypt to Tunisia was the last all-British victory of the war in the European theater. Thereafter, the British always fought alongside one or more of their allies.

During the first week in February word came that the large German forces encircled at Stalingrad in the Soviet Union had finally surrendered. Over 200,000 Axis troops had been killed or captured. For the Axis leaders in Africa this meant that the German High Command would have to continue giving first priority to the eastern front now more than ever. It also meant that not many more German soldiers or Tiger tanks would be available for Tunisia.

ALGERIAN NATIONALISM SURFACES

Algerian nationalist Ferhat Abbas who, in December, had been rebuffed in his attempt to begin a dialogue with the French authorities loyal to Darlan in Algiers, suddenly came to the fore once again. On February 10, 1943, Abbas, taking advantage of Darlan's disappearance from the scene and the weak de Gaulle-Giraud leadership, published his famous "Manifeste du Peuple Algerien" (Manifesto of the Algerian People). This declaration was openly supported by 28 elected Algerian officials within the French administration. In the Manifeste, Abbas challenged the long-standing French policy of "assimilation," the core ingredient of French-Algerian relations which raised up selected Algerians to the level of French culture, political thinking and religion. Those Algerians left unassimilated remained in the status of lower class colonial subjects. Abbas claimed that this was inherently unfair to the great majority of Algerians and that Moslem society was being reduced to "the most complete servitude." Abbas's Manifeste also objected to the country's political administration, army, and press being under the control of a minority. Furthermore, Abbas called for the universal franchise of all citizens of Algeria and eventual self-determination. The Manifeste did not challenge the current French position in Algeria but clearly indicated that its tenure was not permanent.

Of course, the new French leadership had no intention of giving in to Abbas's demands, but neither did they dare reject them outright for fear of creating political unrest while the military question in North Africa was still undecided. Abbas's timing was excellent. The de Gaulle-Giraud leadership was not prepared to deal with such an issue. After some foot-dragging, the French leaders in Algiers agreed that the Manifeste might become the basis for future discussions. With this concession to their credit, the nationalists now pressed for talks, while the French leaders found reasons to delay. It would be several months before the two factions agreed to meet.

In the meantime the Algiers regime took measures to free North Africa's Jews from the anti-Semitic actions of the Vichy government. On February 17, Algiers decreed that Jews could enlist for military service in the French Army and during March the hated Jewish Affairs Bureau was eliminated.

FIGHTING SOLELY IN TUNISIA NOW

At this time, the only fighting in all of Africa was concentrated in one country, Tunisia, and it would last for four more months. That fighting would be marked by determined resistance by the German forces and frequent counterattacks which would result in temporary gains. But, with the Allies' resources in men and equipment more numerous at all times, it was the Allies who prevailed. Rommel and his Italian allies fought in southern and central Tunisia while von Arnim and his Italian allies fought in the north.

On February 4, Eisenhower was given command of all Allied forces in North Africa. Montgomery served under him. On the 7th the port of Tripoli became serviceable for the Allies and became Montgomery's main port of supply.

On February 14, the Germans launched a major attack in the area of the Kasserine Pass that lasted for eight days. Rommel was in command. Using their powerful Tiger Tanks the attackers decimated much of the American 2nd Corps. Reserve and other Allied units rushed to the area and, in very hard fighting, stopped the German drive.

On February 23, the German command in Tunisia was unified. Rommel became commander-in-chief of Army Group Africa with General von Arnim his deputy. General Giovanni Messe became commander of the Italian First Army.

On February 25, the Americans recaptured the Kasserine Pass, but on the 26th the Axis forces struck again in the Beja and Medjez el Bab area west of Tunis. This attack was stopped by the British after three days of fighting which resulted in considerable losses to the Axis forces.

On March 6, the Germans launched an unsuccessful attack at Medenine in southern Tunisia and lost fifty of their 150 tanks. On March 18, American General George S. Patton, recognized for his skill at directing armored units and his aggressiveness, was promoted to commander of the American 2nd Army Corps, replacing General Lloyd Fredendall. Three days later Rommel was recalled to Germany on a pretense to keep him from being sacrificed or suffer the final defeat that was now inevitable. General von Arnim replaced him.

On March 17, Patton launched an attack in central Tunisia in the Gafza area and advanced as far as El Guettar taking that city on the 18th. El Guettar was only sixty miles from the sea and Patton's troops threatened to split the Axis forces in the north from those in the south.

On March 20, in a coordinated attack, the British 8th Army launched a major attack on the Mareth Line while the American 2nd Corps attacked at Maknassy in central Tunisia. For the next week there was costly fighting in both areas but the Allied forces prevailed. By the 29th the Axis troops abandoned the Mareth Line and retreated beyond Gabes with the British in close pursuit. The British occupied Gabes without a struggle.

On April 2, the Axis defenses stiffened along a dry river bed known as Wadi Akarit, fifteen miles north of Gabes. There the 8th Army paused to rest and resupply. To the west was now a mountain range that confined the fighting to the coastal plain.

Meanwhile, the Allies had finally gained air superiority over battle areas and the naval blockade of Tunisia was virtually impenetrable. The Axis forces in Tunisia suffered major shortages of fuel, food, and ammunition.

On April 6, the British 8th Army attacked the Axis defenses at Wadi Akarit while the Americans attacked again in central Tunisia, threatening to close the Axis escape route. The tactic was successful. The Axis troops abandoned the Wadi Akarit line and retreated to their next defense line at Fondouk. On the 7th American troops and British troops linked up in front of the Fondouk Line. The next day they attacked the line together and it quickly collapsed. The Axis troops resumed their retreat to new positions north of Sousse known as the Enfidavill Line at the neck of the Cape Bon Peninsula.

On April 12, the Allies took Sousse and as they came out onto the broad coastal plain west of Tunis they made contact with the French, British, and American forces that had been fighting in that area since January. The Allies now had a solid line of troops stretching from the neck of the Cape Bon Peninsula on the east coast to a point on the north coast 25 miles west of Bizerte. The Axis forces were more concentrated too, but with their supplies dwindling rapidly their fate was inevitable.

The Allies prepared for the final assault which, they hoped, would push the remaining Axis forces into the sea.

On April 15, General Patton was relieved of command of the 2nd Corps and assigned to the planning staff which was secretly preparing for the invasion of Sicily. General Omar Bradley assumed Patton's old command.

ALLIES WINNING THE SEA WAR IN THE MEDITERRANEAN

The months of December and January showed that the Allies were gaining the upper hand in the Mediterranean Sea off North Africa. One Allied convoy after the other steamed through Gibraltar and deposited troops and equipment at the various French North African ports. German sea and air attacks were infrequent and did little damage.

During February, the Allied warships, primarily British submarines, began concentrating on Axis shipping off Sicily and southern Italy in an effort to interdict the Axis seaborne supply lines further north and prepare those waters for the coming invasion of Sicily. Thus, during February and the months that followed, the sea war moved away from the North African coast. Accordingly, Axis ship losses increased around Sicily and southern Italy and decreased along the North African coast.

During February the Allies lost fifteen ships, including one mine layer while the Axis lost only ten vessels, but three of them were submarines. On February 7, the British sub "Unison" accidentally sank the Spanish sub "General Mola" east of Gibraltar.

During March, the Allies lost fourteen ships, all merchant men, while the Axis lost three merchant men off North Africa and many more off Sicily and southern Italy. They also lost two more subs.

Still the Allied convoys arrived bringing more men and material. Some of the men were scheduled for the invasion of Sicily and were not sent to Tunisia. Rather they were sent to a number of Advanced Amphibious Training Bases along the coast to train for the invasion of Sicily. Bases were established at Port Lyautey, Morocco; at Nemoirs, Tenes; and at Benisaf and Mostaganem, Algeria.

During April 1943, the Allies lost another five merchant ships in the waters off North Africa while the Axis lost three.

THE "PALM SUNDAY MASSACRE"

Sunday April 18, was Palm Sunday. That day the Luftwaffe organized a massive air lift of supplies from Sicily to Tunisia which consisted of nearly 100 transport planes escorted by fighters. The Allied air forces knew of this plan thanks to Ultra and were prepared. As the Luftwaffe air fleet passed over the waters of the Mediterranean they were met by wave after wave of British and American fighters. In ten minutes 51 of the transports and sixteen of the defending fighters were in the sea. Seven of the Allied aircraft were lost. This action went down in the history books as the Palm Sunday Massacre. The next day, the Luftwaffe sent a second but smaller fleet of transports, and the results were similar.

Two days later, the Germans evened the score at Oran when the sub U–565 torpedoed and sank the French merchant ship "Sidi Bel Abbes" and the American merchant ship "Michigan." Aboard the Side Bel Abbes, was a battalion of Senegalese infantrymen who were en route to Tunisia. Five hundred sixty seven men were lost.

THE LAST PUSH IN TUNISIA

On April 20, the Allies launched what they hoped would be their last major offensive in North Africa. American tanks smashed through the mountains north of Medjez el Bab and advanced to the Tine River Valley. From there to the sea, the land was flat and ideal for tank warfare—and by now the Allies had superiority in the number of tanks. And the powerful German Tiger tanks were still too few in number to be a major factor.

On April 22, other attacks began. The American 2nd Corps headed for Bizerte and the British 5th Corps for Tunis. To the south the British 9th Corps, the French 19th Corps, and the British 8th Army made limited attacks. The fighting was hard and proceeded day after day. On the 28, the Germans launched a three-day counteroffensive which gained some ground but was then halted. It was to be the last major German attack in North Africa.

By now the Axis Powers had abandoned conventional convoys to Tunisia, which faced certain destruction, and began running men and supplies across the Mediterranean by destroyers, which had a fair chance of fighting their way through the Allied naval blockade. But this too failed. One of the last attempts to run the Allied blockade occurred on April 30, when two Italian destroyers and a German destroyer tried to get 600 German troops and fifty tons of ammunition through to Tunisia. Two of the ships left from the Naples area and the third from Trapani, rendezvoused at sea under strong air support, and tried to race through the blockade. They almost made it. Just after noon, American aircraft caught up with the three ships as they approached Tunisia. The Americans brushed aside the air cover and sank one of the Italian destroyers and badly damaged the German destroyer, both within sight of land. Of the 280 soldiers on the Italian destroyer 156 were rescued. The damaged German destroyer made it under her own power to the port of Korbus, but was so badly damaged that she was later scuttled. At 5:00 p.m., the American planes caught up with the remaining Italian destroyer off Ras Mustafa and badly damaged her, setting her afire. She was carrying the bulk of the fifty tons of ammunition and sank at 5:35 p.m. that evening.

On May 1, the Americans scored a major breakthrough in the north and the Axis forces began to retreat en masse. On the 3rd, the Americans took Mateur, twenty miles southwest of their objective, Bizerte. On the 5th the British broke through the Axis lines east of Medjez el Bab and on the 6th occupied the town of Massacault sixteen miles southwest of Tunis. On May 7, Axis defenses crumbled and the Americans raced into Bizerte while the British raced into Tunis. At Bizerte, 41,000 Axis troops surrendered, including six generals. At Tunis, though, the bulk of the Axis forces and their commander, General Arnim, withdrew successfully to the Cape Bon Peninsula. But their strength was broken. They were unable to establish a successful defense line and were eventually chased down and captured, unit-by-unit, by the British. On May 12, the last of the Axis forces, including General von Arnim, surrendered unconditionally at the tip end of the Cape Bone Peninsula. The next day Italian General Messe, who had been promoted to Field Marshal hours earlier, surrendered unconditionally. In all, the Axis lost a total of over 300,000 men with some 238,000 German and Italian troops having been taken prisoner. In the number of troops, it was a disaster comparable to Stalingrad. The Allies suffered some 75,000 casualties.

Von Arnim's and Messe's surrender ended all organized fighting in Africa.

The next day, May 13, Churchill's deputy Prime Minister, Clement Attlee (Churchill was in Washington), officially announced that the campaign in North Africa had ended in a complete Allied victory.

On May 7, General Charles Mast had been appointed Governor-General of Tunisia and on May 15, the Bey Al-Moncef of Tunis, the native ruler of Tunisia, was ousted from power for collaborating with the Axis Powers. This left Bourguiba, still in Rome, the undisputed but absent leader of the Tunisian nationalists. Sidi Alim Pasha succeeded Moncef as Bey but soon found his position untenable and resigned in July.

Of the three French North African colonies, two had contributed significantly to the Allied victory by supplying soldiers for the French Army. By the end of the fighting, some 3,000 Moroccans had become casualties along with about 1,200 Algerians. There were very few Tunisian casualties because they did not have the opportunity to fight with the Allies. Most of the Tunisian casualties suffered were on the Axis side.

On May 17, a large British convoy entered the Mediterranean at Gibraltar and traveled to the Suez Canal, the entire length of the Mediterranean, without incident. The convoy stayed close to the North African coastline. This was the first time an Allied convoy was able to do this since Italy entered the war in June 1940.

The North African coast was not yet entirely safe. German and Italian subs were still operating there, and during May they sank four Allied merchant ships. On May 21, the U.S. destroyer "Nields" sank the Italian sub "Gorgo" off Algeria and the German submarine, U–414, was lost on the 25th off Algeria to the British corvette "Vetch."

On May 12, the Allies established another Advanced Amphibious Training Base at Bizerte and on the 22nd another at Tunis. Allied troops were trained at these facilities for the coming invasion of Sicily.

On May 25, Roosevelt and Churchill concluded their thirteen-day meeting in Washington, the "Trident Conference," during which they agreed on the next major campaigns of the war. It was secretly agreed that Sicily would be invaded in July using North Africa as a staging area. This would be known as "Operation Husky" with a target date of July 10. After Sicily was secured, Italy would then be invaded. It was also decided at Trident that Allied planes would bomb the Ploesti oil fields in Romania from North African air bases. Those oil fields were Germany's main source for oil.

Another decision made at Trident was to proceed with a cross-channel invasion of northern France, "Operation Overlord," which would be scheduled for May 1, 1944 (later changed to June 6, 1944).

Upon returning from Washington, Churchill flew to Algiers to confer with de Gaulle on political and military matters. There de Gaulle and Giraud were in the process of establishing a unified command to conduct the future of the French war effort. During the first days in June, they reached agreement to restructure de Gaulle's National Committee for Liberation and become co-Presidents.

On May 31, French Admiral Godfroy, Commander of the neutralized French ships at Alexandria, Egypt, announced that he, his men, and his ships would join the Allies.

Chapter 16
ELSEWHERE IN AFRICA (SEPTEMBER 1942–MAY 1943)
WARTIME CONDITIONS CONTINUE

As the fighting raged across North Africa, so did the war in Africa's coastal waters, but that war would last much longer. South of the Sahara there was relative calm, but wartime conditions still dominated virtually all activities, and political change was upon the land.

THE SEA WAR—ATLANTIC

The Atlantic waters off Africa continued to be relatively productive hunting grounds for Axis submarines. During September 1942, Axis subs sank fourteen Allied merchantmen with no German subs lost. Four of those ships, including the Laconia (sunk September 12) were sunk by groups of submarines known as the "Eisbaer" (polar bear) group on their way to carry out a submarine blitz in the waters off South Africa.

On September 10, the raider Michel captured and sank the American freighter "American Leader" west of the Cape of Good Hope. Forty-seven crewmen were taken captive and eventually taken to Singapore to become prisoners of the Japanese. Fourteen Americans perished in the attack.

SUB BLITZ OFF SOUTH AFRICA

Admiral Doenitz had concluded from various reports that the waters off South Africa were one of the few areas left within the range of German submarines where Allied antisubmarine activities were still weak. With the advent of his new Milch Cows, he could sustain the operational patrols of subs at that greater distance for a period of two months or more. To this end, he organized the Eisbaer group consisting of six subs; U–68, U–156, U–159, U–172, U–179, and U–504, and sent them off to test his theory. The results were immediate and outstanding. The first two subs, U–172 and U–159, arrived on station off Cape Town during the first week in October, after refueling from Milch Cow U–459 south of St. Helena Island. On October 7, the first day of operations, the two subs sank three Allied merchantmen, all sailing alone and unescorted. The next day more Eisbaer subs arrived after refueling and a total of seven more ships were sunk. That was ten Allied ships sunk in two days. On that day, though, the Allies scored a victory when the British destroyer "Active" encountered and sank U–179 off Cape Town with several volleys of depth charges. On October 9, U–172 boldly penetrated Cape Town harbor but found no targets worthy of an attack and departed. That same day three more ships were sunk by the Eisbaer subs and one each on the 10th, 13th and 17th. By now the South Africans and other Allies were so alarmed that all ships in the areas were ordered to remain in port if at all possible. Realizing what had happened, the subs moved eastward and began operating off Port Elizabeth. And once again they found easy, unescorted, targets. On October 23 and 26, one ship was taken each day. On the 29th two ships were sunk and on the 31st, three.

Doenitz was so pleased with the results of the Eisbaer group that he organized a second group called the "Paukenschlag" (Drum Roll) to continue the attack as the Eisbaer subs ended their patrols and returned home.

Meanwhile, other Axis subs were doing their bloody business in Africa's Atlantic waters. During October, north of the South African blitz area, 24 more Allied ships were sent to the bottom. Two of these were the British corvette "Crocus" sunk on October 6 by U–333 60 miles southwest of Freetown, and the British light cruiser "Phoebe" sunk by the Italian sub

"Achilles" six miles off Pointe Noire, French Equatorial Africa. During October no Axis subs were lost in the area.

THE BATTLESHIP THAT WAS NOT THERE

On October 6, the Italian sub "Barbarico" reported that it had attacked and sunk an American battleship of the "Mississippi" class off Liberia. This was taken at face value by both the Italian and German submarine commands and when Barbarico returned to Bordeaux the captain and crew were met by the Italian ambassador and lavishly entertained by the Germans. Unfortunately for the Axis, the report was false. No American battleship was in the area at the time. The ship the Barbarico attacked was the British corvette "Petunia" which survived the attack unharmed.

On November 1, the first Paukenschlag sub, U–178, arrived in South African waters and promptly sank the British cargo ship "Mendoza" off Durban. A second Paukenschlag sub arrived and sank a Greek merchantman off Cape Town on the 2nd. That same day, Eisbaer sub U–172, on its way home, sank another British ship south of St. Helena Island. On November 3, another Paukenschlag sub, U–181, arrived and sank an American cargo ship while the departing U–504 sank a Brazilian ship. And so it went throughout the rest of the month. Between November 4 and 30, hardly a day went by when one or more ships were sunk by the departing Eisbaer group or the newly arrived Paukenschlag group. During that time, a total of 23 Allied ships went to the bottom in South African waters. The Italian sub "Cagni" added to the toll by sinking a British merchant ship off Cape Town on November 29. Furthermore, the sub menace in the South African waters had disrupted the Allied supply lines to the Middle East and forced the temporary closing of several harbors in southern Africa.

During November 1942, other Axis subs and some of the returning Eisbaer subs took another nineteen Allied merchantmen and troop transports and four warships in the waters off western Africa. Nine of the merchantmen and troop transports were sunk off Morocco during the American invasion there. Fortunately for the Allies virtually all of the troops had disembarked from the transports before they were sunk. All four of the warships were sunk off the Moroccan coast during the period of November 11–15. They were the American destroyer "Hambleton" sunk on November 11 by U–173, the British destroyer "Marne" and destroyer tender "Hecla" sunk on the 12th by U–515, and the British escort carrier "Avenger" sunk on the 15th by U–155.

During the American invasion of Morocco on November 8, several French vessels challenged the invaders and were damaged or sunk. They were the French battleship Jean Bart which was badly damaged at anchor in Casablanca harbor, the cruiser "Primauget" which was damaged by gunfire and beached at Casablanca; the destroyers "Fougueux," "Brestois Frondeur" and "Boulonnais" all sunk at Casablanca; and the flotilla leaders "Milan" and "Albatros" both damaged and beached.

The Americans were quick to utilize the French airfields in Morocco to begin antisubmarine patrols off the northwest coast of Africa. Airfields at Casablanca, Agadir, and Port Lyautey were in use as early as November 10. Together with Allied ships operating offshore, these land-based aircraft became a part of the newly-formed Moroccan Sea Frontier Command, which became responsible for the security of the waters off northwestern Africa.

The Moroccan Sea Frontier Command's first success came on November 16, when three American destroyers, "Woolsey," "Swanson" and "Quill," located and sank the German sub U–173 fifty miles off Casablanca. She was the ninth German sub to be sunk in African Atlantic waters.

Because of the efforts of the Moroccan Sea Frontier Command and the strong convoy escort forces now available to the Allies, the coastal waters off Morocco became relatively safe for a distance of up to 200 miles out to sea.

Eventually the Moroccan Sea Frontier Command was given over to the Fighting French, who continued the aggressive sea and air patrols.

During late November 1942, French ships operating out of Dakar, now in Allied hands, began antisubmarine patrols into the Atlantic. This made four navies, the American, British, Brazilian and French, who now patrolled the mid-ocean gap between West Africa and South America and the waters south of the Equator.

December 1942 saw the Paukenschlag group still working the waters of South Africa, but by then Allied antisubmarine activities had increased, keeping the subs more often on the run than on the attack. Also, more convoys were being utilized by the Allies. Nevertheless, the Paukenschlag subs succeeded in sinking four more ships before mid-December when they were obliged to break off the campaign and return home. Back at Submarine Command in Germany, Doenitz was not discouraged. The Eisbaer—Paukenschlag campaign had cost the Allies 54 ships. He would send his subs again to South Africa.

Elsewhere along the Atlantic coast, submarine activity was greatly reduced. Only two ships were sunk during December. On December 3, U–552 sank the British freighter "Wallsend" between the Canary Island and the Cape Verde Islands, and on the 17th U–432 sank the French trawler "Poitou" off Morocco.

On December 27, the German raider Michel, working the South Atlantic, sank the British freighter "Empire March" out of Durban for Trinidad.

MORE OF EVERYTHING FOR THE ALLIES

The dawn of the new year, 1943, did not bring good fortune for the Axis naval operations in the mid and South Atlantic. The Allies' antisubmarine and anti-blockade runner patrols were getting more of everything. Most significant was the arrival of the baby flat tops, small aircraft carriers usually converted from fast merchant ships. These vessels formed the nucleus of the newly-created "Hunter-Killer Groups" (H-K Group) specifically designed for antisubmarine and anti-blockade runner activities. An H-K Group usually consisted of a baby flat top and two or more small fast ships such as destroyers, destroyer escorts, corvettes, trawlers, etc. With the baby flat top's aircraft searching the sea for more than a hundred miles around, and with the latest in radar and sonar scanning the surface and the depths of the water, the H-K Group could locate any vessel on or below the surface within a considerable range. Once an enemy submarine or blockade runner was spotted, it was very unlikely that it would get away. The H-K Group had the wherewithal to maintain contact with the enemy vessel, day or night, until it was destroyed.

The baby flat tops were also used to deliver aircraft to West Africa. On January 19, Ranger delivered another batch of P–40 fighters from her deck to the airport at Accra. These planes then went on across the Cannonball Route to North Africa. On February 24, Ranger was back again to deliver a second batch of P–40s.

Allied land-based air coverage was also improving significantly. Long-range Catalina flying boats and B–24 bombers were rolling off the production lines in America at amazing rates, and were now plentiful enough to be sent to the most remote war fronts. With such planes based out of West Africa, South Africa, Ascension Island, and Brazil, most of the waters of the Central and South Atlantic came under Allied air surveillance. In addition, there was Ultra and the new Huff-Duff system. The latter, officially known as the "High Frequency Direction Finding" system (HFDF), was a system of very sensitive land-based radio receiver stations on both sides of the Atlantic that could pick up the radio transmission of Axis subs and, by triangulation, spot their location.

BLOCKADE RUNNERS IN TROUBLE

The increased Allied surveillance and attack capabilities in the Atlantic spelled big trouble for the Axis blockade runners. For most of their journey, the blockade runners had wide open seas to travel where Allied air and sea patrols were rare or nonexistent. But, when the runners reached the heavily patrolled mid-ocean gap in the Central Atlantic they were now hard to miss. Heretofore, most of the blockade runners made it. Beginning in 1943, most of them did not.

THE NEW YEAR IN THE CENTRAL AND SOUTH ATLANTIC

Despite the growing Allied strength in the Central and South Atlantic the Axis subs had a relatively good month in January 1943, sinking seventeen Allied ships, fourteen of them in convoys. Most of those sunk were north of the Equator among or between the three island groups; Cape Verdes, Canaries, and Azores. No ships were sunk off the South African coast. One outstanding feat was pulled off by the ten-sub "Delphin" group operating in the Central Atlantic. Between January 8 and 11, they attacked an Allied convoy of nine tankers out of Trinidad for North Africa. The Delphin group was joined by several other German subs and together they simply overwhelmed the convoy's four escorts, a destroyer and three corvettes. Seven of the nine tankers were sunk and seriously hampered the Allied activities in Tunisia for a period of time. No German subs were lost.

February was another successful month, with 24 Allied ships sunk. Thirteen of the ships were sailing in convoys. Four of the others, all sailing alone, were sunk off South Africa where Doenitz had sent three submarines. Allied antisubmarine activity off South Africa was stronger but still not as strong as elsewhere. Plus there were fewer convoys in South African waters. These conditions affected Doenitz's strategy for the month of March.

On February 23, another U–boat was lost. She was U–522 sunk south of the Azores by the British Coast Guard cutter "Totland." During February, Doenitz sent another group of six submarines, called the "Seehund" (Seal) group, to carry out another submarine blitz in South African waters. To his great pleasure they sank a total of nineteen ships between February 10th and April 5, twelve sailing alone and six in one convoy, DN–21. Doenitz was so pleased that he organized "Seehund II" to succeed Seehund.

To put together both Seehund and Seehund II, Doenitz had to pull some of his subs away from the African west coast. As a result, sinkings during March there dropped to a total of nine, four of which were sunk by Italian subs.

Once again, the Germans lost another sub in the West African waters during this time. She was U–524, which was sunk south of Madeira Island by an American B–24 bomber.

STILL MORE ADVANTAGES FOR THE ALLIES

During the spring of 1943, the Allies increased the speeds of their convoys. This was made possible by the fact that many of the slower ships had been sunk or sent off to safer waters, and because newer and faster ships, especially the mass-produced American "Liberty Ships," were becoming available. For the submariners this meant that convoys were now harder to catch, harder to keep up with, and at sea for less time.

Another change made by the Allies was, with more ships available, the British and Americans divided responsibility for convoy protection and became more efficient. The British and Canadians took responsibility for northern convoys while the Americans took responsibility for southern convoys.

On March 15, the American ships in the Atlantic were designated as the United States 4th Fleet. The new fleet had five light cruisers, 75 destroyers, dozens of smaller vessels, and a growing number of baby flat tops. The 4th Fleet was designed for one purpose—to sink submarines and blockade runners.

APRIL AND MAY IN THE CENTRAL AND SOUTH ATLANTIC

April in the Central and South Atlantic proved to be another good month for the Axis submariners. Fifteen Allied ships were sunk between April 8 and May 1. Seven of the ships were sunk by U–515 acting alone, attacking an eighteen-ship convoy, TS–37. The convoy was lightly guarded by only one British corvette and three trawlers. Adding to U–515's success was the fact that the British experienced communication problems during the attacks.

One of the fifteen ships in the monthly total was sunk by an Italian sub "Archimede." Another of the lost Allied vessels lost was the British submarine, P.615. She was an early-war submarine originally built by the British for Turkey, but taken over by the British when war started. She was torpedoed and sunk on April 18 by U–123 off Liberia.

Off South Africa, Doenitz's Seehund II group arrived in mid-April and began taking ships as fast as the Seehund group had done before it. Serving alongside the German subs off South Africa was the Italian sub "Da Vinci." During April the Axis subs sank five ships and during May, eight ships. Da Vinci sank four of the five ships in April and then departed.

April, though, cost the Germans another sub in African waters. U–167 had been badly damaged on April 5 in an attack by two RAF planes and put in at the Canary Islands where the German supply ship Charlotte Schliemann was anchored in the harbor. It was determined by personnel from both U–167 and the supply ship that the sub was too badly damaged to make it back to Europe. Therefore, it was taken out of the harbor and scuttled in Spanish waters on April 6. The sub's crew was lavishly entertained by the Spanish authorities and given a tour of the islands. British agents photographed the Germans on tour. Then, the crew was smuggled out of the islands at night on U–455 and returned to France. Later, most of them became the crew for the new sub, U–547.

During May the Charlotte Schliemann left the Canary Islands because of British diplomatic pressure on the Spaniards and headed south. Her new assignment was to operate out of Penang, Malaya, a soon-to-be acquired base for German warships.

Also during May 1943, the German subs took another eight Allied merchant ships in West African waters, all of them were sailing alone. Off South Africa the score was also eight and all of them sailing alone. These numbers reflected a negative development for the Axis subs in that the primary targets for submarine, the convoys, were not attacked. Indeed, with Allied antisubmarine activities on the increase, convoys now appeared as though they might be untouchable.

During May, the Germans lost two subs in West African waters. The first was U–447 sunk May 7 off Morocco by RAF aircraft. The second was U–182 sunk May 16 northwest of Madeira Island by the American destroyer "C." U–182 had been part of the Seehund group and was returning home.

"BLACK MAY"

The submarine activity off West and South Africa did not reflect accurately what was happening in the other ocean war zones in May. During May 1943, the Germans lost a staggering total of 43 subs worldwide out of the 100+ subs at sea. The month before it was 17 and a year ago, May 1942, it was four. Because of this sudden upsurge in losses, near panic gripped Germany's U–boat command. Doenitz issued the very unusual order on May 24 recalling the great majority of the subs at sea until the problem could be analyzed and corrective measures taken. Most of those subs recalled were from the North Atlantic where the seagoing traffic was the heaviest and the new Allied antisubmarine measures had been applied first and in greatest intensity.

Another part of the problem for the Germans was that several of the subs sunk during May were Milch Cows. The Milch Cows had been doing what they were intended to do, but this, in turn, created yet another problem for Doenitz. Because the Milch Cows were at sea for such long times, the morale of the crews tended to decline making them less efficient. This, together with the huge losses in May, sent the morale of the entire German submarine branch into a downward spiral. It was so severe that the British detected it through their Ultra intercepts.

"FIDO"

What the Germans did not know, and would not discover throughout the remainder of the war, was that the Americans had a new and very potent antisubmarine weapon dubbed "FIDO" (as in the dog that can sniff things out). This was an air-dropped acoustic torpedo which, when dropped close to a submarine, would home in on the sub's propeller noise. It was proving to be a very successful weapon and one that the Americans took great measures to keep secret. Ironically, the Germans were, at this very time, in the final stages of producing an acoustic torpedo of their own to be launched from submarines. When Doenitz gave the order again for the subs to return to the North Atlantic many of the subs would be carry those torpedoes.

THE SEA WAR—INDIAN OCEAN

The sea war in the Indian Ocean from September 1942 to May 1943 was considerably less than that in the Atlantic because the Axis nations sent fewer submarines there. The Japanese, the primary threat in the Indian Ocean, were on the defensive after their defeat at Midway, trying to protect their newly-won empire and needing the subs closer to home. Therefore, they greatly reduced the number of subs they sent to remote areas such as the western Indian Ocean. Furthermore, the Japanese no longer had the wherewithal to carry out large-scale amphibious operations, so the threat of invasion throughout the whole Indian Ocean region was greatly reduced. The Allies, of course, could not be absolutely sure of this and continued to keep up their guard.

During September 1942, the Japanese did dispatch one submarine, I–29, to African waters and she sank four ships off the coast of Italian Somaliland. No Japanese submarines, though, appeared during October.

BLOCKADE RUNNERS AGAIN

Between October 1941 and March 1942, the summer months in the southern hemisphere, the Germans and Italians had succeeded in sending eleven blockade runners from the Far East to Europe via the Indian and Atlantic Oceans with vitally needed supplies. Of the eleven ships, nine made it. Beginning in October 1942, they hoped to repeat that success. During that month, the first of sixteen blockade runners left Japanese waters for Europe. But the Allies were much better prepared now and the program would end in disaster. Over the southern summer months four blockade runners would be forced to turn back, eight would be sunk along the way, and only four would make it to Europe.

VERY LITTLE NAVAL ACTION IN WESTERN INDIAN OCEAN

During November and December 1942, there was very little naval action in the western Indian Ocean. In November, the Japanese sub I–29 returned to its hunting-ground off Italian Somaliland and sank one British cargo ship, and in December it sank a Norwegian tanker.

Further to the south the German raider Michel was a patrolling off Madagascar and on November 29 sank the American freighter "Sawolka." The Sawolka was out of Cape Town bound for Colombo, Ceylon and was able to get off an alarm before it sank. Michel then departed the area but not before taking aboard the survivors of the Sawolka as captives.

An American–made "Catalina" seaplane in the service of the RAF over the Indian Ocean. This aircraft was one of the best antisubmarine weapons in the Allied arsenal.

On November 28, Fighting French forces landed on Reunion Island, about 500 miles east of Madagascar, and took control of that strategic island. The island's administration, heretofore loyal to Vichy, answered Darlan's call to join the Allies. Reunion was of very little strategic value to the Allies because the British-held Mauritius Islands were nearby, and there were already two Allied air bases there.

On November 30, the Italians took note of the lack of naval activity in the western Indian Ocean, and they made statements to the effect that part of the blame for the Axis defeat at el Alamein had to be borne by the Japanese for their failure to interdict the massive amounts of supplies that had reached the British in Egypt via the Indian Ocean sea routes. The Japanese responded to this in December by offering the use of Japanese bases in South East Asia to warships of the European Axis nations for operations in the Indian Ocean. The Germans were very interested in this proposal. The Germans had, by now, lost most of their submarine supply ships and were fast losing the Milch Cows so the prospect of having reliable naval facilities in the Indian Ocean appealed to them. Doenitz and his staff studied the proposal carefully.

Meanwhile, the British and South Africans, in response to the German submarine blitz in South African waters, took steps to increase air surveillance over that area by making use of new American-made Catalina flying boats that were becoming more available through Lend-Lease. A base for those planes was established at St. Lucia Lake, 150 miles up the coast from Durban from which most of South Africa's waters could be covered far out to sea. Durban's harbor had been considered, but it was so crowded with ship traffic that no place could be found for the big seaplanes.

Facilities for Catalinas were also established at Port Elizabeth. Some of the air crews were Dutch—a planned move by the British to win over the hearts and minds of the Afrikaners.

PENANG

In February 1943, the Germans accepted the Japanese offer of the use of their bases in South East Asia for German vessels. The Indian Ocean was still fertile hunting-ground for Axis submarines, because few convoys operated there and Allied antisubmarine defenses were still weaker than elsewhere. There was yet another advantage for the Germans in that the German vessels from the Far Eastern ports would be operating on Japanese oil, which was plentiful, and thereby helped to relieve the critical oil shortage in Europe. Furthermore, the Japanese had a few fast tankers which were equipped to refuel submarines at sea.

Several bases were made available to the Germans; Penang and Singapore in Malaya, and Batavia and Sourabaya on the island of Java. Penang was the most important. This was a very modern naval base on an island off the southern shore of the Malaya Peninsula and at the mouth of the heavily-traveled Strait of Malacca. Penang was the western-most of the bases on the rim of the Indian Ocean and could supply the needs for most vessels, including dry dock services. This base became the German's port of choice.

Over a period of months, four German supply ships arrived at Penang with large stores of torpedoes, spare parts, radio equipment, radar and anti-radar devices, etc. They brought no stores of food or fuel because those items were plentiful in Japanese-occupied South East Asia. Two of the German ships that arrived were the Charlotte Schliemann and Brake, both of which had operated out of the Spanish-owned Canary Islands in the Atlantic. It was planned that they would operate out of Penang, supplying German submarines operating in the Indian Ocean. Milch Cows would also operate out of Penang. The other two German ships, the "Quito" and "Bogata," would be used to gather supplies throughout the Japanese Empire, as far north as Japan itself, and bring those items to the Germans at Penang and the other bases.

During April, the German Navy established a headquarters operation at Penang known as the 8th Submarine Squadron. One of the first measures taken by the new headquarters was to work out areas of the Indian Ocean with the Japanese in which their respective submarines would operate. The Germans acquired much of the western and southern Indian Ocean, while the Japanese acquired the northern and eastern parts. Neither party was restricted to their own areas and often did operate in the other's area.

During April, the subs of Seehund II began operating off South Africa and they, unlike their predecessor, now had the option of using Penang especially when they needed repairs or ran out of torpedoes. Throughout their tour of duty, which extended into early August 1943, several of the Seehund II subs made use of Penang.

Captain Max Schley, center, Commander of the German sub U–178, a member of the Seehund II group, embraces two of his Japanese comrades-in-arms at Penang.

VIP TRANSFER IN MID-OCEAN

At a prearranged spot in the Indian Ocean south of Madagascar, the German sub U-180 and the Japanese sub I-29 met on April 26 for the purpose of transferring three individuals from the German sub to the Japanese sub. They were Subhas Chandra Bose, a militant Indian nationalist leader and his secretary; Abid Hassan, and Bose's German-born wife. Bose did not believe that peaceful civil disobedience, promoted by Mahatma Gandhi, would bring independence to India. He supported and engaged in military and terrorist activities. Bose had been arrested by the British in India but escaped to Germany, where he helped organize a small Indian Legion for the German Army. When Japan entered the war and India fell within their sphere of influence, it was obvious that Bose's services would be more valuable to the Japanese than to the Germans. Thus, the transfer was initiated. The captain of U–180 had strict orders to avoid all combat until Bose was transferred. After that U–180 became a part of the Seehund II group.

Bose was taken to Singapore and went on to establish the Provisional government of India and the Indian National Army with the help of the Japanese. The Provisional government was recognized by most of the Axis nations as the independent government of India and established a nominal political capital in the Andaman Islands in the Bay of Bengal, the only Indian territory occupied by the Japanese. But Bose and his army operated out of headquarters in Rangoon, Burma. The Indian National Army (INA) was comprised mostly of Indian soldiers who had been in the British Army and were captured by the Japanese in South East Asia. The INA was stationed in Burma, along with the Japanese forces there to pose a constant threat to India's eastern border.

MAY 1943 IN THE INDIAN OCEAN

It will be remembered that this was Black May in the North Atlantic for the German submarine fleet. In the Indian Ocean, though, things were quite different. The few German and Japanese subs that operated there did so with relative impunity compared to what was happening in the Atlantic. During May, two brand new German subs arrived at Penang, which had been traded to the Japanese government in exchange for supplies. Along the way these subs had been refueled by a Japanese tanker in the Indian Ocean. The two subs went on to Japan, where they were studied carefully by Japanese naval engineers and some of their features copied. At this point in time, the Japanese were known for their propensity of copying the industrial advances of the West. Later in the war a third German sub was traded to the Japanese for supplies.

During both April and May, Japanese submarine activity in the Indian Ocean was minimal. Two Allied ships were sunk by Japanese subs in the eastern Indian Ocean, but no Japanese subs ventured into its western waters.

In North Africa, as we have already seen, the Allies had become victorious over the Axis forces there in early May, and by the end of May, Allied convoys were again traversing the Mediterranean Sea. This reduced, to a great degree, the need to send convoys around the southern tip of Africa and through the Indian Ocean. The South Africa route was still important to the Allies, though, for several reasons. It was still safer for single, unescorted ships to sail around Africa than to traverse the Mediterranean, plus the convoys in the Mediterranean, because of their size, tended to create sudden areas of congestion at ports and important waterways such as Gibraltar and the Suez Canal. Also, it was still believed by the Allies that ships and convoys rounding South Africa could do so with fewer escorts. And finally, it was not much further for ships to travel from the United States to the Far East via South Africa than to do so through the Mediterranean. Therefore, many Allied ships and convoys continued to sail around South Africa.

ROOSEVELT VISITS LIBERIA

On his return from the Casablanca Conference in January 1943, President Roosevelt stopped for a visit in Monrovia, Liberia to meet with Liberian President, Edwin Barclay. Liberia was still neutral but cooperating openly with the Allies. The country's main contribution to the Allied war effort was the leasing of airfields and parts of Fisherman's Lake for seaplanes to the Allies as a part of the Allied trans-African air system. Furthermore, the United States was, as it had long been, Liberia's main trading partner. Liberia was one of America's better wartime sources for natural rubber. In the prewar years, the Firestone Tire and Rubber Company had planted 75,000 acres of rubber trees, of which 45,000 were now producing. This source, coupled with the production of Liberian-owned plantations and wild rubber gathered by natives provided the United States with 35,500,000 pounds or rubber a year. Some 23,000 Liberians were employed by Firestone.

More recently, American mining interests had invested in Liberia and by this time the country was exporting bauxite and high-grade iron ore from mines near Mount Nimba.

The American expeditionary force, which had landed in Liberia in 1942, was the strongest military force in the country and the one the Liberian government would depend upon to defend the country if attacked. Even the small Liberian militia had been put under American command.

The meeting was most cordial and Barclay was invited to come to the United States. He did so in May 1943, met again with Roosevelt again, and addressed Congress. Barclay also came to the United States for medical treatment and an operation.

VICHY LOSES OUT IN WEST AFRICA

Admiral Darlan's call for the Vichy-controlled colonies of the French Empire to join the Allies brought about one of the most profound changes in Africa during the entire war. In a matter of days the French colonial administrators in Africa responded favorably to that call and about 20% of the land mass of Africa abandoned the neutralist and pro-Axis policies of Vichy and reentered the war on the side of the Allies. The greatest French colonial holding was, of course, French West Africa. With that colonial federation's adherence to the Allies the great western bulge of Africa, from the Mediterranean to the Gulf of Guinea became Allied territory.

This produced enormous advantages for the Allies. The great natural wealth of the French African colonies, so long dormant, could now be mobilized for the Allied war effort. Several million people would now work for the Allied cause, while the French armed forces could be revitalized and able to draw on the huge manpower sources of the colonies. French West African seaports, airfields, military bases, roads, and railroads, some of which had served the Axis, would now serve the Allies.

Furthermore, the British could lift their naval blockade of the former Vichy colonies and use those important resources elsewhere. Intercolonial trade could resume between the French colonies and those of the Allies reducing the need for border controls and smuggling. What is more, the vast coastline of the French lands bordering the Atlantic made it possible for Allied armed forces to establish bases from which they could more aggressively pursue the sea war in Africa's Atlantic waters.

Politically, the leadership of the newly-acquired colonial holdings still had to be worked out, but it was never in doubt that these areas would, in the end, benefit the Allies.

In still another advantage to the Allies, the loss of the African colonies by Vichy reduced that government's control and influence to insignificance outside of Axis-occupied France.

The Allies had made preparations for all this by announcing, on several occasions, that any French colony that switched over to the Allied side would be held in trust and remain a part of the French Empire until such time that a newly recognized government of France was in place and able to resume control of the colonies. That was a pledge the Allies intended to keep.

The Vichy government had, inadvertently, facilitated the great transformation by announcing, a few weeks before the Allied invasion of French North Africa, yet another unpopular concession to Germany. That was an agreement which had been reached between Vichy and Berlin whereby one French POW, from the 1940 campaign in France, would be released for every three Frenchmen who agreed to go to work in Germany. Those workers were to come from both occupied and unoccupied French territories and there were indications that conscription might be used to recruit workers. This new policy made it much easier for Frenchmen and natives alike throughout the Empire to reconsider their loyalty to Vichy.

BOISSON AT DAKAR A PROBLEM

Despite the Allied invasion of French North Africa, High Commissioner Pierre Boisson was still the man who ruled French West Africa from his headquarters in Dakar; and he was the man the Allies had to deal with to bring French West Africa over to them. Unfortunately for the Allies, though, Boisson did not like the British and hated de Gaulle. With regards to de Gaulle, the feeling was mutual. It had been Boisson who brought about de Gaulle's failed attempt in September 1940 to bring Dakar and French West Africa back into the western alliance.

Boisson could see that the Allied demand for French West Africa to join them would soon be forthcoming, so he quickly surveyed the governors of the colonies that made up the federation of French West Africa and discovered that they all agreed that there was little choice but to go along with the Allies.

President Roosevelt was very anxious to bring French West Africa into the Allied camp, and he instructed Eisenhower to send an American emissary to Boisson to make any concession that was reasonable to gain his support. Therefore negotiations began during the second week in November between Algiers and Dakar. When Darlan's position was clarified, he too joined in the negotiations. The British, however, were not included in the negotiations but had given the Americans authority to negotiate on their behalf. And, of course, de Gaulle took no part in the talks.

As the talks were underway, the crew of the French battleship Richelieu, which was demobilized, damaged and anchored in Dakar harbor, declared for the Allies, but not necessarily for de Gaulle. This put some pressure on Boisson to hasten an agreement with the Allies. On November 23, it was announced that an agreement in principle had been reached for French West Africa to join the Allies, and on the 28th Boisson went to Algiers to work out details with Darlan and Eisenhower. On November 30, when Darlan formed his Imperial Council, Boisson became one of its members. On December 7, 1942, a final agreement was reached and French West Africa officially joined the Allies and reentered the war. The agreement called for the naval and other military facilities at Dakar to come under the command of American Admiral William A. Glassford and that the British would also have access to those facilities. Boisson would stay on as High Commissioner, retain his civil authority, and cooperate with Darlan in Algiers on military matters. In an attempt to improve relations with Boisson the British offered to buy the entire production of French West Africa's vegetable oil production and cooperate with Dakar in reestablishing the traditional trade relations between French West Africa and the British West African colonies.

Surprisingly, Roosevelt took a liking to Boisson although he had never met the man, and it was noted that Admiral Glassford and Boisson got along well. De Gaulle's people resented this and rumors started, possibly instigated by the Fighting French, that there were secret talks going on between the Americans and the French leaders at Dakar; that a postwar arrangement was being worked out whereby the Americans could obtain permanent concessions at Dakar in exchange for a part of Libya acquired by French-controlled Tunisia. This was, of course, denied by Washington but it was not the end of the story. At the Casablanca Conference in January 1943, Roosevelt confided in several of his close aides that he favored reducing the size of the French Empire after the war and specifically mentioned Dakar as an area that might be taken from the French. News of this leaked to de Gaulle, but nothing was discussed openly on the issue. These things served only to widen the distrust that had long existed between Roosevelt and de Gaulle and muddy the already fragile and complex French political question.

THOSE "PUSHY" AMERICANS

Another problem of sorts with the Americans developed in the newly-acquired French territories. As the Americans moved into French West Africa, they began, with much gusto, to build and improve all sorts of facilities such as airfields, harbors and roads, etc. This American penchant for building things soon came to be resented by the French because they did not have the financial resources to keep up with the "pushy" Americans. The British had already experienced this and had solved the problem by avoiding joint ventures with the Americans because they would, with their lesser resources, be automatically relegated to the status of a junior partner. Now, the French took up this attitude too and avoided joint ventures with the Americans. There was another aspect for the British and French in that in their own colonial lands they did not want to appear to the native population as playing a secondary role to the Americans.

But there was also a positive side to this arrangement in that everyone got to build what they wanted, their way, without the interference of partners. And the British and French knew that after the war the Americans would, in all likelihood, walk away from their newly-built projects, leaving them to benefit the local communities.

AFTER DARLAN

When Darlan was assassinated in late December and de Gaulle entered the French political scene in Algiers, the relationship between Dakar and Algiers deteriorated rapidly into a state of political non-contact. But by then the Americans and British had control of the military assets of French West Africa, and the French political problems had become less important to them. However, the French political situation was still of importance enough that in January 1943, the British sent a mission to Boisson in an attempt to improve relations between Dakar and Algiers. After meeting with Boisson, the British had reason to concluded that he would continue to cooperate with the Allies and strive toward a working relationship with Algiers. This honeymoon did not last long. Boisson, for reasons of his own, sabotaged the new trade agreements with the neighboring British colonies which hindered the recovery of the West African economy and upset both French and British business interests. Furthermore, Boisson continued to maintain visible ties to Vichy. For example, every government office in Dakar still prominently displayed a picture of Petain and Radio Dakar ended each broadcast day with the slogan "Vive le Marechal!" As time passed the British became convinced that Boisson was both undemocratic and unyielding. During this time de Gaulle's people began a bitter anti-Boisson propaganda campaign on the air and in print, some of it coming from the adjoining British colonies. De Gaulle took it upon himself to send emissaries to the various colonial governors in French West Africa seeking their support and undermining that of Boisson. This effort was generally successful because the governors could see that de Gaulle's movement, having the support of the major Allies, was on the rise and that Boisson's position had no future.

As for the natives of French West Africa they were, almost universally, anxious to cooperate with the Americans and British because it meant jobs, a revival of the economy and, hopefully, relief from the repressive Vichy regime represented by Boisson. Some of the natives decided not to wait for the white men to work out their political problems and continued the process of migrating into the neighboring British colonies where economic conditions were already good. This was facilitated because border restrictions had been relaxed. The influx of French West African natives was particularly strong into the Gold Coast; this caused colonial administrators there concern lest they flood the labor market and upset the economic status quo. Officially the British government claimed that the outflow of natives from French territory was a French problem, but behind the scenes the British encouraged their border guards to cooperate with the French border control people to stem the flow of migrants.

For the first few months of 1943, the problems with Boisson lingered on, but by the spring of 1943, it was clear that the forces operating against him were gaining dominance and that his continuance in office was only a matter of time.

Meanwhile, American and British military activities progressed rapidly and Dakar became a vital Allied naval and air base as well as a link in the Allied air supply system in Africa. The battleship Richelieu and three French cruisers Glore, "Montcalm" and "Georges Leygues," long dormant at Dakar, were sent to the United States for refurbishing and eventually joined the reconstructed French Navy. Other French warships at Dakar that were serviceable began cooperating with the British and Americans on antisubmarine activities.

FRENCH EQUATORIAL AFRICA

In French Equatorial Africa, the main Gaullist stronghold in Africa, the events in French North Africa and French West Africa proved disappointing to the Fighting French leaders in Brazzaville. With Boisson still in power in neighboring French West Africa conditions along their common border still remained tense. Equatorial Africa, quite naturally, became one of the bases from which anti-Boisson propaganda was generated. This effort was augmented in the spring of 1943, when newer and more powerful radio transmitting equipment was acquired from the United States and installed in Equatorial Africa. Once it became operational Gaullist propaganda was broadcast to all parts of French West and North Africa.

BRITISH WEST AFRICA

The political changes in French West Africa had a positive effect on the British West African colonies of Nigeria, Gold Coast, Sierra Leone and Gambia in that trade and communications with their French neighbors reopened and returned to normal despite Boisson's effort to the contrary. The respective economies of the British colonies continued to be strong and such places as Freetown, Takoradi, Accra, Lagos, and Bathurst became very busy centers of trade and industry. The British government in London looked upon these colonies as making important contributions to the Allied war effort in both war materials and men.

During late 1942 and early 1943, the British military planners in London were preparing for campaign in Burma and turned to the British West African colonies as a source for troops. The West African Frontier Force, which was comprised of men from all four British colonies, had performed well during the 1941 East African campaign and it was decided that the West Africans should be called upon again for service in Burma. The British, therefore, set about creating two new divisions, the 81st and 82nd (West Africans). The divisions were organized in West Africa, and plans called for them to be sent to Ceylon for jungle training and then to Burma for combat duty. The 81st (WA) Division was comprised of the 4th Nigerian, 5th Gold Coast, and 6th Nigerian Brigades, and one each Gambian and Sierra Leonean battalions. The 82nd (WA) Division consisted of the 1st Nigerian, 2nd Gold Coast, and 7th Gold Coast Brigades and an extra Sierra Leonean battalion. The independent 3rd Nigerian Brigade was also formed along with artillery, Pioneer, reconnaissance, and rear-echelon units.

During this period the local nationalists in British West Africa were weak, and poorly organized and posed no challenge to the British plans. In Nigeria, the British position was aided by the emirs of the north who continued to support the British and the war effort. One reason for this cooperation was that the emirs had no desire to see the black nationalist of the south gain an upper hand in Nigeria.

TOGO

The African colony of Togo had been a Germany colony up to the time of World War I, populated mainly by Ewe tribesmen. After the war, it was divided roughly in half with the western half attached to British-controlled Gold Coast and the eastern half to the French-controlled colony of Dahomey, a part of French West Africa. The Ewe people resented the division of their homeland but were too backward and poorly organized to do anything about it. In 1941, though, a native organization called "Comite de l'unite Togolaise" evolved in Dahomey, calling for the reunification of Togo under French control. In Gold Coast, in 1943, a competitive organization was founded entitled the "Togoland Union" which called for reunification, but under British control. Neither organization was militant nor had much political clout during the war. Nevertheless, the seeds were sown for the postwar struggle that would, in the long run, result in the reunification of Togo and its eventual independence.

AIR ROUTES EXPANDED IN NORTH AND WEST AFRICA

With the adherence of French North and West Africa to the Allied cause, this entire region of Africa was ripe for the expansion of Allied air supply routes. Only the few Spanish possessions in the area were still closed to the Allies but this caused no major problems.

Once again, Dakar figured into the new equation for the Allies. With that city in Allied hands some Allied aircraft, with enough range, began flying directly to Dakar from Brazil thus cutting several hundred miles off of the flights to Sierra Leone and Liberia. By October 1942, the new four-engine Douglas C–54 transports were available and these were one of the aircraft in the American arsenal that could easily make Dakar from Brazil.

From Dakar, planes could continue on north to either Marakesh or Casablanca, both of which were important links in the Allied air supply system.

Marakesh quickly became an important Allied air link, too, because of the excellent year-around flying weather that prevailed in the area. From Marakesh and Casablanca, aircraft could easily reach points to the east such as Oran and Algiers. Most of the existing airfields needed expansion and modernization, and several new fields had to be built. This was undertaken by the Americans, who hired thousands of local workers and thereby helped to revive the depressed economies in some parts of the former Vichy-controlled French Empire.

As the Axis forces were chased into the northern corner of Tunisia additional north-south air supply routes opened up across the Sahara Desert, connecting points in North Africa with air stations along the Cannonball Route of central Africa. As early as November 17, 1942, only nine days after the Allied invasion of North Africa, an air link was established across the Sahara Desert between Oran and the Accra/Takoradi area in Gold Coast. A second trans-Saharan route soon followed between Kano, Nigeria and Oran.

In south-central Africa, the ATC opened a circular route; Lagos, Nigeria–Brazzaville–Salisbury, Southern Rhodesia–Nairobi and Mombasa–Khartoum.

As the military air operations moved on, the commercial air line companies followed in their wake. During December 1942, American Airlines Company established scheduled domestic airline service across the Atlantic from Brazil to West Africa. In early 1943, the company extended that service all the way to India.

Throughout French North and West Africa there already existed commercial air service via Air France. The Allies encouraged Air France's operations to continue and made it possible for that airline to obtain new equipment and expand its services for both military and commercial purposes.

As more military resources became available to the USAAF that service became less dependent on the commercial airline companies they had engaged earlier in the war to conduct ferrying operations of military aircraft. At this time, the USAAF sought to terminated those contracts and take over the ferrying operations themselves. A case in point was the Pan-American Air Ferry Service (PAAF) contracted in 1941 to ferry military aircraft from the United States to points in Africa. In late 1942, the USAAF terminated its contract with PAAF and took over the company's ferrying operations. But PAAF had done its job well. By the time the contract ended, PAAF had ferried 464 military aircraft to Africa and points beyond.

After the collapse of the Axis forces in Tunisia in early May 1943, air routes were extended to Tunis and other Tunisian cities from both east and west. This gave the Allies, for the first time since June 1940, unhindered east-west air service across the entire length of North Africa. As the Allied buildup for the invasion of Sicily got underway supplies and personnel could be brought into the staging areas by air from the west, the east, and the south.

As might be expected, the air routes across North Africa rapidly became crowded in preparation for the invasion of Sicily, so the Cannonball Route across central Africa retained its importance and continued to carry the major load of ferrying operations to the Middle East and on to India and China. The Allied needs in the China–Burma–India (CBI) theater had steadily become more demanding because of the British preparations for military action against the Japanese in Burma and because the AAF's Air Transport Command (ATC) established, in May 1943, a massive airlift operation over the Hump (Himalaya Mountains) from India to China.

EAST AFRICA

Conditions, for the most part, had stabilized in East Africa by the summer of 1942. The British occupation governments in Eritrea and Italian Somaliland were functioning well, Ethiopia was peaceful and on the road to recovery, The Sudan was prospering, and normalcy had returned to British East Africa albeit on a wartime footing.

The faithful KAR forces were reassigned where needed. Some patrolled the blockaded border of French Somaliland, others assisted in the relocation and resettling of Italians and POWs and still others were positioned in strategic military locations in Kenya and Tanganyika. Some KAR units stayed on in Madagascar as occupation forces and several new KAR Pioneer units were formed. The East Africans were dependable workers, so many of the newly-formed Pioneer units were sent off to work on projects in such places as Basutoland, Bechuanaland, Swaziland and the islands in the Indian Ocean.

Neutral Saudi Arabia was now free of German and Italian influences and was cooperating with the Allies. The development of the oil fields on the Persian Gulf was well under way by the American oil companies, and Washington extended Lend-Lease to Saudi Arabia to strengthen its military.

Saudi Arabia's southern neighbor, Yemen, also saw the handwriting on the wall. Heretofore, Yemen had been an unofficial ally of Fascist Italy and after the fall of Italian East Africa many Italians took refuge here. Now, as a friendly gesture toward the Allies, the Yemeni government interned those Italians along with the few German citizens in the country.

"AFRICANIZATION"

The British government in London realized that, as a result of the war, Africans in general would be more worldly, better educated and more politically sophisticated as a result of the multitude of experiences and changes thrust upon them. Consequently, they would want more say in matters of interest to themselves and to their respective homelands. Therefore, a plan for "Africanizing" the various colonial administrations was adapted, which authorized the colonial governors to assist local chiefs and other local leaders to create provincial councils and a central colonial advisory council. The main purposes of the councils would be to offer advice on colonial matters at both the provincial and colonial levels. Members of provincial councils would be partly appointed and partly elected. Those councils would then appoint representatives to serve in the colonial council.

The Sudan, jointly administered by Britain and Egypt, was one of the first colonies authorized to carry out the new plan. Therefore, during 1943, the colonial administrators in Khartoum assisted the local chiefs and other leaders throughout the colony to form the provincial councils and the central council. The new system was well-received by the colonial subjects and showed promise. It would soon be authorized by London for other British colonies.

ALLIED INVASION OF NORTH AFRICA SPARKS EVENTS IN EAST AFRICA

In East Africa, a new event was sparked by the Allied invasion of North Africa in early November 1942. This concerned the Vichy-controlled colony of French Somaliland. Heretofore, that colony was one of Vichy's most loyal territories but, when the French North and West African colonies switched over to the Allied side and Admiral Darlan called upon all Frenchmen to reenter the war, loyalties in French Somaliland became sharply divided. French morale and loyalty to Vichy had already been eroded before the Allied landings in North Africa because of the loss of Madagascar and the on-going stream of negative decrees coming from Vichy.

After the Allied invasion of French North Africa the Vichy-appointed governor of the colony could see turmoil coming and flew off to Vichy ostensibly on leave but he did not return. This left control of the colony in the hands of an acting governor, General Edmond DuPont. But DuPont was still loyal to Vichy and not likely to capitulate easily to the Allies.

On November 28, a French Army colonel named Raynal took unilateral action and crossed over into British Somaliland at Zeila along with his regiment of Senegalese troops and declared for the Allies. Raynal's force represented about one-third of the armed forces of the French colony. Also, with Raynal went most of the colony's artillery and a lot of its other military equipment.

Realizing that Vichy's control over her African colonies was nearing its end, acting governor DuPont sent a delegation to Aden to negotiate with the British on the transfer of authority in the French colony. Negotiations dragged on, mainly because of DuPont's reluctance to have anything to do with de Gaulle, whose authority was soon to be installed in nearby Madagascar and on the French islands in the Indian Ocean. Furthermore, it was de Gaulle's Fighting French troops that were participating in the blockade of French Somaliland and, upon entering the colony, would bring de Gaulle's authority. Then on December 24, Darlan was assassinated and Generals de Gaulle and Giraud jointly assumed authority in Algiers. This only stiffened DuPont's reluctance to declare for the Allies.

The British and Fighting French had, even before Darlan's assassination, decided to force DuPont's hand by invading French Somaliland from Ethiopia with Colonel Raynal's Senegalese the lead element. In preparation for this, Colonel Raynal's force had been brought from Zeila and staged at the border town of Douance, Ethiopia along the railroad leading to Djibouti. British intelligence reports from inside French Somaliland indicated that Raynal was now something of a hero and that many individuals in the French colony would support his return. On December 26, Raynal's force invaded French Somaliland followed closely by British troops and supported in the air by the RAF. The British intelligence reports were correct; Raynal and his Senegalese were greeted as heroes. As they marched on Djibouti, other French soldiers, and some entire units, joined them. The Raynal force reached the outskirts of Djibouti on December 28, and that day acting Governor DuPont promptly sent word to his British contacts that he was ready to declare for the Allies. Wisely, DuPont did not obey standing orders from Vichy to destroy Djibouti's harbor and rail facilities. Raynal's Senegalese then entered the city, arrested the members of the Italian Armistice Commission and various individuals known to be still loyal to Vichy, but made no attempt to arrest DuPont.

During the next few days Raynal's force and the British troops went on to secure the rest of the colony. The British blockade was then lifted and the rail line from Djibouti to Addis Ababa was reopened.

On December 31, General Legentilhomme, the Fighting French High Commissioner for French possessions in the Indian Ocean theater, and General Pratt, British commander in East Africa, journeyed to Djibouti and, in formal ceremonies, accepted acting Governor DuPont's offer to join the Allies. Following that a temporary joint British and French military government was established and a local French Somali Guard force was formed to do police work to replace the French military units, which would soon leave for other assignments. Unfortunately, there were not enough uniforms available in the area to outfit the new Somali Guard so they were given captured Italian uniforms. Several month later the British were able to come through with proper Allied uniforms.

ETHIOPIA

With the swift Allied advances in North Africa Haile Selassie concluded, as did many other people, that the Allies would soon win the war in Africa. That being the case, Selassie wanted his country to be on the winning side. So on December 1st his government declared war on Germany, Italy and Japan. This was almost totally a political gesture because Ethiopia could offer very little in the way of military help. What this action did, though, was to assure Ethiopia a seat in any future peace talks and a voice in the future boundary settlements with regards to the neighboring territories of Eritrea and the Somalilands. Furthermore, there were indications circulating that any nation that had participated on the Allied side during the war would become a founding member of the soon-to-be-formed United Nations Organization.

In addition, the "Lion of Judah" was still not the master of his own domain because of the strong British presence in his country. So here again, a declaration of war gave him an opportunity to communicate with any and all of the other Allied nations in an effort to build favorable relationships that, in the long run, might provide Ethiopia with some political counterweights against the British. That prospect, however, lay in the future.

With developments in French Somaliland heading toward a favorable conclusion the British would, at least for the near term, continue to dominate both militarily and politically within the region. But if and when French Somaliland became Allied territory, the Fighting French would increase their influence in the region, which would be of benefit to Ethiopia. To this end, the Fighting French, with the Ethiopian government's full cooperation, opened a legation in Addis Ababa with its immediate objectives that of liberating French Somaliland and regaining control of the French-owned Addis Ababa-to-Djibouti Railroad.

Then the long-suffering Haile Selassie received another hurtful blow from his erstwhile Allies. The British and French opened bilateral talks on the future of the Djibouti-to-Addis Ababa Railroad excluding the Ethiopians altogether despite the fact that Selassie had asked that they be included. The Anglo-French talks resulted in the railroad's restoration to total French control just as it had been before the Italian invasion of 1935.

Then there was another setback for Ethiopia. After the declaration of French Somaliland for the Allies, the British refused to withdraw their forces from Northern Ethiopia which had heretofore been placed there as part of the British blockade of French Somaliland. The retention of those forces in Northern Ethiopia now became a purely political issue and not a military one. This was because, in London, the idea of creating a Greater Somalia was still being seriously considered by the British Colonial Office and others in the government. The creation of such a new colonial entity would take time and, in the view of the Colonial Office, it would only be logical that Greater Somalia should become a British protectorate until such time as the new country of Somalia could stand on its own. In creating a Greater Somalia there were age-old border disputes that would have to be worked out before firm borders could be fixed. Therefore, the British position was that the areas in question, which not only included northern Ethiopia but the Ogaden region as well, had to remain under British control until the question of Greater Somalia was resolved.

The Ethiopians were painfully aware of all this but were assured by the British with promises that Ethiopia's interests, such as gaining an access to the sea and Ethiopia's own territorial claims, were being favorably considered. To further ease relations the British government concluded an agreement with Ethiopia to provide quarterly cash grants to the Addis Ababa government over the next four years. In exchange, the Ethiopians agreed to appoint British officers to important posts in the army, police, courts and other governmental jobs. The British also helped improve schools and education throughout the country as well as medical services. The grants aided Haile Selassie's government in another way in that he did not have to raise local taxes.

The strong British presence in the region, though, provided fuel for the various nationalist organizations slowly gaining strength in the Somalilands and in Eritrea.

OTHER EVENTS AND PROBLEMS IN EAST AFRICA

As the Americans became involved militarily in Tunisia they began, for the first time in the war, to acquire large numbers of Axis POWs. Coincidentally, a large-scale program was under way to send several hundred thousand current and future POWs to the United States where food, housing, medical care and the like were readily available and could easily be provided by the strong home economy. Furthermore, transportation was readily available because so many ships returned to America empty. Furthermore, incentives for POWs to try to escape would be relatively meaningless because of the difficulty escapees would encounter getting back across the Atlantic to Europe. A system on this type had been in place for several years in Canada and had worked well.

East Africa benefited from this program because, so many Italian soldiers had been captured that their on-going incarceration there did pose problems of manpower and logistics for the British. So, the Americans agreed to take 25,000 Italian POWs from East Africa as transportation to the United States became available. The first shipments of Italian POWs from East Africa to America began in the spring of 1943.

Another benefit befell East Africa because of the general expansion of air routes. Several new air routes were established in East Africa especially in Kenya and Tanganyika. Kismayu, Italian Somaliland also acquired scheduled air service and Lake Victoria became a base for seaplanes flying the air routes.

During 1943, a food shortage developed in Italian Somaliland as the result of a deal made between the British occupation government and various clan chieftains in 1942. At the time, tracts of irrigated land, formerly owned by Italians, were turned over to local clan chieftains in exchange for labor performed by clan members on behalf of the occupation government. The Somalis, however, mismanaged the land terribly which resulted in the food shortage of 1943. The British occupation government had to step in and assign agricultural experts to the clans to put the land back into production.

A famine also developed on the island of Socotra during 1943 and the British had to rush food to the island to keep the Bedouin tribes people from starving.

HAIR-BRAINED SCHEMES

In London there were, as always, some members of the government who advocated the demise of the colonial system and were ever ready to hasten that event. One such individual was a junior minister named Harold Macmillian who suggested that the British government buy out all of the white settlers of Kenya, repatriate them, and prepare Kenya for early independence within the British Commonwealth. Macmillian's scheme was not adapted but the junior minister continued to be heard from on this and other matters and eventually he became Prime Minister of England.

Another individual of the same ilk was Colonial Secretary Oliver Stanley. He suggested that the government purchase all the mineral rights from British mine owners in the Rhodesias and Nigeria and use the profits from the mines for the benefit of the local people. This proposal was rejected also.

NATIONALISM EMERGES IN SOMALILAND

On May 5, 1943, the second anniversary of the liberation of Ethiopia, an organization called the Somali Youth Club (SYC) was founded in Italian Somaliland by a group of Somalis who supported the union of Italian Somaliland with Ethiopia. Members of the club looked upon Haile Selassie as their leader and called for Somali unity under his leadership. They also promoted increased education, an end to tribal frictions, and denounced a tax increase that had recently been imposed by the British occupation government. The British, of course, were opposed to the SYC's positions because their program would upset the Greater Somalia scheme currently in vogue in London. Nevertheless, in a demonstration of democracy, the British allowed the SYC to operate openly and espouse its beliefs. This was also another sop to the long-suffering Ethiopian government of Haile Selassie.

In the postwar years, the SYC would evolve into one of Somaliland's more prominent nationalist movements thanks, in no small part, to Britain's political tolerance.

OFF TO BURMA

In London the British military planners were preparing for their return to Burma. In searching the Empire for soldiers they once again turned to the King's African Rifles (KAR) in East Africa (two British West African divisions had already been designated for service in Burma). Many of the KAR men were veterans of the campaigns in Italian East Africa and Madagascar and were currently assigned to noncombat duties. Furthermore, the KAR 22nd Brigade had already been selected for use in Burma and was already in training in Madagascar. Therefore, it was decided to create one large KAR unit, the 11th (KAR) Division, for service in Burma.

To this end, existing KAR units, currently scattered about East Africa, and new recruits were assembled during February 1943 at a training camp at Moshi, Tanganyika. The British plans called for the division to be organized at Moshi and then sent to Ceylon for jungle training. It was anticipated that the 11th (KAR) Division would then be ready for combat in early 1944.

In March the first large unit, the 21st (KAR) Brigade, departed for Ceylon.

Continued recruiting throughout East Africa increased the overall size of the total KAR commitment to 28 battalions, the largest ever. By comparison, the KAR consisted of seven battalions at the start of the war.

NO MORE CAMELS

In early 1943, the London military planners decided that it was time to modernize the exalted Somaliland Camel Corps in British Somaliland. Therefore, the camels were retired and the men equipped with armored cars. This was a very unpopular development as far as the corpsmen were concerned. They loved their camels. But as good soldiers they tried to adapt to the new situation although the old esprit de corps was no longer there.

THE ISLANDERS MADE THEIR CONTRIBUTIONS

North and west of Madagascar are several island groups generally associated with East Africa. They are the Seychelles Island Group (1939 population 34,000) and the Mauritius Island Group (1939 population 396,000), both British possessions, and 150 miles southwest of Mauritius Island, the French Island of Reunion (1939 population 210,000).

When war started in 1939, all of these island groups contributed soldiers and support personnel to the respective armed forces of their colonial masters. No Seychellian, Mauritian, or Reunion units were formed as such. In 1940, some 4000 Mauritian and 400 Seychellian Pioneers were sent to serve with the British forces in Egypt where they served during the Italian invasion of Egypt and O'Connor's advance into Libya.

During April 1941, another 800 Mauritians served briefly at Tobruk. Twenty six of these men were killed and 48 wounded when their ship, carrying them into Tobruk, was bombed. About 400 Mauritians returned to Tobruk in the spring of 1942 and were all captured when the city fell in June.

Other islanders served with the British at El Alamein and in the advance across Libya and into Tunisia.

The British established air bases in the islands, one at Port Victoria, Seychelles and one each at Port Louis and Tombeau Bay, Mauritius. RAF aircraft from those bases took an active part in antisubmarine activities in the western Indian Ocean.

The British also used the islands as places of exile for political prisoners. In 1940, the Pro-Axis former Premier of Yugoslavia, Milan Stoyadinovich, was exiled to Mauritius and in 1943, the militant nationalist Archbishop Makarios of Cyprus was sent to Seychelles.

Reunion also contributed soldiers to the French Army in 1939 and 1940, but after the collapse of France the island remained under Vichy control and took on a neutral stance. As described above, though, Reunion was occupied by Fighting French forces in November 1943 and reentered the war on the Allied side.

SOUTH AFRICA

By early 1943, South Africa was very much at war. One out of every three white males between the ages of twenty and sixty had volunteered for full-time military service. This amounted to a total of 190,000 men by May 1943. There were 66 military camps in South Africa and twenty military hospitals. South African industry was a major supplier to the other Allies of bombs and ammunition of all types, armored cars, antitank mines, steel, gold, industrial diamonds, timber, raw materials, army blankets, boots, and food. The South Africans produced almost all of their own artillery pieces and, by 1943, were able to export small numbers of their guns to Burma.

In South Africa during this time, there were two important concerns for the South Africans; their own soldiers deeply involved in the fighting in North Africa with the British 8th Army, and the German submarine blitz off the coast. As for the former the government and populace subscribed to the universal feeling of the times that the best thing they could do for the men at the front was to fully support the war effort at home. As for the submarine menace, the South

Men of the 1st South African Division being welcomed home in Cape Town. Many of these men would be transferred to the soon-to-be-created 6th South African Armoured Division.

Africans committed every airplane and ship they could find to antisubmarine and rescue activities at sea. And they asked for more aid from both Britain and the United States. They also began operating convoys along their coast when escort vessels and aircraft could be found.

The men who had fought in Madagascar were welcomed home and Smuts had another military victory to strengthen his political position. This one was especially sweet since Smuts had been one of the strongest proponents favoring the occupation of southern Madagascar. During October 1942 Smuts journeyed to England and was given a rousing and highly publicized welcome by Churchill and, on October 21, addressed a special assembly of Parliament. This was good politics at home for Smuts because he faced a national election in July 1943. While Smuts was in England word came from El Alamein that the 1st South African Division was in the forefront of the four-division attack on October 23 that had been successful in meeting its goal in only two hours of fighting. Then, on the 25th, word came again that the South Africans had captured some 600 Germans, mostly from Rommel's 9th Light Division. Smuts left England and returned home covered with accolades.

On November 12, 1942, South African troops participated in the capture of Tobruk. But by this time the South Africans had been in the line for a long time and had suffered considerable losses; 2,104 killed, 3,928 wounded, and 14,847 missing and presumed captured, so the 1st and 2nd South African Divisions were taken out of action and returned to Egypt and eventually to South Africa.

Once back in South Africa the two infantry divisions were disbanded and many of their members combined into a newly structured armored unit, the 6th South African Armoured Division. The Division was commanded by South African Lieutenant-General William H. E. Poole and equipped with newly-arrived American-made Sherman tanks under Lend-Lease.

During November, J.B.M. Hertzog, the former Prime Minister of South Africa, who had been unseated by Smuts in September 1939, died of natural causes. By the time of his death, Hertzog was a bitter man and had espoused far right-wing politics and become one of the political right's leading figures.

On December 12, the South Africans suffered another loss in the person of Major General Daniel H. Pienaar, Commander of the disbanding 1st South African Infantry Division. He and twelve others were killed when their plane crashed into Lake Victoria on their way home. Smuts gave the oration at Pienaar's funeral.

WAR WITH CHINA

On January 9, 1943, South Africa acquired one more enemy when the Republic of China at Nanking declared war on the United States, Britain, and the British Commonwealth. This Chinese regime was a puppet government set up at Nanking, China by the Japanese in 1940 under the leadership of Wang Ching-wei, a defector from Chiang Kai-shek's Republic of China regime in Chungking. At that time the Japanese had declared Chiang's regime militarily defeated and established the Nanking regime as the new government of China. Wang's government was utterly powerless and the declaration of war was simply a political maneuver.

SOUTH AFRICA'S RIGHT WING IN TROUBLE

During 1942 and 1943, after months of internal wrangling, the political right once again came apart at the seams—another Broedertwis. The military failures of the Axis Powers in North Africa and the Soviet Union were deciding factors in the current disintegration. Oswald Pirow, leader of the "New Order" party and former Foreign Minister in the Hertzog government, had a falling out over ideological issues with Daniel Malan, leader of the National Party. This was due, in part, to the fact that Malan had formed an organization within his party called the "Afrikaner Unity Committee" and, as it's chairman, appointed himself "volk-leader." Pirow resented this attempt by Malan to designate himself as South Africa's leader (fuhrer) and, thereafter, would not have anything to do with the committee or Malan. The militant right-wing OB organization also resented Malan's move and threatened to destroy Malan's committee by force—a threat that never came about.

During 1943, though, the OB was able to expand its domain into a new direction by gaining control of the "Afrikaanse Nasional Studentebund" (ANS—Afrikaner National Student Union), a politically right-of-center organization founded in the 1930s. Now, under OB control, the ANS espoused the OB's more radical right-wing philosophy to both students and teachers. Also, there were rumors—again—that the OB was planning a "putsch," this time in Natal. But, like the rumors of other OB-planned coups, nothing came of it.

With his former colleagues now so bitterly against him, volk-leader Malan and his National Party made a new political deal with Smuts and the United Party. It called for the two organizations to work together to root out and destroy any and all "subversive" movements in the country. This clearly was a move designed against Malan's former colleagues and payment for Malan's new-found cooperation with Smuts and the United Party. But little real action was taken against the subversives.

Nonetheless, it was a new political ball game in South Africa with Malan and Smuts now working together, and it served to demonstrate that South African politics was still a very volatile thing.

Adding to the complexity of South African politics was the growing influence of the African National Congress (ANC), the nation's leading black political organization. New leadership was coming to the fore within the organization including two individuals who would eventually become the ANC's driving forces, Oliver Tambo and Nelson Mandela. In 1942, an ANC "Youth League" was formed and quickly became the most militant faction within the organization, eager to carry out demonstrations and other acts of civil disobedience. But the more moderate leaders of the main body were able to keep the youthful radicals under control, at least, for the moment.

At the ANC's annual conference in 1943, that organization adopted several far-reaching resolutions that would set the course of action for them for years to come. One resolution proclaimed the ANC's support of the Atlantic Charter and another resolution called for a sweeping "Bill of Rights" for South Africa's black people. The latter called for the abolition of discriminatory legislation, a redistribution of land, African participation in collective bargaining, and universal adult suffrage. This type of rhetoric was seen by the white South Africans as dangerous and even revolutionary and set the ANC squarely on a collision course with the white-dominated "Establishment." The Smuts government rejected the ANC's demands out-of-hand. From the ANC's point of view, however, these were issues that, one day, would have to be addressed in South Africa and that now was an advantageous time to bring them to the fore; the country badly needed the labor of black people and many blacks were serving honorably as service personnel in South Africa's armed forces. By making immediate demands now, the ANC hoped to gain a measure of sympathy and support among the white community, especially from the progressives and liberals.

The ANC's plan had some positive results. A few moderate whites recognized that at least some of the things the ANC advocated would eventually have to be reckoned with in a fair manner. One such individual who spoke out in this vein was Jan Hendrik Hofmeyr, a leading member of the United Party and seen by some as Smuts's heir-apparent. Hofmeyr said on several occasions that at sometime in the future the blacks would become sufficiently advanced to a point where they would have to be included in the nation's political process. This, coming from a man as influential as Hofmeyr, caused some whites to take notice of the ANC's call, while other whites cringed at the prospect Hofmeyr suggested. So, once again, as a result of the ANC's demands, a new division in South African politics began to develop.

IN THE MINES

Another area of black discontent was in the mines. The vast majority of miners were black and worked long and hard hours for the war effort, which brought forth a feeling among the miners that, during and after the war, their worth and importance should be better recognized and appreciated. Quite understandably, the miners had long been drawn to liberal share-the-wealth politics and to the concept of unionism with its promises of better things for the working classes. Throughout the mining regions talk of the miners becoming unionized was widespread. In Nyasaland, at this time, black miners took action and made an attempt to organize a union and strike, if necessary, to press their demands. But the effort failed. White management, of course, was bitterly opposed to the creation of a union and there was a general lack of support among the miners themselves, many of whom felt that it was an unpatriotic act to strike in time of war.

In one area of mining, though, South Africa was falling short. That was in the production of chromium ore. The mines in South Africa and the Rhodesias could not meet the demands of the Allies, especially the United States. As a result the Americans began a crash program to find new sources of chromium which resulted in the discovery of a large deposit in the state of Montana. This meant that after the war, when the use of chromium would most likely decline, the South Africans would face a new and advantageously located competitor for the North American chromium market.

SOUTH AFRICA BREAKS WITH VICHY

On the international scene, South Africa broke diplomatic relations with Vichy on April 23, 1943, thus putting itself into a position to recognize the rapidly-emerging Gaullist regime. This was also a popular move for the Smuts government in view of the coming July elections. The general population of South Africa had lost all respect for the Vichy regime for having opposed South African forces fighting in Madagascar and supposedly supplying Japanese submarines in Madagascar's ports.

With this move, and the strong economy and the overall favorable military picture of the war, the Smuts government was predicted to win the elections.

IN THE RHODESIAS

Both Rhodesias were enjoying continued prosperity with mines and farms producing at full capacity. A new cold-storage facility was built in Livingston, Northern Rhodesia to accommodate the large amount of meat products coming to market, which needed to be stored prior to export. With prosperity came good tax collections, and the Southern Rhodesians were able to make a no-interest war loan to Britain of three million pounds. Also, in the self-governing colony of Southern Rhodesia, the colonial parliament voted itself an additional twelve months in being. This had the effect of postponing an upcoming election.

Another battalion of Rhodesian African riflemen was sent to East Africa during 1943 to serve with the KAR. Most Rhodesian whites in uniform were serving as volunteers in British or South African forces.

PORTUGUESE AFRICA

By far the most important Portuguese real estate in Africa at this time was the Azores Islands. The Azores were within the ocean "air gap" of the Central Atlantic where Allied land-based aircraft could not patrol. This being the case, the waters of the Azores made good hunting grounds for Axis submarines. Furthermore, Germany's new Milch Cow submarines often operated in these strategic waters supplying German subs operating in the North Atlantic, South Atlantic and Western Hemisphere. This amounted to dozens of German subs constantly coming and going in the waters around the Azores.

The Allies, naturally, wanted to do something about this, so the British, with their long history of friendship with Portugal, sent out secret feelers to the government of Premier Antonio Salazar in Lisbon on the possibility of the Allies leasing air and naval bases in the Azores for antisubmarine work. This British request was met with some interest in Lisbon so secret negotiations were begun.

In the Cape Verde Islands, the air gap problem did not exist after French West Africa's adherence to the Allied cause. Allied planes out of Dakar could adequately patrol the entire island group and its surrounding waters. But economic conditions in the Cape Verde Islands were bleak, because the islands had been experiencing drought conditions since 1940. During the latter part of 1943 the rains came again but not before the government counted some 20,000 dead as a result of the three-year-long drought.

Many Cape Verdeans were able to support themselves by continuing the long-standing policy of seeking work abroad. Fortunately, wartime conditions made such jobs plentiful.

There was a fledgling nationalist movement in the Cape Verde Islands but the Portuguese administrators suppressed it at every opportunity so it survived only as an underground organization.

In contrast, there was virtually no nationalist activities in the Azores because the people there were mostly of Portuguese descent and considered the Azores as an integral part of the mother country.

SPANISH AFRICA

Spain's African colonies were relatively quiet during this period and following a policy of strict neutrality dictated from Madrid. Spanish Morocco, however, had become a strategically important area as a result of the Allied invasion of French North Africa in November 1942. A glance at the map reveals that any sizable military force in Spanish Morocco could threaten the American's northern flank in French Morocco as well as the Strait of Gibraltar. In late November and early December 1942, the Germans and Italians made plans to approach Spain and possibly use Spanish Morocco for that purpose. At the time the Axis Powers were pouring men and material into Tunisia with the hope that the British and Americans could be pushed back to the Atlantic Ocean. If that were the case an Axis force in Spanish Morocco would be very beneficial to Axis military operations. Furthermore, having troops in Spanish Morocco would give the Axis Powers an opportunity to establish strong forces on the southern shore of the Strait of Gibraltar and thereby contest control of the Strait with the British at Gibraltar. But the Axis troops in Tunisia were unable to push the Allies back to the west, so Madrid was not approached.

The Allies could see the possibility, too, of Spanish Morocco becoming hostile territory. Therefore, they devised a plan, called "Operation Backbone," to occupy Spanish Morocco if necessary. This plan was never implemented.

GERMANY

The Nazi government wanted to keep the prospect of Germany returning to Africa before the public, so the German people were subjected to another Germany-in-Africa propaganda campaign which included a movie, called "Germanin." This movie utilized the usual theme of glorifying Germany's former colonial rule in Africa. Its main theme was similar to previous movies in that the British and French are shown as cruel colonial masters while the Germans are shown as being compassionate overseers much loved by the natives. The movie was produced by Max W. Kimmich, Joseph Goebbels' brother-in-law. Since there were very few black actors in Germany many of the movie's "extras" were black African POWs.

At Hitler's quarters, though, there were no illusions. Hitler told his commanders on March 14, 1943, "The loss of Tunisia will also mean the loss of Italy." At that time the Germans could see themselves having to make a determined stand in the Alps against Allied forces advancing into northern Italy. Military wisdom dictated that to make such a stand the Germans must control Switzerland. Therefore, Hitler ordered that advanced planning be undertaken to occupy Switzerland. Occupying Switzerland was not a new concept in Nazi Germany. Plans for such an eventuality called "Case Switzerland" had been drawn up years earlier. These plans were now taken from the files and on March 20, General Eduard Dietl, an experienced commander of mountain troops, set up an office in Munich to update them and plan for the possible invasion of Switzerland. Dietl's operation in Munich, called the "Switzerland Command" was supposed to be secret, but Swiss agents soon learned of it. This caused great concern in Switzerland and the Swiss Army was ordered on the alert. This period in time was known in Switzerland as the "Marz Alarm" (March Alarm). Allen Dulles, Chief of America's OSS operations in Switzerland, also learned of the German plans and informed Washington. In the days and weeks that followed, no German military activity was noted that appeared as a threat to Switzerland so the fears there slowly subsided.

The loss of Tunisia had yet another far-reaching effect for Germany, this time on the Arabs. By evacuating North Africa the Germans and Italians lost physical contact with the Arab world. Furthermore, German propaganda began speaking of "Festung Europa" (Fortress Europe) which automatically excluded the Arabs. This appeared to many Arab leaders as abandonment by Germany. The few Arab leaders in occupied Europe who had sided with the Axis Powers earlier in the war still called for favorable pronouncements from Berlin and Rome on behalf of the Arabs, but their influence was now greatly diminished and they, themselves, became increasingly ignored by the Axis leadership.

More or less, then, the Axis Powers abandoned the Arabs to the Allies by default. This propelled Britain into the position of being the most influential foreign power among the Arabs with the Fighting French having an increasing important secondary role. The Americans, due to their oil interests in the Middle East and Lend-Lease operations, also had an important role in the Arab world. Mussolini, the self-proclaimed Protector Of Islam, had lost out altogether. Now, he had only a few thousand Moslems in Albania and the occupied Balkan countries to "protect."

THE UNITED STATES

In the United States the patriotic mood was very upbeat. American fighting men had had their baptism of fire in North Africa and had performed very well. Generals Eisenhower and Patton had become household names. Everyone knew that the Americans would play a major role in the next major campaign in Europe, wherever it might be. Also people were proud of what was accomplished on the home front. Everyone knew that it was the appearance of American tanks, planes, and other weapons on the battlefields, and American warships and cargo ships at sea, that made the Allied victories possible. Gone were the days of the post-Pearl Harbor fears that the Axis Powers were unstoppable. Everyone knew now that with Africa won, Europe would be next and the Americans would win the war.

Hollywood picked up on the theme of the victory in Africa and produced a cascade of films with upbeat African themes. In "Casablanca," refugees from Europe and a Czech underground hero outwit the Vichy officials and the Gestapo and escape to the West with the help of an American expatriate who runs a night club in Casablanca. In "White Cargo," an American rubber plantation manager finds it difficult to keep his mind on business and is able to overcome all obstacles in face of the temptations thrust upon him by a beautiful jungle princess named Tondelayo (Hedy Lamarr). In "Five Graves to Cairo," British spies destroy Rommel's (Erich von Stroheim) secret supply dumps. In "Secret Service in Darkest Africa" an American secret agent infiltrates the Gestapo and unmasks a plot to convert Arabs to the Nazi cause. And in "Tarzan Triumphs," the famous ape-man foils a Nazi plan to acquire oil and tin from his jungle domain.

In real life, though, the Allied victory in Africa brought renewed hope to those who favored decolonization. But the Roosevelt Administration kept this subject in the background for the good of harmony among the Allies. To do otherwise would be politically unhealthy, because decolonization was also promoted by the Communists.

It was during this time that some of the horrors of the Nazi concentration camps were becoming known in the West. In New York City, during the spring of 1943, a group of Jewish organizations rallied at Madison Square Garden and passed resolutions calling on the American and other Allied governments to take steps to help Europe's Jews. One resolution adapted brought up the often-mentioned proposal of finding a sanctuary for Europe's Jews somewhere in Latin America or in Africa.

Chapter 17
AFRICA AS A STAGING AREA (JUNE–DECEMBER 1943)
ON TO SICILY AND ITALY

With the Allies now in control of the North African coast, all of Axis-controlled southern Europe was militarily threatened. The initiative was with the Allies. The Allies could strike at dozens of places in southern Europe and had adequately demonstrated their ability to do so by successfully carry out large-scale amphibious operations elsewhere. From the German perspective, such operations in southern Europe were now to be expected. The main question for the Axis leaders was where: southern France, Italy, Greece, the Balkans, or one or more of the Axis-held islands; Sicily, Sardinia, Corsica, Crete...?

Another question was when? That answer was simple; soon.

With the bulk of the German Army tied down in the Soviet Union, Germany had very few forces left to defend the entire length of their southern European frontier, which stretched from Spain to Turkey. They could only station their limited forces at the most vulnerable points and depend upon their allies, primarily Italy, to defend the rest.

As has already been stated, in January 1943, at the Casablanca Conference, the decision was made that the next Allied offensive would be the invasion of Sicily, followed by the invasion of southern Italy itself. The main Allied effort in the Mediterranean would then be concentrated in Italy to force that country out of the war, advance to the Alps, and threaten Germany from the south. A second invasion of Europe would be conducted the following year, May 1944, with a cross-channel invasion of France and a drive into Germany from the west. It would be left to the Soviet forces to drive into Germany from the east.

This, then, was the Allied grand strategy in Europe for the latter half of 1943 and all of 1944.

For the moment, though, the task at hand was the invasion of Sicily. It was obvious that the staging area for the invasion would be North Africa. There were plenty of fine ports, airfields, army, and naval bases now in Allied hands able to receive and accommodate the ships, planes, and thousands of tons of material that would be used in the invasion, as well as house the tens of thousands of men required to carry out the invasion. After the invasion of Sicily commenced, Allied planning called for North Africa to become the main supply base for the advancing Allied forces.

To these ends, a tremendous amount of military activity developed all across North Africa. Actually, preparations for the invasion had begun even before the last Axis soldier laid down his arms in Tunisia. By early June, though, every North African seaport, from Casablanca to Cairo, became involved in some manner in the staging operations. Convoys from the west brought in men, tanks, artillery, ammunition, and thousands of other items to be stored in the available warehouse space at the respective ports. When the warehouses filled, the war material was stored in the open. The men moved into existing army barracks, requisitioned hotels and resorts and when those filled they moved into tent cities. Allied warplanes to be used in the invasion flew in and crowded the parking ramps at both military and civilian airfields awaiting the call to action. Ships arrived, especially landing craft, and quickly took up all the available wharf space in some of the main harbors. Ships that followed had to be anchored wherever space could be found in the crowded harbors.

After Tunis and the other Tunisian ports were captured and cleared of mines and wreckage, they became the primary staging ports because of their proximity to Sicily.

Equipment and supplies brought in by ship from America and elsewhere are transferred onto Landing Ship Tanks (LST) for the actual assault on Sicily.

on future operations in the Mediterranean and on June 5, Churchill returned to London.

During this time General Giraud was in Washington conferring with American political and military leaders on integrating the rejuvenated French Army into the Allied war effort. Before he left, Girard had a commitment from the Americans to provide weapons and equipment to arm 300,000 French soldiers. Technically these were not Lend-Lease goods because the Americans did not yet have a Lend-Lease agreement with the French leaders in Algiers. At the Casablanca meeting, however, the Americans agreed to send military aid to the French until a formal agreement could be written.

In Algiers, the Committee took direct political control of the three colonial entities of French North Africa, French Morocco, Algeria, and Tunisia, and attempted to extend their influence over the stubborn Boisson in French West Africa.

In Libya, now occupied by the Allies, the British set up an occupation government in the northern part of the country while a French occupation government administered southern Libya. In both areas, all fascist political and educational organizations were abolished, and Allied military courts were set up to deal with violence, sabotage, and cases of looting. Jews and others living in internment camps were set free.

There was a food shortage in northern Libya, because the retreating Axis forces had taken the food with them as they retreated. The worst conditions were in Cyrenaica since most of the Italian farmers were gone, having departed with the Axis forces.

In Tripolitania, many of the Italians from Cyrenaica, plus those from Tripolitania, eventually fell under British control and most were returned to their homes and farms. Those Italian farms that remained vacant were turned over to Libyans to work.

Some 4,000 Italian administrators had fled, but those that remained were retained in their jobs by the British. The lire continued to circulate along with the new British military script.

On June 11, the heavily-fortified Italian island of Pantelleria, strategically situated in the Sicilian Channel, surrendered after enduring more than a month of Allied bom-

THE GERMANS GUESSED WRONG

Fortunately for the Allies, the German High Command had discounted the possibility of the Allies invading Sicily and southern Italy and concluded, by June 10, 1943, that the Allied assault would most likely be against the islands of Corsica or Sardinia. Subsequently, some of their limited forces were sent to those islands. This decision was made, in part, because of a clever British deception called "Operation Mincemeat." The British had planted the body of a dead British naval officer on a beach in Spain with detailed, but phony, plans for the Allied invasion of Sardinia and Northern Italy. The plans reached Hitler's headquarters, as the British knew they would, and the Fuhrer and his staff took the bait.

PRELIMINARY EVENTS IN NORTH AFRICA

Many preliminary events took place in the weeks preceding the invasion. On June 3, the competing French political factions in Algiers finally came together and established the "National Committee for Liberation" to direct the French war effort and serve as a political governing body and, hopefully, a future provisional government for the entire French Empire. The next day both de Gaulle and Giraud addressed the French people over radio detailing the new arrangement. Churchill, returning from a conference in Washington with Roosevelt, was on hand to witness the new arrangement and give his approval. The American Chief of Staff, General George Marshall, was also traveling with Churchill. While in Algiers, Churchill and Marshall conferred with Eisenhower

bardment. The next day, the nearby Italian island of Lampedusa surrendered after an Allied bombardment. The Sicilian Channel was now safer for Allied shipping.

On June 12, Britain's King George VI arrived in North Africa to visit the British troops. His presence served to demonstrate that North Africa was fully secured and firmly in the Allied camp.

On June 15, the Turkish government, concerned that the coming military activity in the Mediterranean might somehow effect their country, affirmed its neutrality and friendship treaties with both the Soviet Union, in the Allied camp, and Germany, in the Axis camp. Turkey's neutrality was based on a policy of placating both sides.

On June 18, targets in Sicily were heavily bombed by Allied aircraft operating out of North Africa. In the days that followed, these raids continued and intensified.

NORTH AFRICANS FIGHTING FOR THE GERMANS

During the long North African campaign the Germans acquired a large number of North African natives as POWs. Moroccans comprised the largest number taken but there were also Algerians, Tunisians and Egyptians. Some of these men held strong nationalistic beliefs or, for one reason or another, resented the Allies and/or favored the Axis. The Germans were able to capitalize on this by offering these individuals release from the prison camps if they would serve in the German Army. Several hundred men accepted the offer and were sent to occupied Greece for training and incorporation into the "Deutsch-Arabische Lehrabteilung," an all-Arab unit commanded by German officers and serving in the German Army. Eighty of the most loyal men were formed into a paratroop unit while some 600 others were trained primarily as guards. For the time being all of the men were retained in Greece. The eighty paratroopers, however, would see combat near the end of 1944.

MEDITERRANEAN SEA STILL A BATTLE GROUND

Even though the Axis troops had been ousted from North Africa, the Axis submarines were still very active along the North African coast. And there were plenty of Allied ships for them to attack. Most Allied ships, though, sailed in convoys, making attacks difficult. In addition to the convoys bringing in men and supplies to North Africa, there were also convoys passing through the Mediterranean on their way to the Persian Gulf and Far East. Many of those convoys carried supplies for the Soviet Union—supplies that used to go via the Arctic. With the clearing of the Mediterranean, this sea route was now safer than the Arctic route. That route which arched around the North Cape of Scandinavia and was constantly plagued with bad weather, the threat of German air attacks from occupied Norway and attacks by three German battleships ships, "Tirpitz," "Scharnhorst" and "Lutzow" stationed in Norwegian waters. In the Mediterranean the weather was much better and there was no threat from large German warships. Air attacks were still a problem as were the Italian capital ships, although most of them had withdrawn to the north. Both the Arctic and Mediterranean routes were subjected to Axis submarine attacks, but in the Mediterranean help was always close at hand in the form of Allied naval and air support from nearby bases in North Africa.

THE SEA WAR IN THE SOUTHERN MEDITERRANEAN

As in previous months, Axis submarines, primarily German, continued to press their attacks against Allied shipping in the Mediterranean. During June, German subs sank two Allied merchant ships off Algeria, two LSTs (Landing Ship Tanks) off Tunisia, two merchant ships off Libya, one off Egypt and three off Palestine/Lebanon. One German sub was sunk off Haifa, Palestine by a British aircraft.

During July, German and Italian subs sank five merchant ships off Algeria, one off Libya, one off Palestine/Lebanon, and one off southern Sicily. This was the month the Allies invaded Sicily and in conjunction with the invasion the Allies lost the American destroyer "Maddox" and minesweeper "Sentinel" on the 10th, the British light cruiser "Cleopatra" on the 16th, and the British light cruiser "Newfoundland" on the 23rd. On July 16, German planes bombed an Allied convoy that had just arrived at Algiers and hit two ammunition ships, both of which exploded with tremendous force damaging several other ships and causing a large number of casualties.

The Italians lost the minesweeper "Oriole" in an air attack near Augusta on July 10, the mine layer "Durazzo" to the British sub "Safari" off Corsica on the 22nd, and the corvette "Cicogna" in an air raid at Messina on the 24th. During July, the Germans lost three subs in the Mediterranean; U–409 sunk on the 12th off Algiers by a British destroyer, U–561 sunk the same day in the Strait of Messina by a British Motor-Torpedo boat, and U–375 sunk on July 30 off Tunisia by an American patrol craft.

During August, one Allied merchant ship was sunk off Algeria, three off Tunisia, one off Egypt, three off Palestine/Lebanon, and on the 11th the American light cruiser "Philadelphia" was sunk by the German sub U–73 off the north coast of Sicily. On August 3, the American destroyer "Buck" sank the Italian sub "Argento" off Tunisia. On the 13th German planes damaged two American freighters in a convoy off Algeria and on the 16th damaged the American transport "Benjamin Contee" off Bone, Algeria. This ship was carrying 1,800 Italian POWs of which 264 were killed in the attack and 142 injured. There were no casualties among the crew. The ship did not sink and made it to safety under her own power. The next day German planes sank an American LCI (Landing Craft Infantry) off Bizerte.

On August 22, the Germans lost another sub, U–458, sunk off Tunisia by two British destroyer escorts. The next day, U–380 torpedoed and damaged a American freighter as it left Bizerte for Sicily. The ship was towed back to Bizerte.

THE ITALIANS GUESSED RIGHT—SICILY

Unlike their German ally the Italian High Command believed that the next Allied effort in the Mediterranean would be the invasion of Sicily or, perhaps, southern Italy. In response to this, the Italian government, on June 20, ordered the evacuation of large numbers of civilians from all cities and large towns in Sicily and the Naples area on the mainland.

This action came just in time, because the Allied air campaign against Sicily and Italy was beginning to increase.

There was a new development in the air war against Sicily and Italy—shuttle bombing. Allied planes would fly from England, bomb targets in Italy or Sicily, and land in North Africa. Then they would reverse the process by flying from North Africa to bomb Italian targets again, and return to England.

On June 25, Messina, the strategic port in northeastern Sicily just across the Strait of Messina from the toe of Italy, was bombed very heavily by Allied planes. Harbor and transportation facilities were targeted. This was another indication to the Axis that Sicily would be the invasion point, because any reinforcements coming from the Italian mainland to Sicily would normally pass through Messina.

During these days, Allied bombing raids were carried out on Naples, Palermo, Catania, Leghorn, the naval base at La Spezia, and targets on Sardinia.

MALTA TO BE INDEPENDENT

On July 7, London announced that after the war the Island of Malta, which had been so mercilessly pounded by Axis planes and warships for two years, would be given its independence. This was an attempt to gain the favor of the Italian people because there was a sizable minority of Italians on the island and Italy had long wanted Malta removed from the British Empire. It was hoped that this concession would lessen the resistance of the Italians to the invasion of Sicily.

Throughout Africa the various nationalist groups viewed the British declaration with great interest.

On July 4, British Commandos operating out of North Africa carried out a hit-and-run attack on the Axis-occupied island of Crete. This was a diversionary attack to draw Axis attention away from Sicily.

SICILY INVADED

On the night of July 9, 1943, British and American paratroopers descended on targets in Sicily in preparation for the amphibious landings that were to take place a few hours later. It was a bad beginning. Due to bad weather and poor navigation some of the paratroops were dropped as far away as fifty miles from their objectives. As the paratroopers began their overland treks, some 3000 vessels, many of them landing craft loaded with men, tanks, and artillery pieces, were approaching the southern shore of Sicily.

At 2:45 a.m., on the morning of July 10, British and American army troops began landing on the southern coast of Sicily. Operation Husky was underway. The major Allied units involved were the U.S. 7th Army and the British 8th Army which, together, consisted of a total of twelve divisions, all of which had come from North Africa. Defending the southern coast was an Axis force of almost equal size, consisting of ten Italian and three German divisions. But, quite remarkably, the defenders were taken by complete surprise. The Allied soldiers streamed ashore against very little opposition. Secure beachheads were quickly established and the landings continued with considerable efficiency. By the end of the day, the Allies had 160,000 troops ashore, 1,000 artillery pieces and 600 tanks. The Allies were on the island to stay.

Landing with the Americans was a regiment of 6,000 Moroccan Goumiers, mountain fighters, which had been recruited and trained in French Morocco. There were mountains in the path of the American advance and the American Army was short of trained mountain troops, so the Moroccans filled that void. As the advance progressed, the Goumiers proved themselves very well in the mountains and the American came to depend upon them.

The day after the landing, July 11, the Allied troops fanned out and encountered some Axis resistance but, by the end of the day, had moved inland and achieved all of their objectives.

On July 12, a determined German counterattack, spearheaded by 100 tanks, was turned back in hard fighting. Also that day, the Allies captured six airfields and the port of Syracuse. These facilities were soon put to use by the Allies and marked the beginning of the phase down of the North African bases as staging areas.

On July 13, British commandos and paratroopers carried out a second amphibious landing on Sicily's east coast between Syracuse and Catania. They quickly captured the coastal road, cutting off supplies—and the best route of retreat—for the Axis forces to the south. By this time, the Allies were gaining air superiority over the island.

On the 14th Messina was heavily bombed again and on the 16th President Roosevelt addressed the Italian people by radio urging them not to resist the Allies and to overthrow their Fascist government. Roosevelt concluded his address by telling the Italian people that they had two choices, to "die for Mussolini and Hitler, or live for Italy and civilization."

That same day, Americans captured Porto Empedocle on the southern coast of Sicily—a usable port of supply for the Allies. This reduced further the Allies' dependence on North Africa.

At this time, Hitler and Mussolini met at Feltre in northern Italy to discuss the situation in Sicily. Mussolini, though, had a secret—a secret he dared not share with the Fuhrer. Before leaving for Feltre, Mussolini had been told by his military advisers that the Italian armed forces were incapable of stopping the Allies and that Italy might have to drop out of the war. These were words Hitler did not want, to hear so Mussolini put up a brave front, telling his German ally that the Allies would be stopped.

On July 22, American troops under General Patton took Palermo, the capital of Sicily, on the northwestern coast of the island. It became yet another supply port for the Allies. Now more than half the island was in Allied hands.

MUSSOLINI OUSTED FROM POWER

On July 25, 1943, Mussolini was voted out of power by an organization that he, himself, had created, the Fascist Grand Council. This Council was made up of his closest and oldest supporters and was so loyal to him it had not met in years, thus giving Mussolini free reign to rule Italy as he saw fit. But things had changed and the old loyalties had disappeared. The Council was convened at the insistence of several of its members to consider the possible removal of Mussolini from office. When the vote was taken it was nineteen to seven in favor of removal. This was a tragic blow for Mussolini. His old friends had deserted him. Mussolini was obliged by law to report to King Victor Emmanuel III and submit his resignation as Premier of Italy. Upon arriving at the palace, the King had him taken into protective custody by the Royal guards because, at this point, a civil war was very possible. With Mussolini in the King's custody that would be less likely to happen.

The news of Mussolini's fall was devastating to the Italian Armed Forces. The will to resist by the troops at the fronts in Sicily all but evaporated. Many individuals and some whole units defected to the Allies.

Mussolini's fall was also devastating news for Hitler, but not altogether unexpected. The signs that Mussolini was in political trouble had been evident to the Germans for some time. With regard to the military situation, though, the disintegration of the Italian armed forces meant that Germany's southern border was now more threatened than before. Hitler decreed that the defense of that border must take place as far south in Italy as possible. To this end, he ordered the German forces already in Italy to hold on as best they could and made arrangements to rush in reinforcements. To command the troops and save Italy, Hitler called again upon Rommel and gave him command of the German buildup in northern Italy. In southern Italy, General Albert Kesselring would remain in command.

On July 26, the King appointed Marshal Pietro Badoglio as the new Premier of Italy. Badoglio had been a hero of the First East African War in Ethiopia and became Chief of Staff of Italy's armed forces. Upon assuming power, Badoglio declared martial law throughout Italy and banned the Fascist Party along with all other political activities. He also announced that Italy would continue the war as an Axis ally. This was a political untruth and virtually everyone knew it. It was a foregone conclusion that Badoglio would take Italy out of the war at the first opportunity. By the end of July, the Axis forces on Sicily had been forced back into a pocket on the northeastern tip of the island with Messina and the escape route to Italy to their backs. The fall of Sicily and invasion of Italy were imminent. Allied broadcasts from Algiers on July 2 confirmed that fact to the Italian people.

Meanwhile, secret surrender talks had begun in Lisbon on August 2 between the Italian ambassador to Portugal and Allied representatives. On August 6, strong German forces began pouring into northern Italy and sped southward to meet the anticipated Allied invasion of southern Italy. On August 12, German troops began evacuating Sicily.

On August 16, the last German troops evacuated Sicily via Messina. The next day American troops occupied the city and the fighting in Sicily ended.

THE QUEBEC CONFERENCE

Between August 14 and 24, Churchill and Roosevelt met again at Quebec, Canada in what was known as the "Quadrant" Conference. They discussed many aspects of the war including several that affected Africa. This included a decision to invade the islands of Corsica and Sardinia with troops that would stage from Africa. Burma was also discussed including the previously agreed upon decision to use troops from British East and West Africa in that campaign.

At the conference, with Churchill's urging, Roosevelt reluctantly agreed to recognize the French National Committee for Liberation in Algiers as the government representing France's overseas possessions. Roosevelt was still distrustful of de Gaulle, but he had to admit that de Gaulle and Giraud were succeeding in bringing the French back into the fight and that recognition of that fact by the United States was both appropriate and inevitable. Heretofore, Roosevelt had instructed Eisenhower to have as little contact as possible with the Committee regarding political matters, so as not to imply American de facto political recognition of de Gaulle's and Giraud's Committee.

BACK IN NORTH AFRICA

With the war steadily moving northward, staging activities in North Africa came to an end and the ports and military bases took on the new role as supply depots supporting the advancing troops. Many of the ships operating out of Tunisian and other North African ports now took mostly supplies to Sicily and returned with wounded servicemen and POWs. The only large Allied unit left in North Africa was the British 78th Division held in reserve, but it did not stay long. Because of the rapid advances the 78th departed to Sicily on July 20.

FRENCH RECLAIM TUNISIA AS A PROTECTORATE

As has been stated, a few days after the fighting ended in Tunisia, the French authorities from Algiers arrested and deposed Bey al-Moncef of Tunisia on the grounds that he had collaborated with the enemy. Arrests of collaborators, nationalists, and individuals who had harmed French nationals continued under the new Resident General, General Charles-Emmanuel Mast. Eventually these arrests reached some 10,000 individuals and angered large segments of the Tunisian people.

All Vichy-era anti-Jewish legislation was repealed and the needs of the Jewish refugees were attended. A program of repatriating Libyan Jews back to Libya was begun. The prewar "Jewish Council of Tunisia" was allowed to resume functioning and printing its official publication "La Revue Juive." At the same time, several anti-Semitic Arab publications were shut down.

Mast, with blessings from Algiers, reimposed all of the old prewar laws of the Protectorate, many of which were discriminatory against the Tunisians. Beginning in July 1943, he also transferred to his own office, by a series of decrees, the few powers the Bey's office had retained. Eventually all of the Bey's powers were acquired by the Resident General's office, reducing the bey's office to a political nonentity. It was at this time that the new Bey resigned in protest and Mast made no effort to replace him.

As a result of Mast's high-handed methods, the populace grew evermore resentful of the French and supportive of the nationalists who were now represented in the person of Habib Bourguiba. Also in the process, the imprisoned Bey al-Moncef became something of a martyr symbol.

From Rome, which was now under the Badoglio government, Bourguiba tried to improve the image of the nationalist by calling upon the Tunisian people to support the Allies. This appeal, though, fell upon deaf ears in Tunisia because the die had already been cast. For the rest of the war Tunisia would remain a political powder keg.

NORTH AFRICA STILL PARTICIPATING IN THE WAR

Even though the ground war had ended in North Africa, the North African airfields were still taking an active part in the fighting. From these airfields Allied planes regularly bombarded targets in Sicily and Italy.

On August 1, American long-range B–24s operating from Benghazi, Libya reached deep into Eastern Europe and bombed the oil fields at Ploesti, Romania again. The raid was costly. Of the 178 planes that participated 41 were shot down and thirteen lost to other causes, but the raid temporarily knocked out about 40% of the area's oil production. Other air raids into the Balkans were made from Alexandria.

In the ports and military camps in North Africa, during August, the staging of troops and equipment started all over again. Coming now to North Africa were the British and American forces of "Operation Avalanche," that would invade the western coast of the Italian peninsula at Salerno and "Operation Slapstick," that would invade the toe and heel of Italy. Operation Avalanche was commanded by American General Mark Clark, while Operation Slapstick was commanded by British General Montgomery. Both operations were planned for early September and were to be launched from North Africa. The staging numbers this time were not as great as for Operation Husky, but they were still substantial. The main facilities utilized were the military bases at Oran, Bizerte and Tripoli.

In Algiers, the French leadership was finally resolved in favor of de Gaulle. In a mutual agreement with his co-president of the French National Committee for Liberation, General Giraud, it was agreed that de Gaulle would take charge of all political matters and Giraud would assume command of all French armed forces.

On August 26 and 27, the new arrangement was confirmed when most of the major Allied nations, including Britain and the United States, extended formal recognition to the National Committee for Liberation as the provisional government of France. By this time the Committee, having gained control of taxes collected throughout the French colonies in Africa and elsewhere, had become self-supporting and was no longer financially dependent on the British to finance its basic day-to-day operations. They had also repealed most, but not all, of the Anti-Jewish legislation passed by Vichy. All of the major Allies sent representatives to Algiers including the United States and on September 25, the United States extended Lend-Lease to the French in ceremonies at Algiers.

ITALY INVADED AND SURRENDERS

On August 27, 1943, British reconnaissance teams landed on the toe of Italy (Calabria Province) to test the Axis defenses. They found them very weak. On September 1 and 2, military targets, especially airfields, in Calabria were bombed by Allied planes and on the 3rd, strong elements of the British 8th Army landed on the toe of Italy under an umbrella of Allied air cover. Only light opposition was offered by the Italian units guarding the beaches. There were no strong German units to oppose them. The Germans were building their defenses further north.

Joining the African contingents already fighting with the British 8th Army came some 800 Mauritian Pioneers who landed in Italy on September 3. Some of them were veterans of the North African campaign.

That same day two surrender documents were signed by the chief Italian negotiator, General Giuseppe Castillano. The First document assured the Allies that the Italians were surrendering, but that fact was not to be made public lest the Germans use it as an excuse to accelerate their takeover of Italy. The second document was the one that would be used to publicly announce the surrender at the appropriate time.

HOLD THE AFRICANS

At the time of the Italian surrender, the Badoglio government sent orders to all of its POW camp commanders to release all of the Allied POWs if they could not be relieved in a reasonable time by Allied troops. There was one exception, however. Black African POWs were to remain incarcerated.

On September 5, the main forces of Operation Avalanche left their staging areas in North Africa by ship for the invasion of Salerno.

Meanwhile, British forces advanced rapidly through Calabria, delayed only by Italian rear-guard actions. By the evening of September 5, the British had advanced 150 miles and captured most of the toe of Italy. The Italian defensive forces in their path were in full retreat. The next day the port of Messina in Sicily became operative and became the Allies' advanced supply base.

At 6:30 p.m. September 8, Italy's surrender was announced from Algiers by General Eisenhower and an hour and fourteen minutes later General Badoglio went on Italian radio to confirm the surrender. He ordered that Italian armed forces cease resistance and that ships and planes should proceed to designated locations to surrender to the Allies.

From Berlin came the pronouncement that Italy's surrender was a treasonable and treacherous act and praised Mussolini saying that he was "...too great a person for a nation like that."

The next day, September 9, American and British troops landed at Salerno—Operation Avalanche. That same day a British force landed near Taranto on the heel of Italy. General Kesselring had anticipated such moves and the Allied assault troops at Salerno were met by strong resistance from the German 16th Panzer Division. In the days that followed the battle for Salerno would be hard and bloody. Caught up in this fighting were some 800 Pioneers from Mauritius and Seychelles who closely followed the landing troops onto the beaches. Their primary duty was unloading and distributing ammunition. For three weeks straight they worked under nearly-constant enemy fire.

On the heel of Italy, in the Taranto area, the troops of Operation Slapstick met no opposition while landing and quickly captured the town and the Italian naval base, including all of the Italian warships at anchor there. Once the Taranto area was secured, the British troops advanced up the eastern side of the Italian peninsula.

On September 10, the Germans occupied Rome and the Badoglio government, along with the King and the royal family, fled to the Allied-occupied area in the south.

On September 12, Mussolini was rescued by the Germans in a daring operation carried out at a resort near Abruzzi where forces loyal to the King had Mussolini in custody. Mussolini was taken to Germany, conferred with Hitler, and then returned to northern Italy to establish a reconstituted Fascist regime, which became known as the "Salo Republic" because Mussolini's new headquarters were at the town of Salo on Lake Garda.

EVENTS IN NORTH AFRICA

The ports and bases of North Africa were used once again as a staging area in mid-September. This time it was for the 8th Indian Division which had been sent on to Italy to become a part of the British 8th Army advancing up the east coast of Italy.

In naval actions during September German subs sank three merchant ships off Algeria and one off the southern coast of Sicily. On September 6, U–617 sank the British destroyer escort "Puckeridge" off the Mediterranean coast of Spanish Morocco. This was to be her last victim, because on September 12, U–617 was sunk in the same area by a combination of British aircraft and destroyers. On the 22nd, the U.S. freighter "Richard Olney," sailing in convoy, hit a mine off Bizerte and had to be towed into port. On September 25, the American minesweeper "Skill" was sunk off the southern coast of Sicily by U–593—but her days were numbered, too.

By early October, the Allied advance in Italy appeared to be going so well that the Allied leaders believed Rome would fall within the next week or so. Eisenhower, still operating from his headquarters in Algiers, made plans to move to Rome by the end of the month. Before the month was out, though, the Allied drive stalled before a series of massive German defense lines south of Rome. Those defense lines would not be penetrated by the Allies until January 1944.

French Moroccan troops entering Ajaccio, Corsica.

Meanwhile, Rome remained in German hands and Eisenhower remained in Algiers.

MOROCCANS HELP LIBERATE CORSICA

A very strong French resistance movement existed on the island of Corsica, fighting the German garrison troops that had occupied the island in November 1942. In August, the resistance fighters on Corsica asked the National Committee for Liberation in Algiers for assistance in liberating the island. This coincided with the decision at the Quebec Conference that also called for the liberation of the island. With Eisenhower's approval, the Committee responded by sending a regiment of the 4th Moroccan Division which landed on the island on September 15, from French ships and protected by French aircraft. General Giraud, the Committee's co-president, personally oversaw the operation. The Moroccans soon linked up with the resistance fighters and together they attacked the German force occupying Ajaccio, the capital city on the southwestern coast of the island. The attack succeeded and on the 17th the Moroccans and resistance fighters occupied the town.

Another 6,600 Moroccans then landed, along with some French regulars and an American Ranger unit, and in a series of battles, succeeded in liberating the rest of the island. On October 3, the last German defenders abandoned the island. This was the first department (province) of metropolitan France liberated in the war and, appropriately, it was liberated primarily by French forces.

THE SEA WAR ALONG THE NORTH AFRICAN COAST

Off the North African coast the sea war continued during October with German subs sinking four Allied merchant ships off Algeria, one off Libya and two warships, the British minesweeper "Hythe" and the American destroyer "Bristol," off Algeria. On October 4, German planes attacked an Allied convoy twelve miles off Cape Tenes, Algeria and damaged an American freighter. On October 21st German planes attacked another Allied convoy fifteen miles off Cape Tenes and managed to sink an American cargo ship. On that same day, though, the Germans lost U–431, sunk off Cartagena, Spain to a British bomber.

On November 2, the German sub U–73 sank a French cargo ship off Oran. Then there was a long lull in submarine activity off North Africa until the second week of December. German aircraft continued to attack Allied shipping. On November 6, German aircraft sank the American destroyer "Beatty" off Philippeville, Algeria and on the 11th fifty German planes attacked an Allied convoy east of Oran and sank three transports and one tanker. On November 26, the Luftwaffe scored a major victory by sinking a fully-loaded British troops transport off Bougie with a glider-bomb. Over 1,000 British soldiers and seamen perished. The Germans lost eight attacking aircraft.

In December, German subs reappeared off the North African coast and on the 11th, the German sub U–223 sank the British frigate "Cuckmere" off Algiers. The next day, U–593 sank two British destroyer escorts off Algiers. These sinkings would be U–593's last. On December 13, she was sunk off Bone, Algeria by the American destroyer "Wainwright" and the British destroyer escort "Caple."

On that same day U–380 sank a French destroyer leader off Algiers and U–73 sank an American cargo ship off Oran. This would be U–73's last sinking. Three days later, U–73 was sunk off Oran by the American destroyers "Trippe" and "Woolsey."

Following these losses, the Germans withdrew their subs from the North African waters because they were too dangerous. This resulted in another extended lull in submarine activity well into the new year—but the Germans would eventually return.

On December 7, the various Allied commands in the Mediterranean, except for strategic bombing, were unified under Eisenhower. This would be temporary, though, because Eisenhower had already been selected to command Operation Overlord, the cross-channel invasion of northern France scheduled for May 1944. The official announcement on that decision came on December 24, and soon afterwards Eisenhower left Algiers and moved to London. British General Henry Maitland Wilson replaced Eisenhower as Supreme Commander in the Mediterranean.

ITALY DECLARES WAR ON GERMANY

On October 13, at 3:00 in the afternoon, the government of Marshal Badoglio declared war on Germany. This had repercussions in Africa because tens of thousands of Italian soldiers were scattered about the continent as prisoners of war. Suddenly, these soldiers were on the Allied side. With time, a system was worked out whereby these men were designated as "co-belligerents," which erased the label of prisoner of war but yet implied something less than fully recognized Allied soldiers. Under the co-belligerent status the Italian soldiers were screened, and those who showed a willingness to cooperate with the Allies were relieved of their POW status and organized into various types of service units to work on a wide variety of projects. As POWs they could not work on Allied military projects under the guidelines of the Geneva Convention, but as co-belligerents they could work on anything. Therefore, the Allied in Africa gained a large number of workers that could serve the military, as well as domestic needs. This helped considerably in relieving the manpower shortages that existed in many places. Some of the Italians were moved to new locations for work projects, while others remained in their former POW camps and operated from there. In both cases the men were given more freedom of movement. Those few Italians who refused to cooperate with the Allies remained as POWs. Very few former Italian POWs were organized into combat units, and those that were were used sparingly in combat roles.

THE CAIRO CONFERENCES

Between November 22 and 26, 1943 Churchill, Roosevelt, and Generalissimo Chiang Kai-shek of China met in Cairo, Egypt to discuss mutual issues related to the war in the Far East. One of the decisions made was to reconquer northern Burma and reestablish ground communications with Chiang's government in Chungking, China. When the conference ended, Churchill and Roosevelt traveled to Teheran, Iran to meet with Stalin and Chiang returned to China.

On December 4, Churchill and Roosevelt were back in Cairo, this time to meet with other important leaders and their own commanders. They first met with President Inonu of Turkey on the prospect of inducing Turkey to cooperate with the Allies and using Turkey as a staging area for Allied troops, which would eventually enter Greece and the Balkans.

Also discussed at this second Cairo conference was a timetable for the war in the Pacific against Japan and the planned invasion of southern France, "Operation Anvil," to be conducted soon after the cross-channel invasion. The conference concluded December 7.

From Cairo Roosevelt and his party flew to Dakar and on December 9 departed for home aboard the U.S. battleship 'Iowa.'

DE GAULLE BECOMES DOMINANT IN ALGIERS

For most of the year, it had been de Gaulle who made the political decisions on behalf of the French Committee for National Liberation in Algiers while his co-president, General Giraud, took charge of military affairs. By November 1943, this arrangement had become standard procedure and only de Gaulle was consulted by the Allies and others on political matters, although Giraud still held the title of co-president. All knew that this unorthodox arrangement could not last long.

FRENCH FORCES FROM AFRICA MOVE TO ITALY

By November 1943, the Allied forces fighting their way up the Italian peninsula were in bad need of rest and rehabilitation. To replace them, the French forces, veterans of Tunisia and still in North Africa, were selected as part of the replacement force. These forces were redesignated as the "French Expeditionary Force," and on November 25 moved from North Africa to Italy. The French were to replace American units on the western side of the peninsula and become a part of the American 5th Army.

The first major French unit to take its place at the front was the Moroccan 2nd Infantry Division which replaced the American 34th Division on December 8. In addition to the 2nd division, six battalions of Moroccan Goumiers arrived as reinforcements to serve as mountain troops. Many of the Moroccans were veterans of the Tunisian campaign. They participated in their first major attack on December 15, in the San Pietro area, and performed very well.

DE GAULLE MAKES CONCESSIONS TO NORTH AFRICANS

With North Africans going into battle in Italy, de Gaulle chose this time to make a major political speech directed at the population of French North Africa, offering them a number of concession for the postwar era. De Gaulle spoke at

Constantine, Algeria on December 12, and promised that an increased number of North Africans, based on an expanded category system, would be granted French citizenship, while others would receive a wide variety of additional privileges. In this way, de Gaulle hoped to defuse the ardent Arab nationalism which was so visibly on the rise. The Algerian nationalist leaders, though, were not impressed. They resented the continuation of the old prewar policy of their people being categorized by the French, which would continue to keep a large number of Algerians in the status of colonial subjects. De Gaulle's speech made little impact on the political atmosphere in Algeria and anti-French tensions remained high.

SEA WAR—ATLANTIC

During June 1943, German submarine activity in Africa's Atlantic waters was greatly reduced and subs continued to be lost. On June 4, U–594 was sunk 150 miles northwest of Casablanca by British aircraft.

The Germans, though, were still having successes in Atlantic waters off the coast of South Africa where the Seehund II group was still operating. That group took four Allied merchant ships during the month.

Up the Atlantic coast other German subs were able to sink only three Allied ships. U–214, however, laid a string of mines at Dakar early in the month that resulted in the loss of one ship and, on June 6, the German raider Michel sank the American freighter "George Clymer" south of Ascension Island. She was out of Portland, Oregon bound for Cape Town with a full cargo and 24 airplanes on her deck. The Germans lost one sub, U–105 off Dakar, sunk on June 2 by a French plane. On the 20th, the American freighter "Santa Maria" hit a mine laid by U–214 five miles off Dakar and was damaged. She remained afloat and was towed to Dakar.

During July 1943, Seehund II's score jumped to twelve ships while in other Atlantic African waters the toll was eight ships. One of these ships, the British armed merchant cruiser "Asturias" was sunk by the Italian sub "Cagni" on July 25. This was the last Allied ship to be taken by an Italian sub in African waters, because thirteen days later Italy's surrender was announced.

The Germans lost six operating subs in African waters during July and one Milch Cow. These were serious losses for the German U–boat Command. The first operating sub lost was U–160 sunk July 14 south of the Azores with a FIDO homing torpedo by an aircraft from the "Santee" hunter-killer group. The second and third subs lost were U–135 and U–509, both sunk on July 15. U–135 went down off the coast of Rio de Oro by depth charges from three British warships and an American Catalina flying boat. U–509 was sunk between the Azores and Madeira Island by a FIDO from an American plane from the Santee hunter-killer group. U–509 was on her way to work out of Penang, Malaya. Subs four and five, U–527 and U–613, were both sunk on July 23 within a few miles of each other south of the Azores. U–527 was destroyed with depth charges by planes from the American "Bogue" hunter-killer group while U–613 went down after being hit with depth charges from the American destroyer "George E. Rogers." On July 30, planes from the Santee group sank U–43 southwest of the Azores. She was on her way to lay mines at Lagos, Nigeria. The Milch Cow lost was U–487 sunk off the Azores on July 13 by aircraft from the "Core" hunter-killer group.

At this point in time the Americans had 29 baby flat tops operating in the Atlantic. Some were used for convoy escort and others like Core, Bogue, and Santee were used as nucleus ships for hunter-killer groups.

When the need came for the hunter-killer groups to refuel and resupply many of them used West African ports such as Casablanca and Dakar. These became the two most-often used ports.

END OF THE MILCH COWS

U–487 was one of the last Milch Cows in the German inventory. They had proved to be too big and slow and, therefore, vulnerable to the increased Allied antisubmarine tactics. The Allies found Milch Cows relatively easy to locate thanks to Ultra intercepts, Huff-Duff, radar and sonar. Because of this, no more Milch Cows were being built. From this time on, until the end of the war, the Germans would convert some of their faster operating subs and mine layers into submarine tankers. They were still relatively easy for the Allies to locate, but when attacked, their greater speed gave them an increased chance of escaping.

In addition to the converted sub-tankers, an intricate system of sharing fuel at sea was worked out between the operating subs.

In early August two more Milch Cows were sunk as they tried to exit the Bay of Biscay on their way to refueling stations off the Azores. This necessitated U–boat Command ordering several subs home early from West African and Caribbean waters.

Also in early August, Doenitz issued two new standing orders for the operating subs at sea. One order stated that the American baby flat tops were now top priority for attacks and the second order was to stop sending so much bad news because it was having a demoralizing effect on the entire command. Reports of bad news were to be sent only via the officers' cipher code rather than the sub's regular cipher code.

During August, Seehund II's score in South African waters was a respectable seven ships, the last sunk on the 19th. After that, the last of the Seehund II subs departed for home and South Africa's waters became peaceful once more.

Along the rest of the African west coast, only one ship was taken during August. Four German subs, U–604, U–468,

U–403, and U–197 were sunk—another hard blow to U-boat Command.

The next four month's submarine activities in Africa's Atlantic waters reflected the worldwide difficulty the German subs were having in combating the rapidly increasing Allied antisubmarine campaign. September saw no ships or subs lost in those waters. On September 26, American hunter-killer groups began operating out off Natal, Brazil. This gave the Allies more intense coverage of the central and South Atlantic. Heretofore, only American aircraft had operated out of Brazil.

On October 8, U. S. Naval Air Facility, Dakar was established. This meant that U. S. Navy planes would now be patrolling the Atlantic narrows in increased strength from both the African and South American coasts.

On October 27, a very unusual event occurred. An American Catalina, on submarine patrol out of Agadir, French Morocco, was attacked and fired upon by Spanish airplanes as it passed near the Canary Islands. The next day, two more American aircraft, flying in the same area, were attacked again by Spanish planes. No damage was done in either attack but the message from Madrid was clear—the Spaniards were carefully watching the American military buildup in West Africa and wanted to get the message across that American aircraft would not be allowed to fly over what the Spaniards considered their air space. The Americans took heed of the warning and avoided flying over the Canary Islands.

During October, the U–boats returned to African Atlantic waters and three Allied ships were sunk with no subs lost. In November two ships were taken, but three German subs were lost.

On November 1, U–103 deposited eight mines off Takoradi. These were a new type of magnetic mine identified as "TMC." Their main feature was that they would not explode until passed over a preset number of times by ships. This made them very difficult to sweep.

On November 25, U–boat Command sent a message to all subs operating in the central and South Atlantic to cease attacks on single unescorted ships for a period of days because a wave of blockade runners from Japan was coming through. The British picked up this message on Ultra and alerted Allied forces in the area. As a result only one blockade runner got through to Europe.

During December, three more Allied ships went down along with two more German subs. By now Africa's Atlantic waters had become extremely dangerous for German subs for its entire length from French Morocco to South Africa. These last months of 1943 proved to be a turning point in the sea war along the west coast of Africa. Dangerous conditions there would persist for German subs for the remainder of the war, and German submarine activities would steadily decline.

On a worldwide basis the situation also looked bleak for German subs. Between September and the end of December 1943, German subs sank only 67 Allied ships while losing 62 of their own. Furthermore, all ten of the original Milch Cow subs had been sunk.

AZORES BASES LEASED TO BRITISH

On August 17, 1943, after lengthy negotiations between London and Lisbon, the Portuguese government agreed to lease naval and air facilities at two locations in the Azores to the British and Commonwealth nations under a 600-year-old treaty of alliance between England and Portugal. Those facilities were at Lagens on the island of Terceira and Rabo de Peixe on the island of Sao Miguel. As part of the agreement, the British guaranteed to come to the defense of Portugal and/or the islands if they were attacked by any of the Axis powers or by Spain. Furthermore, if Portugal was attacked by Spain the British promised to give serious considerations to declaring war on Spain. The Anglo-Portuguese agreement also promised military aid to the Portuguese. Some of that aid began arriving in late August, and was widely publicized by the Portuguese government as a warning to the Axis Powers. One of the most important items given to the Portuguese was a large number of British-made antiaircraft guns, which the Portuguese used to protect the islands' cities and their own military installations.

British soldiers and sailors were scheduled to arrived in the island on October 12. The day before, the Portuguese administrators in the islands conducted civil defense exercises to prepare the local citizens for the arrival of the British. As the British came ashore on the 12th, Churchill announced the fact publicly to Parliament and promised that the British forces would withdraw after the war. In Lisbon, Salazar made a similar announcement and emphasized the defensive nature of the agreement. Both Churchill and Salazar stated that the agreement did not, in any way, jeopardize Portugal's neutrality.

Also as part of the agreement, the Portuguese received a number of modern fighter planes. Those soon arrived and were given to the Portuguese Air Force both in the islands and on the mainland. Under the Anglo-Portuguese agreement the Portuguese were, in theory, buying these war supplies for fifteen million pounds, but that debt was to be paid for in future goods and services provided to the British from any and all parts of the Portuguese Empire. Other concessions made by the British included promises to help Portugal obtain fuel and food from outside sources and to militarily protect Portuguese merchant and fishing vessels. Furthermore, a Portuguese military delegation was invited to London to discuss further military cooperation with the possibility that additional military aid to Portugal would be forthcoming.

Neither the Americans, nor any of the other Allied nations, were included in the arrangement.

The Portuguese government was taking a considerable risk with regards to German retaliation, and insisted that only British forces operate in the islands for a period of time to keep the Allied presence in the islands to as small a profile as possible.

With British aircraft operating out of the Azores, a vast area of the North and Central Atlantic now came under Allied air surveillance and made it all but impossible for the Germans to continue their refueling and resupply efforts in that part of the Atlantic. It was another serious blow to German sub operations in the central and South Atlantic and the Caribbean.

The Allies gained another advantage in that air and naval protection now available from the Azores meant that convoys could be routed to a more southerly route where the weather was better and, in some instances, distances shorter. Furthermore, the Allies were allowed to install valuable meteorological and navigational stations in the Azores as well as air-sea rescue facilities.

ITALIAN SHIPS PATROLLING FOR THE ALLIES

During October, two Italian cruisers, the "Duca degli Abruzzi" and "Duca d'Aosta," began operating out of Freetown, Sierra Leone participating in Allied antisubmarine patrols and anti-blockade running activities. This made the sixth Allied navy operating in the South Atlantic; American, British, French, Brazilian, South African, and Italian.

SEA WAR—INDIAN OCEAN

With the Mediterranean now open to Allied shipping, more convoys and unescorted cargo ships now poured out of the Gulf of Aden into the northern Indian Ocean. Together with the sea traffic coming up from the east coast of Africa and the existing local traffic the northern Indian Ocean became a heavily traveled sea. Both the Germans and Japanese recognized this but the Germans, after losing their Milch Cows, had little chance of sending submarines there from Germany. Sending subs from Penang, though, was within their capabilities.

The Japanese, hard pressed in the Pacific, were still able to send a few subs into the Indian Ocean. Those subs, however, were not sent as far west as the Gulf of Aden because there were plenty of targets in the eastern Indian Ocean, off southern India and in the Bay of Bengal.

To better protect the northern Indian Ocean sea lanes the British committed an additional number of Wellington bombers to the area. In this respect, the RAF air base at Khormaksar, Aden became a principle base of operations for antisubmarine activity.

During June, the Seehund II submarines were operating off the South African coast and, having been at sea since March, were in need of fuel and supplies. Therefore, the supply ship Charlotte Schliemann, operating out of Penang, was called upon to resupply those subs. One of her first missions was to supply six subs at one time. This was efficient but somewhat risky. The ship and subs gathered at a location in the Indian Ocean south of Madagascar beginning on June 21. All six subs came to the supply ship the same day, representing the largest accumulation of German warships in the Indian Ocean during the war. During the refueling operation all six of the sub captains dined together aboard the Charlotte Schliemann with the ship's captain, while the submarines' crewmen came aboard for showers, hot meals, and rest. The refueling operating went off as planned, but the Germans were lucky. The British knew of the rendezvous beforehand, thanks to Ultra, but did not have any ships or planes available to make an attack.

After the six-sub refueling operation the Charlotte Schliemann remained in the same general area refueling other Seehund II subs, one at a time, until all of the Seehund II group returned home in early August.

Also during June, one German sub out of Penang, U–511, and one Japanese sub, I–27, were patrolling Africa's east coast. I–27 was operating off the entrance to the Gulf of Aden and sank the American freighter "Montanan" there on June 3 and, on June 24, sank the British tanker "British Venture," in the same general area. I–27 took another Allied ship in the Persian Gulf area in early July and then returned to her base in Southeast Asia. U–511, operating southeast of Madagascar, sank the American freighter "Sebastiano Cermeno" on June 27 and then departed the area to operate further east.

Two of Seehund II's subs left South African waters and ventured into the Indian Ocean during July. U–181 sank the British cargo ship "Hoihow" on July 2 off Mauritius Island and U–177 took the Canadian merchantman "Jasper Park" on July 6th southeast of Madagascar.

When the Japanese sub I–27 departed for home, another Japanese sub, I–29, took up station at the entrance to the Gulf of Aden and on July 12 sank the British freighter "Rahmani."

Back in Germany, Admiral Doenitz had decided, by early July, to send about twenty German subs to operate permanently out of the newly-available Japanese bases in the Far East. The subs would be sent in two waves, "Monsun I" and "Monsun II." In Monsun I, eleven operating subs left Europe during July accompanied by two Milch Cows which would accompany them part way and refuel them in the South Atlantic. All the operating subs carried extra torpedoes, spare parts, tools and other items not readily available in the Far East. Of the eleven operating subs only five made it to Penang. Five were sunk en route and the sixth was diverted to the Caribbean. Also, one of the Milch Cows was sunk.

Along the way, though, the eleven operating subs sank 21 Allied ships.

ALLIES BUILDING ANTISUBMARINE STRENGTH IN INDIAN OCEAN

The Allies were also building up their strength in the Indian Ocean at this time, especially in the air. More Catalina flying boats arrived from America and began flying out of existing bases at Dar-es-Salaam, Diego Suarez, Durban, and St. Lucia. Furthermore, B–24 bombers, which had been so successful in the Atlantic in antisubmarine work, began operating out of Ceylon. As still more Allied aircraft became available, they began operating out of Madagascar and the island groups in the western Indian Ocean. More Huff-Duff, directional-finding equipment was also installed at strategic locations along the western rim of the Indian Ocean. More small ships were put into operation by the British Navy, the French Navy, and the South African Navy. With time, the waters of the western Indian Ocean became much better patrolled, but not to the extent of those on the other side of the African continent in the Atlantic Ocean. Conspicuously absent in the Indian Ocean were Allied hunter-killer groups.

AXIS SUBS APPEAR IN NORTHERN INDIAN OCEAN

By September 1943, some of the Monsun I subs were ready to operate out of Penang. During mid-September, U–188 left Penang and invaded the waters in the Gulf of Aden area and on September 21, sank the American freighter "Cornelia P. Spencer" off the coast of Italian Somaliland. The Japanese sub I–10 was also working the area and on September 24 sank a second American freighter, the "Elias Howe" in the same general area.

During October, U–188 and I–10 were joined by another German sub, U–168, also out of Penang, and two Japanese subs, I–27 and I–37. I–27 had been there before, in June and July. The five Axis subs succeeded in sinking four Allied ships along the East African coast in October and three in November.

December saw only two Japanese subs, I–26 and I–27, working East African waters where they took four Allied ships. All but one of the ships sunk during October, November and December were in the Gulf of Aden area.

FRENCH AFRICA

By June 1943, time had run out for Vichy-appointed High Commissioner Boisson at Dakar. He resigned on June 3. A de Gaulle appointee, General Pierre Cournarie, took over and the atmosphere in Dakar changed rapidly from one of obstructionism to one of cooperation with the Allies. Cournarie had a free hand to administer French West Africa as a colonial entity separate from French North Africa. This had been the standard prewar arrangement.

French West African trade benefited greatly under Cournarie's guidance, especially with regard to the neighboring British colonies and with Britain herself. The main items sent to Britain were vegetable oils and ground nuts.

Trade with the United States also increased in vegetable oils and other foodstuffs, and raw materials. But, here again, the French were reluctant to do too much business with the Americans and avoided all joint ventures with them because of the fear that the Americans tended to take control of cooperative ventures. There was also genuine fear that a strong influx of American dollars would undermine the existing, and rather fragile, economy. Furthermore, America's anticolonial attitude was resented by the French who did not want that type of thinking clouding the minds of the West African people and encouraging nationalist sentiments. Also, there was a political faction in Washington that advocated putting all of the French colonies under some sort of international control after the war. Because of these feelings toward the United States, the French attitude was that if there were products to be sold or bought, they would, if at all possible, be sold to or bought from Britain or others before they would be sold to or bought from the Americans. This arrangement suited de Gaulle well because he was aware of President Roosevelt's animosity toward him. In Washington, this attitude did nothing to improve Franco-American relations. The Americans saw it as a slap in the face in view of the fact that the United States was quite generous with the French with regards to Lend-Lease.

The French animosity toward the Americans, though, helped bring the French and British closer together. Several joint projects were undertaken by the French and British, such as an insect control program that benefited both French and British West Africa and a mutual support program designed to increase the production of Cocoa.

In French North Africa, the city of Tunis had now become a hub of Allied activities and planning because of its proximity to Sicily and Italy. On Christmas Day 1943, top Allied commanders met in Tunis and agreed to a plan for another amphibious landing on the coast of Italy to take place in the latter part of January 1944. This would be the landing at Anzio.

MORE BLACK SOLDIERS FOR THE ALLIES

Under Vichy rule, which was subject to the limitations of the 1940 armistices, no significant military forces could be raised among the native population of French West Africa. Now that all changed, and French Army recruiters spread throughout West Africa seeking recruits. They found a warm reception. The West Africans had a long history of serving honorably in the French armed forces and were respected by the French as good soldiers. Collectively, the black soldiers of French West Africa were known as "Senegalese" no matter which colony they were from. The young men of West Africa saw military service as an honorable profession and, like young men everywhere, a chance at adventure, travel, education, and possibly a pension. As a result of this positive attitude toward soldiering, thousands of West Africans joined the new French Army. They were virtually all trained in West Africa and then dispatched to the various parts of the French Empire and to Italy. In Italy, they served in both combat and service roles. From late 1943, and until the end of the war, over 100,000 West Africans would serve in the French armed forces.

The Germans took note of this surge of black men being taken into the French armed forces and used it in their propaganda. As they had done before, the German propagandists stressed that the French Army was an army of nonwhites whose mission was to plunge deep into white Europe.

COLONIAL LOYALTIES TO DE GAULLE SURGE

In early June, de Gaulle established a "Consultant Assembly" in Algiers to serve as an advisory body to his Committee for National Liberation and as a preliminary parliamentary body. Accordingly, all the French colonies were invited to send representatives to serve in the new Assembly. This was a very popular move among the French colonial administrators and they promptly dispatched representatives to Algiers. The notable exception was French Indo-China which was under Japanese domination and, technically, still loyal to Vichy. Because of this great show of loyalty to his regime, de Gaulle now took the opportunity to purge his administration of Vichy holdovers. As a result, hundreds of high and low level officials were dismissed—punishment for not having gone with de Gaulle in 1940. Boisson at Dakar was one of these victims, as was Marcel Peyrouton, the former governor-general of Algeria at the time of the Allied invasion. Furthermore, on August 12, the Committee set up the "Commission of Purification" to punish those who had been the most ardent collaborationists and were subjects for legal prosecution. The Commission proceeded to arrest dozens of men and women, charging them with treason and other crimes. De Gaulle's wrath for Boisson and Peyrouton was particularly deep, so they were among the first arrested. Both were placed in prison under less-than-comfortable conditions. This action angered both Roosevelt and Churchill, because they had given their personal guarantees of protection to both Boisson and Peyrouton. Roosevelt went so far as to send a very terse note to de Gaulle which stated, in part, "...you are directed to take no action against Peyrouton or Boisson at this time!" De Gaulle ignored the note and proceeded with his purges. Roosevelt was not pleased.

Along with these developments and purges came a wave of new enlistments in the French armed forces from the various French colonies. Most of those volunteering for military service were, once again, nonwhites. From Metropolitan France came word that the French Resistance movement wholeheartedly backed the work of the Commission as an example to those in France who were still collaborating with the Germans.

As the collaborators in French Africa were arrested, the political prisoners jailed by Vichy were released. On October 14, Algiers announced that they had freed 7,100 men and women. On October 21, the 1870 Cremieux Decree, making all Jews in Algeria French citizens, was reinstated after having been canceled by the Vichy regime. Furthermore, all other remaining Vichy-created anti-Jewish legislation was repealed. The Cremieux Decree reinstated some 144,000 Algerian Jews as French citizens. This was good news for the Algerian Jews but bad news for the Algerian Moslems, who still had no easy way to rise from colonial subject to citizen.

The United States, for the good of the war effort, welcomed the wave of new recruits and, despite the differences with de Gaulle, increased France's share of Lend-Lease accordingly so that the new recruits could be adequately equipped and utilized.

THE DAY WILL COME—

During November 1943, the French West African administration changed the rules regrading trade. Suddenly, large quantities of vegetable oil and ground nuts were no longer available for export to the British or anyone else. The explanation given by the French was that those products, and others, were being stockpiled for the day when they would be badly needed in liberated Metropolitan France. This decision, which could not have been made without de Gaulle's approval, hurt England most of all. Also, it was another barb in the Allies' relations with de Gaulle. In London, Harold Macmillan, an outspoken member of Parliament, called this action the "gifts and bribes" approach by the Gaullists to win the favor of the Metropolitan French away from Vichy when the opportunity presented itself. Macmillan, though, had to admit that it was good for the postwar reunification of the French people even though it hurt Britain.

This action of stockpiling had negative repercussions in West Africa because the resulting downturn in the colony's international trade made it more difficult for the Dakar administration to acquire foreign capital to buy items abroad. Foremost among these items were consumer goods which had long been in short supply during the Vichy years. Now, the purchase of consumer goods from England and other nations all but dried up. The end result of all this was that it was the native peoples of West Africa that suffered the most. Black markets and smuggling reappeared and the general economy of French West Africa once again began to slump.

MADAGASCAR

By the latter part of 1943, the Gaullists had consolidated their position on Madagascar except for the strategic port of Diego Suarez at the northern end of the island which was still under British control. Altogether, there were still some 1,800 British and 12,000 KAR troops on the island.

The island's economy had improved with the reopening of world markets, but there was one ominous development during the summer of 1943 in that there was insufficient rain. Drought conditions soon developed in some areas of the island and food shortages appeared. As the year ended there was still no end to the drought in sight.

BRITISH EAST AFRICANS AND WEST AFRICANS GO TO BURMA

During the late summer of 1943, the 11th KAR Division and the 25th and 26th KAR Brigades joined the 21st KAR Brigade in Ceylon for training. The 11th KAR Division and its attached brigades consisted of one battalion from British Somaliland, two from Kenya, three from Tanganyika, three from the Rhodesians, and four each from Uganda and Nyasaland.

Also sent to Ceylon for training at this time were the two West African divisions, the 81st and 82nd Divisions. By late October, some of the African troops completed their training so, in early November, the KAR units and the 81st West African Division were sent off to Burma. They were integrated into the 15th Indian Corps, which consisted of both British and Indian units and was operating along the Burmese coast which was known as the Arakan Coast. Their main opponent was the Japanese 55th Division, a component of two Japanese armies in Burma that were threatening to invade India. The British knew that the Japanese had plans to invade India and that that invasion would occur about 200 miles to the north in the Imphal area. The mission of the 15th Corps was to help foil that invasion by threatening the Japanese southern flank and rear. The 15th also posed a threat to the Burmese capital, Rangoon, which was the Japanese's main port of supply.

The KAR and West Africans first saw action in late November as the 15th Corps advanced into western Burma along the Arakan Coast on both sides of the Mayu Mountain Range. The KAR units were on the coastal side of the range and the West Africans were on the interior side. The reconnaissance battalion of the West African 81st Division was detached from the main body and participated in raids on other Japanese facilities along the coast.

The advance progressed slowly due to the difficult terrain and Japanese delaying tactics. By the end of December, the 15th Corps had reached a point a few miles north of the Burmese port of Maungdaw where the Japanese had established a strong defense line. There the advance halted while the Japanese defenses were probed and studied.

EAST AFRICA

Back in British East Africa, fewer African young men were being recruited for military service than previously due to the acute manpower shortage. Those who were recruited were usually put in the British Army's Pioneer units for service both at home and overseas. Some were sent to Sicily and later to Italy, while others went to the Middle East and some to North Africa. Those who were sent overseas were all volunteers.

On the domestic scene the British government had spent about twenty million pounds during the year in grants to Kenya under the Colonial Development and Welfare Act. That money went for such things as soil conservation, African housing, improved water supplies, education, agricultural projects, reforestation and combating the tsetse fly.

When the sisal, rubber, and pyrethrum crops came to harvest there were not enough laborers available so the British authorities had to resort to drafting laborers to bring in the harvests. Again, because of the labor shortage, European women between the ages of 25 and forty were called up for colonial service work.

In Uganda, the economy was still prosperous and the cotton crop was excellent. The British government made arrangements with the local growers to buy all of Uganda's cotton until the end of the war. Celebrations were held in Uganda during the year honoring the colony's fifty years of British rule.

In Tanganyika, several old rubber plantations were put back into production and a survey of known coal deposits was taken with the intent of putting some of them into production. The all-important sisal harvest was good and, as usual, most of it was sent to the United States. Sisal was so important to the U. S. Navy that a permanent U. S. naval commission was established in Dar-es-Salaam to oversee the production and distribution of the Navy's share of the crop. That commission constantly urged growers to grow more and more sisal.

In the Mauritius Island Group, the colonial government undertook a program to increase food production. This provided work for the many newly-arrived Jewish refugees in the islands who were instrumental in making the program a success. By the end of 1943, over one-third of the cultivated land in the islands was producing food.

In Kenya, Uganda and Tanganyika some 21,000 Polish refugees arrived during the year and were placed in refugee camps. Most of these people fled Poland via the Soviet Union, Iran, and India. Over 1,000 Greek refugees also arrived during the year and were placed in camps in British East Africa and Ethiopia.

In occupied Italian East Africa, most of the agricultural lands had been brought back under responsible management during 1943 and the food shortages there eased. Most food produced, though, was consumed locally so there was little to export and bring in much needed foreign revenue. This, coupled with an on-going fuel shortage, required the British government to heavily subsidize the occupied lands.

By mid-1943 virtually all of the British Commonwealth and colonial forces had left Italian Somaliland. To replace them, the British occupation government raised an armed police force of 3,070 Somalis commanded by 120 British officers. This force had two missions; to maintain law and order throughout the occupied colony and, after having received some additional military training, serve as a defense force against a possible Japanese invasion.

A small mobile KAR force, officered by white settlers from British East Africa, remained in Italian Somaliland to patrol the disputed Ogaden Desert region. This was a task that could not be allotted to the Somalis because of their long-standing hatred for the Ethiopians, some of whom lived in the disputed area.

In Ethiopia, word came from Italy, on November 30, that the Badoglio government had stripped the King of Italy of his title of Emperor of Abyssinia (the Italian name for Ethiopia). This ended one of Italy's last claims on the domain of Haile Selassie. Ironically, Badoglio was still wanted in Ethiopia for war crimes he allegedly committed during the Italian invasion of 1935–36.

In the Gulf of Aden, area the RAF air base on the strategic island of Socotra had became more important to the Allies in their antisubmarine efforts. During September, the first two RAF Catalina flying boats, manned by Dutch crews, arrived at Socotra to participate in finding and sinking enemy subs. More Catalinas soon followed.

BRITISH WEST AFRICA

British West African troops were serving in Burma and Italy but at home the main focus of the colonial administrations was more domestic than war-related. British Secretary of State for Colonies, Colonel Oliver F. Stanley, toured the four main colonies discussing current and postwar issues with both European and African leaders. He asked each colonial administration to draw up plans for the postwar era and submit them to him for funding under future Colonial Development and Welfare Acts. A commission of both European and African members was formed to recommend improvements in education while a second commission was formed, with headquarters in Gold Coast, to establish cultural institutions in each of the colonies.

In Nigeria, a government committee was created of both Europeans and Africans to recommend individuals who might be appointed to administrative posts in the colonial government. This was in line with London's new Africanization program for the colonies. A labor board was also formed to study wage scales and make recommendations.

In Gold Coast, a new town council was created for Accra with the majority of the members being elected. Achimota College received a large grant under the Colonial Development and Welfare Act for three new departments, and a commission was established to guide the college toward full university status. Improvements were made in various educational facilities and teachers' wages and pensions were improved. Work was begun to address the problem of the "swollen root" disease that affected cocoa plants.

In Sierra Leone, the capital city, Freetown, was a beehive of activity, primarily because of the importance of its harbor to the Allied war effort. The on-going program of improving harbor facilities continued throughout 1943 and the population of the town continued to grow due to the influx of both Europeans and Africans.

High grade iron ore was flowing steadily from Sierra Leone's mines and the overall economy was good. A sizable grant was given to Fourah Bay College from the Colonial Development and Welfare Act and additional monies were provided to improve the education of women. A number of African women teachers were sent to England for further training.

In Gambia, the Colonial Development and Welfare Act provided money for improvements in Bathurst's harbor, an important harbor to the Allies. Other funds went to improve education and to further train teachers. The British government agreed to purchase the colony's entire groundnut production for the year 1943–44, thereby guaranteeing economically sound conditions in that important industry. A government plan was also worked out for the equitable distribution of grains and other food staples to prevent shortages and black market activities.

AIR ROUTES

With more long-range bombers and transport planes available to the Americans, flights across the North Atlantic were becoming routine. A long-range aircraft could leave the New York City area, refuel at Gander, Newfoundland and be in England in twenty hours flying time. It was then ten more hours to Casablanca.

Planes flying from the Miami, Florida area via Brazil and West Africa required seventy hours flying time to reach Casablanca. When the Azores opened up to the Allies in October 1943, that shortened the air route from North America to North Africa even more than via England. Therefore, air traffic from North America to North Africa via West Africa diminished during the latter part of 1943. The U.S.–Brazil–West Africa–Cannonball Route was still important, though, for short-range aircraft and for aircraft flying on to the east.

On October 19, 1943, the Third London Protocol was signed between the United States, Britain, and the Soviet

Union which promised that 5,100,000 tons of war supplies would be sent to the Soviet Union up to June 1944. Since some of this war material included aircraft, the continued importance of the Cannonball Route was assured.

In November 1943, the Naval Air Transport Service (NATS) created a new wing called the Naval Air Ferry Command (NAFC) to ferry naval aircraft to various parts of the globe, much as the AAF had been doing. Quite understandably, NAFC began using the existing air routes throughout Africa. Many of the planes ferried by NAFC were destined for antisubmarine service around Africa's coasts.

By December, the AAF's Air Transport Command (ATC) began treating the North African air routes separately from the central African air routes, and on December 15, the ATC established separate commands for both; the North African Wing and the Central African Wing.

In Eritrea, the American maintenance and assembly center at Gura was no longer needed. It was dismantled and sent to India. The aircraft assembly center at Takoradi, Gold Coast, continued in operation.

MAURITIANS A PROBLEM

During 1943, the British decided to recruit another unit of Mauritian young men from the Mauritius Island Group and send them, along with the KAR, to Madagascar for training and eventually service in Burma. This venture did not turn out well. Many of the Mauritians were reluctant to leave their islands and when they arrived in Madagascar they were not well-received by the local people. Furthermore, their training camp, near Diego Suarez, was plagued with unpleasant jungle creatures such as snakes, scorpions, cockroaches, and large centipedes. Morale at the training camp was very low. When a fire broke out in the adjoining jungle, the Mauritian recruits were ordered to help put it out. They refused and disorder followed. British and KAR troops had to be rushed in from Diego Suarez to restore authority. After this, the British gave up all hope of using these men in combat. After their training was completed, the Mauritians were divided up into small groups and dispersed into various other colonial Pioneer units.

SOUTH AFRICA

On July 17, 1944, South Africa held national elections. Smuts and his allies campaigned on the fundamental issues of the day; continued participation in the war, cooperation with the Allies, and remaining within the British Commonwealth. Malan and his followers preached their somewhat weathered doctrines of ending the war, bringing the troops home, and abandoning the British Commonwealth in favor of an independent republic. As for a peace settlement with the Axis Powers, Malan said that depended on both parties. Malan's supporters also raised the "Red Scare," predicting that if the Soviet Union won the war the communists would impose their system on a large part of the world. The recent activities of the ANC gave the Red Scare theory some additional credibility among the right-wing voters.

When the white voters of the country finally went to the polls they returned Smuts and his United Party to power by a small popular majority. This was a strong showing in an election in which half a dozen political factions were contesting for power. The United Party took 89 seats, up from 71 and, together with their allies, the Labour Party and the Dominion Party, could count on 110 seats, or 60%, of the Parliament. Malan's National Party took 43 seats, up from forty seats previously. The late General Hertzog's Afrikaner Party won sixteen seats. The few OB candidates who stood for election were badly defeated as were the nine communist candidates. Election prospects were so bleak for the far right that sixteen ultra-rightists of Malan's National Party refused to stand for reelection. This was another sign that Malan's National Party was moving more toward the political center. Oswald Pirow's New Order Party boycotted the election because, as early polls showed, it would make a miserable showing. The remaining two far right organizations, the Grey Shirts and the Afrikaner National Party won no seats at all.

The 1943 election proved to be a turning point for both Malan's National Party as well as the OB. Malan's distancing himself from the far right proved to be beneficial in that his party won more of the popular vote and gained more seats in Parliament. He would continue this process in the years to come and by so doing keep the National Party closer to the political center.

As for the OB, it now dominated the far right but, at the same time, had reached its zenith. At this point, the OB claimed to have over 100,000 supporters. But without the support of Malan, the OB's future was bleak. Never again would it claim such numbers. As the war progressed in favor of the Allies and the horrors of the Nazi concentration camps and other atrocities became known the far right factions in South Africa steadily lost supporters. Most of them moved toward the National Party thus strengthening Malan's hand. This would have a dramatic effect in the next national election scheduled for 1948.

The newly-restructured South African 6th Armoured Division participated in the Allied invasion of Sicily and saw its first action in August 1943. They continued fighting with the other Allied units as they moved into Italy. Attached to the 6th Armoured Division was a contingent of 1,500 white Rhodesians, several South African road building units, and several Pioneer units from Bechuanaland and Basutoland. By late 1943, the battle front had moved into the mountains of southern Italy and the weather had turned cold and wet.

Mountains and muddy mountain roads were not inviting conditions for armored vehicles, so the South Africans were not called upon to fight in the front lines. They were held in reserve and saw little action during the latter part of 1943.

The Pioneer units from Swaziland and Basutoland that had landed with the Allies at Salerno in September 1943 had come under heavy fire, as did all the other Allied troops. Before the situation was stabilized 139 Swazis had been killed. When the Allies broke out of the Salerno beachhead, the Swazis and Basutolanders followed close behind.

The South African Air Force (SAAF) expanded considerably during 1943 thanks in large part to American Lend-Lease. SAAF units continued serving out of North Africa under the command of the RAF and participated, along with the other Allied air forces, in the invasions of Sicily and Italy. The SAAF also took on an expanded role in antisubmarine activity off the South African coast, and in parts of the South Atlantic, and the western Indian Ocean. Like the 6th Armoured Division the SAAF had a contingent of white Rhodesian pilots and mechanics.

With the war moving away from South Africa, domestic issues came to the fore once again, including the long-standing interest of the Smuts government to extend its political and economic influence over its neighbors. The South African economy was, by far, the strongest economy in southern Africa and it was only natural that many in South Africa, especially the industrial leaders, wanted to extend their markets and sources of raw materials into the immediate area. South Africa already exerted a dominant influence in southern Africa which, in turn, created an informal Rand Bloc (the Rand being South Africa's monetary unit). There was some positive sentiments for this in the Rhodesians, Bechuanaland, Basutoland, and Swaziland, but not necessarily in London because those colonies were still under the crown. With the ever-present threat of South Africa breaking away from the British Commonwealth, the British did not want the Rhodesians and other colonies going, too.

The Portuguese and Belgians were also concerned lest South Africa become so economically and politically strong that the status quo was threatened in their respective colonies. This same feeling was expressed by the de Gaulle regime in Algiers with respect to Madagascar. The Smuts government made no concrete moves toward establishing a formal Rand Bloc, but it was a factor that affected all of southern Africa and one that might become more of a problem in the postwar years.

In July, the Smuts government sponsored the first "South African Labour Conference" in Johannesburg to discuss ways and means by which all phases of the South African labor movement could be unified into one organization. The conference was chaired by Smuts's Minister of Labour, and delegates from the Rhodesias and the Belgian Congo were invited. This was an attempt by the government to gain some controls over one of the most liberal segments of South African society. At the conference, the government leaders tried to put forth a resolution favoring a large increase in "selected productive immigrants" after the war. This phrase was taken to mean the immigration of white people and a ploy to "whiten" South Africa. This, and the overall tone of the conference, did not impress the independently-mined labor leaders nor the political left, and the results of the conference were nil.

The small "South African Labour Party," a self-proclaimed spokesman for the labor movement, offered its proposal for the future of South African labor and for the benefit of the soon-to-returning service man. It called for radical land reforms and the creation of collective farms as well as a collective system of the distribution of farm products all the way to the final markets. To the political right wing, and many moderates, this smacked of communism and, not surprisingly, was completely ignored by every political figure except those on the far left.

During September 1944, another political party was formed in Johannesburg, the "Socialist Party of South Africa." Its platform called for an end to "racialism," "starvation wages," and, ultimately, the end of "the present system of capitalism" and the creation of a "democratic and classless" society. The Socialist Party gained few adherents but its message was not popular. Its creation, though, along with the stirrings of labor and other elements of the political left gave a clear indication that the leftists in South Africa were growing and becoming more aggressive. Both the Smuts government and the political right could take comfort, however, in that the leftists were still not unified—at least for the time being.

During October, Smuts made another trip to England where he took a seat in the British War Cabinet to participate in the Allies' future war planning. Before leaving South Africa, Smuts made a speech in which he made a strict distinction between Nazi Germany and "...another and better Germany." This was a message to both South Africa's Afrikaner population and the German people that South Africa would present a conciliatory attitude toward the German people after the defeat of Germany.

On October 23, 1943, South Africa acquired yet another enemy in the war when the Free government of India declared war on the United States, Britain, and the British Commonwealth. This was a Japanese-supported Indian government, located in Singapore, under its leader, Subhas Chandra Bose. Bose was the militant Indian leader who was one of the individuals transferred from a German sub to a Japanese sub in the waters south of Madagascar in April 1943. With Japanese support Bose had formed the provisional government and raised a small Indian army to fight along side the Japanese for the liberation of India.

Since the South African government did not recognize the Free government of India as a legitimate political entity, the declaration of war was ignored.

During November 1943, provincial elections were held throughout the country resulting in a strong victory for the pro-government parties. Smuts and his supporters won 122 of the 170 seats in Parliament. Reflecting the decreasing war influences in South Africa, it must be noted that the main issue during the election was not about war-related matters but an issue concerning schools.

With regard to schools, the Smuts government applied all of the taxes collected from the natives in South Africa during 1943 toward improving native education and to fund a program under which every school-age child got at least one good meal each day at school.

SOUTH WEST AFRICA WANTED IN

During the year the legislative council of the mandated territory of South West Africa passed a unanimous resolution asking that their territory be incorporated into the Union of South Africa as that nation's fifth province. The Smuts government declared that such a move would require approval from the League of Nations. Since the League of Nations was all but defunct, the Smuts government was really saying that this issue had to be postponed until after the war. Furthermore, since the majority of voting whites in South West Africa were right-wing, and even pro-Nazi, German-speakers they would, after union, very likely become the political allies of the right-wing Afrikaners. This, in turn, could reduce the tenuous majority that Smuts' coalition of moderate and liberal Afrikaners and English-speakers currently enjoyed. It was Smuts' hope that, after the war, with Nazi Germany defeated and Hitler out of the picture, the strong pro-Nazi sympathies in South West Africa would moderate. This would bring centrist and leftist political figures to prominence who would be more apt to ally themselves with Smuts's coalition than with his opposition. Furthermore, absorbing South West Africa at this time would certainly be controversial in England and with the other members of the British Commonwealth. Clearly, Smuts was in no hurry to change the status quo under which his government ruled South West Africa through the League of Nation's mandate.

DISASTER AT BARI, ITALY

On December 2, 1943, disaster struck a large number of Pioneers from Bechuanaland when two munitions ship at Bari, Italy suddenly blew up after a German air raid. The Pioneers, members of the British 8th Army, were unloading the ships at the time. To make the disaster even more deadly, some of the shells that exploded were loaded with poison gas. The blast was so powerful that it sunk seventeen additional vessels and damaged eight others. Several hundred Bechuanalanders were killed in the blast and many more were injured along with Britons, Americans, and Italians. The total death count was over 1,000. Some Bechuanalanders risked their lives to save others and were later rewarded for their bravery.

BELGIAN CONGO AND URANIUM

By the summer of 1943, the Manhattan Project was getting under way in the United States and General Leslie Groves, who headed the program for the U.S. Army, wanted to learn more about the Project's main source of uranium, the Shinkolobwe Mine in the Belgian Congo. This mine's ore was far richer in uranium content than either of the Project's other two sources in Canada and Colorado. Groves wanted to know if the mine could meet the Project's demands, whether or not transportation facilities were adequate, and if there were any other exploitable uranium deposits in the area. To this end, he sent a team of Army geologists and scientists in September 1943, under Captain Philip L. Merritt, to the Congo to report on the situation. Merritt's team explored the area and reported back that the Shinkolobwe Mine was the only known deposit of exploitable uranium in the area. Merritt reported that in some of the mine's tailing dumps, the tailings were richer in uranium content than either of the ores from Canada or Colorado.

As for transportation, Merritt reported that the rail line leading west from the mine to the port of Lobito in Portuguese Angola was adequate and that there were other routes by which the ore could be transported from the Congo. A second, but longer, route was via a system of rail lines which led to the east and terminated in the ports of Beira or Lorenco Marques in Portuguese Mozambique. If there was ever any political problems with the Portuguese, the ores could be shipped via a third route to the south through South Africa.

PORTUGUESE AND SPANISH AFRICA

As has been related, the Portuguese allowed the British to use air bases in the Portuguese-owned Azores Islands in October. The Americans wanted to make use of the bases also, but the Lisbon government was reluctant to extend those privileges. The Portuguese were fearful of German retaliation as well as America's long-standing anticolonial foreign policy. Nevertheless, negotiations began between Lisbon and Washington. By the end of 1943, with Italy out of the war and Germany clearly on the defensive, the Portuguese became less fearful of German retaliation and agreed to let the Americans use the Azores. In the agreement, signed in late December, the Americans agreed to respect the integrity of the Portuguese Empire, especially the Azores, both during and after the war, and to withdraw their military forces from the Azores after the war.

The Americans made yet another concession to Portugal by upgrading their diplomatic mission in Lisbon from a charge d'affaires to an ambassador. Years earlier, the United States had developed serious misgivings about the dictatorial nature of the Salazar regime and had down-graded that mission. The necessities of war had obviously changed the attitude of the Americans toward dictatorships.

As a compensation to the Germans, the Salazar government assured Berlin that shipments of Wolfram ore (tungsten) from Portugal to Germany would continue.

In Spain, the lease of bases in the Azores was met with little reaction. The Portuguese had kept the Spaniards fully informed during the negotiations with Britain and the United States, and Madrid understood Portugal's position in the matter. Madrid could see that it was a no-win situation to condemn or support the arrangements. Spain, too, was now trying to distance herself from Germany and make amends to the Allies. To condemn the Azores agreements would have been a show of support for Germany and work against Madrid's disengagement policy while, on the other hand, a show of support for the Azores agreements might cause a drastic reaction in Germany. The Spaniards were mindful that there were still German troops on Spain's northern border in occupied France. Furthermore, the Spaniards had dealt the Germans an unpleasant surprise only recently, on September 7, when they interned a German submarine, U-760, under international law. U–760 had put in at the Spanish port of Vigo with engine failure and the Spanish authorities prohibited it from leaving. This was the first time in the war the Spaniards had done such a thing. It was a clear signal to Berlin that German subs would no longer be welcome in Spanish ports.

A German artist's rendering of a propaganda painting showing men of three races fighting against Germany and captured in Italy.

With the internment of U–760 at Vigo, Doenitz had to alter his policy with regards to his subs seeking refuge in Spanish ports. Therefore, orders went out to all subs at sea that the days of German subs putting into Spanish ports had ended. Doenitz ordered that if a sub was in grave trouble and could not make it back to its base in Europe, the crew could scuttle the sub in Spanish waters and then surrender themselves to the Spaniards, telling them that the sub had been sunk by enemy action. There was still some hope in Germany that submarine crews would be returned through diplomatic efforts.

On December 2, Madrid drew another step closer to the Allies by making an agreement with the United States which allowed American commercial aircraft to operate in Spanish territory. The operation of American military aircraft on Spanish soil was still forbidden.

GERMANY AND JAPAN AND THE AZORES

The Azores arrangements were bitterly denounced in Germany on October 14, the day the Anglo-Portuguese agreement became known. Berlin condemned the Portuguese government for a flagrant breach of its neutrality and warned the Portuguese that the British were now in a position to take over the Azores as a colonial possession of their own. The Germans could not admit to their people that the Azores arrangement was brought about by Germany's military weakness. Rather, they blamed the situation on mythical reports of a poor harvest and food shortages in Portugal and that the Portuguese were forced into the arrangement to get food.

The next day, October 15, the German ambassador in Lisbon presented a note to the Salazar government stating that Germany was now forced to reevaluate its position with regard to Portugal's neutrality and reserved the right to take any action it saw fit with regard to Portuguese interests. This sabre-rattling was also backed up by German radio broadcasts and a similar note and pronouncements from Japan.

In the days that followed, though, neither Germany nor Japan took any military or diplomatic actions against Portugal. As for the Germans, they desperately needed Portugal's wolfram ore and did not want to jeopardize that arrangement. As for the Japanese, they had already taken about all the actions they could against Portugal when, early in 1942, they had occupied the only two Portuguese enclaves in the Far East, Macau and Timor.

The Portuguese had to accept the fact that the Germans might take some military action against the British bases in the Azores and that Portuguese ships might not now be as safe at sea as before.

GERMANY AND OTHER AFRICAN MATTERS

The German propagandists took note, once again, of the racial makeup of some of the Allied troops fighting against them in Italy, and they lashed out against the Allies for employing inferior races as soldiers and bringing them to Europe to threaten the racial purity of the white race. Articles and cartoons with this theme appeared throughout occupied Europe during 1943.

During the third week in June an ugly race riot occurred in Detroit, Michigan, which provided more grist for Germany's racist propaganda mill. German propagandists reported on the riot in great detail, with accompanying Nazi commentary, and broadcast it to as many parts of Africa as they could reach.

Chapter 18
"OVER THERE" (JANUARY–JUNE, 1944)
AFRICANS FIGHT IN EUROPE AND ASIA

As the war moved away from Africa, African soldiers followed it. North Africans and various units from sub-Saharan Africa were part of the Allied forces fighting in Italy, while East and West Africans were a part of the Allied forces fighting in Burma. For the remainder of the war, Africans would be fighting abroad.

Additionally, the sea war continued all around the African continent, but here the Allies were slowly gaining the upper hand. The first African waters to be freed of almost all enemy activities were those along the North African shore.

NORTH AFRICA

North Africa was still very deeply involved in the war during the first months of 1944. Its Mediterranean ports and military facilities continued to serve as staging areas, supply depots, POW camps, hospitals, operational bases for aircraft bombing southern Europe, and antisubmarine forces patrolling the Mediterranean Sea.

FRENCH NORTH AFRICA—STRONGHOLD OF THE FIGHTING FRENCH

By January 1944, the Fighting French were in both political and military control of French North Africa and gaining strength in all respects. De Gaulle was the dominant political figure and had lost his image as a dependent of the British, and had acquired the image of a national leader on his own. This was made apparent on January 9, 1944 when Churchill came to meet with him at Marrakech, Morocco. The purpose of the meeting was to discuss the forthcoming cross-channel invasion of France scheduled for May 1944—only four months away. De Gaulle assured Churchill that the Fighting French could take an active role in the invasion, and they would rally the growing French resistance movement inside Metropolitan France to cooperate with the Allies. All indications were that de Gaulle could accomplish what he promised. Both men agreed that at an appropriate time, which would be associated with the massive Allied invasion of France, de Gaulle should proclaim his National Committee for Liberation to be the provisional government of France and that it should be quickly recognized by the major Allies.

With Churchill's approval and cooperation de Gaulle eagerly set out to accomplish these goals.

But first, there was some housecleaning to be done and certain problems to be solved to strengthen his political base and his armed forces. The housecleaning centered in the person of Pierre Pucheau, the former Vichy Minister of the Interior, which had fallen into the hands of the Fighting French. As Minister of the Interior he controlled the French police who, under Vichy's direction, carried out a number of hideous crimes against the French people. Pucheau was tried in Algiers before a military court, convicted of war crimes and gross collaboration with the enemy, and sentenced to death. Pucheau was the first French war criminal to be brought to justice by the Gaullists and it sent a clear message to other Frenchmen who might, in the future, commit war crimes in the name of Vichy.

Another of de Gaulle's problems was in French Morocco where, in January, the "Istiqal" (Independence) Party issued a manifesto calling for an end to the French protectorate and complete independence for all of Morocco in the near future. Several disturbances broke out in the cities of Rabat, Fez, and Sale in support of the manifesto, and the Gaullists deemed it necessary to arrest several of the Istiqal leaders. The disturbances were quelled by troops loyal to de Gaulle, but the

French Moroccan Resident-General, Gabriel Puaux, was authorized, in an effort to defuse the situation, to announce a number of reforms. Puaux did this but, at the same time, also increased taxes.

Another problem for de Gaulle was food. There had been a bad harvest in North Africa during the 1943–44 season and in some places there were plagues of locusts. De Gaulle was able to obtain emergency grain shipments from the United States, but vegetables, meat, milk, and other basic foodstuffs were in short supply. A system of rationing had to be introduced and, of course, a blackmarket arose. Conditions were especially bad in Tunisia which was already a hotbed of anti-French sentiment.

In an effort to improve the situation in Tunisia, the French colonial administration there offered certain educated Tunisians an opportunity to participate in the colonial government by holding examinations, open to both Frenchmen and Tunisians, for 536 government posts, 100 of which were senior posts. This improved the situation in Tunisia to some degree, but the French still had a long way to go to win over the hearts and minds of the Tunisian people.

On April 4, de Gaulle ended the unworkable arrangement of having co-presidents of the National Committee for Liberation by acquiring the approval of the French National Assembly in Algiers to promote his co-President, General Giraud, "upstairs" to be Inspector-General of the French armed forces—a mainly ceremonial position. Also, with the Assembly's approval, de Gaulle took over Giraud's former position as Commander-in-Chief of the Fighting French armed forces, worldwide. Giraud realized that his association with de Gaulle had come to an end and that he had lost out. He resigned his post and retired from the Army on April 14.

There was yet another problem that de Gaulle had to face in the French armed forces. With their rapid growth, servicemen, formerly loyal to Vichy, were beginning to outnumber the original Free French volunteers—men who had risked their careers and the likelihood of ever returning home again to join de Gaulle. In numerous cases, the former Free Frenchmen were being asked to serve under former Vichy officers and NCOs. This was a situation that had no quick solution and would plague the French armed forces for years to come. De Gaulle's approach was to manage the situation as carefully as he could by being fair and, at times, placating those who felt offended with promotions or other amenities. Fortunately for both de Gaulle's Algiers administration and the Allies, the French armed forces were still more African than European and the Africans were less sensitive to this than the Europeans. For the moment, de Gaulle seemed to have the situation under control because the French armed forces were functioning well.

Another action de Gaulle took to get his political house in order was to make a concession to the Soviet Union by appointing two French Communists to his ruling Committee. This was done in expectation that Moscow would extend recognition to his provisional government at the appropriate time.

A recruiting poster for the KAR used in East Africa.

During May, a second French war criminal, Admiral Edmond Derrien, was prosecuted in an Algiers court. He was found guilty of collaborating with the enemy and was sentenced to life imprisonment.

THE BRAZZAVILLE CONFERENCE

De Gaulle saw the need, while he was still headquartered in Africa, to address the increasing wave of nationalism that was emerging throughout French Africa. He had a plan for the future of the African empire which he wanted to present in hopes that it would satisfy the various nationalistic groups and preserve the empire as an integral unit in the postwar years. To this end he called together representatives from throughout Africa to a conference at the site of his first political triumph, Brazzaville, French Equatorial Africa. The conference

Governor-General Felix Eboue, left, and General Charles de Gaulle at the Brazzaville Conference.

took place between January 30 and February 8, 1944. Governor-General Felix Eboue, the first colonial governor to declare for de Gaulle and the Free French in 1940, hosted the conference and it was chaired by Rene Pleven, de Gaulle's Commissioner of Colonies. The conference was known officially as the "French Africa Conference" but has gone down in the history books as the "Brazzaville Conference."

Most of the representatives invited were de Gaulle appointees and supporters, so it was a given that de Gaulle's plan would prevail. Care was taken so that no Communists were in attendance.

Just before the Conference began, de Gaulle travelled from Algiers to Brazzaville via a roundabout route, making goodwill stops in support of his plan as he went. De Gaulle then went on to Brazzaville to be present at the opening of the conference. He gave the opening speech and presented his plan to the assembled delegates. De Gaulle stressed the importance of strengthening the French Empire as a political and economic entity for the future and for the mutual benefits of all its inhabitants. He defined the role of France as being a "civilizing" mission and the unifier of the great and newly-structured empire that would emerge in the postwar era. De Gaulle than returned to Algiers leaving the delegates to debate and finalize the plan. As expected, the Conference produced a resolution adapting the plan pretty much along the lines that de Gaulle wanted.

The Brazzaville Plan called for a general consolidation of the entire colonial system under a federalized, representative-operating colonial administration to be based in Paris. Voting rights with regards to public affairs and the holding of public office would be expanded among the colonial subjects but were to be granted only to those who were deemed politically sophisticated enough to handle them. This, of course, favored the white settlers and native elite.

The Plan further called for a general increase in education by training more teachers and building more grade schools, high schools and trade schools. No universities were planned at this time. The overall goal was to provide at least a grade school in every village where fifty or more students could be accumulated. The teaching of French would be mandatory as a unifying factor for all the people of the empire. A target date for the completion of this village school program was set for 1995—a fifty-year program.

The Conference also resolved that local native customs should be preserved, labor conscription abolished after the end of the war, the lot of women improved, the "indigenat" cast-like system that existed in some colonies gradually abolished, the creation of a uniform penal code, and a general improvement of health conditions, with a medical school being built somewhere within the empire.

Various economic measures, such as industrialization and tariff reform, were addressed to increase intercolonial trade and the living standards for all colonial subjects. The Conference recommended that industrialization in the colonies be carried out by private enterprise with government assistance in research, development, and pilot projects.

By prewar French colonial standards, the Plan was quite generous, but it remained to be seen whether or not it would satisfy the many and varied nationalist groups that were now emerging.

In the months that followed the Brazzaville Conference, several concrete steps were taken by the Algiers regime to activate the Plan. One of the first steps was the creation, by Colonial Minister Pleven, of a special department within his Ministry to oversee and implement the Plan. Then in March, the de Gaulle administration addressed a long-standing problem in Algeria by decreeing that Moslems could now become French citizens without having to formally renounce Koranic law. This was the fulfillment of a promise de Gaulle had made in December 1943. Unfortunately, it was met with only a lukewarm response by the Algerians. Clearly, they wanted more and were not afraid to ask for it.

Later that month, Algerian leaders met at Setif, Algeria in what they called the "Congress of the Friends of the Manifesto (February 1943) and of Liberty" to discuss Algeria's future relationship with France. Previously, Algerian nationalists, led by Ferhat Abbas, had formed a political organization called "Friends of the Manifesto and of Liberty." At the Congress, the delegates professed their continuing loyalty to France but called for Algeria to become an autonomous republic associated with France in a structure something like the British Commonwealth. The Algerians had hopes that this proposal would be successful in that they were dealing from a relatively strong position, considering the fact that a large percentage of de Gaulle's army consisted of North African Moslems. This made little difference to the French leaders in Algiers and the congress's proposal was all but ignored. During April, the Algiers regime adapted a more uniform tax code system throughout the French Empire, with one of its main features being the elimination the long-standing practice of payment in kind. Chickens and goats would no longer be accepted as payment for taxes.

In other parts of the French African empire, nationalist were inspired in that the Brazzaville Conference ushered in a new relationship between France and her colonial subjects. Native leaders now came together in many places to determine how to address the reforms that were offered. This resulted in the formation, during 1944, of two more neo-political organizations within the French Empire, one in Ivory Coast called the "Syndicat Agricole Africain" and one in Senegal called the "Bloc Africain."

Unfortunately for all concerned, de Gaulle's loyal follower, Felix Eboue, did not live to see many of the Brazzaville reforms come to pass. He died of natural causes on May 17, 1944. Eboue had represented an important bridge between blacks and whites. Now that bridge was gone. He was replaced by Ange Bayardelle.

JUIN—ONLY SLIGHTLY TAINTED

Alphonse Pierre Juin was born in Bone, Algeria c. 1888, attended St. Cyr Military Academy and became a highly respected professional soldier. He was captured by the Germans at the time of France's defeat but later released, at Pierre Laval's request, to take over as French military commander in French North Africa at the time of General Maxim Weygand's forced retirement. When the Allies invaded North Africa in November 1942, it was Juin that gave the order to resist. But, after sixteen hours, with Darlan's consent, Juin ordered a cease fire and was later captured by the Allies. Juin was soon released to work closely with Darlan in bringing over the French African colonies to the Allied cause. Five days after Darlan's assassination, on December 29, 1942, General Giraud restored Juin to his post as Commander-in-Chief of all French forces in North Africa. This was not popular with the Gaullists, but capable generals were sorely needed and since Juin was one of the least Vichy-tainted generals available he was confirmed in his post.

THE PROVISIONAL GOVERNMENT OF FRANCE COMES INTO BEING

On June 2, four days before the Allied invasion of Normandy, de Gaulle took the step he had long been waiting for but was, in effect, a violation of his agreement with Churchill made in Marrakech in January. Without consulting Churchill, de Gaulle declared from Algiers that his National Committee for Liberation was, henceforth, the "Provisional Government of France." This was greeted with considerable joy throughout the French Empire, but not necessarily in the capitals of de Gaulle's allies. Both the British and Americans had warned him that the time was not yet right for such a proclamation, because as the Allies saw it, there was still some question as to de Gaulle's popularity in Metropolitan France. But de Gaulle, ever the individualist, ignored the advice of his Allies and proceeded with the declaration. The response by the Allies was to withhold formal recognition of the provisional government until such a time as they felt it to be appropriate. Thus, de Gaulle's independent action introduced yet another point of disagreement in his political alliances but, fortunately, it did not carry over on the battlefield. His forces fighting in Italy under General Alphonse Juin continued to cooperate closely with the Americans and British on military matters.

IN OTHER PARTS OF NORTH AFRICA

With the war having moved away from its borders, the Egyptian government ended blackout practices and the country returned to somewhat normal. The economy was good but, as usual, the country's political scene was still turbulent. Stimulating the economy were the exports of cotton and food which, together, exceeded imports, thereby producing a favorable balance of trade. Inflation, though, continued to erode the Egyptian pound. Tax collections were up and the government was repaying its foreign debts.

A malaria epidemic plagued Upper Egypt early in the year affecting 110,000 people and killing 11,000. Britain and America sent in medical aid.

A political opposition bloc of five parties was formed in January, but together they were still very weak in comparison to the powerful Wafd Party. The bloc controlled only thirty seats in Parliament while the Wafd Party controlled 230. As always, the opposition accused the Wafd Party leaders of corruption and a former Wafd Minister of Finance, Makram Ebeid Pasha, who was now in opposition, wrote a tell-all book naming names and giving details about Wafd corruption. Makram was arrested in May for slandering the government.

During 1943, some 2000 Greek refugees had sought sanctuary in Egypt and were now living in temporary refugee camps mainly in the Cairo area.

Libya, like Egypt, was peaceful and prospering under British occupation in the north and French occupation in the south. The British allowed the Senussi clan, which had risen up against Italian rule and been expelled from the country, to return to their home territory in Cyrenaica. There, they became a rallying point for Libyan nationalists.

The sea war off North Africa continued, because German submarines had become active there again and the Luftwaffe was still active. During January 1944 no Allied ships were sunk off North Africa by the German submarines although the U.S. freighter "Daniel Webster" was damaged by a German aerial torpedo off Algeria. She was towed to port and later scrapped. Then, during February, German planes sank two American merchantmen off eastern Algeria. On January 24, though, U.S. and RAF planes sank the German sub U–761 as it attempted to transit the Strait of Gibraltar.

During March, German planes sank another American and a Dutch merchantman off eastern Algeria, and U–371 ventured into the eastern Mediterranean to sink an American freighter off Tobruk. On March 6, a New York City-to-Alexandria convoy strayed into an Allied mine field off Tunisia and two cargo ships were sunk. Three days later the American freighter "Clark Mills" hit a mine off Bizerte and had to be beached. She was later declared a total loss. On March 16, another German sub, U–392, trying to transit the Strait of Gibraltar, was sunk by US aircraft, a British destroyer and a frigate.

On April 11, the Luftwaffe made another appearance in the western Mediterranean when a German torpedo plane damaged the American destroyer escort "Holder" northeast of Algiers. The ship did not sink and was towed to Algiers but was not repaired. On April 20, the Luftwaffe returned to the Algiers area and torpedoed and sank the American destroyer "Lansdale."

South African troops searching a tobacco factory at Carroceto, Italy, a scene of hard fighting.

On April 16, U–371 sank another American cargo ship off Tobruk. Then on April 20, German planes attacked an 87–ship Allied convoy off Algeria with deadly effect. The American freighter, "Paul Hamilton," which carried ammunition, was hit by an aerial torpedo and disintegrated in one tremendous explosion. There were no survivors among the 47 crewmen, 29 armed guards, and 504 troops aboard. Also sunk in the attack was the U.S. destroyer Lansdale. Three other Allied cargo ships were damaged.

On May 2, U–371 sank the American destroyer escort "Menges" off eastern Algeria, but then, on the 4th, U–371 was discovered and attacked by a force of four Allied warships. She managed to sink one of her attackers, the French destroyer escort "Senegalais," but was, herself, sunk in the process.

U–616, U–960, and U–967 were also operating in Algerian waters during May and sank two Allied ships in the Oran area, one on the 5th and the other on the 14th. But then, on May 17, U–616 was caught off Cartegena, Spain by a hunter-killer force of eight American destroyers and smaller ships. Working in cooperation with the RAF, the ships depth charged U–616 to the surface and sank her. On May 19, U–960 met a similar end when she was caught by a force of two American destroyers and several RAF planes northwest of Algiers.

This was the grand finale for the German subs in North African waters. In late May they were withdrawn, never to return.

IN ITALY—A "UNITED NATIONS FORCE"

The United Nations Organization was still an idea on paper but the phrase "United Nations," which referred to the Allied nations, had become widespread. In Italy, for example, the conglomeration of national forces fighting there were often referred to as the "United Nations Forces." In hindsight, this wartime phraseology portended what was to come in the postwar years when the United Nations Organization sanctioned multinational coalition forces to address various problems around the globe.

Basically there were three Allied armies operating in Italy, and within their ranks were a wide assortment of humanity with Africans well represented. The British Army under General Montgomery, which advanced up the east coast of the Italian peninsula, consisted, at various times, of Britons, Canadians, South Africans, Australians, New Zealanders, Indians, Poles, Greeks, Rhodesians, West Africans, East Africans, Jews, Maldavian Islanders and Bechuanalanders. Virtually all of these units were ground units but some of the larger Allies, such as the South African, contributed air contingents.

The French Army under General Juin, advancing up the center of the peninsula, consisted of Frenchmen, Moroccans, Algerians, Tunisians, Senegalese, and Foreign Legionnaires.

The American Army, under General Mark Clark, advancing up the western side of the peninsula, was the most homogeneous of all consisting almost entirely of Americans. Being a segregated army, though, there were separate black American combat units as well as black service units. Later in the war, there would be Japanese-Americans and Brazilians fighting under American command. Virtually no Africans fought under American command.

In addition, all three armies had Italian units, mostly service units operating in the rear.

AFRICANS IN ITALY

On January 9, the 3rd Algerian Division, which now contained a regiment of Tunisians, relieved the American 45th Division south of the Rapido River. At 20,000, men the 3rd Algerian was one of the largest divisions in Italy. With their arrival, this part of the front came under the command of General Juin. On January 12, the 3rd Algerians, together with the 2nd Moroccan Division, launched successful attacks toward Sant' Elia Fiumerapido north of Naples and held the ground they gained. On the 14th, the 2nd Moroccans assaulted German positions along the Rapido River and, in five days of fighting, succeeded in crossing the river and taking the strategic town of Monte Il Lago.

Then on January 25, the 3rd Algerians, after fighting their way up snow-covered slopes near the headwaters of the Rapido River, captured Colle Grosso and Monte Belvedere from the Germans after a bloody 48-hour battle. But two days later, the Algerians were driven off Monte Abate by a determined German attack. This sector of the front then fell silent until May.

In late January, when the Allies invaded Italy at Anzio, no large African formations were involved but several black African Pioneer units participated as part of the British force.

During February, March, and April 1944 there was little progress by the Allies in Italy due to strong German resistance along the formidable "Gustav Line" and cold, rainy winter weather that made military operations particularly difficult. This weather was exceptionally hard on the African troops and during this time some of them were rotated to the rear and given rest and relaxation.

In late March, with warmer, and drier weather on the way, the Allies prepared for a major assault on the powerful Gustav Line. As part of the preparations, General Juin's entire French Expeditionary Corps, including his African divisions, moved into the western part of the Italian peninsula and replaced the American 2nd Corps in the front lines. Juin's forces had just been reinforced with the arrival of the 4th Moroccan Division. This was another large North African division of 19,652 men equipped for mountain fighting. By taking over part of the American front, the Americans could then concentrate their forces for a more powerful attack on a narrower front.

On May 12, General Juin's troops launched a major attack on the Gustav Line south of Sant' Ambrogio. There was fierce fighting, but by 3:00 p.m., troops of the 2nd Moroccan Division had smashed through the German defenses and taken the village of Monte Faito. The next day, the Moroccans scored another major victory by capturing two more key German positions in the Abruzzi Mountains and opening a breach in the main German defenses. In the process, they captured over 1,000 Germans and opened the way for a general Allied advance. These were very important victories for the Allies. Meanwhile, troops of the 1st Moroccan Division, operating to the north of the 2nd Division penetrated the Gustav Line to reach the Liri River. The 4th Moroccan Division and the 3rd Algerian Division then poured through the holes in the line and captured the towns of Castelforte, Damiano, and Monte Ceschito. On other sectors of the front, American and Polish forces broke through the Gustav Line and the road to Rome was open even though large segments of the Gustav Line still held out.

On the May 15, Moroccan troops were instrumental in clearing the Ausonia defile and other key points along the Gustav Line. The next day, other Allied forces crushed the eastern hinge of the Line and a general advance began toward Rome. French troops, after overcoming strong German rear-guard actions, took the town of Pico on May 22, 63 miles south of Rome. The next day, the French penetrated the hastily-built "Senger Line" south of Rome, forcing the Germans to withdraw other units within the line lest they be outflanked. The Senger Line then collapsed altogether.

The 3rd Algerians soon captured Belvedere Hill and moved on to retake Monte Abate on May 26, which they had lost in January.

By June 3, Juin's forces were rapidly advancing on Rome along highway Six southeast of the capital. By nightfall of that day, they were about thirty miles from Rome. To the west the Americans were slightly ahead of them, advancing along the coast.

On June 4, American troops entered and secured the open city of Rome. The next day, the French troops filed through the city on their way north. Still other French troops, and most of the British forces, bypassed the city to the east.

While the Americans were taking Rome, British forces, marching parallel to the French, crossed the Tiber River north of Rome on June 6. The South African 6th Armoured Division, now responsible for an important part of the British front, smashed through German defenses at Viterlo on the 5th and on the 6th they encircled a large German force at Monte Fiascone, which surrendered the next day. Then in a swift and surprise attack, the South Africans occupied the town of Civita Castellana 25 miles north of Rome. After securing the city, they led the next British advance to the north toward Orvieto, an important rail junction. The advance was slowed by strong German rear-guard action and by a determined German defense at Bagnoregio.

On June 11, the 3rd Algerians captured Valentano but the South Africans were stopped at Bagnoregio. Two days later, though, the South Africans broke through the Germans defenses at Bagnoregio and continued their advance on Orvieto, which they occupied on the 14th.

On June 17, the French 9th Colonial Division (Senegalese) and elements of the 4th Moroccan Division made an amphibious landing on the important island of Elba, 120 miles north of Rome. After two days of fighting, they secured the island.

On June 20, a major change was made within the French Expeditionary Force when one of Juin's best divisions, the French 1st Motorized Division, was withdrawn from him in preparation for its being used in "Operation Anvil," the forthcoming invasion of Southern France. Taking its place was the 2nd Moroccan Division.

On June 21, the South African 6th Armoured Division reached the town of Chiusi but could not occupy it because of strong German opposition. There the South Africans paused to bring up supplies. They were now ninety miles north of Rome and approaching the next major German defense lines, the "Arno River Line," and behind it the more substantial "Gothic Line." On June 26, the South Africans launched at attack at Chiusi, broke through the German defenses, and occupied the town. Beyond Chiusi, German resistance evaporated and the South Africans quickly advanced to the next town, Chianciano. The next day, they reached Aquaviva and Montepulciano and began mopping up operations along the eastern shore of Lake Trasimene.

DE GAULLE LEAVES ALGIERS AND RETURNS TO FRANCE

On June 6, massive Allied forces invaded Normandy in northern France and after several days of hard fighting established a firm beachhead. On June 14, General de Gaulle ceremoniously returned to French soil and began making preparations for transferring his Provisional government from Algiers. It had already been decided that the Provisional government would remain in Algiers until Paris was liberated. In the meantime, de Gaulle would work to build a favorable relationship with the French people and the French resistance leaders. The attitude of the French people, in particular, was a major question in the minds of de Gaulle and the other Allied leaders. These people had lived under Vichy's rule for four years and had been subjected to intense anti-de Gaulle propaganda all that time.

Fortunately for de Gaulle—and for the Allied cause—early signs indicated that both the French people and the French resistance leaders inside France were willing to cooperate with, and take orders from, de Gaulle's Provisional government.

THE SEA WAR—ATLANTIC

By January 1944, almost every part of the North and South Atlantic Oceans had become dangerous waters for German submarines because virtually all of the Allied ships and planes now had the most modern antisubmarine devices and were constantly fed intelligence information about German submarine and blockade runner activities through Ultra.

The Allies were quick to demonstrate their new strength in African waters. Between January 3 and 5, Allied hunter-killer groups sank three German blockade runners off West Africa. All three were heading for German, from the Far East. This was the last straw for the Germans. Henceforth, all blockade running from the Far East would be done by submarines.

As for West African waters, there was no German submarine action during January and most of February 1944 along the entire length of western Africa, with one exception. That exception concerned the Milch Cow U–544 which was operating off the Azores, refuelling German subs operating in the North Atlantic and Caribbean. On January 16, the Milch Cow was located and attacked by aircraft from the "Guadalcanal" hunter-killer group while in the process of refuelling U–516. Both subs, however, escaped undamaged.

During late February, U–66, which had made its way secretly to the Gulf of Guinea, sank the British merchantman "Silvermaple" off Gold Coast. U–66 took the captain of the British ship prisoner. U–66 then went on to sink three more Allied ships during March, all in the Gulf of Guinea.

During the second week of February, U–852 arrived in the area; operating several hundred miles west of U–66, it sank the Greek freighter, "Peleus," off Liberia on the 13th. As the ship broke apart some of its cargo floated on the water and there were survivors on three rafts. The sub's captain, Lieutenant Commander Heinz Eck, ordered that the survivors, rafts and floating cargo all be destroyed with machine gun fire and grenades to eliminate all traces of the ship's sinking. Such debris, Eck reasoned, would give away the fact that his sub was in the area. This was a flagrant violation of the rules of war, and both Eck and his crewmen knew it.

The attempt, though, was unsuccessful. One raft and three of Peleus' crewmen survived the attack and were picked up by a passing Portuguese ship and taken to Cape Town. There they related the atrocity to the South African authorities, and the facts were forwarded on to the Allied authorities tracking war crimes.

After the war, war crimes charges were brought against Eck and four of his officers for the Peleus incident. All five were tried at the same time before a British Military Court in Hamburg and found guilty. Eck and two of his officers were executed by firing squad, the fourth officer received life imprisonment, and the fifth fifteen years.

At this time, another German sub, UIT–22, made it undetected to South Africa's waters. UIT–22 was the former Italian sub "Alpino Bagnolini" captured by the Germans at

Bordeaux at the time of the Italian surrender. On March 11, however, she met her end before she could sink any Allied ships. On that date, UIT–22 was discovered south of Cape Town by two RAF Catalinas out of Langebaam, South Africa and sunk with depth charges.

On March 17, yet another German sub, U–801, was caught by planes and ships of the "Block Island" hunter-killer group west of the Cape Verde Islands and disabled with a FIDO torpedo. U–801 was forced to the surface and sunk with naval gunfire.

On March 19, the Germans lost the Milch Cow U–1059 southwest of the Cape Verde Islands. The sub was outbound for the Far East but was temporarily on station in this area to refuel two subs operating in the Atlantic. Foolishly, her captain allowed several of the members of the crew to go swimming on this bright and sunny day as they waited for the operating subs to appear. U–1059, with crewmen in the water, was spotted and quickly attacked by planes of the Block Island hunter-killer group and sunk by the first bomb dropped. Gunners on U–1059 were, however, able to bring down one of the American planes. Eight sub crewmen, out of 55, were rescued as was the lone American pilot.

The carnage of March 1944 was not over yet for the German submariners off West Africa. On or about March 27, U–851 mysteriously disappeared without a trace somewhere in the South Atlantic. She was on her way to operate in the Indian Ocean out of Penang.

April was another bad month for the Germans off West Africa. On the 9th, U–515 was spotted northwest of Madeira Island by planes of the Guadalcanal hunter-killer group and set upon by both planes and ships. She was sunk in a hail of depth charges and rockets. The very next day, the Guadalcanal group struck again and sank U–68 in the same general area. No Allied ships were lost off West Africa during April.

In May, the sinking of German subs continued. On the 6th, U–66 was spotted by aircraft from the Block Island group west of the Cape Verde Islands and sent to the bottom after being depth-charged, hit by artillery fire, and rammed.

On May 13, a very unique sub was sunk west of the Cape Verde Islands by the American destroyer escort "Francis M. Robinson." She was a new German prototype identified as XU–1224 but manned by a Japanese crew. Germany had given the sub to the Japanese to take to Japan and copy. There were no survivors.

GERMANS GET REVENGE IN WEST AFRICAN WATERS.

On May 29, U–549 scored a major naval victory in the waters south of the Azores by torpedoing and sinking the American baby flat top Block Island. She also succeeded in torpedoing and damaging the American destroyer escort "Barr" which was later towed safely to Casablanca and repaired. Only six crewmen aboard the Block Island were killed while 951 were rescued.

The crewmen of U–549, though, paid the ultimate price for their victory. Their sub was located and attacked by two other American destroyer escorts from the Block Island's group and sunk with all hands aboard.

JUNE 1944—AN EVENTFUL MONTH IN WEST AFRICAN WATERS

Within a week of the sinking of the Block Island, another dramatic event occurred in West African waters west of Dakar. Ships of the Guadalcanal group succeeded in capturing at sea, intact, the German sub U–505. Capturing an enemy sub intact was a rare event in the sea war of World War II. U–505 had been damaged by depth charges and was forced to the surface, whereupon her captain surrendered the crew, but not the sub. The Germans had opened the sub's sea cocks and she was slowly sinking. The Americans soon realized this, and several very brave American seamen went into the sub to close the sea cocks. They did so just in time. U–505, half flooded and low in the water, was then towed to Bermuda where she was carefully studied by Allied submarine experts. After the war, U–505 was put on permanent public display at the Museum of Science and Industry in Chicago.

On June 6, 1944, the Allies invaded Normandy, France and within a few days were threatening to advance down the French Atlantic coast where the bulk of the German submarine pens were located. Doenitz could see that the pens would soon be overrun and on June 12 sent word to all subs at sea that the French ports might no longer be available to them and that they should conserve enough fuel to reach Bergen, Norway. During July, the Allies did, in fact, overrun all of the French submarine pens. Those German subs that were in the ports and serviceable were sent to sea or to Norway, while those that were not serviceable were scuttled. For German subs now operating south of France, it was now another 1,000 miles back to their home port.

Also in June 1944, U–547 appeared in the Gulf of Guinea and on June 14 sank a British trawler and a French merchantman. Then on June 22, the American freighter "Pierre Gibault," hit a mine southeast of the Azores and sank. These were the only Allied ships lost in West African waters during June.

On June 24, American airplanes spotted a strange sub on the surface southwest of the Azores and went to investigate. The sub quickly dived as the planes approached. The Americans dropped sonabuoys and 500 lb. bombs into the subs's path, and the sonabuoys promptly recorded the sound of a submarine breaking up. The next day 65 bales of raw rubber were found floating in the sea near where the sub had gone down. The Americans did not known it at the time, but their victim was the Japanese sub, I–52, which was on its way to Germany with rubber, tin, tungsten and other supplies from the Far East. Aboard was a German navigator who had been transferred to I–52 days earlier from the German sub U–530. He was to guide the Japanese sub in European waters.

SEA WAR—INDIAN OCEAN

By the beginning of 1944, the German Monsun I submarine group was established at Penang and the other Japanese bases in South East Asia and the subs of the Monsun II group were in the process of arriving. By January and February, subs from both groups were raiding into the Indian Ocean along with Japanese subs, but only a small percentage of these raids were carried out in African waters. With Allied antisubmarine defenses still relatively weak throughout the entire Indian Ocean area, there were still plenty of targets for the Axis subs closer to their Far Eastern bases in the waters off India, Burma, the East Indies, and Australia. There was little need to travel to faraway Africa.

During this time, the Allies were able to commit their first hunter-killer group, a British force, to the Indian Ocean. Others, though, were being organized.

On January 2, 1944, the Japanese sub I–26, which had been operating in the Gulf of Aden area since December, took its last victim, an American freighter, and then departed for the east. I–26's place was taken by the German sub U–188, which sank six more Allied merchantmen, all in the Gulf of Aden area, between January 26 and February 9. U–188 then departed. U–510 soon arrived in the area and sank three ships out of an Allied convoy on February 22 and a ship sailing alone on March 7. U–510 departed and a lull of several months then followed in the Gulf of Aden area.

By the end of January, the British finally had enough warships in the Atlantic Ocean to spare a few for operations in the Indian Ocean. During this time, a powerful force of large capital ships assembled at Colombo, Ceylon. They consisted of the battleships "Queen Elizabeth" and "Valiant," the battlecruiser "Renown" and two aircraft carriers "Illustrious" and "Unicorn." These ships would not be used in African waters but rather in the waters of the eastern Indian Ocean to support operations in Burma and the East Indies. Their presence in Ceylon, though, provided an effective shield against Axis penetration into African waters.

THE END OF THE CHARLOTTE SCHLIEMANN

The German supply ship Charlotte Schliemann, that had been stationed in the Canary Islands for long periods of time during the early part of the war, was now operating out of Penang. A second German supply ship, the "Brake," was also operating out of Penang. The Allies were well aware of both ships at Penang and were tracking their every move through Ultra. In mid-January, Charlotte Schliemann left Penang to supply Axis subs and blockade runners operating in the western Indian Ocean. This was discovered through Ultra and the British launched a well-organized campaign, called "Operation Thwart" to intercept the German ship. Planes from Ceylon, East Africa, Socotra, Mauritius and Aden cooperated in the search. At about 3:00 p.m. on the afternoon of February 11, an RAF Catalina from Mauritius spotted the Charlotte Schliemann in the process of supplying U–532 just east of Madagascar. The Germans also spotted the plane and the submarine quickly dove before the plane could get close enough to attack. The Catalina, though, radioed the find to its base and remained in the area circling the ship but out of range of her guns. The Catalina, running low on fuel, had to break off contact about 4:30, but by then the British destroyer "Relentless" was fast approaching and soon had the Charlotte Schliemann on radar. Relentless tracked the German ship through the night and by noon on the 12th was in a position to attack. The Germans, knowing they were outgunned, set scuttling charges, then stopped and abandoned the ship as the Relentless opened fire. The German ship was hit by both artillery fire and torpedoes. Then the scuttling charges went off and the ship sank quickly. Relentless, fearing that there might be Axis subs in the area, stopped only long enough to pick up forty survivors. This left four lifeboats still in the water with the other survivors. One lifeboat was soon picked up by a British freighter and a second reached Madagascar. The other two, though, were never seen again. The prisoners from the Charlotte Schliemann were all sent to a POW camp at Londiana, Kenya.

KAR TROOPS LOST AT SEA

On the same day the Charlotte Schliemann went down, the Japanese sub I–27 attacked an Allied convoy off the southern tip of India and sank the British troop ship "Khedive Ishmail." She was one of five troop ships out of Kenya bound for Ceylon and had 1,527 people aboard, including 850 KAR troops, a large number of nurses, and a contingent of sixty WREN (the British Navy's Women's Royal Naval Service). The ship sank quickly and 1,134 people were lost, including 736 of the KAR men. Only two of the sixty WRENS survived. Also lost was a large number of artillery pieces destined for the 11th KAR Division in Burma. Later that day, British destroyers tracked down I–27 and sent her to the bottom.

THE END OF BRAKE

On March 10, the German supply ship Brake left Penang with orders to supply Axis subs and blockade runners deep in the southern Indian Ocean, about 1,000 miles south of Mauritius. The British learned of this through Ultra and, since the Brake's operational area was beyond the range of most land-based aircraft, quickly put together a hunter-killer group of five warships based around the escort carrier "Battler." RAF Catalinas out of Madagascar were to assist the force within their range of operation. The Battler force assembled at Durban, South Africa and set out into the southern Indian Ocean with hopes of intercepting Brake when she came on station.

At 10:32 a.m. on March 12, an airplane from Battler located Brake which was in the process of refuelling U–188. It was Sunday morning and most of the crewmen were not at their battle stations, but were on deck attending religious services. The British plane radioed the location of the two vessels, and the British destroyer "Roebuck," which was not far away, raced to the scene and soon had Brake on radar. U–188 dove and got away, but Brake was now a sitting duck. Brake tried to make a run but the British destroyer began closing rapidly and opened fire at thirteen miles. The Germans knew the end was near, so they set scuttling charges and abandoned the ship. As Roebuck approached, her shells began to hit Brake and four Germans were killed. The remaining 135 crewmen got off safely into lifeboats. The scuttling charges sent off and Brake sank slowly, finally going under at 1:20 p.m. Roebuck, fearing the presence of U–188, did not stop to rescue survivors but sped off to safer waters. Actually, there were two German subs in the area, the other being U–168, which was to refuel from Brake after U–188. U–168 rescued the Brake's crew but was attacked as it sped away from the scene by planes from Battler. U–168 dove quickly and deep and managed to escape. Ten days later, she disembarked the Brake's survivors to Batavia, Java.

THE MONSUN GROUPS COMETH

On April 1, U–852, a member of the Monsun II group and the sub that had machine-gunned survivors of the freighter Peleus in February, was on its way to the east. South of Cape Town, U–852 sank a British freighter but, this time, did not attack the survivors. She went on then, without incident, to Penang.

By early May, U–852 was back again in African waters operating south of Socotra Island when, on May 2, she was discovered by RAF planes and depth-charged repeatedly. She was damaged by the charges and forced to the surface but still had power. The British destroyer "Falmouth" joined in the chase which lasted for two days. On May 3, the sub was able to beach herself, and the surviving crew of 59 then blew up their boat and surrendered. They were taken to Aden. Seven Germans had been killed in the attacks. U–852 had not been able to sink any Allied ships in the Indian Ocean.

MAN-LIFTING KITE

Upon inspecting the scuttled U–852, the British discovered a device they had not seen before. It was a man-lifting helicopter-type kite (bachstelze) used to send a man aloft as a lookout. The device was taken to Kenya and successfully tested off the windy cliffs near Mombasa.

On June 16, U–198, another member of the Monsun II group on its way to the east, sank a South African freighter in the waters off Cape Town. U–198 then went of safely to Penang and would operate later in the Indian Ocean.

MORE ALLIED SEA POWER FOR THE INDIAN OCEAN

During April, additional Allied warships arrived at Colombo, Ceylon to strengthen the Allied naval forces that had arrived there in January. This time the French battleship Richelieu, which had been idled at Dakar for over two years, joined the force as did three British escort carriers. With regards to Africa, the three escort carriers were, perhaps, the most important because they were to be used to escort convoys and could become the nuclei for future hunter-killer groups operating in the Indian Ocean.

EVENTS IN BRITISH WEST AFRICA

By 1944, thousands of British West Africans were fighting in Burma in the 81st and 82nd West African Divisions while other West Africans were serving, primarily in service units, in Italy.

The British West African colonies remained a vital part of the Allied war effort, supplying the Allies with raw materials and food, and as a result, their economies continued to prosper. One of Nigeria's mineral resources, columbium ore, had become very important to the Allies in that columbium was an important alloying metal used in the construction of jet engines.

In Lagos, Nigeria, the colonial government, with London's approval, appointed more Nigerians to administrative posts as a part of the British government's long-range plan to increase the Africanization of the Nigerian colonial government. This was also done in recognition of Nigeria's contribution to the war in that two-thirds of the men fighting in Burma in 81st and 82nd West African Divisions were Nigerians.

During 1944, two more nationalist oriented organizations were founded by Nigerians. They were the "Nigerian National Council" and "Egbe Omo Oduduwa." This brought the number of Nigerian-controlled, politically-oriented organizations to four in that country; the other two being the Nigerian Reconstruction Group founded in 1942 and the "Trade Union Congress of Nigeria" founded in 1943.

In Sierra Leone, a large-scale irrigation and drainage program was begun to increase rice production. In the field of education, several hundred local women teachers were sent to England for further education along with a contingent of young women who were to study nursing. At home, the various missionary schools, with government assistance, increased their effort to decrease adult illiteracy.

In Gambia, as in Nigeria, the Africanization of the colonial government progressed with the restructuring of the four-man legislative advisory council. Henceforth, one white member would be elected while one white member and two black members would be appointed by the governor. Another facet of Africanization was the establishment of a government-sponsored annual meeting of the local tribal chiefs to discuss and give advice on matters of local concern.

EAST AFRICA

In early 1944, the 11th KAR Division left East Africa for service in Burma. By late June, they were on the India/Burma border ready to advance into Burma.

In British East Africa, region-wide planning got underway for the eventual demobilization of the KAR to take place after the war. Emphasis was put on the reintegration of the ex-servicemen back into the peacetime economy.

An intense two-month-long eradication program was conducted against a recent locust outbreak, and labor conscription was introduced in certain areas to bring in the sisal crop.

In Kenya, the British Africanization of that colony's government got off to a very modest start with the appointment of only one Kenyan, Eliud Mathu, to the Kenyan Legislative Council. Mathu had enthusiastic backing from Kenya's black elite who formed, on their own, the Kenya African Union (KAU), for the sole purpose of supporting and advising Mathu and any successor.

FROM MODEST BEGINNING TO REBELLION

The Kenya African Union (KAU) would grow more nationalistic with time. In 1947 it would be taken over by Jomo Kenyatta, a militant nationalist, and become the political instrument from which the infamous Mau Mau Rebellion would spring.

The overall economy of Kenya was very good, but inflation was a factor and some strikes occurred as workers sought higher wages. Those strikes were generally resolved by giving the workers cost-of-living bonuses.

Two new agricultural and teacher-training schools were opened with a 50,000–pound grant under the latest Colonial Development and Welfare Act from London. Also, the day-to-day administration of grade schools in native areas was turned over to the local native councils. A further grant of 500,000 pounds was used to help provide native housing in Nairobi.

In Uganda, a six-year, five-million-pound general development plan was instigated to improve the colony's infrastructure, and a new department of the colonial administration, the Social Welfare Office, was created to coordinate African social services.

In Tanganyika, sisal production increased and the growing of pyrethrum, a plant producing natural insecticides, was expanding rapidly. Also, plans for native agriculture, soil conservation, stock breeding, water supply, new roads, new airfields, and increased native housing in Dar-es-Salaam were progressing. The production of coffee, cotton, and groundnuts was adversely affected by unfavorable weather conditions.

In British Somaliland, favorable rains helped make 1944 one of the best harvest years on record. New date plantations were begun at Horo, Hedle, and Zeliah. Advances were made in education and a welfare program for native women was instigated. The conduct of the Somali Camel Corps, though, provided a major problem for the colony. Having been forced to give up their camels in favor of armored cars, the morale of the unit was still very low. When rumors circulated in June that the Corps might be sent out of Somaliland, about 150 members of the Corps mutinied, stole arms and ammunition from the arms magazine, and disappeared into the bush. Some local civilians joined in looting the magazine and barracks. Later, 69 of the corpsmen returned or were captured and court-marshaled. By now, though, the value of the Corps was very much in doubt. The Corps was reconstituted with assurances that it would not leave British Somaliland, but a decision on its future usefulness was remanded to the British War Office in London. Two major complaints from the Corpsmen were that they feared their religion and life-style would be forcibly altered by serving in foreign lands and, furthermore, they thought their uniforms were degrading compared to the uniforms of other colonial forces.

In the Mauritius Island Group, a hurricane in April damaged the sugar cane crop which had already been diminished because so much sugar cane land had been converted to the use of growing food. Strikes had plagued the local economy, so a new labor law was enacted establishing labor courts to settle such problems. A new factory for the production of yeast was established with government funds.

In the Seychelles Island Group, plans were underway for an expected increase in postwar settlement and a land reclamation program was underway at Port Victoria. Educational and medical services were also increased.

ETHIOPIA AND OCCUPIED ITALIAN EAST AFRICA

In Ethiopia, the government of Haile Selassie was now quite stable and the economy beginning to prosper. Exports, especially coffee, increased to a level higher than that before the Italian occupation. The Ethiopian police were functioning efficiently and the armed forces were loyal to the government and slowly modernizing. In this respect, the United States gave the Ethiopian Air Force four new aircraft under Lend-Lease. Also, an American economic mission arrived with the goal of modernizing the Addis Ababa–Djibouti Railroad. It was hoped in Addis Ababa that the Americans might, one day, take control of the railroad from the French.

In British-occupied Eritrea, efforts were underway to make this, the richest of the former Italian colonies, once again economically self-sufficient. Most of the original agricultural and industrial enterprises were operating again and new ventures were in the offing. In western Eritrea, bandits became a problem so the Sudanese Defense Force, one of the main occupation forces in the colony, conducted a well-organized sweep of the area during June to restore law and order. Several hundred Eritreans were arrested and sentenced for bandit-related activities.

In British-occupied Italian Somaliland, the economy had also stabilized and efforts were underway to make that colony, like Eritrea, self-supporting. Agricultural production, heretofore a problem, had improved to the point where very little food now had to be imported. Some 4,000 Italians remained in the colony and had been successfully integrated into the economy. To improve the colony's infrastructure and communications, roads to Kenya and British Somaliland were improved and new ferries were established across the Juba River.

With regards to electronic communications, which had long been inadequate in this part of East Africa, the British Army established a very unique organization called the Somaliland Signals Squadron. "Somaliland Signals," as it was called, was based in Mogadishu and was responsible for establishing and operating radio and telephone communications throughout the region, connecting points as far away as Aden and Nairobi. They also extended such services into remote areas such as the Ogaden Desert. Because of the many different nationalities and languages encompassed in their communication system, the Somaliland Signals was, of necessity, one of the most ethnically mixed units in the British Army. Within its ranks were British, Frenchmen, Italians, South Africans, Rhodesians, Canadians, Somalis, Ethiopians, Kenyans, Adenese, and Mauritians. At Hargeisa, British Somaliland, one of the communications systems' hubs, there were four separate mess halls to accommodate the diets of the different nationalities working there.

In The Sudan, nationalism was stirring ever more forcefully. During 1944, a radical political organization was formed called the "Sudan Movement for National Liberation," known to the Sudanese as "Ashiqqua." This marked the second nationalist group in the colony, the first being the "National Unionist Party" founded in 1942. Neither of these organizations were welcomed by the joint British and Egyptian colonial administration.

JEWS TO AFRICA—AGAIN

On June 28, 1944, the British government in London announced that it was considering a plan to create a new homeland for European refugees somewhere in the former Italian African colonies. This was greeted with mixed emotions in Eritrea, Italian Somaliland, and Libya. As did other schemes before it, this one also came to naught.

BURMA

In the Imphal area of west-central Burma, that front was relatively quiet during the first three months of 1944, although the Japanese were expected to make a major effort there soon in an attempt to invade India.

Further north, American General Joseph Stilwell's two American-trained and equipped Chinese divisions were slugging their way through rugged mountains and jungles, building a road as they went from Ledo, India. Their objective was to eventually connect that new road with the old Burma road and open, once again, a land supply link to China. Meanwhile, the only supplies reaching China were flown over the "Hump" by American transport planes.

During June 1944, the 3rd West African Brigade was sent to Stilwell and participated in the attack on Sahmaw, which was occupied in late June. They then accompanied the British 36th Division in its difficult southward advanced toward Indaw which was not taken until December.

In the south along the Arakan coast, the 81st and 82nd West African Divisions were engaged in combat as components of the British 15th Corps under General Philip Christison. Attached to the West African divisions were several KAR battalions from East Africa. Those troops included two regiments and a battalion from the Rhodesias, four battalions from Nyasaland, four from Uganda, three from Tanganyika, two from Kenya, and one from British Somaliland. Also attached to the 15th Corps was a specialized unit called the "East African Scouts." They were primarily Nyasalanders who, using their natural instincts, were trained as jungle scouts to operate on the flanks of, and in advance of, the main force. They would be separated from the main body for days at a time and have to maneuver and survive on their own. Their white officers had been specially selected because they spoke the Nyasalanders' language and had had experience commanding askaris in the past.

Christison's 15th Corps had been inching its way along the Arakan coast since November, fighting difficult terrain, stubborn Japanese rear-guard actions, and the fact that many white officers had become sick with tropical diseases. Their main objective was to capture the port of Akyab and its airfields, eighty miles distant from the India/Burma border. From Akyab, Rangoon could be bombed. A large-scale amphibious operation along the Arakan coast had been planned by the Allies which would link up with the advancing 15th Corps and, together, march on to possibly capture Rangoon. But in mid-January this ambitious plan was called off because of a shortage of landing craft. All available Allied landing craft were needed for the cross-channel invasion of Europe scheduled for May 1944. This relegated the advance under way by the 15th Corps to a lesser importance in the overall Allied planning in Burma. From this point, on the 15th Corps would serve, as it had originally, as a diversionary force drawing Japanese troops away from the other fronts in Burma and being a threat to Rangoon.

On January 9, the men of the 15th Corps captured the small port city of Maungdaw, sixty miles from Akyab. In three month's effort they had advanced only twenty miles.

On February 6, the Japanese launched a strong counterattack at Maungdaw by circling around the Allies' front and striking the 15th Corps in the rear. For a while they were able to surround a large part of the Allied force at the village of Sinzwey. But the Allies, supplied only by air drop, held out. Up to this time the West Africans had suffered no combat casualties, but on the 20th a company commander and several askaris were killed in action along the Pi Chuang River. On February 25, the 81st West African Division attacked the Japanese at the village of Kyauktaw, threatening their flank; on the 26th, the Japanese called off their attacks and withdrew. The encirclement of Sinzwey was broken. This was a significant victory for the men of the 15th Corps. On February 29, the important Ngakyeduak Pass was taken and on March 2, the 81st West Africans attacked and captured the village of Apaukwa. The Japanese counterattacked, though, and the men of the 81st were driven out of Apaukwa. Along the Pi Chuang River the East African Scouts were badly mauled in several fierce clashes with Japanese forces and reduced to a little over 100 men. The survivors were withdrawn from combat and sent to Ceylon where the unit was disbanded. No more scout units were formed because it was determined that they were too vulnerable.

On March 5, Christison's Corps had recovered enough to resume the offensive and that day began an advance south from Maungdaw toward the mouth of the Naaf River.

On March 8, strong Japanese forces launched their long-anticipated invasion of India in the Imphal area 200 miles north of the Arakan front. The main activity on the Burma front was now focused there. For the next three months, a complex series of battles erupted throughout the Imphal area during which the British forces and their Indian allies were successful in thwarting the planned Japanese invasion of India. This was accomplished by mid-May, but the Japanese did not withdraw and fighting there continued well into July.

All the while the 15th Corps was advancing slowly on the Arakan front. On March 11, the Corps' 7th Indian Division took Buthidaung a few miles inland from Maungdaw and the next day routed the Japanese from Razibil. The 15th Corps then advanced in a line paralleling the coast in three columns, with the 25th Indian Division on the coast, the 82nd West African Division in the center, and the 81st West African Division on the left flank. The Allied advance again progressed very slowly. In late March, the Japanese launched a strong counterattack that forced the Allies to give ground. For a while the result of the battle was in doubt, and there was genuine fear that Christison's Indians and Africans could not hold on. If the Japanese broke through the 15th Corps's defenses, there was nothing to stop them from advancing all the way into India and threatening the important Allied supply base at Chittagong. But the men of the 15th held the line and the Japanese attack eventually petered out. By the first week in April the Arakan front had stabilized. The fighting at Imphal, though, was at its height and at this time the 15th Corps' 7th Indian Division, which was held in reserve, was suddenly air lifted to Imphal to meet an emergency situation there. This reduced the strength of the 15th Corps by about 25%. Now reduced in strength the Corps halted its advance and set up a defensive line.

Then, in early June, the annual monsoon rains began again and military activity over most of Burma decreased. But the 15th Corps was again ordered on the attack to make what progress they could, considering the weather and the fact that the 7th Indian Division had not, as yet, been returned. Their objective, once again, was Akyab.

AFRICANS BECOME "CHINDITS"

There was yet another Allied force operating in Burma officially known as the "British Long-Range Penetration Group" but nicknamed the "Chindits" after a mythical Hindu figure. This force was made up of specially selected men and commanded by General Orde Wingate, a specialist in unconventional warfare and guerilla operations. Wingate had commanded irregular troops, most of them Africans, in Ethiopia in 1941. Wingate and his Chindits didn't fight on any of the Burma fronts. Rather, they were airlifted into the interior of Burma, usually by gliders, captured airfields and used them as bases of operation to spread out in different directions to cut Japanese lines of supply and communications.

In February, the 3rd Nigerian Brigade was attached to the Chindits and given a rapid training course in their way of fighting. In mid-March, half of the unit, the 6th Battalion, was airlifted deep inside Japanese-held territory to Aberdeen Air Field and given the task of guarding that base. In early April, they were again airlifted to White City Air Field and charged with guarding that post. At White City they promptly became involved in a three-day fire-fight with attacking Japanese forces and, together with Gurkha troops, successfully fought off the attacks. On April 11, the other half of the 3rd Nigerian Brigade, the 7th Battalion, arrived at White City as reinforcements. The next day, the Nigerians and Gurkhas counterattacked and forced the Japanese out of the nearby village of Mawlu. On the 14th, the Japanese attacked again but were beaten off with the help of Allied aircraft.

In early May, the 3rd Nigerian Brigade marched overland to another Chindit base at Hopin and took up defensive positions at a strategic location ten miles from the base. On May 14, the Japanese attack the Hopin base and the Nigerians made a forced march overland to help drive off the attackers. The same thing happened on May 23 and the Nigerians, once again, came to the rescue. By July, however, most of the other Chindit units that had been in the field longer were decimated by military losses and tropical diseases and were flow out. That left the 3rd Nigerians and a British brigade to defend Hopin alone. Fortunately, the Japanese did not attack this relatively weak force and they were flown out on August 18. This ended the association of the 3rd Nigerians with the Chindits.

AIR ROUTES ACROSS AFRICA

The two main east-west air routes across Africa, one across North Africa and the other the old Cannonball Route across central Africa, continued to be important links in the worldwide Allied supply and communications system. On February 6, the

American's Army Air Transport Command (ATC) announced that it was now providing regular scheduled military air service all the way from New York City to Calcutta, India. Both of the African routes were a part of this system.

The U. S. Navy's Naval Air Transport System (NATS) was also using the trans-African routes more, and as more military transport planes became available to both ATC and NATS, contracts with American commercial carriers were terminated. This was not always the case, though. In June, Eastern Air Lines' Military Transport Division was awarded a contract to provide scheduled military air service on the Natal-Ascension Island-Accra route. This lasted only five months, however, when the military services took over the route.

Nigerian natives swinging their axes in unison as they work on a construction project at an ATC airfield in Nigeria in 1944.

The British and French, too, were continually expanding their air services in Africa and new airports were built and existing ones were expanded.

SOUTH AFRICA

The political scene in South Africa was now the most stable it had been during the war. The November 1943, provincial elections had given Smuts and his supporters a strong majority in Parliament, and with the Allies winning on all fronts and the South African economy strong, there were few troublesome foreign policy questions to address. When the new Parliament met in January, most of the issues brought before it pertained to domestic affairs.

Prime Minister Smuts, now 74 years old, relinquished some of his authority to his Deputy Prime Minister, J. H. Hofmeyr, who was both legally and politically Smuts' designated successor. Smuts, with his worldwide fame and international connections, retained control of foreign policy and military affairs, while Hofmeyr took over most of the domestic issues.

The economy was still very strong and getting stronger. This was due, in part, to the fact that the South Africans received a significant amount of new business supplying war materials to Burma.

Race relations were good. With many blacks in the work force and prosperity upon the land, a mutual dependency and respect evolved that was quite rare within South African society. This was reflected in sports, in which white teams now played against black teams—a phenomenon that was unheard of before the war. There were still no integrated teams in South Africa, though.

Furthermore, the blacks were getting a larger share of the government's handouts, although, as usual, not in proportion to their numbers. In the cities, now crowded with black

President William Vacanarat Shadrach Tubman of Liberia. Tubman was elected in 1943 and took Liberia into the war. He was also credited with greatly improving the country's economy and remained President until his death in 1971.

war workers, the government provided some new and improved housing, and on the reservations, several land reclamation projects were started.

On the other side of the coin, though, it was noted that blacks were becoming more skilled and urbanized and that a problem would almost certainly arise after the war in trying to get them to return to their rural homes and prewar way of life. The white radical right lamented this development; they warned that Communist influences were on the rise among the blacks and that the purity and political control of the white race were in danger.

In South Africa's neighboring territories, the economies were good too, but not as good as in South Africa. Therefore, there was a flow of workers from these territories into South Africa seeking better jobs. This was seen by the colonial administrators as a potential postwar problem in that those who went to South Africa, and witnessed the higher standard of living there, would return home demanding reforms.

In Bechuanaland, the Colonial Development and Welfare Act provided funds for a three-year water survey, the creation of new livestock centers to assist the cattle industry, and a program to control the tsetse fly.

In Swaziland, the British government purchased 230,000 acres of European-owned land and combined it with 135,000 acres of crown land to provide new homesteads for some 27,000 landless natives. Money was also spent on roads, water supply, and other improvements preparing the land for habitation.

For the moment, nationalism was dormant in the neighboring states, except for Nyasaland. There a group of educated and reform-minded blacks formed the Nyasaland African Congress (NAC) to press the British authorities for reforms and more native participation in internal affairs. The leaders of the NAC had modest goals and were not political radicals seeking independence or even autonomy.

The Colonial Office in London, which administered Nyasaland, met some of the NAC's requests. One of the most important was that the chiefs and other local leaders in the colony's two provinces were allowed to establish local councils and, once this was accomplished, to proceed to form a unified council for the entire colony. The role of the unified council was to advise the governor on colonial matters.

BELGIAN CONGO

The economy of the Belgian Congo was still booming because of the export of minerals and other raw materials. The mineral tantalite, from which the alloy tantalum is extracted, was in greater demand than supply, so new mines were started at known deposits with the financial assistance of the colonial government. A new tin mine was also opened at Kasese.

The colonial government raised an army field hospital company which was sent to Burma to serve under British command. At Luluabourg, however, the local Congolese garrison mutinied during March over local issues, threatening both whites and educated blacks. This was strictly a local matter and there were no nationalist overtones. Educated blacks, though, did use the occasion to petition the colonial administration to recognize them as a higher class of colonial subjects.

As was happening all over Africa, the population of the Congo's major cities was increasing dramatically—in some cases doubling. But, unlike elsewhere, nationalism did not follow. There were some small strikes but, in general, the newcomers were content with the political and economic conditions that existed and were happy to have good jobs.

The first of the year saw several hundred Greek refugees arrive in the Congo. For the past three years, small numbers of Greek refugees had trickled into the Congo and were housed, at the expense of the colonial government, in a temporary refugee camp.

LIBERIA GOES TO WAR

On January 26, 1944, Liberia declared war on Germany and Japan. This was a political gesture more than anything because Liberia's small 400–man army was unable to contribute militarily to the Allied cause. Actually, the country had been contributing to the Allied cause for several years by allowing Allied forces on its soil to conduct air and antisubmarine activities. The main Allied installation in the country was Roberts Air Field operated by the Americans.

With Liberia's declaration of war that left only the Spanish and Portuguese colonies in Africa, and Egypt, not at war. The rest of the continent was firmly committed to the Allied cause.

Liberia's 400–man Army parades past the presidential residence in Monrovia, the nation's capital.

SPAIN BEGINS TO COOPERATE WITH THE ALLIES

The leaders in Madrid could see the handwriting on the wall and the fact that they should begin to make amends with the Allies. Furthermore, the Allied invasion of France had forced the Germans to withdraw all German forces from the northern Spanish border, making Spain much less vulnerable to German pressures. The British and Americans welcomed the new attitude in Madrid but the Franco government was still reluctant to begin negotiations. So the Allies forced Franco's hand and, in January 1944, cut off shipments of all oil products to Spain. Within a few weeks Spain's transportation system was virtually paralyzed. The Spaniards got the message and secret negotiations began between Spanish and Allied diplomats in Madrid soon afterwards. By late April, a series of agreements had been worked out. The Spaniards agreed to recall the last remnants of the all-volunteer Spanish "Blue Division," which had been fighting on the eastern front since 1942, and to end recruitment in Spain for the German Army's Spanish Legion, which also was fighting in the east. Furthermore, Spain agreed to turn over to the Allies twelve of the fourteen Italian merchant ships interned in Spanish harbors at the time of the Italian surrender. The remaining two ships were leased to the Spaniards for a time. Disposition of the six Italian warships (one cruiser, three destroyers, and two torpedo boats) would be determined at a later date. Spain also agreed to reduce shipments of wolfram ore (tungsten) to Germany.

Pertaining to Africa, the Spaniards agreed to close the German consulate at Tangier and ask its staff, along with the Japanese Military Attache there, to leave Spanish territory. Other known Axis spies and agents in Tangier, Spanish Morocco, and other Spanish territories would also be expelled.

It was further agreed that these concessions would not be revealed in either the Spanish or Allied medias and that the Spanish people would be told only that Madrid and the Allies were negotiating on economic matters. Giving credibility to this claim economic issues were addressed within the framework of the negotiations, which opened up certain business opportunities to the American, but not to the British.

In June, the Spaniards made further concessions, allowing Allied military aircraft to overfly all Spanish coastal waters and all of Spanish Morocco and the Canary Islands pursuing their antisubmarine activities. Furthermore, all Spanish commercial airports were opened to American air line companies.

In return for these concessions, American and British oil began to flow once again to Spain and the Allies agreed to respect Spain's neutrality.

MOSLEM AFRICA

In the Moslem parts of Africa, there was a noticeable change of attitude among the local leaders and the population in general. In 1940–41, the attitude of most Moslems in both Africa and the Middle East favored the Axis. This was stimulated by the fact that the Axis armies were victoriously on the march against the Moslem world's traditional oppressors, and the Axis countries were actively wooing the Arabs with propaganda and had given sanctuary to several of their prominent leaders. Anti-west sentiment was also increased in the late summer of 1941, when the Westerners forged an alliance with godless communism.

By 1944 this had changed. The Axis was in retreat and no longer propagandizing the Arab world. Furthermore, it was becoming clear that the Allies would win the war and that the old colonial system would remain, more-or-less, intact. What's more, the Arab lands were relatively prosperous and the colonial powers were showing a new willingness to make meaningful concessions beneficial to their colonial subjects. And finally, Arab nationalist leaders and organizations were coming to the fore promising better things for the future. The attitude of the Moslem world in 1944 could be summed up as one of being more hopeful of positive changes in the near future.

UNITED STATES AND AFRICA

In early 1944, the State Department created an African Department in recognition of the emerging importance of that continent. The department was headed by Henry S. Villard, an experienced diplomat with considerable knowledge of Africa. This, of course, was welcomed by nationalists all over Africa but looked upon with some concern by the British, French, and other colonial powers.

Also about this time, President Roosevelt made an offhand remark that he felt the French would be better off if they gave up their colonial empire after the war. This comment was repeated in the press and was most unwelcome by the French. It proved to be one more barb in the relationship between Roosevelt and de Gaulle. In fact, it strengthened de Gaulle's position at home because most Frenchmen felt, like de Gaulle, that giving up the empire was unthinkable and that the Americans should mind their own business.

On June 5, the day after Rome fell, Roosevelt went on American radio giving his first Fireside Chat of 1944. In describing the fighting in Italy, he praised the efforts of the Americans and British and went on to mention the various Allies; "... the gallant Canadians. The fighting New Zealanders from the far South Pacific, the courageous French and the French Moroccans, the South Africans, the Poles and the East Indians." It was noted in various parts of Africa that he left out the Algerians, Tunisians, and all of the black Africans.

Chapter 19
WAR ABROAD, PROSPERITY AND POLITICS AT HOME (JULY–DECEMBER 1944)
THE STIRRING OF AFRICAN NATIONALISM

The latter part of 1944 saw Africans fighting in Italy and Burma and, as of August 1944, in France.

In Africa, there was a high degree of prosperity and many Africans of all races were enjoying a level of economic well-being that they had never seen before. This phenomenon was especially dynamic for Africa's blacks because jobs, educational opportunities, and worldly experiences had opened to them on a broad scale. They had flocked to the cities in large numbers to take war jobs and acquire new skills and, in the process, learned of amenities and opportunities that were nonexistent in their villages and rural homes. Nearly everyone could sense that this was an irreversible trend, and that the future of postwar Africa would be very different than before. For the moment, the main focus of most individuals was still to win the war, but there were those in Africa who were planning ahead.

ITALY

By July, the fighting in Italy was north of Rome and the Germans were still strong and capable of establishing one major defense line after the other. Each one had to be breached by the Allies with steel, courage, and blood.

On July 2, troops of General Juin's French Expeditionary Corps, now veterans of one year of combat in Italy, captured Sovicille and continued their advance on Siena. To their east, the South African 6th Armoured Division, a part of the British 8th Army, occupied Sinalunga.

On July 3, General Juin's 3rd Algerians captured the major city of Siena. But southeast of Leghorn, German opposition stiffened and the Allied advance slowed. The German defenses in Italy were somewhat weaker than before because several important units had been withdrawn to northern France to counter the Allied invasion at Normandy.

After taking Siena, the 3rd Algerians were withdrawn from the front and sent to Naples for rest and rehabilitation. They would not return to the Italian front. Shortly, Juin's entire French Expeditionary Force would be withdrawn from Italy and made ready for "Operation Dragoon" (formerly Operation Anvil—the name had been changed because the Allies believed the Axis had learned the meaning of Anvil), the invasion of southern France. The 3rd Algerians were replaced in the line by the French 4th Mountain Division. That division then participated in the Allied advance and on July 13, captured the town of San Gimignano. The 2nd Moroccan Division, working closely with the 4th Mountain Division, advanced on Castellina, south of Leghorn, and captured the town on the 15th. On July 17, 18 and 19, Juin's entire force advanced all along the line, and on his right flank the British 8th Army kept pace.

On July 20, the main body of Juin's force began to withdraw from the front and were taken to Naples and/or the Taranto/Brindisi area. There they were given rest and rehabilitation and made ready for Dragoon. This ended the presence of the North Africans in Italy. With the French went one-third of the U.S. 5th Army's artillery which was also needed for Dragoon.

That same day the 6th South Africans captured two strategic towns in central Italy, which opened the way for other troops of the British 8th Army to surge into the strategic Arno River Valley.

An American Lend-Lease Sherman tank being used by the South African 6th Armoured Division in Italy crosses a river in Italy on an American-made Lend-Lease Bailey Bridge.

By August 25, all was ready for the attack on the "Arno River Line," which was to be led by the Canadian 1st Corps and the Polish 2nd Corps of the British 8th Army.

To replace the withdrawing French forces, elements of the 6th South Africans and the 2nd New Zealanders temporarily took over their positions at the front.

The advance continued without the French and on July 22, the 6th South Africans took two strategic heights near the Greve River and established a bridgehead on the other side. During the last days of July, the South Africans fought a protracted battle with the Germans at Improneta, just south of Florence. The South Africans prevailed and on August 4 they reached the southern suburbs of Florence—the first Allied unit to enter that city. The South Africans continued to advance through the city's streets and were then able to secure the portion of the city south of the Arno River. In a stroke of good fortune, a bridge across the Arno was captured by the South Africans when advance units chased off the German demolition crew that was about to destroy it. South African tanks raced across the bridge and established a small bridgehead on the northern bank in the heart of the city.

But there, along the Arno, the Allied advance halted. The Germans had build yet another strong defense line, and behind it, the more formidable Gothic Line. In face of such defenses, the Allies had to halt, regroup, and bring up reinforcements before attempting to resume the attack. Brought into the line at this time was the all-black U.S. 92nd Infantry Division. They were assigned to a segment of the front formerly held by the French.

AUGUST 15, 1944: SOUTHERN FRANCE INVADED

On August 15, the long-awaited invasion of Southern France, Operation Dragoon, began. It was a massive operation consisting of over 2,000 transports and landing craft, 300 warships, tens of thousands of troops, and thousands of aircraft.

French Moroccan Commandos and American Army troops landed in the first waves in the Cannes–Toulon area under the command of American General Alexander M. Patch. Patch's command, the U.S. 7th Army, consisted of the U.S. Army's 6th Corps , the U.S. First Airborne Task Force, a force of French Moroccan Commandos, and the French Army "B" under General Jean de Lattre de Tassigny. The latter consisted of the 1st French Armoured Division equipped with American tanks, the 2nd and 4th Moroccan Infantry Divisions, 3rd Algerian Infantry Division with Tunisian detachments, and the 9th French Colonial Infantry Division consisting mostly of Equatorial and West Africans.

The Allies had air and sea superiority and the German coastal defenses were almost nonexistent. The only significant German opposition came from a patrol boat which sank the American destroyer "Somers" in the darkness hours on the morning of August 15. Upon landing the first wave, Allied forces established a secure beachhead and the next day Tassigny's forces came ashore. The Allied forces then fanned out to the east toward Nice, to the west toward Toulon and Marseilles, to the northwest toward Avignon in the Rhone River Valley, and to the north toward Digne. In the big cities and in some rural areas French resistance fighters harassed the German defenders, attacking their supply columns, disrupting communications, and performing other guerilla-type activities. Opposing the Allies was the weak and outnumbered German 19th Army under General Friedrich Wiese. Wiese's Army was the only major German force in southern

France and was spread out very thinly from the Spanish to the Italian border.

The overall Allied plan was for Patch's force to secure the French Mediterranean ports of Toulon, Marseilles, and Nice as ports of supply, then march northward through central France, forcing the weak German garrisons on either side of them to withdraw or be bypassed and cut off. Once in the north, Patch's 7th Army would link up with the Allied forces coming in from Normandy, and at that point, de Tassigny's French forces would be detached from Patch's force, join with the French forces operating in the north, and take over the southernmost portion of the massive Allied front as it marched into Germany. At that point, American forces would be on de Tassigny's northern flank and the Swiss border on his southern flank.

By August 17, Patch's 7th Army had enlarged their beachhead along the southern coast of France to a width of fifty miles, and his troops were advancing against light opposition on Toulon and Marseilles. French Moroccan forces were in the lead.

On that same day, in northern France, General Patton's 3rd Army had succeeded in forcing a large-scale German retreat from the Falaise Pocket and had reached a point forty miles west of Paris. About this time the French 2nd Armoured Division, under General Leclerc, equipped with American Lend-Lease tanks, had come ashore at Normandy and was rushed to the front to participate in the liberation of Paris. It would be this force that would eventually link up with de Tassigny's force east of Paris.

By August 20, de Tassigny's forces reached the outskirts of Toulon and on the 22nd a combined force of American, Frenchmen, Moroccans, and Algerians entered the suburbs of Marseilles and prepared for a final assault on the city center. It was here that the Germans put up their strongest opposition.

On the 21, the Germans forcibly removed Marshal Petain and his government from Vichy and took them to Belfort, France and later to Germany. By now, Petain's government had very little authority in France, but what authority it did have the Germans wanted to retain unto themselves. With Allied forces now in southern France there was the possibility that Petain might flee to the south and join the Allies.

On August 23, the German garrison on the offshore island of Proquerolles surrendered to a U.S. Naval force that was poised to bombard the island. The Americans were surprised to find that many of the "German" soldiers were, in fact, Armenians, who had joined the German Army when German troops were deep inside the Soviet Union. The enemy soldiers were removed and a contingent of French colonial troops occupied the island.

On August 25, Paris was liberated by General Leclerc's 2nd French Armored Division and the U.S. 4th Infantry Division. That evening de Gaulle entered the city to a tumultuous welcome by the citizenry. That same day, American troops under General Patch captured Avignon, 55 miles northwest of Marseilles.

Troops of the 3rd Algerian Infantry Division marching northward from Marseilles. There was no appreciable German opposition so they could march in formation.

By the 28th, both Toulon and Marseilles were in Allied hands after some hard fighting at both locations. At Toulon it was the 9th French Colonials that led the attack and accepted the German surrender while at Marseilles the 3rd Algerians, accompanied by the 1st American Armored Division, worked together to defeat the German defenders there. While mopping up operations were being undertaken in Toulon and Marseilles, the main body of Patch's 7th Army began to march in force northward up the Rhone River Valley. The American forces marched up the east bank and the French forces up the west bank. There was very little German opposition.

While most of Patch's forces were marching up the Rhone, a smaller force captured the port city of Nice on September 1. The capture of the French Mediterranean ports all but ended the need of the ports in French North Africa to continue serving as supply ports.

On September 2, de Tassigny's troops, marching in the lead of Patch's troops, liberated the city of Lyon, 165 miles north of Marseilles. And the march up the Rhone River Valley continued.

To the east, along the French-Italian frontier, six newly arrived battalions of French West and Equatorial Africans were stationed to guard Patch's eastern flank. This was a quiet front and neither side expected the other to launch a major attack here. In December, when the harsh winter weather set in, the Africans were relieved and given occupation duties on the French Riviera.

In northern France, Allied forces had entered Luxembourg and, for the first time, on September 11, crossed the German border at the village of Stalzemberg. That same day, lead elements of Patch's 7th Army linked up with elements of Leclerc's 2nd French Armoured Division at the village of Sombernon about 150 miles southeast of Paris. The Allied plans were proceeding as scheduled. A new Allied Army group, under the command of American General Jacob Devers, was created. It would be centered in the Belfort area of France and covered the Allied front down to the Swiss border. This new force, designated as the American 6th Army Group, was activated on September 15 and was made up primarily of Patch's 7th Army and de Tassigny's French Army B, which would be reinforced by Leclerc's 2nd French Armoured Division and redesignated the French 1st Army. De Tassigny was replaced by French General Jean de Lattre. Within days, the 6th Army Group was in position anchoring the southern end of the Allied front and ready to advance eastward. It appeared that Africans would soon be fighting in Germany.

COLONIAL POWS RELEASED BY WESTERN ALLIES AND SOVIETS

During July and August, both the Western Allies and Soviets advanced so rapidly into Europe that the Germans did not have time or the resources to transport prisoners of war to the rear. Subsequently, these men were liberated by the advancing Allied armies. In France, several thousand French colonial soldiers were liberated in both northern and southern France. On one occasion 400 French colonial soldiers were liberated by the French resistance when they commandeered a train near Salbis in southern France. The soldiers temporarily joined the resistance fighters until contact was made with Patch's troops.

The colonial soldiers were reincorporated into their respective armies but not used in combat, because most of them had been incarcerated for four years and did not have adequate training in the latest weapons and tactics. Some of them were put into labor battalions and others simply released and sent home or allowed to drift to Paris. Still others were made POW camp guards. This proved to be a misfortune for the German POWs, because now the colonial troops retaliated in kind against the German POWs for the treatment they had received at the hands of their German captors. This, of course, was done while their officers and other guards were not watching.

The few colonial soldiers liberated by the Soviets were all put into labor battalions and, according to later accounts, were treated as badly as they had been in German captivity.

NORTH AFRICA

To support Operation Dragoon, North Africa was once again used as a staging area. Only the ports in the Oran area of Algeria were used for this operation. To get the men and equipment of Operation Dragoon to southern France, six convoys were created. Two of those convoys originated from the Oran area, two from Italy, and two from the Corsica/ Sardinia area. The Oran convoys carried the French 2nd Corps. By now, threats to such convoys by enemy submarines were almost nonexistent. Having lost most of their safe ports in the Mediterranean, all of the remaining German submarines had been withdrawn from the Mediterranean, never to return.

At the other end of the Mediterranean the Germans found their position in Greece untenable due to the advances of the Soviet Union's Red Army to the north, so on August 26, Hitler gave the order to evacuate all of Greece. Once this became known to the Allies, the British quickly gathered forces in Egypt and the Middle East to send to Greece in the wake of the German withdrawal. Therefore, the ports of Egypt served one last time as staging areas. In the occupation of Greece, however, there were no large African units involved.

During the latter part of September, the Germans evacuated the Mediterranean island of Crete and the Greek Aegean Islands. These actions lessened further the threat of enemy actions toward North Africa.

ALGIERS

During July and August, the Provisional government of France still resided in Algiers even though large tracts of Metropolitan France had been liberated by the Allies. The French plans were to not move the government until Paris was liberated. In the meantime there was some fence-mending to do with the Americans. De Gaulle was well aware of Roosevelt's negative opinion of him personally but, in the last year, de Gaulle's star had soared. He had become the undisputed leader of the Fighting French and his armed forces were growing stronger by the day and proving their worth on the battlefield. Therefore, de Gaulle could now deal with the Roosevelt Administration from a position of strength. Under these conditions, de Gaulle went to the United States in early July, and on July 6 met with Roosevelt and other American leaders in Washington. It was a difficult meeting for both sides, but each realized they needed the other for the good of the cause. Despite their personal differences Roosevelt and de Gaulle came to several agreements. These agreements were that the United States would continue to supply the French with large amounts of Lend-Lease materials, and the American government would extend de facto recognition to de Gaulle's Provisional government as the government of France in the immediate future; they would extend formal recognition once the government was installed in Paris. De Gaulle then departed and returned to Algiers via Canada and England. Accordingly, on July 11, the United States extended de facto recognition to de Gaulle's government. Other Allied governments soon followed suit.

Having gained recognition for the United States and others, the French Provisional government in Algiers, on August 9, declared the Vichy government of Marshal Petain null and void. The liberation of Paris was near and this action legally cleared the way for the Provisional government to take over the reigns of power. On August 25, Paris was liberated and on the 31st, de Gaulle's government began its transfer from Algiers.

EGYPT—YUGOSLAVIA—GREECE—PALESTINE

During the summer of 1944, some 35,000 Yugoslav refugees fled to Italy as the Axis Powers began to lose their grip on Yugoslavia. About 27,000 of these people were sent to Egypt and placed in refugee camps in and around Cairo where it was easier to care for them than in war-torn Italy. They remained there until after the war under the care of the recently formed United Nations Relief and Rehabilitation Administration (UNRRA).

In Cairo, the Greek government-in-exile, which had been in the city for about a year, was in trouble. In March 1943, a group of moderate and left-wing Greek politicians in German-occupied Athens produced a manifesto stating that King George II must not return to Greece after the war until a nationwide referendum was held on that issue. King George had created some bitter enemies among the moderates and leftists in Greece in the late 1930s when he appointed a right-wing and ultra-royalist military leader, General Joannes Metaxas, as premier. Metaxas then created an oppressive right-wing dictatorship. When Greece was invaded by Italy in October 1940, Metaxas had successfully united the Greeks, albeit temporarily, to oppose the Italians. Greece, though, was conquered by the Axis and King George fled to Africa. Metaxas died of natural causes in January 1941. Under the occupation, the Greek political scene fell into disarray and the Axis partners who occupied Greece (Germany, Italy, and Bulgaria) were happy to keep it that way. From their point of view, it was better that the Greeks fought each other than be united against the Axis. Thus, when it came time to withdraw, the Germans allowed the manifesto of March 1943 to be written and published, knowing it would cause further damage to the Greek political scene.

In early 1944, when it became apparent that the Germans would, in all likelihood, evacuate Greece, a civil war erupted in Greece as the most powerful guerilla force in the country, the communist-controlled ELAS, made a bid to gain control of the government. Again the Axis powers did nothing to prevent this, because an attempted communist takeover in Greece would cause major problems for the Allies. The British would have to send large numbers of troops to Greece to try to prevent a civil war and, on the international scene, the action by ELAS would pit the Soviet Union against the Western Allies. Therefore, the various factions in Greece were allowed a considerable measure of political freedom and, as expected, created a very volatile political situation in Greece. ELAS took advantage of this on March 26, 1944, by announcing the creation of a "Committee of Liberation," a forerunner to a communist provisional government. In Cairo, five days later, communist members of the government-in-exile (who had been brought into the government in an effort to gain some sort of unity) announced their support for the new Committee and demanded that the current Greek Premier, Emmanual Tsouderos, resign and that the King abdicate in favor of a regent. This, of course, split the Greek government-in-exile apart and the shock sent political reverberations down through the entire Greek political scene in Cairo and into to the Greek armed forces stationed in Egypt. The Greek soldiers and sailors, too, were bitterly divided and fought among themselves. For several days, a mini-civil war raged in Egypt among the Greek factions until the British sent in troops to restore order. Several people were injured but, fortunately, no one was killed.

As the British restored order, King George drastically restructured his government-in-exile during April in an attempt to bring about some sort of reconciliation. Tsouderos resigned and George Papandreou, leader of the leftist Social Democrat Party, was brought from Greece to become Premier. Most of the ministerial posts were assigned to individuals still in Athens. This satisfied many of the political moderates but not the communists who threatened to take control of the government by force. This and subsequent negotiations brought about a temporary truce with the Papandreou government in charge and all parties agreed to work together as long as German and Bulgarian forces remained in Greece (the Germans and Bulgarians had taken over the Italian zones of occupation at the time of Italy's surrender in 1943).

In early October 1944, the Germans evacuated Greece and British forces landed in the south of Greece. On the 12th the Germans evacuated Athens and the next day British paratroopers occupied the city. On October 16, the Papandreou government left Cairo for Athens. But during the next six weeks the situation in Greece went from bad to worse, and in early December a full-scale civil war broke out that would keep large numbers of British troops deeply engaged in Greece until well into the postwar years.

Before the Germans evacuated Greece, they sent eighty Moroccan paratroops, members of the "Deutsch-Arabische Lehrabteilung" unit formed by the German Army in 1943, on a desperate and suicidal mission into Palestine. It was hoped that they would spark a three-way rebellion there among the Palestinian Arabs, the Jews, and the British authorities. The Moroccans were, however, very demoralized and no longer eager to sacrifice themselves for the Axis cause. Upon landing in Palestine, most of them surrendered to the British.

Back in Egypt, Arab nationalism was stirring in another way. Various influential Arab leaders called an all-Arab conference together during September and October at Alexandria to pursue the long-standing dream among the Arab peoples of finding some sort of political unity. Leaders from Egypt, Iraq, Syria, Lebanon, Trans-Jordan, Saudi Arabia, and Yemen attended the conference. The delegates found enough common ground to pursue the matter further and made plans for further meetings which, in a relatively short time, would result in the creation of the "Arab League," a multi-nation organization with a strong nationalistic agenda. The Arab League was to play a major role in bringing about the independence of several Arab lands in the postwar years.

EGYPT GAINS STATUS

During the course of the war, the country of Egypt had taken on a new importance on the world economic and political stage. One thing that brought this about was the fact that Cairo had become the political crossroads of the Arab world and that the Egyptian government's independent, and often troublesome, stand against the British had become admired by Arabs in other colonial lands. Furthermore, Cairo had emerged as the most important air hub in the Middle East, which brought a new measure of economic importance to that city. All through the war the airfields around Cairo had been of great importance to the Allies. The Americans had aided in this endeavor by building a large new airfield, Payne Field, to help handle the increased air activity. Now, with the Axis forces pulling out of the Balkans as well as being forced back in Italy, air traffic from Cairo to Europe increased. This brought the Egyptians into political and economic contact with more governments, people, and markets than ever before and it was especially true with regard to the Soviet Union. It was becoming obvious that the Soviet Union would, in the postwar years, become much more influential in the Balkans and the Middle East and that Cairo would become the Soviet Union's gateway to all of Africa. This was a bittersweet revelation in Cairo because the Egyptian government had, ever since it gained independence in the 1930s, avoided establishing diplomatic relations with the godless communist. But now, circumstances dictated that that position had to be changed. Therefore, in the latter months of 1944, the Egyptians and Soviets began a series of negotiations that led to the establishment of normal diplomatic relations. At the same time, the two parties concluded a treaty guaranteeing not to interfere in each others' internal affairs.

On November 6, an ugly incident occurred in Cairo when two assailants shot and killed Lord Walter E. G. Moyne, the British Resident Minister for the Middle East. Moyne was gunned down as he stepped out of his automobile at his residence. The gunmen, Palestinian Jews, were apprehended and convicted of the crime. Zionist organizations disavowed the assassins and expressed regret for the incident. This act was an offshoot of the political turmoil that was beginning to brew in Palestine.

THE "JEWISH BRIGADE" AND "THE INDEPENDENT ARAB BRIGADE"

Small Jewish units had, for several years, fought with distinction in the British Army, so during September 1944 the British created an enlarged all-Jewish unit known as the "Jewish Brigade." Most of its members were Palestinian Jews. The Brigade was commanded by a Jewish Brigadier General and all of its members wore the Star of David. This action was very unpopular in the Arab world because the British were obviously providing Jews with military training that could benefit the Jews of Palestine in any future struggle with the Palestinian Arabs. It was also one of the factors that brought about the all-Arab conference in Alexandria later that month.

The Germans saw in the British action a way to enhance their standing among the Arabs by creating a counter-organization, an all-Arab unit, within the German Army. Small Arab units had already existed within the German Army, so during November these units, along with new Arab recruits, were formed into an enlarged unit called "The Independent Arab Brigade." The all-Arab unit had more propaganda value than military value in that the Germans could now show that they, along with their Arab allies, stood together against a British-sponsored Jewish takeover of Palestine.

BURMA

In far away Burma, the battle for Imphal had, by July, been won by the Allies and the Japanese were in retreat into the mountains of eastern Burma. Lord Louis Mountbatten, Supreme Allied Commander in Southeast Asia, ordered most of this troops to break off contact and take a well-deserved rest. At the same time, though, he ordered the 11th KAR Division, the 5th Indian Division, and the irregular Lushai Brigade to pursue the Japanese, harass them, and gain as much ground as possible to the east of Imphal in preparation for a planned counteroffensive into central Burma. The Japanese retreated down the mountainous road southeast from Imphal and made no attempted stands in the mountains. But, as they emerged into the eastern foothills, they made a determined stand at the town of Tamu on the Kabaw River, 45 miles southeast of Imphal and on the India/Burma border. This was on August 5, with the monsoon rains coming down. The 11th KAR, 5th Indian and Lushai brigade went on the attack and, against suicidal Japanese resistance, managed to occupy the town on the 6th. This was an important victory. From the nearby mountain tops the Allied troops could see into the great central plain of Burma. Tamu provided an ideal jumping-off point for the forthcoming British offensive.

General Slim, Commander of the British 14th Army, ordered the men of the Tamu force to dig in and hold it for future use. Unfortunately, by now the monsoon rains had made the mountainous road leading back to Imphal impassible, cutting off all supplies. The troops at Tamu, therefore, had to be supplied by air drops and could not count on receiving any significant number of reinforcements. The weather and occasional Japanese raids made conditions at Tamu miserable. Sleep was hard to come by and the prolonged exposure of the KAR men to the elements increased the number of malaria and scrub-typhus cases. During August, about 1,000 KAR men became medical casualties at Tamu. Their suffering did not go unnoticed. On August 31, General Slim's order of the day praised the men of the 11th KAR for their fighting quality.

By early September, the Tamu force had been sufficiently resupplied and reinforced and was now ordered to advance southward, despite the monsoons, down the Kabaw Valley road in order to secure more land for the coming offensive. All indications were that the Japanese had abandoned the valley. On September 8, the KAR men crossed the 500-yard-wide rain-swollen Kabaw River, a tributary of the Chindwin River, becoming the first Allied troops to do so.

The Chindwin River is a major eastern tributary to the Irrawaddy River, the main north-south river of Burma which, in turn, is the main north-south transportation and communications channel of all Burma. An Allied advance down the Chindwin to the Irrawaddy would cut the main north-south communications and supply link for the Japanese in northern Burma.

On September 20, the 26th Brigade of the KAR force was taken out of the line and ordered back to Tamu for rest and refitting. To get there they had to build sections of corduroy (log) roads because the valley road had become impassible in places due to the rains. The remainder of the KAR unit, along with the Indians and the Lushai Brigade, continued to advance down the Kabaw Valley, all the while being supplied by air drops. Japanese resistance was very light. General Kimura, Commander of the Burmese Area Army, was conserving his strength and planning to make a stand at a time and place of his own choosing. He too, like the Tamu force, had been cut off from his main source of supply but not by the monsoon rains. Kimura's Burmese Area Army, as well as most other major Japanese units in Southeast Asia, had been cut off from Japan due to the very successful activities of the U.S. Navy in the western Pacific. American submarines, warships, and aircraft had all but halted Japanese sea traffic south of the home islands.

The rain and mud in west-central Burma made movement by both sides very difficult and some Japanese units were unable to retreat. Since they were stuck in the mud and relatively harmless they were simply bypassed by the advancing Allies. Some of the enemy units encountered by the Tamu force were from the Indian National Army (INA) of the Provisional government of India, which was headed by Subhas Chandra Bose. It will be remembered that Bose formed the Provisional government of India and the INA with Japanese help and, on October 23, 1943, had declared war on the British Empire.

DECISION TAKEN ON BURMA AT QUEBEC

On the other side of the globe, at Quebec City, Canada, Churchill, Roosevelt, and other Allied leaders were meeting during September to plot the future course of the war and Burma was on the agenda. Subsequently, one of the decisions made at Quebec was that Burma should be liberated as soon as possible. Orders from the Joint Chiefs of Staff soon went out to Mountbatten's headquarters to that effect. The leaders at Quebec understood the difficulties encountered with regard to the monsoon rains and did not expect much activity until November 1944, when the monsoons subsided. This applied more to the northern front and the Arakan front along the coast, because on the central front the Tamu force was making such good headway, despite the rains, that Mountbatten ordered them to continue their advance.

ADVANCES IN BURMA

The Tamu force advanced slowly but steadily down the Kabaw Valley throughout October. In this part of western Burma the Kabaw River parallels the Chindwin with a low mountain range in between. In early November a segment of the Tamu force crossed a mountain pass and occupied the town of Mawlaik, which was on the Chindwin River. This was on November 6 and that action was unopposed. These were the first Allied troops to reach the Chindwin River. The Tamu force then continued down the Kabaw Valley and on November 8 fought a sharp engagement with a Japanese rear guard force at the village of Mushi. The Japanese were forced to retreat and the Tamu force occupied the village. The Allied force resumed its march and on the 14th took the town of Kalemyo. There the 11th KAR linked up with an Indian Division coming in from the west and by now the monsoons had ended, improving the ability to maneuver. Also, the roads back to Imphal would soon be open again and the Tamu force could receive reinforcements and supplies by ground transportation.

At Kalemyo, an all-weather road led to the east to Kalewa on the Chindwin and then on to Mandalay, the largest city in central Burma. At Kalemyo the 28th KAR Brigade and the Lushai Brigade separated from the main force and advanced

Troops of the 11th KAR on the march in the Kalemyo area.

southward down the Manipur River Valley, a tributary to the Kabaw River, in the direction of Gangaw. The remainder of the Tamu force took the road to the east, and on December 2, occupied the town of Kalewa without incident. There they crossed the Chindwin and continued down the east bank of the river to take Schwegyin a few days later. Schwegyin had been badly damaged by the retreating Japanese. On December 19, the 11th KAR Division was relieved by the 19th Indian Division and the recently-arrived 28th KAR Brigade. The 11th KAR was sent to the rear for a well-deserved rest.

On the Arakan Front, the 81st and 82nd West African Divisions had, in contrast to the 11th KAR Division, seen little action due mostly to enemy inaction and the monsoon rains. During July the 81st was withdrawn and sent to the rear for rest and rehabilitation. They had suffered 431 killed and wounded and another 100 sick. The 82nd continued its slow advance down the Arakan coast in conjunction with Indian forces despite the monsoon rains.

On September 28, General Christison's British 15th Corps headquarters on the Arakan front received official orders to go on the offensive with the first objective to be the capture of the Naaf River estuary and the port of Akyab.

With the monsoons ending in November the 15th Corps began a slow overland advance toward their objectives. Once again, the Indian troops advanced along the coast while the 82nd West Africans, still operating alone, advanced on a parallel line further inland on the other side of the coastal mountains. During October, the 82nd encountered a 2,000–man Japanese garrison at Mowdok and forced them to give up the village. The 82nd then advanced to the village of Taung Bazaar, where the Japanese were waiting, and launched a surprise attack. The main West African force held off the attackers while a small unit scaled a 3,000–foot mountain and attacked the Japanese on their flank. This forced the Japanese to retreat and the West African won the day. By December 12, the 82nd West Africans had penetrated the Kalapanzin Valley near Buthidaung, while the 81st, which was now back in the line, engaged Japanese rear guard units at Kyauktaw. On the 15th men of the 82nd captured Buthidaung. During this battle, a Gold Coast unit surged through the Japanese defenses in an act of great bravery and rescued a surrounded Indian artillery unit.

On the coast, Christison's 25th Indian Division was making faster progress than expected advancing on Akyab. The Japanese decided not to defend Akyab and on December 24 began to withdraw from the entire Akyab Peninsula. On January 4, Christison's Indian troops occupied the port of Akyab, unopposed, in an amphibious operation.

Meanwhile, some 25 miles inland, the 81st and 82nd West Africans continued advancing overland toward their next objective, the seaport of Myebon.

BACK IN ITALY

During August, the 6th South African Armoured Division was withdrawn from the front and sent to the western part of Italy for rest and rehabilitation and to serve as a reserve unit for the Americans 5th Army.

On September 1, British troops finally, after weeks of hard fighting, broke through the German's Gothic Line. Other segments of the line were penetrated, but then the Allied advance was, once again, hampered by bad weather. Nevertheless, by September 10, Allied forces were breaking out onto the southern edge of the Po River Valley, the heartland of northern Italy. The South African 6th Armoured Division, now back at the front, was in the forefront of the attack and on September 11 captured the city of Pistoria. A few days later the newly-arrived Brazilian forces were placed in the front lines in the area previously covered by the French. The Allied front now had to be widened due to the geography of northern Italy.

On October 3, the South Africans reached Lagaro and on the 6th began a prolonged series of battles against a formidable German unit, the 11th SS Panzers. These battles would last more than two weeks and be the most difficult period of battle for the South Africans so far in the war. The battlefield was the snow-covered mountainous area along the southern rim of the Po River Valley. The hard-fighting South Africans managed to advance slowly, capturing Grizzana on October 14. By the 19th, they were approaching Monte Salvaro and on the 24th they captured the strategic Passo del Termine. On October 26, heavy rains again stalled the Allied advance and a lull fell over the battlefield once more.

THE SAAF AND AFRICAN PIONEERS IN ITALY

During the latter half of 1944, the SAAF (South African Air Force) had 25 squadrons of war planes in Italy. This was the largest Commonwealth air force in Italy outside the RAF. SAAF planes not only supported the Allied ground troops in Italy but were sent on missions into the Balkans and as far north as Austria.

During the last half of 1944, African Pioneers continued to serve in Italy with virtually all of them being attached to the British 8th Army. And, additional Pioneers continued to arrive. For example, in the fall of 1944, 400 Pioneers from the Indian Ocean island of Rodriguez arrived, bringing the total number of islanders from Rodriguez, Mauritius, and The Seychelles to 2,000 men. During the battle for Casino, the Mauritians were cited, as a unit, for bravery under fire.

In late 1944, eight companies of Swazi Pioneers arrived in northern Italy to serve with the British 8th Army. They were assigned to aid the British build up for the planned spring offensive.

In early November, the Allied command structure of the Italian front was altered and the 6th South Africans were placed under temporary command of the U. S. 5th Army. This was the first time in the war that South Africans served under American command. In late November, heavy rains again slowed the Allied advance all along the front, and in mid-December, it was slowed further by strong German opposition.

NORTHERN FRANCE

As the summer months waned, the Allies continued to press forward in northern France and, in a few places, penetrated into the German Rhineland. This front was now known as "the Western Front." At the southern end of the front, the French were fighting in the Belfort area of France and had not yet entered Germany. But the French had taken the offensive and were forcing the Germans to retreat toward the Rhine River.

On October 14 the 23, Algerians reached Cornimont and on the 16th they and the French 1st Armoured Division launched an attack on German positions in the Vosges area.

In early November, the Allies launched a general offensive on the Western Front and de Lattre's 1st French Army was very much a part of it, although its part of the offensive was delayed until November 14. Nevertheless, the 3rd Algerians were still on the move and on November 5 took the towns of Rochesson and Menaurupt. On November 14, the French 1st Army began its offensive in the south with its primary objective the town of Belfort. The 2nd Moroccans spearheaded the attack, with close support provided by the French 2nd Armoured Division on their left and the 9th Colonial Division on their right. The advance progressed well and on the 18th the Frenchmen were fast approaching Belfort. The 2nd Moroccans and 2nd Armoured Divisions threatened the city from the north and west while the 9th Colonials, now supported by the French 1st Infantry Division, advanced to a point six miles beyond Belfort to the southeast, placing themselves between Belfort and the Swiss border and threatening the German's rear. About 6:30 p.m. on the 19th lead elements of the 9th Colonials reached the west bank of the Rhine River at a point just north of the Swiss border. On the other side was Germany.

On November 20, the French 2nd Armoured Division crossed the Saar River, and that same day the Moroccans entered Belfort after experiencing some sharp clashes with the Germans. The Germans were determined to hold Belfort, and bitter house-to-house fighting continued for several days. The Germans, though, could not hold their flanks, and lead elements of the French 1st Armoured Division, operating to the north, reached Mulhouse twenty miles east-northeast of Belfort, threatening to surround that city.

The Germans finally abandoned Belfort and fled to the Colmar area northeast of Belfort, where a determined defense was planned to keep the French from crossing the Rhine. The French pursued the retreating Germans, and the fast-moving French 2nd Armoured Division managed to circle around the Colmar area and reach the Rhine, at a point northeast of Colmar and ten miles south of Strasbourg. The Germans were now in a pocket with the French on three sides and the Rhine River to their back. On November 24, the 2nd Armoured occupied Strasbourg, closing the ring around Colmar even tighter.

At this point, the Allied High Command assigned the reduction of the Colmar pocket to de Lattre and his French 1st Army, and on December 2, the U.S. 76th Infantry Division was sent to de Lattre as reinforcements. On December 7, the French launched their attack on the Colmar pocket, but the same day the Germans also launched a strong counterattack from inside the pocket. The two attacks clashed head on and hard fighting ensued with little progress made by either side. It was clear that the reduction of the Colmar pocket would not be easy. The German 19th Army, defending the pocket, was strong, well-entrenched, and determined to keep the French from crossing the Rhine into Germany. Fighting continued for days, as the bitter cold of December made life miserable for the troops on both sides. The French managed to take the village of Mittelwihr on December 9 and on the 10th, the 2nd Moroccans took the town of Thann, while the 9th Colonials eliminated the last German bridgehead on the west bank of the Rhine between Colmar and the Swiss border. The Colmar front fell silent for several days and then, on the 15th, the French launched another major attack but it made little progress.

The next day, all hell broke loose in the north. The Germans launched a major offensive in the Ardennes area of Luxembourg and France which was to develop into the infamous "Battle of the Bulge." The German tanks broke through a thinly-held sector of the American line and were soon rolling across undefended terrain in the direction of Antwerp, Belgium. This was a major setback for the Allies, and all priorities now went to containing and stopping the German offensive. All of the Allied units along the western front were ordered to go on the defensive in their respective areas and be prepared to rush some of their units to the Bulge area to help stop the German drive if called upon to do so. This, of course, applied to the French in the Colmar area. For the next two weeks, the Colmar area, and other areas of the western front not directly involved in the Battle of the Bulge, fell silent. By December 29, the German offensive had been stopped and contained. Now, an eerie quiet developed all along the entire Western Front. It was clear that the Germans had spent the greater part of their strength on the Ardennes offensive and that the initiative had passed to the Allies. The French and others along the front now waited for word to resume their attacks.

THE SEA WAR—ATLANTIC

During the last six months of 1944, German submarine activity off the Atlantic coast of Africa dropped to a new low. Only two Allied ships were sunk during July. On July 2, the Germans lost another sub, U–543, sunk by aircraft from the "Wake Island" hunter-killer group, southwest of the Canary Islands. The American planes used depth charges and FIDOs.

No Allied ships were sunk off West Africa during August, September, and October, but on September 9, the Germans lost U–1062 south of the Cape Verde Islands to the American destroyer escort "Fessenden" which was part of the "Mission Bay" hunter-killer group. U–1062 was a blockade runner returning from the Far East with a load of rubber and other supplies. U–1062 was trying to rendezvous with U–219 to get additional fuel to make it to Norway, but ships and planes from two American hunter-killer groups, Mission Bay and "Tripoli," harassed both subs constantly so they could not get together on the surface long enough to carry out the fueling operation. U–1062 had the unhappy distinction of being the last German sub sank in Africa's Atlantic water in the war.

U–219 was lucky. She was a blockade runner too, outbound for Penang with a cargo of radio equipment, spare parts, and medical supplies. She was able to elude both hunter-killer groups. The Tripoli group, however, continued to pursue U–219 and caught up with her again on October 30 off South Africa. U–219, though, eluded the Americans once again and disappeared into the Indian Ocean eventually making it to Penang.

On November 8, U–1227, patrolling off French Morocco, attacked an Allied convoy and sank a tanker. This was the last Allied ship sunk in West African waters for the remainder of the year.

THE SEA WAR—INDIAN OCEAN

By late June, all of the German subs of Monsun I and II had reached Penang and were seeing action in the Indian Ocean. Four of the subs, U–198, –859, –861, and –862 went on patrol in the western Indian Ocean. The others operated in the central and eastern part of the ocean.

Off East Africa U–198, was the first to strike. On July 15, she torpedoed and sank a British freighter at the southern end of the Madagascar Channel. She then moved to the north end of the channel and, operating off the coast of Tanganyika, sank another British cargo vessel on August 6, and another on August 7. These would be U–198's last victims. The British "Force F" hunter-killer group, operating out of Ceylon, was hot on the trail of U–198, thanks to distress messages sent by the sinking ships and information received via Ultra.

SURVIVORS' ORDEAL—"EMPIRE CITY"

The ship sunk by U–198 on August 6 was the British freighter "Empire City" and two of its crewmen later wrote of their ordeal. Seaman Donkeyman Smith recorded:

"Then the U–boat surfaced and came alongside the lifeboats into which we were crowded. The submarine Commander told us he had heard our wireless operator sending out his SOS messages and we judged from that they would be picked up by a friendly station. He asked if we had enough provisions and we told him we had provisions and water that should last till we reached land. We were 120 miles from the coast of East Africa.

One of our men asked the German captain, who spoke good English, if he had any cigarettes to spare for us, but the commander told us he had not as he was too far from home. He said, "goodbye" and wished us, "good Luck" before he left us."

Seaman William Corkhill also wrote of the ordeal:

"The (life)boat I was in with the Irish 3rd mate, was the first to reach the mainland in about forty hours. We had been met about two or three miles offshore by some native villagers in outriggers who did not speak English. Nor did they appreciate the chocolates we threw into their boats, for they dumped them overboard and retained only the shiny tin boxes. They led the way into a sandy beach behind which was a small village, where women and children were leaving their huts and heading into the trees.

A fire was lit on the beach and in a very short time a delicious meal of rice and goats' flesh was served on a thirty-inch diameter brass tray, and we enjoyed sitting cross-legged on the beach."

SURVIVOR'S ORDEAL—"RADBURY"

The ship U–862 sunk on August 13 was the British freighter "Radbury." Her survivors had quite a different ordeal than those of the Empire City. The Radbury's survivors made it to a small uninhabited island known as Europa Island in the middle of the Mozambique Channel. There was no fresh water on the island but there were wild chickens, goats, and turtles. The ship's Chinese engineer rigged up a water still out of a lifeboat buoyancy tank and was able to distill sea water, so that each man had at least one cup of fresh water per day. Otherwise they lived off the island's wildlife. There was enough combustible debris on the island so that they could build a signal fire each day, but for days on end no savior arrived.

Finally on October 26, an RAF Catalina, out of Diego Suarez, spotted them and dropped food, water, first aid kits, cigarettes, and a note saying that a ship had been summoned. The next day, the Catalina returned bringing more supplies and on the 28th, a British warship picked up the survivors and took them to Mombasa. They had been on Europa Island for 73 days.

In the search for U–198, planes from Force F's two escort carriers as well as land-based planes from Diego Suarez, Madagascar and Mombasa, Kenya were searching every square mile of ocean both day and night. U–198 was spotted and unsuccessfully bombed by planes from Force F on both August 10 and 12 in the waters between the Comoros Islands and the Seychelles. On the 12th, though, an Indian sloop and a British frigate from Force F located the sub, gave chase, and sank her with a volley of hedgehog depth charges. Another sub from Penang, U–862, then moved into the Madagascar Channel and on August 13, 16, 18 and 19 sank a British merchantman each day.

Another German sub, U–861, was operating off South Africa and on August 20, sank a British cargo ship and a British tanker. Up north, U–859 was patrolling off the Gulf of Aden and on August 28, sank the American merchantman "John Barry" out of Philadelphia. This ship, which sank in 8,500 feet of water, was carrying 300 million dollars worth of gold and silver. It was not until 1994 that salvage technology reached the point where treasures of this type could be salvaged at such depths. In that year, some, but not all, of the treasure was salvaged.

On September 1, U–859 sank another ship, a British freighter, in the Gulf of Aden area and on the 5th U–861 scored again, taking a Greek ship off Kenya.

This flurry of sinking was to be the last hurrah for the German submarines in the Indian Ocean. There were no more sinkings by German subs during the remainder of September and all of October. In November, only one Allied ship was sunk by a German sub and that was in the eastern Indian Ocean.

Back in Europe, Doenitz was forced to accept the fact that, from recent losses, it was now too costly to try to get supplies to the Far East. Without spare parts and torpedoes, the German subs there would be useless. In December, he made the hard decision to recall all of his subs in the Far East back to Europe. The first subs left in late December and the rest followed in early 1945.

The Japanese sub menace in the Indian Ocean had also greatly diminished. With the war going badly for the Japanese in the Pacific, they had very little resources to dedicate to the Indian Ocean. During the last six months of 1944, Japanese subs sank only three Allied ships in the Indian Ocean, all of them in eastern waters.

The Allies soon recognized that the waters of the western Indian Ocean were much safer, and they began moving some of their antisubmarine air and sea patrols from East Africa and Madagascar further east to Ceylon and points in India and Australia.

EAST AFRICA

The rigors of war had created a rather unique situation in certain parts of East Africa in that many men had postponed marriage until after having served in the armed forces or in war jobs. By mid–1944, with the economies returning more to normal, there developed an excess of single men and a limited supply of brides. The problem was especially acute in The Sudan, where the price of a bride's dowry demanded by the bride's parents soared to as high as $400 for the most choice ladies in question. Even the less-desirable ladies were going for $100. Both prices were far above the price the average man could pay. To the rescue came Sir Sayed Rahman el Mahdi Pasha, a bearded, rich, and British-knighted political and religious leader. During July 1944, he organized a bride-buying fair at the city of Omdurman in northern Sudan. Several large tents were erected in which the brides and their parents took up residence and the prospective suitors went from tent to tent selecting the lady of their choice and making the best deal possible with the parents. When a deal was made the future bridegroom paid the parents $8.00 and Sir Sayed picked up the balance of the dowry. At the end of the fair, some 300 couples were married in a mass wedding ceremony.

In British Somaliland, the now-motorized Somaliland Camel Corps, which had become unruly and mutinous, was still proving to be a problem unit and was finally disbanded by the British colonial authorities in September 1944. Those men who were still reliable and wished to continue their military careers were transferred to the Somali Scouts. The others were discharged from the service. It was a sad ending for a unit that had served the British for over thirty years.

There were other problems, too, in British Somaliland. During 1942–43, two battalions of Somalis, the 71st and 72nd Somalis had been formed to serve in the KAR. The 71st Battalion was sent to Burma and served honorably there. The 72nd, however, was sent to Kenya to become a training unit for new KAR recruits. During September 1944, a dispute erupted between the Somalis of the 72nd Battalion and their British superiors, and 63 men deserted the unit. Others were deemed unreliable and disarmed. In February 1945, the 72nd Battalion was disbanded.

In Ethiopia, the British loosened, somewhat, their reigns on the Ethiopian government. On December 19, a new Anglo-Ethiopian agreement was signed in which the British agreed to withdraw their troops from Diredawa, in the north, and from along the Addis Ababa-to-Djibouti railroad. The latter was conditional, depending upon when the French company that owned and operated the railroad could get it functioning normally again.

As for the Ogaden Desert, whose control had long been disputed between Ethiopia and Italian Somaliland, the British acknowledged that the Ogaden belonged to Ethiopia but that British troops would remain as peacekeepers in certain parts of the area for the near future. In the meantime, both the Ethiopian and British flags would fly side-by-side in those areas and the British headquarters would remain in Mogadishu, occupied Italian Somaliland.

In occupied Italian Somaliland the British were still having troubles with the local Somalis. The British-trained Somali police force had become very unpopular with the civilian population because many members of the force had become corrupt and repeatedly took advantage of their authority. The British occupation authorities had, by now, come to realize that they had an on-going problem they had to live with. Once again, they weeded out the corrupt and abusive policemen and took steps to keep the rest in line.

Another problem arose concerning the recently-formed Somali Youth League, which purported to speak for the Somali people on matters of reform and self-determination. The League worked closely with the British occupation authorities—too closely for most of the population's liking—and was not very well supported. Because of this, a political void developed in occupied Italian Somaliland, which tended to strengthen personal loyalties of the people to their traditional clan leaders. This, in turn, worked against the concept of national unity and in favor of a potential state of anarchy.

Eritrea's future still remained a question mark for all concerned, so for the time being, the British occupation government continued to function as a caretaker administration only, unable to promise anything to the Eritrean people in the way of a future government. The political scene in Eritrea was further complicated by the emergence of the "Party of Unity with Ethiopia" (PUE). But, unlike the name implied, the PUE favored ending the British occupation of Eritrea and replacing it with a British trusteeship for an indefinite period. They also advocated attaching a large part of the Ethiopian province of Tigre to Eritrea, which the Italians had done. These ideas, of course, were not welcome in Addis Ababa.

In London, certain anti-colonialists in Parliament were pressing the Churchill government on the future of the former Italian East African colonies. They stressed that under the Atlantic Charter, Britain promised not to seek territorial aggrandizement and asked if the government intended to live up to that pledge. Anthony Eden, the Foreign Secretary, stated on October 4 that the colonies would, under no circumstances, be returned to Italy, but beyond that he could offer no advice.

In the British part of East Africa, the political situations were stable and the colonies were still prospering from the wartime economy. For Kenya, the London government made a grant of 500,000 pounds toward the construction of new homes for Africans in a new native township of Nairobi to house the many Kenyans who had come to the city for war work. In Dar-es-Salaam, Tanganyika a new native township was created for the same purpose but received lesser funding.

BRITISH WEST AFRICA

In the rich and productive lands of southern Nigeria, both old and new problems were festering. At the heart of the old problems was land. With the need to produce more and more food for the war effort, many whites and some Nigerians wanted to buy land and start, or expand, farming operations. But ancient tribal traditions dictated that tribal lands should never be sold to non-tribal members. Such land could only be leased. This was not a satisfactory arrangement because the lessees often needed to build permanent and sometimes specialized structures on the land and, quite naturally, wanted to own the land upon which the structures stood. Furthermore, there were still generations-old disputes between the tribes themselves over land ownership.

Another problem that affected both Nigeria and Gold Coast were labor strikes. Local union leaders, who were usually black, had learned to work the system for the advantage of their members and themselves. In addition, the union leaders had legitimate complaints because creeping inflation had eroded the buying power of many black workers whose wages tended to be static. Demands for wage increases where usually what sparked the strikes.

In northern Nigeria there were strikes and some tribal conflicts in the vital Enugu coal mining area. This caused the local authorities some major problems as well as lost coal production.

In western Nigeria, a popular, and very independent-minded black political leader, Alake of Abeokuta, was removed from office by the colonial administration. But the local people came to his support and he was later restored to his position in an effort to prevent local unrest.

American-built Cazes Air Base at Casablanca, French Morocco had become the most important Allied air hub in northwestern Africa by late 1944.

In late 1944, the London government squeezed an additional 120 million pounds out of its national budget for the city of Nairobi. This was over and above Nigeria's annual allotment and was used to improve selected areas of infrastructure and community services, such as streets and utility services, that were both needed and would enhance Britain's image as a colonial master.

In Nairobi and other cities in British East Africa, many white and some black specialists and technicians were brought in by the colonial government and the military and given jobs for which many local people felt they were qualified. Fortunately, for the moment, the booming economy and manpower shortages made it possible for virtually any skilled worker to find a good job, but this problem of bringing in outsiders smoldered just under the surface.

PORTUGAL ALLOWS AMERICANS TO USE AZORES

During July 1944, the Portuguese government in Lisbon gave the Americans permission to use the existing airfield at the Portuguese naval air station at Lagens in the Azores Island for military operations. This, of course, was another violation of Portugal's neutrality, but the Lisbon government was willing to take the risk in order to further befriend the Allies who were clearly winning the war. In addition, the Portuguese could see some benefits for themselves in the deal.

Up to this time, only the British military had been allowed to use the islands' air facilities. By making concessions to the Americans the Allies gained significantly in two ways. It meant that American war planes would now join in the antisubmarine activities in this vital area of the Atlantic, and that American military cargo and transport planes could fly direct from the United States to the Azores and then on to points in northwest Africa. This was a much shorter route across the Atlantic than the route used since the beginning of the war via the Caribbean, South America, South Atlantic, and West Africa.

The Portuguese did not want the Americans to use the Lagens airfield permanently because they needed it for their own military purposes. Therefore, part of the American/Portuguese agreement called for the Americans to build a new field on Santa Maria Island which the Allies would use for the duration of the war and then turn over to Portugal after the war for commercial use. USAAF and Pan American Airways technicians worked together to pick a site on Santa Maria that would suit both the current military and postwar commercial needs. Construction began during November 1944.

AIR ROUTES

During the later part of 1944, the Cannonball Route across central Africa was beginning to lose its importance due to the opening of the Azores to the Americans and the advent of longer-range cargo planes, especially the American-build Douglas C–54. This four-engine transport plane could easily fly from the United States, via the Azores, to Casablanca, French Morocco, and other cities in northwestern Africa.

C–54s also used the Cannonball Route, but when they did they bypassed may existing airfields. This, in turn, further reduced the importance of the Cannonball Route.

By mid 1944, commercial air routes to West Africa had become, by mid 1944, a permanent operation. Pan-American Airways was crossing both the North and South Atlantic Oceans on a regularly scheduled basis now using land-based planes. The great expansion of new airfields built by the Americans and others in Latin America and Africa negated the need for seaplanes.

SOUTH AFRICA

On July 26, 1944, one of South Africa's more important political exiles died of natural causes. He was Riza Khan Pahlavi, the former Shah of Iran and brother-in-law of King Farouk of Egypt. Pahlavi was forced to abdicated as Shah of Iran under Allied pressures in September 1941, when he opposed the use of his country as a conduit for Allied supplies flowing to the Soviet Union. Assuming the throne was Pahlavi's 22 year-old son, who agreed to cooperate with the Allies. Pahlavi was then exiled to Mauritius Island and then to South Africa.

In neighboring Portuguese Mozambique, a buildup of Portuguese military forces was noted during the latter part of 1944. The Portuguese government could see that the Japanese would almost certainly be defeated and when that occurred they needed to be in a position to send troops as soon as possible to reoccupy their island colony of Timor, in the East Indies. Timor had been under Japanese occupation since early 1942.

BELGIAN CONGO

The Belgian Congo's mobile field hospital unit, formed earlier for use in Burma, was still at the front and performing well. It served under British command and followed closely behind the advancing front line troops, tending to the wounded.

In Europe, on September 3, 1944, British Armoured units liberated Brussels, the capital of Belgium. Five days later, the Belgian government-in-exile moved from London to Brussels and proclaimed themselves the legitimate government of the country. This was most welcome news throughout the Belgian Congo and the colonial officials were quick to reaffirm their loyalty to the Brussels government.

Also in Belgium, on September 8, a small group of American nuclear scientists and Army officers, known as the "ALSOS Team" and secretly working for the Manhattan Project, discovered eighty tons of uranium ore from the Belgian Congo at the Union Miniere Company plant in Oolen, Belgium. That company had been, before the war, the world's largest processor of uranium ore. Examination of the company's records revealed that most of the ore had remained at Oolen untouched during the war and that another large quantity of ore, described as "three freight cars full," was at Toulouse, France and also had not been utilized. These were significant finds for the Americans in that they told the members of the ALSOS Team that the German nuclear scientists had not used much of the ore and therefore had not produced any significant amount of fissionable uranium that might be used in an atomic bomb. Simply put, Germany was nowhere near producing an atomic bomb.

The ore in both locations was confiscated by the Americans as war booty and sent on to Oak Ridge, Tennessee to be processed and used in America's atomic bombs.

GERMANY

In Germany, Hitler and his closest aides were grasping at straws. One of the scenarios they hoped might come to pass would be the collapse of the British and American alliance which, Hitler felt, might be sparked over colonial issues. On December 14, 1944, Hitler told his associates:

> *"On the one hand (there is) Britain, a dying empire; on the other, the United States, a colony eager for its inheritance. Each of these partners joined the coalition in the hope of realizing their own political ambitions and to cheat the other out of something. America wants to be England's heir (while) England tries to hold on to her possession."*

POLITICAL STIRRINGS IN TUNISIA

By late 1944, the political situation in Tunisia had gone from bad to worse. The de Gaulle government's attempts to reestablish the prewar protectorate status over the country was fomenting almost unanimous resentment among the Tunisian people. Since the liberation of the country in May 1943, many new political groups and trade unions had been formed, all with some sort of nationalistic agenda. The most formidable of these groups was the "Union Generale Tunisienne du Travail" (UGGT). During November 1944, the UGGT and some of the other groups banded together to produce the "Manifesto of the Tunisian Front" which called for, at the very minimum, internal autonomy for the Tunisian people. This was not at all what the Paris government had in mind for the future for Tunisia and it was becoming clear that that government and the Tunisian nationalists were on a collision course.

RETURNING FRENCH COLONIAL SOLDIERS A PROBLEM IN WEST AFRICA

During the latter part of 1944, thousands of French colonial soldiers were returned to their homes, primarily in West Africa.

The French, perpetually short of seagoing transportation, were very slow in getting these men home and had to rely on the British and Americans to help transport them. In the process of being transported many of the colonial soldiers were shipped to England to await transportation. There, they waited with little to do and became angered by the slowness of the process. When transportation finally became available, they virtually all were shipped to Dakar, West Africa's main seaport. There they waited again, in very crowded and uncomfortable holding camps, until local transportation became available. To complicate matters the French authorities were slow to come through with back pay and other promised forms of compensation.

The French government in Paris recognized the problem and France's Minister of Colonies, Rene Pleven, wrote to the Governor-General of West Africa, warning him that many of the colonial soldiers, "...have acquired European habits and a different mentality… this confused situation has been bad for morale."

On December 1, the lid blew off at one of the crowded camps at Thiaroye, a few miles from Dakar. Some 1,200 colonial soldiers, most of them former POWs, mutinied and took over the camp. Police and troops had to be sent to quell the riot, and in the process 35 people were killed and scores injured. This was a wake-up call to the French authorities. Immediately, they sped up the payment of back pay and other compensations and gave the returning soldiers as much priority as they could on transportation home. Furthermore, they reduced the crowded conditions in the camps by slowing the flow of men from Europe and also avoided concentrating too many ex-POWs in any one camp. This, though, slowed the whole process all the way up the line of returning the colonial soldiers to Africa. More colonial soldiers now accumulated in England and France, thereby building even more resentment. The end result was that many of the returning colonial soldiers came home angry at the French and became easy recruits for the nationalist movements springing up all over West Africa.

The feelings of the soldiers were expressed, at the time, in a famous poem centering on the Thiaroye Mutiny which stressed the oppressive conditions the returning veterans suffered at the hands of the French. In 1980, a movie of the Thiaroye Mutiny was made with the same theme as the poem—that of condemning the French.

Chapter 20

VICTORY ATTAINED IN EUROPE (JANUARY–JUNE 1945)

POSTWAR PROBLEMS IN SIGHT

The first half of 1945 brought victory for the Allies in Europe and prospects of victory in the Far East. In both Europe and the Far East, African fighting men served to the end.

Also during this time African waters became safe again, ending wartime hostilities directly affecting Africa. And the African colonial economies continued to boom. Beneath the surface, though, lay a smoldering and ever-growing resentment of colonialism among the African people, accompanied by a newfound belief that, having contributed significantly to the war effort, they deserved more than they had had before. Most believed that the time to address these issues was at hand. But first, there was the war.

ITALY

From January to early March 1945, the Italian front was relatively quiet. Allied troops were poised in positions stretching across the northern part of the Italian peninsula along the mountains on the southern edge of the Po River Valley. The winter weather was bad and the Allies were biding their time and building their strength for a spring offensive—and the Germans knew it. The German leaders in Italy also knew they were not strong enough to match what was coming.

During this time, the men of the 6th South Africans were rotated to the rear for a well-deserved period of rest and relaxation in the town of Lucca.

Also during this time, the Germans took the opportunity to move most of their Allied prisoners of war from Italy to Germany. Some of them, of course, were Africans. This was a difficult time for such individuals because the weather was more severe in Germany and the Germans allotted POWs only the bare minimum of food and fuel. Furthermore, many of the German camp guards were very abusive to the black Africans.

During March, another nationality entered the potpourri of nationalities fighting in Italy, the Jewish Brigade. They were attached to the British 8th Army and took a section of the front in northern Italy along the Montone River front. In their first action, on March 7, they successfully crossed that river and secured a bridgehead on the other side.

By this time the South African 6th Armoured Division was back in the fray in full strength and positioned in the west-central part of Italy under American command.

To the west, along the French/Italian border, six French colonial battalions had been brought up during March to reinforce the French forces there. During April, that force crossed the border into Italy driving toward a linkup with American forces advancing into northwestern Italy.

As the beginning stages of the Allied spring offensive got underway, the German commander in Italy, Field Marshal Kesselring, realized that the strength of the Allied forces was overwhelming and made contact with America's OSS (Office of Strategic Services) chief, Allen Dulles, in Switzerland for the purpose of ending the fighting. Talks were held in Bern, Switzerland between Dulles and SS General Karl Wolff, Kesselring's deputy. The Germans offered to evacuate all of northern Italy if they could be allowed to return to Germany and, together with the Allies, continue to fight against the Soviets. The Americans, as did the British, flatly refused this proposal, but the talks continued. So did the fighting.

During the second week in April, the American 15th Army launched what the Allied commanders hoped would be the last major offensive in Italy. The Americans attacked along a lengthy part of the front in west-central Italy in the general direction of Bologna in the heart of the Po River Valley. The 6th South African Armoured Division was one of the units that went on the attack with the Americans. This great Allied force was irresistible. It smashed forward, overcame relatively strong German defenses, and advanced northward across the flat farm lands of the great valley in a northerly direction. The role of the 6th South Africans was to advance on a due-northerly course and flank Bologna on the west to facilitate the direct American attack on the city itself.

The day after the Americans launched their attack the British launched their attack in the east. They crossed the Senio River and spread out on a fan-like front up the Adriatic coast toward Venice, to the north-northwest toward Ferrara and to the northwest toward Bologna. Together with the Americans the Allied front was 85 miles wide and advancing everywhere. It was also a United Nations event. Pushing into the Po River Valley were Americans, British, South Africans, New Zealanders, Canadians, Poles, Greeks, Brazilians, Indians, Italians, and Jews. Following closely behind were the African Pioneer units and other service units from many parts of the British Empire. As the South Africans advanced on Bologna, they were forced to fight another difficult battle at Monte Sole, a strong defensive position southwest of Bologna manned by elite German mountain troops. American forces came to aid the South Africans and, having control of the air, superior artillery firepower and dogged determination, helped the South Africans overcame the defender's positions by April 16. The German mountaineers, though, were not yet beaten. They retreated in order toward another defense line, the "Genghis Kahn Line," south of Bologna, which stretched eastward to the Adriatic coast south of Argenta. This proved to be a very weak defensive line and the powerful Allied juggernaut quickly broke through in several places.

On April 21, Bologna fell to American and Polish troops. The South Africans passed to the west of the city as planned and continued to advance northward with the 91st American Division on their right flank and the 88th American Division on their left. In the east, the British took Argenta and continued to advance up the Adriatic coast.

Meanwhile Allied planes, including planes of the SAAF, were pounding the mountain passes through the Alps destroying highway and railroad bridges, tunnels, and other facilities to cut off the German's lines of retreat. Also in the Alps, anti-Fascist Italian partisans units were building in strength.

By April 23, the South Africans had reached the center of the Po River Valley at a point 38 miles north of Bologna and just south of the Po River. They had crossed over the path of the 91st American Division and now had the 6th British Armoured Division on their right.

On April 25, British forces, including the South Africans, crossed the Po River at Ferrara and advanced rapidly throughout the eastern part of northern Italy. German resistance was sporadic and weak, but the South Africans had to fight another engagement at Finale Santo Campo. No one knew it

This racist cartoon appeared in one of the Italian Fascist publications in northern Italy in early 1945, and was an admission, of sorts, that the "liberation" of Italy was at hand. Its caption read: "Well, Italian, what did you do before the liberation?" "I was a university professor."

at the time, but this would be their last engagement of the war. The German defenders of Finale Santo Campo were overcome and the South Africans continued on to enter the undefended city of Treviso, 25 miles north of Venice. Then, they were suddenly ordered to turn about and race to the west where two German divisions were holding out in the Milan area. Before the South Africans could make contact, however, the Germans there surrendered. Therefore, the last days of combat in northern Italy saw the South Africans charging across the Po Valley toward a battle that did not happen.

Along the American sector, the Germans had abandoned almost all of western Italy and on April 26, Italian partisans occupied the cities of Milan and Genoa. On the 27th, the American troops of the all-black 92nd Infantry Division entered Genoa. To the west, the French troops were marching in from the French-Italian border toward a linkup with the Americans.

On April 28, Mussolini, in the company of his mistress, Claretta Petacci, was captured by Italian partisans. The next day, they were executed, along with other Fascist leaders, and their bodies taken to Milan where they were displayed to, and desecrated by, angry mobs. On the 28th the British occupied Venice and on that same day the German forces in northern Italy surrendered unconditionally. Some isolated and die-hard German units continued to fight on until May 2. On the 30th, troops of the 92nd American Infantry Division took Turin in the west and linked up with the French forces advancing from France. During the first days of May, Allied troops entered the Alps via the Brenner Pass moving northward for an eventual linkup with Allied troops in Austria and southern Germany.

As the Allies mopped up the last of the German positions in northern Italy, they liberated several prisoner of war camps. Thousands of other Allied prisoners were liberated, including 173 South African officers and 2,405 white and 450 black South African enlisted men.

For the 6th South Africans and the many other Africans in the Pioneer and service units, the war in Italy was over. Many of these men had fought the full length of Italy, from the southern coast of Sicily to the Alps.

LAURELS FOR THE SOUTH AFRICANS

On May 3, the 6th South Africans held their own victory parade at the Monza race track near Milan. In attendance was Frederick Sturrock, South African Minister of Transportation and acting Minister of Defense. Prime Minister Smuts could not attend the ceremony because he was on his way to San Francisco, California for an important United Nations conference.

Sturrock promised the men of the South African troops that they would be returned home as soon as transportation became available, warning, however, that transportation for the war in the Pacific had priority. He added that the war in the Pacific might require their services once again, but only after all of them had returned home for an extended stay.

American General Mark Clark was also in attendance at the parade, and awarded General W. H. E. Poole, the commander of the 6th South Africans, the American Legion of Merit. The South Africans had lost men 753 killed and 4,423 men wounded in the Italian campaign.

On May 4, the South Africans participated in a second and much larger multi-nation victory parade in Milan.

THE WESTERN FRONT

There was no lull on the Western Front during the winter of 1944-45 as there was in Italy. After the last remnants of the German forces had been pushed out of the Bulge, the entire western front came alive again as the Allies resumed their march into Germany.

On January 5, the Americans relinquished control of Strasbourg to the French because the American troops were needed further north. This stretched the French sector by about fifty miles.

The areas around Strasbourg and Colmar were still contested by the Germans, and heavy fighting soon broke out between German units and the 3rd Algerians north of Colmar. The Algerians were forced onto the defensive but

Algerian troops in a defensive position in the Colmar area.

Moroccan troops on the move in the Colmar area.

were able to beat off several German attacks and hold their positions.

On January 20, the forces of the 1st French Army, reinforced with four American divisions from General Devers' 6th Army, launched a major attack on the Colmar pocket. This was the largest area of French soil still held by the Germans.

The Allied attack began on the southern perimeter of the pocket with the 4th Motorized Moroccan Division and the 2nd Moroccan Infantry Division leading the attack, supported by tanks of the 1st French Armored Division. The Germans put up a strong defense and the weather was bad but, on January 23, the Moroccans were able to force a crossing of the Ill River, and penetrate the German's main defense line. The next day the bridgehead was extended. On February 1, the Moroccan and Frenchmen reached their objective, the village of Ensisheim.

While the attack on the southern perimeter of the pocket was underway, the Allies attacked the northern perimeter on January 22 between the villages of Selestat and Ostheim. This force consisted of the 2nd French Armored Division, the 1st Moroccan Infantry Division, the 5th American Armored Division, and the 3rd American Infantry Division. From the west, the 28th American Infantry Division carried out diversionary raids against the western perimeter of the pocket. Then, on January 25, the American 21st Corps, following up in the wake of the 28th's diversionary attacks, smashed into the pocket's western perimeter. At this point three powerful Allied columns were attacking simultaneously into the Colmar Pocket.

On January 26, the 1st Moroccans cut the road between Jebsheim and Illhausern at a point six miles north of Colmar, and on the 30th, cleared an important wooded area east of Illhausern.

Fighting was very difficult for both sides due, in part, to the winter weather conditions, but the Allies were not to be denied. French units led in most of the attacks and on January 31, the first French units reached the outskirts of Colmar. The Germans fought hard for the city but without success. On February 2, Colmar was in French hands. Moroccan troops surged forward and on February 5, linked up with American troops at Rouffach, cutting the Colmar pocket in two. By February 6, the Germans in the pocket were in general retreat. That day the Americans took the old fortress town of Neuf-Brisach, and the U.S. 12th Armored Division and the French 5th Armored Division eliminated a German force which was cut off in the Vosges. At the same time, the Moroccan 2nd Division crossed the Ill River and advanced east of the Rhine Canal to take Hirtzfelden. The 9th French Colonial Division captured Ensisheim and sent a force toward Baldersheim, while the 4th Moroccan Motorized Division blocked the escape of the remaining German troops in the Vosges.

Daily fighting continued in the pocket and by February 8, the Germans held only four small villages west of the Rhine. The next day, those villages were taken and German resistance along the west bank of the Rhine south of Strasbourg ended. Also, the existence of the German 19th Army came to an end. It had been a bloody struggle. The Allies suffered 18,000 men killed, wounded, and missing while the Germans suffered 25,000 casualties.

A six-week lull then followed along this sector of the front but not to the north.

THOUSANDS OF AFRICAN SENT HOME

During the lull, thousands of black Africans and some North Africans were sent home. The official explanation given was that they had fought well and deserved a rest and that the winter weather had been exceptionally hard on them. These were valid reasons but only a part of the story. It was widely believed that the French wanted to "whiten" their army as they moved into Germany. It must be remembered that the German people had been fed a steady diet of racial hatred for over ten years and the French did not want to give the Germans cause to fight harder, or resist the coming occupation because of racial issues. There was some validity to this argument because on December 11, 1944, eleven black American soldiers had been murdered at Wereth, Belgium by German SS troops. The black soldiers had been betrayed by German-speaking Belgians. Furthermore, it was widely rumored but officially denied, that the French did not want their African subjects to see the terrible destruction that had been wrought by the white people of the Allied nations on the white people of Germany. This, the rumors held, would tend to dispel the image of unity and superiority of the white race that the colonialists had tried to foster in Africa for decades. Yet another reason was that black African soldiers would come into contact with black Americans, whom they viewed as having more of everything including more equality and independence. And finally, there was the lingering memory of the "Rhineland Bastards."

THE "RHINELAND BASTARDS"

In the early 1920s, the French sent troops to occupy the German Rhineland in an effort to force the Germans to pay the war reparations due France as a result of World War I. Some of the troops used in the occupation were black Africans. The troops stayed for several years and as a result of fraternization, several hundred mulatto children were born to German women. These children were seen as a great embarrassment to the German people of all political persuasions and were dubbed the Rhineland Bastards. The Nazis and other right-wing political organizations in German, used the French occupation and the Rhineland Bastards as political fodder for their racist rhetoric and to stir the pot of hatred against the French.

When the Nazis came to power in 1933, the Rhineland Bastards were young adolescents approaching puberty. To prevent their seed from spreading further among the German people, the Nazis had the children forcibly sterilized.

This very unpleasant episode in German-French relations was within living memory of many Germans, and the French did not want it repeated.

FIGHTING RESUMES ALONG THE RHINE

On March 7, American troops unexpectedly crossed the Rhine River at Remagen when they captured a railroad bridge still intact. American troops then raced up and down the east bank of the Rhine securing places where other Allied forces could cross.

French forces moved north, up the west bank of the Rhine past Strasbourg and, with American forces coming down the east bank of the Rhine from the north, forced a crossing of the River at Germersheim, 55 miles north of Strasbourg. This was March 29, 1945, and for the first time in the war French and African troops were fighting on German soil.

The French forces made contact with the American forces south of Heidelberg on April 1 and then turned south, taking Karlsruhe on the 4th. At Karlsruhe, the French forces split into two columns. One continued down the east bank of the Rhine, occupying Baden Baden on the 12th and advancing as far as Frieburg, in the heart of the Black Forest only thirty miles north of the Swiss border. The other French column struck out in a southeasterly direction toward Tubingen, twenty miles southwest of Stuttgart. With additional French forces advancing from Strasbourg, that column and the column from Karlsruhe easily took Tubingen. From Tubingen the French force divided into three columns; one marched north to help take Stuttgart in a pincers action with American forces moving in from the north. The second column marched due south toward Lake Constance and the Swiss border, and the third advanced to the southeast toward Ulm on the Danube River.

On April 20, the French reached the southern suburbs of Stuttgart and found the city well defended. The French attacked and after several hours of hard fighting fought their way further into the city's suburbs. The next day they captured the city center. A few days later, the Americans and British asked the French to allow them to set up the occupation administration for the city, but de Gaulle, as independent as ever, refused. The capture of Stuttgart represented an important French victory and the city remained in French hands.

On April 25, 280 miles to the northeast, American and Soviet forces met for the first time at the town of Torgau seventy miles south of Berlin. Nazi Germany was cut in two.

By now the end was near. German propaganda, however, had proclaimed that strong German forces would make a prolonged last stand in what they called the "National Redoubt," the mountains of Bavaria and northern Austria. To this end, the German forces trapped in the Black Forest area of southwestern Germany attempted to break out, on the 25th, to the east toward Bavaria. In doing so they hit the right flank of the French forces advancing on Lake Constance. The French had to halt their advance and turn to the west to address this new attack. The German forces were weak and the troops demoralized, so the attack was stopped by the French and the Germans were beaten back into the Black Forest. The French then resumed their drive to the south. The next day they reached the northern shore of Lake Constance, further trapping the Germans in the Black Forest. They then advanced down the northern shore of the lake and on April 30 crossed into Austria near Bregenz, Austria.

HITLER COMMITS SUICIDE

On April 30, 1945, Hitler turned over his office of President of Germany to Admiral Doenitz, his office of Chancellor to Joseph Goebbels, and his position as head of the Nazi Party to Martin Bormann and then committed suicide. Goebbels committed suicide soon afterwards without leaving a successor and Bormann disappeared, most likely killed while trying to escape encircled Berlin. This left Doenitz as the legal and undisputed leader of the German government. Doenitz had not expected this "honor" but saw his duty clearly—to end the war.

BACK ON THE FRENCH FRONT IN GERMANY

On April 30, the day Hitler committed suicide, units of the 4th and 28th Moroccan Divisions crossed into Austria, the land of Hitler's birth.

On May 1, the French units to the northeast secured the town of Bregenz and again split their force into two columns. One column moved due south to secure the Aarlberg Pass in the Alps, and the other column moved southeastward toward the Oberjoch Pass. As they advanced, the French took the Austrian towns of Obersdorf and Goetzis on May 2.

On their left flank, the American 7th Army had also crossed into Austria and was moving into the mountains to secure other passes, including the famous Brenner Pass.

GERMANY SURRENDERS UNCONDITIONALLY

The fighting in Germany went on for another week after Hitler's death, but on May 7, the Germans surrendered unconditionally. General Alfred Jodl signed the documents of surrender on behalf of President Doenitz at Allied headquarters at Reims, France. The terms of the surrender set the time of one minute past midnight May 9 as the end of hostilities.

With the German surrender came the liberation of all Allied POWs held in Germany. When the final tally of POWs was taken, it was discovered that black Africans had suffered considerably more at the hands of the Germans than had other POWs. Of the 16,000 black soldiers in the French Army captured during the fall of France, only about half of them had survived their four years of captivity.

ON THE FRENCH FRONT

With the end of hostilities, the French forces in southwestern Germany and western Austria halted their attacks. By that time, they were on the northern slopes of the Alps. The African units in Germany at the time of the surrender were the 1st and 2nd Moroccan Infantry Divisions, the 4th Moroccan Motorized Division, the 3rd Algerian Infantry Division, and the considerably reduced 9th Colonial Infantry Division. Other Africans were serving further north with the British Army as service personnel and Pioneers.

BURMA

During the first days of January, Indian troops of General Christison's 15th Corps had taken the port of Akyab on the Arakan coast of Burma. The British 3rd Commando Brigade then landed at Myebon on the 12th, and secured a beachhead thirty miles southeast of Akyab. Inland the 82nd West African Division relieved the 81st West African Division and together with the 25th Indian Division moved parallel to the coast toward the new beachhead. In doing so they met considerable Japanese resistance, which was overcome. The Africans and Indians then succeeded in linking up with the British commandos and then proceeded along the coast toward several smaller coastal villages, including the ancient capital of Arakan, which they occupied on January 25.

On January 21, the 71st Brigade of Christison's 26th Indian Division leap-frogged along the coast to conduct another amphibious landing on the northern end of the large island of Ramree. The Japanese force on the island was known to be sizable, so the landing areas were bombarded beforehand by American planes from the U.S. Strategic Air Command and by ships from the British Navy and the Royal Indian Navy.

The next day, the 3rd British commandos landed at Kangaw, on the mainland, in an effort to cut off the retreat of the Japanese forces which were being pursued by the 25th Indians and 82nd West Africans along the coast.

On Ramree Island, as expected, the Japanese fought hard, but the 26th Indians brought over tanks which turned the tide of battle. The town of Ramree, on the southern end of the island, was finally captured on February 9. An all-weather airfield was rapidly built on the island, which put all of southern Burma, including Rangoon, within range of even the shortest-range British aircraft. Meanwhile, the 82nd West African Division continued down the coast in an effort, now, to keep up with the Indians moving down Ramree Island.

On the mainland, the 81st West African Division was back in the line and advancing with the 82nd West Africans and the 25th Indians on the new commando-held beachhead at Kangaw. On January 26, the 81st West Africans occupied Myohaung, and on January 30, the 25th Indians overcame strong Japanese resistance and linked up with the British commandos in the Kangaw beachhead. The 82nd West Africans then struck out and resumed the advance to the south.

In central Burma, large British and Indian forces there had crossed the Chindwin River at several places and spread out onto the central Burmese plain in six columns. In the southernmost column was the 28th KAR Brigade that had helped lead the advance down the Kabaw Valley. On January 2, the

KAR troops occupied the town of Yeu, an important rail head. Then, two larger and more powerful Indian divisions, the 7th and 17th Indian Divisions, which followed in the wake of the KAR force, arrived and took the lead for the next advance. The Indian units had tanks, armored cars, and heavy artillery, which could now be used effectively on the flat lands. Also, it was known that the Japanese had tanks and heavy artillery, and at some point, would make a stand. This relegated the KAR infantry troops to a supporting role. On January 7, the Indian and KAR column took the town of Shwebo, 55 miles northwest of Mandalay, and on the 20th, they took the town of Gangaw, on the Myittha River. The force then split into two smaller column, with a part of the Indian 7th Division striking out across county toward the lower Chindwin River and the remainder of the force, including the KAR troops, continuing down the Myittha River Valley. The objectives of these two columns was to converge on several towns and villages along the Irrawaddy River south of Mandalay, thereby cutting the city's river communications with lower Burma and Rangoon. Other British and Indian columns to the north advanced on Mandalay and points north and south of there.

About this time, the 28th KAR Brigade was transferred north to assist other British forces in their attack on Nyaungu. During Feburary the 28th successfully engaged Japanese forces at Letse, just west of Nyaungu, and then participated in the general advance toward Meiktila which was taken in early March.

On January 22, the Indians and KAR troops took Tilin at the headwaters of the Myittha River and then marched overland, in a southeasterly direction, toward the Irrawaddy River valley. On the 26, that force took the town of Pauk and there split into three columns, all heading for the Irrawaddy. With the Indian units that had formed a separate column at Gangaw also marching on the Irrawaddy, that made four columns of Allied troops all heading for the same objective—the Irrawaddy River in order to cut the Japanese communications between Mandalay and Rangoon.

A study in inter-Allied cooperations. A wounded African soldier being received at an Indian aid station after having arrived in an American airplane.

On February 14, the southernmost column out of Pauk, which included the KAR troops, reached the town of Seipyu, on the west bank of the Irrawaddy River. The river was very wide there and the Allied troops were unable to cross. Further north, though, the Indian column out of Gangaw reached the river that same day and was able to cross and establish a bridgehead on the east bank. This successfully severed Japanese communications and accomplished the Allied objective in this area. There, the Indian and KAR troops halted and rested while other British forces, marching in from the north and west, advanced on Mandalay. During the next few weeks, the Japanese attacked the Irrawaddy bridgehead, but the Indians held. Holding the bridgehead aided the Allied advances on Mandalay, because Japanese reinforcements and supplies could not reach Mandalay, via the Irrawaddy River valley, from the south.

Along the Arakan Coast, the West Africans had secured the Kaladin, Kalapinsin, and Mayu Valleys and reached the area of the mainland opposite Ramree Island. On February 16, a brigade of the 25th Indians carried out yet another amphibious landing on the mainland across from Ramree Island. They soon linked up with the 82nd West Africans and the 25th Indians, advancing from the north, and together secured the vital An Pass which led over the mountains into the Burmese central plain. The Taungup Pass, which led southward to the port of Taungup, was also taken. The Indians and West Africans then advanced on Taungup, but the advance was slowed again by dense vegetation, wide and rapidly flowing mountain streams, mangrove swamps and strong Japanese resistance. On March 5, the West Africans and Indians captured the port of Tamandu.

During March, the Arakan front was reinforced with the arrival of the 22nd KAR Brigade, comprised of Northern Rhodesians and the Rhodesian African Rifles. With their arrival, both East Africans and West Africans were fighting side-by-side in Burma.

Meanwhile, to the north, Mandalay fell to the British forces in late March, after a bitter two-week battle that cost the Japanese one-third of their total strength in Burma. After giving up the city, the remnants of the Japanese forces retreated southward toward Rangoon via the Sittang River valley, the only remaining route to the south. The Sittang River valley paralleled the Irrawaddy River valley to the east. Both valleys converged in the Rangoon area.

To the west, the Indian and KAR troops on the Irrawaddy likewise began an advance southward down the Irrawaddy River valley.

Once Mandalay was secured, the British regrouped and a powerful British force began marching southward down the Sittang River valley in pursuit of the retreating Japanese. The force marching down the Sittang, which had no African troops, was the most powerful of the all the British forces now in Burma and made rapid progress. On April 10, this force captured Meiktila, seventy miles south of Mandalay and by April 26 had advanced 215 miles down the Sittang Valley to the Schwegin area only 95 miles north-northeast of Rangoon. In contrast, the Indian and KAR force marching down the Irrawaddy River valley reached the river city of Thayetmyo on April 28 and were still 190 miles from Rangoon. The Arakan force too, which occupied Taungup on February 28, was still far from the Burmese capital. It was therefore decided by the Allied commanders that the Sittang force would be given top priority to attack Rangoon from the north, in conjunction with another amphibious landing to be carried out at Elephant Point at the mouth of the 25 mile-long channel leading inland from the sea to Rangoon. The amphibious landing, labeled "Operation Dracula," would be carried out by the 26th Indian Division from the Arakan front which was equipped for, and experienced in, amphibious operations. It had been the 26th Indians who had landed at Akyab in January and on Ramree Island in February.

During the last days of April 1944, the Sittang force, now on the flat coastal plain of southern Burma, struck out in a southwesterly direction along an all-weather road and a rail line toward Pegu, one of Burma's largest cities, and only 48 miles northeast of Rangoon. On April 30, this force secured Pegu and continued its march on Rangoon. On May 2, the 26th Indians landed at Elephant Point without resistance and marched northward toward the Burmese capital. Aiding in Operation Dracula were the 2nd and 3rd Gurkha Parachute Battalions, flying in from Akyab, which dropped inland from the invasion beach to secure roads and bridges.

The Japanese had decided not to fight for the capital and offered only delaying actions. On May 3, the 26th Indians and Gurkha paratroopers occupied Rangoon from the south and on the 6th, linked up with the Sittang force at a point midway between Rangoon and Pegu. The Japanese forces retreated down the panhandle of Burma and into Thailand. Thus ended the battle of Burma.

Meanwhile, the British force in the Irrawaddy River Valley and the remainder of Christison's 15th Corps on the Arakan front, both of which had African troops, made only small advances and were still many miles from Rangoon when the end came. Rangoon was captured just in time, because in late April the monsoon rains began again.

By May 10, troops from the Arakan front had marched inland to link up with the British forces in the Irrawaddy Valley, thus securing southwestern Burma. They then marched toward Rangoon and linked up with British forces in the Rangoon area on May 14.

As the British troops mopped up in Burma preparations were being made at Mountbatten's headquarters for the next phase of the war in Southeast Asia—the invasion of Malaya. By mid-May, those plans were well-advanced and had been labeled "Operation Zipper." Most of the British forces that had been used in Burma would be used again, including the 81st and 82nd West African Divisions and the 11th KAR Division. But first, the great victory of the re-conquest of Burma was to be savored. On June 14, a massive victory parade was held in Rangoon in which the West and East Africans participated. Mountbatten and other dignitaries were on the reviewing stand, saluting the units as they passed by. Unbeknownst to the men on parade, though, their next date with combat had already been set for September 9 on the Malayan Peninsula.

THE LAST OF THE SEA BATTLES IN AFRICAN WATERS

By 1945, the waters all around Africa had become unsafe everywhere for Axis submarines. With radar in virtually every Allied ship and many Allied planes, and hundreds of ships and thousands of planes in operation day and night, there was virtually no place in the Atlantic Ocean, the Indian Ocean, or the Mediterranean Sea where a German sub could sail for long without detection. The development of the air-breathing "snorkel," which allowed a submarine to remain submerged while charging its batteries, helped the German submariners survive, but it was not the total answer. Newer models of radar were coming into use that could detect even the snorkel's small exposed snout. And even underwater the German subs were not as safe as before because of improved sonar detection and improved means of underwater weaponry, such as the acoustic torpedo and the multiple-head depth charge device known as the "hedgehog." Furthermore, the German subs now had to stay close to home, having lost their at-sea refueling capabilities and their French bases.

All this meant that in the Atlantic Ocean German subs could travel southward only as far as the coast of Morocco. They could not reach the Indian Ocean and had given up operating in the Mediterranean Sea.

During January 1945, U–870 was the only German sub operating off Morocco. But on the 3rd, she was able to sink the American freighter "Henry Miller" which was part of a convoy. There were no more attacks off Morocco until, on February 17, U–300 sank two Allied merchantmen out of another convoy. U–300 would not escape, though. She was sunk just five days later, on February 22, by British ships off Cadiz, Spain as she stalked Allied ships at the western entrance to the Strait of Gibraltar.

Surprisingly, there were still some blockade runners that attempted to make the run from Europe to the Far East. One such ship was the Japanese tanker "Yashima Maru." She was spotted by American planes off the Azores on February 2, attacked, and forced to ground herself on Flores Island.

On February 23, the last Allied ship to be taken by a German submarine along the Atlantic coast of Africa was the Canadian freighter "Point Pleasant Park." She was sunk by U–510 off the Atlantic coast of South Africa. U–510 was one of the German subs returning to Europe after having given up their base at Penang. U–510 returned safely to northern Europe.

On February 28, sub U–869 met her end off the coast of Morocco when she was attacked and sunk by the American destroyer escort "Fowler" and the French sub chaser "L'Indiscret." The French ship was an American-built ship given to the French under Lend Lease.

In the greater part of the Indian Ocean all was calm. All German and Japanese submarines had been withdrawn. The only Allied ship losses in the Indian Ocean occurred off the coast of Burma because of the amphibious operations there. Those losses were caused by enemy actions other than submarines. Allied ships, though, plying the Indian Ocean, continued to sail in convoys and the British hunter-killer groups continued to patrol in case the enemy returned.

This persisted until May 28, when the Allies made a joint pronouncement that after this date convoys would be discontinued in the Atlantic, Arctic, and Indian Oceans. War conditions remained, however, in the Pacific. The Allied pronouncement contained the glorious statement, "burn navigation lights at full brilliancy."

Although the submarines were gone from African waters, the mines were not. Ships continued to run into these devilish devices of war well after the shipping lanes were declared safe. A case in point was the disaster that befell the American freighter "Pierre Gibault" out of Ismir, Turkey with a cargo of tobacco, licorice root and fuel oil bound for Oran, Algeria. On June 22, 1945, the Pierre Gibault stuck a mine in a shipping channel off Kythera Island that had previously been swept for mines. The bow of the ship was blown off and three crewmen were killed and seven injured. An international effort was made to save the ship when a Greek escort destroyer, a British salvage ship, and a South African Navy whaler, with a Greek salvage crew aboard, all came to her aid. Their efforts were fruitless, however. The ship was declared a total loss. Fifty-five people survived the ordeal.

THE DEATH KNELL OF COLONIALISM

Around the world the old colonial system was rapidly crumbling, especially during the last year of the war. The reasons were many and varied, but generally it was due to the awakening of the colonial peoples that the old world order was not likely to return and that they, by their own efforts and the circumstances of war, were now positioned to take charge of their own destinies.

Japan, ironically, had been in the forefront of wartime decolonization as a part of their major war aim, which was to create a large Japanese-dominated East Asian economic bloc, known as "The Greater East Asia Co-prosperity Sphere." Under this program, the Japanese leaders planned to militarily conquer the British, French, American, Dutch, and Portuguese colonies of Southeast Asia, and then set most of them up as independent nations allied to Japan militarily and economically. To this end, Tokyo had, by 1945, "granted" independence to Burma, the Philippines, Laos, and recognized the Provisional government of India. They had also given assurances of independence to local leaders in Viet Nam, Cambodia, and the Dutch East Indies. If the Japanese had not suffered a major defeat at Midway in 1942 and been successful in conquering the Hawaiian Islands as they had planned, they would have eventually granted Hawaii its independence and incorporated it into The Greater East Asia Co-prosperity Sphere.

Coincidentally, and independent of Japan, a great independence movement was well under way in India, and in the Middle East both the Vichy French and Fighting French had granted independence to Lebanon and Syria. And, as has been mentioned, the British had acknowledged that Malta would become independent after the war.

These developments were keenly noted by all of the nationalist leaders in Africa. But, so far, no African colony had yet been promised independence. To be sure, reforms had been promised and some of them implemented, but independence was still an illusive goal. It was a goal, though, that many Africans believed was attainable—by one means or the other.

DECOLONIZATION DISCUSSED AT YALTA

The Yalta Conference of January/February 1945 produced a curious political alignment on the subject of colonies. Here Churchill, Roosevelt, and Stalin discussed the future of the mandated and conquered colonies, and Roosevelt and Stalin sided with each other against Churchill. Both Roosevelt and Stalin wanted the colonies in question to be turned over to the soon-to-be-established United Nations Organization to serve as trustee, until a firm and definite program could be worked out to bring independence to each colony in question. Wording to this effect was worked into the Conference's final declaration. Neither Churchill nor de Gaulle, who had not been invited to Yalta, were sympathetic with this plan. Churchill and de Gaulle, therefore, drew closer together on this issue with Roosevelt and Stalin standing in opposition. The latter alliance, though, was not all that strong. Roosevelt fully realized that granting independence to inexperienced and politically unsophisticated peoples opened the door to Communism, and that such programs should not be rushed and would have to be carefully managed by the western powers. This fear, though, was not publicly acknowledge at Yalta nor during the closing months of the war in order to preserve, as much as possible, the harmony within the East-West alliance.

For the various nationalists in Africa and elsewhere, this split between the victorious Allies at Yalta was seen as yet another weakness in the old colonial masters—a weakness that could be exploited.

FRENCH AFRICA

As has been related, strong independence movements had arisen in French North Africa; Morocco, Algeria and Tunisia, and there were others emerging elsewhere within the French Empire. In North Africa, those organizations were spurred to action by an unforeseen and most unwelcome event—famine. The food crops of late 1944 and early 1945 had failed in varying degrees all across North Africa and food shortages began to appear in early 1945. Algeria was especially hard hit.

In February, de Gaulle personally addressed the food problems in North Africa in a meeting with his government's committee on North African affairs. It was decided at that time to send various individuals and investigative teams to North Africa to report on the situation and make recommendations.

While the Paris bureaucracy was studying the food problem in North Africa, the country's largest nationalist organization, "The Congress of the Friends of the Manifesto and of Liberty," which had been formed in the spring of 1944, met again in March. The food shortage was angrily debated and, not surprisingly, the French were blamed for being too slow to react and were doing little or nothing to provide relief. One of the Congress's most radical leaders, Messali Hadj, head of the outlawed and now underground Algerian Peoples' Party (PPA) and recently released from jail, emerged as the Congress's leading personality. With the support of most of the Congress delegates, Messali encouraged the Congress to pass resolutions ending French rule in Algeria. The resolutions stating categorically that the existence of an Algerian republic within the framework of the French Empire was unworkable, and that Algeria should become an all-Moslem, socialist-oriented, independent nation with close ties to Egypt and the newly-formed Arab League (which had been formed in Egypt the month before).

Secretly Messali, and others, were planning an armed insurrection to begin at Setif, a Moslem separatist stronghold and, at that time, declare Algerian independence. Clearly, this would mean civil war in Algeria.

The French could not let this challenge of the Congress go unanswered and soon learned of the Setif plot. Thus, they arrested Messali and deported him to French Equatorial Africa.

By April, the French government's reports on the problems in Algeria had been submitted and analyzed, along with other information coming in from other parts of the French Empire. The reaction by de Gaulle and the other French leaders was to create a new department for the administration of the colonies within the Paris government, with the aim of providing more autonomy, over and above what had been promised at the Brazzaville Conference. From the point of view of the leaders in Paris this was a very generous concession. Their new program called for limited self-government for some colonies and larger elected native assemblies for others—but all within the framework of the empire. The concept of limited self-government would be applied to Algeria but not to the protectorates, Tunisia, and Morocco which already had existing governments. Nor did it apply to French Indo-China where a revolution was under way. To emphasize this new relationship of France with her colonies, all references to those lands being "colonies" was dropped from the official rhetoric and replaced by the phrase "France overseas."

These changes were not unwelcome in North Africa, but did nothing to relieve the great problem of the hour that affected everyone—the food shortages. In some parts of North Africa, primarily in Algeria, conditions were reaching famine conditions. Then the lid blew off.

On May 8, a spontaneous and bloody food riot erupted in Setif, instigated by the hungry Algerian populace. Riots quickly spread to Algiers, Oran, Canrobert, Bougie, Philippeville and Blida. The French authorities were forced to call out the Army, which included many black African troops, to quell the unrest. It proved to be a very difficult job. As soon as one riot was suppressed, another sprang up somewhere else. A large part of the Moslem population of Algeria was in general revolt while, surprisingly, other segments of the Moslem population remained quiet.

During the riots, which lasted until June, some 200 Frenchmen were savagely massacred, while an estimated 1,500 Algerians were killed (some estimates run as high as 8,000) and another 4,500 injured. Some Algerian extremists were arrested and tried, and a few condemned to death. The Egyptian government tried to intercede on behalf of those condemned to death but to no avail. Meanwhile, the slow-moving bureaucracy in Paris did nothing to relieve the food shortages.

The riots and harsh reprisals by the French opened the door for the Algerian nationalist, to take action. They now saw their opportunity to gain the support of the Algerian people. But the French moved first and arrested the two leading nationalist figures, Ferhat Abbas and Dr. Saadane and dissolved the Friends of the Manifesto organization. This successfully blunted the efforts of the Algerian nationalist organizations for the time being.

Meanwhile, the French settlers of Algeria reacted bitterly to the riots, which badly disrupted the Algerian economy and condemned Algerian Governor Chataigreau for being too lenient on the rioters and their leaders. Through their representatives in the Algerian Assembly, the settlers rammed through a new Algerian constitution, allowing the French Algerian administration to clamp down more forcefully on dissidents and nationalists. The message was that if Paris would not do it, the French settlers would do it themselves. Surprisingly, the rapidly reemerging French Communist Party sided with the settlers, because the Communists viewed the radical Algerian nationalists as neo-fascists.

So bitter was the resentment of the French settlers that vigilante-type groups soon came into being called "colons" or "Pieds Noirs." On their own, these groups carried out counter-riots and assassinations against Arab extremists.

As a sop to the Algerian people, the new constitution opened the door for some 60,000 Algerians to become French citizens. Also, the word "natives" was purged from official use. Not surprisingly, these measures satisfied no one.

Thus, a highly-charged political atmosphere developed in Algeria, with the native population and French settlers bitterly polarized and the Paris government seemingly unable, or unwilling, to resolve the major issues.

During June, though, the Paris government diverted shipments of cereals intended for France to Algeria to help relieve the food shortage. Also in June, the Paris government sent its Minister of the Interior, Adrian Tixier, to Algeria to make yet another report. This resulted in a program whereby certain Algerian workers were given government allowances with which to buy food.

But these were only stop-gap measures. Furthermore, all indications were, by the end of June, that the crops for 1945 would fail again. And in July, new municipal elections were scheduled with more Algerians than ever before being allowed to vote.

No one knew it at the time, but the riots of May 1945 had become the breaking point in the relationship between the French and Moslem populations of Algeria. The breach begun at that time proved to be unreconcilable and ultimately led to a long and bloody war of liberation.

In Tunisia, the 1944 harvest was bad but not as bad as that in Algeria. Still, bread was rationed to 250 grams per person per day. Some disturbances occurred but were not bloody and were easily suppressed.

On the positive side, the ports of Sfax and La Goulette were relinquished by the Allied military authorities in April and returned to civilian control. Otherwise, Tunisia was relatively quiet and everyone, Tunisians and Frenchmen alike, were busy trying to rebuild the war-torn nation.

On March 26, 1945, the Tunisian nationalist leader, Habib Bourguiba, arrived clandestinely in Egypt and made contact with Egyptian leaders, as well as leaders of the other Arab nations. He concentrated on befriending those involved in the new Arab League. Bourguiba could not return to Tunisia because he would be arrested by the French for having collaborated with the Axis. Therefore, for the next four years he traveled about the Arab world establishing political support for himself and for the cause of Tunisian independence.

In Morocco, the food shortage had affected some two million people by March and some demonstrations had occurred, but not as bad as those in Algeria. To prevent further troubles, the French administration banned pubic meetings. As in Tunisia, bread was rationed to 250 grams per person per day.

In late June, Sultan Side Mohammed ben Youssef visited battle sites in France and Germany where Moroccan troops had fought. This was a goodwill gesture toward his people and the French.

In French West Africa, there was no food shortage and nationalist activities were mild. The economy, though, was not strong and many blacks were unemployed. Many of them roamed aimlessly about the cities, where they became easy prey for radical union leaders and nationalists. Paris made some effort to improve economic conditions in West Africa by announcing that a large hydroelectric dam would be built at Richard-Tollin, Senegal. A new sawmill was built in the Ivory Coast to increase exports of lumber—the primary customer being the United States. Airline expansion allowed air mail service to be offered for the first time, every other day, to the United States and North America. At Dakar, the French decided to build a new and modern air and naval base. This provided many construction jobs now, and ongoing permanent jobs later, for the local people.

These efforts made only a dent in the unemployment picture and suffering still persisted.

In French Equatorial Africa, there was, also, no food shortage and, in contrast to West Africa, the economy was relatively good. Increased meat production and exports helped the economy. Unlike French West Africa though, the Paris government had no significant plans to make sizeable investments in the colony's economy.

The economic picture in Equatorial Africa was not universal. In early 1945, unemployment increased in the port city of Duala and a series of riots erupted there, led by trade unionists and the unemployed.

On Madagascar, the British relinquished their control over Diego Suarez during January 1945 and returned it to the French.

At Tananarive, the capital, a colonial administration comprised of both French and Malagachies, was established during February. This was the first such administration in the history of French Madagascar. The government had a governor and a sixty-member assembly with thirty members elected and thirty appointed. The new governor answered to the colony's Paris-appointed Governor-General who retained control of the northern part of Madagascar and a few other areas not incorporated into the local administration.

In French Somaliland, conditions had returned to normal. The colony's economy was strong and the French-owned Djibouti-to-Addis Ababa railroad was functioning well, making the port of Djibouti, once again, Ethiopia's main outlet to the sea. There was no interest in, and even considerable resistance to, the British scheme for a Greater Somalia, in which the three Somalilands would be united into one country. This was not surprising, because of the three Somalilands, French Somaliland was the most prosperous.

On the island of Reunion the peacetime economy had resumed, but the island was devastated by a strong cyclone in January, which did much damage.

BRITISH AFRICA

Virtually all of the British colonies in Africa continued to prosper during the first half of 1945 and there was less African nationalism evident compared to other places in Africa. This was certainly due to the British policy of Africanizing the colonial administrations. And, here too, the nationalists felt the need to continue cooperating with the British because many East and West Africans were still engaged in combat in Burma.

In London, Parliament passed the annual Colonial Development and Welfare Act of 1945 which greatly increased funding for the colonies over the previous war years. This, too, had a moderating effect on African nationalism within the British colonies.

British Colonial Secretary, Oliver Stanley, reconfirmed the Churchill government's intentions of holding the empire together when, on March 19, he stated publicly that, "the division of the British Empire into component parts would not serve world peace."

In British West Africa about seven million pounds in aid had been granted under the Colonial Development and Welfare Act of 1945, and plans were made to reabsorb the West African soldiers back into the economy after the war ended.

In all four major colonies, natives were appointed as judges, and in all major cities, city planning proposals were posted and opened to discussion by the local residents.

During June, a lively debate raged over whether or not to build a third college for the natives of British West Africa at Ibadan, Nigeria equal to the others, or whether that college should be one of higher education and the others become feeder colleges to it.

In Sierra Leone, a steel mill had been built by the British and was now producing steel. This provided well-paying, long-term jobs for many natives and promised to enhance the importance of the port of Freetown as a modern shipping center, where ships could now be repaired, converted, and even built thanks to the availability of steel. Furthermore, steel became another export item for the economy of Sierra Leone.

In Nigeria, the British had also built a tin mill, which had similar positive effects on the Nigerian economy, and a palm oil research station in Benin Province. An eleven-year development plan was announced estimated to cost some forty million pounds which would improve roads, water supplies, schools, and up to sixty new hospitals.

On March 22, major political changes took place in Nigeria when the colonial legislative council approved a new constitution for Nigeria. Before it could go into effect it had to be approved by London, but indications were that that would occur. The new constitution created three regional councils, all in the northern part of the country, which would serve as electoral colleges for the main council. They would also address local matters concerning budgeting and regional legislation. Many technical services,formerly provided from Logos, would be transferred to the respective regions. State control of minerals was also included in the constitution, as was a process for the structured election of tribal chiefs.

Not surprisingly, the new constitution was criticized by many of the better educated and more politically sophisticated leaders in southern Nigeria, because it took some political and economic controls away from them and disbursed them to the peoples of the north. This sparked to life another long-smoldering grievance in the south—high inflation and the lack of wages to keep up with the cost of living. This grievance soon took center stage and brought about a strike of skilled workers in the south. The strike was supported mainly by railway workers and promised to be long and bitter.

In Gold Coast, a grant of 173,000 pounds was received from London under the Colonial Development and Welfare Act providing for teacher training, and plans were made for a general education survey in the south. During March, a new system of four grades of native courts was established and in May, a youth center was created. Also that month the colony's first retail co-operative was established. During June, the Town and Country Planning Ordnance was passed, granting the right of eminent domain to local planning commissions throughout the colony.

On the negative side, a scheme to open land in the north for the resettlement of returning soldiers failed, and an epidemic of polio broke out in the northern districts of Wa and Lawra.

In British East Africa, the status quo was the order of the day during the first months of 1945, except in Uganda. There, wages had not kept up with inflation and riots broke out in several Ugandan cities in January. The local police suppressed the riots and imprisoned some individuals. Modest wage adjustments were granted and the colony became peaceful again, although tensions lingered. Five month later, investigations into the riots revealed that nationalist elements had had a hand in instigating them in an attempt to embarrass, and possibly oust, a new young Kabaka (tribal head man) and an unpopular finance minister. In this respect, the riots failed. The Kabaka and finance minister retained their posts.

In all of the British East African colonies the war economy was still booming, and the colonial administrations, as well as the general population, were supporting their men at the front in Burma. News of the increase in funding for the Colonial Development and Welfare Act of 1945 was well-received throughout British East Africa. The greater part of this money was, as in British West Africa, directed toward civilian needs.

A series of inter-colonial meeting, were held to deal with the problems of the returning soldiers. By May, a plan was worked out which called for a number of new training centers, mostly in Kenya, whereby veterans could be taught peace-time skills. Furthermore, an inter-colonial directorate of demobilization was formed to aid the returning veterans in many ways. The African branch of the British Legion veterans organization was charged with preparing an after-care program for veterans who, after receiving government assistance, still had problems.

There was good news in Tanganyika in that a new and sizeable diamond deposit had been found in the Shinyanga area, and in May the colonial governor announced a comprehensive program for the improvement of the colony's infrastructure. This included some 3000 miles of new roads, the creation of an agricultural development fund, a new cotton seed mill at Dar-es-Salaam, and experiments in spraying the new insecticide DDT from low-flying aircraft. An experienced mining consultant was also being sought to exploit the new diamond finds.

On the island of Mauritius, the local population suffered three serious natural disasters. The first and second disasters were two cyclones which hit the island, one after the other within a few weeks of each other. Then, in the spring, a bad outbreak of polio occurred during which about 1,000 people died and many more were crippled.

On the positive side, though, the colonial government undertook measures to bring more natives into the administration of the colony and to widen the franchise. A new and modern 300-bed hospital was built at Floreal, and a British trade union expert was brought from Britain to act as an advisor to the colony's trade unions.

In May, with the war having ended in Europe, some war-related orders fell off in the British East African colonies, and for the first time in more than five years employers stopped hiring new employees and began cutting back on overtime. On a few rare occasions, layoffs occurred. All could see that the boom days were coming to an end, and the blacks expected that they would be the first to be let go.

In occupied Italian East Africa, the political future of those colonies was still on hold pending the creation of the working body of the United Nations Organization.

In occupied Italian Somaliland, some Italian land owners returned hoping to reclaim their land and began farming again. Not surprisingly, the Somali people resented this and refused to work for the Italians, because under the pre-war Italian regime Somalis had been forced to work on Italian-owned farms at very low wages. That bitter memory was still strong and the Italians were resented for it. The British had no intention of allowing the Italian-style forced labor programs to resume, but the British did have in place a quota system which was a more moderate form of forced labor. During their brief tenure as occupiers of Italian Somaliland, the British had learned, as had the Italians before them, that if some sort of work program was not forced on the people many able-bodied Somalis simply would not work at all.

BRITAIN—POLITICAL CHANGES

With the defeat of Nazi Germany, signs of major political changes appeared in London when, on May 21, the Labour Party announced that it was discontinuing its participation in the wartime coalition government with the Conservative Party. This forced the Churchill government to call general elections, the first since 1935. They were scheduled for July.

The Labour Party was now quite far to the political left and contained some strong socialist and neo-socialist elements which saw the empire as an economic burden on the British working classes as well as a deterrent to the economic, social, and political development of the subject peoples themselves. All realized that if, per chance, the Labourites should win power in July, the colonial policies of Britain would most likely be dramatically altered. This fact was well known to the various nationalist leaders throughout the British Empire.

ROOSEVELT AND CHURCHILL IN AFRICA AGAIN

Following the Yalta conference, Roosevelt and Churchill stopped over in Egypt once again. Roosevelt went to the Suez Canal and on February 13 and 14 met, in turn, with Egypt's King Farouk, Ethiopia's Emperor Haile Selassie, and Saudi Arabia's King Ibn Saud aboard an American warship in the Great Bitter Lake (a part of the Suez Canal system).

Little of substance concerning the war resulted from the meetings with the three heads of state, except that the world stature of all three leaders was enhanced by having met with one of the world's most powerful men. Both Egypt and Saudi Arabia were, at the time, contemplating declaring war on one or more of the Axis nations and Roosevelt, of course, encouraged that action and held out the possibility of their receiving Lend-Lease.

Roosevelt and Haile Selassie meeting in Egypt on February 14, 1945, aboard the American cruiser "Quincy."

Churchill was less than pleased with the meetings. He and other British leaders saw them as Americans meddling into matters within the British spheres of influence, especially with regard to Egypt and Ethiopia. This slight dent in Anglo-American relations was seen, though, in a positive light by Farouk and Selassie because both lived under strong British influences. It was also seen in a positive light by many black African nationalist leaders because it demonstrated that the United States still had an on-going interest in African affairs.

Roosevelt's meeting with Selassie made good political fodder for home consumption because many black Americans, who traditionally voted for the Democrat Party, now saw Haile Selassie as a great war hero.

Roosevelt then sailed to Alexandria harbor and, on February 15, met with Churchill. Events would dictate that this would be their last face-to-face meeting. At this meeting, Churchill assured Roosevelt that the British would pursue the war in the Pacific against Japan with full vigor after Germany was defeated. De Gaulle had been invited to this meeting but, miffed at not having been invited to Yalta, declined.

Roosevelt then departed for home but Churchill went on to Cairo and on February 16, met with Haile Selassie, and on the 17th with Ibn Saud and King Farouk.

After Roosevelt was safely back in Washington the American government announced the meetings in Egypt on February 20. Little information was given except that the announcements stressed the intended increase in American-Egyptian trade during the postwar years.

A TIME TO DECLARE WAR—ONCE AGAIN

The major Allied powers, planning the creation of the new United Nations Organization, had decreed that only those nations at war with one or more of the Axis Powers before March 1, 1945, could become founding members of the U.N. The multi-national conference that would bring the United Nations Organization into being was scheduled for September 1945 in San Francisco, California. In the weeks preceding the March 1 deadline more than half a dozen nations around the world declared war. One of those nations was Egypt. On February 24, Egypt declared war on both Germany and Japan. The Egyptian government, though, had no intention of sending Egyptian soldiers to the war fronts as either combat soldiers or support personnel. Furthermore, with the battle fronts now far from Egypt's borders and the Axis nations very weak, the Egyptians expected no enemy action against their territory. Negative effects of Egypt's declaration fell upon those few Egyptian citizens in German and Japanese controlled areas who were now enemy aliens and subject to internment. Also, Egyptian assets would be frozen by the Germans and Japanese, and Egyptian ships at sea would become legitimate targets for the enemy's armed forces. These sacrifices were deemed acceptable, though, because Egypt would gain founding-member status at the U.N. conference in San Francisco, a seat at the eventual peace conferences, and the good will of the soon-to-be-victorious Allied nations.

With Egypt going to war, every part of the African continent now, with the exception of the Spanish and Portuguese colonies, was at war.

On March 1, 1945, the last day of the deadline, Egypt's neighbor, Saudi Arabia, also declared war on Germany and Japan.

Declarations of war went the other way during March, too, in that Japan declared war on France. This came about because French forces were building up in Southeast Asia and the de Gaulle government had announcement that France intended to recover its colony of French Indo-China.

Taking advantage of the state of war between Japan and France Emperor Bao Dai, heretofore a political figurehead in Indo-China, declared Viet Nam an independent nation on March 11. Bao Dai, of course, had the support of the Japanese. This action represented still one more problem the French would have to deal with in order to save their empire. And, as history has recorded, Bao Dai's action started a chain of bloody events that would some take twenty years to resolve.

TROUBLES IN EGYPT AND THE CREATION OF THE "ARAB LEAGUE"

Egypt's declaration war on Germany and Japan came at a turbulent time in Egypt. A hotly-contested general election on January 8 had brought a new coalition government to power under Prime Minister Ahmed Maher Pasha. Strikes, riots, and street demonstrations followed the election and were believed to have been sparked by the losers, the Wafdists.

Another important development in Arab politics was taking place in Egypt during this time in Cairo. On February

14, while both Roosevelt and Churchill were in the country, the Arab leaders, who had met at Alexandria during September and October 1944 at the all-Arab conference, met again and formed the Arab League. Founding members were Egypt, Iraq, Syria, Lebanon, Trans-Jordan, Saudi Arabia, and Yemen. This conference lasted until March 3, and demonstrated an unusually strong show of unity among the Arab nations that portended a dramatic increase in Arab influence on world politics.

From London came pronouncements of support for the Arab League and statements that the British government wanted to work with it. The British, of course, had many interests in the areas involved and it was no secret that London wanted to keep both the Soviets and the Americans out of the region.

It was in this highly-charged atmosphere the Prime Minister Ahmed Maher Pasha announced Egypt's declaration of war. This action was so bitterly resented by some factions and individuals in Egypt that Maher was assassinated hours after making the announcement and while still in the parliament building. The assailant, who was captured and eventually executed, was an Egyptian lawyer who still believed that the Axis Powers would win the war.

Maher's Foreign Minister, Mahmoud Fahmy el-Nokrashy Pasha, was elevated to Prime Minister and Egypt's coalition government remained intact. Tensions, however, remained high throughout the country.

On February 26, the Egyptian Parliament ratified the declaration of war, but declared that Egypt had entered into a state of "defensive war" only.

Also accompanying these turbulent events was a noticeable change in the attitude of the Egyptian people. Sensing their newfound importance in world affairs, the Egyptian people became more nationalistic and openly anti-British than ever before. This resulted in an increase in harassments and attacks on British service personnel and civilians by ordinary Egyptian citizens. There were now many places in Egypt where British individuals and small groups of Britons were not safe. And since the Egyptians could not always distinguish Britons from other westerners, they too were endangered. In addition, an increase in anti-Semitism was noted due to the on-going troubles in neighboring Palestine.

Egypt was to receive a bitter disappointment, however, when the Allied powers ruled that Egypt's "defensive war" was not a sufficient enough commitment to allow that nation to become a founding member of the United Nations Organization. Some saw this as a retaliation, of sorts, by the Western powers against Egypt's rapid increase in anti-Western activities. Now there would be no seat for Egypt at the San Francisco Conference in September, and the Egyptians had yet another reason to be angry with the West.

AIR ROUTES

During the first half of 1945, both of the east-west military air routes across Africa, the Cannonball Route and the North African route, were still heavily used by the Allies. Most of the planes, men, and cargo flying across Africa were headed for Southeast Asia and the Far East.

BELGIAN CONGO

During April 1945, colonial Governor-General Pierre Ryckmans went to Brussels to discuss colonial matters with the Belgian government's colonial minister, Edgar de Bruyn. Ryckmans had brought with him good news. The mines and plantations of the Belgian Congo were still producing at record rates and the tax coffers in the colony were full. Furthermore, sizeable sums of money were flowing to Belgium, where that money became an important factor in rebuilding Belgium's war-torn economy. In both Leopoldville and Brussels, the mood was to keep this good thing going as long as possible. Therefore, there was little thought given to change and little tolerance for those who spoke of it. And most of all, there was no tolerance whatsoever in the halls of the Belgian government for those who spoke of autonomy and/or independence for the Congo.

One nationalistic organization that had emerged in the Congo, the "Ethiopianists," spoke out on some issues regarding native rights and the uplifting of natives in matters of politics and the economy. The colonial government, often aided by the Catholic Church, worked together, though, to suppress the Ethiopianists and their leaders. The Catholic Church's interest was in maintaining control of the colony's educational system, which it had created over the years through its many missions. The gentlemen's agreement between the government and the Church was that four years of primary education was sufficient for the general population, along with certain selected educational programs designed to produce a steady supply of skilled native workers, primarily for the mining industry. The missionaries also provided some medical services for the natives.

For the most part, though, the natives seemed satisfied. Their wages were as high as they had ever been and there were still plenty of jobs for those who wanted them. Unfortunately, not many of the profits generated during the war years went into social improvements for the natives or for the colonial infrastructure. The Belgian colonial administrators felt that this was unimportant and were counting on the old pre-war colonial structure to be maintained for many years to come. Also, since the Belgian Congo sent so few servicemen overseas, the colonial administration would not be plagued with large numbers of young men returning home with new and radical ideas.

There was a small problem among the Europeans in the Congo, though, in that inflation, and the recent fall in value of the Belgian franc, had adversely effected their living standard. Some influential Belgians believed that the solution lie in having Brussels grant the white-ruled colonial administration more political and economic power.

SOUTH AFRICA BRINGS THE BOYS HOME

In South Africa, the tenuous political unity that the South Africans displayed during the war began to deteriorate once again as victory neared and the old problems of nationalities and race reappeared. On the surface, though, things appeared to be rosy. Prosperity was upon the land; foreign investment in South Africa, mainly from Britain and the United States, were at an all time high and there had been no significant problems with labor—either black or white. Prime Minister Smuts had become a world-renowned figure and was taking a leading role in the founding of the United Nations Organization and South Africa was sharing in the glory of being on the winning side of the war with the knowledge that South Africans played a significant role defeating the European enemies. Furthermore, for good or bad, Smuts's United Party had produced a liberal wing under Smuts's acknowledged successor, J. H. Hofmeyer, and even Smuts spoke in more liberal tones of the coming postwar years. To an outsider it might have appeared that South Africa was on the verge of a new era of prosperity, enlightenment, and unity.

Beneath the surface, though, it was the same old South Africa. There had been no labor problems because blacks were forbidden to strike by law and the whites were enjoying good wages with minimal inflation. Also, blacks were relatively content because, for the moment, conditions for them were as good as they had ever been and their services were still needed.

Despite the necessities of war, there still existed an inequality in job assignments between blacks and whites which had been maintained throughout the war years.

In the cities, the shanty towns of the blacks had grown so large that they now abutted white residential districts and ugly racial incidents had occurred. This was a problem that government leaders realized could not be easily resolved. But the radical Afrikaners offered a solution. In late 1944, yet another Afrikaner racist organization, "Blanke Werkers se Berskermingsbond" (White Workers' Protection Society—BWB) was born and rapidly gained strength claiming to be the spokesman for the white working man. Its main agenda declared that the blacks who had been elevated in the work place because of the necessities of war, should now go back to their rural homes and lifestyles. This would reduce the number of blacks in the cities and open up jobs for the returning white servicemen.

Malan's National Party, having outmaneuvered or pushed aside all of its major rivals during the war, was strong, too, and claiming still to speak for the Afrikaners and the political right wing. The activities of the BWB, which was considered one of Malan's fellow-travelers, complimented the National Party's platform but posed no threat.

With regard to military events in South Africa, the men of the 6th South African Armoured Division began arriving home in Lotte and early 1945, even though the unit was still heavily engaged in Italy. This was made possible because many replacements had been trained in South Africa, and the men of the 6th Armoured, having fought the entire length of Italy, deserved to be relieved and sent home. Also serving in the British 8th Army at this time in Italy was a unit of South African road builders who had become the longest-serving unit in the entire 8th Army. These men, and others like them, were also rotated home.

Furthermore, the SAAF had acquired enough American-made C-47 transport planes through Lend-Lease that it was able to establish its own scheduled air route between South Africa and Italy. Therefore, a steady flow of replacements went to Italy and a steady flow of veterans returned home.

Once returned home, a large percentage of the veterans were discharged from service. This proved to be a very popular move by the Smuts government. By the end of February, 19,560 veterans had been discharged and returned to their

VERY FEW JEWS TO SOUTH AFRICA

Jewish immigrants had never been particularly welcome in South Africa, but when they came, they came in waves. The typical pattern would be that immigration policies would be relaxed, Jews would flow in, there would be a negative public reaction, and the immigration policies would tighten again. There had been three distinct waves of Jewish immigration into South Africa in the twentieth century up to the time of World War II. The last wave peaked in 1936, when 3,330 Jewish immigrants arrived, most of them fleeing Nazi Germany. Jewish immigration then declined steadily, and in 1945 reached an all-time low when only 49 Jews were allowed in. It appears to have been the policy of the Smuts government to suppress Jewish immigration as a concession to the Afrikaners and political right in exchange for their on-going support of the war effort.

With the war ended in Europe, Jewish immigration was relaxed somewhat and 688 Jews were accepted in 1947. In the next year, Smuts's United Party fell from power, the political right wing came to the fore, and the immigration door closed once again to Jews.

pre-war jobs, which had been preserved for them by law. Another 8000 discharged veterans had been placed in new jobs. Several government-sponsored educational programs and financial help schemes were available to the veterans to help them make the transition back to civilian life. In addition, there was a government-sponsored emergency housing program in place for the veterans. Similar programs, although funded with less money and many restrictions, were available to black South African veterans.

From a military point of view, the "shelving" of the 6th South African Armoured Division was not a major problem for the Allied planners. Even though the men of the 6th had been told that they would be called on again for action in the Far East, it would not happen soon. The next major British offensive in East Asia was the planned invasion of Malaya and southern Thailand scheduled for September 1945. The terrain of those areas was mostly jungles and mountains and not conducive to tank warfare. The next foreseeable use for an armored division, such as the 6th, would be in Japan itself and that invasion was not likely until late 1945 or early 1946. By that time, a whole new compliment of men could be trained for the division.

On March 14, 1945, the South Africans received a welcome news report from the North Atlantic describing how the South African frigate HMSAS "Natal" had sunk the German submarine U–714 in the North Sea. There were not many South African ships fighting in the northern waters and this was the first report of its kind.

When the end came for Hitler's Germany in May, there were still some 80,000 South Africans serving abroad. The largest percentages were in the 6th South African Armoured Division and the SAAF.

In May, with Europe at peace, the old Afrikaner ties with their distant homeland were demonstrated when an Afrikaner organization created a nation-wide program to collect money to help the people of Holland. Large sums of money were collected and sent to the Afrikaner's distant kinfolk in Europe.

BRITISH SOUTHERN AFRICA

In the self-governing colony of Southern Rhodesia, the government set aside 1.5 million pounds for the rehabilitation of white soldiers. This included a scheme whereby the veterans could acquire farms on a seven-year lease.

In Northern Rhodesia, various schemes were proposed to improve the colony's economy by building, with governmental assistance, such facilities as a foundry, a fish dehydrating plant, a leather works, some clothes factories, and a fiber plant. All of these would make use of native labor and, hopefully, keep the economy of the colony strong. Also, a plan was put forth to increase tourism after the war. Yet another plan was proposed to aid native farming and provide a state-controlled central marketing system for the farmers' produce.

In neighboring Nyasaland the local economy was still good with union and political strife minimal. The political calm was due, in part, because the "North Nyasaland Association," which by now had emerged as the leading organization speaking out on the rights and well-being of Nysalanders, was still cooperating with the British colonial administration.

In the protectorates of Basutoland and Swaziland, a grant of one million pounds had been provided from the Colonial Development and Welfare Act for a variety of projects over the next ten years. In Roma, Basutoland, a new Catholic university came into being, the first on African soil. Education in Basutoland was firmly in the hands of missionaries. In Swaziland, a grant of 100,000 pounds was received for the upgrading of the educational system.

UNITED STATES

In the United States, there was a new awareness of Africa. American men had fought and died there, American-built airfields stretched across the continent, Africa had become a supply source for much-needed war materials, and, most important of all, Americans were aware that Africans had fought gallantly on the side of the Allies. It must also be noted that America's president met with African leaders Haile Selassie, Prime Minister Smuts, King Farouk, the Sultan of Morocco, and President Tubman of Liberia. And Roosevelt had been to Africa several times. During peacetime, such meetings and journeys to Africa by an American president would not likely have happened.

This new American connection with Africa was somewhat muted when, on April 12, President Roosevelt died suddenly at his vacation home in Warm Springs, Georgia. His successor, Harry S Truman, had not accompanied Roosevelt on any of his trips to Africa and had met only Smuts and President Tubman during the course of the war.

Less than two weeks after Roosevelt's death, African leaders came again to the United States to participate in the conference at San Francisco to draw up the Charter for the soon-to-be-created United Nations Organization. Delegates arrived from Ethiopia, Liberia, and South Africa with Prime Minister Smuts himself leading the latter delegation. The meeting would last until June 26.

During the conference, a plan to administer certain African territories under United Nations' trusteeship was agreed to after much debate. It was noted with some concern that the Soviet Union was a strong proponent of this plan which clearly revealed that the communist nation intended to take a new and concerned interest in African affairs in the postwar years. Proposals put forth by the Soviet Union spoke repeatedly of future independence for those territories. This attitude was not lost on the various nationalist leaders throughout Africa. They also noted with interest that India, still a British colony but aggressively pressing for independence, had been invited to the San Francisco conference.

By the time the San Francisco conference adjourned on June 26 the Charter for the United Nations Organization had been created and signed by the representative nations taking part. The matter of administering colonial lands was resolved in an article of the Charter which created the "United Nations Trustee Council." The new council was charged with the responsibility of administering territories turned over to it by the powers that currently occupied those territories. The territories in question were defined as:

1. Territories held under League of Nations mandates.
2. Territories which may be detached from enemy states as a result of World War II.
3. Territories which may be voluntarily placed under the trusteeship system by states responsible for their administration.

Almost immediately, objections to this formula were heard from responsible leaders in two African territories. They came from Eritrea, where the political mood at the moment was leaning toward union with Ethiopia, and from Libya, where hopes for securing independence in the near future were high. The representatives at San Francisco did not attempt to deal with these specific problems at this time. First of all, the proposed Charter had to be ratified by the governments of the member states and then the occupying powers had to be consulted on any objections raised, such as those posed by the Eritreans and Libyans.

Chapter 21
PEACE RETURNS TO AFRICA—TEMPORARILY (JULY–DECEMBER 1945)
THE "GIANTS" AND THE "PYGMIES"

During the last months of 1945, international peace returned to most of the world, and for a short while relative peace reigned throughout the continent of Africa. History was to reveal, though, that this was only a lull before the storm of a new kind of conflict that would endure on the continent much longer than had World War II.

Africa was a continent of people on the move, as tens of thousands of Africans returned to their homes from overseas and from war jobs. Large numbers of them now had experiences, education, and cultural insights that they did not have before the war. More Africans had been trained for military service and war-related jobs than during any other time in history.

Greeting the returnees at dockside, in the city streets, and in the home villages were tens of thousands of other Africans who also had had new and enlightening experiences by just observing what had gone on during the last few years. African soldiers, who had now become accustomed to accepting, as well as commanding, discipline, mingled with the farmer who had become a lathe operator, the laundress who had become an assembly-line worker, and the hunter who had become a truck driver. They soon discovered each others' newfound accomplishments and also discovered that, together, they had a new and powerful collective strength. From this point on there was no turning back. The masses were ready to move forward and the search was on for new leaders who could show them the way.

But as always, there are two sides to every story. The old colonial powers, primarily Britain and France, and to a lesser degree the United States and Belgium, had other ideas about the future of colonial lands and their people. They could point to the fact that they had fought long and hard to save their colonial subjects from becoming slaves of the racist and evil empires of Germany, Italy, and Japan. Furthermore, they had made significant improvements in virtually every colony during the war, provided hundreds of thousands of jobs, increased the skills, education, and medical well-being of tens of thousands of people and were now offering meaningful postwar reforms. Most importantly, the postwar reforms would provide for closer ties to the mother countries and the other entities of the empires which, together, would assure every member of the empire a large measure of economic opportunities, social advancements, and internal as well as external military security against the new world villain, communism. Their argument was that integration into, and cooperation with, a large marketing bloc would be more beneficial to the individual colony rather than going it alone.

As the history of the next few years would show, this argument fell on deaf ears. The glitter of becoming independent, self-governing nations was too powerful to resist.

EUROPE

With the war having ended in Europe, most of the victorious Allied nations gave top priority to bringing their men home as soon as possible. Africa was no exception. Usually, men with the longer service were the first to leave and the others, awaiting their turn, became occupation troops. Eventually, replacements arrived to take their places and all of the veterans came home. Thus it was, in Africa, that tens of thousands of men returned home during June, July, and August 1945. Similarly, there was a cross flow of businessmen between Europe and Africa who were anxious to reestablish their pre-war markets and search for new ones. To a lesser degree there was also a cross flow of businessmen between Africa and North America for the same reasons.

During July Truman, Stalin, and Churchill (later replaced by Clement Attlee) met at Potsdam, Germany to make plans for the final assault on Japan and for the postwar era. Among the many decision made at Potsdam was one in which a "Council of Foreign Ministers" would be formed to prepare peace treaties with the lesser Axis allies, Italy, Bulgaria, Romania, Hungary, and Finland. As part of their mission, the foreign ministers would also make recommendations as to the future of the Italian colonies. There was an immediate reaction in Rome to this development. The Italian government sent an urgent message to the Allied leaders, claiming that Italy's retention of her colonies was essential to the Italian economy. There was little sympathy for this claim in the Allied capitals and it was almost a certainty that Italy's colonies would not be returned to her.

Concerned, too, were the Ethiopians. They were afraid that changes in the former Italian colonies in East Africa might adversely effect them. In August, the Foreign Ministers' Council dispatched a representative to Addis Ababa to personally assure Haile Selassie that Ethiopia's interests would be given the utmost attention regarding any changes in that region.

BURMA

In Burma, the bulk of the Japanese troops fled the country and were pursued by British forces. By mid-June, the last of those troops crossed over into Thailand, and on the 16th, British troops entered Thailand and occupied a small area of land along that country's eastern border. The British then halted their pursuit. There was still a large Japanese force in Burma that had been bypassed and plenty for the British troops to do.

The Japanese force in question consisted of about 10,000 troops who were cut off in the Pego Yoma area about midway between Mandalay and Rangoon. On August 4, these troops did what so many other Japanese troops did in the latter stages of the war when the situation was hopeless; they carried out a massive suicide attack. It was a bloody affair. The Japanese soldiers, lead by General T. Koba, carried out a massive suicide attack against the British troops that surrounded them. Some 8,300 of the Japanese perished in the attempt. The rest were wounded or surrendered.

This ended organized enemy resistance in Burma, and the British were free to give their troops a well-earned respite. The troops also needed additional training for the coming invasion of Thailand and Malaya, scheduled for September, so a rotating program of rest and training was implemented. These plans affected the African troops in Burma, some of whom would be given expanded roles in the coming campaign. As an example, the 22nd KAR Brigade and other units of the 11th KAR Division were sent to Ranchi, India and were trained in crossing wide rivers. They used the Ganges River as their training ground. These skills would be needed in the areas in which they were scheduled to operate in Southeast Asia. Not all the time at Ranchi was spent on military matters. The British also gave the soldiers opportunities to learn new skills that would be useful when they returned to civilian life. Classes were offered in masonry, carpentry, gardening, agriculture, and other endeavors. A large sports program was organized and the men participated in several parades.

Some of the British troops were not given rest but were sent into the delta region of the country to quell a local war that had erupted between Burmese civilians and their age-old rival, Karen tribesmen. This conflict erupted anew during the brief period when neither the British or the Japanese were in control of that area. It would not be an easy conflict to stop. It quickly degenerated into a guerrilla-type war and would last well into the postwar era.

With the re-conquest of Burma, many of the old political problems also resurfaced. Burma had been given its independence under the Japanese and there was now, more than ever, a strong feeling among the Burmese leaders that the British should do likewise. The British showed their willingness to accommodate this popular feeling so long as Burma remained a dominion within the British Commonwealth. Few Burmese accepted this concept, and a prolonged political struggle began within Burma as to its future.

Also with peace came the return of the Burmese Indian population who, before the war, had been the small businessmen, the land owners, and the hated money lenders. These people were most unwelcome in Burma, and the Burmese politicians were quick to blame the British for permitting their return. All of these things made the British position in Burma more difficult; they indicated that the days of the old style British rule in Burma were numbered.

As for the African troops in Burma, the political stirrings by the Burmese people were fully noted and this experience would be carried back to Africa. In addition, the egos of the black soldiers were stroked by a steady stream of African tribal chiefs and other black African leaders, who now came to Burma to praise and congratulate their fighting men. When the black African soldiers finally departed for home, many of them had a new image of themselves.

CHURCHILL GOVERNMENT FALLS IN BRITAIN

During the month of July, the war-weary British people went to the polls and, in one of the most surprising developments of World War II, voted the Churchill government out of office. They voted into office a new government headed by Clement Attlee, leader of the socialist-leaning Labour Party. This portended very significant changes for Great Britain. The

Labourites had long campaigned on a platform of nationalizing much of Britain's industry, expanding public welfare programs, and—of interest to all in the colonies—pursuing a policy of bringing about more self-government for the respective British colonies. This meant that the British colonial empire would decline and, hopefully, the British Commonwealth would expand. The Labourites admitted that they had no definite plan in place for this as they took office and that the process would, almost certainly, be slow and orderly and tailored for each colony. Domestic and postwar-related issues, the Labourites insisted, took priority. Nevertheless, the die was cast for major changes to take place within the mighty British Empire. This very significant change in British colonial policy brought about a new alignment of political forces throughout the empire. The London government and most of the nationalist organizations throughout the empire were now allies of sorts and the old colonial administrators, virtually all of whom had been installed by the Conservative governments, were required to accept the new arrangement. Furthermore, the Labourite leaders in London now depended heavily upon the colonial administrators to advise them on the course of action needed to bring about the respective self-governing bodies.

FRANCE

In France, the de Gaulle government was firmly entrenched and continuing to pursue a policy of retaining as much of the French Empire as possible. There was talk of colonial reform and economic expansion in Paris but no mention of self-government, as there was in London.

Serious troubles, though, were brewing in Algeria and French Indo-China, and the resurgence of the French Communists at home soon added another controversy. The French Communists had experienced a strong resurrection after the liberation of France and now had a say in the de Gaulle government, thanks to de Gaulle's policy of seeking rapprochement with the Soviet Union. The French Communists used this newfound platform to create a colonial department within the French Communist Party, whose mission was to spread communist doctrine throughout the French Empire. De Gaulle and most of the other French leaders were opposed to this activity but did little to stop it lest they upset relations with the Soviet Union. Fortunately for de Gaulle, the French Communists were under-financed and their efforts to spread communist doctrines throughout the empire were minimal. The Soviet Union, likewise, wanting to continue good relations with France, refrained from financing the French Communist's efforts in the colonies.

The French Communist Party was the only Communist party in the Western world that made any attempt, at this time, to spread its doctrines into its colonial empire. The communist parties in the other Western colonial nations were either too weak or too caught up with matters at home to devote money and time to the colonies. The feeling at the time throughout the communist world was that Communism, with its great appeal to oppressed peoples, would spread of its own accord through the old colonial empires. Furthermore, Moscow still wanted good relations with the West. The war with Japan was still raging and Stalin had promised the United States and Britain at Yalta that the Soviet Union would enter that war and cooperate with the Western allies in defeating Japan.

SOUTH AFRICA

During the summer of 1945, the last large body of the South African troops had returned from Europe but South Africa was still a country at war. The armed forces were maintained at full strength, ready for the call to fight in the Far East, and South African industry was still on a wartime footing. So far, South African losses in the war, as of August 1945, were 6,496 men killed, 14,078 wounded and 14,583 prisoners of war and missing. The war had cost the South Africans 600 million pounds which had been financed by war loans and increased taxes.

Furthermore, South Africa was the temporary home of 93,376 enemy prisoners of war, a relatively large number for a country its size. Throughout the war the POWs had been employed in agriculture,forestry, road building, and other non-military activities as allowed by the Geneva Convention.

The Smuts government was participating actively in the new United Nations Organization and Smuts, who had long sought such an organization to replace the old League of Nations, was personally in the forefront of U.N. activities.

GERMAN BABIES TO SOUTH AFRICA

During the summer of 1945, a steady stream of German babies and pre-school children arrived in South Africa for adoption. Many of these were children from the infamous "Lebensborn" (Fount of Life) organization that had been created in Nazi Germany to increase the nation's birth rate. That organization established "homes" to which pregnant Aryan women, married or not, could go to have their babies. Indeed, German women were actively recruited for the homes. Upon having the baby, the woman could keep the child and receive a small pension, give it up for adoption, or allow it to go to a Lebensborn orphanage where it would be raised by the state.

When the Allies conquered Germany, they found thousands of these children in the homes and orphanages. Sadly, the children were looked upon as outcasts by German society and placement of the children within Germany was difficult. Furthermore, the German economy was in such bad shape that many families did not relish the idea of having one more mouth to feed. In Germany they were called "Orphans of Shame."

Fortunately, charitable organizations took charge of the children and found homes for them in other countries. South Africa, with its large Afrikaner population, was one of the countries that welcomed the children.

BELGIAN CONGO

By summer 1945, the Belgian government was functioning again in Brussels and struggling with the problems of rebuilding the country's economy and war-torn infrastructure. Also, still festering in Belgian politics was the split between King Leopold and the elected Belgian government. These questions took center stage in Belgium and little attention was given to the Congo. Most of the Belgian leaders, as well as most of the Belgian people, still looked upon the Congo as they had before the war that the Congo was a prized Belgian possession that existed primarily for the benefit of the mother country. Fortunately for the Belgians, there were few problems in the Congo during 1945 to upset this thinking in Brussels. There were no organized nationalistic groups in the Congo strong enough to cause the colonial officials concern and the colonial economy was still strong. This translated into high employment for the natives, minimal problems with the worker's unions, profits for the Belgian corporations, and generous tax revenues for the government.

Much of the peaceful conditions in the Congo could be attributed to the enlightened administration of Governor-General Pierre Ryckmans. Ryckmans had served in his post throughout the war and proved to be a good organizer who had created an efficient administration. He was also stern, but at the same time he was benevolent. Under his leadership, some progress was made in providing more services for the natives. This included advances in medical care, education, and public utilities. He also helped native farmers acquire land. In regards to education, Ryckmans opened the door, during 1945, to Protestant missionaries to come to the Congo and establish schools. Heretofore, the Catholic Church had had a monopoly on native education.

Ryckmans had an ally in Brussels, Colonial Minister Robert Godding. Godding was a progressive politician who urged the Congolese people to take some matters of public interest into their own hands. Specifically, Godding recommended that native leaders establish village-level councils, to administer some of their own local affairs, as well as native workers' councils. He also encouraged the natives to start their own newspapers. Even though these doors now opened to the Congolese people little progress was made. There simply were not enough well-educated and/or experienced Congolese to step forward to become effective leaders. As a result, the colonial administration had to continue managing many of the native's affairs. In 1946, after these programs for the natives had had a chance to work, it was noticed that little progress had been made by the natives. This was a disappointment to Ryckmans who would lament in a report, "The mass of (Congo) natives (are still) badly housed, badly nourished, illiterate; destined to sickness and premature death."

In the Belgian-mandated territories of Rwanda and Urundi the situation was different. These were heavily-populated areas on the eastern border of the Congo and had only moderate resources, so they did not contribute significantly to the economy of Belgium. They had been given to Belgium by the League of Nations after World War I with the understanding that Belgium would, at some unspecified time in the future, help these territories become self-governing. It was now certain that the United Nations Organization would take over the mandate responsibilities from the League of Nations and that the future goals for Rwanda and Urundi would still be the same. Through the years the two major tribes that inhabited the area, the Tutsie and Hutus, had proven capable of managing many of their own affairs as well as providing for their own fundamental needs with regard to food, housing, and public order.

With these conditions in place and the United Nations soon to take over, Brussels decided that the time had come to begin the process of leading these two territories toward self-government. Subsequently, a program was devised which would bring about that goal, in stages, over a number of years. No such program, though, was prepared for the Congo.

In August 1945, when the Americans dropped the two atomic bombs on Japan, only a handful of people in Belgium and the Congo knew that most of the uranium and plutonium used in those bombs had come from the Belgian Congo. Suddenly now, that fact was known world-wide, as well as the fact that half of the entire world's production of uranium came from the Congo.

This near-monopoly would not last long, however. Before the year was out a frantic world-wide search was under way for new uranium deposits. Two of those new sources were being explored in Africa, one in Tanganyika and the other in South Africa. Before long dozens of sources would be found around the world but, fortunately for the Belgians, few would measure up to the richness of the ore produced in the Congo. The Congo would continue to be a major source for this awesome product of nature during the early postwar years. In Brussels the Congo's uranium gave the Belgian government yet another reason to maintain tight reigns on that colony.

During September, native railroad workers went on strike, seeking better wages and working conditions, but the railroad owners refused to meet their demands. Worker demonstrations, and eventually riots, occurred, shattering the tranquility in the Congo that seemed to be so well under control. Large numbers of police had to be rushed to the scene to restore order. But before the strikers could be contained, disorder broke out in other parts of the colony and escalated from economic issues to racial issues. At one point, the Ryckmans government urged whites in some parts of the colony to arm themselves. Suddenly, the Congo was on the verge of a colonial war.

The unrest was eventually put down, but the incident served as a wakeup call to both the Ryckmans government and the government in Brussels that all was not was well in the Congo as had been believed.

PORTUGUESE TROOPS IN MOZAMBIQUE

In Mozambique, the Portuguese continued their troop buildup until, by late summer, there were two army divisions stationed in and around Lourenco Marques. Portuguese warships also gathered in the harbor. Their mission was to recover the Portuguese colony of Timor in the East Indies, which had been occupied by the Japanese in early 1942. They also would be used to recover Macau, the Portuguese enclave on the east coast of China, when the timing was right. Until then they would wait in Mozambique.

AT SEA

There were no more Axis submarines plying African waters but there were a few Axis blockade runners still trying to make the extremely dangerous passage between Europe and the Far East. One such ship, the Japanese freighter "Eigyo Maru," which had fled Europe at the time of the German collapse, was encountered by Royal Air Force planes and sunk off the western shore of Flores Island in the Azores.

The Allies were still experiencing ship losses in all the world's oceans due to renegade mines. Mines had a tendency, after a while, to break free from their anchors and drift aimlessly about the oceans. Occasionally ships would run into them or they would wash up on distant beaches. This was a phenomena that lasted for years.

In African waters, for example, it happened on June 22, when the American freighter "Pierre Gibault" hit a mine southeast of the Azores. Ten months later, in April 1946, a second American merchantman, the "Park Victory" would strike a mine in the same general area.

In the Indian Ocean, there was still something of a threat from German subs, which were now in the hands of the Japanese. When Germany surrendered in May 1945, six German subs were trapped in the Far East: two at Kobe, Japan; two at Singapore, and one each at Batavia and Soerabaya, Dutch East Indies. The Japanese confiscated these subs and began converting them for their own use. Those conversions, however, were not completed by the time hostilities ended so the subs were not used.

SUDDENLY THERE WAS PEACE

On August 6, the Americans stunned the world and changed the course of history by dropping an atomic bomb on the Japanese city of Hiroshima. That one bomb obliterated the city. On August 8, the Soviet Union declared war on Japan and invaded Japanese-held territories on the Asian mainland and the smaller Japanese home islands in the north of Japan. The next day, the Americans dropped a second atomic bomb, this time on the city of Nagasaki.

These events spelled doom for Japan's war effort. There was no way they could continue the fight against such overwhelming developments. On August 10, the Tokyo government announced that it was willing to surrender as long as the status of the Emperor remained unchanged. The Allies responded within hours, saying that the Emperor could stay

JAPAN HASTENS DECOLONIZATION

On August 7, the day after the first atomic bomb was dropped on Hiroshima, the Tokyo government activated a plan that had been made for the eventuality that Japan could no longer hold on to their newly-conquered possessions in Southeast Asia. That plan called for Japan to hasten the independence of both French Indo-China and the Dutch East Indies as soon as possible. Both of these lands had been promised independence at some unspecified future date by the Japanese as a part of Tokyo's overall plan to create a huge economic bloc in the Far East known as "The Greater East Asia Co-prosperity Sphere." Now that dream was shattered, but Tokyo still had the wherewithal to "liberate" those two large colonies from their European masters.

That same day, August 7, Japanese Field Marshal Terauchi, Supreme Japanese Commander for Southeast Asia, headquartered in Saigon, French Indo-China, received orders from Tokyo to summon nationalist leaders from Indo-China and the Dutch East Indies to Saigon immediately and cooperate with them in the proclaiming of independence for their respective nations. Terauchi's order went out and the nationalist leaders eagerly responded. They began to arrive in Saigon within the next 48 hours. In conferring with Terauchi, the nationalists were assured that they could proceed with proclaiming their nations' independence with the full backing of the Tokyo government. Furthermore, the Japanese armed forces in their lands would cooperate in keeping order and turn over the reigns of government to the newly created regimes.

but would be subject to Allied authority. Then the Japanese hesitated, and on the 13th the Americans sent 1,600 bombers over Tokyo to pulverize the city once more with conventional weapons in an effort to force the Japanese hand. Unbeknownst to the Japanese and the rest of the world, the Americans did not have their third atomic bomb ready to drop. If they had, they might very well have used it.

On the 14th, American bombers hit the cities of Kumagaya, Isesaki, and Akita, all with conventional weapons. While these raids were in progress, the Tokyo government announced that it would accept the Allied terms. The Allies agreed and proclaimed the next day, August 15, a day of world-wide celebration—V-J Day.

On September 2, representatives of the Japanese government signed the documents of surrender aboard the American battleship "Missouri" in Tokyo Bay and World War II ended. The war that had raged for almost six years ended in a 28-day series of dramatic events. Suddenly there was peace.

INDONESIA AND FRENCH INDO-CHINA IN TURMOIL

On August 17, Indonesian nationalists proclaimed the Dutch East Indies an independent nation to be known, henceforth, as Indonesia. The Dutch government in The Hague denounced this action but had no means by which to counter it. Out of desperation, they turned to the British and asked them to send troops into the East Indies to help save their colony.

During the last days of August, the Viet Namese nationalist leader, Ho Chi Minh, a communist, and his guerrilla forces took control of the city of Hanoi in French Indo-China without opposition from the Japanese. On September 2, the day the Japanese surrendered, he proclaimed the eastern region of Indo-China an independent nation to be known as the Republic of Viet Nam. The de Gaulle government in Paris rejected Ho's bold move outright, and announced that they would send troops to oust the communist rebels. Unfortunately, there were no French troops available to enforce the Paris government's will. So they, like the Dutch, asked the British to intervene and occupy the southern part of Indo-China up to the 16th parallel until French troops arrived.

Provisions for the British to occupy the southern part of Indo-China, and the Chinese Nationalists to occupy the northern part, had been made at Potsdam. Both the British and Chinese agreed to cooperate with the French but could not do so immediately because of other commitments in Southeast Asia.

The Chinese Nationalists, facing a looming civil war with the Chinese Communists, showed little interest in committing resources to Indo-China but did manage to send a modest force into northern Indo-China early in September. The Chinese soldiers were, however, very poorly disciplined and many of them harbored communist sympathies. Ho's forces, considerably smaller but well-disciplined, resisted the Chinese as they poured in and were able to defeat them at every turn. The Chinese troops usually fled at the first sign of combat. Some deserted, others turned to looting, and still others sold their weapons to the Vietnamese. In all, the Chinese incursion was a failure.

To add to these miseries, pirates reappeared in the country's many waterways and along the coast and some tribal feuds resumed.

In the south, British forces finally arrived unopposed during the first and second week of September. They disarmed the Japanese and freed the French POWs and administrators who had been incarcerated by them. They also assisted those freed administrators in beginning the process of reconstituting the French colonial administration. On September 12, a small contingent of French administrators and military officers arrived at Saigon by air from Ceylon to assist in this effort.

HO WAS PREPARED

Ho Chi Minh was unique in the colonial world. There was no other colonial nationalist leader who was as well-prepared for a war of liberation at this stage of the war than he. Ho had long prepared for this day—September 2.

Years earlier, Ho had formed a guerrilla band and throughout the war carried on a low-level guerrilla war against the Japanese using his forces very sparingly. Ho could see the big picture and, as the war turned against the Japanese, he saw that the French would be his real enemy. Therefore, he organized his forces to be ready for the day when Japan collapsed and a political and military vacuum would develop in Indo-China for a short while before the French could return. That was the time he would strike with maximum effort. By the time that day came, Ho had an army of 10,000 men, well-trained and adequately armed to carry out the task assigned to them. Upon capturing Hanoi and other parts of Indo-China Ho acquired large stores of Japanese war materials, at times with the acquiescence of the Japanese themselves, and from that point on was able to carry on an effective guerrilla war for many years to come. Not surprisingly, Ho would become a role model for those revolutionary leaders who would later try to emulate his success.

Ho had many followers in the south who resented the return of both the British and French. They were willing to take up arms on behalf of his revolution. Thus, local guerrilla-type warfare broke out in the south between the Vietnamese on the one hand and the British and French on the other. In some instances, the British allowed the Japanese to keep their arms in an effort to maintain order.

This was a most unwelcome development for the British, who were now obliged to commit British lives and money to a struggle to save someone else's colony. As a result, the British went on the defensive to protect themselves but, at the same time, to secure Saigon and provide enough safe territory from which the soon-to-return French could operate militarily against the insurgents. Unfortunately for the British, the French would be very slow to returning in force and these difficult conditions would drag on for weeks. The main reason for this delay was that the French were desperately short of ships.

To complicate matters further in Indo-China, the Americans opposed the return of the French to the colony and, instead, hoped to create a joint American, British, and Chinese commission to administer the colony until its future could be determined.

In short, the political and military situations in Indo-China had become an international political football and one giant mess. And, as history has recorded, it would take decades to resolve.

ELSEWHERE IN ASIAN COLONIES

After September 2, Japanese garrisons throughout Southeast Asia, the Pacific, and on the Asian mainland began surrendering en masse. As a result, political vacuums were created in some areas and local resistance groups, many of them nationalistic and/or communist in makeup, jumped into the voids which were created to take control of their local areas. In other areas, political factions and guerrilla groups began fighting among themselves for control, and in still other areas there was no one to take control. In some instances, the Allies asked the Japanese to retain their arms and keep the peace until Allied troops could reach them.

These actions once again demonstrated that, in many instances, the old colonial powers were weak and inept when it came to rescuing their colonial subjects. The most obvious example of this, perhaps, was demonstrated in the Dutch East Indies. As a part of the Japanese surrender terms, the Dutch military authorities, stationed in Australia, sent orders to the Japanese garrisons throughout the Dutch colony to continue to maintain order until Allied troops could arrive. The Indonesian people took this as a great insult in that the Dutch now trusted the former enemy rather than their own colonial subjects.

The recovery of the Philippines proved to be no major problem for the Americans, because most of that nation had, by war's end, already been reconquered. Also, the Americans had the manpower, ships and planes readily available to spread throughout the islands to accept the surrender of the various Japanese garrisons and quickly establish local controls. Furthermore, there was little incentive for dissident forces to attempt to take control because the Americans had announced that they would proceed with granting the Philippines full independence in 1946. That independence had long been promised for 1945 but was postponed due to the war.

MALAYA AND SINGAPORE

As for Malaya and Singapore, the British reaction was swift. The British were in the final planning stages of "Operation Zipper," the planned invasion of Malaya, and had combat forces, landing craft and warships ready and waiting at Rangoon, Burma. When the Japanese surrendered, these forces where hastily mobilized and, during the first days of September, were able to land at strategic points along the western coast of Malaya and at Singapore. They quickly spread out across the peninsula and secured almost all of Malaya and Singapore. The Japanese garrison at Singapore surrendered to the British on the 12th. The British went on then to reoccupy the British possessions on the island of Borneo.

The British re-conquest of Malaya, Singapore and the Borneo possessions was facilitated by the fact that the Japanese had not encouraged the local nationalist leaders there to proceed with plans to make their lands independent, as had been the case in Indo-China and the Dutch East Indies. The nationalist organizations in these British colonies were poorly organized and, almost certainly, could not survive once the British returned. Furthermore, some of the nationalist organizations were led by communists. Therefore, the Japanese opted to let the British recover their colonies rather than create a situation for the local people that was destined to fail and for which Japan might later be blamed.

The recovery of Malaya did not go peacefully, though. communist-led guerrilla forces in the interior of the colony, which had been fighting the Japanese, had political aspirations of their own and now began to resist the British. Furthermore, the people of Malaya and Singapore had been fed a steady three-year diet of anti-western propaganda by the Japanese, so in many quarters the British were less than welcome. This resulted in a large part of the population being sympathetic to the guerrillas in the bush. As a result, the British were able to reoccupy only the major cities,which the Japanese had already secured, but were not able to gain control of much of the interior. This unhappy situation would prevail for years, resulting in yet another prolonged colonial war.

Further to the east, British, Australian, and New Zealand forces were quick to reoccupy the many British island possessions in the western Pacific. Here again, there were no viable nationalist groups so the occupations proceeded without incidents. On August 30, British naval forces peacefully reoccupied Hong Kong.

In the meantime, the British found the means to respond favorably to the request from the Dutch to help them recover the Dutch East Indies. On September 29, British and Indian forces landed on the main island of Java and occupied the colonial capital of Batavia. They also landed on the other major islands of Sumatra and Borneo. The Indonesians, though, had had enough time to put together a small ragtag army and they resisted. The Indonesian People's Army, as it was called, was equipped with captured and donated Japanese weapons as well as some pre-war Dutch weapons. This demonstrated to the Dutch that when they arrived they could be expected to walk into a full-blown colonial war.

The Indonesian insurgents were no match for the British forces and were easily routed whenever encountered, but the British found themselves caught up in yet another situation, as in Indo-China, whereby they were expending British lives and money to reconquer someone else's colony. They, therefore, did in Indonesia as they were doing in Indo-China; occupied only the areas they deemed necessary for their own security and that would be needed by the Dutch to establish a secure foothold in the colony.

TIMOR PEACEFULLY RESTORED TO PORTUGAL

On August 17, the Tokyo government announced that its troops would withdraw from the Portuguese colony of Timor and that the Portuguese would be free to return. There was no attempt by the Japanese to promote independence for the people of Timor.

When this news reached the Portuguese forces waiting at Lourenco Marques, Mozambique, they departed at once by ship for Timor. During the first week in September, enough Portuguese troops and officials had arrived in Timor for the Japanese to relinquish control to them. More arrived at the end of September. By then the Japanese forces had withdrawn to Indonesian territory on the western portion of the island and surrendered to the Australians.

COLONIAL WAR ERUPTS IN INDONESIA

During the first two weeks of October, Dutch forces and administrators returned to Indonesia in considerable numbers and began to restore their old colonial system throughout the islands. The Dutch, having landed in the enclaves prepared for them by the British and Indian troops, were able to do this peacefully at first because the British forces continued to maintain order. The rebel Indonesian government, of course, had every intention of contesting the return of the Dutch, but for the moment offered only limited resistance. Their People's Army was no match for the combined British and Dutch military strength arrayed against them. It was almost certain that the British would soon withdraw and then the odds would be more even.

In the meantime, the Indonesian government, acting as the independent government it claimed to be, formally declared war on Holland. This was October 13, 1945.

Soon afterwards the British did withdraw and yet another colonial war erupted in East Asia. It would last until 1949 and result in a complete victory for the Indonesians. But, it would then be followed by a bitter civil war which would last until 1961.

INDIA TO BE SELF-GOVERNING

Perhaps the best news for Africa's nationalists was the fact that India was, after years of non-violent struggle, on the road to independence. This was the direct result of the British elections of July 1945 when the Labour Party came to power in London. The Labourites had long campaigned on a platform of granting India self-government with the hope that she would remain in the British Commonwealth, become a friend to Britain, and become a valued trading partner with the other Commonwealth nations.

The Indian leaders, of course, welcomed this development, but they did not necessarily support the idea of remaining within the British commonwealth. Nevertheless, the Indians realized, as did the British, that there were major problems to be overcome before any form of self-rule could be granted. The main problem was that the Hindus and Moslems, who made up the greatest percentage of the population, had long had problems living together and there was a real threat that India might split into two or more nations based on religion. All sides agreed that this should not happen if it could be prevented and agreed to work together toward a solution.

Then too, the Indians were showing that they would follow a foreign policy of their own which was not always compatible with Britain's. Indian leaders had already expressed opinions that Burma and Ceylon should be set free and had developed their own policies toward China, the Soviet Union, and the Middle East. Now, on September 21, the Indian leaders jumped into the colonial fracas of Southeast Asia. On that date, the leaders of the All-India Congress Party, meeting in Bombay, called for an end to the "imperialist domination" of all the colonial lands of Southeast Asia. This action increased the polarization among the wartime Allies that was now developing over colonial policies in that region. Arrayed on one side were the United States, the Soviet Union and now India favoring decolonization in Southeast Asia, and on the other side were Britain, France, The Netherlands, and Portugal determined to reestablish their colonial empires there.

THE AFRICANS WATCH

The African people and their leaders all over the continent watched the dynamic developments occurring in the East with great interest. Nearly every day brought news of some new dynamic development in a far-away colony. From their point of view, it was clear that the old colonial system was changing rapidly and often in a difficult and, at times, bloody way. Indo-China was of particular interest because here was a worst-case-scenario in the making. The respective nationalist leaders in Africa could not have helped fearing that such things might happen in their land when the time came for them to make their bids for freedom. The tragedies unfolding in Indo-China and Indonesia, and the difficulties in Malaya and India, could not have helped but act as deterrents for those African leaders who might otherwise have taken hasty and poorly-planned actions.

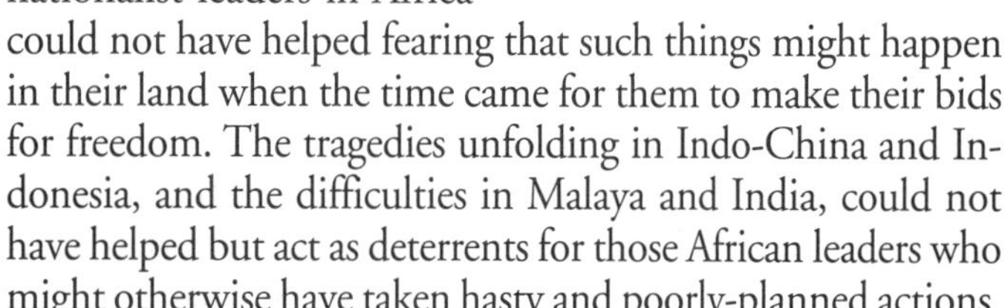

Leaders of the Arab League at a meeting in Cairo in May 1946. Left to right: Seif al Islam Abdullah of Yemen; Sheikh Bishara al Khoury, President of Lebanon; Shukri el Quwatli, President of Syria; King Farouk I of Egypt; King Abdullah of Trans-Jordan and Emir Saud, Crown Prince of Saudi Arabia.

RELATIVELY PEACEFUL IN AFRICA BUT NEIGHBORS IN TURMOIL

As 1945 came to a close, Africa was relatively peaceful, with its old colonial system still very much intact. There was only one colonial war underway in Africa—that being in Algeria. But there were signs of change all around and some unpleasant turmoil in lands close by. In the Middle East, the French had given up all attempts to reestablish their colonial mandates over Lebanon and Syria and in early June withdrew the last of their forces from those countries. That the countries of Lebanon and Syria had successfully attained independence and thrown off the last vestiges of French influence in a relatively short time was an encouragement for the African nationalists—but there was also bad news.

In Palestine serious trouble was still brewing. Jews were streaming in, many of them illegally, to the British mandate with the expressed purpose of establishing an independent Jewish state. The Palestinian Arabs, of course, opposed this and hoped to establish an independent Palestinian state. The British showed every sign that they wanted out from under their mandated responsibility, but they were morally bound to try to maintain order in Palestine until some solution could be found. Furthermore, with regard to Palestine, it was revealed on August 13 at a World Zionist conference that as early as May 1945 a plan to establish a Jewish state in Palestine had been secretly, and favorably, reviewed by the British government in London.

The nations of the newly-formed Arab League, anxious to flex their muscles on the world scene, announced that they would aggressively oppose the establishment of a Jewish state in Palestine with force of arms if necessary. Thus, a new war loomed in the Middle East over Palestine—a war in which Egypt, and possibly other African states, might become involved.

EGYPT ASKS THE BRITISH TO LEAVE

With the return of peace and the relaxation of wartime restrictions, the squabbling political factions of Egypt found a common issue upon which they all could agree; that the British should leave Egypt. The general feeling among the Egyptian political leaders was that the much-hated Anglo-Egyptian treaty of 1936, which permitted virtually unlimited British military presence in Egypt, must be abolished and there were still hard feelings about Britain's having forced unwanted governments on the King and the nation during the war. On September 23, the government of Premier Mahmoud Nokrashy responded to this feeling and leveled two demands on Britain. The first was that Britain withdraw all her armed forces from Egypt, thereby negating the 1936 treaty, and the second was that the joint British and Egyptian control over The Sudan be terminated and it be annexed by Egypt. London rejected both of these demands and the struggle between the two countries continued. The Egyptian/British relationship would see-saw back and forth over the next few months and years. In the long run, though, Britain would have its way. The British would remain in Egypt until 1954, and The Sudan would become an independent nation in 1956.

On October 8, the Egyptian government lifted the "State of Siege" decree that had been imposed on October 12, 1939. With this, martial law was lifted.

On October 31, well-armed Jewish terrorist groups launched a co-ordinated attack on the British in Palestine with the hope of driving them out of Palestine and establishing the Israeli state. Tensions arose throughout the Arab world, and suddenly the Arabs were supportive of the British because they were now fighting the Arab's enemy, the Jews.

During the first week in November, this crisis spilled over into Egypt and Libya. On November 2, the anniversary of the Balfour Declaration, there were nation-wide anti-Zionist protests throughout Egypt. An angry mob raided the Jewish quarter in Cairo and torched Jewish shops and a synagogue. Over a hundred people were injured. The next day, a much more deadly anti-Zionist riot erupted in Tripoli, Libya, in which 74 people were killed and 183 injured.

On November 12, King Farouk make a major speech which had a conciliatory tone to it with regards to the British. In keeping with the new liberal thinking in London and the British action in Palestine, Farouk announced a number of far-reaching economic and social reforms in Egypt long favored by Britain. One of the reforms called for the distribution of some 50,000 acres of land to small farmers. Farouk also called for an excess profits tax of 50% on war profits and an income tax which would be levied on the rich for the benefit of the poor. And, as another sop to the British, he abolished the import permits system with regards to all goods coming from the sterling bloc. These concessions appeared to be an attempt by the King to mollify tensions between Egypt and Britain, for on December 20 the Egyptian government formally asked the British government to renegotiate the 1936 military treaty.

As 1945 ended, Egypt was plagued by many issues; troubles with the British, troubles in neighboring Palestine, the corruption of the ruling Wafdist Party having been exposed, the rise of the politically radical and religiously fundamentalist Moslem Brotherhood, disorder in the streets, the King's independent attitude, and the question of the annexation of The Sudan. In the new year, the Nokrashy government would last only two months and give way to a new government heavily influenced by the "Moslem Brotherhood." Egypt's political scene would remain turbulent until 1952, when a military coup took control of the government and brought a measure of stability, albeit at the cost of political freedom.

THE UNITED STATES ANGERS THE ARABS

During November 1945, the British and Americans formed a joint committee to study the problems in Palestine. This upset the Arab community in that the United States had now thrown its lot in with the British. To the Arabs it appeared that Britain was setting the stage to renege on its White Paper of May 1939, in which the British government promised the creation of an Arab state in Palestine.

Further adding to the anti-Zionist sentiments in North Africa and the Arab world was the fact that the United States government, on its own, was becoming very supportive of the Zionist cause in Palestine. This was made very clear on December 17, when the U. S. Senate passed a resolution calling for the establishment of a Jewish "commonwealth" in Palestine and the free and unlimited entry of Jews there. This was like a stab in the back to the Arabs. All of the goodwill built up by the United States in North Africa and the other Arab lands during the war now evaporated into thin air.

As the Palestine situation worsened, Palestinian Arab leaders called for a boycott of Jewish goods and services throughout the Arab world. This call was acknowledged by all of the Arab nations but was not fully implemented until the summer of 1946.

TANGIER

Then there was Tangier. On August 22, the four major Allied powers, Britain, France, the United States, and the Soviet Union, announced that they intended to reestablish the old international status of the city of Tangier on the northern coast of Morocco. This, of course, was in direct conflict with Spanish interests because Spain, during the war, had unilaterally occupied the city and attached it to Spanish Morocco.

The Spanish government, now an outcast within the world community, was in no position to resist the Allied demands. Therefore, Madrid reluctantly agreed to give up control of Tangier and allow the old order to be reestablished under agreements dating back to the 1920s. There were several changes, however, in the administration of Tangier. The United States and the Soviet Union would now become participants, and Italy would be excluded for the time being. Also, at the insistence of the Soviet Union, the Spanish government would be excluded from participation in the Tangier administration so long as the Franco regime remained in power in Madrid. On October 11, the Spanish troops withdrew from Tangier and an international police force replaced them.

This action by the Allied nations was seen as a setback for the African nationalists in general and for the Moroccan nationalists in particular. Both of these factions hoped to see the Spanish and French protectorates of Morocco abolished and Morocco become, once again, an independent nation with Tangier an integral part. The parting out of Tangier as a separate political entity made that process more difficult.

LONDON MEETING ON U.N. TRUSTEESHIPS

On September 14, 1945, the foreign ministers of the Four Power Commission (U.S., Britain, France, Soviet Union), established by the United Nations Organization, met in London to work out the details of setting up trusteeships for the former Italian colonies in Africa. Representatives from Canada, Australia, New Zealand, South Africa, and India were invited to present their views. Representatives from the colonies in question and from Ethiopia and Egypt were not invited.

Almost immediately the meeting was deadlocked over the principle question as to how the former colonies should be administrated. The three western powers advocated a collective trusteeship arrangement for the colonies under United Nations supervision but the Soviet Union advocated individual trusteeships by the four powers and expressed interest in themselves being given jurisdiction over Libya and Eritrea. This was a condition the western powers could never agree to, because it would open the door to the introduction of communism in Africa. To complicate matters further, a memo was received from the Ethiopian government asking that the foreign ministers give their consent to the union of Ethiopia and Eritrea.

The meeting ended in deadlock, with all parties assigning second-level diplomats to continue to meet and work on the problems. In the meantime the British continued their occupation of Eritrea and Italian Somaliland, and along with the French, their occupation of Libya.

It was not until 1946 that guidelines were established by the UN for the Italian colonies. They provided for four options. The colonies could; 1) opt for independence; 2) opt for incorporation, or partial incorporation, into neighboring territory; 3) remain a trustee of the UN, any of the Four Powers, or of Italy; and 4) if none of the above options were exercised the Four Powers would decide on the future of the colony in question.

When the peace treaty with Italy was signed on February 10, 1947, Italy gave up all rights to Libya, Eritrea, and Italian Somaliland and paid Ethiopia $25 million in reparations.

UN ADDRESSES THE QUESTION OF NON-SELF-GOVERNING AND TRUSTEE TERRITORIES

On September 26, the founding meeting of the United Nations Organization came to an end, having produced its Charter. Within the Charter, the member nations addressed the question of non-self-governing territories as well as territories to be taken under UN trusteeship. Chapter XI of the Charter addressed non-self-governing territories and stated "Members of the United Nations which have or assume responsibility for the administration of territories whose peoples have not yet attained a full measure of self-government... accept as a sacred trust the obligation to... develop self-government (in those territories), to take due account of the political aspirations of the peoples, and to assist them in the progressive development of their free political institutions..."

Chapter XII outlined the UN's trustee systems, stating, "The United Nations shall establish under its authority an international trusteeship system for the administration and supervision of such territories as may be placed thereunder... The basic objective of the trusteeship system... shall be... to promote the political, economic, social and educational advancement of the inhabitants of the trust territories, and their progressive development toward self-government or independence..."

With these words the death knell of colonialism was pronounced in principle by the world body. By accepting the UN Charter, each member nation accepted these conditions and gave its approval that the old colonial system, which the world had known for over 100 years, would eventually end with each and every colony eventually given "self-determination or independence."

LEFTIST GOVERNMENT ELECTED IN FRANCE BUT EMPIRE POLICIES UNCHANGED

When the Constituent Assembly was established in Paris at the end of hostilities, it was agreed that general elections would be held as soon as possible. In the meantime, the Constituent Assembly would serve as the nation's legislative body. That body, however, would be slow and reluctant to address many of the major problems of the moment. This included the promises put forth to France's colonial subjects in the Brazzaville Plan of February 1944. The Assembly did manage, though, to abolish forced labor throughout the empire, to improve civil rights in general, and make it easier for certain colonial subjects to become French citizens. Also, higher education opportunities in France was extended to more colonial subjects.

On October 21, 1945, the first national elections since the war were held in France. In this election French women could vote for the first time. As some had predicted, the French electorate did what the British electorate had done four months earlier—they brought to power a leftist government. The French Communists emerged in the multi-party contest with the strongest vote count, and, were followed closely behind by the Socialists and Popular Republicans.

The coalition government thus formed was considerably left of center. This was good news for the nationalist leaders throughout the empire, because it raised their hopes that self-determination for their respective lands might now be easier to accomplish than before.

These hopes were soon dashed, however, when in late October the new government announced that it would pursue the policy of recovering Indo-China by force and that it would be a top priority for the French nation until victory was achieved. Other policies concerning the empire would, likewise, remain basically unchanged. This was the work of de Gaulle, now serving as President of the newly reconstituted government of France, now known as the Fourth Republic. De Gaulle still wielded enormous power in the French political arena, and in order for the winners of the election to have formed a coalition government they had to make concessions to the President. One of the concessions made was that de Gaulle's policy of trying to preserve the French Empire would continue.

During October, the first significant number of French troops arrived in southern Indo-China in two borrowed British transports escorted by French warships. At that same time, Chinese Nationalist troops had managed to reach Hanoi in the north and liberated many French military men and colonial administrators that had been held captive by the Japanese. In both cases, the French and Chinese Nationalists were able to quickly occupy the cities, ports, and most communications facilities. In the countryside, though, the Vietnamese rebels reigned supreme.

During November, more French troops arrived in the south, including several units of colonial troops from West Africa and Algeria. Once again Africans were to be used by the French Army. On December 19, the French launched their first major offensive against the Vietnamese rebels and a second full-scale colonial war in the French Empire was under way.

In Paris 33, colonial representatives had been elected to the new Assembly, which, in Africa, was perceived with mixed feelings. While it was a step forward in having African representatives in Paris, it was obviously a continuation of the Gaullist policy of integrating France and the empire into one global political entity. Translated, this meant that independence for the respective French colonies was still not an option.

The political integration of Metropolitan France and the empire was formalized in October 1946 when the Second French Constitution was promulgated. It retained the old colonial system of centralized control although certain colonies were elevated to a newly-created status as a "federal" colony. Also, colonial subjects were offered a new form of citizenship, somewhat less than the citizenship enjoyed by those in Metropolitan France.

The new constitution was not well-received in the greater part of the French Empire and in some areas it was deeply resented. Consequently, and not surprisingly, France was on the threshold of a long period of colonial strife.

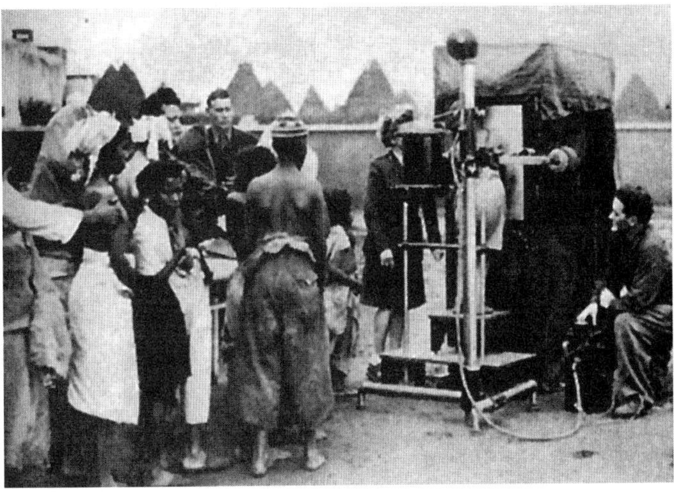

As part of the new liberal French government's concern for colonial subjects, many natives in French Morocco were given free X-ray scans to reduce tuberculosis and other diseases.

FRENCH AFRICA

Algeria was a land at war. Algerian nationalists were carrying out sporadic attacks on Frenchmen, French settlers, and French institutions. Many French settlers had armed themselves by now, and the French Army was in Algeria in strength to combat the rebels. Also, the famine continued and in some parts of the country people were starving.

In the midst of this, municipal elections were held in mid-July, with results similar to those in Metropolitan France. A left-wing coalition called the "France Combattante," which included communists, socialists and former resistance fighters, took 31 offices; Moslem factions took 15, and the conservatives took 5.

In French Morocco, there was famine too, but not as bad as in Algeria. Moroccan nationalists were active and pressing their agenda, but there was no great threat that they would take up arms, as their compatriots had done in neighboring Algeria. It must be remembered that French Morocco was a protectorate, meaning that it had been independent once before and would likely be independent once again. The great hope of the Moroccan leadership and the Moroccan people was that independence could be attained relatively soon and peacefully. And the signs were good. The Sultan and his shadow government were respected by the people and had cooperated with the French and the other Allies throughout the war. Furthermore, the new left-wing government in Paris was likely to subscribe to a more lenient colonial policy than the conservative governments before it. Supporting this contention was the visit to Morocco during August by the new French Foreign Minister, Georges Bidault. Bidault offered a package of reforms favorable to the Moroccan people, including reforms of the antiquated legal system that, heretofore,

Top left: Sultan Mohammed V of Morocco. Bottom left: Habib Bourghiba of Tunisia. Right: bey Sidi Mohammed al Amin of Tunisia.

had favored Frenchmen over Moroccans. He also promised the elimination of all statutes discriminating against Moroccans and favoring Frenchmen. Bidault further promised financial aid in education, and he praised the recently-begun construction on the hydroelectric dam at Bi Al Quidan as an example of future Moroccan-French cooperation.

Added to this detente between Morocco and the West was the undeniable fact that Moroccan troops had fought loyally and hard for the Allied cause and that the United States had shown it was a friend to the Moroccan people, evidenced by President Roosevelt having visited with the Sultan when he was in Morocco for the Casablanca Conference in January 1943. And what's more, there was no strong communist or radical political activities in the country.

Another positive factor for the Moroccans was the fact that Spain was now politically isolated in the world community as well as being militarily weak. These things boded well for the possibility that Spain, under several possible scenarios, might be persuaded to relinquish its protectorate status over Spanish Morocco and accept some form of Moroccan self-rule.

In Tunisia the political situation was not as bad as in Algeria, but not as good as in Morocco. There was famine to some degree and people, as well as the economy, were suffering. Bread was still rationed.

Tunisian nationalists, most of whom were working underground, were quite active pressing their views within the country and were remaining loyal to their long-time leader, Habib Bourghiba, who was living in exile in Egypt. Bourghiba was now recognized throughout the Arab world as the dominant leader of the Tunisian nationalists, and he had valuable connections with other Arab leaders who would be in positions to support Tunisian nationalist objectives.

In July, Bey Sidi Mohammed al-Amin and his son visited battlefield, in France and Germany were Tunisian soldiers had fought. This was, of course, a goodwill gesture toward the French as well as the Tunisian people. The Bey also made a public display, pleading with the French authorities to spare the lives of those Tunisians who had collaborated with the Axis forces and been condemned to death by French military tribunals during the latter part of the war.

About this time, though, there were some anti-French disturbances and the French Resident-General, General Charles Mast, decreed a ban on meetings at Sfax and Gabes where some of the disturbances had occurred. He also threatened those spreading Anti-French rumors with punishment under martial law.

During September, anti-French demonstrations flared again and were put down by the police.

During November, some 1,200 Italian families who had been identified as having been actively pro-Axis during the war were expelled from Tunisia by the French authorities.

In French West Africa all was peaceful. There were no threats from local nationalist or other radicals and the economy was relatively good, with the traditional trade with Metropolitan France having resumed. One favorable factor was that the grain harvests had been good and the French West Africans found a ready market for their crops in famine-plagued French North Africa.

In French Equatorial Africa, the situation was much like that in West Africa. The local economy was good and sales of meat and grain to Metropolitan France and French North Africa were good.

All was quiet, too, in French Somaliland in East Africa. The economy had returned to normal with the port of Djibouti thriving as an important regional trade center.

On the island of Madagascar, the French administration was functioning in Tananarive and elections were held for thirty of the sixty members of the newly-formed Representative Council. The other thirty members were appointed by the French governor. The Council convened in September to address local issues.

There were still relatively large numbers of British troops on the island, and both Paris and Tananarive were urging them to leave. But, as in Ethiopia, the British found reasons to stay on and did not fully withdraw until 1946. This inability of the

French to eject the British was seen by the Malagachy people and their leaders as a weakness on the part of the French.

THE FIFTH PAN-AFRICAN CONGRESS

During October, some of the world's leading black leaders came together to organize the "Fifth Pan-African Congress" for the purpose of furthering the process of decolonization. The four previous Pan-African congresses had been held in various places between the war years. For this congress, the African leaders picked a friendly country, Britain, and a friendly city, Manchester, a primarily working-class and heavily socialist city.

The principle organizers of the Congress were Kwame Nkrumah, an expatriate from Gold Coast; Jomo Kenyatta, an expatriate from Kenya; W.E.B. Du Bois, an American author and executive of the National Association for the Advancement of Colored People (NAACP); George Padmore of Trinidad, and Mrs. Amy Jacques Garver, the Labourite Mayor of Manchester.

Nkrumah was, at the time, something of a celebrity, because he had just written a popular-selling book entitled "Declaration of the Colonial Peoples of the World," in which he urged colonial peoples, world-wide, to unite to throw off the yoke of colonialism. As expected, the Congress passed resolutions calling for an end to colonialism and unity among colonial peoples to attain that goal. The Congress stressed "political non-alignment," a phrase that would become very prominent in the coming years. Defining "political non-alignment," the resolution read in part "...as free nations they (the former colonies) would stand united to consolidate and safeguard their liberties and independence from the restoration of Western imperialism as well as the danger of Communism."

Jomo Kenyatta at the Pan-African Congress. Kenyatta would return to Kenya in 1946 after having lived abroad for fifteen years.

THE "THIRD WORLD"

The non-alignment policy of the Fifth Pan-African Congress was one of the first expressions of the political concept that would, a few years later, result in the coining of the phrase "Third World"; the "First" world being the western democracies, the "Second" being the communist nations, and the "Third" being the non-aligned nations.

The Congress also called for native control of Africa's economy, equality with whites, separation of religion and politics and a wide array of social programs.

Information about the Congress quickly spread throughout the colonial world, giving the various nationalist groups in every colony encouragement and a sense of increasing power.

History would show that the hoped-for pan-Africanism would be an impossible goal, because there were simply too many differences between the peoples of Africa country-to-county and tribe-to-tribe. The great black leaders soon recognized this and, for the most part, abandoned pan-Africanism as a workable goal.

AMERICAN POLICY TOWARD COLONIALISM CHANGES

As it became more obvious to America's leaders that the new threat to the security of the Western nations was communism American policy toward colonialism changed. This was in the latter months of 1945. It was then seen in Washington that if there was a sudden upsurge in the number of small independent countries around the world some of those countries would turn communist. Rather than have this happen, it seemed more prudent to postpone decolonization and let the colonial lands continue to be ruled by friendly western nations, at least so long as the Soviet threat existed. This was part of the newly emerging "Truman Doctrine," which called for the containment of communism.

AIR ROUTES

With hostilities ended in the Far East, there was no need to send large supplies of men and material across Africa by plane. Thus, the military routes across both North and central Africa gradually closed down. Many of the planes returned to their home countries, taking with them military personnel, much of their equipment, and an occasion cargo of Lend-Lease material being returned to the United States.

What they left behind, though, was of great value to all who lived in Africa. There were well-built and modern airfields all across the continent where there had been none before. And commercial air travel was rapidly expanding all over the world as aircraft plants were retooled from making military planes to producing bigger, faster, and more comfortable commercial aircraft. Furthermore, air travel was no longer the plaything of the rich and the status symbol of the public servant and the politician; it had become a necessity in international communications and commerce. Consequently, the former military airfields throughout Africa were rapidly converted to commercial use and, more often than not, became regional airports serving several communities for many miles around.

BRITISH WEST AFRICA

In British West Africa, Nigeria and the Gold Coast were the most politically and economically advanced colonies; they quickly gained the attention of the new Labour government in London as candidates for an early transfer to the status of self-governing colonies. Sir Arthur Richards, Governor of Nigeria, was instructed by London to propose a new constitution for that colony which would bring about self-government within a few years. This was accomplished during the latter part of 1945. The new constitution was approved by the colonial Legislative Council and by both houses of Parliament in London and scheduled to be promulgated in 1946. It called for a federal Legislative Council to be created in Lagos, 91% of whose members would be appointed either by the governor or by the traditional native authorities. In addition, each of the three major regions of the colony would have their own legislative council, which would serve as advisory bodies to, and electoral colleges for, the federal Legislative Council in Lagos. In the eastern and western regions of Nigeria the councils would be unicameral with 60% of the members by the governor and 40% by tribal councils. In the north, the councils would be bicameral with a House of Assembly and a House of Chiefs with members similarly appointed.

The new constitution also revised provincial boundaries, and it provided machinery for existing local and tribal authorities to be integrated into a unified provincial structure. The purpose of this was to stimulate a sense of nationhood among the Nigerian people which was essential if the colony was to become, and remain, a united political entity. Ordinances accompanying the new constitution called for state control of all minerals and closer controls over the elections of tribal chiefs.

From its inception, though, the new constitution had its critics. It was drawn up without consultation from native leaders and without any test of public opinion.

As 1945 ended, the contents of the new constitution were still being digested by the Nigerian people and their leaders. And, as time passed, criticism mounted as unanswered questions arose and individuals, small groups, and tribal leaders came to understand the changes that were about to be wrought. As 1946 dawned, prospects for the new constitution did not look good.

In the Gold Coast, a new constitution for that colony was drawn up during the latter months of 1945 by the colony's Governor, Sir Alan Burns and his associates. It was scheduled to be announced in 1946 and would not be a carbon copy of the Nigerian constitution but one tailored for Gold Coast. One of its main differences was that it called for more elected native leaders. Most of the non-elected government officials would be appointed by native organizations and only a few by the colonial administration. For the times, the new Gold Coast constitution promised to be one of the most progressive new constitutions yet presented in the colonial world. But native control would not yet be absolute. The existing colonial administration and a London-appointed governor would remain in place, and the governor, aided by these advisors, also appointed by London, would have the final say and veto power over any political matter concerning the colony. As the year ended the constitution was still being drafted.

Earlier, in September, the various unions of the colony, most of them newly formed, met together in what they called the "First Trade Union Congress." The purpose was to find common ground and solidarity for their many and varied labor and political agendas. This was not a welcome event for the colonial administration in that labor would, in all likelihood, now become a more powerful and organized force and that strikes and work stoppages would be more likely.

During the latter months of 1945, a natural disaster of major proportions began in Gold Coast in the form of a plant disease called "swollen root." This disease struck, and eventually killed, cocoa trees. During the next year, it would devastate the colony's cocoa industry. This, in turn, would bring unemployment, inflation, shortages of imported goods, black markets and the shattering of the dreams of many of Gold Coast's returning service men.

AFRICANS RETURN FROM BURMA

During November and December 1945, the West African and East African fighting men returned home from Burma. They were sent home on a quota system based on length of service and age. Their arrivals were, for the most part, unceremonious, but later, parades and other ceremonies were organized on their behalf. A few units were selected to go to Britain to participate in ceremonies there.

Then, after being mustered out of the service, the great majority of the men returned to civilian life in their respective colonies where they found many changes and new challenges. A relatively large number of these men, building on their wartime experiences and education, became men of vision and leaders within their communities. In general, these veterans were looked upon as men of wisdom and experience by their peers.

EAST AFRICA

The people of British East Africa took pride in knowing that they had made a major contribution to the Allied victory in the war. Their King's African Rifles (KAR) forces had grown from seven battalions before the war to 44 at the end of the war. This accounted for over 100,000 combat fighting men having served the Allied cause. In addition, Kenya supplied about 160,000 porters and pioneers to the Allied forces. Tanganyika had contributed 87,000 fighting men to the war; Uganda 70,000, Nyasaland 30,000. Of these numbers some 50,000 East Africans were killed or wounded during the war. Also during the war, the British had conscripted laborers in East Africa at various times for service from two to fifteen months. In Kenya and Tanganyika alone, this amounted to some 160,000 individuals. The labor conscription laws were still on the books in late 1945 but were rescinded in 1946.

Another great mass of humanity in East Africa were Axis POWs. By the end of the war, some 70,000 Axis prisoners were incarcerated in British East Africa. Repatriation of these men began in late 1945 and carried through during 1946.

The people on the home front had done their share, too. The general mood of the people in British East Africa during the latter part of 1945 was one of pride, optimism, confidence, and hope. The future seemed positive, and it was obvious that there was no going back to the subservience of the past. Leading the way in this thinking were the Kikuyu and Luo tribes of Kenya. These were two very large tribes of intelligent and ambitious peoples who were eager to adopt western knowledge and technology. They populated the Kenyan highlands—the heart of the country—which had been heavily populated by Europeans and East Indians over the decades. In the past the Kikuyu and Luo people had been traditional enemies who had allowed themselves to be exploited by the newcomers for their labor and their land. The tribesmen had resented these actions as they happened and they resented them now. But now, things were different. They felt they had ways to rectify the situation.

The British were not oblivious to what was happening in East Africa and made attempts, as they did elsewhere, to improve the lot of the native peoples. Accordingly, a number of five and ten-year plans got underway in late 1945 on internal development projects.

One of the many schemes the British planned was to build a road across central Africa which would connect British East Africa with British West Africa. Up to now, no such road existed. During the war a military dirt road had been pushed through from Nigeria to the Nile Valley in The Sudan, but it stopped there. Now, London announced that parts of that road would be used to build a new 3,000 mile all-weather road from Lagos, Nigeria to Mombasa, Kenya. The road would open new markets for East African goods all throughout West Africa, Western Europe and the Western Hemisphere. Also, in the field of transportation, BOAC and East African, Airways rapidly expanded their services throughout East Africa using war surplus military aircraft and the many new airfields built during the war.

In Uganda, the mood of the people was similar to that in Kenya but Uganda had not been exploited by the Europeans and East Asians to the extent that Kenya had and the Ugandan people were not as well advanced in the ways of the west. The largest tribe in the country, the Ganda, were, like the Kikuyu and Luo in Kenya, well organized and receptive to western ways. Thus, the incentive and mechanics were present for the Ugandan people to become more self-reliant, but it was generally accepted that this would take time.

In Tanganyika, the political future of that former League of Nations mandate had been pre-determined with the creation of the United Nations Organization. Tanganyika would become a trust territory of the UN and would be guided to eventual self-determination. Therefore, the political organizations in Tanganyika busied themselves with gaining members, constituents, and power bases so that they could position themselves to take part in the orderly political process that was planned.

In Nyasaland, the people had remained peaceful and cooperative throughout most of the war, except for a few small strikes instigated by the fledgling labor unions. During the war, though, little capital improvement had been made in this heavily-populated colony. The wartime economy functioned much as it had before the war, with small farmers producing crops for themselves with small surpluses for the domestic market and for export. Because of the lack of jobs,

Nyasalanders continued, as before the war, to emigrate in large numbers to work in the surrounding territories. Eventually these men returned home, bringing with them money, skills, and western ideas. As a result, signs of nationalism began to stir. Leading this trend among the Nyasalanders was the North Nyasaland Association, which, by 1945, had evolved into a larger organization known as the "Nyasaland African National Congress" (NANC), patterned after the African National Congress (ANC) in South Africa. And like the ANC, the NANC was more nationalistic and demanding. As yet, though, the NANC had caused no trouble for the colonial authorities nor the relatively small white settler population.

In Ethiopia, Haile Selassie was still pressing the British to give up the areas they controlled around French Somaliland and in the Ogaden Desert. To counter the British influence and to show the British that he intended not to be drawn any further into their orbit, Selassie turned to the Americans. In September, he concluded a business deal with America's Sinclair Oil Company, under which Sinclair was given a fifty-year oil-prospecting concession within Ethiopia. Also at this time the Ethiopian government contracted with America's Trans-World Airlines to help develop a new state-owned airline company to be known as Ethiopian Airlines. In yet another business arrangement, Ethiopia was flooded with six million American-made Lucky Strike cigarettes at very competitive prices—a ploy to capture the cigarette market for the Americans.

Back in the United States, especially in Harlem in New York City, a pro-Ethiopian movement was underway which advocated closer ties between Ethiopia and the United States. The Ethiopian government made this fact well known throughout the country.

To counter these American inroads into Ethiopia, the Attlee government in London let it be known in Addis Ababa that Britain supported Ethiopia's claim to all, or at least part, of Eritrea and they would press for this at the coming Peace Conference scheduled for July 1946.

These events must certainly have made the wily old Emperor smile. Now he had two of the world's great powers bidding for his attention. But the British were a determined lot and would remain in the Ogaden and some of the other occupied areas of Ethiopia until 1954.

HAILE SELASSIE'S FATE

Haile Selassie's last years would not be happy ones. In 1960, he survived a bloody coup attempt while he was away on a state visit to Brazil. In 1973, a severe famine devastated Ethiopia and in 1974, after serving more than fifty years as Emperor, he was deposed and arrested by a group of young military officers who imposed a communist regime on Ethiopia. The next year, Selassie died of natural causes at the age of 82. The country's new ruler, Mengistu Haile Mariam, fearful that Selassie's burial place would become a shrine for his opponents, had the Emperor's body secretly buried beneath the floor of his office in the Grand Palace. The disappearance of Selassie's body, though, only led to rumors and speculation. Some believed that he had not died and was in hiding. Others believed that the saintly Emperor had been assumed into heaven and would return someday to lead his people once again.

In 1991, Mengistu was overthrown and the truth learned about Selassie's secret burial. His body was exhumed in 1992 and given a proper Christian burial in the chapel of the Grand Palace. In November, 2000, it was moved again and reburied in the Holy Trinity Cathedral in Addis Ababa.

COMMUNISM IN AFRICA

There was still very little communist penetration in Africa at this time. The first priority of the Soviet Union was to rebuild the infrastructure and social order within its own borders and within its newly conquered lands in eastern Europe. Exporting communism to Africa was a low priority for Moscow. Communism would filter into Africa slowly via individuals who had been abroad, by news media reports of communism spreading in China and other lands and by small groups of Africans who had espoused the theories of Marx, Lenin, and Stalin.

BRITISH SOUTHERN AFRICA

As the war ended, the economy of South Africa remained strong because of the pent-up demand for consumer goods and a still-strong export market. South African industry quickly changed over to manufacturing consumer goods, and wartime taxes were repealed. The Smuts government predicted a bright future for the South African economy in manufacturing and provided financial subsidies to certain industries, especially iron and steel. The country's foreign debt had been greatly reduced during the war, making the South African rand a strong currency world-wide.

During November, Smuts' United Party's two coalition partners in the government, the Labour Party and the Dominion Party, withdrew from the coalition, which had been organized primarily for the pursuit of the war. The two parties each had one cabinet member, both of whom resigned and were replaced by members of the United Party. The parting of the ways was friendly and the United Party still had enough strength in Parliament to continue in power without new elections being called.

With the defeat of the Axis nations came a similar defeat for the Afrikaner organizations and individuals who had produced the voluminous amounts of pro-Axis propaganda throughout the war. The OB and other small pro-Axis organizations had diminished in size and importance, and they no longer regurgitated their Axis-inspired rhetoric. Instead, they reverted to the old and worn themes of racial superiority and right-wing politics.

Daniel Malan, head of the National Party, was one of the Afrikaner leaders who changed with the times. No longer did he mention the Draft Constitution, which would have taken South Africa out of the war and out of the British Commonwealth. Instead, he distanced himself from the Draft Constitution, claiming that it had been the work of others. Malan's overall political views had moved noticeably toward the center and concentrated more on domestic issues. His, and the National Party's, foreign policy now came down on the communists and their fellow travelers. A favorite political theme of the National Party became that the Smuts government had been an active ally of the Soviet Union, which had opened the door to communist thinking and activities within the country and Africa.

With India on the road to independence, the Indian population of South Africa, who had long suffered from discrimination and oppressive laws, now became more organized and vocal. Located mostly in Natal Province, these people appealed to both the Indian government and the United Nations for support. At the UN the Indian government actively took up the cause of the oppressed Indians in South Africa and bitterly criticized South Africa. This action found many supporters within the UN and dashed South Africa's hopes for become a major force within that international body. It was a disappointing blow to Smuts and his foreign policy. To make matters worse, the Indian government withdrew its High Commissioner to South Africa and officially sponsored a world-wide boycott of South African goods.

Not surprisingly, the UN became very unpopular in South Africa, especially with the Afrikaner population. It was seen by them as an organization controlled by liberal states who intended to promote the uplifting of the lesser peoples of the world at the expense of white people. The UN became even less popular in South Africa when it rejected the South African government's request that South West Africa be incorporated into South Africa. This attack was led at the UN by India. Also, the South Africans did not relish the idea of South West Africa becoming a UN trust territory. The various factions within the South African government warranted on this point and would fight to hold on to South Africa's mandate over the territory as long as possible. The UN did not, at this time, force its trusteeship on South West Africa but required the South African government to make periodic reports on the mandated territory, as had been required by the League of Nations.

On other issues concerning South Africa, the Smuts government took note of the many Europeans displaced as a result of the war and made it an official policy to encourage the immigration of European white people into South Africa. Jews, communists, orientals, and people of color were, of course, not welcome.

Another problem for the Smuts government were the shanty towns which housed the tens of thousands of blacks who had come to the cities to work in the war plants. Fortunately for the blacks, but not so fortunately for the whites, was the fact that the economy was still strong enough to keep most of the blacks employed. From the viewpoint of the whites, this indicated that there would be no great exodus of blacks back to their rural homes and that the shanty towns were likely to remain for a long time to come. This situation made ample political ammunition for the National Party and they exploited it with a vengeance, calling for more strict laws separating the races now that they were living closer together.

The Smuts government, too, wanted to see blacks return to their villages and instigated a scheme to entice them to do so. The scheme included opening new areas of land for black settlement and reclaiming some of the black lands that had been exhausted by intensive farming. As for the latter, attractive wages were offered to blacks who would return to the exhausted land areas, work on its reclamation, and remain there.

APARTHEID

Apartheid is an Afrikaner word meaning "separateness" and would, in the near future, come to refer to the planned, legislated and clearly defined separation of the races in South Africa. In 1945, though, it was not yet in use. It would come into general use after the National Party won the 1948 elections and enacted rigid segregation laws.

The National Party also zeroed in on jobs, claiming that now, with the many veterans returning from the armed forces, the blacks were taking jobs from the whites. Some credibility was given to this claim, because many employers were reluctant to discharge their black workers because they were, by now, trained and competent workers and usually worked for less money than whites. To protect the returning veterans, the Smuts government had decreed that no white service man or woman would be discharged from the service until they had a job or some other suitable arrangement. Keeping these people in service, therefore, created a major governmental expense, thereby giving the National Party yet another issue.

As 1945 ended, there were signs that the country's wheat and corn crops, both important export items, were in trouble. By the end of the South African "summer" in the spring of 1946, this was confirmed. Both crops were poor. The blow fell hardest on the blacks and in some areas of the country, food rationing had to be imposed. Nation-wide restrictions were placed on the use of white flour in order to provide as much wheat as possible for export.

On the positive side, though, gold was discovered in the Orange Free State in 1946, giving the South African economy a welcome boost.

As for the native population, the ANC was growing in strength especially among urbanized blacks. These city people now working at steady jobs and pursuing urban ways were slowly becoming de-tribalized. Therefore, it was relatively easy for them to transfer their loyalty away from their tribes and to an organization like the ANC. The leaders of the ANC could see that these changes strengthened their position considerably and began making plans to actively press their demands on the Smuts government. Then too, the other oppressed people of South Africa, the coloreds (people of mixed race) and the Indians, were gathering their strength and uniting. Quite naturally, it was inevitable that they would ally themselves with the ANC, and the coming year, 1946, would be the year during which the ANC emerged as a serious factor in the political arena of South Africa.

Pressures for South Africa to become a republic, independent of the British Commonwealth continued after the war and in 1960, when the National Party was in power, that step was taken.

In Southern Rhodesia, both the black and white populations contributed significantly to the Allied war effort and the economy was still strong. As a self-governing colony, the white ruling class had made virtually no attempt to improve the lot of the blacks during the war other than what occurred naturally as a result of the wartime economy. Nor had they made significant plans to alter the status quo for the future. This sparked a mounting resentment in the black population and was reflected in the fact that the leading black political organization in the country, the "Bantu Congress of Southern Rhodesia," founded in the late 1930s, changed its name to "Southern Rhodesian African National Congress" (SRANC) in imitation of, and as a show of unity with, the ANC in South Africa. Like the ANC, the SRANC increased its demands on the white government, especially with regards to labor reform. During late 1945, the SRANC carried out several well-orchestrated and disciplined strikes. The SRANC also devised a collective insurance plan for black workers and their families. It would be the SRANC that, in 1950, would come under the control of Joshua Nkomo who, together with Robert Mugabe, would instigate a bloody civil war that would eventually lead to the independence of the country.

In the meantime, the white rulers of Southern Rhodesia imitated the action taken by South Africa and opened the door of immigration for white settlers. Three large tracts of government-owned land were set aside for homesteading, and many white Europeans came to Southern Rhodesia to settle.

In Northern Rhodesia, the mining industry was still in full production, there was high employment, and the political scene was quiet as it had been throughout most of the war.

As yet no black nationalist organization of note had emerged in the colony. The most significant black organization in Northern Rhodesia was the large Barote Tribe, which had been granted self-rule in 1938 similar to the large tribes in Nigeria. By late 1945, the Barote leaders were still satisfied with the status quo and offered the colonial authorities no trouble. This would change in 1946, when several black welfare associations merged into the "Northern Rhodesian Congress" and in 1948 changed its name to the "Northern Rhodesian African National Congress" (NRANC) in imitation of the National Congresses in the neighboring territories. In 1951, Harry Nkumbula would become leader of the NRANC and lead Northern Rhodesia to independence.

In the British protectorates of Basutoland, Bechuanaland, and Swaziland there was no nationalist movements to speak of and no formalized segregation. These protectorates had long been recognized as black homelands and had been ruled by black councils under supervision from London. The South African government accepted this arrangement with regard to Basutoland and Swaziland, but had long-standing hopes of one day gaining control of mineral-rich Bechuanaland. The new Labour government, though, had no intentions of changing the existing arrangements. They did have, however, new ideas on how the ruling councils of the protectorates might be liberalized to more accurately reflect the aspirations of their own native workers. To that end, the Labour government began negotiations, in late 1945, with the Basuto Council in Basutoland, the most heavily populated of the three protectorates, with hopes that the Council would be restructured so that fewer members were appointed and more elected.

For most of the people in the three protectorates, these political proposals were of secondary importance, because all three had been suffering from drought conditions off and on over the last few years, with 1945 having been one of the worst. This had brought hard times to the protectorates' economic mainstays of agriculture and cattle raising.

In Bechuanaland, the South African government, anxious to expand its influence there, sent a team of engineers and agricultural experts into the protectorate to inspect the possibilities of creating large-scale irrigation projects using the waters of the Chobe and Okovango Rivers. The team reported back that some four million acres of land could be irrigated and would become "possibly the finest ranching land in South Africa." They also recommended that South Africans be given the opportunity to develop and manage the projects. These proposals were sent on to London where they met with little support.

London, instead, wanting to maintain its influence in Bechuanaland, countered the activities of the South Africans by inviting young King Seretse Kahma, head of the large Bamwangwato Tribe, to London for a state visit.

PORTUGUESE AFRICA

The end of the war brought several internal changes to Portuguese Africa but no political changes. Those colonies continued to be managed from Lisbon much as they had been before the war.

In the Cape Verde Islands many of the war workers returned home from the United States and elsewhere bringing with them their nest eggs of money. This sparked a brief period of prosperity in the islands, but when the money was gone the bulk of the people became poor again. With time, the next generation of young men went abroad as migrant workers and the cycle continued.

In the Azores, the American military stayed on long into the postwar era. This was welcomed by the Portuguese because it pumped American dollars into the economy and provided military protection for the islands during the Cold War.

In Mozambique, the Portuguese government engaged a British firm to install a radio-linked communications system throughout the colony. Here, as in the other Portuguese colonies, with the exception of the Azores, telephones were a rarity.

In all of their African colonies the Portuguese made some effort to improve roads, bridges, harbors, schools, and hospitals.

Nationalist organizations slowly emerged within the Portuguese colonies but were vigorously suppressed by the Portuguese authorities when they became a threat to the status quo. Lisbon maintained, more often than not, that the natives living under Portuguese control were generally satisfied and that nationalist and subversive activities were the work of outsiders and communists. This fiction eventually wore thin, and during the 1960s, with virtually all of Africa's colonies gaining, or having gained, their independence, the home-grown nationalists in the Portuguese colonies gained the upper hand. Because of Lisbon's delaying tactics, though, the Portuguese colonies were among the last in Africa to gain their independence. It would not be until the 1970s that this would be achieved and then only after very long and bloody colonial wars in Angola and Mozambique.

Winston Churchill

CHURCHILL SAID IT...

As the hostilities of World war II ended, Winston Churchill could see the postwar turmoil that was certain to erupt in the colonial world. He discussed this in his last letter to Franklin Roosevelt dated March 17, 1945. Roosevelt died a few weeks later on April 12. In his letter, Churchill commented on the strife that was coming in the world's colonies and told Roosevelt, "...when the war of the giants is over the wars of the pygmies will begin."

INDEX